Digital Enterprise Technology
Perspectives and Future Challenges

T0189485

CIRP-The International Academy for Production Engineering

CIRP[1] is a scientific Academy organized along the lines of a number of Scientific Technical Committees (STCs) and Working Groups (WGs), covering many areas of production science and technology. CIRP has Fellows, Associate and Corporate members from 46 different countries and it's aims in general at:

- Promoting scientific research, related to
  - manufacturing processes,
  - production equipment and automation,
  - manufacturing systems and
  - product design and manufacturing;

- Promoting cooperative research among the members of the Academy and creating opportunities for informal contacts among CIRP members at large;

- Promoting the industrial application of the fundamental research work and simultaneously receiving feed back from industry, related to industrial needs and their evolution.

CIRP was founded in 1951 with the aim to address scientifically, through international co-operation, issues related to modern production science and technology. In the late 1940s it was becoming increasingly clear that the development of new production techniques was being hampered by the lack of appropriate analysis methods and it was realized that, in view of the importance and scale of the problems to be tackled, only international cooperative action would be effective. Therefore it was decided that efforts should be made to bring together research workers studying the application of scientific methods to production technology. This initiative led to the foundation of the International Institution for Production Research (CIRP), named today "The International Academy for Production Engineering".

The flagship event of CIRP is its annual General Assembly with keynote and paper sessions and meetings of the Scientific and Technical Committees. CIRP also promotes a number of conferences within relevant topics. Also CIRP members organize a variety of conferences, under the sponsorship of CIRP.

The main publications of CIRP are the CIRP Annals under ISI standards with two volumes; Volume I, with refereed papers presented in the GA and Volume II with refereed keynote papers. There are also other relevant publications such as CIRP proceedings which include technical reports, special issues, reports and internal communications, proceedings of CIRP seminars and conferences.

---

[1] Acronym of "College International pour la Recherche en Productique". To see more follow the link www.cirp.net.

Digital Enterprise Technology
Perspectives and Future Challenges

edited by

Pedro F. Cunha
Instituto Politécnico de Setúbal
Setúbal, Portugal

Paul G. Maropoulos
University of Bath
Bath, United Kingdom

 Springer

Pedro Filipe Cunha
Escola Superior de Tecnologia
Instituto Politécnico de Setúbal
Campus do IPS
Estefanilha
2910-761 SETUBAL
PORTUGAL
Email: pcunha@est.ips.pt

Paul G. Maropoulos
University of Bath
Department of Mechanical Engineering
BATH
UNITED KINGDOM BA2 7AY
Email: p.g.maropoulos@bath.ac.uk

Digital Enterprise Technology: *Perspectives and Future Challenges*
Edited by Pedro F. Cunha and Paul G. Maropoulos

ISBN-13: 978-1-4419-4322-4   e-ISBN-13: 978-0-387-49864-5

Printed on acid-free paper.

9 8 7 6 5 4 3 2 1

springer.com

CONTENTS

INTERNACIONAL COMMITTEE

ORGANIZING COMMITTEE

Pedro F. Cunha, IPS/ESTSetúbal (Chair)

Aires de Abreu, OGMA

António Ramos Pires, IPS/ESTSetúbal

Caldeira Duarte, IPS/ESTSetúbal

Cláudio Sapateiro, IPS/ESTSetúbal

Elsa Henriques, IST

Ferdinand Schultz, ATEC

Fernando Cunha, IPS/ESTSetúbal

Fernando Valente, IPS/ESTSetúbal

Hernani Mourão, IPS/ESCESetúbal

Jaroslav Holeček, VW-Slovakia

Joaquim Filipe, IPS/ESTSetúbal

João Falcão Neves, GM Portugal

Jorge N. R. Vilhena, IPS/ESTSetúbal

José Dionísio, IDMEC/IST

José Simões, IPS/ESTSetúbal

Julius von Ingelheim, VW-Autoeuropa

Luís Esteves, IPS/ESTSetúbal

Luís M. Camarinha-Matos, New University of Lisbon

Paulo Anacleto, IPS/ESTSetúbal

Patricia Macedo, IPS/ESTSetúbal

Teresa Sequeira, New University of Lisbon

Vera Santos, IPS/ESTSetúbal

PREFACE

Digital Enterprise Technology: Perspectives and Future Challenges

Manufacturing industry and the associated services are undergoing a period of considerable and sustained change, facilitated by the rapid growth of large Asian economies, such as the Chinese and Indian, the incorporation of Easter European countries into the European Union and the development of new production capabilities and consumer markets in many other parts of the world. Sustaining innovation and the rapid development of new products and services are key elements for ensuring the competitiveness of manufacturing companies, in a global context.

Digital engineering methods and systems are vitally important for performing key technical and business functions in a distributed and collaborative manner. The product design and engineering systems are gradually being developed to include a variety of tools for DfX as well as incorporate aspects of digital manufacturing. Product Data Management and Product Lifecycle Management systems are now more seamlessly integrated with product design systems, allowing connectivity and management of the global design, production and service processes, across the product lifecycle.

There is growing realisation that the competitiveness of industrial companies in today's global environment is closely associated with the efficiency and performance of its production networks and the logistics of the supply chain operations. These are areas of considerable promise for the development of novel digital modelling and optimisation methods for large and complex systems and networks.

New applications, such as systems integration software for product verification and validation and RFIDs, are having a major impact on the way product quality can be assessed during manufacturing and assembly and on how logistic functions can be executed in industry, respectively. The importance and potential impact of such infusion of digital technologies have not been fully realised as the integration of associated systems and services is still incomplete. These are, therefore, areas in which research and development effort from the academic community should be channelled to deal with the new and challenging areas of digital enterprise technology.

This book contains papers accepted and presented at the 3rd CIRP sponsored International Conference in Digital Enterprise Technology (DET'06) held in Setubal, Portugal, in September 2006. DET 2006 follows on the success of the two previous meetings held in Durham, UK, and Seattle, USA, in 2002 and 2004 respectively. The papers presented represent relevant examples of current state-of-art in the development and use of systems and methods for the digital modelling of global product development and realization processes, in the context of life cycle management.

The presented papers are thematically related to the five technical areas of Digital Enterprise Technology namely;

- *Distributed and Collaborative Design*

- *Process Modelling and Process Planning*

- *Advanced Factory Design and Modelling*

- *Physical-to-Digital Environment Integrators*

- *Enterprise* Integration Technologies

The integrated vision to design and management of products, processes and production systems was introduced in DET'06 through the session in *Production System Evolution* (SPECIES). The relevance of this theme comes from the presentation and discussion of techniques and methods devoted to determining the most appropriate evolution strategy for production systems.

The five keynote papers provide valuable insights on the future trends and challenges of digital enterprise technology. These papers make an important contribution to the definition of perspectives for developing technologies and systems to address the digital design of products, factories and networks.

The Editors and Joint Chairmen of DET'06 would like to gratefully acknowledge the contribution of all colleagues who participated in the meeting with the submission of high quality papers. We would also like to formally thank all those who assisted in any way with the preparation and delivery of DET'06, including the distinguished members of the International Scientific Committee and of the Local Organising Committee, as well as the Publishers of the scientific output of DET'06. We would also like to acknowledge the great contribution of our referees, whose valuable comments improved the quality of papers and consequently enhanced the academic quality of this book.

Finally, we are deeply grateful to the many sponsors of DET'06, whose financial support was essential for the success of the meeting and the outcomes obtained, such as the present book.

The future of the International Conferences in *Digital Enterprise Technology* is well established with the organization already assured for the next events. These meetings will address novel digital technology developments, particularly on novel digital methods and systems for the Design, Modelling, and Verification of Complex Products, Systems and Nertworks.

Professor P.F.Cunha   Professor P.G. Maropoulos
Instituto Politécnico de Setúbal   *University of Bath*
Portugal   *UK*
Editor and DET 2006 Chairman   Co-Editor and DET 2006 Co-Chairman

SPONSORS

Edition partial funded by:

FCT Fundação para a Ciência e a Tecnologia
MINISTÉRIO DA CIÊNCIA, TECNOLOGIA E ENSINO SUPERIOR

KEYNOTE PAPERS

DIGITAL MANUFACTURING
IN THE GLOBAL ERA

Engelbert Westkämper
Fraunhofer Institut IPA
Universität Stuttgart, Germany
wke@ipa.fhg.de

The global era of manufacturing is going on. Digital Manufacturing is one of the core strategies of the European Manufuture vision and strategic agenda towards the knowledge based production. It is driven by the application and standardization of information and communication technologies and the increasing demand for the efficiency of operations in global networks. The environment of manufacturing is turbulent and requires permanent adaptation of the manufacturing systems. Manufacturing Engineering covers wide scales from networks to processes and from real-time to long-term operations. The tools of future engineering and management of manufacturing are digital and distributed. Strategic aspects and the potential and the needs of research and development are the main positions of the presentation.

1. INTRODUCTION

Manufacturing is the backbone of our economy. More than 27 million people are employed in 230,000 companies. The total added value of these industries is about € 1,300 million in Europe. Manufacturing has a long tradition and its role is adding value for the economies and their prosperity. But now there is a strong change caused by globalisation and internal changes of technologies.

More than 80 years ago Taylor formulated the paradigms of scientific based manufacturing: "Analysing the manufacturing work on elementary processes with scientific based methodologies gives benefits to the economic efficiency of companies and their workers" (Taylor, 1983). Today the so called "Taylorism" is still today the dominant paradigm of manufacturing in practice. The methodologies have changed and computers are used in nearly all processes. Manufacturing is on the way to a knowledge-based and digital era.

2. DRIVING FORCES AND CHALLENGES

Global networks of communication and the diffusion process of electronics and information systems characterise the environment, in which peoples live, business and manufacturing is done. The world of manufacturing of this century is a networking information world – inside and outside of enterprises and linked to all participants of markets.

2.1   Migration of production and consumption

Beside economic aspects the fast and global transfer of information and open markets is the main driver of changing the global structure of manufacturing.
Comparing manufacturing of the last decades of the 20th Century to the actual situation we have now, it is evident that new requirements are driving forces for the global changes of the manufacturing area:
- Migration of production and consumption of industrial products to developing regions,
- Turbulent environment and influencing factors – only robust and transformable enterprises survive,
- Global networking in engineering and manufacturing on a global quality level.

The migration of production and consumption towards global manufacturing and especially to growing economies accelerated. Figure 1 shows the general development from the Triade to the developing countries.

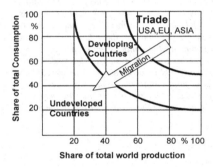

Figure 1 - Production and Consumption of technical Products.

The migration creates value and prosperity and in the origins unemployment. In the technical view we notice the equalisation of technologies and quality and a new challenge for acceleration of innovation.

Innovation for adding value may solve unemployment problems by generating new products and processes. In this century innovation is driven by basic knowledge and can transform manufacturing towards a knowledge based new Taylorism – using the digital manufacturing systems (Westkämper, 2005).

2.2   Objectives of Manufacturing Development

New technologies and the adaptability of the manufacturing structures are challenges for our future. The EU initiative Manufuture demands as objectives of future development towards 2020:
Competitiveness of European manufacturing industries
- to survive in the turbulent economic environment
- to compensate migration and consumption of technologies
- to have more and better jobs

          - to stabilise economic results (growth)
          - to ensure welfare and social standards of living

Leadership in manufacturing technologies
          - to support innovative products and platforms
          - to lead manufacturing with global standards
          - to guarantee human and social standards of work

Environmentally friendly products and manufacturing
          - to reduce the environmental losses
          - to change the consumption of limited resources
          - to maximise the benefits of each product during its life cycle.

All of these objectives are focused on the innovation of the manufacturing industries. They require an innovation culture inside the companies to quickly implement and permanent transform the manufacturing structures.

2.3   Adapting to changes in a turbulent environment

Flexibility can give companies enormous advantages in customer and market oriented innovation, as the structures of present companies are usually only adaptable up to a certain extent. The external and internal factors of manufacturing are changing permanently and re-quire the dynamic change in operations, organization and structure, as is shown in figure 2.

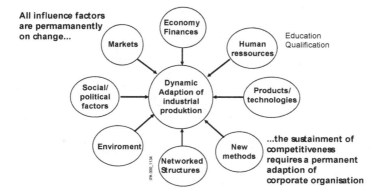

Figure 2 - Turbulent Influences - Dynamic adaptation of structures.

The problems are associated with time-related transformation when altering structures concerning property and possession, personal resources and established methods in the information system. Adaptability has a temporal aspect. It is not a question of whether the management is prepared to change, but it must be strived for permanently by all responsible persons in management. The crucial factors when carrying out an alteration are the time required and expenses involved (Wiendahl, 2003; Warnecke, 1999; Arai, 2000).

3. DIGITAL MANUFACTURING FOR INTELLIGENT PRODUCTION

3.1 European Manufacturing Platform "Manufuture" and global Cooperation

European Technology Platforms are a newly introduced concept that aims to bring together all interested stakeholders to develop a shared long-term vision, create roadmaps, secure long-term financing and realise a coherent approach to governance. The Technology Platform specifically designed for the manufacturing will mobilise and concentrate a critical mass of research and innovation efforts in a mission-oriented plan with actions that will provide practical benefits to enterprises actively operating in this sector.

The MANUFUTURE Initiative of the EU is oriented to a Vision of Manufacturing in 2020. Just like Taylor's view, the vision's bases are science and technology implemented in holistic networking manufacturing and managed towards sustainability and welfare. The MANUFUTURE Initiative has 4 levels: global, European, national and regional.

Figure 3 shows the main and strategic orientations of Manufuture – following a CIRP Model for the new age of manufacturing. Its focuses are business models, advanced industrial engineering and emergent technologies for High Adding Value (Fig. 3).

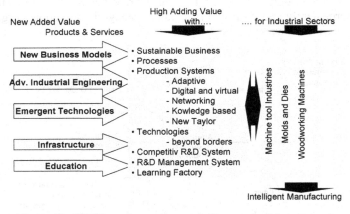

Figure 3 - EU Manufuture Strategic Research (Manufuture).

The knowledge generated by research has to be transferred to application by efficient R&D and education. All of these pillars take into account the full availability of IT and networked manufacturing. Therefore it can be stated, that this initiative is oriented to the digital manufacturing of the future.

Product engineering, production processes and the management of industrial enterprises need a common base for realising the goals of European Manufacturing and maximise the synergy towards the 2020 Vision. This frame indicates the industrial sectors on the one side and the need of research in Engineering, Production Processes and enterprise management.

3.2   Paradigms for Manufacturing

The following theses are contributions to the manufacturing vision and development of research on a global level.

Life Cycle Orientation
The new paradigm of manufacturing is oriented to the optimization and value creation of products during their whole life. This includes understanding the requirements and usage of products (customization), manufacturing, product-near services and recycling. Basic information and communication technologies are used to follow products throughout their life from engineering to the end of life. This understanding allows manufacturers to follow each product's life and to maximise the benefits of each product.

The success factors of manufacturing industries are mainly based on high diversity and high-skill personnel at all levels. The new developments will change the structure of future work in the life cycle of technical products.

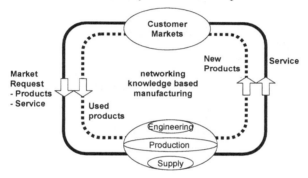

Figure 4 - Life Cycle Orientation.

Sustainable Business
In order to manage and optimise the life cycle it is necessary to develop new business models. Business models which activate and add value have to transform the conventional relationship between manufacturers and users. Sustainable business for life cycle takes into account the responsibility for the environment and the consumption of natural resources as well as social standards of work.

There is another aspect of sustainable business: To maximise the profit more and more companies operate in short business dimensions and invest only a minimum in R&D. Many of them see the responsibility for R&D with governments or suppliers. Business models of the future will take into account even long-term strategic R&D for manufacturing as part of the sustainable business (Bullinger, 2002).

Global networking
Manufacturing processes used to be linked together in a line; today these processes are usually part of complex manufacturing networks that span across multiple companies and countries. By using manufacturing networks, it becomes possible to integrate manufacturing processes into dynamic, cooperative manufacturing and value-added networks and also to remove them from those networks if necessary.

Efficient networking requires standards and management systems for the networking in engineering and logistics based on global communication standards. In the future the flow of materials from origin to the end of life has to be documented.

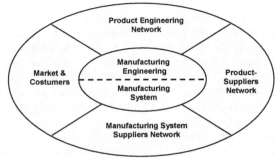

Figure 5 - Networking in Manufacturing: Activating Potentials of Synergy.

Emergent Technologies and Manufacturing Engineering

Manufacturing technologies are permanently developing towards new dimensions of efficiency and overcoming existing technical limits. The common objectives are to summarize as to how to overcome limits in manufacturing by the activation of theoretical potentials of technologies to save time, materials and energy with innovative solutions.

The fast activation of technological potentials in manufacturing technologies is a prerequisite to achieve advantages in the competition of manufacturing industries and users in a broad field of industries. The main potentials to overcome existing limits are:

- high performance technical processes (time, precision, cost)
- reduction of energy and material consumption
- reduction of time and increase of utilization of machines
- reduction of waste and emissions (clean manufacturing)
- zero defect manufacturing

There are diverse new technologies for manufacturing, which promise high potentials to overcome existing limits.

Theoretical boarders are defined by natural (physical, chemical, biological) laws. The degree of utilization caused by the technical solutions, the influencing factors and the uncertainness of the processes can be increased by research and experiments. Knowledge about the processes is the main success factor towards higher efficiency. Beside the traditional goals like time, cost and quality, there are some with a higher future impact, like the reduction of energy consumption and material. Another interesting aspect is the efficiency of integrating functionalities into parts and components, as it seems to be possible with surface technologies. And last but not least, the methodology is a backbone of economic efficiency.

Technological limits of processes are not reached. High quality, zero defects, high precision, high productivity and high reliability of complex systems are to be realised by overcoming existing limits of technologies. These goals must be reached by activating the potentials of materials, processes and cognition. The basic understanding of processes and the evaluation of critical areas can activate potentials for a high level of manufacturing. This includes the manufacturing of low value parts and components for high end products.

Manufacturing Engineering itself is the key-technology for innovative manufacturing. Engineers work in digital and virtual environments. They need highly developed tools like CAD/CAM, digital products and digital manufacturing. Development and Innovation of industrial products and processes is experience oriented. Experiments and experiences are the basics for reliability. In the knowledge-based industry, the "costs of experience" – loss of productivity and time – can be reduced by modelling all manufacturing processes.

4. NEW TAYLORISM INTEGRATED IN DIGITAL MANUFACTURING

Taylor defined the basic paradigm for manufacturing management more than 80 years ago. The tayloristic organisation characterises the organisation model of nearly all manufacturing processes and systems. Taylorism divides work for humans based on elementary processes. Work of humans is planned in detail by using basic methodologies like MTM or REFA. Global operating companies in the automotive and other sectors use this methodology to calculate, to compare and to standardise processes worldwide.

This methodology is contradictory to the paradigm of a socio-technical system following knowledge-based manufacturing, manufacturing in networks or principles of self-organisation and self-optimisation. Even the integration of knowledge into machines and systems is not to be combined with detailed process planning for human work. Therefore manufacturers need a new type of Taylorism, which takes into account dynamic change and adaptation, the specific human skills and the requirements of cooperation in networks. A new European standard of manufacturing takes into account the social culture of regions.

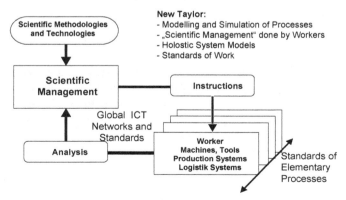

Figure 6 - Taylorism and Production Systems (Taylor, 1983).

The factors accounting for the success of manufacturing industries are mainly related to the great diversity and skills of personnel at all levels. Harnessing these abilities in the factories of the future will be vital to the economies. It will be essential to adapt the structures as quickly as possible, aided by research into all aspects of manufacturing. Rapid evaluation of change under practical conditions, monitoring the success in meeting the demands of markets, and exchanging knowledge are the keys to growth.

4.2 Innovative Manufacturing – adaptation of resources and processes

Experts discussed the reliability and the potential of new manufacturing concepts, which are based on the integration of new technologies in products and their realisation in the production area.

Intelligent Manufacturing's vision are holistic systems operating in parameter fields of high performance and managed by highly skilled workers. They can be adapted by plug and produce and are linked in a digital and virtual engineering and management IT. Some aspects of this vision are to be explained now.

Adaptive manufacturing recombines new and innovative processes, uses intelligent combinations and the flexible configuration of products and manufacturing systems to overcome existing process limitations, and transfers manufacturing know-how using completely new themes or manufacturing-related themes.

- Adaptive manufacturing takes into account the engineering and manufacturing of functional (or adaptive) materials and intelligent manufacturing technologies.
- Adaptive Manufacturing includes the field of automation and robotics. Robots as assistants of humans, hybrid assembly, service robots.
- Adaptive manufacturing includes new solutions of automation by integrating new methods of cognitive information processing, signal processing and production control by high speed information and communication systems.

4.2 Factories are Products – adapted by Manufacturing Engineering in a Digital Environment

Factories are complex and long life products which have to be adapted to the needs of markets, production programs and technologies.

For the adaptation of the resources and the optimisation in early phases companies need a new and advanced competence in manufacturing engineering, which operates in a digital environment and uses tools to adapt the resources and processes. There are 7 layers of structure which have to be adapted in planning processes. All of them are on permanent change (Wiendahl, 2003; Arai, 2000).

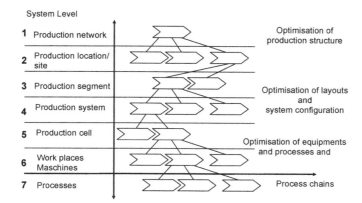

System Level

1 Production network
2 Production location/ site
3 Production segment
4 Production system
5 Production cell
6 Work places Maschines
7 Processes

Optimisation of production structure

Optimisation of layouts and system configuration

Optimisation of equipments and processes and

Process chains

Figure 7 - Factories are products.

The basis of integrated manufacturing systems is a system theory concept which permits the modelling of complex technical systems. Figure 7 shows a fundamental concept for depicting complex technical and organizational processes which seems to be suitable for portraying assembly systems. The system is made up of separate interrelated elements. In an assembly system, these elements may be workplaces or other technical equipment. Interrelations are created as a result of material and information flows. A single element of the assembly system, e.g. an assembly workplace, may be a sub-system which is in turn composed of further elements (Daenzer, 1999; Marks, 1999). It already becomes clear at this point that mechanisms of cooperation and interfaces are decisive features of configurability. Using modern information and control technology, practically all elements can be linked with one

4.3 Advanced Manufacturing Engineering

Alteration processes in manufacturing systems are planned on an elementary basis. For example, alterations to a construction will directly lead to alterations in processes and documents. For the employee executing operations or for the machines, this leads to alterations in such elementary processes as movement, position or function. This also affects digital tools and the fitting and ergonomic design of individual work stations. The corresponding superior level has the function of management and optimization.

Digital manufacturing uses a wide range of engineering and planning tools, software, and information and communication technologies to integrate new technologies into manufacturing processes as quickly and efficiently as possible (Masurat, 2004; Delmia Digitale Fabrik; UGS Digital Manufacturing). The main area of research is the development of integrated tools for industrial engineering and the adaptation of manufacturing, taking into account the configurability of systems.

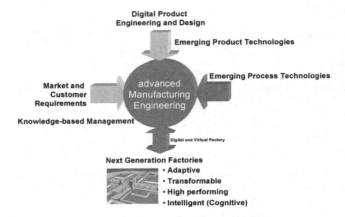

Figure 8 - Advanced Manufacturing Engineering.

Digital manufacturing is the most important technology of the future. It requires:
- distributed data management
- tools for process engineering
- tools for presentation and graphic interfaces
- participative, collaborative and networked engineering
- interfaces to reality

Starting from the digital picture of the factory/manufacturing and by deploying *virtual manufacturing technologies* consisting of simulation tools and specific applications/systems, as well as components of the advanced Industrial Engineering, the planners deal with the factory and manufacturing processes in their dynamicity, by having the reflection of the "as is" and the state in the future "to be", which we call in our approach the *virtual factory/manufacturing*.

Engineering is a key technology. In the German manufacturing industry about 16% of the employees are engineers. They need tools for efficient work, which allows for the quickening of engineering processes and simultaneous work. Digital and virtual manufacturing is able to support manufacturers' work, if these tools are close to reality and linked to manufacturing as it is.

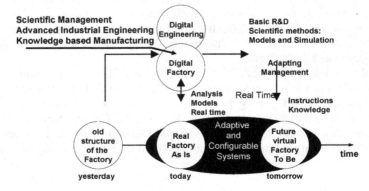

Figure 9 - Digital Manufacturing.

R&D is driven by the vision of fully digital engineering and multi-scale modelling of the dynamic behaviour of products in their whole life cycle. This way it seems to be possible to activate potentials in the utilisation to optimise the life time and to reduce environmental pollution. At present, the developmental activities associated with the digital factory/manufacturing focuses on the planning of factories, production plants, new logistic systems, and of the manufacturing processes. Two advanced digital factory/manufacturing concepts are currently offered by Delmia and Tecnomatix, a few solutions from other companies are also available on the market. These are based on a similar concept: various software tools are mutually networked by a central data management system which constitutes the core of the integrated solutions incorporated in the product spectrum of the respective software supplier. The object of the endeavour is to ensure that all planning results are always completely up-to-date and are available to the authorised users at any time. With these concepts and by using a large spectrum of simulation application/systems, a virtual and scalable system constitutes the platform for a high-end visualisation of the planning results and thus facilitates interdisciplinary communication among various experts, despite differences in specialised terminology.

4.4 The Real-Time Factory

Everyone knows that intelligent manufacturing systems can also be linked up to communications technology networks to assure real-time adaptation. For the future new technologies like RFID, MES, Wireless, Grid Computing and others lead to the vision of a real-time factory or Smart factory.

From here, it is possible to proceed to networks, factories, manufacturing segments and systems integrated in a ubiquitous information supply. We call it "Smart Factories". As a result of these developments, value-adding structures are changing in companies manufacturing and using holistic production systems. This opens up new potentials for manufacturers and users alike. The machines and equipment delivered by them remain within information technology networks for service reasons, for monitoring the operation status (tele-presence) and for technical consulting purposes when reconditioning and optimizing operations.

5. SUMMARY

This presentation is based on the challenges of global manufacturing and driving forces. The global era of manufacturing is influenced by economic and technological factors to increase dynamic innovation and adaptation to the turbulent environment. Digital manufacturing is a key for adaptation and based on modern tools and techniques for engineering, control, supervision and management in a network. The vision of manufacturing towards Manufacturing of the Future has been formulated in the European Manufacturing Platform (Manufuture).

Taking into account the dynamics of markets and innovation the industrial engineering has a key role in the fast adaptation and complexity when factories are seen as scalable products. Optimisation of systems, data management and knowledge are new challenges for engineers and their work. It will be done in a digital world linked by global information systems. This is the new era of manufacturing – the digital manufacturing.

6. REFERENCES

1. Bullinger, Warnecke, Westkämper: Neue Organisationsformen in Unternehmen, Berlin, u.a.: Springer 2002
2. Daenzer, W. F./Huber, F. (Hrsg.): Systems Engineering – Methodik and Praxis. 10. Aufl. Zürich: Verlag Industrielle organization, 1999
3. http://www.delmia.de
4. http://www.manufuture.org
5. http://www.ugs.com/products/tecnomatix
6. Taylor, Frederick W.: Gesellschaft für Sozialwissenschaftliche und Ökologische Forschung: Die Grundsätze wissenschaftlicher Betriebsführung: Nachdruck der Original-Ausgabe von 1919. 2. Auflage, München: Raben Verlag, 1983
7. T. Arai (1), Y. Aiyama, Y. Maeda, J. Ota Agile Assembly System by "Plug & Produce"; Annals of the CIRP 2000
8. Marks, S.: Gemeinsame Gestaltung von technology and organization in soziotechnischen kybernetischen Systemsn. Düsseldorf: VDI-Verlag, 1999
9. Masurat, T.: Open Digital Factory, White Paper: Available at: http://www.sim-serv.com/wg2.php, 2004
10. Nyhuis, P., Elscher, A.: Process Model for Factory Planning. In: Proceedings of the 38th International Seminar On Manufacturing Systems, Florianopolis, Brazil, 16-18 May, 2005
11. Warnecke, H.J.: Aufbruch zum fraktalen Unternehmen, Berlin: Springer 1995 Daenzer, W. F./Huber, F. (Hrsg.): Systems Engineering – Methodik and Praxis. 10. Aufl. Zürich: Verlag Industrielle Organization, 1999
12. Westkämper, E., Hummel, V.: The Stuttgart Enterprise Mode. Integrated Engineering of Strategic & Operational Functions. In: Proceedings of the 38th International Seminar On Manufacturing Systems, Florianopolis, Brazil, 16-18 May, 2005
13. Wiendahl, H.-P., Heger, C. L.: Justifying Changeability: A Methodical Approach to Achieving Cost Effectiveness. In: 2nd International Conference on Reconfigurable Manufacturing, Ann Arbor, USA, 20-21 August, 2003

GLOBAL MANUFACTURING – CHALLENGES AND SOLUTIONS

Hans-Peter Wiendahl
Institut für Fabrikanlagen und Logistik
Leibniz Universität Hannover, Germanyr
wiendahl@ifa.uni-hannover.de

The design and the operation of global supply chains has become a new challenge for many production enterprises, additional to the existing problems in everyday practice.
However, with increasing success followed up by growth the weak points often show up in the order execution process. This becomes apparent in a bad delivery performance, increasing inventories and frequent special actions.
The consequences are that the essential business processes, product design, process design, production and order fulfillment must be reviewed in a comprehensive cooperative process.
The classical single step order partially turns around due to the market priority of fulfilling customer wishes within short delivery times. Local optimization in a single enterprise can even be counterproductive.
The requirements for products, processes, production equipment and logistics in global supply chains require pliable solutions. These solutions have to take into account costs for material and added values at the respective production place, local conditions concerning knowledge and local content, currency relations between production locations and markets, commercial law terms, as well as protection from imitation.
The paper describes the challenge more from a scenario point of view, giving first solutions from industrial practice and formulating new fields of research in the production science.

1. PITFALLS IN GLOBAL SUPPLY CHAINS

The operation of global supply chains is a new challenge for many manufacturing companies. This does not only apply to the automobile industry and its suppliers but meanwhile also to medium-sized enterprises which serve international markets with high-quality special products.

With increasing success and the growth connected with it, weak points frequently appear in the order handling. Bad delivery performance and frequent special actions are typical. The main reasons are the wrong planning methods besides the bad customers and supplier connections, the use of insufficient control models, bad forecast quality, and missing logistic monitoring. In the operative phase too little attention is given on a consistent target system for punctuality, inventory, utilization, and delivery time. Also, regular checks of the planning parameters, such as plan lead time, lot sizes, and capacity are not being performed (Wiendahl et al. 2005).

Since global supply chains are naturally subject to quick changes, further weaknesses show up in the design of the products with regard to the variants. The manufacturing and assembly processes are inflexible at larger quantity changes.

In the past product development and order handling were regarded as primary processes whereas the order fulfilment and distribution were seen more as auxiliary functions. But nowadays the reliable delivery has a highest priority in globally distributing markets. This priority has to subordinate the development of the products, processes and production facilities to logistics.

The new requirements can be summarized in the following points:

- The arrangement of business processes and supply chains must be primarily carried out from the view of the market demand distributed globally.
- Instead of central factories with high production depth close to the market, adaptable and perhaps temporary production units are required.
- The production logistics must act in harmony with the purchasing and distribution logistics.
- Different order types in the same factory must be mastered with different planning and control procedures within the same planning system.
- Product structures must quickly adapt to the changing requirements of an internationally distributed production.
- Production and assembly methods must take into account local points of view with regard to know-how, labour costs and local-content regulations.

2. UNDERSTANDING THE SUPPLY CHAIN

The design of global supply chains follows a systematic procedure, the main rules of which are:

Supply Chain is a customer-oriented and value increasing design, planning and control of the global enterprise network for the processes "customer order to payment receipt" and "supply order to payment". It follows the principles integral, process-oriented, simply, transparent and time-optimized based on standards, and summarizes the responsibility for all material, information and value streams for the fulfilment of the customer orders (Nyhuis, 2006).

As an example for the purchase process altogether 6 models were defined based on the SCOR model, figure 1.

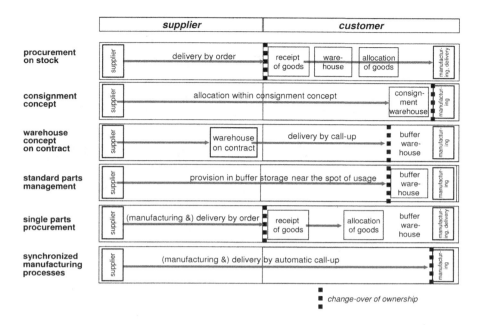

Figure 1 - Standard Procurement Models (SIEMENS AG).

Figure 1 starts with the classical individual procurement on stock, consumption near stocks such as the consignment concept and standard part management, then followed up by the automated call concept of the synchronous production. The aim is to minimize the inventory risk of the buyer at a maximum supply safety.

Models were also defined in the same way for the production process. The division defined originally by the company Philips has largely proved itself into three order types.

On the one hand it is distinguished, whether it is a series product or custom designed product and on the other hand whether a specific engineering effort is still required. The case "engineer to order" is typical of the machines and facility industry. A real supply chain in the classic meaning does not exist in the case of engineered orders because it is either a single or even a unique product. The two other cases "make to stock" and "make to order" are the standard cases in practice.

A producer would ideally like to manufacture and store (make to stock) finished products as little as possible because of the obsolescence risk and the capital binding. But if he makes the product only when an order arrives (make to order), the internal lead time is usually too long compared with the desired delivery time figure 2 illustrates such a case at the example of a multistage product on the left side. The overall lead time (here called replenishment time) is considerably longer than the usual market delivery time.

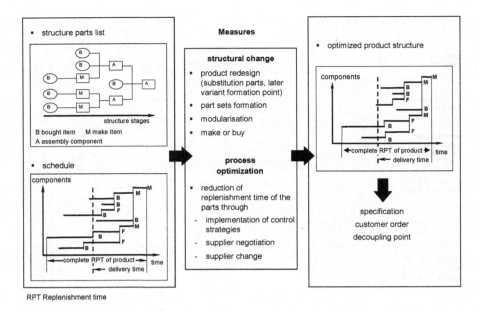

RPT Replenishment time

Figure 2 - Optimisation of a product structure (Nyhuis, 2006).

As a first step in order to solve that problem the number of stages of the product would be reduced and modules would be used. In the second step the transition time of the components would be lowered by optimization of the plan lead times and lot sizes or by negotiation with suppliers. These measures often do not suffice however, and a subdivision of the product must be carried out into order-neutral and order-specific components. This takes place at the so-called variant decoupling point.

In such a case far-reaching design considerations are required for the products in a global supply chain. One will often try to manufacture the order neutral components with a high automation level at the home place while the order-specific additions are configured as closely to the market as possible in short time to the desired end product.

An impressive example of such an approach is a module system developed by the company Sartorius in Göttingen for laboratory scales. The central component consists of the so-called monolith; it replaces the previous lever construction by one single work piece which is milled from an aluminium block. Figure 3 compares the old and the new design. It was possible to reduce the number of parts for the whole system by 27%. Based on this component manufactured in Göttingen and completed to a measuring cell it is possible to offer very different scales in the design and in the application.

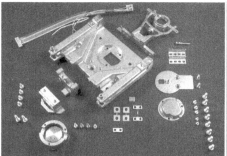

Figure 3 - Example of a product re-design (Sartorius AG).

The following logistics oriented design rules for products are suitable in global supply chains:

- Apply as few as possible product stages.
- Avoid long delivery times in low product stages.
- Create variants in product stages as high as possible.
- Separate the product into subcomponents with high and low wage share.
- Develop modules and platforms
- Consider technical copy protection

3. CHANGEABILITY ENABLERS OF SUPPLY CHAINS

As a next step after the redesign of the product it has to be looked at the manufacturing and assembly systems, and even at of the entire factory and its operative control. Because of the various influences from product design and market requirements, new technologies as well as currency and trade regulations it is no longer possible to fix a stable product range in the long run. The mandatory conclusion arises that the more unsafe the forecast is the more adaptable a production site must be. An exhibition hall in which heterogeneous events like a machine tool fair, a consumer goods fair, or a rock concert take place can be regarded as a vision of a highly adaptable factory.

The capital expenditure connected to such an approach can usually not be provided by a manufacturing company. However, it has been very successful to pay attention to the so called changeability enablers (Wiendahl 2002).

The outstanding enabler is modularity. A modular design allows a high rate of reuse for all objects of the supply chain and at all levels in different applications. The changeability quality of an object is further marked by its universality to accomplish different tasks. For example, the laser beam is universal for the production of metal parts unlike a form-bound punch die. Scalability permits extending or reducing the output of a resource economically, by e.g. a flexible working schedule. As the fourth enabler the mobility of a resource allows shifting quickly both within a site and between production sites. Mobility requires a self-supporting construction without foundations and a quick dismantling and refurbishing into standard transport units. Finally, the compatibility of machinery and also standardized interfaces of software secure the fast networking of facilities (Koren 2005).

These enabling features generally do require additional costs compared with conventional non-changeable solutions. However, these costs are frequently overestimated because also the manufacturers follow a similar strategy to be able to adapt their products to the special customer wishes. The additional costs contrast with the increased changeability in form of shorter downtimes. In any case it is rewarding at every new investment – is it production or logistics facilities, a building or software – these five enablers should be questioned systematically for every object (Wiendahl Heger 2004).

Some examples of adaptable facilities are introduced to production, assembly, and at factory level in the following which shall serve as a suggestion for projects of their own.

Manufacturing

In the production one has always tried to reuse production components as much as possible by a far-reaching application of modules. This reduces the design effort, decreases the functional risk and shortens the delivery time. In the context of the order handling in a supply chain, however, not only pure technical aspects have to be included. Figure 4 shows a systematic approach which starts out from the idea of a production module completely able to work autonomously (Drabow 2006).

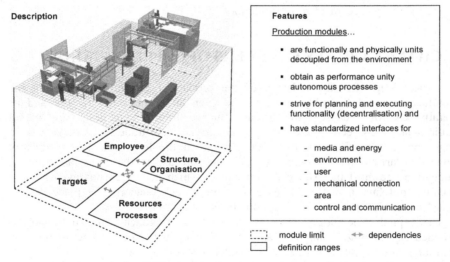

Figure 4 - Definition of production modules (Drabow, 2006).

Besides the real resources for the fulfilment of a process it is also looked at the targets, employees, as well as the inner module structure and the connection to the superior organization. The listed qualities of production modules in the figure make obvious, that the approach has great similarity to the concept of segments, holons or fractals. However, the depicted module aims at allowing a fast reconfiguration to whole production systems on the shop floor level.

An interface definition which permits a computer-aided design and quick reconfiguration of production systems is therefore included. Special interface types have been developed which include soluble interfaces for a quick reconfiguration besides the "classical" ones. Those soluble interfaces correspond with the change-ability enabler "compatibility". Altogether, the approach is not unproblematic because the interfaces need a high precision and stiffness. This means noticeable additional expenses. And the manufacturer must guarantee a long-standing subsequent delivery of single modules.

Assembly

The mentioned problems of reconfigurable production systems are by far not as serious at assembly systems because the supplier industry offers modular scalable and mobile assembly systems for many years already.

For the application in global supply chains the changeability qualities of assembly systems still must be enlarged regarding the degree of automation. It is then possible, depending on the location of the assembly, to change the deployment of personnel. These so-called hybrid assembly systems combine automatic stations with manual stations. With respect to diversity of variants, productivity, and flexibility they are positioned between the manual assembly and automated assembly system (Lotter, 2006).

Figure 5 shows an example of such an assembly module with one assembly operator being employed. His activities are supplemented by three automatic stations for impressing, grease, and final test. The system is highly economic because the share of non value adding so-called secondary operations can be reduced to a minimum.

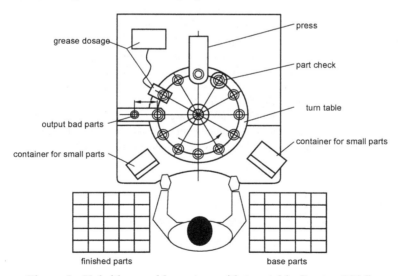

Figure 5 - Hybrid assembly system with turn table (Lotter, 2006).

A special advantage lies in the scalability of the system. This permits an expandable output in little steps which is achieved on the one hand by the automation of single operations and on the other hand by the combination of several modules to a system. Figure 6 shows the rough layout of the system. (Lotter, 2006).

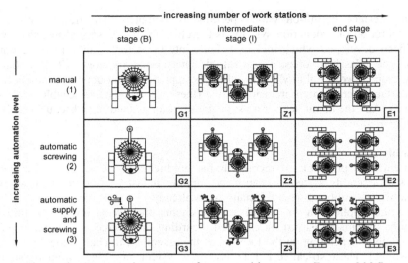

Figure 6 - Construction stages of an assembly system (Lotter, 2006).

In the basic stage B1 the complete pre and final assembly is carried out at an individual assembly table by hand. Automatic system stations are provided merely for the press fitting operation. In a first step, the screws are inserted automatically at the automated stages, see case B2. At the following construction stage G3 the supplying of the screws is automated with vibration bowl feeder's at all rotary work piece holders. The individual pre-assemblies and the final assembly spread out on three assembly tables in the intermediate construction stages I1 to I3. And the assembly spreads out with increasing volume to be produced on four individual assembly tables in the end stages E1 to E3.

The pure assembly costs of an automated system were compared with a modular hybrid assembly system in a specific example (Lotter, 2006). A quantity range had to be covered between 1,000 and 10,000 products per day. Target costs of EUR 0.21 per piece were predefined. Figure 7 shows the corresponding cost curves which reveal that the assembly automat reaches the target costs of the modular system only at a production rate of 6,000 to 9,500 pieces per day whereas considerable additional costs of the automatic system can be expected below these quantities.

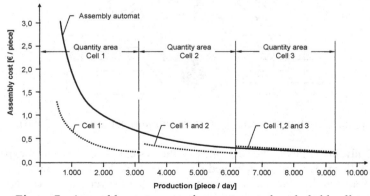

Figure 7 - Assembly cost comparison automated vs. hybrid cells.

In addition, a noticeable employment effect is connected with the cell solution, because 2 workers are employed per cell and shift.

Such concepts are therefore particularly suitable for quickly variable products and quantities because:

- the investment is considerably lower compared with an automated system designed for the final quantity,
- the risk of a bad investment is lower as well,
- the assembly unit costs are already in the target area of a final construction stage with use of the first construction stage,
- in the context of the actual development of the demand the development can gradually be carried out and
- single assembly cells can be used differently at decline in the demand.

4. PARADIGM OF THE GLOBAL PRODUCTION SYSTEM

The outlined problems and examples are far away from a closed system approach and do not lay the claim of a complete scientific penetration of the global production. The effect on the real operative control of such supply chains and the optimization connected to that was not treated. For example questions of an adequate training of the employees planning as well as the consideration of an adequate technical copy protection still have to be deepened.

A combined project called "global variant production system", short GVP, supported by the BMBF (German Ministry of Education and Research) therefore investigates the systematic penetration of these and broader problems with 6 companies and 2 research institutes being involved (GVP 2006). The goal is the development and proof testing of a highly flexible production system for high-quality mechatronic products which are producible manually or automated in variable quantities and in high a diversity of variants at different global locations. Figure 8 shows the project structure.

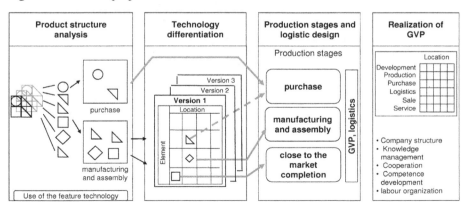

Figure 8 - The global variant production system GVP.

5. CONCLUSION

The explanations about the consequences of global supply chains have shown that for technical products the essential business processes product construction, process design, production and order fulfilment must be reviewed in a cooperative process starting with the customer order fulfilment at the highest priority. The requirements on products, processes, production facilities, and logistics in global supply chains require adaptable solutions under consideration of:

- costs for material and creation of value of the respective production place,
- local conditions with regard to know how and local content,
- currency relations between production locations and markets,
- boundary conditions referring to commercial law as well as
- technical copy protection.

Furthermore it is clear, that the quick and nevertheless economic change ability of all required resources is an important conducting principle.

6. REFERENCES

1. Drabow, G.: Modulare Gestaltung und ganzheitliche Bewertung wandlungsfähiger Fertigungssysteme.
2. Diss. Universität Hannover 2006
3. GVP Globales Varianten-Produktions-System: http://www.gvp-projekt.de/. Read out July 12, 2006
4. Koren, Y.: Reconfigurable Manufacturing and Beyond (Keynote Paper). In: Proceedings 3rd International CIRP Conference on Reconfigurable Manufacturing, University of Michigan, Ann Arbor, Michigan, 11.05.2005, p. 1-6
5. Lotter, E.: Hybride Montagesysteme. In: Lotter, B. u. Wiendahl H.-P. (Hrsg.) Montage in der industriellen Produktion. Ein Handbuch für die Praxis. Springer Verlag 2006
6. Nyhuis, P.: Gestaltung und Betrieb von Logistiksystemen. In: Executive MBA in Technologie-management und Logistik St. Gallen 09.01. – 13.01. 2006
7. Wiendahl, H.-H.; Cieminski G. von; Wiendahl, H.-P.: Stumbling blocks of PPC: Towards the holistic configuration of PPC-Systems. Production Planning & Control, Vol. 16, No. 7, October 2005, 634-651
8. Wiendahl, H.-P.; Heger, C.L.: Justifying Changeability – A Methodical Approach to Achieving Cost Effectiveness. In: The International Journal For Manufacturing Science & Production, Vol. 6, No. 1/2, 2004, p. 33-39
9. Wiendahl, H.-P.: Wandlungsfähigkeit – Schlüsselbegriff der zukunftsfähigen Fabrik. In: wt Werkstatttstechnik online, Jahrg. 92, Nr. 4, 2002, S. 122-127

EMERGENT SYNTHESIS APPROACHES TO BIOLOGICAL MANUFACTURING SYSTEMS

Kanji Ueda
The University of Tokyo, Japan
ueda@race.u-tokyo.ac.jp

This paper introduces the concept of Biological Manufacturing Systems (BMS), and then provides details of emergent synthesis. Next, it describes emergent synthesis based case studies of BMS: 1) Self-Organisation of Manufacturing Systems, 2) Emergence of Supply Chain Networks, and 3) BMS Introducing Bounded Rationality.

1. INTRODUCTION

Increasing complexity and uncertainty arise from factors such as 1) individualization of lifestyles, 2) diversification of culture, 3) globalisation of industrial activities, and 4) growing consideration toward natural environment. Those factors bring about practical and theoretical difficulties in all domains of artifactual activities, from the planning phase through post-sales activities, such as the combinatorial explosion of possible states, incomplete data and knowledge, dynamic changes in environment, the frame problem, etc. To address such difficulties, biological manufacturing systems (BMS) present a promising concept.

The concept of BMS proposed (Ueda, 1992) is a next-generation manufacturing system which adapts dynamically to *non-predeterministic* changes in both internal and external environments based on biologically-inspired ideas such as self-organisation, adaptation, evolution, and learning. The basic theory for BMS is *Emergent Synthesis* (Ueda, Markus, et al., 2001). Synthesis is a necessary component of problem-solving processes in almost all phases of an artefact's life cycle. It starts with design, continues through the phases of planning, production, and consumption, and ends with disposal of the product. The central question is how we can solve the problem of synthesis: how to determine the system's structure, which exhibits its function, to achieve a purpose under the constraints of dynamic environments and incomplete information.

This keynote paper starts with the concept of BMS, followed by details of emergent synthesis. Subsequently, it describes several emergent synthetic approaches to BMS.

2. CONCEPT OF BMS

Conceptually, BMS was devised in connection with new fields of computer science such as Evolutionary Computation, Artificial Life, and Adaptive Complex Systems (Langton, 1989). It has also been involved in many international projects such as the Intelligent Manufacturing Systems Program.

Biological organisms can adapt themselves to environmental changes and sustain their own life by exhibiting functions such as self-recognition, self-growth, self-recovery, and evolution. These functions of organisms are displayed by expressing two types of biological information: genetic information evolving through progressive generations (DNA-type) and individually achieved information during one's lifetime (BN-type) by learning. Unification of biological information with individuals makes living systems autonomous but adaptive.

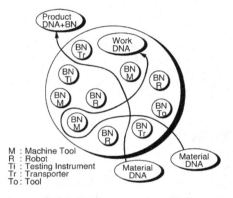

Figure 1 – Concept of BMS for floor level.

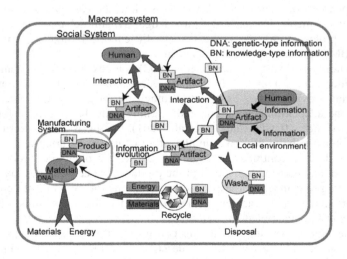

Figure 2 – Extension of BMS concept.

Figure 1 depicts all system elements in the BMS model such as work materials, machine tools, transporters, robots, etc (Ueda, et al., 1997). The illustration resembles that of an autonomous organism. Products develop from raw materials expressing their own DNA-type information. The product continues to learn BN-type information as knowledge through its lifetime. As a result, the product can resolve malfunctions autonomously and can be recycled and disposed of easily. Moreover, its design can be evolved for next-generation products, as shown in Figure 2.

3. EMERGENT SYNTHESIS

3.1 Problem of Synthesis

The use of the term *synthesis* is related to human activities for creation of artifacts, while analysis is related mainly to natural things. Analysis is an effective method to clarify the causality of existing natural systems in fields such as physics. Analysis methods enable us to explore the structure that realises the functions of systems, whether natural or artificial. On the other hand, synthesis is indispensable for creating artifacts that satisfy required functions. The latter type of problem, i.e., from function to structure, should be called the inverse problem, whereas the former, from structure to function, should be called the direct problem. Figure 3 shows the essential problem of how to determine the system's structure to realise its function and thereby achieve a purpose under environmental constraints.

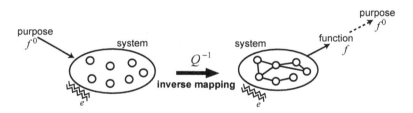

Figure 3 – Problem of synthesis.

The main concern here is when and whether completeness of information can be achieved in the description of the environment and in the specification of the purpose of the artifactual system. With respect to the incompleteness of information on the environment and/or the specification, the difficulties in synthesis can be categorised into three classes (Ueda, Markus, et al., 2001).

- Class I – Problem with complete description: if information of the environment and specifications are given completely, then the problem is entirely described. However, it is often difficult to find an optimal solution.
- Class II – Problem with incomplete environment description: the specification is complete, but the information on the environment is incomplete. The problem is not completely described now. Therefore, it is difficult to cope with the dynamic properties of the unknown environment.

- Class III – Problem with incomplete specification: the environment description and the specification are incomplete. Problem solving, therefore, must start with an ambiguous purpose; human interaction becomes significant.

3.2 Emergence

The traditional, i.e., analytic and deterministic approaches based on top-down principles are unsuitable for solving the above-mentioned problems. Instead, emergent approaches would be more feasible. As figure 4 indicates, the term *emergence* is used here in the following sense: "A global order of structure expressing a new function is formed through bi-directional dynamic processes, where local interactions between elements reveal global behaviour, and the global behaviour results in new constraints on the behaviour of the elements". The important element here is the formation of a stable global order, which is neither fixed, periodical nor chaotic, but rather a complex structure. A stable global order gives a new function. If that function meets the specified purpose, one can adopt it as a solution. The definition given above is fundamentally compatible with that used in Artificial Life and in Complex Adaptive System studies (Ueda, et al., 1999).

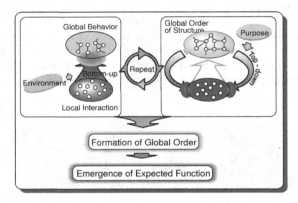

Figure 4 – Concept of emergence.

3.3 Models of Emergent Synthesis

Instead of traditional approaches, which are analytic and deterministic, emergence based approaches are being developed with both bottom-up and top-down features. They include evolutionary computation, self-organisation, behaviour-based methods, reinforcement learning, multi-agent systems, game theory, etc. They are promising for offering efficient, robust and adaptive solutions to the problem of synthesis.

Figure 5 shows a schematic view of conceptual models for emergent synthetic approaches to problems assigned to the three classes discussed above (Ueda, Markus, et al., 2001). For Class I, because the specification of purpose and the constraints attributable to the environment are fixed, the problem is known completely from the very beginning. However, in most cases, too many feasible solutions exist, which engenders combinatorial explosion and creates so-called NP-hard problems. Therefore, it is necessary to develop efficient, robust search methods to find optimal solutions. For this type of problem, evolutionary computation methods have been applied: genetic algorithms, genetic programming, evolutionary strategies, and evolutionary programming. Hence, this class of models can be characterised as fixed, both in its syntax and semantics.

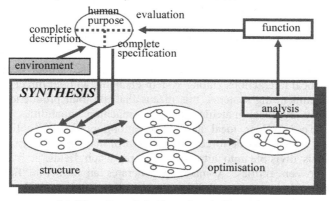

(a) Class I model: Complete information.

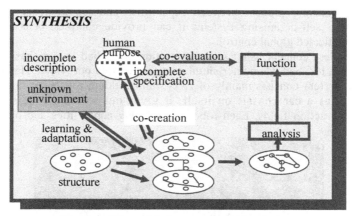

(b) Class III model: Incomplete information.

Figure 5 – Model of emergent synthesis.

In Class II, in spite of the fixed specification, missing information about the environment engenders unforeseen constraints of problem solving. One must unveil these constraints via repeated interactions with the environment. Learning and adaptation based approaches, such as reinforcement learning or adaptive behaviour based methods, are feasible to resolve this class of problems. Fixed semantics and adaptive syntax characterise models belonging to this class.

In Class III problems, in addition to the lack of environmental information, we must cope with the ambiguity of human intention. Problem-solving in this class must include the iterative determination of system structure; moreover, human designers should be considered to include changing specifications. Therefore, to realise human participation in the design of the target system (object) – including the designer itself (subject) – additional emergent properties are essential for this class: e.g., co-creation, co-evolution and self-reference.

4. CASE STUDIES OF BMS

4.1 Self-organisation of Manufacturing Systems

Self-organisation is defined as the process of emerging global behaviour that emerges from local interactions among system elements without direct control from outside. In manufacturing systems, this means that the total production process is provided merely by local matching between machine capabilities and product requirements. To introduce local interaction among production entities, we use potential fields, which provide force as a function of distance between entities. The potential field is divisible into attraction and repulsion fields; it realises spatial interactions between entities. A machine generates an attraction field to get a product according to its own capabilities. On the other hand, an AGV can sense the attraction field and move to the source of field according to the requirement of a product. It gives the product to the machine when the AGV arrives at the machine. This local matching process between capabilities and requirements is the core engine of the self-organising system; it can provide complex behaviour easily without complicated global control.

This line-less concept using self-organisation is applied to car chassis welding processes as a test bed. Computer simulations are carried out (Ueda, Hatono, et al., 2001). The system consists mainly of AGVs and welding robots. In this example, each AGV has a car chassis on itself; it gives out welding requirements by generating attraction fields. Each robot has welding capabilities and moves to an

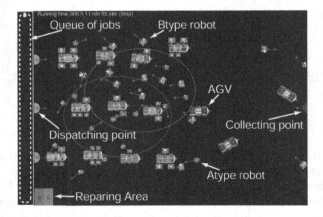

Figure 6 - Snapshot of line-less welding system.

AGV according to the sensed attraction fields. The production floor is 75 m × 50 m. The respective numbers of ATYPE welding robots, BTYPE robots, and AGVs are 30, 35 and 25. The work milieu includes a queue to stock AGVs, three dispatching areas for new product, and a collecting area for finished product.

Figure 6 shows a snapshot of the simulation. Although no order is visible initially in the simulation, a global order, production line like order, are visible in the stable state. The proposed method using self-organisation has been verified in terms of high-variety production, robustness to malfunction, easy system reconfiguration, and cost evaluation.

4.2 Emergence of Supply Chain Networks

The model under consideration consists of a customer, dealer, producer, and supplier agents. The key feature in the method is the autonomous and independent activity of respective agents. Interactions among the agents happen through the products in the direction from producer to customer, and through monetary feedback in the direction from customer to producer.

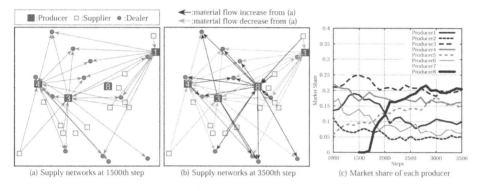

(a) Supply networks at 1500th step   (b) Supply networks at 3500th step   (c) Market share of each producer

Figure 7 – Snapshots of simulation of supply network emergence.

Figure 7 illustrates the emergence of supply chain networks (Ueda, et al., 1999). The simulation starts with the conditions of 800 customers, 12 dealers, 12 suppliers, 7 producers, and 7 kinds of products. The number of producers is changed from 7 to 8 at the 1500th step to elucidate the effect of introducing a new producer (denoted as number 8). Figures 7(a) and 7(b) depict two snapshots of the networks that emerged respectively at the 1500th and 3500th steps. For the sake of clarity, in figures 7(a) and 7(b), we did not plot all the customers, and the four producers with smallest shares at the 1500th step were omitted. figure 7(c) shows the change of the market share of all producers at steps 1000–3500. Because of the participation of the new producer, the structure of the networks changes remarkably: some new networks emerge and others disappear. The amount of material flow at figure 7(b) also largely differs from that for figure 7(a). The new producer rapidly increases its market share and ultimately wins (figure 7(c)). The winning producer is characterised by providing low-cost products with average technical properties and appropriate distances from both suppliers and dealers.

4.3 BMS Introducing Bounded Rationality

This chapter presents a novel approach (Kito, et al., 2004) by introducing bounded rationality as a characteristic of agents to develop their behaviour in BMS.

Clarifying the definition and description of bounded rationality, the approach is implemented in an Ant System (AS) model. The model is intended to handle uncertainty in the perception, action, and inner structure of agents by introducing bounded rationality in their characteristics. Computer simulation demonstrates the effectiveness of the approach by indicating considerable improvement in the performance of the modelled BMS

The AS simulation is presented as a preliminary experiment. Ants exhibit complexly organised behaviour, e.g. forming lines from the nest to food, but each ant has extremely poor capabilities and interacts with other ants locally using a pheromone substance. This section introduces bounded-rational ants into the colony and confirms the improvement of their overall foraging efficiency.

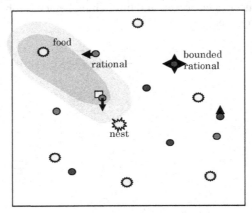

Figure 8 – Model of an ant system introducing bounded-rational ants.

Figure 8 shows that this simulation subsumes a discrete-time model and a discrete two-dimensional finite space as the environment (200 × 200). The agents are 200 ants and the system is an ant group. Ten feeding stations exist in positions that are initially unknown to the ants. Each feeding station has 200 food units. The system goal is to gather all food to the nest in the centre of the environment in the shortest possible time. Each ant has its own goal of gathering as much food as possible, but it remains ignorant of the system goal.

Each ant has four behaviour alternatives: move forward, back, left or right. In the case of a rational ant, the agent moves in the direction of a feeding station if it finds one, or moves where the pheromone density is highest. It selects a behaviour randomly if it can find neither a feeding station nor a pheromone. On the other hand, in the case of bounded-rational ant, it heads in the direction of a feeding station if it finds one, or selects a behaviour randomly otherwise, i.e., it uses no pheromone information.

Figure 9 shows a simulated transition of the average execution time steps of 20 experiments required for gathering all the food according to the number of bounded-rational ants among the 200 ants. This result indicates that the relative performances of systems including several quantities of bounded-rational ants (number of bounded-rational ants is 25, 50, 75 and 100) are greater than for the system including only rational ants (bounded-rational ants are zero).

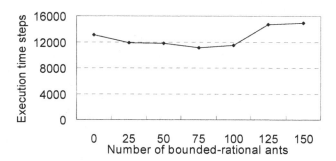

Figure 9 – Transition of performance according to the
number of bounded-rational ants.

The BMS model, which is based on the self-organisation method, verifies the effectiveness of the proposed idea (Ueda, et al., 2006). The jobs supplied from the dispatching point are carried by AGVs toward appropriate machines and are processed. After processing, the finished jobs are carried by AGVs toward the collection point, which is located at the same position as the dispatching point. This process flow is self-organised through matching of job requirements and machine capabilities. Each machine creates attraction fields according to its capabilities, and each AGV becomes sensitive to a particular attraction field according to the work-piece that it is carrying, and moves to the input/output buffer of machines. The rational AGV moves in the direction of the attraction force if it senses an attraction field; otherwise, it takes no action. In the case of a bounded-rational AGV, it stays without action until a certain time has elapsed even if it senses an attraction field.

Figure 10 shows the makespan, which is the time from when the first job is dispatched to that when the last job is collected. This simulation was executed by changing the number of bounded-rational AGVs from 4. This result shows that bounded-rational AGVs contributed to improve system performance. In this case, the makespan was approximately 34% shorter when two AGVs were bounded-rational than when all AGVs were rational.

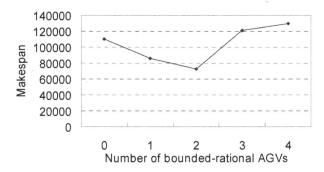

Figure 10 – Transition of makespan according to the number of
bounded-rational AGVs.

5. CONCLUSIONS

This keynote has introduced the concept of BMS, which adapts dynamically to non-predeterministic changes in manufacturing environments based on biologically inspired ideas such as self-organisation, adaptation, evolution, and learning. The basic theory for BMS is *Emergent Synthesis*, by which the central question is how to determine the system's structure to exhibit its function and achieve a purpose under informational incompleteness. With respect to the incompleteness of information about the environment and specifications related to the purpose, difficulties in synthesis can be categorised into three classes: Class 1 problems with complete description of the information of both the specification and environment; Class II problems with incomplete environment description; and Class III problems, with incomplete specifications.

The results presented in this paper also underscore the effectiveness and feasibility of the proposed concepts by showing three examples of emergent synthetic approaches to BMS: 1) Self-Organisation of Manufacturing Systems, 2) Emergence of Supply Chain Networks, and 3) BMS Introducing Bounded Rationality.

6. REFERENCES

1. Kito, T., Fujii, N., and Ueda, K. Co-Creative Decision Making in Artifactual Systems in Consideration of Bounded Rationality. Proceedings of the International Conference on Experiments in Economic Sciences: New Approaches to Solving Real-World Problems; Kyoto, 2004; 303-317.
2. Langton, C. "Artificial Life". In *Artificial Life*, C. Langton ed. Addison Wesley, 1989; 1-47.
3. Ueda, K. A Concept for Bionic Manufacturing Systems Based on DNA-type Information. Proceedings of IFIP 8th International PROLAMAT Conference; Tokyo, 1992; 853-863.
4. Ueda, K., Hatono, I., Fujii, N. and Vaario, J. Line-Less Production System Using Self-Organization: A Case Study for BMS. Annals of the CIRP, 2001; 50/1: 319-322.
5. Ueda, K., Kito, T. and Fujii, N. Modelling Biological Manufacturing Systems with Bounded-Rational Agents. Annals of the CIRP, 2006; 55/1: 469-472.
6. Ueda, K., Markus, A., Monostori, L., Kals, H.J.J. and Arai, T. Emergent Synthesis Methodologies for Manufacturing. Annals of the CIRP, 2001; 50/2: 335-365.
7. Ueda, K., Vaario, J., and Ohkura, K. Modelling of Biological Manufacturing Systems for Dynamic Reconfiguration. Annals of the CIRP, 1997; 46/1: 343-346.
8. Ueda, K., Vaario, J., Takeshita, T., and Hatono, I. An Emergent Synthetic Approach to Supply Networks. Annals of the CIRP, 1999; 48/1: 377-380.

RECONFIGURABLE PROCESS PLANS FOR RESPONSIVE MANUFACTURING SYSTEMS

Hoda A. ElMaraghy
Canada Research Chair in Manufacturing Systems,
Professor and Director, Intelligent Manufacturing Systems (IMS) Centre,
University of Windsor, Canada
hae@uwindsor.ca

This keynote paper focuses on the process plans and planning functions as the important link between the features of generations of products/product families and the features, capabilities and configurations of manufacturing systems and components throughout their respective life cycles. The challenges presented by the paradigm shift in manufacturing systems and their increased flexibility and changeability require corresponding responsiveness in all support functions. Process planning is part of the "soft" or "logical" enablers of changeability in this new environment. New perspectives on process planning for Flexible (FMS) and Reconfigurable (RMS) manufacturing systems in integrated digital manufacturing enterprises are presented. Process plans reconfiguration and their pre-requisites, characteristics, modeling and solution approaches, potential automation, and integration with both products and systems models as they evolve are discussed. New concepts of "Evolving Products Families" and "Reconfigurable Process Plans" are introduced and their ramifications for process planning approaches are outlined. The distinguishing features of process plans and planning methodologies in flexible, reconfigurable and changeable manufacturing systems, for both planned and un-planned products changes, are highlighted. Future research directions and challenges in process planning, being one of the enablers for changeable and responsive manufacturing systems, are presented.

1. INTRODUCTION

Global competition and unpredictable frequent market changes are challenges facing manufacturing enterprises at present. There is a need for reducing cost and improving quality of highly customized products. Responsiveness, agility and high performance of manufacturing systems are driving the recent paradigm shifts and call for new approaches to achieve cost-effective responsiveness at all levels of the enterprise. It is becoming important that the manufacturing system and all its support functions, both at the physical and logical levels, can accommodate these changes and be usable across several generations of products and product families.

Modern manufacturing paradigms aim to achieve these multi-objectives. For example, flexible manufacturing systems (FMS) provide pre-planned generalized flexibility built-in a priori, while reconfigurable manufacturing systems (FMS) aim at providing customized flexibility by offering the functionality and capacity needed when needed. Many enablers are required for the successful implementation of these paradigms and achieving the desired adaptability. The flexibility, changeability and reconfigurability of the hardware components and systems are essential. However, more often what represents the most formidable challenge is the soft or logical support functions, such as product/process modeling, process planning, process and production control strategies and logistics, which must not only be in place but also be adaptable and well integrated for any successful and economical responsiveness to changes in manufacturing to materialize.

2. CLASSIFICATION OF PROCESS PLANNING CONCEPTS

The process planning activities have seen significant growth and development since the nineties, which have been reviewed in a number of publications where details can be found. Planning is concerned with generating the set of steps required to reach a specified goal, within given constraints, while optimizing some stated criteria. Manufacturing process planning seeks to define all necessary steps required to execute a manufacturing process, which imparts a definite change in shape, properties, surface finish or appearance on a part or a product (ElMaraghy, 1993).

A classification of the various process planning concepts and approaches, based on their level of granularity, degree of automation, and scope, as outlined below, is helpful in highlighting the current challenges and future directions.

2.1 Process Plans Granularity

2.1.1 Multi-Domain Process Planning
At the highest level, planning seeks to select the most suitable manufacturing domain or technology for producing a feature, a part or a product (e.g. metal removal, material addition, forming or joining). A planner, for example, would determine whether a certain cavity would be produced by EDM rather than milling. Multi-domain process planning is concerned with this initial choice of manufacturing technology to be used. This type of planning has seen little automation to date.

2.1.2 Macro-Process Planning
It is concerned with selecting the best sequence of multiple different processing steps and set-ups as well as the machines to perform those operations. For example determining the individual operations to be performed for rough and finish machining a cylinder block casting and their sequence. Macro-level process planning, in a high volume dedicated manufacturing system, is carried out once at the system design stage to optimize the overall process. However, in a flexible or reconfigurable manufacturing system, Macro-planning has to be done frequently as the machines/products and their modules are changed.

2.1.3 Micro-Process Planning
At this level, the details of each individual operation are optimized to determine the best process parameters. For metal removal the feed, speed, depth of cut, tools, fixtures, cutting path, etc. are determined to optimize process time, and cost and avoid undesirable behaviour such as tool breakage and chatter. More detailed planning specifies the machining execution instructions and NC program steps.

2.2 Process Planning Automation

2.2.1 Manual Process Planning

Process planners often possess extensive experience and knowledge that are used to establish process plans at any level of granularity. However, manual planning lacks consistency, standardization and optimality and does not lend itself to computerization and automation.

2.2.2 Computerized Process Planning

It capitalizes on the increasing capabilities of computers to facilitate storage, retrieval and use of data, models, and knowledge to speed up computation and allow user interaction and participation in decision-making. This is called Computer-Aided Process Planning (CAPP) and should not be confused with automated process planning.

2.2.3 Automated Process Planning

Automated process planning is by nature also computerized. However, the following classification is more concerned with the type and degree of automation.

2.2.3.1 Retrieval /Variant Process Planning

The variant approach marks the beginning of automating process planning activities, and is basically a computerized database retrieval approach. The fundamental concept is that parts that bare similarity in design or manufacturing features are grouped into part families, a unique Group Technology code is generated for each part, a composite part that contains all the features in the family, and a standard optimized master process plan for each family of parts are developed beforehand. The planning of a new part is performed by identifying and retrieving existing plans for similar parts, using the GT code, and making the necessary modifications.

A *dynamic process planning* system is a retrieval type, which allows adaptation of pre-determined process plans (or portions of) to changes in the manufacturing facilities (machines failure, material and tools shortage, order changes, etc.). This adaptation may be done at both Macro- and Micro- process planning levels.

2.2.3.2 Semi-Generative Process Planning

Semi-generative process planning is the next automation step wherein the "standard master process plan" concept was *augmented* by algorithms capable of making some "*part-specific*" decisions about the operation to be performed and their parameters. It combines both retrieval and algorithmic procedures assisted by CAD models, databases, decision tables or trees, heuristics and knowledge rules. This allowed process plans to be partially customized for individual parts and new features.

2.2.3.3 Generative Process Planning

A totally generative process planning system aims at generating an optimized process plan from scratch given sufficient input about all relevant data. It relies heavily on complete and accurate models of the parts and processes, and their behaviour, constraints and interactions. Automated reasoning, knowledge-based systems and Artificial Intelligence techniques are essential to the success of this approach. Some CAM/CNC applications claim to be moving in this direction in some aspects of metal cutting. However, a truly generative process planning system in any domain is yet to be realized. The major challenge is the complete mathematical modelling of the various processes and their characteristics.

2.2.3.4 Distributed, Web-based, Networked Process Planning
A trend is evolving for distributed and more decentralized process planning systems. These would be a collection of process planning sub-systems, each with a limited function or scope and more specialized nature, which are loosely connected to form a "system of systems" with an overall supervisory system to coordinates their interaction and the flow of control and data between them. These systems could reside on one or more computers and may fall under any of the above classifications according to their degree of automation and level of granularity. There are a number of factors, which motivate this trend including the globally distributed manufacturing facilities, the wide spread use of the Internet, and the application of agent-based techniques.

2.3 Scope of Process Planning

Process planning for metal removal received a great deal of attention due to their widespread use and importance. However, the increased emphasis on reducing the cost of the total manufacturing process, the advent of many new production methods and technologies, and the desire to compete globally highlighted the need to carefully plan all steps of manufacturing. Hence, process planning principles and techniques are now being applied to non-traditional domains such as assembly/ disassembly, inspection, robotic tasks, rapid prototyping, welding, forming, and sheet metal working. Process planning classification, approaches and solution methods are applicable across these domains. However, the process nature, specific knowledge and constraints vary greatly and hence some of the terminology, logic and criteria used in their planning.

Several application programs, using many of the process planning approaches classified in this section, have been developed and used in industry to date. A review of specific systems or solutions is beyond the scope of this paper.

3. EVOLUTION OF MANUFACTURING SYSTEMS

Manufacturing systems have evolved from job shops, which feature general-purpose machines, low volume, high variety and significant human involvement, to high volume, low variety dedicated manufacturing lines driven by the economy of scale. In the eighties flexible manufacturing was introduced for mid-volume, mid-variety production to achieve greater responsiveness to changes in products, production technology, and markets. Similarities between parts in design and/or manufacture, and the concepts of static Product Families and Group Technology were used to achieve economy of scope. Flexible manufacturing systems (FMSs) anticipated these variations and built-in flexibility a priori.

The reconfigurable manufacturing concept has emerged in the last few years in an attempt to achieve changeable functionality and scalable capacity (Koren, *et al.*, 1999 and Fujii, *et al.*, 2000). It proposes a manufacturing system the modules of which can be added, removed, modified, or interchanged as needed to respond to changing requirements. It has the potential, when implemented, to offer a cheaper solution in the long run compared to FMSs, as it can increase the life and utility of a manufacturing system. However, hardware reconfiguration also requires major changes in the software used to control individual machines, complete cells, and systems as well as to plan and control the individual processes and production (ElMaraghy, 2005).

3.1 Manufacturing Systems Life Cycle

In the context of manufacturing systems, one can also envisage a life cycle (ElMaraghy, 2005). It has several phases including the initial system design to implementation, use/operation, re-design/reconfiguration and re-use as well as sale/ retirements of some of its modules. Both "soft" and "hard" reconfiguration and flexibility can be used to achieve capability and capacity scalability and extend the utility, usability, and life of manufacturing system. Hard or physical reconfiguration includes adding/removing machines and machine elements, material handing equipment, buffers and storage devices as well as changing their location and layout. Soft or logical reconfiguration can be achieved in variety of ways including re-programming, re-routing, re-planning, re-scheduling, and capacity changes through sub-contracting, utilization of shifts (time) and operators (human resources).

4. EVOLUTION OF PARTS AND PRODUCTS

The evolution of products is driven by customer demands, innovation, availability of new knowledge, technology and materials, cost reduction, environmental concerns, and legal regulations. Derivatives and variations in function, form and configuration lead to products classes including Series of Products with different Functions, Series of Components with different Configurations and Series of Features with different Dimensional and Time Versions that were developed over time in response to these demands. The result is a product family that contains variants of the product, its components and their configuration. One such example is the family of high bypass ratio turbine fan engine - CFM56, which has been under development since 1970s (www.cfm56.com) and consists of six series (sub-sets).

4.1 Static Parts/Products Families

The classical notion of a parts/products family was established in conjunction with the concept of Group Technology where members of the family have similarities in the design and/or manufacturing features. Flexible manufacturing systems relied on this definition of pre-defined parts/products families with non-changing borders to achieve the economy of scale by pre-planning the manufacturing system flexibility according to the defined scope of variations within the family. In this case, a *"Composite part"* that contains all features of the family members can be considered and a *"Master Process Plan"* is devised and optimized, in anticipation of the pre-defined variations, for use in *"Variant Process Planning"* and other manufacturing related activities. The cylinder block for an automobile engine is an example of a product family with well-defined and pre-planned boundaries, where variations in the number, orientation, size and characteristics of cylinder bores, as well as size, mounting bosses, oil gallery, bolt holes, etc. produce different members of the family such as V6, V8 and V10 cylinder blocks for different vehicles.

4.2 Evolving Parts/Products Families

In the current dynamic and changeable manufacturing environment, the products are frequently changed and customized, and it is possible to reconfigure the manufacturing systems as needed and when needed by changing their modules and hence their capability and capacity. Therefore, the notion of constant parts/products families is changing. This presents new challenges for related activities such as process planning.

We propose a new class of "*Evolving Parts/Products Families*". Since adding, removing, or changing manufacturing systems' modules changes its capabilities and functionality, the reconfigured system would be capable of producing new product features that did not exist in the original product family. This allows it to respond to the rapid changes in products, their widening scope and faster pace of their customization. The features of new members in the evolving families of parts overlap to varying degrees with some existing features; they mutate and form new and sometimes different members or families as shown in figure 1.

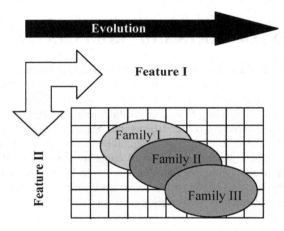

Figure 1 – Evolving parts/products families.

It is suggest that this evolution occurs in two modes (Al Geddawy, 2006):

- Chronological Evolution: It develops gradually over time and represents a unidirectional natural progression as more knowledge and better technology become available. It is unidirectional because as new and better solutions are obtained, there is no need to revert to older inefficient or flawed designs.
- Functional Evolution: It is caused by a significant and major change in requirement, which is normally forced by many factors. It is often selective and discrete although a major overhaul is also possible. This type of change may be bi/multi-directional as the new product fulfils different functional requirements but does not necessarily render previous designs obsolete.

In summary, and to use the natural evolution metaphor:

a) In a Flexible Manufacturing System: The parts family members are closely knit have a strong core of common features, and all variations are within the pre-defined boundaries. The concepts of Composite Parts, Master Plans and Variant/Retrieval Process Planning are both valid and useful. After a few generations, new product families gradually lose their roots (missing features) and develop new and different branches (additional features). The extent of difference between product generations depends of the number and nature of features changes.

b) In a Reconfigurable Manufacturing System: After many and different products generations, new product features and different families/Species emerge with much less resemblance to the original parent family and many of the familiar rules do not apply. The magnitude of change and distance between new and old members of the family significantly influences the characteristics of the process plans in this new setting.

We introduce, in light of the above discussion, the concept of *"Evolvable and Reconfigurable Process Plans"*, which are capable of responding efficiently to both subtle and major changes in *"Evolving Parts/Products Families"* and changeable and Reconfigurable manufacturing systems.

5. RECONFIGURABLE PROCESS PLANS

The process plans and planning functions are important links between the features of various generations of products/product families and the features, capabilities and configurations of manufacturing systems and its components throughout their respective life cycles. The efficient generation and reconfiguration of process plans is an important enabler for changeable and responsive manufacturing systems.

Since the manufacturing resources and their functionalities are becoming reconfigurable, the products variations are increasing in scope and frequency and, the families of manufactured parts are also changeable and evolvable. Hence, the concept of "Reconfigurable Process Plans" applies to Macro and Micro level plans.

There are some key criteria for achieving reconfigurable process plans and commensurate techniques for their efficient regeneration when needed. The multi-directional relationships between the product features, process plan elements and all manufacturing system modules capable of producing them must be clearly established. Modeling methods including classes, hierarchies, reconfiguration rules and knowledge, associations and relationships rules, functions, constraints, tables, and the like must be developed. Process plans representations that would facilitate their reconfiguration should be utilized. Appropriate models should be developed for the representation and use of: parts geometry (models, and design and manufacturing features), parts technological constraints (hierarchies, precedence, association, and datums), static and dynamic manufacturing resources constraints (e.g. capabilities, limitations, capacity, size, number, alternatives, and availability), and process knowledge (mathematical models, rules, heuristics, expert systems, intelligent agents, etc.). New algorithms for re-planning and reconfiguring process plans should be developed to ensure the efficiency of this process. The reasoning to recognize the need for, trigger and achieve a reconfiguration of the process plan in response to both pre-planned and evolutionary changes in the product and/or system must be established. The optimality (time, quality, cost, etc.) of the evolved and reconfigured process plans should also be verified and maintained.

Some examples of newly developed approaches and methods for reconfiguring process plans are presented next for illustration of the proposed concepts.

5.1 Semi-Generative Macro Process Planning for Reconfigurable Manufacturing

A practical semi-generative process planning approach suitable for both reconfiguration of the products and manufacturing systems has been developed (Azab *et al.*, 2006). The macro-level process plan is formulated as a sequence of operations corresponding to a set of features in the part. The interactions between the part's different features/operations are modeled using Features/Operations Precedence Graphs (FPG/OPG). The FPG/OPG graphs of a part family's composite part are modified to account for missing and added features. A random-based heuristic and validation scheme were developed to obtain optimal or near-optimal operation sequences that maintain the precedence relationships and constraints.

The developed method was applied to an industrial example of a single cylinder, air cooled, overhead valve engine front cover family of parts defined by a composite cover and a corresponding master process plan. A new Macro-level process plan for a new cover with different (new, missing and modified) features was generated and the manufacturing system machines had to be reconfigured accordingly.

It has been illustrated that a hybrid system, which is variant in nature yet capable of generating process plans for parts with machining features beyond those present in the current part family's composite part best meets the current challenges.

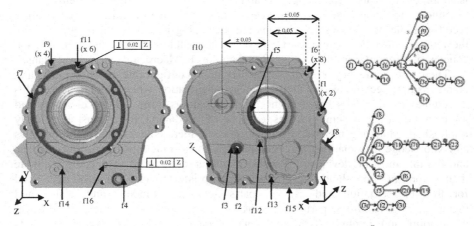

Figure 2 – The composite cylinder front cover, and Feature precedence graph (FPG) - composite & new cylinder covers (Azab et al., 2006).

5.2 Mapping Products Machining Requirements and Machine Tools Structure Characteristics in RMS

A two-way mapping between the features of products and machine tools was developed. The selection of the different types of machine(s) and their appropriate configurations to produce different types of parts and features, according to the required machine capabilities is a fundamental building block in generative planning of manufacturing processes (Shabaka and ElMaraghy 2006). The machine structure is represented as kinematic chains that capture the number, type and order of different axes of motion, which are indicative of its ability to produce certain geometric features. Operations are represented by a precedence graph and clustered according to the logical, functional and technical constraints.

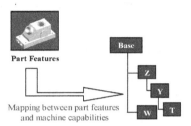

Figure 3 - Mapping between part features and machine capabilities.

5.3 Reconfigurable Process Planning Modelling

A new and novel mathematical model and algorithms for reconfigurable process planning are introduced (Azab and ElMaraghy, 2006). An automated iterative reconfiguration process is devised to account for new, modified or missing features. The reconfiguration logic considers the new part, its precedence graph and corresponding operations precedence graph, the current generation of parts family and manufacturing system and their attributes. An engine cylinder block family for V6, V8 and inline engines is used to test the process plans reconfiguration algorithm. The proposed algorithm is linear in the amount of required modifications whereas re-planning provides global solutions by solving an exponentially growing NP-complete problem, which requires far more computational effort.

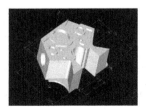

Figure 4 - Cylinder block used in reconfiguring process plans and a geometric model of one of its family members (2 cylinders engine block) (Azab et al., 2006).

6. CONCLUDING REMARKS

Responsiveness, agility and high performance of manufacturing systems call for new approaches to achieve cost-effective adaptability at all levels. It is increasingly important that all support functions, both at the physical and logical levels, are usable across several generations of product families and manufacturing systems.

In particular, process planning and production control strategies and logistics present a formidable challenge in this changeable environment. These must not only be in place but also be adaptive and well integrated at many levels for any successful and economical responsiveness to changes in manufacturing to materialize.

The designers of products, processes and manufacturing systems as well as production planners should be cognizant of the coupling between generations of products and manufacturing systems and capitalize on its potential benefits in improving the productivity of the whole enterprise. The automatic evolution of process plans is an important enabler of effective changeability

A classification of the various process planning concepts was presented. The evolution of manufacturing paradigms, the manufacturing system life cycle and evolution of products were discussed. A new class of *"Evolving Parts/Products Families"* was proposed and contrasted with the traditional notions of static parts families, composite parts and master process plans. The new concept of *"Reconfigurable Process Plans"* was introduced, and the need to link their evolution and reconfiguration to the changes and evolution of both products and manufacturing systems was highlighted. The new rules and challenges of reconfigurable process plans were discussed. Research implementations were briefly described to demonstrate applications of the presented new concepts.

The new manufacturing paradigms and need for responsiveness and adaptability are highlighting the importance of developing new process planning approaches that can support the objectives of the new environment. This paper shed light on the many remaining research challenges and pointed to several potential and exciting opportunities for improving manufacturing productivity and competitiveness.

7. REFERENCES

1. Al Geddawy, T. Private Communication. IMS Centre. Univ. of Windsor, Ontario, Canada; 2006.
2. Azab, A. and ElMaraghy, H. "Reconfigurable Process Planning Modelling". Int. Journal of Production Research – IJPR 2006; (submitted).
3. Azab, A., Perusi, G., ElMaraghy, H. and Urbanic, J. Semi-Generative Macro Process Planning for Reconfigurable Manufacturing, DET'06- 3rd Int.CIRP Conference in Digital Enterprise Technology. Setúbal/Portugal 18- 20 September 2006.
4. ElMaraghy, HA. Flexible and Reconfigurable Manufacturing Systems Paradigms, Special Issue of the International Journal of Manufacturing Systems (IJMS) 2005; Vol. 17, No. 4, pp. 261-276.
5. ElMaraghy, HA. Evolution and Future Perspectives of CAPP, CIRP Annals 1993; Vol. 42(2): 739-751.
6. Fujii, S., Morita, H., Kakino, Y., Ihara, Y., Takata, Y., Murakami, D., Miki, T., Tatsuta, Y., Highly Productive and Reconfigurable Manufacturing Systems. Proc. the Pacific Conf. on Manufacturing 2000; Vol. 2, pp. 970-980.
7. Koren, Y, Heisel, U, Jovane, F, Moriwaki, T, Pritschow, G, Ulsoy, G and Van Brussel, H. Reconfigurable Manufacturing Systems. CIRP Annals 1999; Vol. 48 (2): 527-540.
8. Shabaka, A. and ElMaraghy, H. Generation of Machine Configurations Based on Product Features, Int. J. of Computer Integrated Manufacturing; Published Online on: 26 July, 2006 DOI: 10.1080/09511920600740627.

COLLABORATIVE NETWORKS IN INDUSTRY TRENDS AND FOUNDATIONS

Luís M. Camarinha-Matos
New University of Lisbon, Portugal
cam@uninova.pt

Collaborative networks offer a high potential for survival and value creation in enterprises under turbulent market conditions. Collaboration manifests in a large variety of forms, including virtual organizations, virtual enterprises, dynamic supply chains, professional virtual communities, etc. In order to support preparedness of enterprises for participation in such dynamic coalitions, breeding environments for virtual organizations are being developed in many application sectors. A large body of empiric knowledge related to collaborative networks is already available, but only recently the research community started to focus on the consolidation of this knowledge and building the foundations for a more sustainable development of the area. The definition of reference models and the establishment of a scientific discipline for collaborative networks are strong instruments in achieving this purpose. In this paper a brief survey of the main characteristics of the area is presented, current baseline is discussed, and future trends are pointed out.

1. INTRODUCTION

The implementation of collaborative processes has accelerated in recent years as a consequence of both the new challenges posed to companies by the fast changing market conditions and the new developments in the information and communication technologies sector. In fact, a large variety of collaborative networks have emerged during the last years as a result of the rapidly evolving challenges faced by business entities and the society in general (Camarinha-Matos, Afsarmanesh, 2005). For instance, the reduction of commercial barriers not only gave consumers wider access to goods, but also led to higher demands for quality and diversity as well as a substantial increase in the competition among suppliers and a decrease of the products' life cycle. Therefore, highly integrated and dynamic supply chains, extended and virtual enterprises, virtual organizations, and professional virtual communities are just some manifestations of this trend that are indeed enabled by the advances in the information and communication technologies.

In this context, it became a common assumption that participation in a collaborative network has the potential of bringing benefits to the involved entities, including: an increase in "survivability" of organizations in a context of market turbulence, as well as the possibility of better achieving common goals by excelling the individual capabilities or acquiring more visibility and lobbying power. On the basis of these positive expectations we can find, among others, the following factors: acquisition of a larger (apparent) dimension, access to new/wider markets and new knowledge, sharing of risks and resources, joining of complementary skills and capacities which allow each entity to focus on its core competencies while keeping a high level of agility, etc. In addition to agility through participation in different networks, the new organizational forms also induce innovation, and thus *creation of new value*, by confrontation of ideas and practices, combination of resources and technologies, and creation of synergies.

2. SOME MANIFESTATIONS

Moving from the classical supply chains format, characterized by relatively stable networks with well defined roles requiring only minimal coordination and information exchange, more dynamic structures are emerging in industry. Some of these organizational forms are goal-oriented, i.e. focused on a single project or business opportunity, such as the case of virtual enterprises (VE) (figure 1). The same concept can be applied to other contexts, e.g. government and service sectors, leading to a more general term, the virtual organizations (VO). A VE/VO is often a temporary organization that "gathers" its potential from the possibility of (rapidly) forming consortia well suited (in terms of competencies and resources) to each business opportunity.

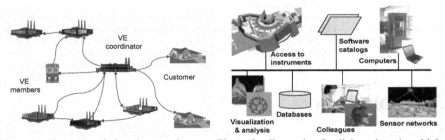

Figure 1 – Example of virtual enterprise.   Figure 2 – Example of collaborative virtual lab.

Other emerging collaborative networks are formed by human professionals that may collaborate in virtual communities of practice and form virtual teams to address specific problems, such as collaborative concurrent engineering or development of a consultancy project.

Fig. 2 illustrates another case of collaborative network, the collaborative virtual laboratory (VL). Here a virtual experimental environment is provided for scientists and engineers to perform their experiments, enabling a group of researchers located around the world to work together, sharing resources (such as expensive lab equipments) and results. It shall be noted that in this case, in addition to the network of involved organizations (e.g. research centers), there is an overlapping network of people. In a research activity most collaboration acts are in fact conducted by researchers that have a high degree of autonomy. Therefore, in this example, it becomes evident the necessity of tools to support human collaboration – groupware tools. A typical VL involves scientific equipments connected to a network, large-scale simulations, visualization, data reduction and data summarization capabilities, application-specific databases, collaboration tools, e.g. teleconferencing, federated data exchange, chat, shared electronic-whiteboard, notepad, etc., application-dependent software tools and interfaces, safe communications, and large network bandwidth. A similar situation can happen in a VE when engineering teams formed by engineers of different enterprises collaborate on some engineering problem.

Figure 3 illustrates another manifestation combining a network of organizations with a network of people for remote assistance of elderly. This case consists of a number of organizations such as care centers, day centers, health care institutions, and social security institutions acting in cooperation with involved personnel e.g. health care professionals, social care assistants, elderly people, and their relatives. When based on computer networks and adequate ICT tools, collaboration among care institutions may evolve towards operating as a long-term virtual organization and the various involved humans will become part of a virtual community.

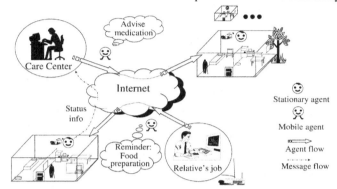

Figure 3 – Example of collaborative network in elderly care.

Many more examples can be found in different sectors. For instance, we can think of networks of insurance companies, networks of governmental institutions, networks of academic institutions forming virtual institutes for joint delivery of advanced courses, networks of entities involved in disaster rescuing, etc. With the development of new collaborative tools supported by Internet and a better understanding of the mechanisms of collaborative networks, new organizational forms are naturally emerging. And yet all these cases have a number of characteristics in common:
- Networks composed of a variety of entities – organizations and people – which are largely autonomous, geographically distributed, and heterogeneous in terms of their operating environment, culture, social capital and goals.
- Participants collaborate to (better) achieve common or compatible goals.
- The interactions among participants are supported by computer network.

Therefore, the term collaborative network, or more specifically collaborative networked organization (CNO) when we think of more organized collaboration processes, is often used as a generic term to represent all these particular cases.

3. BREEDING ENVIRONMENTS

One of the important conditions to leverage the potential of these new organizational forms is the possibility of fast configuration of a consortium well suited to the needs of a business opportunity once this opportunity is identified (figure 4).

Finding the right partners and establishing the necessary conditions for starting the collaboration process have however proved to be a difficult and costly task. Among other factors, the formation of any collaborative coalition depends on its members sharing some common (or compatible) goals, possessing some level of mutual trust, having established common (interoperable) infrastructures, and having agreed on some common (business) practices and values. Achieving these conditions is a pre-requisite for launching a potentially successful and effective collaborative network.

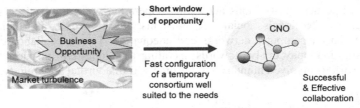

Figure 4 – From business opportunity to a dynamic CNO creation.

Although with some differences, similar challenges happen both in the creation of a network of organizations (virtual organization) or a network of professionals (virtual team). Figure 5 illustrates some of the steps involved in the CNO creation process.

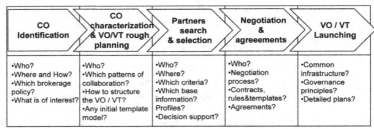

Figure 5 – Main steps in dynamic CNO creation.

As implied in figure 5, the CNO creation process requires several steps that might be a difficult and time consuming activity. The situation is not too critical in the case of long-term collaboration processes not limited to a single business opportunity, such as in the case of stable supply chains. When the perspectives for the operation phase are of long-term the necessary initial preparation effort can be affordable. On the other hand, for some specific niche sectors in which all actors share the same or compatible tools, business culture and practices, it is possible to quickly form a consortium even for a short-term single opportunity.

For the other cases, probably the most typical scenario in current industry, the situation is much more critical. Particularly when the window of opportunity is short, in order to support rapid formation of CNOs it is necessary that potential partners are *ready and prepared to participate* in such collaboration. This readiness includes common interoperable infrastructure, common operating rules, and common cooperation agreement, among others. Any collaboration action also requires a base level of trust among the organizations. For this case a working solution is the creation of a long-term association of entities that prepare themselves to collaborate whenever an opportunity arises. This association of organizations is a **VO Breeding Environment** (VBE) (Afsarmanesh, Camarinha-Matos, 2005) (Camarinha-Matos, Afsarmanesh, 2005) for the creation of dynamic VOs.

A **Virtual organization Breeding Environment (VBE)** is thus an association of organizations and their related supporting institutions, adhering to a base long term cooperation agreement, and adoption of common operating principles and infra-structures, with the main goal of increasing their preparedness towards collaboration in potential Virtual Organizations (Afsarmanesh, Camarinha-Matos, 2005). Traditionally, VBEs are established in a geographic region, in the tradition of industry clusters, with the advantage of having common business culture and sense of community, as well as focusing on one of the specialty sectors of the region. But, this restriction can in most cases be overcome today by an effective information and communication infrastructure. Examples of such organizations are:

- The Virtuelle Fabrik is a network of about 70 industrial SMEs in Switzerland and South Germany in the metal-mechanic sector. The network provides a full range of industrial services and production to the customers. The network enables the SMEs to act in collaboration with other SMEs the same way as a very big industrial company. Virtuelle Fabrik AG is the project management and sales company for this VBE.
- IECOS (Integration Engineering and Construction Systems) is an enterprise that uses the VBE model integrating capabilities and competences of its partners (mainly in metal-mechanic and plastic industry) to satisfy customer requirements in Mexico.
- Swiss Microtech (SMT) is a regional collaborative network created in 2001 by SMEs of the mechanical subcontracting sector to address together new markets and develop new products which are beyond their own possibilities if they would stay alone. SMT has actually 7 members. The very fierce competition on the prices and the importance of the emerging Chinese market led to the creation in 2005 of DecoCHina, an international VBE combining two regional networks, SMT and a new parent Chinese network in the Guangdong Province.
- CeBeNetwork represents a supplier network in the aeronautical industry and a strategic supplier to the main customer Airbus. CeBeNetwork AG is the leader of this network and acts as a broker as well as a member.
- HELICE is the Andalusian aeronautic cluster, which operates under the VBE model, to increase process efficiency and business opportunities while fostering innovation in a sustainable structure. It is registered as a Foundation, linking main contractors (EADS, AIRBUS, GAMESA), 39 auxiliary SMEs and supporting entities (Universities, Research Centers and Regional Government).
- Supply Network Shannon (SNS) is an open network of companies in the Shannon region of Ireland. SNS provides a framework for companies to collaborate in joint marketing, training development and collaborative quotation development for participation in outsourcing networks. As such SNS currently operates as a regional VBE with individual members currently creating sub networks on a global scale.

Many other similar examples can be found in different geographical regions (Afsarmanesh, Camarinha-Matos, 2005), (Galeano, Molina, 2005). Well known examples are given by the industrial districts in Italy. There are also some attempts to transform traditional science parks and enterprise incubators into a kind of VBE, i.e. moving from a simple sharing of basic infrastructures and services to a co-operative business context. Based on an empirical analysis of current VBEs, Table 1 shows an attempt to define a VBE typology.

As in the case of organizations, a similar long term association can be formed with professionals, in which case it is called a **Professional Virtual Community (PVC)** (Afsarmanesh, Camarinha-Matos, 2005), (Crave, Ladame, 2005). One example could be an association of free-lancer knowledge workers (e.g. engineers,

consultants). When a business opportunity happens (e.g. a design project or con-
sultation activity), similarly to the VO creation, a temporary coalition of experts – a
Virtual Team (VT) – can be rapidly formed according to the specific needs of that
business opportunity.

Table 1 – A typology of VBEs.

VBE Types	Membership	Overlapping of competencies	Support institutions	Market access
A1 **Customer induced** (to qualify as a supplier)	•Enterprises & other •Highly selective	•Possible	•Limited	•Extremely focused
A2 **Capacity induced** (too big a "problem" / market for 1 company)	•Organizations in same domain/sector	•Mostly	•Limited	Focused on a domain (in general)
A3 **Complement competencies** (new markets, new products, also dimension)	•May cover various sectors •Basic adhesion rule	•Possible, limited (regulated)	•Limited	•Generic (as possible)
A4 **Regional ecosystem** (to preserve local specificities, tradition, culture ... and benefit from government incentives)	•Specific sector (mostly) •Regional basis	•Possible	•Strong	•Generic, with regional focus

Figure 6 illustrates a taxonomy of collaborative networks considering both the
long-term breeding environments (strategic alliances) and the goal-oriented networks.

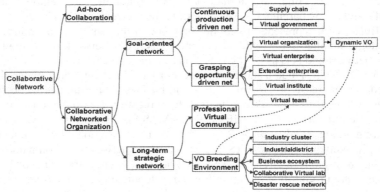

Figure 6 – A taxonomy of collaborative networks.

Although a main motivation for the establishment of a breeding environment is to
give its members preparedness to benefit from collaborative business opportunities,
once a VBE is established other benefits can arise to its members. Some of these
benefits are summarized in Table 2.

The initial attracting factors are not exactly the same that keep members happy in
the long run. For instance, knowledge acquisition can be a major attracting factor in
the initial phase but rapidly fades as some leveraging of knowledge is achieved.
Table 3 shows some of the most relevant factors, according to empirical observation,
that might keep participants together in a VBE. Nevertheless a current challenge
is the development of suitable performance indicators that provide objective and
explicit representation of the benefits. Most past efforts in performance management
were focused on a single enterprise. Other works such as the SCOR framework
developed indicators for supply chains. It is now necessary to elaborate on a set of

appropriate indicators for collaborative networks in general. This research is however still in its infancy (Alfaro et al., 2005), (Folan, Browne, 2005). One example can be found in (Galeano, Molina, 2005) that suggested a preliminary set of indicators based on the creation of networks of benefits.

Table 2 – Some benefits of participation in a breeding environment.

Market-related reasons	Organizational reasons
•Coping with market turbulence •Increase chances of survival •More chances to compete with larger companies •Lobbying and market influence (branding / marketing) •Easier access to loans •Cheaper group insurance •Better negotiation power (e.g. Joint purchasing) •Prestige, reputation, reference •Access to explore new market / product (e.g. Multidisciplinary sector) •Expand geographical coverage •Increase potential for innovation •Economies of scale •Achieve (global) diversity •...	•Management of competencies and resources •Approaches to build trust •Improve potential of risk taking •Support members through necessary re-organization •Learning and training •Shared bag of assets •Organize success stories and joint advertisement •Help in attaining clear focus / developing core competencies •... **Preparedness** •Agility for opportunity-based VO creation •Effective common ICTR infrastructure •Mechanisms, guidelines for VO creation •General guidelines for collaboration •Increase chances of VO involvement •...

Table 3 – Some reasons to stay in a VBE.

Long-term attraction factors
•Profit from businesses •Benefiting from the existing infrastructure •Better marketing possibilities (fairs, cheaper admission costs, better publicity/visibility (better location) ...) •Better strategic position through the VBE •Easy access to complementary skills •Explore new market / new product (multi-disciplinary sector), expand geographical coverage •Potential for innovation •Continue profiting from the opportunities only available through the VBE •Fight against a common enemy •Better negotiation power •Existing success stories and advertising •Gain higher rank for more opportunities •...

ECOLEAD project. A large number of research projects are carried out worldwide and a growing number of practical cases on different forms of collaborative networks are being reported. However, many of these initiatives have a limited focus and, as a result, lead to a fragmented research panorama. Aiming at providing a more holistic approach the ECOLEAD integrated project was launched in 2004 as a 4-year initiative, involving 27 industrial and academic organizations from Europe and Latin America. The fundamental assumption in this project is that a substantial increase in materializing networked collaborative business requires a comprehensive holistic approach. Given the complexity of the area and the multiple inter-dependencies among the involved business entities, social actors, and technologic approaches, the substantial breakthrough cannot be achieved with only incremental innovation in isolated areas. Therefore, the project addresses three most fundamental and inter-related focus areas – constituting pillars – as the basis for dynamic and sustainable networked organizations including: VO breeding environments, dynamic Virtual Organizations, and Professional Virtual Communities and Virtual Teams.

As the main focus of work, the VBE pillar addresses the characterization of these networks, namely in terms of structure, life cycle, competencies, working and sharing principles, value systems and metrics, the governance principles and trust building processes, the VBE management, and VO creation. The dynamic VO area is mainly focused on the VO management and governance approaches, performance measurement, and VO inheritance. PVC addresses the characterization of these communities in terms of the socio-economic context, governance principles, social and legal implications, value systems, metrics and business models, as well as the support platform for collaboration. Interactions and synergies among these three entities, namely in terms of business models, value creation and corresponding metrics, are a major issue of integration. In addition to the three pillars, two horizontal areas complete the scope of ECOLEAD: Theoretical foundation, which focus on reference models and soft computing applied to CNOs, and Horizontal ICT infrastructure, which develops a service-oriented infrastructure for collaboration.

4. MODELING FRAMEWORK

As identified by different studies, one of the main weaknesses in the area of collaborative networks is the lack of appropriate theories, consistent paradigms definition, and adoption of formal modeling tools. In an attempt to contribute to the establishment of a sounder theoretical foundation for CNOs, a comprehensive modeling framework was proposed by the ECOLEAD projects – the ARCON (A Reference Model for CNOs) framework (Camarinha-Matos, Afsarmanesh, 2006). For the purpose of modeling the CNO components, at the highest level three perspectives are identified and defined in the proposed ARCON framework (Fig. 7).

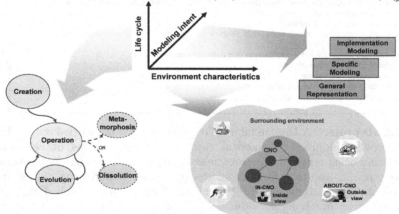

Figure 7 – Modeling perspectives in ARCON.

The first perspective addresses the timing cycle for different CNO stages, to capture the diversity and evolution of CNOs during their entire life cycle (CNO-Life-Cycle – vertical perspective). The following main stages are considered:
- *Creation phase*, which can be divided into two phases, namely (i) initiation and recruiting, dealing with the strategic planning and initial incubation of the CNO; (ii) foundation, dealing with the constitution and start up.
- *Operation phase*, the main phase of the life cycle where the goals of the CNO are in fact achieved.

- *Evolution phase*, covering potential changes needed during the operation of the CNO such as changes in roles, replacement of partners, etc.
- *Dissolution or Metamorphosis*. A temporary CNO such as a VO will typically dissolve after accomplishing its goal. In the case of a long-term alliance such as a VBE, considering its valuable bag of assets gradually collected during its operation, its dissolution is an undesirable situation. Instead, it is much more probable that this CNO goes through another stage, that we call the *metamorphosis* stage, where it can evolve by changing its form and purpose.

A second perspective focuses on capturing the CNO environment characteristics (as a horizontal perspective). This perspective includes two subspaces (points of view) to comprehensively cover, the internal (**In-CNO**) characteristics as well as the external (**About-CNO**) characteristics that are related to the logical surrounding of the CNOs. From the In-CNO point of view the following dimensions are considered:

- *Structural dimension*, addressing the structure or composition of the CNO's constituting elements (namely its participants and their relationships) as well as the roles performed by those elements and other compositional characteristics of the network nodes such as the location, time, etc.
- *Componential dimension*, focusing on the individual tangible/intangible elements in the CNO's network, e.g. the resource composition such as human elements, software and hardware resources, information and knowledge. Furthermore, the componential dimension also consists of ontology and the description of the information/knowledge.
- *Functional dimension*, addressing the "base functions/operations" available at the network, and time-sequenced flows of executable operations (processes and procedures) related to the different phases of the CNO life cycle.
- *Behavioral dimension*, addressing the principles, policies, and governance rules that drive or constrain the behavior of the CNO and its members over time. Included here are elements such as principles of collaboration and rules of conduct, principles of trust, contracts, conflict resolution policies, etc.

Table 4 illustrates the application of these dimensions for the case of a VBE.

From the About-CNO point of view 4 dimensions are also considered in ARCON:

- *Market dimension*, covering the issues related to both the interactions with "customers" (or potential beneficiaries) and "competitors".
- *Support dimension*, covering the issues related to support services provided by third party institutions (outside the CNO).
- *Societal dimension*, capturing the issues related to interactions between the CNO and the society in general.
- *Constituency dimension*, focusing on the interaction with the universe of potential new members of the CNO, i.e. the interactions with those organizations that are not part of the CNO but that the CNO might be interested in attracting.

The third perspective (diagonal perspective) is related to different intents for the modeling of CNOs:

- *General concepts level* – that includes the most general concepts and related relationships, common to all CNOs independently of the application domain (e.g. all kinds of VBEs independent of the area).
- *Specific modeling level* – an intermediate level that includes more detailed models focused on different classes of CNOs (the CNO typology).

- ■ ***Implementation modeling level*** – that represents models of concrete CNOs.
Further details on the ARCON reference modeling framework can be found in
(Camarinha-Matos, Afsarmanesh, 2006).

Table 4 – In-CNO perspective for VBEs.

Dimension	Sub-dimension	Examples
Structural	Actors / relationships	VBE members (business entities, non-profit institutions, support institutions), collaboration links, trust links, coordination links, etc.
	Roles	VBE member, VBE administrator, Broker, VO planner, VO coordinator, VBE advisor, etc.
Componential	Hardware resources	(Domain specific) machines, ICT infrastructure
	Software resources	Common software tools, VBE specific services, commercial tools with special agreement with VBE, etc.
	Human resources	Human actors performing a role in the VBE.
	Info / Knowledge	Directory of members, Record of past performance, Directory of running VOs, Ranking and Ratings, Patents, etc.
	Ontology resources	Common ontology, Profile and competencies ontology, etc.
Functional	Processes	VBE creation processes (initiation & recruiting, foundation), Trust management process, Competency management process, Marketing & promotion process, VO creation process, Metamorphosis process, etc.
	Aux. processes	Assets management process, VBE Monitoring process, Incentive creation process, Competencies assessment process, etc.
	Methodologies	Conflict resolution procedure, Performance management procedure, Members registration procedure, Competences and Profiling management approach, etc.
Behavioral	Prescriptive behavior	Membership eligibility principles, Brokering principles, Decision-making principles, Rewarding and Sanctioning principles, Leadership principles, Commitment rules, etc
	Obligatory behavior	Bylaws, VBE behavior rules (Ethical code and culture), Governance policies, etc.
	Constraints & conditions	Constraints imposed by the external environment, Constraints on the use of some resources, Constraints on timing for interactions (when partners in different time zones), Legal constrains to VBE due to differences in government laws among countries, possible cultural constrains, etc.
	Contracts & agreements	VBE adhesion contract, VBE cooperation agreement, Contract templates for VOs, etc.

Figure 8 combines the three mentioned perspectives into a single diagram.

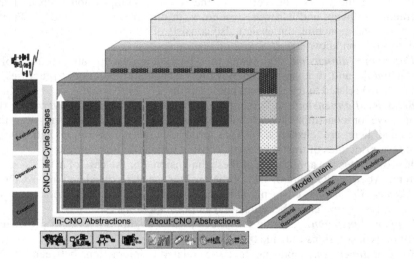

Figure 8 – The ARCON modeling framework for CNOs.

Lack of reference models for collaborative networks or even to some of their
manifestations (such as virtual enterprises) is a common concern found in the
literature, being also pointed out as an obstacle for a more consistent development of
the area. The difficulties are found namely in the terminology and associated
meanings, what leads to frequent misunderstandings among members of the
community which often possess different original backgrounds.

A reference model is a generic abstract representation for understanding the
entities and the significant relationships among those entities of some area, and for
the derivation of other specific models for particular cases in that area. Preferably a
reference model is based on a small number of unifying concepts and may be used

for education, explaining concepts, and systems' development. A reference model for Collaborative Networked Organizations (CNOs) is thus a generic conceptual model that synthesizes and formalizes the base concepts, principles and recommended practices for collaborative networked organizations. It is intended as an authoritative basis (guide) to streamline or facilitate the creation of focused models for the various manifestations of CNOs as well as architectures and implementation models for particular systems development. On the other hand it is important to have in mind that a reference model is generic and not directly applicable to concrete cases but rather provides the basis for the development (derivation) of other models closer to those cases.

With reference to figure 8, a reference model for CNOs will cover basically the first layer, i.e. the General Representation layer. In terms of representation, a generic tool like UML, or another standard representation formalism (like an ontology representation language) that is proper for human understanding can be adequate for representation of the general concepts level. An effort in this direction is currently being made in the ECOLEAD project (Camarinha-Matos, Afsarmanesh, 2006).

5. CONCLUSIONS AND CHALLENGES

The emergence of a large diversity of collaborative organizational forms in industry shows that CNOs are recognized in society as a very important instrument for survival of organizations in a period of turbulent socio-economic changes. It is also being recognized that a new discipline of collaborative networks is being founded. Breeding environments play a fundamental role in creating the conditions for the rapid formation of consortia to respond to business opportunities. Once a VBE is established, a number of additional benefits of these long-term alliances are also becoming evident. With the geographical relocation of some industrial activities, collaborative networks can also be an instrument to help in dynamic reorganization of local capacities and competencies in a given region. It is however necessary to invest more on the theoretical foundation for collaborative networks.

Acknowledgements. This work was supported in part by the ECOLEAD project funded by the European Commission. The author also thanks the contributions from his partners.

6. REFERENCES

1. Afsarmanesh, H.; Camarinha-Matos, L.M. – A Framework for Management of Virtual Organization Breeding Environments, in *Collaborative Networks and their Breeding Environments*, Springer, 2005.
2. Alfaro, J.; Rodriguez, R.; Ortiz, A. – A performance measurement system for virtual and extended enterprises, in *Collaborative Networks and their Breeding Environments*, Springer, 2005.
3. Camarinha-Matos, L. M.; Afsarmanesh, H. – Collaborative networks: A new scientific discipline, *J. Intelligent Manufacturing*, vol. 16, N° 4-5, pp 439-452, 2005.
4. Camarinha-Matos, L.M.; Abreu, A. – Performance indicators based on collaboration benefits, in *Collaborative Networks and their Breeding Environments*, Springer, 2005.
5. Camarinha-Matos, L. M.; Afsarmanesh, H. – Towards a reference model for collaborative networked organizations, in *Information Technology for Balanced Manufacturing Systems*, Springer, 2006.
6. Crave, S.; Ladame, S. – Professional Virtual Communities (PVC) inside Networks of firms, in Proceedings of ICE 2005, Munich, June 2005.

7. Folan, P.; Browne, J. (2005) – A review of performance measurement: Towards performance management. Computers in Industry, vol. 56, pp 663-680.
8. Galeano, N.; Molina, A. – Core Competence Management in Virtual Industry Clusters, in *Proceedings of 16th IFAC World Congress*, July 4-8, 2005 Prague, Czech Republic.

SESSION 1

ADVANCED FACTORY DESIGN
AND MODELING

A LOGISTICS FRAMEWORK FOR COORDINATING SUPPLY CHAINS ON UNSTABLE MARKETS

Péter Egri and József Váncza
Computer and Automation Research Institute
Hungarian Academy of Sciences, Hungary
{egri,vancza}@sztaki.hu

In this paper we discuss the difficulties of customized mass production in case of high manufacturing setup costs and unstable markets, where due to high service level requirements and demand volatility the risk of remaining obsolete inventory is significant. We propose a two-level logistics framework for coordinating supply channels in such production networks and methods for medium-term lot sizing decisions considering uncertainty.

1. INTRODUCTION

Growing customer expectations and *mass customization* induce large complexity and uncertainty in the consumer markets. Such markets are typically served by *supply networks* where demand is met by a focal manufacturer who operates in a network, together with suppliers of components, sub-assemblies and packaging materials. The common goal of each network partner is to provide high service level towards the customers of end-products, while, at the same time, keeping production and logistics costs as low as possible. However, these requirements are conflicting: high service level can only be guaranteed by *inventories* (of components, packaging materials, end-products). Furthermore, in mass production technology lower costs can be achieved with larger lot sizes, which involve, again, higher product and component inventories as well as increased work-in-process. On the other hand, markets of customized mass products are volatile. If the demand unexpectedly ceases for a product, then accumulated inventories become *obsolete* and cause significant losses. Most difficult is the situation with non-standardizable components (e.g., packaging materials of customized products): due to an unexpected change or cancellation of demand the product may *run out*, leaving obsolete inventories behind.

We are interested in *coordinating* production of supply networks. The particular motivation of this work comes from a large-scale national industry-academy R&D project aimed at realizing real-time, cooperative enterprises. The actual network has to meet ever-changing, hardly predictable, complex demand on a market of customized mass products. A further challenge is that all network partners are *autonomous*, and those in the supplier's role take typically part in other network relations as well.

For solving the network coordination problem, we suggest a generic *logistics framework* that links the planning and control functions of the manufacturer and its suppliers. The aim of this framework is to facilitate the exchange of information that is essential to minimize overall costs in the chain while guaranteeing high service level. In particular, it provides channels for exchanging, matching and adjusting both medium- and short-term demand of the manufacturer and corresponding production and delivery plans of the suppliers.

An integral part of supply chain management is to decide whether and how much to produce from particular products and components at a given moment. This is essentially a *lot sizing problem* (LSP) that is well studied in the literature. The most widespread standard models are the Economic Order Quantity (EOQ) and the Wagner-Whitin methods. However, while these models are easy to solve, realistic variants of LSPs are usually NP-hard problems (Brahimi, 2006). Stochastic inventory policies can handle *uncertainty* in case of demand volatility (such as the (s,S) policy) and one-period uncertain demand (*newsvendor* model) (Hopp, 1996), but the unforeseeable termination of the demand is still missing. Recently, there was also proposed a distinction between the two types of uncertainty (Grabot, 2005). However, in this model uncertainties are attached to orders and not to product. Furthermore, for handling uncertainties, a fuzzy logic approach is taken.

According to our experience, the run-out of products is an exogenous property of the market that must be taken into account when making supply decisions. In our previous work, we have identified two types of demand uncertainty: (1) quantity fluctuation and (2) the run-out (Váncza, 2006). While the former one can be handled with traditional approaches (safety stocks, time fences, rolling horizon planning), the latter should be included in the lot sizing model. Hence, after presenting outlines of a coordination platform, we give novel methods for lot sizing that concern all main cost factors, including the cost of expected obsolete inventories. Furthermore, we also present results of comparative simulation experiments run on historic data sets.

2. COORDINATION FRAMEWORK

Planning tasks of enterprises are usually categorized according to their horizons into three levels: long term, medium term and short term (Fleischmann, 2003). Consequently, a supply coordination model should cover all of these levels. The purchasing of raw materials can be planned relatively easily in the long term exploiting economies of scale, forasmuch the bulk of them are standard materials and the demand of the end products can be aggregated. In the framework proposed below we do not tackle this issue. The production-related decisions (plans, lot sizes) have to be made in medium term aligning the conflicting aims of flexibility and economic efficiency. In short term, the challenge is to organize smooth operation of the network, i.e., production as planned should not stop anywhere due to material shortage.

Following the above requirements, we propose a *logistics framework* for coordinating the manufacturer's and the supplier's decisions along a supply channel. The aim of this framework is (1) to minimize overall costs including setup, inventory holding and expected obsolete inventory costs, while (2) providing extremely high (98-99%) service level towards the customers. The key idea is to establish a *one-point inventory system* between companies, whose management needs coordination, truthful information sharing, and optimization. The logistics framework consists of two levels:

1. On the *scheduling platform*, the supplier meets the exact, short-term component demand of the manufacturer. This demand is generated from the actual production schedule of the manufacturer in form of *call-offs* and is satisfied by direct, just-in-time delivery from the inventory. On this platform, decisions are made on a daily basis, with a short term (1-2 weeks long) horizon. With this short look-ahead, demand uncertainty is hedged by appropriate safety stocks.

2. On the *planning platform*, the supplier builds up and maintains the one-point inventory. So as to be able to do that, the supplier receives information from the manufacturer concerning demand forecasts and the chances of product run-outs. The component demand is generated from the *master production plan* of the manufacturer that determines its planned output for a longer horizon. On this platform, decisions are made in a weekly cycle.

Note that this framework detaches the two main, conflicting objectives and makes both of them manageable: while service level is tackled at the scheduling platform, cost-efficient production is the main concern at the medium-term planning platform.

3. LOT SIZING CONSIDERING RUN-OUT

This chapter presents a portfolio of methods that are aimed to facilitate optimal *planning level* decisions in the above framework. These decisions are basically lot sizing decisions, to be made by the supplier who is responsible for maintaining the one-point inventory. The models consider single components, discrete, finite (medium-term), rolling horizon component forecast and no inventory limits. We also assume infinite production capacities at the supplier's side, and that lead-time of components (manufacturing plus shipment) fits into one planning time unit.

The *component forecast*, which is derived from the manufacturer's medium-term master production plan, is the basic input for supplier's lot sizing problem. This plan is uncertain, but does not provide valid statistical information (such as standard deviation). Hence, the uncertainty of component forecast is captured by the *probability of run-out*. Since the models consider only one product, there are no "speculative motives": it is always preferable to produce at a later period than producing earlier and holding stock.

3.1 Wagner-Whitin with run-out (WWr)

The standard, widely applied Wagner-Whitin inventory handling method uses a dynamic programming approach to minimize the total cost in the given horizon and to determine the times of the necessary setups (Wagner, 1958; Hopp, 1996). Here, we introduce the probability of run-out to this standard model. Since this model is discrete, we assume the *Wagner-Whitin property*, which can be derived from the lack of speculative motives: for every time unit of the horizon either the production is zero or the expected inventory carried to the next time unit is zero. Our model differs from the standard one in several ways: (1) we consider the probability of run-out and the cost of obsolete inventory, (2) we include one time unit for lead-time and (3) we consider linearly decreasing inventory within a time unit. The parameters and variables of the model are the following:

Table 1 – Notation.

n	length of the horizon
F_i	forecast for time unit i
h	inventory holding cost per piece per time unit
c_S	setup cost
c_p	production cost per piece
p	probability of run-out in an arbitrary time unit

Let's suppose that we produce in time unit $t \in \{0,...,n\text{-}1\}$ for the time units $\{t+1,...,t+j\}$ for some $j \in \{1,...,n\text{-}t\}$. This implies two things: (1) the expected inventory at the beginning of time unit $t+1$ is zero (from the Wagner-Whitin property) and (2) the product has not run out until the beginning of the time unit t (which has a probability $(1-p)^t$). Fig. 1 presents this situation.

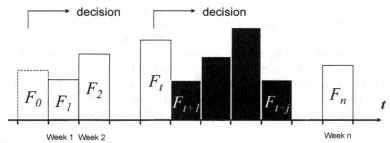

Figure 1 – Planning horizon.

Then for every $i \in \{1,...,j\}$ the expected storage cost in time unit $t+i$ is

$$SC(t,j,i) = (1-p)^i h \left(\sum_{k=i+1}^{j} F_{t+k} + \frac{F_{t+i}}{2} \right),$$ where $(1-p)^i$ expresses the probability that

the product is still saleable in the time unit i. The cost of obsolete inventory can be

determined similarly: $OC(t,j,i) = p(1-p)^{i-1} \sum_{k=i}^{j} F_{t+k}$, where $p(1-p)^{i-1}$ is the proba-

bility of running out the product in time unit i. To measure the loss in case of a run-out, the production cost of the obsolete inventory should be included into the total cost—it may represent both material and labor costs, and could be reduced with salvage value, etc. By summing up storage, obsolete inventory and setup costs, we get the total cost for time units $\{t+1,...,t+j\}$: $C_{tj} = c_s + \sum_{i=1}^{j}(SC(t,j,i)+OC(t,j,i))$. Then we can compute for every $t \in \{0,...,n-1\}$ the optimal total cost TC_t in the $\{t+1,...,n\}$ horizon by the following recursion: $TC_t = \min_{j\in\{1,...,n-t\}}\left\{C_{tj}+(1-p)^j TC_{t+j}\right\}$ and $TC_n := 0$. The optimal total cost for the whole horizon will be TC_0. Furthermore, if we note down the optimal j values, we can easily compute both the optimal lot size at the actual time unit and the expected number of setups on the horizon.

3.2 Heuristic approaches

Earlier, we have presented two different heuristics for the lot sizing problem (Váncza, 2006). Both of them compute only the first lot size and disregard the less trusted remote forecasts that used to fluctuate intensely. One of the heuristics minimizes the cost average by the quantity; the other minimizes the cost average by the expected consumption period. This latter one resembles the so-called Silver-Meal heuristic (Silver, 1973). We now recall these methods and analyze their behavior in a nutshell.

The parameters are the same as in the Wagner-Whitin case (see Table 1), but the decision variable x is the length of the expected consumption period which can be any real number between 1 and n. We use some further notations: $S_k := \sum_{l=1}^{k} F_l$ is the accumulated forecast of the first k time units, $i := \lfloor x \rfloor + 1$ and $y := \{x\}$ (the integer part of x plus one and the fractional part of x, respectively). The lot size can be calculated as the forecasted quantity until x: $q(x) := S_{i-1} + yF_i$ (the total amount of the first $(i-1)$ time units and the y fraction of the forecast of time unit i).

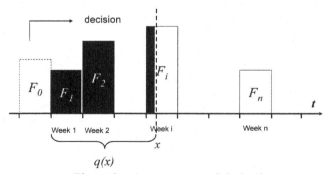

Figure 2 – Average cost minimization.

If there were no run-out, then the storage cost in the first l $(l < i)$ time units would be $SC(l,x) = h\sum_{k=1}^{l}\left(q(x)-S_{k-1}-\frac{F_k}{2}\right)$. With run-out, the expected storage cost will be the following:

$$SC(x) = \sum_{k=1}^{i} \left(p(1-p)^{k-1} SC(k-1,x) \right) + (1-p)^i \left(SC(i-1,x) + h\frac{y^2 F_i}{2} \right)$$

and the expected cost of obsolete inventory is:

$$OC(x) = c_p \sum_{k=1}^{i-1} \left(p(1-p)^{k-1} \left(q(x) - S_{k-1} \right) \right) + c_p p(1-p)^{i-1} y F_i.$$

Thus we obtain piecewise continuously differentiable average cost functions $AC_x(x) = \left(c_s + SC(x) + OC(x) \right)/x$ and $AC_q(x) = \left(c_s + SC(x) + OC(x) \right)/q(x)$ which can be minimized by searching through the roots of their derivative and the borders of the intervals.

3.3 Choosing the appropriate method and parameter

There are two fundamentally different situations: (1) run-out can occur with a certain possibility, but no further details are known and (2) the fact of the run-out and its date are known, but the demand forecast is uncertain. In the first case—which is the usual situation—one can use both WWr and the AC heuristics with an appropriate p value. In case of the known date of run-out, we distinguish whether the date is *near* or *far*. We regard the date near, if the previous methods (especially WWr) suggest that all forecasted quantities have to be produced immediately in one lot. If the date is far, then the previous methods can be used henceforward. Additionally, the formulas can be used with different probabilities in various time units.

However, if the date is near, then finding the appropriate lot size is much more subtle: over-planning leads to obsolete inventory, while under-planning may lead to costly additional setups. In this case, the horizon can be considered one period long; hence we propose a variant of the standard *newsvendor* model (Hopp, 1996) which minimizes the expected total cost in one period with uncertain demand. Naturally, this requires more/different information than the other situations.

While forecasts and most of the parameters are easily accessible in existing enterprise data warehouses, the probabilities of run-out are hard to estimate in general. Fortunately, in typical real-life production plans—where planned manufacturing of a product is sparse and involves large volumes—quantity is almost everywhere zero and the formulas are not too sensitive to the uncertainty. To measure this sensitivity, we propose that an interval around p should be examined instead of only a single value. Any of the methods can compute how changes in p influence the optimal lot size in the specific situation, thus we can get a measure for the *robustness* of the result. The less robust the proposed lot size, the more care is needed from the human experts who reconsider the results.

4. EXPERIENCES WITH INDUSTRIAL DATA

The above methods have been tested together with the industrial partners. The focal manufacturer—who is still responsible for the inventories—has provided the actual data weekly: component forecasts on 9 months long horizon with one week's time unit, inventory levels, production costs, approximated setup and inventory holding costs.

We have computed the proposed lot sizes with respect to probability of run-out in the interval $[0, 0.15]$—which took only a few seconds—and discussed the result with the experts of the factory. All the three methods were similar in that with relatively small p values (around 0.05) they have given nearly the same lot sizes calculated by the rules of thumb of the experts. In the other cases, either the forecasts were incomplete, or the experts had some extra knowledge about the demand of the specific product. An interesting further research direction would be to automatically filter out these extreme situations.

Another conclusion is that the result of WWr is more useful, since it can also tell the expected number of the setups on the horizon, which is important practical information. Furthermore, in some cases the heuristics have proposed too large quantities, since they have disregarded the efficiency on the whole horizon.

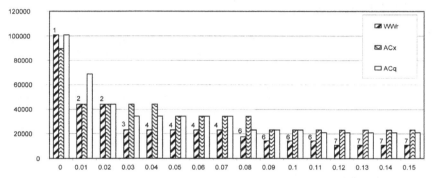

Figure 3 – Lot sizes in function of probability of run-out.

An illustrative example of the results can be seen on Fig. 3. The x axis represents the probabilities of run-out, while the y axis indicates the proposed lot sizes according to the different methods. In case of WWr, expected numbers of setups are indicated, too. Note that changing p can cause changes in the lot size, in the number of setups, in both or in neither. In this specific case, the human experts have proposed a lot of 40000 pieces, which was close to our results using $p = 0.02$.

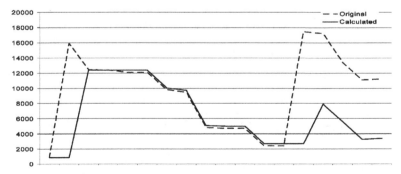

Figure 4 – Original and calculated inventory levels.

We have also simulated the methods with historic data sets on a five months long horizon. The goal of these "what-if" experiments was to explore the long-term effect of the novel lot sizing methods, and to compare the hypothetical and the historic inventory levels. When calculating lot sizes, we used 1% run-out probability and a predefined amount of safety stock. Fig. 4 shows a characteristic example comparing the original inventory levels with the simulation of a heuristic method. According to the simulations, calculated hypothetic curves never run under zero—i.e., the novel methods did not cause material shortage.

Due to the promising results, the focal manufacturer has just started to test a pilot software, which also contains the implementation of WWr. In addition, to better analyze the effects of the novel methods and to validate the complete logistics framework, we have defined a multi-agent organizational model of the network (Egri, 2005) and are going to make extensive simulation experiments over the complete data of the previous year's production and inventory histories.

5. CONCLUSIONS

We have suggested a two-level logistics framework for facilitating coordination between enterprises of a supply network and proposed methods for supporting decisions at the planning level. While the industrial deployment of the framework is underway, we extend our research to multi-item supply channels and finite capacities at the suppliers. Since our model is based on information sharing, assumes truthfulness of the partners. As a future work, we will examine the supply relationships with game theoretical tools and design such coordination mechanisms, which inspire enterprises to cooperate in pursuing mutual benefit.

6. ACKNOWLEDGEMENTS

This work has been supported by the VITAL NKFP grant No. 2/010/2004 and the OTKA grant No. T046509.

7. REFERENCES

1. Brahimi, N., Dauzere-Peres, S., Najid, N. M., Nordli, A.: Single Item Lot Sizing Problems. European Journal of Operational Research, 168, pp. 1-16, 2006.
2. Egri, P., Váncza, J.: Cooperative Planning in the Supply Network – A Multiagent Organization Model. In: Multi-Agent Systems and Applications IV (eds. Pechoucek, M., Petta, P., Varga, L. Zs.), Springer LNAI 3690, pp. 346-356, 2005.
3. Fleischmann, B., Meyr, H.: Planning Hierarchy, Modelling and Advanced Planning Systems. In de Kok, A. G., Graves, S. C. (eds): Supply Chain Management: Design, Coordination and Cooperation. Handbooks in Op. Res. and Man. Sci., 11, Elsevier, pp. 457-523, 2003.
4. Grabot, B., Geneste, L., Reynoso-Castillo, G., Vérot, S.: Integration of Uncertain and Imprecise Orders in the MRP Method. Journal of Intelligent Manufacturing, 16, pp. 215-234, 2005.
5. Hopp, W. J., Spearman, M. L.: Factory Physics – Foundations of Manufacturing Management. McGraw Hill, 1996.
6. Silver, E. A., Meal, H. C.: A Heuristic Selecting Lot Size Requirements for the Case of a Deterministic Time-varying Demand Rate and Discrete Opportunities for Replenishment. Production and Inventory Management, 14, pp. 64-77, 1973.
7. Váncza, J., Egri, P.: Coordinating Supply Networks in Customized Mass Production—A Contract-based Approach. Annals of the CIRP, 55/1, 2006, in print.
8. Wagner, H. M., Whitin, T. M.: Dynamic Version of the Economic Lot Size Model. Management Science, 5, pp. 89-96, 1958.

FEDERATIVE FACTORY DATA MANAGEMENT AN APPROACH BASED UPON SERVICE ORIENTED ARCHITECTURE

Reiner Anderl and Majid Rezaei
Department of Computer Integrated Design (DiK)
Technische Universität Darmstadt, Germany
{anderl, rezaei}@dik.tu-darmstadt.de

The current situation in product development, production scheduling and factory design is characterized by collaborative engineering, participative factory design and fragmentation of value-added chains. According to this trend, new challenges are to meet around this field. From increasing use of multiple IT tools (creation, verification and information management systems) a distributed heterogeneous IT-landscape is growing which affects all processes and leads to financial risks. Regarding this, product development and factory design require a transparent and redundancy-free information flow in order to accomplish this complexity. A federative FDM (factory data management) provides a federation of PDM and FDM-systems as well as distributed applications. It builds a solid foundation for acquisition and propagation of factor-related data. It enables efficient integration and aggregation of data to support technical and economical decisions for downstream phases of factory planning and to overcome the prevailing deficits. The vision and approaches are described in this paper, based on SOA technology and on a reference information model as a common ontology to overcome the semantic and syntactic heterogeneities of all involved domain-specific applications and multiple systems in this surrounding field.

1. INTRODUCTION

Today's situation in the interdependent field of product development and factory planning is characterized by acceleration of innovation cycles while reducing time-to-market and time to SOP (Start of Production). Regarding this, Fleischer et al. indicates in (Fleischer, 2005) that the number of SOPs by Daimler Chrysler increased from seven to ten and the development cycle has been shortened around four years. Additionally, we are observing a globalisation of markets more and more and a globalisation of dynamical enterprise structures which is the outcome of global corporate merges. Consequently, a global fragmentation of value-added chains, a spatially distributed collaborative engineering in product development and participative factory planning and production organization result from this current trend. In particular, the integration of suppliers and development partners in early phases of factory planning activities (Greenfield, Brownfield, Lean field and Streamlining) becomes more important and is indispensable. Additionally we can presently identify an increasing digitalization and virtualization of all processes and information within the factory planning and the production scheduling. A 3D-geometry-oriented and simulation-based factory design and planning are replacing conventional alpha-numerical production scheduling (Eißrich, 2005). Regarding this situation, every cross-domain department which is involved in product development and factory planning, uses different isolated IT applications and systems and generates domain-specific partial models. Generally, product development and production planning processes require transparent information flow by means of innovative tools in order to accomplish the complexity of all processes. This paper proposes a federative approach based upon SOA-technology with loosely coupled services and an information model to overcome these prevailing situations.

2. STATE OF THE ART

EXISTING SYSTEMS
Principally an integrative realization of a virtual factory is possible with today's available commercial tools (creation, verification- and information management systems). Nevertheless one can ascertain that especially in the field of information-acquisition and -propagation there is still a lot of improvement necessary. Today's PDM-Systems focus on the management of product related data. Accordingly the underlying data models base in the same way on product data management and not on factory data management. Hence it is necessary to extend these data models with generic characteristics of factories. According to (Frankel, 2005) the extended to factory-planning-needs adapted data models overcome the present situation and allow integrated management of product-related as well as production related data. There already exists a series of data management systems for managing manufacturing related data which allow integrated product, process and resource planning. Nevertheless commonly available systems often build upon a central database with monolithic data models in order to offer a holistic integration of all relevant data. According to this, such integration solutions are inflexible in particular with respect to future modifications and extensions. Furthermore, a distributed engineering collaboration can not be supported efficiently.

EXISTING DATA MODELS
The essential requirements for the realization of integrated virtual factory planning are a) bidirectional associability between domain-specific partial models and b) interoperability between different user systems. The implementation of an integrated PLM approach by using a common platform is proposed in (N.N.-CIMdata, 2005). However the use of common software package by all suppliers and system partners is rather a nonrealistic case. Therefore it is less significant for every involved department to agree on the use of the same software than it is to agree on the communication between these systems. According to (Anderl, 2005) a standardizing of communication, coordination and collaboration contributes to harmonizing all process within factory planning and production scheduling. A coherent standardized representation of data adds to the homogenization of the in many cases heterogeneous environment. A standard like STEP (standard for the exchange of product data) and IFC (industry foundation classes) for factory planning and production scheduling harmonizing the information flow doesn't currently exist.

Presently, a series of approaches from researchers and the industry exists which depend on STEP or comparable monolithically information models. But STEP is not compatible with today's web-based technologies. A large deficit of STEP is the lack of a fine granularity interface to access product-related data over the internet (Nowaki, 2003). Figure 1 depicts that numerous applications exist within digital factory planning which often generate proprietary models. Therefore the creation of a uniform monolithic data model for the fine grain data integration of these tools is very complex and needs for agreement between different software-vendors.

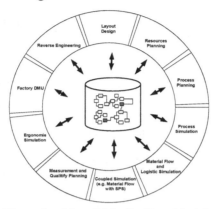

Figure 1 – Monolithically Data Model.

SERVICE ORIENTED APPROACHES
In order to avoid communication barriers between different systems coherent representation of relevant data is necessary as well as coherent services which provide the access and the possibility to modify essential data. Therefore in addition to the representation forms, a standardized interface is necessary in order to access distributed data. In order to access data being managed in various PDM's, "PDM Enabler" was developed in the nineties, which was very little accepted by the OEM's. "PLM Services" as a new standard of OMG (Object Management Group) provide a promising solution (within the product development at present time). The specification of PLM Services depends on standards (STEP AP214, XML, WSDL and SOAP) and enables distributed data exchange and communication between heterogeneous systems (OMG, 2005).

3. REQUIREMENTS AND OBJECTIVES

From the previously described situation it becomes evident that most of the worldwide operating companies are exposed to a dynamic change of structure which is also reflected in these companies' IT-infrastructure. Derived from this background is the necessity for an environment which enables distributed engineering collaboration. It should be considered that single domains keep their local autonomy regarding the administration of their data and are consolidated to a DV-network through a federative environment. A federative layer is in charge of bringing the necessary information together from different source systems without the necessity of the user operating single source systems individually or having to deal with the architecture of these systems. Furthermore a synchronous and asynchronous data sharing and data exchange using the federative environment shall be possible over the internet. Also a fine-grain data sharing shall be reached, not only at the file level but also at the object level. The federative approach as described in this paper has to harmonize dynamic processes at the inter-enterprise and intra-enterprise level and assures the interoperability between the interdisciplinary isolated applications and data management systems, particularly throughout all phases of factory planning considering appropriate standards. The Major challenge in this context is transformation of data formats, resolving technical and semantic differences and the *integration and aggregation of data* from multiple (decentralized) systems.

4. APPROACH: FEDERATIVE FACTORY DATA MANAGEMENT

4.1 Components of federative infrastructure

The federative environment consists of tree substantial components (Meta Data, Services and Transfer Protocol) which will be envisaged in this section.

META DATA
The federative infrastructure is based on virtual integration of data and information from different autonomous sources systems (e.g. PDM, ERP, FDM, etc.). Therefore it makes sense not to exchange the entire product and factory data of different applications at this point, but only the relevant data or only parts of the data (meta data). The federative environment is based on the exchange of meta data of the native data. Meta data are one of the substantial components of the federation environment. These data describe native data (documents) and contain, in addition to identifying and classifying data (e.g. document number, version counter, ID, etc.), logical interconnection data about native data (e.g. information about location of physical files). They can also contain defined technical data. Some of the data management systems provide configurations to define technical meta data as common (interface) data which can be shared from two or more applications. For example, a set of common data which are used by simulation and process planning tools in order to facilitate integrative factory planning. In order to assure the access to meta data without much programming efforts, XML (eXtensible Markup Language) technology can be used to describe these data. Thereby, XML files can be generated from meta data of databases, so that for each version of partial models (e.g. simulation models) a set of meta data exists which contains results of a simulation (e.g. cycle times of machine tools, production line utilization and etc.). A process planner uses these data as raw data for his planning activities (figure 2).

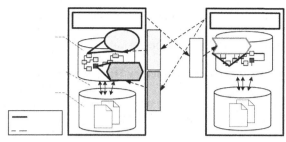

Figure 2 – Distributed data sharing between different systems.

SERVICES FOR META DATA

In order to access to meta data, services are required which allow queries and manipulation of data on different heterogeneous systems (figure 2). They provide a transmission of data between different data sources and mapping of semantic and syntactic of source data to target (system specific) data. Hence the technical realization of federative environment by means of SOA technology (services oriented architecture) appears to be convenient. What distinguishes the SOA from other architectures is the loose coupling of services. Loose coupling means that the user of a service is essentially independent of the service. Loose-coupled applications are more flexible as tightly-coupled applications. Services can be implemented as web services which encapsulate native operations on the back-end systems. They can be published on the internet for other users through WSDL (Web Services Description Language) files. WSDL files contain information about the identification and localization of services as well as information about semantic and syntactic of input- and output data which will be exchanged.

COMMUNICATION PROTOCOL FOR EXCHANGE OF MESSAGES

It is also significant to ensure the transfer of meta data between heterogeneous systems. Therefore, SOAP (Simple Object Access Protocol) as a standardized transport protocol is dedicated to this approach. By means of this technology data are packaged (encapsulated) into a SOAP message (figure 3). According to this, consumer of services for meta data doesn't have to worry about the operating system and language as well as a component model used to create or access the services.

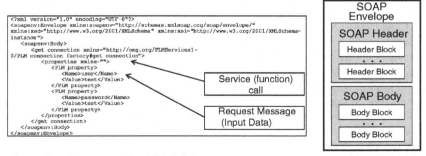

Figure 3 – Construct of a SOAP-Message as a request-message (OMG, 2005).

Exchanged data are meta data, data for operation invocation and information about services (e.g. port, server, binding, etc.). The new specification of SOAP allows exchange of files (xml or non-xml) as attachments of SOAP messages.

4.2 System Architecture of Federative Factory Data Management

The IT architecture of FFDM (see figure 4) builds upon four layers: front-end layer, federation layer, interface layer and back-end layer.

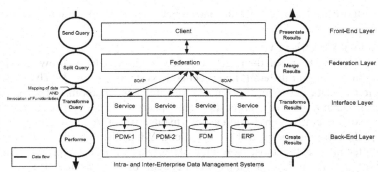

Figure 4 – Virtual Federative Environment.

I) FRONT-END-LAYER
The presentation layer or front-end can be realized as a web browser that accepts the request (input) of a user and presents merged response data of back-end systems.

II) FEDERATION LAYER
Due to federative characteristics, the client sends queries to a central point. This central point or node is defined at the federation layer. Thus, the client doesn't need to send his query to several PDM's or FDM's individually. The federation layer is a central component of virtual integration intention and performs integration tasks similar to the splitting of client queries and the merging of results in compliance with algorithm guidelines that are stored on a repository. Federation layer communicates with other services and can be regarded as a communication layer between front-end and back-end systems. This layer defines a communication interface between loosely coupled services and manages communication and cooperation behaviour of objects.

III) ACCESS INTERFACE LAYER
The access interface layer is defined by services (they can be called as connectors). The services act as a wrapper which envelop data and connects this encapsulated data as a SOAP-Message to the federation layer. They are the interface to the back-end system which provides methods to create, update, delete and query data on the respective systems. The services accept client queries and transform these queries to native operation invocations of respective systems, map results to the information model conformal data of federation and delegate them back to the client.

IV) BACK-END LAYER
Back-end layer includes back-end systems similar to engineering data management systems (PDM, FDM, ERP, and MES) and data basis (Oracle, DB2, SQL, etc.).

4.3 Meta model for Representation of Meta Data

For each defined meta data between two or more applications on different systems one or more services can exist, so that a huge amount of services can arise without a coordination between different domain specific departments. Thus, redundant services are materialized which have various semantic and syntactic. Furthermore, users have to integrate all services on an integration layer in order to homogenize queries. Hence the definition of an information model (meta model) for the federation can contribute to describe a common terminology. According to this meta model as a reference model all meta data can be defined and the mapping process can be performed based on this model. This reference model provides a foundation for the development of new (standardized) services and corresponding WSDL files. Thus, uniform semantic and syntactic of request- and response data as well as operation invocation can be achieved. An additional conversation of queries can be avoided. Regarding this approach, all system-vendors have to adapt the communication behaviour of their data management systems to this reference model.

4.4 Scenario: Composition of virtual factory structure and related factory data based on federative approach

A virtual factory structure can be composed through structure data of production lines with the corresponding factory components (machine tools, roboter, handling systems, process plan, simulation models and results, etc.) on the client layer (e.g. Browser). The Federation layer merges all project-related (physical distributed) data as a puzzle to one (virtual) result and delegates them to the client. By means of structure and referenced native data (e.g. factory DMU and simulation data) a virtual factory can be generated through distributed data. Also a re- and configuration of factory by using different structures and components can contribute for next generation of factory plans. The federative environment allows arbitrary combinations of various distributed data. By federation of relevant data, it is possible to carry out analysis and evaluation of the factory from different views (technical, economical and ecological views) and if necessary for each phases of factory planning and along the factory life cycle.

5. RESEARCH PERSPECTIVE

In the context of a common project of IFF-Stuttgart (Institute of Industrial Manufacturing and Management) and DiK-Darmstadt (Department of Computer Integrated Design) a standardized collaborative environment for factory life cycle management based on existing standards is intended. The vision of this project is a) the consideration of factory as a product and realization of FLM (factory life cycle management) and b) integration of all concerned domain applications within the factory design and production scheduling in an open and standardized environment (Constantinescu, 2006).

6. OUTLOOK AND CONCLUSION

Manufacturing companies are facing the trend of distributed value-added chains and collaborative engineering processes as a result of the increasing globalization of markets. Participative factory design and production planning are especially arising from this situation reflected in heterogeneous IT-landscape and a spreading process chain increase the complexity of factory data management. Product development and production planning require transparent and redundancy-free information flows in order to handle this complexity. Currently (isolated) IT-solutions in the surrounding field of factory design and planning have not been designed yet in order to allow a fast and flexible integration of upstream and downstream phases within an overall concept. The approach of "Federative Factory Data Management (FFDM)" that is described in this paper, aims at providing a solution to avoid these deficits by harmonizing the factory data. It covers the development of a coherent IT framework that binds different data processing systems of factory planning and design and product data management systems, while taking available standards (e.g. Web Services, XML and SOAP) into account. This framework is based upon the approach of the SOA-technology and web services. It realizes the integration of back-end systems easily within and outside the enterprise boundaries efficiently. Therefore, the considering manufacturing plants as independent complex systems (Westkämper, 2004) whose life cycles are significant for the future factory planning, the introduction of the FFDM system is a sine qua non.

7. REFERENCES

1. Anderl, R., Trippner, F.: "STEP (Standard for the exchange of product data): Eine Einführung in die Entwicklung, Implementierung und industrielle Nutzung der Normenreihe ISO 10303 (STEP)". B.G. Teubner Stuttgart – Leipzig, 2000.
2. Anderl, R., Rezaei, M., Pfouga, A. J.:"A new holistic approach for virtual manufacturing". International PACE-Forum in Darmstadt. 2005.
3. Constantinescu, C., Hummel, V., Westkämper E.: Fabrik Life Cycle Management. Kollaborative standardisierte Umgebung für die Fabrikplanung (KOSIFA). In: wt Werkstattstechnik online, Springer-VDI-Verlag, wt-online Issue 4-2006.
4. Eißrich, R.: "Die Vernetzte und integrierte Planung durch die digitale Fabrik", Intelligenter Produzieren, VDMA Verlag GmbH, 2005/1, 2005.
5. Fleischer, J., Wawerla, M., Ender, T., Nyhuis, P., Heins, M., Großhenning, P.: "Digitaler Serienlauf beschleunigt den Markteintritt". Intelligenter Produzieren. VDMA Verlag, 01/2005.
6. Frankel, A.: "Advanced Tooling Solution".10° Seminário Internacional de Alta Tecnologia, SCPM, UNIMEP, Piracicaba, Brazil. 10/2005.
7. Nowaki, S., Von Lukas, U.: "Föderation von PDM-Systemen auf der Basis des PDTnet-Schemas". ProduktDatenJournal. Ausgabe Nr.1. 2003.
8. N.N.: "The Value of digital Manufacturing in a PLM Environment". A CIMdata Case Study: Fiat Auto S.p.A. 03/2005.
9. N.N.: "Product Lifecycle Management Services". Convenience Document of OMG. dtc/05-03-08.
10. Westkämper, E., Constantinescu, C., Hummel, V.: New paradigms in Manufacturing Engineering: Factory Life Cycle. In: Annals of the Academic Society for Production Engineering. Research and Development, XIII/1, Volume XIII, Issue 1, 2006.

ENGINEERING CHANGE IMPACT ANALYSIS IN PRODUCTION USING VR

Jan C. Aurich and Martin Rößing
University of Kaiserslautern, Germany
{aurich, roessing}@cck.uni-kl.de

The market conditions that manufacturing companies are currently exposed to, leads to high demands in terms of flexibility in production and thus to a high number of engineering changes in production. In this paper, an approach will be presented to support engineering change processes, to identify the change impact within production and to process multiple engineering changes simultaneously. Therefore, the elements of production systems as well as their attributes and relations will be represented by using UML. These are used in VR to identify potential impact on other elements when changing an element. After this, a change impact matrix is deduced and a similarity analysis between changes is conducted. The measure of similarity will be used to combine multiple engineering changes to engineering change projects.

1. INTRODUCTION

Globalization creates an increasing number of companies struggling for customers. To ensure competitive advantage, companies are forced to individualize products and services and to quickly place them into the market. Thus, the market character has changed from a supplier driven market to a customer driven market (Aurich, 2004a; Monostori, 2003). This market character continuously leads to altering challenges in production systems, which imply a permanent demand for engineering change. To be successful, companies have to quickly react on challenges by precisely adapting their production system to new demands (Wirth, 2000). The result is a high number of engineering changes (ECs) that have to be processed simultaneously. Another important characteristic of today's production systems is their high complexity (Suh-Nam, 2005). This complexity arises from the number of elements in production systems such as machines, workplaces or logistics elements and the number of their relations. This complicates the implementation of ECs into production. Consequently, while the number of ECs and the complexity of production systems are increasing, the time that is available for the implementation of ECs is decreasing.

The aim of this paper is to present a concept to quickly adapt the elements of a production system to new demands and to cope with multiple ECs simultaneously. Therefore, the paper is structured as follows: in section 2 some general aspects of EC management in production will be presented; based on these, an object model of EC management will be developed in section 3, which is the basis for the usage of VR to support engineering change, which will be presented in section 4. This will be used to analyse the engineering change impact, to determine the similarity of ECs and to derive engineering change projects for the simultaneous implementation of multiple ECs in production in section 5. Section 6 will conclude the paper with a few remarks on further research directions.

2. EC MANAGEMENT IN PRODUCTION

Engineering Change Management (ECM) plays an important role in manufacturing companies since it is time consuming and costly. Industrial case studies proved that it is a serious problem within manufacturing (Huang and Mak, 1999). To handle ECM three general types of approaches can be differentiated (Do, 2002):

- The *document-oriented* approach focuses on adjusting the documentation, which is associated to the change object. It usually uses electronic document management systems to process engineering change requests and to keep the consistency of the documentation with the change object. Moreover, the documentation is separated from the change object.
- The *process-oriented* approach focuses on implementing standardised processes to manage EC and its data. The aim is to enhance EC lead time and to secure the involvement of all departments that are affected by the EC.
- The *structure-oriented* approach uses the structure of the change object including its relations to other objects to store and to manage the information of ECs. In this approach, the status of the change object and its documentation is tightly integrated.

Engineering change is inevitable in manufacturing companies; in fact, to eliminate it is both undesirable and unrealistic since this would inhibit the chance to improve (Tavčar and Duhovnik, 2005; Clark and Fujimoto, 1991). Therefore, the objective in ECM must be to ease the processing of changes that occur. The focus in this paper is put on supporting change execution by combining a process-oriented approach and a structure-oriented approach to handle ECs.

Engineering change processes usually are divided into specific phases. In literature, many reference processes for ECM exist. Examples can be found at Chen, Shir and Shen (2002), Huang and Mak (1999), Terwiesch and Loch (1999) or at Lindemann (1998). Based on these, a generalized model of an EC process in production systems can be divided into an initiation, realization and a post-processing phase (Aurich, 2004b).

- The *initiation* phase includes the detection of EC demands, the identification of change impact and the planning of the EC realization by developing work packages for implementation. The goal is to gather as much information as possible in an early stage of the EC process.
- During the *realization* phase, work packages are defined and carried out to introduce the EC into the production system. The goal is to implement ECs while still delivering products and thus to avoid or reduce downtime. The information that was acquired in the initiation phase is used here.

- In the *post-processing* phase the knowledge that was gained during the EC process is identified. This will be stored as a documentation of the current EC process and can be used in future EC processes.

Such a reference process describes a framework for the management of EC in industrial practice. Although it is a sound basis for EC management, it contains some major deficits. The critical success factors for EC management, which are the easy identification of change impact, the coordination of multiple ECs and the efficient usage of knowledge during the EC process are not well-supported by such a process. Therefore, this process-oriented part of the approach presented in this paper has to be complemented by a structure-oriented part.

3. OBJECTS IN ENGINEERING CHANGE MANAGEMENT

The structure-oriented part is based on an object model for EC management. The model was developed by using the notation of the Unified Modelling Language (UML). It comprises several classes and associations (see figure 1). A class is defined as the attributes and the operations of objects. Attributes are describing data of classes; operations are services that can be obtained from a class. An association represents the linkage that exists between classes. It is described by an association name and a reading direction. Each class represents a set of information, thus its purpose is to collect and to store data. UML in these cases speaks of so called entities (Booch, 2005).

In the representation, the main entity is the *engineering change* class, which describes the engineering change, the person responsible for it, the trigger, the goal, and the status of the change. During the initiation phase of an EC process, the *company strategy* evaluates an engineering change that occurs in terms of its compliance with the company goals. The engineering change in turn realizes the company strategy and goals if it is implemented in production.

The production itself embodies several *production objects*. These are represented by a textual description, their location, and their version. Each production object has a *history*, which arises from the originally constructed production in conjunction with the ECs in the past. Once an EC is implemented, the production object is updated and the history of the production object is expanded. In addition to the corresponding EC, the history class contains the proceeding of the EC, the results and the critical success factors for the update of the production object. Thus, the history can be characterized as knowledge, which is connected to the production object and that is stored during the post-processing phase of the EC process. Apart from its history, each production object also has relations to other production objects. These are represented in the *relation* class. A relation is characterized by the relation type, a textual description, its direction, and the relation intensity. Once an EC is implemented in production, it influences the relations of the production objects.

An *EC Project* is generated by combining multiple ECs during the realization phase. In addition to the ECs, the EC Project class comprises the start and end dates of the EC Project, a textual description, a responsible person for the EC Project and a project status. An EC Project affects the production objects when the ECs that it comprises are implemented in production. The combination of ECs to EC Projects is defined by the relations of the production objects (see Section 5). The ECs and the EC Project is supported by the knowledge that is stored in the History class.

This object model is the basis for the usage of VR in EC management. VR plays an important role for the analysis of the EC before its realization. This will be described in the next section.

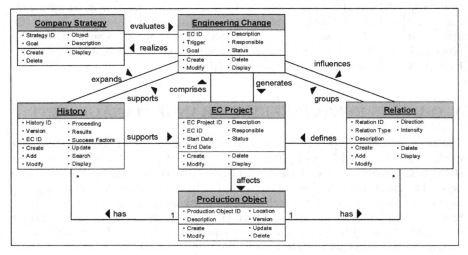

Figure 1 – Engineering Change Class diagram.

4. VR IN ENGINEERING CHANGE

VR-technology is already used in various industrial applications related to the early stages of the life-cycle of production systems. Examples are design for assembly, simulation, evaluation and visualization of planned production systems or training of employees (Wicker, 2004; Zachmann, 2001; Neugebauer, 2004). VR-technology can be characterized by the immersion of the user into the virtual environment, the interaction with it and the three-dimensional real-time simulation (Wiendahl, 2002). Based on these characteristics, VR-technology has the potential to support EC processes in production especially during the initiation phase. The results are helpful for planning the implementation and to gain as much knowledge on the EC as possible before its implementation. This information particularly comprises the impact of the EC as well as the necessary steps that have to be taken to implement an EC.

To achieve this, the classes as they are described before are stored in a VR database. This VR database also comprises the three-dimensional models of the production objects. Based on this, the virtual environment in VR consists of a realistic three-dimensional visualisation of the production objects. Apart from their geometry all the information that is stored together with an object can be displayed in the virtual environment. Also, the relations of the object as well as the object's history are accessible. When pointing at a production object, this information is shown as textual object information (see figure 2).

The benefit from this approach is threefold:

- The user gets a *support* during the EC analysis. He can access all relevant information that is stored together with an object such as technical data or the object's location. The information about the object's history prevents him from implementing solutions that have been proved to be unsuccessful in former EC processes.
- The access to all the relations of the production objects helps to identify the *EC impact*. Each relation potentially implies an EC impact. By displaying the relations of objects, their types, directions, and intensities the user is prevented from overseeing EC impact.
- The realistic visualization of the production objects supports the *deduction of steps* for implementation since the user gets a realistic impression of dimensions. The identified steps are the basis for the definition of work packages for implementation. An additional support for the definition of work packages is the object's history with its lessons learned from former EC processes.

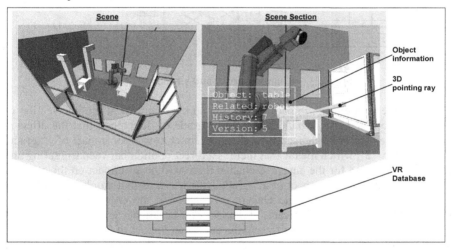

Figure 2 – VR in engineering change.

The results of the VR analysis are the basis for the further processing of ECs, which will be developed in the following sections. Since the number of ECs is increasing, it has to support the implementation of multiple ECs. In subsection one a change impact matrix and a similarity analysis is presented. These are the basis to define engineering change projects by combining ECs in subsection two.

5. IMPLEMENTATION OF MULTIPLE ECs

5.1 Change impact and similarity analysis

Based on the VR analysis, a change impact matrix is deduced. Change impact matrices allow the capture of change relations between production system elements

Digital Enterprise Technology

and are a compact visual representation of change impact (Keller, 2005; Clarkson, 2001). The column headings show the triggering production elements. The row heading show the affected production elements. The affected elements will be changed on an engineering change of the triggering elements (see figure 3).

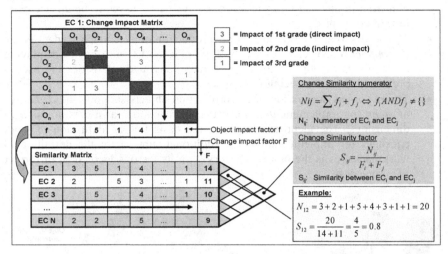

Figure 3 – Change impact and similarity analysis.

An engineering change impact is represented by a number at the intersection of two production elements, which indicates the grade of directness, that the affected production element is influenced by a change. Direct impact, or impact of 1st grade, is indicated by '3', which means that there is a direct relation between triggering and affected objects and for the analysed change there will be an impact on the affected objects. '2' indicates an impact of 2nd grade, which means that an object is affected via an impact of 1st grade. The change propagates in the objects- and relations-structure. '1' consequently indicates an impact of 3rd or higher grade when an object is affected by an object that itself was affected by an impact of 2nd grade. For better visualization and to easily identify the critical relations, the numbers are red, orange and green respectively. The sum of each column is the object impact factor, which represents the grade of impact for each object. The higher the object impact factor, the stronger this object is affected by the engineering change and the more it has to be considered during the implementation phase.

To realize the implementation of multiple ECs, the grade of similarity between ECs is calculated. For this purpose, the object impact factors of the ECs are transferred into a similarity matrix. To determine the similarity between two ECs, three numbers have to be calculated. First and second are the change impact factors for both ECs, which is the sum of all object impact factors of both ECs respectively (horizontal sums in the similarity matrix). The third number is the change similarity numerator. The change similarity numerator is calculated by adding up those object impact factors that have a positive value for both ECs. If the change impact factor is zero or empty in one of the ECs, this object is ignored, even if it has a positive value in the other EC. The change similarity factor then is calculated by dividing the change similarity numerator by the sum of both change impact factors. The change similarity factor is transferred into the "roof" of the similarity matrix at the intersection of the both ECs that are treated.

5.2 Engineering Change projects

The results of the change impact and similarity analysis enable the definition of EC projects. An EC project is generated by combining multiple ECs depending on the similarity factor of ECs. A similarity factor of zero indicates that two ECs affect different production objects so that it doesn't make sense to combine them. As soon as the change similarity factor is above 0.5, the combination of two ECs in one EC project should be considered. This project can additionally be compared with other ECs in terms of their similarity and their potential to be combined.

The grouped ECs are the basis for the further definition of the EC project. Each EC represents one work package. These can be divided into single tasks, which are represented by the production objects that are affected. For each task a start- and end-date is defined and an employee is assigned to it as the responsible person. The work packages are scheduled by using a combination of forward- and backward scheduling. A special focus has to be put on those tasks that affect objects with a high object impact factor and that are part of several ECs. Due to their close relation to other objects and ECs an error that happens during implementation at these objects potentially can affect the integrity of the production system or other work packages in the EC project. This can be avoided by assigning the same employees for the tasks affecting this object or by implementing an intensive information exchange between work packages that comprise this production object.

During the implementation phase the methods of project management are used to track the activities of the tasks and work packages and to intervene in case of deviations. This could be the adaptation of the schedule or of the tasks in the work packages.

In the post-processing phase the knowledge that has been gained during the EC process is saved for future EC. Therefore, the experiences of the employees that have been involved in the EC process are gathered and written down as textual information. This information helps to expand the history of the production objects and supports future ECs.

6. CONCLUSION

The high number of engineering changes in production due to fast altering market conditions is both, time-consuming and expensive. Although there are many approaches and processes to deal with engineering change, the identification of change impact and the processing of multiple engineering change requests simultaneously are still challenging.

An engineering change impact and a similarity analysis have been outlined in this paper. These are based on an object model that describes the objects of engineering change management in production and which is modelled in UML. In the next step, the use VR to analyse the EC and to evaluate the impact of the change on the elements of the production system was presented. To realize the similarity analysis the change impact matrix has been developed, which shows the relations between the production system elements affected by the EC. By using simple mathematical equations the degree of similarity was conducted as a basis for the processing of multiple ECs simultaneously.

The method presented contains some assumptions and will be applied in a research project. However, the need for and the possible success of the method seems clear.

7. REFERENCES

1. Aurich, JC, Drews, O, Wageknecht, C: Competency based production planning in dynamic production environments. ICME, CIRP International Seminar on Intelligent Computation in Manufacturing Engineering, 4, 2004a, 47-52.
2. Aurich, JC, Rößing, M, Jaime, R. Änderungsmanagement in der Produktion. In ZWF – Zeitschrift für wirtschaftlichen Fabrikbetrieb, Vol. 99, No. 7/8, 2004b: 381-384.
3. Booch, G, Rumbaugh, J, Jacobson, I. Unified Modelling Language User Guide. Upper Saddle River, NJ, Munich: Addison-Wesley, 2005.
4. Chen, YM, Shir, WS, Shen, CY. Distributed engineering change management for allied concurrent engineering. In International Journal of Computer Integrated Manufacturing, Vol. 15, No. 2, 2002: 127-151.
5. Clark, KB, Fujimoto, T. Product Development Performance: Strategy, Organization and Management in the World Auto Industry. Cambridge: Harvard School Press, 1991.
6. Clarkson, JP, Simons, C, Eckert, C. Predicting change propagation in complex design. In Proceedings of DECT 01. ASME 2001 Design Engineering Technical Conferences and Computers and Information in Engineering Conference. Pittsburgh: 2001.
7. Do, J, Choi, IJ, Jang, MK. A Structure-Oriented Product Data Representation of Engineering Changes for Supporting Integrity Constraints. In The International Journal of Advanced Manufacturing Technology, Vol. 20, No. 8, 2002: 564-570.
8. Huang, GQ, Mak, KL. Current practices of engineering change management in UK manufacturing industries. In International Journal of Operations & Production Management, Vol. 19, No. 1, 1999: 21-37.
9. Keller, R, Eckert, CM, Clarkson, PJ. Multiple Views to Support Engineering Change Management for Complex Products. In Proceedings: Third International Conference on Coordinated and Multiple Views in Exploratory Visualization (CMV 2005), London, UK, 5 July 2005. Los Alamitos, USA: IEEE Computer Society, 2005: 33-41.
10. Lindemann, U, Reichwald, R. Integriertes Änderungsmanagement. Berlin, Heidelberg: Springer, 1998.
11. Monostori, L, Váncza J, Márkus, A, Kádár, B, Viharos, ZJ. Towards the Realization of Digital Enterprises. Proc. 36th CIRP International Seminar on Manufacturing Systems, June 03 – 05 2003, Saarland University, Saarbrücken, Germany.
12. Neugebauer, R, Weidlich, D, Kolbig, S, Polzin, T. Perspektiven von Virtual-Reality-Technologie in der Produktionstechnik – VRAx. In Neugebauer, R. (ed.): Tagungsband 4. Chemnitzer Produktionstechnische Kolloquium. Zwickau: 2004, 333-347.
13. Suh-Nam, P. Complexity in engineering. Annals of the CIRP, 54 (2005) 2, 581-598.
14. Tavčar, J, Duhovnik, J. Engineering change management in individual and mass production. In Robotics and Computer-Integrated Manufacturing, Vol. No. 3, 2005: 205-215.
15. Terwiesch, C, Loch CH. Managing the Process of Engineering Change Orders – The Case of the Climate Control System in Automobile Development. In Journal of Product Innovation Management, Vol. 16, No. 2, 1999: 160-172.
16. Wicker, K. The virtues of virtual reality. In Power, Vol. 148, 2004: 59-62.
17. Wiendahl HP., Harms T, Fiebig C. Virtual Factory Design – A New Tool for a Cooperative Planning Approach. In Proc. 1st CIRP(UK) Seminar on Digital Enterprise Technology. September 16 – 17 2002, University of Durham, UK, 193-196.
18. Wirth, S (ed.). Flexible, temporäre Fabrik – Ergebnisbericht der Vordringlichen Aktion. Karlsruhe, 2000.
19. Zachmann, G. Virtual Reality in Assembly Simulation. Darmstadt: Zentrum für Graphische Datenverarbeitung e. V., 2001.

VIRTUAL FACTORY FRAMEWORK: KEY ENABLER FOR FUTURE MANUFACTURING

Paolo Pedrazzoli, Marco Sacco, Anders Jönsson and Claudio R. Boër

TTS srl, Italy
pedrazzoli@ttsnetwork.com
ITIA-CNR, Italy
marco.sacco@itia.cnr.it
ETHZ, Switzerland
joensson@imes.mavt.ethz.ch
ICIMSI, Switzerland
claudio.boer@icimsi.ch

The global market with increasing competition calls for new strategies that strengthen the future manufacturing systems. This paper presents the underlying models and ideas enabling a new conceptual framework for the next generation of Virtual Factory implementations. The approach fosters four pillars: a standard extensible data model; decoupled functional modules, based on an object oriented Virtual Factory paradigm; an event driven paradigm at the core of abstract objects management; the integration of knowledge at different layers for the decoupled functional modules. The implementation of a Virtual Factory based on the presented framework, points to the usefulness when developing future manufacturing systems.

1. INTRODUCTION

A primary concept highlighted in the "Manu*future* Strategic Research Agenda" is the innovating production. The idea includes new business models and approaches to industrial engineering that need to be supported by ground-breaking Information and Communication Technologies (ICT). This paper fosters a new framework for the key enabling instrument for the factory of the future: the Virtual Factory (VF).

The implementation of a holistic, integrable, up-gradable, scalable VF carries high cost savings in the implementation of new manufacturing facilities thanks to the effective representation of buildings, resources and products. The ability to simulate dynamic complex behaviour, over the whole life cycle with scalable level of details, is the fundamental cornerstone to achieve time and cost savings while increasing overall performance in the design of new facilities and in the management, evaluation and evolution of existing ones (Jönsson 03, VDI 04).

This paper presents the underlying models and ideas at the foundation of a new conceptual framework for the next generation VF implementation, consistent with the Manu*future* vision, meant to lay the basis for future works and applications in this research area.

The presented approach identifies four pillars:

I - *Standard Extensible Data Model* for factories, taking into account the needs of a holistic and scalable modelling, of real time management of manufacturing data and of collaborative engineering networks.

II - *Decoupled Functional Modules,* based on an object oriented VF paradigm meant to facilitate modelling of complex behaviour through natural mapping abstractions and modular code development.

III - *Event Driven Paradigm* at the core of abstract objects management. This structure enables a centralized synchronization (not control) of the external decoupled modules, thanks to the internal transition system of the core, enabling the second pillar and fostering unparalleled performances (see section 5) and increased quality in the environment representation.

IV - *Integration of Knowledge* at different layers as engine for the modules. The primary objective is to achieve tools which can model a wider range of complex systems and support greater comprehension of the modelled phenomenon. Moreover, the integration of knowledge throughout the VF has the potential to deliver fundamental advisory capabilities as a companion to product, process, plant development and life-cycle management.

The Virtual Factory Framework (VFF) presented lays the basis to simultaneously address all interrelated aspects of product, process and plant life cycle, from design to disposal/recycling, supporting engineers, operating in networks, using knowledge intensive ICT tools based on standardised platform.

2. MANU*FUTURE* & FRAMEWORK PROGRAM 7

The Manu*future* strategic research agenda identifies two fronts of intense and growing competitive pressure on Europe: on one hand, in the high-tech sector we see other developed countries and, on the other hand, in more traditional sectors we face low-wage countries. Moreover, these last countries are rapidly modernising their production methods and enhancing their technological capabilities. To face this challenge, the Manu*future* initiative promotes a response based on an industrial transformation meant to strengthen Europe's ability to compete in terms of high added value, because cost-based competition is not compatible with the goal of maintaining the Community's social and sustainability standards. Manu*future* promotes a response in terms of five main points and their associated new enabling technologies: 1- new, added-value products and services; 2 - new business models; 3 - new advanced industrial engineering; 4 - new emerging manufacturing science and technologies; 5 - transformation of existing R&D and education infrastructure to support world-class manufacturing. The hereby proposed approach is meant to empower those points promoting a successful European innovative industry that will be adaptive, digital, networked and knowledge-based (Westkämper, 2005).

One of the four "applications research", identified in the proposal of the European Parliament and of the Council concerning the seventh framework programme, is the ICT supporting manufacturing industry towards rapid and adaptive design, production and delivery of highly customised goods, digital and virtual production and modelling & simulation, in a dynamic networked collaborative work environment. The development of a knowledge-based Virtual

Factory Framework, based on the new paradigm hereinafter presented, is seen as a concrete response to those research needs and as a major strategic priority for European manufacturing enterprises in all sectors.

3. THE R&D FRAMEWORK AND STATE OF THE ART

Thus rapid product, process, enterprise realization and integration through an effective virtual tool have been identified among the imperatives for enabling the next generation manufacturing. This paper proposes a VF approach meant to support these imperatives that take into account past results and framework proposals.

Several approaches have been fostered by national and international research programmes and the idea of a reference framework has been introduced by (Krolak 96, Jain 95). Most of the previous projects, ManuFuturing (Boër 97), MPA (Sacco 04, Boër 00), IRMA (http://www.virart.nottingham.ac.uk/Projects_Irma.htm), exploited an existing suite (VEGA Multigen + Arena, or ad hoc application + Quest) for developing VF applications. These projects realized very good applications, but they lacked flexibility and reusability. Moreover integration was achieved on ad hoc basis. In the just started projects DiFac and CoSpace, a clear architecture for a seamless, flexible and up-gradable solution for developing the VF is not apparent or emerging. This topic is also highlighted as crucial in the NoE INTUITION. One of the main problems everybody is facing, in the development of a VF, is the availability of proper tools and framework (Mueller 02, Waller 02, Zhai 02).

Most of the previous projects and approaches focus either on the use of commercial tools (Superscape, DigitalMock-up, WorldToolkit) either on more low level software (Vega, Performer, OpenGL directly or customized set of libraries, such as the Unifeye SDK). The first approach faces the problem of excessively rigid tools for developing a complete factory and its functionalities, or too simple to have realistic results. The second, besides the problem of starting from scratches, confronts with the need to offer complex simulation functionality, thus implying the integration of existing tools whose interface has to be studied and adapted.

Lastly, several projects are demonstrating the possibility to democratize the use VR tools, thus making them widespread, such as the IP KoBaS (Pedrazzoli 04).

The VFF represents a fundamental cornerstone for the next generation virtual manufacturing that addresses the issues discussed related to previous approaches: the VFF will be used as an object oriented framework to support single and group work in an immersive and interactive way, for concurrent product design, proto-typing and manufacturing (Schuh 03), as well as worker training, providing support for data analysis, visualization, advanced interaction, presence within the virtual environment, and collaborative decision-making. In this context, the VFF must confront with the five technical strands of the DET Framework (Maropoulos 03) to have their relationship evaluated and analysed.

4. VIRTUAL FACTORY FRAMEWORK

The VF is defined as an integrated simulation of major activities and systems of a factory, that considers the factory as a whole and provides an advanced planning, decision support and validation capability (Jain 2001). The VFF implements the framework for a object oriented collaborative virtualized environment, representing a variety of factory activities meant to facilitate the sharing of factory resources, manufacturing information and knowledge and supports the simulation of design, planning, production and management among different participants.

4.1 The event driven Core of the VFF

Figure 1 presents the Core as the funding building block of the proposed paradigm: it is the manager of all the objects of the virtual environment. It is based on an event driven architecture (pillar III), further detailed later, supported by a common data model (pillar I), and can be divided into three major parts: scenegraph, action manager and event manager. These modules deal with the three most important functions of managing information, incoming actions and outgoing events.

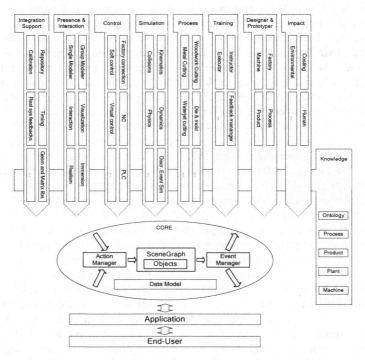

Figure 1– The Virtual Factory Framework – VFF.

The scene graph is the repository of the data objects describing each element composing the environment and their relations. This module guarantees data consistency performing internal checks every time an object is created or destroyed. The action manager is taking care of the first phase in the transition-notification paradigm verifying that concurrent actions on shared objects are correctly queued and processed. The event manager handles all the events generated inside the objects that completed a state transition. Each event can be scheduled on two different queues that represent current and next state and that are swapped every time a dispatch occurs. The notification mechanism can be accessed by the core user in order to control the dispatching phase.

This structure enables a centralized complete synchronization (not control) of the external code with the internal transition system of the core (pillar II). In a multi threading context this synchronization reduces the risk of deadlocks or racing situations, by concentrating actions and event responses into defined phases. The common and extensible data model provides a significant impact on the possibility for real time multi-user multi-disciplinary modules to synchronously collaborate.

Starting from this cornerstone and adopting the proposed framework, it is possible to identify several macro-modules (pillar II), fitting into this paradigm, dealing with the various features and potentiality of the virtual factory: Figure 1 presents a non exhaustive scenario of interacting modules in the VFF.

Besides providing a common ontology (VRL-KCiP NoE fosters an effective approach www.vrl-kcip.org), the integration of a horizontal knowledge-based support (pillar IV) offers functionality to model a wider range of complex phenomenon and support greater comprehension of those systems.

The Core and the cooperating modules are to be regarded as a library framework that will be used to create and deploy complex customized VF applications, which will be interacting with the end-user.

4.2 The internal architecture of the event driven Core

Figure 2 represents a more detailed view on the internal architecture of the core and some possible related modules using a standard UML Component Diagram. The three most important parts of the core, the action manager, the scenegraph and the event manager, are described in terms of functional components and dependency.

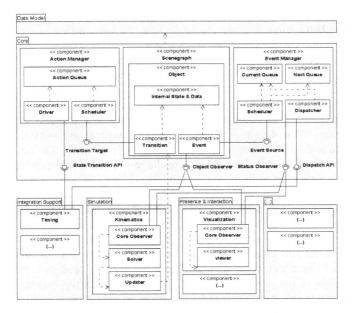

Figure 2 – Internal architecture of the event driven core.

The scenegraph is composed by a list of object elements representing the logical image of the real objects. Each object contains an internal set of data, which is defined inside the data model, and a related internal state. The transition component is responsible for maintaining the consistency of the internal information. When an external action is requesting a modification of an object, a new transition element manages the request, scheduling it in the action manager as a transition target and preventing the internal state to be immediately modified. The scheduler of the action manager takes care of the transition targets produced by all the scenegraph objects, queuing them inside a dedicated action queue which works as a FIFO buffer. The action queue is managed by the driver component which exposes an API that allows to control when to flush all the queued transitions, applying the new values to the objects data and performing a state transition of the entire scenegraph.

When a new value is applied, a new event is generated inside the object to notify the object observer components that something changed in the internal data. Nevertheless the event is not immediately notified but it is scheduled inside the event manager as an event source. The scheduler of the event manager takes care of queuing the event sources inside the current state queue or the next state queue. The decision about the correct buffer where to store the event source depends on the type of the generated event. The moment the events are notified can be synchronized from outside the core through the API exposed by the dispatcher component of the event manager. During the notification phase, the dispatcher flushes the current state queue releasing all the contained events and swapping it with the next state queue. At the end of this process, the dispatcher notifies the status observers with the end of the notification phase. Figure 2 bottom line shows examples of components interacting with this mechanism, showing how each single module can use the core in different ways, controlling the transition-notification as the timing does, or acting on the objects like the kinematics or just listening for changes like the visualization.

4.3 The Core Data-Model

The common data model can be considered as the shared "language" providing a common understanding and unified definition of the information that will be held by the core and elaborated by the external components.

Thus the modules can exactly know how to perform actions on the object instances available in the scenegraph, being able to access interfaces, method and fields definitions. The data model has to be as complete as possible concerning contained data and easily extensible from a design point of view. The object oriented approach, its principles of class design, package cohesion and package coupling must be extensively used to fit these requirements (Viganò 02) as shown in figure 3.

In order to support the event driven paradigm, the data model must not only define the VF elements data and interfaces but also the events and observers interfaces used by the scenegraph objects. Figure 3 shows a UML class diagram of an advanced data model suitable for the VF. The schema covers just relational, geometrical, visual and kinematics issues, along with additional information related to basics of collision detection definition and production process simulation. The proposed design is not supposed to be exhaustive but it represents a good and structured example and starting point for the required extension.

The proposed architecture, along with the data-model and the described centralized state control enables a high level of data consistency while granting a total decoupling of the external modules thanks to the event paradigm. From the performance point of view, this architecture fits well in the current trend of multi-core processors: multiple threads can be issued to independently perform intensive calculations and the synchronization points are well defined and exposed.

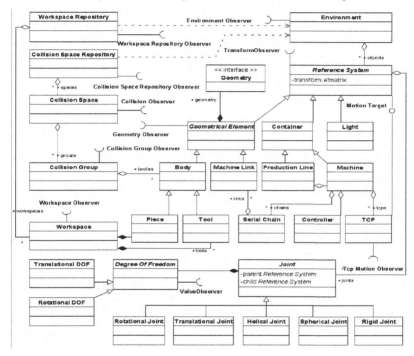

Figure 3 – The Core Data Model (internal information of object definitions have been omitted in order to make the picture more readable).

5. DEMONSTRATION

An example application exploiting the basic concepts and ideas has been developed at TTS. An innovative 3D environment solution based on the VFF principles has been deployed (the scene description is based on (Mancini 04)). The simulation environment can reproduce manufacturing machines and production lines in a virtual environment and mimic the system behaviour. The performances in terms of visualization frame-rates and CPU usage are dramatically better than current applications. In this demonstration, a PC with P4 – 3.0 GHz – NVIDIA 6800 – 256 Mb and a 3D model with 770.000 triangles were used. A comparison is done using Cosmo Player which is a high-performance, cross-platform VRML 2.0 client designed for fast viewing of virtual worlds. Cosmo reaches 13 FPS and 50% usage while the VFF based software reaches 49 FPS and 11% CPU usage. Moreover, both kinematics and visualization engines have been coupled with the core through the event driven approach, demonstrating the feasibility of the overall concept.

6. EXPECTED BENEFITS AND CONCLUSIONS

The implementation of a Virtual Factory, consistent with the VF Framework vision presented, carries high cost savings and increase in manufacturing performances, thanks to the effective support in design, monitoring, management, evaluation, evolution of product, process and plant.

It has been highlighted that, to achieve such objectives, the VF must be holistic, scalable, open, integrable, up-gradable, adherent to reality and must bring high performances. The answer to these challenges is seen by the authors in terms of four pillars, presented within this paper, providing the needed framework.

Finally a software application based on this concept has been created and tested, demonstrating the results of the application of such a framework.

7. REFERENCES

1. Boër CR, Jovane F, Sacco M, Imperio E. Virtual Reality as a Tool for Sustainable Production in the ManuFuturing Model. CIRP International Symposium – Advanced Design and Manufacturing in the Global Manufacturing Era, 1997.
2. Boër CR, Sacco M, Viganò G, Avai A. A Virtual Manufacturing Environment for planning and design of factory layout and equipment. IMCC'2000.
3. Jain S. Virtual Factory Framework: a Key Enabler for Agile Manufacturing. INRIA/IEEE Symposium on Emerging Technologies and Factory Automation 1995; 247-258.
4. Jain S, Choong NF, Aye KM, Ming L. Virtual Factory: an Integrated Approach to Manufacturing Systems Modelling. Int. Journal of Operations & Production Management 2001; 21: 594-608.
5. Jönsson A, Bathelt J, Broman G. Interacting with Real Time Simulations – Virtual Reality in Industry Applications. 9 Eurographics Workshop on Virtual Environments, 2003.
6. Krolak P, Annunziato J, Kosta C, Sodhi M. A Framework for Virtual Manufacturing. Proceedings of the Symposium on Virtual Reality in Manufacturing Research and Education, 1996.
7. Mancini F, Francese C, Viganò G, Liao Z, Sacco M, Boër CR. The Virtual Factory – A Semi-immersive Interactive 3D Environment. 2004 Summer Computer Simulation Conference, 2004.
8. Maropoulos PG, Rogers BC, Chapman P, McKay KR, Bramall DG, A Novel Digital Enterprise Technology Framework for the Distributed Development and Validation of Complex Products, Cirp Annals, 2003.
9. Mueller-Wittig W, Jegathese R, Song M, Quick J. Virtual Factory – Highly interactive visualisation for manifacturing. Proceedings of the 2002 Winter Simulation Conference, 2002.
10. Pedrazzoli P, Boër CR. Knowledge Based Services for Traditional Manufacturing Sectors Provided by a Network of High Tech SMEs. Proceedings of INCOM 2004.
11. Sacco M, Mottura S, Greci L, Viganò G, Boër CR. Experiences in Virtual Factory Prototype: Modular Plants Design and Simulation. IFAC-MIM04, Conference on Manufacturing, Modelling, Management and Control. Proceedings of IFAC 2004.
12. Schuh G, Bergholz M, Westkämper E. Collaborative Production on the Basis of Object Oriented Software Engineering Principles. CIRP Annals 2003; 52; 1: 391-396.
13. VDI 2206: Design Methodology for Mechatronic Systems, Beuth Verlag, Berlin, June 2004.
14. Viganò G, Liao Z, Sacco M, Mottura S, Boër CR. To Build Object-Oriented Virtual Factory based on Virtual Reality and Simulation Tools. DET 2002, 1st CIRP (UK) International Seminar on DET, 2002.
15. Waller AP, Ladbrook J. Experiencing Virtual Factories of the Future. Proceedings of the 2002 Winter Simulation Conference; 513-517.
16. Westkämper E, Gottwald B, Fisser F. Migration of the Digital and Virtual Factory to Reality. CIRP Journal of Manufacturing Systems 2005; 34; 5.
17. Zhai, Wenbin, Fan, Xiumin, Yan, Juanqi, Zhu, Pengsheng, An Integrated Simulation Method to Support Virtual Factory Engineering. China International Journal of CAD/CAM 2002; 2; 1: 39-44.

RECONFIGURABILITY OF MANUFACTURING SYSTEMS FOR AGILITY IMPLEMENTATION
PART I:
REQUIREMENTS AND PRINCIPLES

Goran D. Putnik[1] and Alojzij Sluga[2]

[1]*University of Minho, Department of Production and Systems Engineering, Portugal*
putnikgd@dps.uminho.pt
[2]*University of Ljubljana, Department of Control and Manufacturing systems, Slovenia*
alojz.sluga@fs.uni-lj.si

Implementation agility in Manufacturing Systems (MS) is one of the most important objectives for MS considering the complexity of environment. Agility implementation implies new characteristics as well as new implications not considered by the previous MS concept. These are: the dynamic reconfigurability of MS structure (in the first place), pro-activity, the emergence (as inherent features of agility), and the need for integration of resources outside the original MS. These characteristics imply needs for specific organizational tools and frameworks. The issue is presented in a two-part paper first one presenting the requirements and principles of agility and MS reconfigurability – and the second part presenting two architectures for MS reconfigurability in support of MS agility as well as two applications of the proposed architectures.

1. INTRODUCTION

Implementation agility in Manufacturing Systems (MS) is one of the most important objectives for MS considering the complexity of environment. Although the agility is by most part equal to flexibility, and by other interpretations to adaptivily, it brings into sight new characteristics as well as new implications not considered by the previous concept of FMS and other MS architectures. These characteristics are the need for dynamic reconfigurability of MS structure – in the first place, pro-activity – as an inherent feature of agility, emergence – or self-organization, and the need for integration of resources outside the original MS. These characteristics, i.e. requirements, imply the growing importance and complexity of the integration processes, as well as needs for defining specific organizational tools and frameworks capable to manage them.

The issue is presented in two-part paper of which this is the first part that presents the requirements and principles of agility and MS reconfigurability – while the second part presents two architectures for MS reconfigurability in support of MS agility as well as two applications of the proposed architectures.

The sources on which the paper is conceived are (Putnik *et al.*; 2006), (Putnik; 2001), (Putnik *et al.*; 2005) and (Butala & Sluga; 2002).

2. AGILTY AND RECONFIGURABILITY AS AGILITY ENABLER

2.1 Agility

Agility is a property of an object or a system. To be *agile* means to be "quick-moving, nimble, active" (Oxford Dictionary). We can talk about agility of a company, about agility of a Manufacturing System (MS) as well as about agility of an individual. The company, MS, or individual, can be agile or not, or better, it can have a certain degree of agility, higher or lower.

In (Goldman, Nagel & Preiss; 1995) we can find the following description: "For a company, to be agile is to be capable of operating profitably in a competitive environment of continually, and unpredictably, changing customer opportunities. For an individual, to be agile is to be capable of contributing to the bottom line of a company that is constantly reorganising its human and technological resources in response to unpredictably, changing customer opportunities". In (Kidd; 1994) the agile manufacturing or enterprise is characterized as follows: "the competitive foundations (of the agile manufacturing or enterprise) are continuous change, rapid response, quality improvement, social responsibility and total customer focus". Many other authors share this perspective.

Considering "rapid response" or "rapid adaptability" which is the same, as the premise of agility, then agility is equal to flexibility (as flexibility implies "rapid adaptation" in "response" to the market requirements too). Consequently, if the previous is true, we could say that the "rapid adaptability", flexibility and agility are synonyms.

However, other authors presented other perspectives on agility, i.e. other features of the agility. A good example of a comprehensive definition of agility is given by (Yusuf et al; 1999).

"Agility is the successful exploration of competitive bases (speed, flexibility, innovation, proactivity[1], quality and profitability) through the integration of reconfigurable resources and best practices in a knowledge-rich environment to provide customer-driven products and services in a fast changing market environment."

The question that emerges is: what are, then, the differences between adaptivily, flexibility and agility?

Analyzing the literature sources, the differences between adaptivily, flexibility and agility are interpreted in a different ways, and, we should say, it, there is not a consensus on definitions.

A system is said to be adaptable if it can continue to operate in the face of disturbances changing its structure, properties and behaviour, accordingly to new situations it encounters, considering as disturbance any event not previously specified.

---

[1] Underlined by the authors of this paper

Some authors make a difference between "agility" and "flexibility" saying that the flexibility implies adaptability (only) and the agility implies "fast adaptability". However, by other authors, flexibility requires some additional feature the "pure" adaptability. Within the concept of Flexible Manufacturing Systems (FMS), the *flexibility* is defined as "a capability of the (manufacturing) system to adapt to the new tasks (i.e. to reconfigure, i.e. to reprogram itself in order to satisfy the demand in an optimal way) without interruption of the production (manufacturing) process". The condition "without interruption" implies "fast", or "rapid". So pure "adaptability", or "reconfigurability", is necessary but not sufficient conditions for flexibility (adaptability $\subset$ flexibility). Any system is possible to adapt but we seek for adaptation of the system so fast that the production process will be not affected. Based on these premises, "fast adaptability" or "fast reconfigurability" is a synonym for "flexibility". Consequently, we also state that the *flexibility* is either equal (synonym) to *agility* or is a part of it.

Almost immediately emerges the comparison with the Flexible Manufacturing Systems (FMS). Considering that the concept of flexibility has emerged historically as the underlying concept of the Flexible Manufacturing Systems (FMS) we could conclude that the flexibility is referring to the processes in the manufacturing workshop environment. On contrary, the agility as a concept has emerged considering the wider environment, i.e. considering the processes within the whole enterprise, i.e. the processes in the enterprise and/or business environment.

From the other side, in the agility definition by (Yusuf et al; 1999), we should note the designations "*innovation*" and "*pro-activity*". By our interpretation, these two designations, "*innovation*" and "*pro-activity*", are not present in the "usual" definitions of flexibility[2] and, in fact, could make a "stronger" difference between the flexibility and agility.

Therefore, we could assume, mainly based on (Yusuf et al; 1999), the following: *Flexibility* is a "reactive" concept, i.e. the concept based on reactivity, implying a rapid response to changes, after recognition (detection, identification) of these (changes), the changes whether of the market or of the (workshop, enterprise) internal conditions; while *agility* is a "pro-active" concept, i.e. the concept based on pro-activity, implying anticipating actions, innovation, with the desirable capability of prevision of changes, acting whether on the market or internally in the enterprise (or workshop).

Within the context of this paper, the exact differences between the adaptivily, flexibility and agility are not critical, assuming the positive identification of the need for enterprise or MS *dynamic reconfigurability*, by any of these three requirements designations. However, we will use the agility as the main requirements as it seems a more comprehensive and complex requirement then and has a wider connotation concerning an enterprise then when using only adaptivily or flexibility.

---

[2] For the sake of truth, the concept of flexibility, as well as the adaptibitlity, could be applied on the enterprise level too. Also, by some authors the flexibility includes pro-activity too. However, as these approaches are not "typical" we could understand the differences between the adaptibitlity, flexibility and agility. Otherwise, they are the same – the synonyms.

2.2 Reconfigurability and Dynamics of MS

Adaptability, flexibility or agility, implies the search and selection of new resources (substitute resources) to be allocated to the task to be performed, in order to satisfy the new circumstances (the new tasks, optimization of old tasks, "deadlocks," etc.). When in the system some elements, or resources, are substituted by another elements, or resources, or simply added new elements, or resources, or removed some elements, or resources, we say that the system *reconfigures*. This way, we could say that the adaptation implies *reconfiguration*, and, consequently, that the adaptability implies *reconfigurability*.

Therefore, we will say that the *agility*, is a capability for *fast reconfigurability*, including the pro-activity and the reactivity (fast adaptability), with the objective to explore rapidly the market opportunities and changes or internal innovation potentials (for new products, processes, initiatives).

If any system's, i.e. MS or enterprise, configuration means a system *state*, then the reconfiguration is a process meaning the system's, MS or enterprise, state change. In this way we come to the notion of the (manufacturing or enterprise) *system dynamics*.

"A **dynamic** theory considers primarily *a succession of system's states* … (while) a **static** theory assumes that the state remains constant" (Rapaport, 1972; p49). Webster dictionary (Merriam Webster) defines it as follows: dynamics consists on "a pattern or process of change, growth, or activity".

In our context, dynamics means precisely the intensity of change the MS, or enterprise, is subject of. MS, or enterprise, organizational dynamics considers a succession of MS's, or enterprise's, states along the time, i.e. the *MS or enterprise reconfiguration dynamics*.

2.3 Manufacturing System Reconfigurability

The set of the resources within which the company searches for alignment improvement represents the resources selection domain. If the enterprise searches for resources *"within the company boundaries"* then we talk about *intra-company reconfiguration*. This is the case of the "traditional" organizational paradigm, which, for the problem of reconfiguration, uses the own resources existing within the organization, i.e. *"intra-company reconfiguration"* or *"intra-enterprise reconfiguration"*. On contrary, if the enterprise searches for resources *"across the company boundaries"* then we talk about *inter-company reconfiguration*, i.e. *"inter-enterprise reconfiguration"*, figure 1.

To address the problem of organizational (dynamic) reconfigurability, as one of the competitiveness enablers, there is developed a number of organizational approaches and a number of tools.

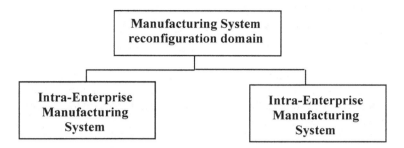

Figure 1 – Manufacturing System reconfiguration domains
(adapted from (Putnik *et al.*, 2006)).

For the "*intra-enterprise reconfiguration*" well-known approaches, or concepts, are (Putnik et al., 2006):

- Flexible Manufacturing Systems (FMS); which later evolved towards Metamorphic and/or Reconfigurable Manufacturing Systems (or Enterprises) (RMS);
- Computer Integrated Manufacturing (CIM), that integrates the disciplines as CAD, CAM, MRP, MRP II, MIS and similar, and, later, the related Enterprise Resource Planning (ERP); in general: Information Systems (IS); which later evolved towards Fractal Factory (or Manufacturing Systems or Enterprises), Holonic Manufacturing Systems (or Enterprises) (HMS) and Intelligent Manufacturing Systems (IMS), Enterprise Integration (EI);
- Total Quality Management (TQM), Business Process Re-engineering (BPR) and, later, Change Management (CM) approach; which later evolved towards Lean Manufacturing (LM) and Agile Manufacturing (AM) (in relation with these approaches is CM discipline); and
- Learning Organization (LO), which later evolved towards Chaordic Enterprise (CE).

For the "*inter-enterprise reconfiguration*" well-known approaches, or concepts, are (Putnik et al., 2006):

- Supply Chain,
- Agile Enterprise,
- Virtual Enterprise,
- Extended Enterprise,
- Virtual Value Chains,
- Smart Organizations,
- Collaborative Network Organization,
- Agile/Virtual Enterprise,
- BM_Virtual Enterprise (BM_VE),
- OPIM model (One Product Integrated Manufacturing),
- Market of Resources (MR) and other meta-organizational structures and environments as Electronic Institutions and Breeding Environments.

3. TOWARDS ARCHITECTURES FOR MANUFACTURING SYSTEMS AGILITY, OR DYNAMIC RECONFIGURATION ENABLING

Based on the previous discussion, and considering that the MS reconfiguration, or restructuring, process is complex in principle, the MS's agility implementation implies the reconfiguration, or restructuring, process management. Or, by (Putnik; 2001) *resources reconfiguration management.*

The resources reconfiguration, or restructuring, process management, as the global task, implies different particular sub-tasks. For example:

1) resource selection;
2) resource integration;
3) resource integration scheduling;
4) resource (dynamic) reconfiguration;
5) resource monitoring and reliability analysis;
6) resource control,

and similar.

For the implementation of the resources reconfiguration, or restructuring, management could be applied the basic, classical, "two-layer hierarchy" organization model, figure 2. Another expressions used for the model are "principal/agent" or "manager/worker" hierarchy, as well as "demand/supply" (Butala, Sluga; 2002). The "principal" is the owner of the vertical structure and the "agent" is responsible for production and affects the principal. The resources reconfiguration, or restructuring, management function is owned by the upper control level i.

But in organizational theory are known higher-order vertical structures as well. The independence of the resource management function corresponds to the "three-layer hierarchy" organization model, figure 3, or, in other words, "principal/ supervisor/agent" or "manager/foreman/worker" or "demand-mediator-supply" (Butala, Sluga: 2002) hierarchy. The main motivation for application of the "principal/supervisor/agent" model is that "the principal, who is the owner of the vertical structure or the buyer of the good produced by the agent, or, more generally, the person who is affected by the agent's activity, lacks either the time or the knowledge required to supervise the agent" (Tirole, 1986).

This type of reasoning implies that the MS reconfiguration could be made/managed more efficiently, which is the indispensable requirement (in order to achieve higher levels of reconfiguration dynamics), i.e. the higher levels of agility, if it is performed by a specialized agent as an independent, and in the certain context autonomous, control level as one of the basic elementary MS control element types, or blocks, or level. This agent will be called *resource manager* or *broker* or *mediator.*

Additionally, the corresponding control level will be called the "Resource Management" function or control level.

In this way, three-layer hierarchy architecture will be considered as an elementary agile MS structure architecture pattern.

This reasoning is in the base of the MS architectures proposed, for agility implementation.

In figure 4 is given an informal presentation of the architecture for MS, or enterprise, reconfigurability for agility implementation.

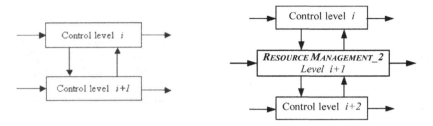

Figure 2 – The basic, classical, "two-layer hierarchy" organizational structural pattern.

Figure 3 – "Three-layer hierarchy" organizational structural pattern with resources reconfiguration, or restructuring, management as an independent layer (Putnik; 2001).

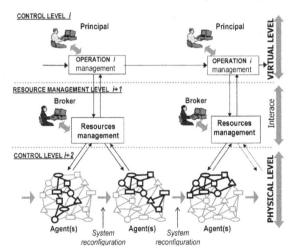

Figure 4 – An informal presentation of the architecture for MS, or enterprise, reconfigurability for agility implementation.
(mapping from BM_VEARM, (Putnik; 2001))

4. CONCLUSIONS

To achieve higher degrees of the MS, or enterprise reconfiguration dynamics, the of MS have to developed many advanced features. The most expected ones are by (Butala, Sluga; 2003) (1) an open multi-level architecture, (2) advanced communication capabilities, (3) decentralized decision making, (4) self-structuring ability, and (5) redefinition of the work systems in terms of autonomy, evolutionary adaptability, re-configurability, cooperativeness, interactivity, task orientation within competence, ability of communication, coordination and co-operation and learning capability, or by (Putnik 2001) and (Putnik *et al.*; 2005) the functionalities (1) integrability, (2) distributivity, (3) agility and (4) virtuality as well as the organizational tools (mechanisms) (1) meta-organizational environments (e.g. Market of Resources), (2) brokers and brokerage functions and (3) virtuality (as the structural architecture pattern.

Implementation of these features, the requirement for the agility implementation, should be heavily based on IT tools. Actually, the requirements are so high that the main "battle-field" for agility is within the computer based environments for simulations, decision makings and control of MS and enterprises. In this sense, we would say that the implementation of the highest degrees of agility in MS and enterprises is practically impossible without its "digitalization".

5. ACKNOWLEDGMENTS

The authors acknowledge the support of

1) I*PROMS NoE – "Innovative PROduction Machines and Systems", Network-of-Excellence, FP6, Contract N°: 500273-2;

2) VRL-KCiP NoE – "Virtual Research Lab for a Knowledge Community in Production", Network-of-Excellence, FP6, Contract N°: FP6-507487-2; and

3) "Adaptive Distributed Manufacturing Systems/Virtual Enterprises", Inter-Governmental Science and Technology Cooperation between Portugal and Slovenia, MCT/GRICES (Ministério da Ciência e do Ensino Superior), University of Minho, University of Ljubljana.

6. REFERENCES

1. Butala, P., Sluga, A. (2002) Dynamic structuring of distributed manufacturing systems, *Advanced Engineering Informatics*, Vol 16 (2002), pp. 127-133.
2. Goldman, S., Nagel, R., & Preiss, K. (1995). *Agile Competitors and Virtual Organizations: Strategies for Enriching the Customer*. New York: van Nostrand Reinhold.
3. Kidd, P. (1994). *Agile Manufacturing: Forging New Frontiers*. Reading, MA: Addison-Wesley.
4. Putnik, G. D. (2001). BM_Virtual Enterprise Architecture Reference Model. In A. Gunasekaran (Ed.), *Agile Manufacturing: 21st Century Manufacturing Strategy* (pp. 73-93). UK: Elsevier Science Publ.
5. Putnik, G. D., Cunha, M. M., Sousa, R., & Ávila, P. (2005). BM Virtual Enterprise - A model for dynamics and virtuality. In G. D. Putnik & M. M. Cunha (Eds.), *Virtual Enterprise Integration: Technological and Organizational Perspectives* (pp. 124-144). Hershey, PA: Idea Group Publishing.
6. Putnik, G. D., Cunha, M. M., Cortes, B. C., Ávila, P. S. (2006) Enterprise Reconfiguration Dynamics and Business Alignment, in Cunha, Putnik, Cortes (Eds.) *Adaptive Technologies and Business Integration: Social, Managerial and Organizational Dimensions*, Hershey, PA: Idea Group Publishing. (forthcoming)
7. Rapaport, A. (1972). The Uses of Mathematical Isomorphism in General System Theory. in Klir G. J. (Ed.) *Trends in General System Theory*, (p. 49). New York: Wiley-Interscience, a Division of John Wiley & Sons.
8. Tirole, J. (1986) Hierarchies and bureaucracies: On the role of collusion in organization, in *Journal of Law, Economics and Organization*, **2** (2), Autumn, 181-214.
9. Yusuf, Y. Y., Sarhadi, M., & Gunasekaran, A. (1999). Agile Manufacturing: The drivers, concepts and attributes. *International Journal of Production Economics, 62*, 33-43.

RECONFIGURABILITY OF MANUFACTURING SYSTEMS FOR AGILITY IMPLEMENTATION PART II: TWO ARCHITECTURES

Goran D. Putnik[1], Alojzij Sluga[2] and Peter Butala[2]

[1]*University of Minho, Department of Production and Systems Engineering, Portugal*
putnikgd@dps.uminho.pt
[2]*University of Ljubljana, Department of Control and Manufacturing systems, Slovenia*
alojz.sluga@fs.uni-lj.si, peter.butala@fs.umi-lj.si

For agility implementation in Manufacturing Systems (MS) the implementation of the mechanisms for dynamic reconfigurability of MS structure, the pro-activity, the emergence (as inherent features of agility), and the need for integration of the resources outside the original MS are required. This paper presents two architectures for MS reconfigurability in support of MS agility as well as two applications of the proposed architectures. This paper is the second part of the two-part paper that addresses the issue of agility implementation in MS (the first part presents the requirements and principles of agility and MS reconfigurability).

1. INTRODUCTION

Implementation of agility in Manufacturing Systems (MS) requires implementation of new characteristics as well as new implications not considered by the previous concept of FMS and other MS architectures. These characteristics are the need for dynamic reconfigurability of MS structure – in the first place, the pro-activity – as an inherent feature of agility, emergence – or self-organization, and the need for integration of the resources outside the original MS. These characteristics, i.e. requirements, imply the needs for defining specific organizational tools and frameworks capable to manage them.

This paper is the second part of a two-part paper that addresses the issue of agility implementation in MS (the first part presents the requirements and principles of agility and MS reconfigurability).

The sources on which the paper is based are (Putnik et al.; 2006), (Putnik; 2001), (Putnik et al.; 2005) and (Butala & Sluga; 2002).

2. TWO ARCHITECTURES FOR MANUFACTURING SYSTEMS RECONFIGURABLITY

Two architectures for implementing agility in MS are presented, namely the *Adaptive Distributed Manufacturing System* (ADMS), (Butala, Sluga; 2002) and *BM*

Virtual Enterprise or Manufacturing Systems (BM VE/MS), (Putnik; 2001), (Putnik *et al.*; 2005). Both approaches, although developed independently, are based on the market mechanism for developing an adequate structure that would be the most competitive for the order considered, and employs the "three-level" hierarchy architecture pattern, see (Putnik, Sluga; 2006 – this volume). The "three-level" hierarchy architecture pattern implies a specialized independent, and in the certain context autonomous, agent as an independent intermediate control level as one of the basic elementary MS control component types, or blocks, or level, for the resources reconfiguration, or restructuring, management. This agent is called *resource manager* or *broker* or *mediator*.

Both approaches to the reconfigurability of the MS consider the MS structure reconfiguration domain.

3. ADAPTIVE DISTRIBUTED MANUFACTURING SYSTEM - ADMS

ADMS, (Butala, Sluga; 2002), is conceived as a distributed MS structured as a network of elementary work systems (EWS), representing the MS building blocks, that act as agents. They (building blocks or agents) can be related in a series or and/or in parallel, and are driven by cooperation and competition on various levels. The agent structure is synthesized through the market mechanism in order to provide self-organization and adaptivity. In order to align with the environment the structure, through the market mechanism, can reconfigure optimizing the overall system's behavior, or performance, in accordance, or aligned, with the environment. A EWS is capable of performing single manufacturing task, e.g. process planning, machining. It consists of hardware elements necessary to implement a work process, work process identification for process control and optimization and a human operator as an autonomous subject for making decisions and synthesis. In ADMS a virtual work system (VWS) is introduced in order to delegate the EWS in a distributed environment. The VWS is an agent and it represents the EWS in a distributed environment. The EWS are interconnected via corresponding VWS agents into a network and thus constitute the ADMS. The agents operate and communicate over the network and coordinate their actions to accomplish complex tasks by exploiting their competences, taking into account their own objectives (inherent to the market mechanism).

The MS structuring is a critical process. For each particular task, the optimal structure has to be built up. It is assumed that the complex tasks are decomposed into less complex tasks, in the limit to the elementary (primitive) tasks. The coordination process implies task decomposition as a recursive task structuring process. The structuring process implies the incorporation of the (elementary) work systems for task execution through the market mechanism.

The market mechanism is characterized by the operation of the self-adjusting forces of supply and demand. The market based dynamic structuring process consists of bidding – negotiation – contracting phases.

Thus contacts between demand and supply are established on the network, resulting in a task-oriented dynamic cluster of cooperating and competing agents, figure 1.

Timing of the dynamic structuring process, i.e. of the task coordination process, figure 2, is a critical factor. The efficiency of dynamic structuring mostly depends on a time lag between the task assignment "milestone" and the time of task execution. The shorter the time gap the more the assumption of a quasi-stable environment is realistic.

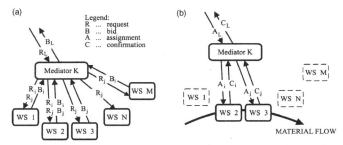

Figure 1 – Dynamic structure of work systems: a) dynamic structure, b) executive structure (Butala, Sluga, 2002).

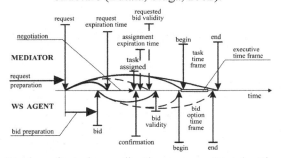

Figure 2 – Timing of a task coordination process (Butala, Sluga, 2002).

Case study

The ADMS approach is demonstrated in an experiment in sheet metal manufacturing on industrial data.

The requested set of tasks was composed of various sheet metal components with different shapes, dimensions and batch sizes. The selected material as well as sheet thickness was the same in order to provide an opportunity for the nesting of different components on the same sheet and, thus, for an optimization of material and time utilization.

Examples of requested tasks (components to be cut) and corresponding basic data are shown in Table 1.

Table 1 - Requested tasks.

TASK	SKETCH	PCS.	S [m²/pc]	L [m/pc]	TIME FRAME BEGIN	END
K 9		50	0,003	0,32	8:30	10:30
K 15		40	0,107	4,39	10:00	13:00
K 10		28	0,071	3,31	9:30	14:30
. . . .						

Examples of the bids are shown in the Table 2. Bids were evaluated by the mediator in terms of: (1) fulfillment of task objectives in terms (in this case it was assumed that the biding work system was capable of performing the task), (2) minimization of costs and (3) fulfillment of constraints (time frame limits). The best bids were selected and corresponding work system assigned as shown in Table 2.

Table 2 - Bidden tasks.

TASK	BIDDER	PRICE	TIME FRAME		ASSIGNED
			BEGIN	END	
K 9	WS 1	13.029	9:30	10:45	¤
	WS 2	13.920	10:30	11:30	
	WS 3	12.314	12:00	13:00	
K 15	WS 1	12.343	10:45	11:45	¤
	WS 3	11.728	13.00	14:00	
K 10	WS 1	10.018	11:45	13:00	¤
	WS 2	10.315	10:30	12:30	
	WS 3	9.695	14:00	15:00	
. . . .					

4. BM_VIRTUAL ENTERPRISE OR MANUFACTURING SYSTEM

The second architecture for dynamic reconfigurability of MS, for agility implementation, we present is an application of the BM_Virtual Enterprise (BM_VE) model for the Manufacturing Systems. BM_VE is a virtual enterprise (VE) in a total or partial conformance with the BM_Virtual Enterprise Architecture Reference Model (BM_VEARM), (Putnik, 2001) and (Putnik *et al.*, 2005).

BM_VE is the VE as a dynamically reconfigurable inter-enterprise network integrated over the global domain, satisfying the requirements for integrability, distributivity, agility, and virtuality as the competitiveness factors.

Therefore, by BM_VE, i.e. BM_VEARM, the reconfigurability domain for MS, concerning the enterprise organizational environment, is primarily *inter-enterprise*.

BM_VE uses three main mechanisms, or tools: market of resources, broker, and virtuality. Virtuality as a tool is a specific organizational structure pattern that contributes to further improvement of agility/reconfiguration dynamics.

Market of resources (MR), that BM_VE uses, is an institution, or enterprise, that serves as a meta-enterprise of the operating VE. It (MR) is an environment to support the VE dynamic reconfiguration, providing a way to overcome (i.e., to minimize) two fundamental networking disablers: "transaction," i.e., reconfiguration cost, and the VE partners' knowledge and rights protection – which are critical reconfigurability dynamics enabling factors for the *inter-enterprise* MS domain, and providing an environment for the market mechanisms.

The broker, as the second mechanism, is described in (Putnik, Sluga; 2006 – this volume). His main role is to be the agent of agility and organization reconfiguration dynamics, acting as an *"MS structure reconfiguration manager,"* or *resource manager* or *mediator*. The second fundamental role of the broker is to be the agent of virtuality. In this role, the broker provides the intermediation services "online" with the operations in a way that the operating agents, the client and the server, are not aware of each other – the client and server are hidden from each other and they communicate through the broker. By this structure, the BM_VE or MS, could be seen as a homomorphism of distributed (software) system architecture (e.g., common object request broker architecture, CORBA[1]).

BM_VE Architecture Reference Model (BM_VEARM) – Elementary Structure

The BM_VEARM (Putnik, 2001) is a reference model to design and control virtual enterprises/manufacturing systems ensuring four fundamental functionalities/ characteristics: integration, distribution, agility, and virtuality.

The BM_VEARM elementary structure, or elementary structural pattern, which is a hierarchical structure, satisfying the above-mentioned fundamental function-alities or characteristics, is represented in figure 3.

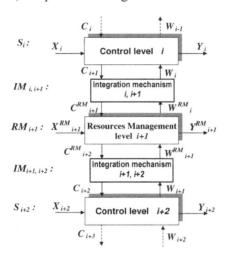

Figure 3 – BM_VEARM elementary structure or structural pattern (Putnik, 2001).

BM_VE Formal Specification and Theory

At the present, BM_VE is rigorously formalized for the structural aspect. For the formalization of the BM_VE structural aspects, an attributed context-free formal grammar, denoted as *GBM* was developed in (Sousa; 2003), (see also (Putnik et al., 2005)). As integration mechanisms can be omitted from the representation of the BM_VE structure (because the integration mechanism acts as an interface between adjacent levels but in implementations it is usually included within those levels), *GBM* deals with only two types of building blocks: control level block (the terminal symbol c_i) and resource management block, or *broker*, (the terminal symbol r_j). Some examples of BM_VE structures synthesized by *GBM* are represented in figure 4.

---

[1] CORBA is "the object bus" architecture that "lets objects transparently make requests to, and receive responses from, other objects located locally or remotely. The client is not aware of the mechanisms used to communicate with, activate, or store the server object. It lets objects discover each other at run time and invoke each other's services" (Orfali et al., 1997, p. 7).

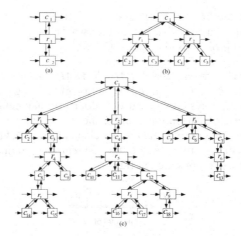

Figure 4 – BM_VE system canonical instances generated
by G_{BM} grammar.

The components of a BM_VE may obviously have their own internal
compositions. The structural, or reconfigurability, dynamics, of the BM_VE or MS
could be presented as in the figure 5.

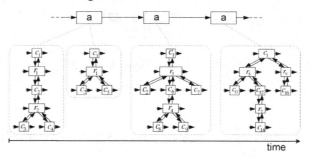

Figure 5 – BM_VE system canonical instances generated
by G_{BM} grammar.

Development of the BM_VE or MS Demonstrator

In order to fulfil the requirements of the project(s) validation, including the VE
reference model, it is implemented a laboratory installation which will serve as a
demonstrator for the VE and MS reconfigurability design and control. The
laboratory installation is conceived as a Distributed/Virtual Manufacturing System
(D/V MS) Cell, named *AURORA 98* (Putnik et al., 1998). In the first period the
laboratory was used for research of distributed manufacturing system. In the second
(present) period the laboratory is extended with the components which are expected
to provide the full demonstration of the VE concept based on the BM_VEARM.

The components of the D/V MS Cell structure which will be used in the first
phase for the VE model validation, based on the *BM_Virtual Enterprise Architecture
Reference Model* and therefore for its validation as well, is composed of, figure 6: 1)
Machine cell: Two machine simulators, Robot SCORBOT ER-VII, vision system,
conveyor system; 2) *Broker*: Computer based remote resource manager; 3) *Control*

center_1: Computer based remote machine cell controller; 4) *Control center_2*: Computer based remote machine cell controller.

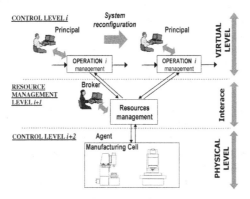

Figure 6 – An informal scheme of the virtual enterprise demonstrator based on the *BM_Virtual Enterprise Architecture Reference Model.*

The cell formal specification (ESTELLE based) is given in the figure 7.

The reconfiguration of the system consists of switching, through negotiation, between two manufacturing cell controllers in accordance with their availability, service cost and quality. The broker performs the function of the system configuration manager. Manufacturing cell controllers, as well as broker, could be located at any point in the world as the system is Internet based.

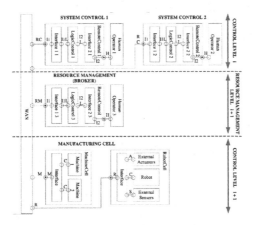

Figure 7 – A formal scheme (Estelle based) of the virtual enterprise demonstrator based on the *BM_VEARM.*

5. CONCLUSIONS

The architectures proposed combines some good properties of hierarchical and heterarchical systems. Actually, the hierarchical and heterarchical structures interchange dynamically through different phases of reconfiguration and execution providing capabilities for the highest degrees of agility (or flexibility, or adaptibitlity).

The heterarchy of the system is especially important during the reconfiguration process, that occurs when new task appears or because of other disturbances or circumstances. The main idea is to build the most adequate MS structure for each task, instead to relay on the previously defined rigid, or with low flexibility, hierarchical structures. For the tasks and time frames defined, the potential resources (not known in advance) for task execution are searched and the MS structure is build through the market mechanism (negotiation). In this way it is provided the emergence, or self-organization, of the MS structure from the actual state of the system and its environment expressed in constraints.

However, there are a number of problems to be positively responded. Some of them are related with a) the complexity that emerges from the dichotomy of the autonomy of an individual work system and the potential synergy rising from cooperation, b) how to control the structuring process if the entire manufacturing system domain is taken into account under the dynamic reconfiguration f the parts of the structure, c) the optimal, or required minimal, reconfigurability domain size, and others. Some aspects of these problems have been already investigated and validated in the real industrial environments, in laboratory environments as well as through the theoretical models, indicated that the approach presented is viable.

6. ACKNOWLEDGMENTS

The authors acknowledge the support of
    1) I*PROMS NoE – "Innovative PROduction Machines and Systems Network of Excellence", Network-of-Excellence, FP6, Contract N°: 500273-2;
    2) VRL-KCiP NoE – "Virtual Research Lab for a Knowledge Community in Production", Network-of-Excellence, FP6, Contract N°: FP6-507487-2; and
    3) "Adaptive Distributed Manufacturing Systems/Virtual Enterprises", Inter-Governmental Science and Technology Cooperation between Portugal and Slovenia, MCT/GRICES (Ministério da Ciência e do Ensino Superior), University of Minho, University of Ljubljana.

7. REFERENCES

1. Butala P., Sluga A. (2002) Dynamic structuring of distributed manufacturing systems, Advanced Engineering Informatics, Vol 16 (2002), pp 127-133.
2. Orfali R., Harkey D., Edwards J. (1997) Instant CORBA, John Wiley & Sons;
3. Putnik G. D. (2001). BM_Virtual Enterprise Architecture Reference Model. In A. Gunasekaran (Ed.), Agile Manufacturing: 21st Century Manufacturing Strategy (pp. 73-93). UK: Elsevier Science Publ.
4. Putnik G. D., Cunha M. M., Sousa R., & Ávila P. (2005). BM Virtual Enterprise - A model for dynamics and virtuality. In G. D. Putnik & M. M. Cunha (Eds.), Virtual Enterprise Integration: Technological and Organizational Perspectives (pp. 124-144). Hershey, PA: Idea Group Publishing.
5. Putnik G. D., Cunha M. M., Cortes B. C., Ávila P. S. (2006) Enterprise Reconfiguration Dynamics and Business Alignment, in Cunha, Putnik, Cortes (Eds.) Adaptive Technologies and Business Integration: Social, Managerial and Organizational Dimensions, Hershey, PA: Idea Group Publishing. (forthcoming)
6. Putnik G. D., Sousa R. M., Moreira J. F., Carvalho J. D., Spasic Z., Babic B. (1998) Distributed/Virtual Manufacturing Cell: An Experimental Installation, in Proceedings of 4th International Seminar on Intelligent Manufacturing Systems, Belgrade;
7. Putnik G. D., Sluga A. (2006) Reconfigurability of Manufacturing Systems for Agility Implementation – PART I: Requirements and principles, in Proceedings of DET 06 – this volume.
8. Sousa, R. (2003). Contribuição para uma Teoria Formal de Sistemas de Produção. Tese de Doutoramento, Universidade do Minho, Braga, Portugal.

SELF ORGANIZATION SHOP FLOOR CONTROL

G. Halevi[1] and P.F. Cunha[2]
[1]Technion - Israel Institute of Technology, Israel
halev@bezeqint.net
[2]Polytechnic Inst. of Setúba/ESTSetúba/CENI, Portugal
pcunha@est.ips.pt

Shop floor control in batch type manufacturing environment is regarded by the current research community as a very complex task. This paper claims that the complexity is a result of the system approach were inflexible decisions are being made at a too early stage in the manufacturing process. It proposes a method that introduces flexibility and dynamics and thus simplifies the decision making in production planning. The SFC method, which is a module of production management system, proposes that in order to introduce flexibility routings should be regarded as a variable. Each expert will generate routine that meets his needs at the time of need and thereby increase dramatically manufacturing efficiency.

1. INTRODUCTION

The turbulence introduced by changing market requirements and technology demands obliges industrial companies to search for new methods to manage operations, fulfil customer orders and meet performance objectives. The amount of data and the manner of processing them is a time critical factor for planning and operation of manufacturing system. (Cunha, 2005)

The planning tasks involve the management of large amounts of dynamic data, which has to be analysed for decision-making, and has to deal with a range of existing options and uncertainty about the impact that some decisions can have on manufacturing systems performance. Thus, the objective of planning tasks is to make sure that the released jobs for a period will be completed on time and in the most economical way. In terms of shop floor the complexity (Halevi, 2004) is caused by the thousands of operations waiting for scheduling, jobs competing over resources, creating bottlenecks and on top of it disruptions that occur such as resource breakdown, tool breakage and unexpected urgent orders. Employing a routing that was defined previously in time (e.g. several weeks/month/years ago) by a process planner which very easily is not a production planner expert, increases the complexity. Assuming that the routing was considered "optimum" by the process planner the efficiency of his work is doubtful. The routing might have been "optimum" at time of devising it with assumed quantity and available resources, however ignoring aspects like shop floor load it is not optimum for ever. Thus, the proposed shop floor control objective should be to employ the routing that will result in meeting planned product mix with no bottlenecks or disruptions at least operation cost. Also, the suggestion is that instead of scheduling at the level of routings that may not be carried out as planned, to schedule by objectives, which means: define a set of product mix that has to be manufactured in each period. Shop floor planning and control must meet this plan. In order to meet the plan, total flexibility must be providing in the form of network of possible routings, while deferring the decision of which routing to use, to a later stage, the stage of actual processing. Furthermore, the routing is allowed to be changed after each technological operation.

The objection of the production scheduling method proposed in this paper is to reduce the shop floor complexity (Guenov 2002; Wiendhal 1994) and disruptions and serve an alternative to the use of priority rules or the development of a very complex planning program (Fitzgeraled 2000; Tinham 2000; Walker 2005; Wallace 2003). It uses the strategy that we (human) do in our daily personal life. The decisions are taken and performance adjusted to the immediate conditions (disruptions), making the resources to search for a job, rather than jobs to be allocated to resources. This is done through a matrix of process alternatives (Table 1) that is created, instead of an additional work of process planning defining routings (Halevi 1999, 2003).

Table 1 - Process plan matrix.

Op	PR	R1	R2	R3	R4	R5	R6
10	00	3.12(*)	3.17	3.68	99	4.02	3.27
20	00	1.15	1.2	1.71	99	2.05	1.3
30	20	1.49	1.53	2.05	99	99	1.64
40	10	1.30	1.35	1.86	1.86	2.2	1.45
50	40	1.28	1.33	1.84	99	2.18	1.43
60	50	1.51	1.56	2.07	99	99	1.66

* - Time to process each operation on available resource.

PR - The priority of sequencing the operations.   00 - Operation that may be processed at any time;
n0 - Operation that can be processed only after   99 - Resource that is unable to process this
     processing operation n0 has finished ;   operation

2. THE CONCEPT AND TERMINOLOGY

The proposed shop floor control approach is based on the concept that whenever a resource is free, it searches for a free operation to perform. A *free resource* is defined as a resource that has just finished an operation and the part that was removed, or is idle and can be loaded at any instant. A *free operation* is defined as an operation that can be loaded for processing at any instant. An example would be the first operation of an item which the raw material and all the auxiliary jobs are available, and is within each of the resources operator. An intermittent operation is one for which the previous operation has been completed and the part has been unloaded from the resource that performed the previous operation, and is within each of the required resource. Example: Process planning of an item is given in table 1. As operations 10 and 20 have the priority of 00, they are both free operation and can be loaded whenever a resource is available. When operation 10 is done, then operation 40 becomes free. When operation 20 is done than operation 30 becomes free. When operation 30 is done, no operation becomes free. Therefore the sequence of operations may be: 20; 30; 10; 40; 50; 60 OR 10; 20; 30; 40; 50; 60; OR 10; 40; 50; 60; 20; 30 and several other combinations as indicated. This shows the flexibility of the system.

The term *operation* has different meaning in production management and scheduling, and in technology. *Production management operation* considers an operation as a set of all the activities done with one resource, from the loading till unloading. It does not give any indication of what are the operations. Production management operations are used for production planning and scheduling. *Technological operation* is an individual processing operation, (for example the 6 operations in table 1) and is used for resource set up, preparing work instructions and job execution. The term operation in the proposed shop floor control approach refers to the meaning presented for a technological operation.

The scheduling cycle starts by scanning all resources in search for a free resource. A free resource scans all free operations and lists them. The best operation for resource can be based on performance objective, such as minimum processing time or cost. This scanning results in a list of candidates for scheduling.

If the list contains only one entry, than that operation is loaded on that resource.

If the list contains more than one entry, then the system allocates the operation with the largest time gap of performing it on another resource.

If the list is empty, this means that there is no free operation available for processing on that resource. Hence the resource becomes idle, waiting for an appropriate operation. Idleness is a waste of time and such time may be used to process a free operation. Despite of increasing processing time, it might be economic. Therefore the system searches for a free operation that the idle resource can perform although not being the best resource for the job, but economically. One method to compute the economics of using an alternate resource is to compute the difference in time between the "best" and the alternate operation and comparing it to the time that the free resource will otherwise be idle. As an example: suppose that the quantity is 100 units, the best processing time is 5 minutes. The alternate resource processing time is 6 minutes and the waiting time is 150 minutes. Then the economic consideration is as follows: i) To produce the operation with the best resource it will take 5 x 100 = 500 minutes; ii) to produce the operation with the alternate resource it will take 6 x 100 = 600 minutes, which 150 out of them are replacing the waiting time. Therefore the actual processing time is 600-150 = 450. Hence using the alternate resource and working "inefficient" will save 500-450 = 50 minutes of elapsed time.

If this next operation is more economical or better in terms of performance for this resource than the following operation is allocated to that resource. Economical or better performance means that this resource is the best for this operation, or that its processing time (or cost) minus a transfer penalty is equivalent or lower then the best time of that operation. *Transfer penalty* is defined as the time/cost to transfer a job from one resource to another. It includes setup time, inspection, storage, material handling, etc.

In case of resource breakdown, no special treatment is needed. It will be marked as busy; hence no scanning cycle will regard it as a free resource.

In case of item being rejected the product structure is consulted to determine if it will hold assembly. If so all items required for that assembly are not needed and will be removed from the list of released jobs for the period.

The figure blows shows how the proposed shop floor control method can be integrated within a production management system.

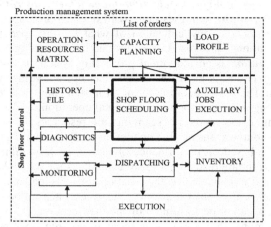

Figure 1 – Implementation of a SFC module in a production management system.

3. THE ALGORITHM AND TERMINOLOGY

Shop floor control starts with a list of jobs that should be processes in the relevant period. Such list may be compiling from the matrix production planning module, or from any other source. The list contains:

Job number and name; Quantity; Sequence priority; Bill of materials of the order.

These jobs are free for execution. However, before job execution can start some auxiliary jobs have to be performed. The auxiliary jobs are:

Fixture design and built; Tool preparation; NC program generation; Material preparation (inventory management and control); Material handling (transport);

Quality control, (preparation of method and tools); Set up instructions; and Set Up Job instruction

Each of the free jobs retrieves from company database the two dimension process plan matrix (as shown in table 1) and construct a 3D matrix process plan as shown in table 2. (3D: Resources - Operations - Items)

The algorithm is based on the following records:

Resource status file keeps the status of the resource throughout of the scheduling period. The data stored is:

Resource number; The loaded item, item and operation; Quantity; A link to the bill of materials; Resource counter; Sequence number of entry in the History file.

Resource counter is a counter that indicates the remaining time for processing the item. When loaded it is set by multiplying the quantity by the processing time, as indicated by the 3D matrix, and it is updated at each scan cycle by the elapsed time from the

History File keeps track of the actual performance on shop floor. It keeps the following data:

Sequence number; Resource number; product, item and operation; Start time; Finished time

The objective of the history file is to store data for management and production control reports. It can be used to compare planning to actual performance. To arrive at actual item cost, resource load etc.

The scheduling module is based on a *sequence cycle* loop that examines all resources, listed in the *resource status file*, loads the free resources and updates the resource counter. The sequence cycle loop starts whenever the processing of an operation has finished. At this point the resource becomes idle and decision has to be made on the next assignment. ***Sequence cycle time*** is the elapsed time between present time and the previous sequence cycle loop. The time is retrieved from running clock that start at the beginning of the scheduling process and advances by the working time.

Shop floor control is based on the concept that whenever resource is free, it searches for a free operation to process. A free operation is identified by scanning the column of "PR" of 3D matrix process plan matrix. Any operation with PR = 0 is a free operation. A free resource is identified by the resource counter is equal to zero (0).

The sequence cycle loop scans all resources and checks the field resource counter.

If the counter is zero it means that it was idle in the last scanning cycle, and will be treated as such (see next case).

If the counter is not zero, the sequence cycle time is deducted from the resource counter. If the result becomes zero it means that the process of the present operation is finished. In this case the priority field (PR) of this operation is marked by X, and the priorities of all operations with this operation number are changed to 00.

Automatically the next operation on that item becomes free and gets priority in processing, if it is economical to do so. This means that this resource is the "BEST" for this operation or that it's processing time/cost minus a transfer penalty is equivalent or lower then the "BEST" time of that operation. The operation is allocated to that resource and its resource status file is updated and its counter is set to the new operating time. As an example: Table 2 represents the shop floor status at a certain time. Item #7 operation 20 was just finished, it was processed on R2, and operation 30 became free. The best resource for this operation is R4 with 7.23 minutes per item. A check is made if it is economical to process this operation on R2 in order to save transfer time. The time to process on R2 is 8.92. The increase in time is 8.92-7.23 = 1.79. If it assumes a transfer penalty of 25 minutes and a quantity of 40 units than the increase in time is 40*1.79 = 71.6 and the saving will only 25 minutes, then it is not economical.

Another case: Item #9 operation 20 was just finished, it was processed on R3, thus operation 30 became free. The best resource for this operation is R4 with 11.4 minutes per item. A check is made if it is economical to process this operation on R3 in order to save transfer time. The time to process on R3 is 11.9 minutes. The increase in time is 11.9-11.4 = 0.4. Assume a transfer penalty of 25 minutes and a quantity of 40 units than the increase in time is 40*0.4 = 16 minutes and the saving will be 25 minutes, then it is economical and R3 will process operation 30.

If it is not economical to process the following operation on the previous resource, or if the resource was idle from the previous sequential cycle, then the system scans the matrices of all parts in this particular resource column, and lists all free operations with a best mark on them. This list includes all free operations that the specific resource can do best.

If the list contains only one entry, then this entry (operation) is allocated to the resource and its resource status file are updated and its counter is set to the new operating time

If the list contains more than one entry, then the system allocates the operation with the biggest time gap of performing it on another resource. This value is determined by scanning the operation row in the relevant matrix, and computing the processing time difference between the best resource and the processing time on different resources. Each free operation will be tagged by this difference value. The free operation with the highest tag value will be the one that will be allocated on this sequence cycle on the idle resource. Table 2 demonstrates this algorithm.

Table 2 - 3D matrix status when R4 is idle.

Op	PR	R1	R2	R3	R4	R5	R6	BES
	I	T	E	M		#3		
10	X	12.5	9.51	5.15	99	4.02	6.54	5
20	X	5.04	3.93	2.55	99	99	2.82	3
30	X	6.28	4.86	2.98	2.53	2.47	3.44	5
40	00	6.38	6.12	7.05	5.78	5.93	6.83	4
50	40	8.24	6.33	3.67	2.96	2.62	4.42	5
60	50	5.15	99	4.02	4.86	2.98	2.53	6
	I	T	E	M		#5		
10	X	3.12	3.17	4.02	3.27	99	99	1
20	00	13.9	10.3	10.8	9.95	12.5	99	4
30	20	4.86	2.98	2.53	4.86	2.98	2.53	3
40	20	6.04	4.68	2.90	99	99	3.32	3
50	40	5.76	4.47	2.8	99	99	3.18	3
	I	T	E	M		#7		
10	X	3.12	3.17	4.02	3.27	99	99	1
20	X	6.15	4.2	8.05	9.3	99	99	2
30	00	8.34	8.92	7.58	7.23	8.76	8.12	4
40	30	2.06	2.11	2.96	2.21	99	99	1
	I	T	E	M		#9		
10	X	4.6	3.60	2.39	99	2.05	2.60	5
20	X	5.96	4.59	2.87	99	99	3.28	3
30	00	11.5	12.8	11.9	11.2	13.1	99	4
40	30	99	99	99	99	1.45	1.72	5

Resource Status File

R4 is the idle resource and there are four free operations for which this resource is the best one. The system scans these operations across all resources and computes the difference between the minimum time (BEST) and the time on each resource. The maximum difference value is on the column marked by Δ. In this case the difference between the BEST resource and the resource processing time of item 5 operation 2 is the biggest (13.9-9.95 = 3.95). Therefore, this operation will be allocated to the R4 resource. Its resource status file is updated and its counter is set to the new operating time.

If the list is empty a "look ahead" feature is used to determine the "waiting time" for a best operation to become "free". This search is done by scanning the idle resource column for a search for a free operation. When such operation is encountered, (it is not the best for that resource) the BEST field of this raw indicates which resource is the best for that operation. The entry in the field *resource counter* of the *resource status file* indicates the waiting time of that resource. Example of this procedure is shown by table 3 which shows the status of the 3D matrix at this stage. R5 is idle and search for a free operation. The free operations (PR = 00). Scanning the "BEST" column of the table finds that none of the free operations calls for resource R5. The BEST for the free item #3 operation 40 is resource R4. Calling the *resource status file* in resource R4 raw indicates that operation 40 is in process and it will take another 25 minutes to end, which means that waiting time for operation 40 is 25 minutes.

The system checks if it will be economically to use the idle resource to process the free operation. One method is to compute the difference in time between the BEST and the alternate operation, and compare it to the time that the free resource would otherwise be idle. If the time spent is lower than the time gained it is economically to do so. The computation is as follows:

Table 3 - Status when R5 is idle.

Op	PR	R1	R2	R3	R4	R5	R6	BES
I	T	E	M		#3			
10	X	12.5	9.51	5.15	99	4.02	6.54	5
20	X	5.04	3.93	2.55	99	99	2.82	3
30	X	6.28	4.86	2.98	2.53	2.47	3.44	5
40	00	6.38	6.12	7.05	5.78	5.93	6.83	4
50	40	8.24	6.33	3.67	2.96	2.62	4.42	5
60	50	5.15	99	4.02	4.86	2.98	2.53	6
I	T	E	M		#5			
10	X	3.12	3.17	4.02	3.27	99	99	1
20	00	13.9	10.3	10.8	9.95	12.5	99	4
30	20	4.86	2.98	2.53	4.86	2.98	2.53	3
40	20	6.04	4.68	2.90	99	99	3.32	3
50	40	5.76	4.47	2.8	99	99	3.18	3
I	T	E	M		#7			
10	X	3.12	3.17	4.02	3.27	99	99	1
20	X	6.15	4.2	8.05	9.3	99	99	2
30	00	8.34	8.92	7.58	7.23	8.76	8.12	4
40	30	2.06	2.11	2.96	2.21	99	99	1
I	T	E	M		#9			
10	X	4.6	3.60	2.39	99	2.05	2.60	5
20	X	5.96	4.59	2.87	99	99	3.28	3
30	00	11.5	12.8	11.9	11.2	13.1	99	4
40	30	99	99	99	99	1.45	1.72	5

Resource Status File

Res.	Item	Op.	Q	Link	Counter	Hist.
R4	#2	40	60	22	25	66
R1	#7	03	100	23	87	68

Processing the free operation, item #3 operations 40 is by resource R4, and it takes 5.78 minutes per unit. However resource R4 will become idle only after 25 minutes. Processing this operation on, the idle, resource R5 takes 5.93 minutes per unit. Suppose that the quantity is 100 units, than by working "inefficient" and increasing the processing time by $(5.93-5.78) * 100 = 15$ minutes gives a savings of $(25-15) = 10$ minutes in throughput time.

Checking the other three open operations indicates that this is the best alternative. Therefore item #3 operation 40 is loaded on R5.

If the finished operation was the last one in processing an item, the data of that item is removed from the 3D matrix, calling the bill of material for another item.

The new item data (item name and quantity) is recorded and it process plan from the two dimension matrix master file is introduced into the 3D matrix.

In case of disruption; the *finish time* on the *history file* will list the time of the interrupt, the *resource counter* of the *resource status file* will be set to 99, which will be set back to zero when the resource will be in working conditions again. A new job for that operation (item and operation number) is opened with the remaining quantity. This procedure is for a single or multi resource disruption.

4. SUMMARY

The job release stage was done in the office with stable conditions. However, conditions on the shop floor are dynamic. Therefore, the decisions on the shop floor must consider the immediate shop floor status, adding flexibility and dynamics in the shop floor control.

This paper proposes a shop floor control method that does not plan in advance the routine for each released job, therefore bottlenecks cannot be created and disruptions are solved automatically. It is allowed to alter the process when necessary.

The matrix (table 1) method is a tool that can generate a process, considering the immediate state of shop floor, and do it within a split of a second.

To validate the flexibility of the proposed system a demonstration program was prepared. For demonstration, 2 orders, 12 items, 35 operations, and 15 resources were considered. Simulation results are shown in table 4.

Table 4 - comparison of scheduling strategies.

Optimization Criteria	No. periods to process	Unit cost
Maximum production	35	162
Minimum cost	32	76.2
Semi flexible	23	131
Outmost strategy	21	102

5. REFERENCES

1. Cunha, P.F. (2005) Knowledge Acquisition from Assembly Operational Data Using Principal Components Analysis and Cluster Analysis, Annals of the CIRP, vol.54/1, pp. 27-30.
2. Fitzgerald-A., (2000), Enterprise resource planning (ERP)-breakthrough or buzzword? In: Third International Conference on Factory 2000. Competitive Performance Through.
3. Guenov, M. D., (2002), Complexity and Cost Effectiveness Measures for Systems Design, Second International Conference of the Manufacturing Complexity Network, pp. 455-466.
4. Halevi, G. (2004), Production planning - Simple or complex, 2004, International Journal of Innovation and Technology Management, Vol. 1, No. 4, December 2004, pp. 369-372.
5. Tinham, B (2000),What place MRPII in the new world. Manufacturing Computer Solutions. Vol. 6, No. 1; p. 14-18.
6. Walker, S.S., Brennan, R.W., Norrie, D.H., (2005), Holonic Job Shop Scheduling Using a Multiagent System, IEEE Intelligent Systems, 20/1: 50-57.
7. Wallace, A., (2003), Sequential Resource Allocation Utilizing Agents, International Journal of Production Research, 41/11: 2481-2499.
8. Wiendahl, H.P., and Scholtissek, P., (1994), Management and Control of Complexity in Manufacturing, Annals of the CIRP, Vol. 43/2, pp. 533-540.

LOGISTIC- AND COST-ORIENTED CROSS-COMPANY RAMP-UP PLANNING

Jörg Hüntelmann, Steffen Reinsch and Adriana Märtens
IPH - Institut für Integrierte Produktion Hannover gGmbH, Germany
{huentelmann, reinsch, maertens}@iph-hannover.de

Shorter product life cycles and quicker innovation cycles entail frequent product replacements or substitutions. Due to additional aspects like a simultaneous engineering beyond company borders, the production ramp-up process becomes significantly important and more and more complex. Existing planning approaches to support the ramp-up process predominantly assume individual cases and are limited to one company or component. Regarding the supply chain as one unit, this approach may lead to logistical as well as economical inefficiencies. Hence, a method is required that enables companies to arrange and to accomplish a logistic- and cost-oriented cross-company ramp-up process in a stable and reproducible manner. A suitable approach for an efficient scheduling is the use of a ramp-up reference model which is described in the following paper.

1. INTRODUCTION

Manufacturing enterprises are supposed to face continuously shorter product life cycles, which are evoked by quicker innovation cycles. Consequently product replacements as well as the substitution of components or single parts occur more frequently. To survive in this cut-throat competition, companies have to enforce their innovation activities and are expected to adapt quickly and cost-effectively to those changes. Due to ongoing outsourcing initiatives, associated with the reduction of the vertical range of manufacturing, simultaneous engineering processes beyond company borders and continuous product changes, the ramp-up phase of a new product becomes highly complex. This needs to be considered as a new challenge along the supply chain.

2. STATE OF THE ART

In order to realise and to keep competitive advantages on a highly competitive market, manufacturing enterprises have to accelerate their innovation activities (Terwisch, 1999; Wildemann, 2004a). In addition to technical and technological innovation, mainly the logistic and organisational processes still have high potentials for improvement and cost-savings. Hence a pervasive comprehension and an ongoing search for continuous improvement and evaluation of these processes are indispensable (Nyhuis, 2003). In order to reduce the time to market the flexibility and speed of the production ramp-up is becoming the main task which is expected to be focused on (Risse, 2002; Risse, 2003; Fleischer, 2004a; Wiesinger, 2002). In this context a conflict of aims occurs as figure 1 shows.

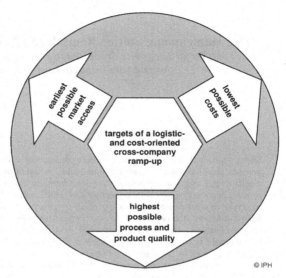

Figure 1 - Conflict of aims of the cross-company ramp-up process.

The production ramp-up process can be considered as an interconnection between product design and mass production. The effects of a rapid and economic cross-company ramp-up process resulting in an early market access are still neglected (Kuhn, 2002). In general manufacturing enterprises do not use an adequate methodical support and or apply appropriate standards. Consequently, the design of the ramp-up processes on one hand and the logistic and economic controlling of the ramp-up on the other hand have to be researched intensely.

The scientific importance of the ramp-up process is consistently emphasised, particularly in the recent few years (Kuhn, 2002; Fleischer, 2004b; Scholz-Reiter, 2004; Schuh, 2004; Urban, 2004; Wildemann, 2004b). Most of the present research work in this field is focused respectively on organisational, economic, qualitative or technical aspects. On contrary, management approaches which consider likewise organisational, logistic and economic aspects as well exist rarely. Thus it is necessary to develop standards, strategy models, tools and methods for an efficient managing of production ramp-ups (Kuhn, 2002). The main aim must be to manage and control complicated cross-company ramp-ups associated with a simultaneous reduction of the ramp-up time and the related costs.

Particularly during the ramp-up of production lines, the late phases of the ramp-up process are characterised by numerous perturbations and related high planning incertitude (Wiendahl, 2002; Nyhuis, 2004; Abele, 2003). Wiendahl et al. as well as

Nyhuis et al. discuss the problems and objectives, define the decisive phases and describe possible fields of action for realising a robust and failure resistant ramp-up of production systems. To resist disturbances technological, organisational and personal aspect need to be considered and optimised. Furthermore the need for reacting strategies to clear the disturbances, which cannot be avoided, is shown. It is pointed out that an independent observation of the separate processes within a comprehensive ramp-up management is essential regarding the complexity, operations network and resulting dependencies.

Fleischer et al. outline a solution concept which focuses on controlling the product quality during the ramp-up phase by means of quality simulation and allows a controlled transfer of a production system to a new series-production operating condition (Fleischer, 2004a). Via a process oriented workflow simulation the production system is modelled, simulated and optimised in an early planning stage.

In addition to quality based and disturbance oriented approaches Schuh et al. (Schuh, 2002) present some basic conditions and requirements for the future production ramp-up management. Flexibility and target-oriented project management are presented as the core of the observation. The explanation of the basic conditions and the formulation of the central challenges of the future ramp-up management focus thereby on the automotive industry. Mainly three central requirements exist:

- For an increasing complexity of planning and control tasks in supplier networks the development of an effective decentralised, cross-company planning and control scenario becomes indispensable. Thereby the cross-company change management is expected to be one of the most important tasks.
- Multi ramp-up scenarios within the affected enterprises and supplier networks have to be supported effectively with tools, methods and supply of services. In addition to the optimised planning and control, it has to be focussed mainly on the guided coordination of the subsequent ramp-ups.
- The third requirement targets the controllability of the increasing number of software and mechatronic systems in the automobile industry. According to Schuh et al. the main objectives are expected to be the development of product appropriate structures for construction design and production scheduling as well as the design of an effective release management.

Amongst other lately released papers, the above mentioned literature shows that numerous approaches already exist to improve some aspects of the production ramp-up. The emphasised ramp-up aspects are product quality, time of the ramp-up process (time-to-market) or costs for example. It needs to be lined out, that the already developed methods are basically aiming at large-scale enterprises like automotive manufacturers, which are able to invest considerable efforts and high costs in accelerating their production ramp-ups (Wildemann, 2004a; Kuhn, 2002; Möller, 2002; Schmahls, 2001).

A suitable methodical support which especially helps small and medium-sized enterprises (SME) to execute their production ramp-ups logistically, economically, rapidly and reliably needs to be developed. Due to the fact that SME had to concentrate in the past on their core competencies, the production ramp-ups and their related planning activities occur nowadays predominantly in a cross-company manner along the supply chain. Hence, it is indispensable for manufacturers to integrate the component-, and equipment suppliers as well as the customers in an early stage. Moreover it is a great challenge to manage simultaneously both the ramp-up process of the forthcoming product and the phase-out of the current product. It is required to develop suitable ramp-up standards, strategy models, tools and methods.

3. DEVELOPMENT OF A RAMP-UP REFERENCE MODEL

The development of a cross-company, ramp-up specific reference model (RRM) for SME presents an effective solution approach. This reference model is supposed to take into account organisational, logistic and economic aspects. Furthermore, it has to consider facilities and manufacturing specific issues. Some of these issues could be for instance:

- How could the start of production of a new product be integrated effectively and without high efforts in an already existing production?
- How could the success of such a ramp-up process be evaluated regarding time, quality and costs?
- How could the gained knowledge be prepared to be used for the following ramp-up process?

In order to answer these questions an appropriate method is required as well as a software tool needs to be developed. The software is expected to be used easily by small and medium-sized enterprises. Within the research project "LogiKoPro" such a method is developed. The approach and the expected results are described below.

3.1 Initial State

The initial state of the current cooperation in a cross-company production ramp-up involves various different enterprises. This comprises the component supplier, the equipment supplier, the manufacturer of the ramp-up product itself and their customers, e.g. the OEM. The network characteristic becomes apparent, particularly due to the fact that usually numerous suppliers are involved in the ramp-up process.

The main objective of the presented approach is the rapid and economic planning and lead-through of the over-all production ramp-up process. Particularly the cross-company ramp-up process needs to be shortened and simultaneously controlled tightly in respect to logistic quality, effort and costs. With this in mind the purpose of the planned ramp-up reference model is designing, configuring and controlling of different types of a production ramp-up along the value chain or supply chain.

3.2 Structure and Appliance of the Reference Model

Figure 2 shows the four steps in the appliance of the RRM. The basic principle is an element-based approach which initially analyses different elements of the production ramp-up process from the three fields: organisation, production system and product. These fields cover organisational, logistic and economic aspects. The analysed coherences between the identified ramp-up elements are used to define different production ramp-up types. For this purpose so-called ramp-up enablers are determined. Then classification criteria for the determination of the production ramp-up types are identified. After that, ramp-up reference process schemes are built for the essential ramp-up types. Each reference process scheme corresponds to one pre-assigned ramp-up type. The process schemes serve for both configuring the over-all ramp-up process and designing the individual ramp-up processes of the respective party in the ramp-up network. In addition to the reference process schemes the RRM considers the support of their configuration, a cross-company cost-benefit-risk-assessment and action guidelines for the cooperation in the ramp-up network. Thus, the planning and execution of production ramp-ups become significantly shortened and due to the reference characteristic reproducible.

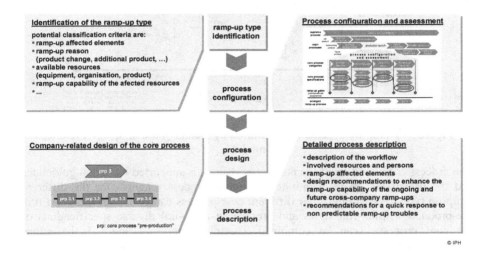

Figure 2 - The four steps in the appliance of the ramp-up reference model (RRM).

The four steps of the application of the RRM are described below:

The first step is the **identification of the ramp-up type**. The classification criteria which are needed to differentiate are the above described ramp-up elements and its values and specifications. While ramp-up-aiding characteristics of the elements can be considered as ramp-up enablers, the repressive characteristics of the elements can be classified as ramp-up disablers. Other classification criteria like the ramp-up reason (product change, additional or new product) or the available time for the ramp-up need to be identified.

The **ramp-up process configuration** defines the second step. After identifying the ramp-up type, the production launch is configured and assessed (cp. figure 3). Within this step the supreme process refers to an ongoing planning and controlling, which is indispensable during the whole production launch. The main processes apply to the different phases of the product life cycles, in which the focus is on the production launch of the forthcoming product.

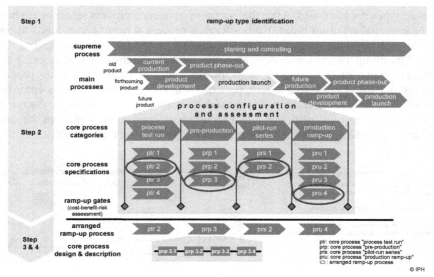

Figure 3 - Ramp-up process configuration by means of the ramp-up reference model.

The process configuration of the production launch is supported by action guidelines and the use of the above mentioned reference process schemes for the different ramp-up types. Based upon four different core process categories (process test run, pre-production, pilot-run series and production ramp-up) diverse specifications of the core processes can be combined. Complementary to figure 3 the return processes, for example of deficient pre-production parts, are incorporated. The assessment is provided by the ramp-up gates, which are described below (chapter 3.3). Thus, the RRM considers organisational and economic aspects as well as logistic and technical conditions. The result is a process configuration that corresponds to the ramp-up type.

The third step contains the **company related design of the core processes**. The core processes of the configured main processes are expected to be designed in respect of the specific requirements of the enterprises. Each partial stage of the core processes design is supported by well-defined action instructions and checklists, enabling a depiction of the designed core processes including input, output, function and resources.

The fourth step comprises the **detailed process description** and contains the following aspects:

- description of the workflow,
- involved resources and persons within the framework of the accordant core processes,
- ramp-up affected elements,
- design recommendations to enhance the ramp-up capability of the ongoing and future cross-company ramp-ups,
- advices for designing a rapid ramp-up production system technology and
- recommendations for a quick response to non predictable or unscheduled ramp-up troubles.

3.3 Ramp-Up Supervision - Controlling as a Comprehensive Task

During the whole cross-company production ramp-up process the supervision of time, quality and cost aspects can be seen as a comprehensive task. Hence, a ramp-up controlling method is required that records data along the value-added chain (supply-chain) on an intra- and interplant wide range. Therefore ramp-up gates will be defined and implemented in the RRM according to the established quality gates in the automotive industry (Scharer, 2002). Yet in addition to quality operating figures, these ramp-up gates analyse cost and time key data and thus allow a cost-benefit-risk-assessment at certain stages of the ramp-up configuration process. By means of this gate based supervision ramp-up participants are given a basis for decisions throughout the whole production ramp-up. Moreover, a platform is provided which enables the possibility to document the gained knowledge and to save it for the forthcoming ramp-ups.

4. SUMMARY

To realise and to keep competitive advantages, manufacturing enterprises have to accelerate their innovation activities. This results in shorter product life cycles and, consequently, the product replacements as well as the substitution of components or single parts occur more frequently. Due to additional aspects like an ongoing outsourcing, the reduction of the vertical range of manufacturing, simultaneous engineering beyond company borders and continuous product changes, the ramp-up process becomes more and more essential and complex. Existing planning approaches to support the production ramp-up generally do not consider the cross-company characteristic and may lead to logistical as well as economical inefficiencies.

By means of the presented integrative ramp-up reference model (RRM) the time-to-market is expected to be shortened substantially due to a rapid logistic- and costs-oriented planning and lead-through of the over-all production ramp-up process. Based on pre-assigned relevant ramp-up elements, previously identified ramp-up enablers and different types of standard ramp-up processes for distinct partners along the supply chain, this reference model supports the process configuration and the process design along the manufacturer's supply chain. In addition to practice-oriented check lists and operation recommendations, the reference model includes an integrated instrument for a cost-benefit-risk-assessment of the proposed ramp-up process configuration. Thus, the reference model is expected to serve as a process management and knowledge system for cross-company ramp-ups and is supposed to provide an efficient tool, particularly for small and medium sized enterprises (SME).

5. ACKNOWLEDGEMENT

The research project "LogiKoPro" is funded by the German Federation of Industrial Research Associations "Otto von Guericke" (AiF). The project is carried out in a cooperation by IPRI (International Performance Research Institute in Stuttgart) and IPH – Institut für Integrierte Produktion Hannover GmbH.

6. REFERENCES

1. Abele, E., Elzenheimer, J., Rüstig, A.: Anlaufmanagement in der Serienproduktion. In: ZWF, Jg. 98, Seite 172-176, Carl Hanser Verlag, München, 2003.
2. Fleischer, J., Spath, D., Lanza, G.: Quality Simulation for Fast Ramp Up. In: 36th CIRP – International Seminar on Manufacturing Systems, 03-05 June, Saarbrücken, Germany, 2004a. pp. 149-153.
3. Fleischer, J., Wawerla M., Nyhuis, P., Winkler, H., Liestmann, V.: Proaktive Anlaufsteuerung von Produktionssystemen entlang der Wertschöpfungskette. In: Industrie Management, volume 20, issue 4, 2004b. pp. 29-32.
4. Kuhn, A., Wiendahl, H.-P., Eversheim, W., Schuh, G.: Schneller Produktionsanlauf von Serienprodukten. Ergebnisbericht der Untersuchung "fast ramp-up", Dortmund: Verlag Praxiswissen, 2002.
5. Möller, K.: Lebenszyklusorientierte Planung und Kalkulation des Serienanlaufs. In: Zeitschrift für Planung, volume 13, issue 12, 2002. pp. 431-457.
6. Nyhuis, P., Wiendahl, H.-P.: Logistische Kennlinien. Grundlagen, Werkzeuge und Anwendungen. 2nd edition, Berlin: Springer Verlag, 2003.
7. Nyhuis, P., Winkler, H.: Development of a Controlling System for the Ramp-up of Productions Systems. In: COMA 04 – International Conference on Competitive Manufacturing, 4 – 6 February 2004, Stellenbosch, 2004. pp. 401-406.
8. Risse, J.: Time-to-Market-Management in der Automobilindustrie, Ph.D.-Thesis of the University of Berlin, 2002.
9. Risse, J.: Zeitorientierte Produktentstehung: Ansatzpunkte und Methoden für das Time-to-Market-Management. In: Baumgarten, H., Wiendahl, H.-P., Zentes, J. (ed.). Logistik Management, Band 2, Berlin/Heidelberg/New York: Springer Verlag, 2003.
10. Scharer, M.: Quality Gates mit integriertem Risikomanagement: Methodik und Leitfaden zur zielorientierten Planung und Durchführung von Produktentstehungsprozessen. Ph.D.-Thesis, Universität Karlsruhe, 2002.
11. Schmahls, T.: Beitrag zur Effizienzsteigerung während Produktionsanläufen in der Automobilindustrie. Dissertation, Technische Universität Chemnitz, 2001.
12. Scholz-Reiter, B. Höhns, H., Kruse, A., König, F.: Hybrides Änderungsmanagement im Serienanlauf. In: Industrie Management, volume 20, issue 4, 2004. pp. 21-24.
13. Schuh, G., Franzkoch, B.: Fast Ramp-Up – Anlaufstrategien, Deviationsmanagement und Wissensmanagement für den Anlauf. In: Zeit gewinnen durch flexible Strukturen, Tagungsband, Leipzig 22.-23.09.2004. VDI-Gesellschaft Fördertechnik Materialfluss Logistik, 2004. VDI-Berichte Nr. 1849, pp. 69-79.
14. Schuh, G., Riedel, H., Abels, I., Desoi, J.: Serienanlauf in branchenübergreifenden Netzwerken. Eine komplexe Planungs- und Kontrollaufgabe. In: wt Werkstattstechnik online, volume 92, issue 11/12, 2002. pp. 656-661.
15. Terwisch, C., Chea, K.S., Bohn, R.E.: An Explanatory Study of International Product Transfer and Production Ramp-Up in the Data Storage Industry, The Information Storage Industry Centre, San Diego: University of California, 1999.
16. Urban, G., Seiter, M.: Fragestellungen zum Produktionsanlauf. In: Industrie Management, volume 20, issue 4, 2004. pp. 57-59.
17. Wiendahl, H.-P., Hegenscheidt, M., Winkler, H.: Anlaufrobuste Produktionssysteme. In: wt Werkstattstechnik, volume 92, issue 11/12, 2002. pp. 650-655.
18. Wiesinger, G.; Housein, G.: Schneller Produktionsanlauf von Serienprodukten – Wettbewerbsvorteile durch ein anforderungsgerechtes Anlaufmanagement. In: wt Werkstattstechnik online, volume 92, issue 10, 2002. pp. 505-508.
19. Wildemann, H.: Optimierung von Anlaufprozessen auf Basis der Schnittstellenanalyse. In: Braßler, A., Corten, H., (ed.). Entwicklungen im Produktionsmanagement. München: Verlag Franz Vahlen, 2004a.
20. Wildemann, H.: Präventive Handlungsstrategien für den Produktionsanlauf. In: Industrie Management, volume 20, issue 4, 2004b. pp. 17-20.

OPTIMIZATION CUSTOMIZED TOKEN-BASED PRODUCTION CONTROL SYSTEMS USING CROSS-ENTROPY

Pedro L. González-R[1]., Jose M Framinan[1], Andreas Dopfer[2] and
Rafael Ruiz-Usano[1]
[1]*Industrial Management School of Engineering, University of Seville, Spain.*
{pedroluis, jose, usano}@esi.us.es
[2]*Production and Industry Department, Univ. of Duisburg-Essen, Germany.*
dopfer@uni-duisburg.de

Customized Token-Based production control Systems constitutes one of the most recent approaches to production control, having shown their effectiveness for different manufacturing environments. Performance optimization of a Customized Token-Based System can be formulated as a multicriteria combinatorial optimization problem, which can be addressed by means of metaheuristics. Among these, the cross-entropy method (CE) has confirmed to be useful for a great diversity of problems, including the NP-hard combinatorial optimization problems. However, its applicability for multi-criteria problems has not still been explored. In this paper we tackle the multicriteria optimization of a customized token-based production control systems using the CE method, and test its suitability for real-life environments in a simulation model extracted from a component automobile factory in Spain.

1. INTRODUCTION

In the production control context, pull systems have been studied by researchers and successfully implemented in practice during last decades. Since the first Kanban approach used in Toyota factory (Monden, 1983) several pull systems (also termed as token-based systems by Gershwin, 2000) have been developed. The most general approach regarding token-based systems are the Customized Token-Based Systems (CTBS) (see e.g. Gaury *et al.*, 2000, or Gaury *et al.*, 2001, or González-R, 2006). CTBS try to control the maximum amount of jobs between each pair of stations by means of cards (control loop), similarly to the Kanban system which try to limit the maximum amount of work by each station. These systems seem to reach better results than other existing pull systems (see e.g. Gaury, 2000), being the main disadvantage its customization, i.e. how to set the control loops to be implemented and the number of cards for every control loop. This problem can be formulated as a combinatorial optimization problem. Besides, it is usual that several objectives -

[1] This research has been supported by the Spanish National Research Plan under DPI2004-02902 project.

such as throughput, work in process (WIP), or service level - must be considered. Therefore, the problem can be regarded as a multi-criteria optimization problem. The Cross-Entropy (CE) method (Rubinstein, 1997) has shown to be useful for a great variety of problems, including some NP-hard combinatorial optimization problems (Alon *et al.*, 2005; De Boer *et al.*, 2005; Rubinstein, 1999; Rubinstein and Kroese, 2004). However, to the best of our knowledge, there are no references on the application of CE to multi-criteria optimization. In this paper, we address the optimization of CTBS using the CE method for multi-criteria optimization.

The remainder of the paper is structured as follows. Section 2 is devoted to the introduction of the CTBS concept, while in section 3 we propose a CE-based algorithm for CTBS multicriteria optimization. Section 4 presents the application of the proposed algorithm to a model based in a real manufacturing line. Conclusions and future research are outlined in section 5.

2. CUSTOMIZED TOKEN-BASED SYSTEMS

2.1 Token-based systems

In token-based systems - such as Kanban or Conwip (Spearman *et al.*, 1990) -, the flow of jobs through the shop is authorized by kanban cards - or tokens -. Consequently, a Single Kanban system has a parameter k_i for each station i, i.e. the maximum amount of work (orders, containers, etc.) allowed in the corresponding station. Thus, the Single Kanban system requires setting n parameters in a shop of n stations (see figure 1).

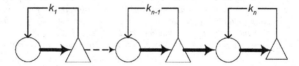

Figure 1 – Single Kanban production control system.

The Conwip system uses a single card count k for all stations in the line. Therefore, the maximum amount of work is limited by the number of cards and one only parameter must be set (see figure 2).

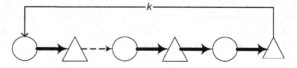

Figure 2 – Conwip production control system.

Kanban systems use only local information about the state of every station. The Conwip system uses global information regarding the complete line, but not for sub-parts of the process. Both Kanban and Conwip are extreme cases of token-based systems. In the middle of these, there exist a great variety of token-based mechanisms, such as Base stock, Double Kanban, Extended Kanban, Generalized Kanban, Generic Kanban, or Hybrid Kanban-Conwip, among others. There are numerous references devoted to the comparison among token-based systems (see e.g. Framinan *et al.*, 2003), and results show that no single system outperforms the others for all possible manufacturing scenarios. However, the currently selection process is neither based on its environmental conditions nor shop conditions. Consequently, its suitability can not be guarantee in that case. Therefore, it would be of interest the design of an *ad-hoc* token-based system for a given shop and manufacturing conditions. This is the approach adopted by the CTBS, which is explained in the next subsection.

2.2 Customized token-based systems description

If we consider all possible card loops - control loops - between all stations in the system, we have the most general token-based system, such as the one shown in figure 3. This type of system is known as Customized Token Based System (CTBS). Every existing token-based system is a particular case of the CTBS. For example, if we only consider the card loop between the first and the last station (and set a high value for the cards in the rest of the loops), we obtain a Conwip system.

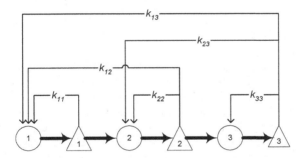

Figure 3 – 3-Station CTBS before optimization.

Hence, a CTBS will initially consider every possible loop between stations. A customization process has to be then carried out in order to simultaneously remove those loops not useful for the specific scenario and to set the proper number of cards for the remaining loops. It has been empirically established that only less than the half of the initial loops is usually necessary to be implemented (Gaury, 2000).

2.3 Search space

The advantages of the CTBS with respect to 'traditional' pull systems have been studied in different works. The CTBS performance was successfully when compared against other pull systems in theoretical and real-life based environments (see e.g. Gaury 2000 and González-R. 2006). Nevertheless, the main problem related to

CTBS lies in determining the useful loops and to set their corresponding card count. This can be formulated as finding a correct integer value for every possible loop according to a set of objectives. If we initially consider all possible card loops between two stations, the total number of loops, m, in one line formed by n stations is:

$$m = n \left(n + 1 \right) / 2 \tag{1}$$

The total search space is given for all combinations of the values assigned to the loops. For a fixed number of cards, K_{max}, for all loops, the size of the search space is the following:

$$\left(K_{max} \right)^m \tag{2}$$

Since the inherent variability of production systems has to be taken into account, the usual way to compute a solution (set of loops and corresponding card counts) is by means of discrete event simulation. In one hand, the complete enumeration of all possible solutions is intractable. On the other hand, alternative exact methods, such as mathematical modelling or queuing theory are useful only for extremely simplistic cases, being unsuitable for most real-life environments. Hence, a heuristic algorithm that obtains good (but not necessarily optimal) solutions within a reasonable computation effort appears to be a realistic approach for addressing the optimization problem.

2.4 Structural properties

In last sub-section, we pointed out that one of the most important drawbacks for the use of CTBS was the enormous size of the search space. Nevertheless, the concept of 'structural properties' can be used in order to efficiently reduce the search space. Although it is not the aim of this paper to fully describe this concept, we briefly introduce it in order to clarify later sections. Structural properties for CTBS were proposed by Gaury (2000) and later generalized by González-R. (2006). Similar works have been done for Kanban systems (see e.g. Tayur 1993 and Ramesh 1997). Structural properties do not depend on particular characteristics of the line, such as time processes, existence of machine breakdowns, set-up times or demand behaviour, but for the number of stations. Regarding the dominance of some solutions with respect to others, it is important to notice that it is possible beforehand to detect whether one solution is dominated by other, or not. The set of dominated solutions is denoted 'set of structurally non-efficient solutions', while the rest form the 'set of structurally efficient solutions'. These dominance relationships among card configurations are termed 'structural dominance' and does not relate, in general, to the performance of the system. For instance, one structural efficient solution and a one solution dominated by the former one may have the same performance for the same system and the same conditions. However, the structural efficient solution depends on less number of parameters than the set of dominated solutions. Therefore, the previous characteristic can be employed to avoid exploring dominated solutions, as it is possible to reach the same performance using a structurally efficient solution. Then, it is possible to detect if one particular solution is a structurally efficient solution or not. The non-structurally efficient solutions are not useful to be explored because the Pareto set of efficient solutions is included in the set of structurally efficient solutions (González-R., 2006). Therefore, structural properties can be used in two different ways: first to simplify a certain solution and second to generate structurally efficient solutions. These aspects will be taken into account in the optimization procedure described in next section.

3. THE CROSS-ENTROPY METHOD

3.1 Description

In many optimization problems in Operations Research the objective function can be evaluated using a closed-form expression. However, there are other types of problems where there is not a known expression for the objective function. In these cases, the objective function must be estimated. Discrete event simulation is a common way to estimate the value of an unknown objective function expression. The CE method (see e.g. Rubinstein and Kroese, 2004) provides a simple and efficient method to solve those types of problems.

The CE method is an iterative process formed by two steps:

1. Generate a set of random data (e.g. variables, or vectors) according to a specific mechanism.
2. Update the parameters of the mechanism in order to produce a better set in the next iteration.

It is possible to show that CE reaches the global optimum for certain cases. Another important aspect is that it provides a unified scheme for simulation and optimization problems. These characteristics make CE a suitable technique for CTBS optimization.

3.2 CE applied to optimize CTBS

A possible solution for the CTBS problem can be characterized by a vector of cards, $\mathbf{k} = \{k_1, k_2, ..., k_i, ..., k_m\}$, formed by m components, being m the maximum number of loops - see equation (1) -. The possible values for every vector component are integer numbers, which represent the number of cards in that loop. In case that one loop is not necessary to be implemented, the same performance can be reached by a closed loop with infinite number of cards (Gaury, 2000). Hence, the domain for the vector components is $1 \le k_i \le K_{max} \cup \infty$.

Every vector of cards will produce different values of throughput/service level and WIP in the system. Then, the problem can be interpreted as a combinatorial optimization problem. The notation used in order to explain the main algorithm steps are the following:

$S(\mathbf{k})$, system performance, objective function

$\hat{\gamma}$, minimal expected throughput for the elite solution

N, population size

ρ, population fraction for elite solutions, usually bounded such, $0.01 \le \rho \le 0.03$ in case that the number of components in the vector is greater than 100, in other case $\rho \approx \ln(n)/n$.

$\mathbf{k}^{(y)}$, certain elite solution vector

$\mathbf{Q}$, is a probability matrix for random set generation

α, smoothing parameter

The main CE procedure for the optimization of the CTBS can be implemented by the following steps:

0. Generate a random set of N cards vectors, $\{\mathbf{k}^{(1)}, \mathbf{k}^{(2)}, ..., \mathbf{k}^{(i)}, ..., \mathbf{k}^{(N)}\}$

1. Select a group of elite solutions according a predefined criterion (e.g. throughput maximization, $\max S(\mathbf{k})$). Usually is done selecting a fraction ρ of the population, i.e. ρN.

2. For each elite solution: record the percentage of the number of times that a certain value is repeated for every component in the vector. This count will be used later to get the best values for every component in one vector. To do so, CE uses a matrix $\mathbf{Q}$, where every component q_{ij} in $\mathbf{Q}$ means the percentage of times that a particular component k_i in a certain elite solution $\mathbf{k}^{(y)}$ obtains the value j. In our implementation, the infinite value is determined by $j = 0$. $\mathbf{Q}$ matrix can be thus interpreted as a probability matrix of the best solutions.

3. Generate a new population using $\mathbf{Q}$. Go to step 1.

The stopping criterion is usually defined by the convergence of the expected response in the elite group solutions ($\hat{\gamma}$ parameter). It is to note that, in order to improve performance of the system, better solutions can be obtained by using the structural properties every time a solution is generated. Consequently, the performance of the algorithm is increased by using 'structurally efficient solutions' on every population generation (details about the generation process can be found in Gonzalez-R. 2006). It is a good practice to smooth the $\mathbf{Q}$ matrix in order to avoid probabilities for some components q_{ij} tending to zero or one in early iterations (Rubinstein and Kroese, 2004). To do so, it is usual to use the smoothed value of $\mathbf{Q}$ for the current iteration t, as follows:

$$\mathbf{Q}_t = \alpha \mathbf{Q}_{t-1} + (1 - \alpha)\mathbf{Q}_t \qquad (3)$$

Usual values for the smoothing parameter, α, are in the range between 0.7 and 1. The initial population is usually obtained by assigning the same probability for every component. In our case it is obtained by setting $1/(K_{\max} + 1)$.

3.3 Multi-criteria CE approach

Gaury (2000) shows three useful objective functions for CTBS optimization, i.e. reaching a target throughput/service level with the smaller WIP by means of a lexicographical approach. However, in a real implementation, the set of Pareto efficient solutions, Ψ, is preferable for a decision making process. In this sub-section we describe an efficient method to obtain the Pareto set based on the CE method previously described. The procedure consists on iteratively updating the Pareto set. In order to avoid exploring several times the same solution, the explored solutions are marked as visited. The procedure contains the following steps:

0. Generate a random solution $\mathbf{k}^{(0)}$ and update the set of Pareto efficient solution, Ψ.
1. Choose the first non-marked as visited solution $\mathbf{k}^{(i)}$ from the Pareto efficient solution set, Ψ, (using a sorting criterion), and set the output as the target throughput/service level, $\theta = S(\mathbf{k}^{(i)})$. If Ψ is empty, generate a random solution. Mark $\mathbf{k}^{(i)}$ as a visited solution.
2. Use the CE algorithm described in 3.2 in order to reach the target throughput/service level, θ. Update the set of efficient solutions, Ψ.
3. Go to step 1 until all solutions in the Pareto set, Ψ are marked as visited, or other stopping criterion is reached.

The sorting criterion we employ is ascending throughput order. An additional stopping criterion (such as the maximum number of iterations) can be established. The proposed algorithm makes an iterative use of the CE method, by means of an intensive search of better solutions from every new solution in the Pareto set. It is important to note that while the algorithm is trying to converge to a certain target value, the probability matrix also explores the neighbourhood of each solution. Therefore, this searching procedure allows identifying new solutions in the Pareto frontier.

4. COMPUTATIONAL EXPERIENCE

In order to test the effectiveness of the algorithm described in sub-section 3.3, we conduct an experiment based on real data of an automobile component factory from Spain. Although detailed data (provided by the production control department of the factory) are not included in this paper for confidentiality reasons, we give the main characteristics of the scenario. The manufacturing system consists of a ten-station line in tandem. Processing times can be considered deterministic, being affected by different variability causes. The model considers 13 important station breakdowns, with mean times between failures (MTBF) exponentially distributed, while mean times to repair (MTTR) follow an Erlang distribution. Additionally, 23 scheduled maintenance labours have been considered. Their frequency and interval have been set as deterministic. Additionally, some short, non scheduled, stops in the processing times were considered. Such stops formed a total of 15 so called 'micro-pauses', with MTBF exponentially distributed and deterministic MTTR. A simulation horizon of 40 days and 10 replicates were used for every experiment in order to get reliable measures. In figure 4 the Pareto efficient solution for the CTBS using the proposed CE methodology for multi-criteria problems is shown. The figure also illustrates those results obtained for the same line if managed by a Conwip system.

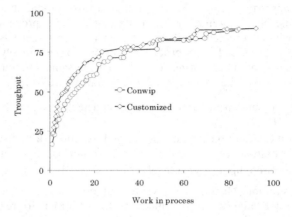

Figure 4 – Pareto frontier for the CTBS and Conwip solution.

Currently, the production line in the factory is controlled by means of a Kanban system, reporting a throughput level of 90% and a WIP of 350 jobs. In contrast, the customized system can reach a 90.17% throughput with only 92.33 WIP. The customized system for the corresponding throughput is shown in figure 5. Circles means machines, while triangles stand for buffers.

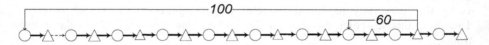

Figure 5 – Customized system for a 90.17% of throughput.

It is to note that the proposed CTBS is easier to control and to put into practice, because it only depends on two parameters, in contrast to the ten parameters used in the currently implemented Kanban system.

5. CONCLUSIONS

In this work we have introduced the CTBS. The customization approach is an alternative method to 'traditional' pull approaches. The main advantage of the CTBS is that environmental and shop conditions are considered. Consequently, efficiency can be higher than other pull systems, because the CTBS is perfectly adapted to the systems needs. In section 3 we have briefly described the CE method and have adapted it to the CTBS optimization under a multi-criteria (throughput, WIP) approach.

In order to test the performance of the proposed optimization algorithm, we test it in a model based on real data of a component automobile factory. Results show that the resulting CTBS reaches better results than a Conwip system for every combination of throughput and WIP. Additionally, it outperforms the production control system currently under operation in the factory.

6. REFERENCES

1. Alon, G., Kroese, D.P., Raviv, T., Rubinstein, R.Y. Application of the Cross-Entropy Method to the Buffer Allocation Problem in a Simulation-Based Environment. Annals of Operations Research 2005; 134(1): 137-151.
2. De Boer, P-T., Kroese, D.P., Mannor, S., Rubinstein, R.Y. A Tutorial on the Cross-Entropy Method. Annals of Operations Research 2005; 134(1): 19-67.
3. Framinan, J.M., González-R, P.L. and Ruiz-Usano, R. The Conwip production control system: review and research issues. Production Planning and Control 2003; 14(3): 255-265.
4. Gaury, E.G.A. Designing pull production control systems: customization and robustness (PhD Thesis, Ed. Center). Tilburg University, The Netherlands, 2000.
5. Gaury, E.G.A., Pierreval, H., Kleijnen, J.P.C. An evolutionary approach to select a pull system among Kanban, Conwip and Hybrid. Journal of Intelligent Manufacturing 2000; 11: 157-167.
6. Gaury, E.G.A., Pierreval, H., Kleijnen, J.P.C. A methodology to customize pull control systems. Journal of Operational Research Society 2001; 52(7): 789-799.
7. González-R., P.L. Design and operation of Customized token-based production control systems. (PhD Thesis). University of Seville, Seville, Spain, 2006.
8. Gershwin, S.B., Design and operation of manufacturing systems_ the control-point policy. IIE Transactions 2000; 32:891-906.
9. Monden, Y. Toyota production system. Industrial Engineering and Management Press, Atlanta, 1983.
10. Ramesh, R., Prasad, S.Y., Thirumurthy, M.V. Flow control in a Kanban based multicell manufacturing: I. A structural analysis of general blocking design space, International Journal of Production Research 1997; 35(8): 2327-2343.
11. Rubinstein, R. Y. Optimization of computer simulation models with rare events. European Journal of Operations Research 1997; 99: 89-112.
12. Rubinstein, R. Y. The cross-entropy method for combinatorial and continuous optimization. Methodology and Computing in Applied Probability 1999; 2: 127-190.
13. Rubinstein, R.Y., Kroese, D. P. The Cross-Entropy Method: A Unified Approach to Monte Carlo Simulation, Randomized Optimization and Machine Learning. Information Science & Statistics, Springer Verlag, NY, 2004.
14. Spearman, M.L., Woodruff, D.L., Hoop, W.J. Conwip: a pull alternative to Kanban. International Journal of Production Research 1990; 28(5): 879-894.
15. Tayur, S.R. Structural properties and heuristic for Kanban-controlled serial lines. Management Science, 1993; 39(11): 1347-1368.

ROLE OF THE INFORMATION AN KNOWLEDGE IN DIGITAL ENTERPRISE TECHNOLOGY

M. Bossmann, H. Bley and N. Avgoustinov
Institute of Production Engineering/CAM, Saarland University, Germany
{bossmann,bley,avgoust}@cam.uni-saarland.de

The globalization and its consequences have driven the competition to a new (probably again temporary) peak: the Internet has made not only the (main) information about every product, but also its comparison with its competitors just a few clicks away. Since the customers' demands for new functionality, high quality, fast delivery, low prices and good service are permanently increasing, for remaining competitive the enterprises have to invest in novel technologies, allowing high quality despite low production costs and good management of their own know-how. Nowadays the know-how and the knowledge around the product development process represent the most important aspects of companies to stay in market. It is essential to speed up product development process with a high quality to get competitive advantages. At present, several methods exist to support the Simultaneous Engineering (SE). The speed and the flexibility of the development process depend on the information, its representation and its transfer. The goal of our new approach is to minimize the waste of time by improving the support for the data transfer of all necessary information between the departments, involved in the development.

1. INTRODUCTION

The goal of our new approach is to minimize the waste of time by improving the support for the data transfer of all necessary information between the departments, involved in the development. So it is possible to automate different activities of the departments by using a standardised information format. A next step towards a better parallelisation is the definition of milestones along the product development process. This concept allows focusing the work on the data exchange at certain stages for reaching a higher stage of maturity. Main advantage of our approach is a shorter development time that is achieved by transparent information management. In doing so, it is possible to produce initial or enhanced information for different tasks in product development. Then, the result is a better integration of all involved departments that gives us also the opportunity to create new knowledge, based on the information flow and on the discussions among the department experts.

2. DEFINITIONS

On the lowest level of all kinds of information and knowledge structures stays the data. Each of the levels above can be viewed as a data derivative. Since these derivatives play an enormous role in the modelling, we shall explain briefly some of them. Under *data* we shall understand *strings of (ordered) symbols*. These symbols are represented in computers by numbers, and in turn, the numbers are represented by binary digits or bits. Apart from bits, the numbers are the smallest "building block" in the representation of data and data derivatives – including algorithms – in a computer. An example of such a string of symbols is "3.1415".

The *information* emerges from interpreting data. The interpreting means that each piece of data and meta-data is connected or put into a relation with already known facts as well as with all other pieces of data. For achieving this, the interpreter (human or machine) should have some *a priori knowledge* – i.e. to be able to read the numbers and to understand the meaning of the sign "<". This knowledge is often called *context* or *background knowledge*.

Since the context always plays a crucial role by gaining the information from given data, another possible definition for information is *data in certain context*.

Another possibility to define the term information is as a combination of meta-data and (groups of) data that are to be connected/related, for instance: $\pi \approx 3.1415$.

Such combination of data and meta-data is usually named an *attribute-value pair*. When representing more complex information it is possible to nest attribute-value pairs by using a given pair as the value of another pair.

When the value of an attribute-value pair contains just data (i.e., there is no nesting), such pair can be named *basic* or *substantial* attribute-value pair. Independently of their representation, basic attribute-value pairs can be viewed as the smallest units of information. The ability to gain new information from already existing information or data shall be called *knowledge*.

The intelligence is a quality that is inherent mainly to human beings. When we say: "this program is intelligent", we mean that in a given situation it behaves or attempts to behave similarly to a human being, which is in the same situation. We shall view a software program as being intelligent if it possesses at least one of the following:

a) Ability to complete maximum tasks with a minimum instructions from the controlling user or program;
b) Ability to guess what action is desired/needed in any given moment and either propose or perform it;
c) Ability to request or find alone any missing or invalid data or information.

It is difficult to think of a way to measure or compute the intelligence of a program that would allow an objective comparison with other programs.

The software models are built-up from data, data-derivatives and (possibly) code. Therefore, many of the model traits depend on the traits of the underlying data and its derivatives, as well as on the chosen representation. Software models can use additional data for specialization (concretization) and communication. Software models can use bound or built-in code (as a special kind of data) for implementing intelligence.

3. INFORMATION MANAGEMENT

The development of every product starts with an idea, which can in extreme case be described by one word only – for instance "car". The amount of data, necessary for representing this word is modest – in our example only 3 bytes – but the information, related to the idea and its related notions could be enormous.

As the idea evolves, though, the information describing and supporting it increases continuously – first the aim is stated, then the requirements are determined, then the functionality is specified, details are described and so on. The information increases – often even exponentially – with each step of the workflow, with each phase of the product life cycle until the product reaches the market and even after that. The objective of a fast development process can be achieved only by an improved information exchange (Alt, 2002; Mäntylä, 1996; Thoben, 1997). For this, milestones by which the relevant information has to be transferred must be defined. Modern CAx Software systems that are used along the product development process make it possible to speed up the special tasks of the different departments (VDI 4499, 2006; Wiendahl, 2002; Schiller, 2002; Westkämper, 2003; Alberts, 2003; Bracht, 2005). The three-dimensional model of the products as well as the use of parametric modelling approaches has performed a decisive step in CAD technology (Bär, 2001; VDI 2218, 1999; Weber, 1996; Cuiper, 1996). New modelling methods make a faster product design possible. The use of feature elements accelerates the process of modelling since routine activities or standard elements can be finished off by bringing in a feature concept. Databases and libraries of standard components can be prepared by suppliers or the own manufacturing to achieve a faster product design. By the use of database elements standardization (von Langsdorff, 2003) of the products is carried out and often synergy effects in the context of orders or the storage of the elements arise. These synergy effects represent the positive factor of a price diminution since discounts are negotiated at larger order quantities or the own production can establish bigger batches, through what the fixed costs of the production can be more distributed on a larger number of products. A faster progress in the information gain has the consequence that the data transfer can be started earlier. The information gain has to be put with the maturity degree of the planning section at once, through what the release and the transportation of the product is achieved faster to a higher level (maturity degree). This gain in time can be used by the enterprises to put faster new product variants on the market to increase the sale and therefore the sales volume of the enterprise. This effect is strongly distinctively performed at products with a short life time and a lot of evolution steps. An example forms the mobile communication industry which had to develop new functionalities and incorporate them in the respective devices in very short intervals during the last few years. For being a market leader it is essential to put new innovations on the market as fast as possible, because the second one is the first loser. Enterprises that want to exist in such a turbulent environment are interested in optimizing their product development to commercialize product innovations faster and take market shares away from the competitors.

So, (Alt, 2002) it is of decisive importance that the tasks of the departments are coordinated with each other and the information importance is indisputable. If the company does not deal with the information as the highest good, then there are information losses that are equate with losses of market shares. The time of no information progress (t_0) must be minimised ($t_0 \rightarrow 0$), so that a maximum time saving can be obtained. Achieving $t_0 \rightarrow 0$ is not realistic, because there are insignificant preparations, they can not eliminate such as the data conversion of the interface file to prepare it for further activities and tasks.

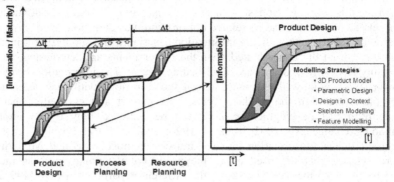

Figure 1 - Product Development Process.

The planning activities must be subdivided into different task classes like the SMED (single minute of the die) of the machine rigging. The tasks get subdivided in sub-tasks that represent a close connection to the product and development maturity with the result that these tasks represent the limited factor of the development process. But there are also tasks that can be worked out in rough structures parallel to other tasks. One can obtain time savings by a good structured organization of the planning tasks. Another advantage by a better preparation for the departments on their tasks is the minimal conversion effort by preparing the input data. Doing so, these method effects no real parallelisation. Therefore the aim is to support planning activities by the product design in a better way. For this reason the tasks of the departments must be subdivided, so that a true parallelization, based on semi finished tasks that represent initial information for other departments, can succeed.

4. STRATEGY FOR PLACEMENT OF INFORMATION AND KNOWLEDGE

All relevant information of a given product is gathered and stored in the so-called product model. In ideal case, the product model is created with the inception of the product and then gradually extended to cover each new need, arisen during the product development.

A product could be so special as to cause the re-development of its production. This process can begin as soon as it is at least partially clear how should the product be manufactured and can give rise to a so-called informational production model. It is derived from the product model and is, therefore, tightly bound to it.

During the product development the product models are usually processed by different CAx-systems. The reason for this is that each of these systems is qualified to solve exclusively tasks, belonging to that phase of the product development cycle for which the system is developed. In (Avgoustinov, 1997), the *phase qualification degree* (QD_{Ph}) of a given CAx-system for a given phase (expressing its suitability to serve all specifics for that phase tasks) is defined as the ratio between the cardinalities of the set of system's relevant functions and the set of phase's specific tasks. T Since due to its exploding complexity no such system is expected to exist in observable time, the processing of each model is performed by several CAx-systems, whereas each system is used for these tasks for which it is best suited.

Despite numerous attempts to establish a common format for representation of the model data or at least for the information exchange, every CAx-system still uses its own format due to historical, strategic, commercial or technical reasons. Therefore, a conversion of the information takes place during (or after) its transfer from one system to the next. When using such conventional workflow for product development, the mentioned transfer and conversion consumes many resources but, at the same time, seems unavoidable. In our view, one of the most prospective approaches for overcoming the problems, arising from the mentioned transfer and conversion, is to re-orient the development process and base it on (model) components. The functionality and properties of any product, which are important for/during most phases of the product lifecycle, deserve special attention. Since they are often used as a core, around which the other characteristics and functionality of the product are formed, they are called *core functionality* and *core properties*, respectively. They are modelled as early in the product development as possible, and are used to build the *skeleton* of the future product or process model. Thus, the exchange and conversion problems of the conventional CAx-system-based development affect at worst the modelling of core properties and functionality. The component-oriented model development would allow to avoid this and to achieve overall improvement.

5. CONCEPT AND IMPLEMENTATION

The design process starts accordingly to the standard with an idea and then it continues with the development of function structures that solve the requirements to the product. In the next step these function structures will be transformed into rough product geometry elements. Numerous function structures give the possibility to start planning activities that get filled progressively based on the development level and additional information about the product. Basic processes can be derived from the function structures (Bley, 2004). On this stage it is already possible to limit the resource choice and to realise first production concepts based on the process plan.

The introduced elements, which standardize the product structure form the general conditions, build the basis for achieving earlier and faster information transfer during the product development. Based on the characteristics of the parts, the manufacturing simulations receive the needed relations and parameters that must be set. Resources, ensuring that given functionality will be produced, must be assigned to the simulations of manufacturing – for instance, component geometry must for the required tolerances.

Afterwards, a tolerance check can be carried out as soon as this parameter is set. In addition, the part production and the assembly planning are also supported by the new elements, since the deposited information represents boundary conditions for the manufacturing and the assembly (Bley, 2004; Bley, 2006). Thereafter, the contact surface matrix, the contact surface graph and first assembly simulations can be built up automatically, without losses of time. Based on automatism, product changes can be analysed faster. Product models and production models represent flexible structures that can be used for analyses in case of product or production changes. The fear of today's organisations generating an effort that perhaps would not bring any progress avoids a realisation of a real parallel development process.

Today, there are a lot of software tools that support the development, but there are only a few methods for realising an integrated workflow with automations, minimising the respective efforts and the risk of waste of time and money (Ehrlenspiel, 1995). As mentioned in the introduction, the enterprises must remain competitive and therefore they must apportion the costs on their products. One way to achieve this is to diminish avoidable effort for being able to produce economically. Therefore, the aim should be to realise concepts and methods that minimise the explained risk and speed up the development process by launching the mentioned planning activities as early as possible and supporting them by automatism. With such an approach it is possible to attain the advantage of a faster information gain in the product development, since the time is minimised without information progress and therefore the consequence will be earlier production start.

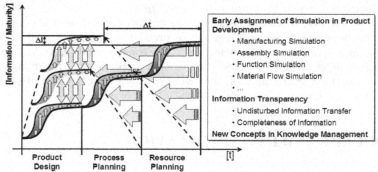

Figure 2 - Optimized product development process.

Due to the integration of control loops in product design and production planning one can expect that the knowledge increase is slowed, but the information quality of the separate processes is higher, since they are coordinated with each other. This leads to a much better information exchange between the departments. This process is also a subject of a learning curve like all other activities, therefore the effort and the time will be reduced at every usage.

The data interchange at earlier times causes a shift of the activities by the design process that have to be subdivided. The final geometry of the product does not represent the maturity level of the advantage of an earlier data transfer. After the design stages, functional modelling, basic geometry and final geometry a data transfer to other departments is probable. So, already the functional geometry definition allows the definition of rough structured process plans and planning tasks. Figure 2 shows the information progress in the individual phases of the product development by the use of simulation tools which have an improved protected stage of development as consequence. Another advantage in the product development is obtained by improved dealing with knowledge and knowledge management, realising an available transparency and storage. If the company uses different tools of different software provider, it is important to prepare a good structured transfer file or transfer medium with all needed information to realise the integrated workflow.

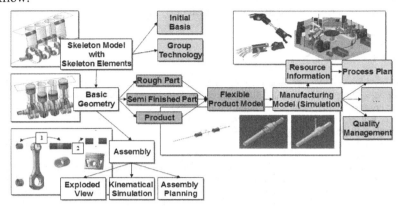

Figure 3 - Information Transfer Concept.

Figure 3 shows the skeleton concept that deals with the requirements. The design phase is standardised with new elements called skeleton elements that represent functional geometry areas of the product. These elements represent also a motion control element based on the global coordinates of the product model and its orientation. Automatism supports the design task by interpreting the skeleton elements into basic geometry that can be derived from the functional model. On the one hand, the basic geometry model can be used in assembly planning to find collision free assembly sequences and to support the positioning of the resources.

This result can be achieved by the three layer concept of collision free assembly planning (Bley, 2006). On the other hand, it is possible to realise a connection between the flexible product model and the process simulation of the manufacturing process, realising a flexible product and process model that can be enhanced by resource information to create a Product-Process-Resource-Model (Bley, 2005). Other advantages of the presented concept are possible enhancements that use the feature structure as an integration platform.

6. SUMMARY AND FUTURE WORK

Information, information transfer and information storage becomes in the last years a competitive factor of the companies. So it is very important to handle information as one of the highest goods of the company. The presented concept achieves a "real" parallelisation of the different task of the product development process by automating routine work of the different departments. Information transfer is based on the first digital product model of the design department, the functional model. Generating the semantic information by using the feature concept and database knowledge represents a possibility to create initial information for the other departments that can start generating rough process plans and simulation models. So the product model can be analysed in different ways by different departments in an early stage of the product development process. The rough process plans and the simulation models will be more detailed during the development process. In doing so, a fast raise of maturation is forced and the waste of time is minimised by the reduction of the effort of the information transfer.

7. REFERENCES

1. Alberts A, Nowicki L. Integration der Simulation in die Produktentwicklung- Neue Möglichkeiten zur Steigerung der Qualität und Effizienz in der Produktentwicklung, Symposium "Simulation in der Produkt- und Prozessentwicklung" 5-7. November 2003 Bremen, pp. 141-147.
2. Alt G, Bill H, Machnig M. Innovation – Technik – Zukunft Die Wissens- und Informationsgesellschaft gestalten, (in German), 2002.
3. Avgoustinov Nikolay. Minimizing the Labour for Exchange of Product Definition Data Among N CAx-Systems. Saarbrücken, Germany, Universität des Saarlandes, 1997.
4. Bär T, Haasis S. Verkürzung der Entwicklungszeiten durch den Einsatz von Skelett-Modellen und Feature-Technologie, VDI-Bericht Nr.1614, Düsseldorf, Germany, 2001.
5. Bley H, Bossmann M. *Automated Assembly Planning Based on Skeleton Modelling Strategy*, Precision Assembly Technologies for Mini and Micro Products, pp.121-131, IFIP International Federation for Information Processing, Springer Verlag, 2006.
6. Bley H, Bossmann M, Zenner C. Flexible Process Models in Manufacturing based on Skeleton Product Models. Preprints of IFAC-MIM Conference on Manufacturing, Modelling and Control, Athens, Greece, 2004.
7. Bley H, Bossmann M, Zenner C. Advances towards an Integrated Product and Production Development Process. Proceedings of 2. German - Israeli Symposium for Design and Manufacture - Advances in Methods and Systems for Products and Processes, Berlin, Germany, 2005, pp. 129-137.
8. Bracht U, Schlange C, Eckert C, Masurat T. Datenmanagement für die Digitale Fabrik, wt Werkstatttechnik online H.4, 2005, pp. 197-204.
9. Cuiper R, Feldmann K, Roßgoderer U. Rechnerunterstütze Parallelisierung von Konstruktion und Montageplanung. ZWF 91 7-8, pp. 338-341, 1996.
10. Ehrlenspiel K. Integrierte Produktentwicklung. München, Hanser, 1995.
11. von Langsdorff P, Rist T. Aufbau innovativer Produktionssysteme durch Standards und Plattformkonzepte, wt Werkstatttechnik online H.3, 2003, pp. 17-181.
12. Mäntylä M, Nau D, Shah J. Challenges in Feature-Based Manufacturing Research, Communication of the ACM February 1996/Vol. 39 No. 2, 1996, pp. 77-85.
13. Thoben KD, Weber F. Information and Communication Structures for product development in the Concurrent Enterprise: Requirements and Concepts, Life-Cycle Approaches to Production Systems- Management, Control, Supervision, the Annual Conference of ICIMS-NOE, Budapest, 1997, pp. 460-467.
14. VDI, VDI-Richtlinie 2218: Feature-Technologie, (in German), 1999.
15. VDI, VDI-Richtlinie 4499: Digitale Fabrik, (in German), Düsseldorf, 2006.
16. Westkämper E, Jovanoski D, Rist T. New Framework for Digital Factory Planning, Proceedings of the 36th CIRP International Seminar on Manufacturing Systems, Saarbrücken, Germany, 2003, pp. 191-198.
17. Wiendahl HP. Auf dem Weg zur "Digitalen Fabrik", wt Werkstattstechnik 4 (in German), 2002, p. 121.

BUSINESS INTELLIGENCE SYSTEM FOR STRATEGIC DECISION MAKING IN MACHINE TOOL SMES

Juan Antonio Arrieta, Itziar Ricondo and Nerea Aranguren
IDEKO Technology Center, Spain
{jarrieta, iricondo, naranguren}@ideko.es

The aim of this paper is to highlight the importance of Business Intelligence (BI) for optimal strategic decision making and, on the long term, for business innovation and competitive advantage. The Business Intelligence System aims at identifying and gathering strategic information from outside and inside the company and communicating it to key stakeholders. It is aimed at the Machine-Tool industry, but it could be applied to other industries where competition is high. The implementation of a BI system will be explained through the development of two competences: component competence and architectural competence.

1. INTRODUCTION

Scarce information on concurrent technology solutions, false estimation of customer requirements, ignorance of the global market situation and future perspectives are some of the issues to which SMEs have to face. Furthermore, the machine tool industry and the whole manufacturing industry operate in a tight competitive environment. The manufacturing industry faces the following external uncertainties (Monostori *et al.*, 2003):

- increasing and diversified customer demands,
- enhancing role of the one-of-a-kind production, fast sequences of new tasks,
- increasing number and speed of communication channels,
- appearance of new technologies,
- frequently changing partnership (suppliers, distributors, customers, purchasers),
- instability of market circumstances.

An adequate information retrieval and capture system is required to provide organizations, particularly SMEs, with the latest information regarding these issues. Companies need to be fully aware of their business environment in order to survive.

Valuable business intelligence involves more than the systematic collection of information. For Business Intelligence (BI), a resource-based theory, to have an effect on performance will depend upon the development of two competences

(Hughes, 2005): component competence (resources) and architectural competence (capability).

Two similar concepts appear in literature: Competitive Intelligence (CI) and Business Intelligence (BI). BI has a broader strategic orientation than mere analysis of competitors. In some cases, CI has been reduced to the analysis of competitors. Throughout this dissertation, the BI concept will be used, understood as "targeting any information in the business universe that affects a firm's ability to compete" (Sharp 2000), but oriented to New Product Development (NPD) decision-making. Some other decisions for BI application are strategy formulation, market entry or exit, corporate restructuring, etc.

Business Intelligence (BI) is related to the concepts of Digital Enterprise Technology (DET) and Engineering as Collaborative Negotiation (ECN). Digital Enterprise Technology (DET) can be defined as "the collection of systems and methods for the digital modelling of the global product development and realization process, in the context of lifecycle management" (Maropoulos & Reiter 2002). Engineering as Collaborative Negotiation (ECN) can be defined as "a socio-technical decision-making activity, where a team of stakeholders with different expertise and mixed motives engage in interactive and joint conflict resolutions to co-construct consensual agreements of some engineering matter" (Lu, 2004). Business Intelligence (BI) is a system for the identification, gathering, storage and diffusion of information for decisions in the early stages of life cycle management, such as the NPD conceptual stage. The BI system establishes the framework for collaborative decision-making in the conceptual stage, when design alternatives are evaluated and configuration decisions made attending to technical and market requirements.

The paper will explain BI methodology and technologies. The implementation of a BI system will be explained through the development of two competences: component competence and architectural competence. Finally, the most relevant achievements regarding the development and implementation of the BI system will be presented.

2. BI METHODOLOGY AND TECHNOLOGIES

Several authors (Bernhardt, 1994; Kahaner, 1997) propose an "intelligence cycle," composed of four stages: (1) Planning & Direction, (2) Collection, (3) Analysis, and (4) Dissemination. In the Planning & Direction stage, the BI needs are established. Collection involves the identification of sources of information and also the access to and retrieval of information. The Analysis stage is the most value-adding activity of the BI system.

BI is supported by a suitable ICT toolkit. Table 1 shows a classification of different technologies according to Hohhof (2000) and Bouthillier and Shearer (2003).

Table 1 – BI technologies. Source: Hohhof (2000) and Bouthillier and Shearer (2003).

Hohhof	Bouthillier and Shearer
E-mail	Profiling/push technology
Text searching software	Filtering/intelligent agent
Profiling/push technology	Web searching
Filtering/agent technology	Text mining
Groupware	Text summarizing
Document management	Text discovering
Imaging software	Groupware
Analysis-oriented software	Document and content management
Portals	Text analysis and structuring
	Multipurpose portals
	Business intelligence/e-business applications
	Analyzing/reporting data
	Information services/vendors

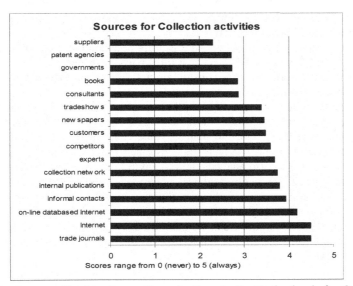

Figure 1 – Sources Used by Large Organizations in the Netherlands for Collection Activities. Source: Lammers and Siegmund (2001).

The most relevant ICT technologies following the stages of the "intelligence cycle" are:

• **Collection**: searchers and metasearchers, intelligent agents, technological alerts, syndication, additional alerts from specialised databases (such as Derwent worldwide patent database) and trade organisations...

- **Analysis**: data miners, text miners, OLAP techniques, data warehouse, summarizers, ontology's, Semantic Web, natural language...
- **Dissemination**: information repositories within I*Net (intranet, extranet), customised portals, electronic bulletins or newsletters, visualisation and militarization tools, graphical representation of key evolution metrics.

The first step in the Collection stage involves the identification of information sources. Figure 1 exhibits the nature and frequency of use of several sources, based on Lammers and Siegmund (2001). ICT tools are then used for information capture and retrieval.

Within these ICT tools, Analysis software programs have a substantial gap for improvement, since many analysis tools only provide visualization alternatives to collected information (Bouhilier and Jin, 2005). Indeed, analysis is mainly based on human effort, and it is argued that "it is almost impossible to build intuition into software" (Nikkel, 2003). On the other hand, the value of automatic analysis depends on the technology and industry specialization. The more specialized (less generic) the technology or industry niches are, the less useful current ICT tools are for analysis.

Accordingly, BI external consultants (without technology know-how) are most valuable when broad and generic BI studies are required, such as the analysis of the whole manufacturing sector, providing generic information from multiple sources. On the other hand, when the BI study area is very focused, topic know-how (component competence) is required, so it is preferable and more valuable that BI be carried out by the company BI team or a third party with technology and industry know-how. Furthermore, external consultants may also support company BI team, providing BI methodology and tools.

Several techniques are usually applied in the Analysis stage (Fleisher & Besoussan), which is the main value-adding stage of BI: Strategic analysis techniques (SWOT, BCG portfolio matrix, value chain analysis), Competitive and Customer analysis (competitor analysis, customer segmentation), Environmental analysis techniques (scenario analysis, macro environmental analysis), Evolutionary analysis (technology life cycle analysis, patent analysis) and Financial analysis techniques. The application of these techniques involves human thinking and reflection, which goes beyond the capability of any software. However, the application of these techniques can be supported by software, involving different levels of intelligence: from simple applications to intelligent software, such as patent analysis software.

3. BI SYSTEM DEVELOPMENT: ARCHITECTURAL AND COMPONENT COMPETENCES

Based on the resource-based theory (Henderson & Cockburn, 1994), the ability of Business Intelligence to have an effect on performance will depend upon the development of two competences: component competence (resources) and architectural competence (capability) (Hughes, 2005). Architectural competence will be gained through the development of information systems, communication channels and information technologies in order to make the best use of the information and build competitive products. Component competence is related to expertise and tacit knowledge, so related work for gaining this competence will be oriented to the adequate identification of knowledge sources (e.g.: technologies and markets) and qualification of people. This section will explain how architectural and component competences have been developed to implement BI within a machine-tool manufacturing group.

3.1 Architectural competence

BI is supported by a suitable ICT toolkit. These tools (meta-searchers, meta-crawlers, data processing tools, web watchers, file repositories, specific-purpose developed software...) are especially useful for the identification, filtering and gathering of information. However, the analysis of information depends heavily on human labour. The machine-tool know-how is wisely applied in this stage.

The main developed information system for communication has been the Business Intelligence Platform (BIP), a Content Management System with the following functionalities (figure 2):

- Document & Content management,
- Personalized portals attending to user,
- Integration with external systems, allowing searches on own databases (e.g.: patents, catalogues, articles, proceedings, books...),
- Subscription service,
- Event manager & calendar,
- RSS Syndication,
- Administration.

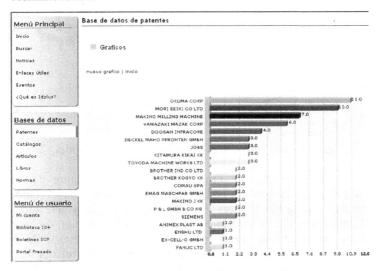

Figure 2 – Business Intelligence Platform.

BI users may get their information in several ways. On the one hand, users can easily access the platform in order to perform specific document searches, get the latest industry news and search databases (e.g.: patents, books, scientific articles...). On the other hand, special templates and procedures have been developed in order to communicate and present the information to the customer. This standardization of the outcome makes it easier for the users to gather and understand the suitable data, establishing some regular information channels: the BI platform, periodic bulletins, periodic face-to-face meetings with BI users, etc.

3.2 Component Competence

BI component competence is gained by the BI service provider through expertise and specialisation in a certain technology, such us turning, milling or grinding. For that purpose, they access state-of-the art sources regarding specialised journals, patents, trademarks, general business information and publications.

Every BI Project Team is composed of a main skilled engineer and some other novice assistants. Machine tool knowledge (technology and market) and competence are gained among assistants through socialization and internalization (Nonaka & Takeuchi, 1995).

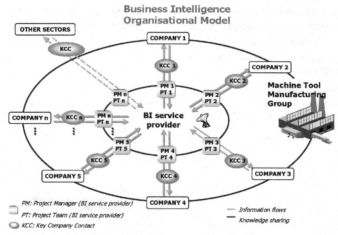

Figure 3 - Business Intelligence Organisational Model.

The shown Business Intelligence Organisational Model (Figure 3) has been established to gather company needs and target BI efforts. The model is based on the close relationship among the BI Project Team (BI service provider) and the Key Company Contact (KCC). Knowledge sharing is two-fold. On the one hand, different BI project teams may enrich from each other's experiences. On the other hand, the information sharing among companies depend on the relationship among them. For example, the sharing of external information among a single industrial group is really valuable, in terms of shared knowledge and economical efficiency.

4. IMPLEMENTATION

This section summarizes the implementation process of BI activities from year 2000 onwards. It is worth pointing out the broadening in scope of these activities. In the beginning, competitive intelligence was focused on mere analysis of competitors' products. The first important milestone took place in 2002, when it was decided to spread the scope out in order to analyze other competitors' areas, such as their financial situation, market orientation and strategic evolution. This approach would fit within the Competitive Intelligence concept. Finally, from year 2004 onwards, it can be said that Business Intelligence has been implemented, which considers more information inputs regarding market (geographical and sector), technology trends, and other relevant information for company competitiveness and product strategy.

In the beginning, the use of ICT tools was focused mainly on collection, to be used by the BI service provider. The tools for collection have been tuned, through periodical updates, to more advanced commercial tools. On the other hand, incremental steps have been taken in order to improve the diffusion of BI. The exposed BI platform is the final result, a Web platform which allows BI users to search and gather information in accordance with their profile.

The next milestones and research areas in BI will aim to:

- Exploit the capabilities of internal BI, through a deeper analysis of some internal key departments, such as sales, technical office, production and assembly, technical assistance service or purchasing.
- Strengthen the use of software tools in the Analysis stage.
- Adapt visual and graphical tools in order to improve the diffusion stage, so that decision-makers can have the most relevant information in a user-friendly interface.
- Measure and quantify BI activity, i.e., to set key indicators that should clearly show both the external evolution in market, competitors and technology, as well as the internal evolution in the different departments within the company.

Consistent with the main components of the BI system, the main success factors are:

- Existence of a target sector and activity for BI application. Fluent communication between the BI service provider and the BI user is necessary.
- Establishment of a BI method, considering both the information transformation process and the organisational aspects, such as communication channels.
- Experience and know-how about the technology and market demands.
- Application of ICT technologies for collection, analysis and dissemination activities for BI efficiency.

5. CONCLUSIONS

This paper has outlined the main elements of a Business Intelligence (BI) system. It enhances the need of such a system in the machine-tool industry and the whole manufacturing industry, characterized by a tight competitive environment. The NPD oriented Business Intelligence system supports decisions made in early design, providing accurate and well-oriented information regarding technological aspects, competitors' evolution, customers and market trends.

The development of the BI system has been explained through the development of two competences: component competence and architectural competence. ICT tools have been made available for companies to index, store and spread out plenty of information in several ways. The critical stage between collection and diffusion is the analysis stage. Analysis involves the extraction of valuable information and knowledge from rough data and heterogeneous sources. Even though there are some ICT tools which support human analysis, this stage remains highly manual, where know-how is wisely applied.

Future activities and challenges in Business Intelligence will be oriented to a higher use of ICT analysis tools through text miners and ontology's, visualization of results and better use of internal information.

6. REFERENCES

1. Bernhardt, D.C. 'I want it fast, factual, actionable'—Tailoring competitive intelligence to executive needs, Long Range Planning, Vol. 27, No. 1, pp. 12-24, 1994.
2. Bouthillier, F., Shearer, K. Assessing Competitive Intelligence Software: A Guide to Evaluating Ci Technology (Hardcover), 2003.
3. Bouthillier, F., Jin, T. CI Professionals and their interactions with CI technology. Journal of Competitive Intelligence and Management, Vol. 3, No. 1, pp. 41-53, 2005.
4. Fleisher, C., Bensoussan, B. Strategic and Competitive Analysis: Methods and Techniques for Analyzing Business Competition. Prentice Hall, 2002.
5. Henderson, R., Cockburn, I. Measuring competence: Exploring firm effects in pharmaceutical research. Strategic Management Journal, Vol. 15, Special Issue Winter, pp. 63-84, 1994.
6. Hohhof, B. The Information Technology Marketplace in Miller, J. (Ed). Millennium Intelligence: Understanding and Conducting Competitive Intelligence in the Digital Age, Cyber Age books, pp.17-44, 2000.
7. Hughes, S. Competitive Intelligence as Competitive Advantage: The Theoretical Link Between Competitive Intelligence, Strategy and Firm Performance. Journal of Competitive Intelligence and Management, Vol. 3, No. 3, pp. 3-18, 2005.
8. Lammers, A., Siegmund, J. Business Intelligence in Nederland. Master's thesis, University of Nijmegen, 2001. In Vriens, D., Information and Communications Technology for Competitive Intelligence. Idea Group Inc, 2004.
9. Lu, S. Engineering as Collaborative Negotiation: A New Paradigm for Collaborative Engineering Research, CIRP Meeting on Engineering as Collaborative Negotiation (WG-ECN), January meeting, 2004.
10. Kahaner, L. Competitive Intelligence. New York: Touchstone, 1997.
11. Maropoulos, P.G. Digital Enterprise Technology – Defining Perspectives and Research Priorities, Proc. of the 1st CIRP (UK) Seminar on Digital Enterprise Technology, DET02, September 16-17, Durham, United Kingdom, Part V: Enterprise Integration Technologies: 3-12, 2002.
12. Monostori, L., Váncza, J., Márkus, A., Kádar, B., Vuharos, Zs. J. Towards the realisation of Digital Enterprises, Proceedings of the 36th CIRP International Seminar on Manufacturing Systems, Progress in Virtual Manufacturing Systems, June 3-5, Saarbrücken, Germany, pp. 99-106, 2003.
13. Nikkel, P. How Can We Determine Which Competitive Intelligence Software Is Most Effective? A Framework for Evaluation, in Fleisher, C.R., Blenkhorn, D.L. (Ed.) Controversies in Competitive Intelligence: The Enduring Issues, Westport, Praeger, 331p. (p.163-175), 2003.
14. Nonaka, I., Takeuchi, H. The knowledge-creating company: Oxford University Press, 1995.
15. Sharp, S. "Truth or Consequences: 10 Myths that Cripple Competitive Intelligence," Competitive Intelligence Magazine, Vol. 3, No. 1, pp. 37-40, 2000.

PRODUCTION MONITORING LINKED TO OBJECT IDENTIFICATION AND TRACKING A STEP TOWARDS REAL TIME MANUFACTURING IN AUTOMOTIVE PLANTS

Olaf Sauer

Fraunhofer Institute for Information and Data Processing IITB, Germany
olaf.sauer@iitb.fraunhofer.de

ProVis.Agent is the first agent-based production monitoring & control system for distributed real-time production monitoring. Its functionality is based on ProVis.NT, the proven object-oriented control system which monitors and controls e.g. the body, paint and assembly shops in DaimlerChrysler's automotive plant in Bremen, Germany. Forming an integral part of the manufacturing execution system (MES), ProVis.Agent for the first time allows to be integrated with other shop-floor related applications. In this paper the author shows a case study of implementing agent-based technology to a classical field of automation and how to use it for interconnection of real time systems.

1. INTRODUCTION

Today's automotive plants are equipped with heterogeneous software systems to support manufacturing operations. These software systems are neither integrated nor do they exchange information that might be of interest for more than one application (see figure 1). Production monitoring and control systems (PMC) play a central role to automation. The main function of these systems is to gather signals produced by production facilities and their programmable logic controllers (PLCs), to combine them to control relevant contexts, to visualize them and to provide functionalities to operate them. While visualization and operation of process signals and contexts are functions of SCADA systems[1], the main work of real time signal processing and interfacing to production plants is done by PMCs (Rao, 1996). Today these PMCs are usually implemented as object oriented systems, interfacing with their environ-ment by standardized protocols, e.g. OPC[2] (Iwanitz, 2006).

The Fraunhofer Institute for Information and Data Processing (Fraunhofer IITB) has an almost 30-years-experience in developing novel PMCs especially in the fields of automotive plants and steel production. In 2005 DaimlerChrysler Bremen ordered

---

[1] SCADA: Supervisory Control And Data Acquisition
[2] OPC: OLE for Process Control

a new generation of PMC for the coming C-type car, starting its production at the beginning of 2007.

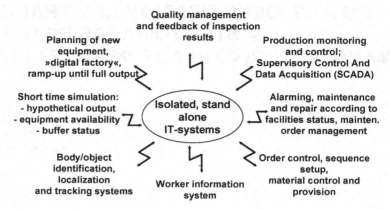

Figure 1 - Current status in automotive factories concerning production related IT-systems.

Shop floor people use PMCs to control manufacturing processes in real time. Today these systems support decisions which are merely based on production quantities. In the case of a facility breakdown or detected quality errors they only know that a certain number of vehicles are affected. They can neither identify the customer orders related to these vehicles nor their options, e.g. color, right or left hand drive, sun roof, etc. due to the fact that PMCs don't hold any product or order related information. To overcome this weak point a new generation of production related IT-systems is going to be established: manufacturing execution systems (MES). Their location within the IT hierarchy is illustrated in figure 2.

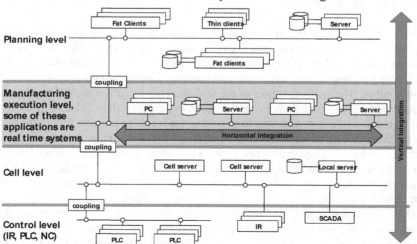

Figure 2 - IT resources on the different manufacturing levels
(source: Betriebshütte, p. 17-19).

2. MOTIVATION

Facing the fact that PMCs usually are operated in highly distributed hard- and software environments, where a continuous connection of all components involved can not be guaranteed, the implementation of each subsystem needs to be able to operate autonomously at least for a certain span of time.

According to the specific needs of a plant PMCs must be able to either follow a central, decentral or mixed control approach. Whereas e.g. DaimlerChrysler's automotive plant in Bremen implements one central control room for each body, paint and trim shop other automotive plants follow a decentralized structure, where visualization and operation are performed directly from the operator panels on the shop floor. Independency from special operating systems becomes more and more important, because in the years to come the traditional Microsoft Windows applications have to be connected to Linux systems and other vendor specific operating systems.

Furthermore the integration of "neighbouring" IT-systems[3], such as quality management, maintenance and repair, sequence scheduling, car body identification, should be made as easy as possible. A connection between these applications leads to both better information to react on unexpected disturbances on the shop floor as well as to higher transparency concerning production related information.

Difficulties arise if these MES systems come from different vendors. Up to now there is no standardized way of communication for such systems leading to problems of misunderstandings about concepts to communicate. The engineering environments of all concurrently running systems are usually specific to the single systems, i.e. there is no common repository for plant specifications, signal types, signal wiring, etc. A large part of the information needed to operate the single systems has to be provided redundantly to the engineering parts of the subsystems. Besides the fact that this leads to an unnecessary engineering overhead, this is a possible source for errors due to manual data input, especially in cases of reconfiguring the plant.

In the years to come many of the assembly lines will be constructed of equipment and PLCs which are self-aware of the functions they can perform and the way they can be parameterized. Some of today's assembly robots e.g. are delivered with web servers allowing to visualize their state and reconfigure them. Assuming that this is a trend for the future, the possibility of 'Plug & Produce' assembly components becomes more and more likely to revolutionize the engineering of production systems. This raises the need for a standardized way of communication among different engineering systems. Fraunhofer IITB's business unit dealing with production monitoring systems is already working on intelligent engineering tools supporting the 'plug & produce' approach (see figure 3).

---

[3] usually subsumed as Manufacturing Execution Systems (MES)

3. CHALLENGES

For production monitoring and control systems have to be able to visualize and operate the state of production facilities in real time, there is a need for very fast communications of signals and operator actions.

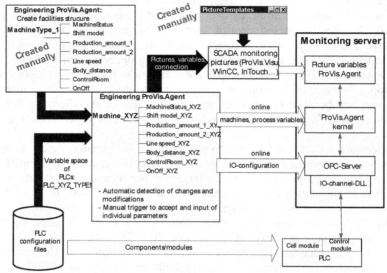

Figure 3 - Tasks during the production monitoring system's engineering.

For certain events, e.g. shift changeover, there is a need to handle a tremendous amount of data and signals in very short time. Several hundred signals per second have to be communicated, gathered, sorted and combined and handed over to subsequent systems like databases for evaluation purposes.

A PMC has furthermore to provide several different protocols[4] to underlying production lines. Having an overall model for process states a PMC has to integrate all this information in real time.

4. INTEGRATION ASPECTS

4.1 General

Given that the development of PMCs can not be regarded as stand-alone systems, it has to take into account that there must be many interfaces to related IT-systems. These systems have usually evolved "historically" in the factories and can - for economical reasons- not simply be replaced by new systems.

Therefore an integration platform for PMC systems with other MES systems is needed. Whereas several vendors provide a platform for their own MES components, e.g. SIEMENS, Wonderware, Rockwell Automation, it is typically not

---

[4] such as OPC, MMS, simple TCP-IP and others

possible to operate systems of different vendors on the same platform. Dedicated interfaces have to be provided for each specific configuration of MES components coming from different vendors.

Here is a challenging need for standardization. In principle there are several ways of integrating concurrent systems. Three possible options will be outlined in the following.

4.2 Vendor proprietary platform

Currently the state of the art for integration of MES systems is to use only MES components from a single vendor. These usually operate via a proprietary integration platform specific for each vendor. Examples for this kind of platforms are the "Industrial Framework" of SIEMENS or Wonderware's Archestra platform.

The main structure of this architecture is shown in option 1 of figure 4. All MES modules reside inside a uniform framework with limited access from outside the framework. The framework itself is designed to optimize interaction of especially the MES modules of this vendor.

Usually the optimization of communication between the in-house components leads to a very high speed of data processing. On the other hand these highly complex frameworks are usually not well suited to integrate third party products. Higher investment for interface implementation is needed whenever a new MES configuration is to be implemented.

4.3 Database centered approach

In contrast to vendor proprietary platforms today the integration aspect is in most cases supported by databases (see option 2 in figure 4). It must be added that a couple of the above-mentioned systems, particularly those for production monitoring, worker information, object identification, etc., require real-time data processing instead of database solutions because they receive a large number of signals from the production equipments' PLCs. For real-time applications database solutions are often not fast enough.

Another disadvantage of integration by means of a data-base is the required data model for all related applications. This data model is comparatively inflexible; especially if changes or extensions of functionalities are required or if new IT systems must be added.

4.4 Integration on agent platform

Today it is evident that new software technologies have to be used to allow a genuine integration of IT systems for production equipment, quality issues, provided parts and shift output and to preserve the existing software functionalities.

A more promising technology for integrating existing software systems and their functionalities and to add assistant systems for the shop floor staff is to be found in software agents (Sauer, 2005) (see option 3 in figure 4). In the academic field, agent technologies have a long tradition, but their use in production and real-time applications has been very limited yet. Describing the state-of-the-art for agent-based systems we concentrate in the following on practical applications, especially in automation applications.

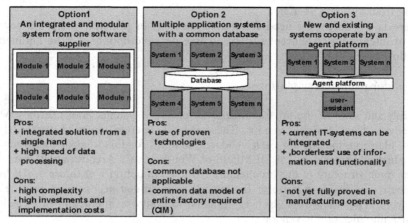

Figure 4 - Options to integrate different software systems (simplified).

One of the first promising applications is described by authors from DaimlerChrysler (Bossmann, 2003; Sundermeyer, 2001) who have implemented a manufacturing cell for cylinder heads and other engine parts that is completely controlled by a software-agent-based system.

The control logic developed in this project by the PLC-supplier (Colombo, 2001) is offered for further industrial applications. Most authors refer to this example to prove agent-technology being applicable on the shop floor. A summary of the application of software agents in production is given in the STC 'O' keynote paper during the CIRP general assembly 2006 (Monostori, 2006).

5. AGENT BASED PRODUCTION MONITORING

Fraunhofer IITB has decided to use software agents for the means of integration when developing further PMCs or other MES components.

Figure 5 shows the architecture of such a new production monitoring and control system (ProVis.Agent) which is now open for connection to IT systems related to logistics. The central monitoring server consists of a collection of cooperating software agents. Each of these agents covers one piece of functionality. It contains the functional treatment of different types of signals, e.g. switches, analog values, distances, etc., as well as shift models, alarming and statistical data.

The I/O-agent encapsulates different types of I/O-channels (OPC, MMS-Light and pure TCP/IP) and allows the Control Room Server to have a uniform look on all the signals delivered by underlying systems. A visualization agent is used for interfacing with a variety of commonly used SCADA systems (WinCC, FactoryLink, etc.) as well as with Fraunhofer's new real-time visualization tool ProVis.Visu. The operating agent always provides the operating context for single signals or complex actions. This context may either be only the name and operating mode of a single underlying plant, but it may also be a combination of several signals of different types coming from several sub-plants. The main objective of the operating agent is to provide the operator with all information needed to perform even complex operations, such as changing the working time model for different plants. The operator must be able to correctly evaluate the consequences of his actions. A variety of special agents is used for interfacing to existing subsystems The Web-Server agent interfaces the PLC to a statistical analysis system. The Archive-Server agent reports production relevant information to an archive database, where it is stored and condensed for quality checks and future planning. The information agent finally handles the connections to the Media Server and the radio server as well as to special assistance components.

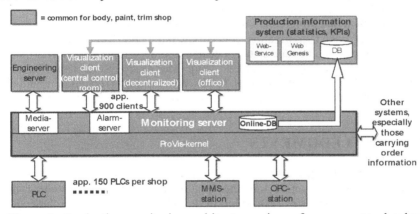

Figure 5 - Production monitoring architecture using software agent technology (ProVis.Agent).

All agents contained in ProVis.Agent communicate via an ontology based communication schema. The ontology is open for neighbouring systems to access any of the data contained in ProVis.Agent.

Fraunhofer decided to base ProVis.Agent on the FIPA[5] standard. All agents have been implemented on top of the agent platform JADE[6] (Bellifemine, 2003). The communication ontology has been developed using Protégé[7] (Stanford, 2000).

6. CONNECTION TO OBJECT IDENTIFICATION, LOCALIZATION AND TRACKING

None of the production monitoring systems on the market especially for large distributed systems is able to view both facilities behaviour and the product flow and thus aspects of logistics, such as (just-in-sequence-) material provision, sequence planning and incremental resequencing. The missing link between the two 'worlds' of automation and logistics is identification information about the products, the car bodies and build-in material. Due to increasing requirements concerning real time

---

[5] FIPA: Foundation for Intelligent Physical Agents ; see www.fipa.org
[6] JADE: Java Agent DEvelopment framework
[7] Protégé is a free, open source ontology editor

information about both facilities status' and car body status in body, paint and trim shop, in rework and distribution Fraunhofer IITB has launched a project to connect production monitoring and object identification. Due to the fact that currently used identification technologies have several weakpoints themselves, the IITB team decided to go for localization technologies instead of simple identification.

Additional objectives for the connection between production monitoring and object tracking are:

- reading id/positioning patterns and matching them with product options and/or manufacturing orders,
- distribute id/positioning data to concerned IT-components on the different levels, e.g. PLC, planning systems, etc.,
- hand over manufacturing orders from planning system to the PLC and its buffer,
- provision of linked information concerning production status, facility status, id/position of car bodies and status of customer orders, if possible in real time.

A new software component, called 'Ident Monitoring System' fulfils these requirements and thus connects **ProVis.Agent**, the real time production monitoring tool to a sequence setup system to prove the new software component's benefit.

7. ACKNOWLEDGMENTS

The authors like to thank the DaimlerChrysler unit in the Bremen plant that is in charge of planning production monitoring systems (FP SNT 5). Without their innovation related mind the realization of ProVis.Agent would not have been possible.

8. REFERENCES

1. Bellifemine F., Caire G., Poggi A., Rimassa G.: JADE - A White Paper. http://jade.tilab.com/, version from September 2003.
2. Bussmann, S., Schild, K.: Self-organizing manufacturing control: an industrial application of agent technology. Proceedings of the 4th International Conference on Multi-Agent Systems, 2000.
3. Colombo, A.W., Neubert, R., Schoop, R.: A Solution to Holonic Control Systems. Proceedings of the 8th IEEE International Conference on Emerging Technologies and Factory Automation, ETFA Oct. 18, 2001.
4. Iwanitz F., Lange J.: OPC, Fundamentals, Implementation and Application. Hüthig, 2006.
5. Monostori, L., Vánczal, J., Kumara, S.R.T.: Agent-Based Systems for Manufacturing. Keynote paper STC 'O', to be published in the annals of CIRP 2006.
6. Rao B.K.N.: Handbook of Condition Monitoring, Elsevier, 1996.
7. Sauer, O.: Agent technology used for monitoring of automotive production. In: Pham, D.T., Eldkhri, E.E., Soroka, A.J.: Intelligent Production Machines and Systems. 1st I*PROMS Virtual International Conference. Oxford: Elsevier 2005, S. 147-153.
8. Stanford University: Protégé-2000 Users Guide. http://protege.stanford.edu/doc/users.html.
9. Sundermeyer, K., Bussmann, S.: Einführung der Agententechnologie in einem produzierenden Unternehmen – ein Erfahrungsbericht. Wirtschaftsinformatik, Vol. 43, No. 2, pp. 135-142, April 2001.

MODELING SERVICES IN INFORMATION SYSTEMS ARCHITECTURES

Anacleto Correia[1] and Miguel Mira da Silva[2]

*[1]Instituto Superior Técnico, Technical University of Lisbon; Escola Superior de Tecnologia –
Polytechnic Institute of Setúbal, Portugal
accorrei@est.ips.pt
[2]Instituto Superior Técnico, Technical University of Lisbon, Portugal
mms@tagus.ist.utl.pt*

*Twenty years ago, Zachman proposed a framework – the Information Systems
Architecture – that was certainly one of the main contributions to the
Enterprise Architecture research area.*

*More recently, the concept of service was proposed and largely adopted, thus
introducing another but fundamental perspective on how organizations not
only operate internally but also relate with stakeholders.*

*In this paper we propose an extension to the Zachman framework that
incorporates the concept of service.*

1. INTRODUCTION

The concept of service has been used for long in the economic and business context
and more recently in the information system field. Simply stated, a service generally
involves a need by one of the parts, the consumer, which is accomplished by the
other part, the provider. A part could be a person, a system or an organization.

In the business context we naturally mention services as inter-organizational
relationships those with clients (e.g. selling products and services) or with suppliers
(e.g. buying raw materials and services for subsequent transformation). Inside the
organization, i.e. intra-organizational relationships, we could also think of services
when a set of persons or organizational unit provides some input for transformation
and subsequently delivers an output (with added value) to another one. Those
transactions are also recorded as costs and benefits, in accounting records.

Computer systems have been using the *service* metaphor in a wide range of
situations. To name but a few, we can think of protocol layers and their service
models in computer networks and the internet (Kurose, 2005), objects and components offering services throughout interfaces (Jacobson, 1999) and, more recently,
Service Oriented Architecture (SOA) and Web Services used for integration of
software systems (Mira da Silva, 2003).

The Internet services (i.e. providing a service using the Internet) are becoming
increasingly popular but they represent just another sign of the growing importance
of the service concept for the enterprise architecture.

In this paper we introduce the concept of *service* for enterprise architectures and
why they are important in this context. We claim that the concept of *service* plays a

structural role, as important as other core concepts in the Information Systems Architecture (ISA) such as, data, functions and locations (Zachman, 1987).

A unified and integrated vision of services in the enterprise architecture could increase the organization's agility when dealing with its internal strengths and weaknesses, external threats and opportunities.

For instance, a possible server's failure is a weakness for which impact and risk could be anticipated (Jonkers, 2004). With a unified and integrated model of services, it would be possible to predict which services would be unavailable, which business processes were interrupted, the undeliverable services to customers, and finally business objectives affected. Therefore, confronted with this information, a manager could assess how critical and risky might be the impact of the technical failure and how it should be prevented, namely with a contingency plan.

The launch of a new product on the market is another opportunity which requires the assessment of available internal services, and eventually the organization needs to increase and/or adapt some of them, such as production capacity, human resources, applications and server's capacity.

We start the paper with an overview of enterprise architectures frameworks and then present a meta–model to generalize the existing frameworks. Next we underline the importance of the service concept in the present stage of organizations from both an internal and external point of view.

Faced with the lack of explicit service representation on existing frameworks, we then propose to add a new column (the service view) to the Zachman framework.

2. ENTERPRISE ARCHITECTURE FRAMEWORKS

Enterprise architecture is the model of the organization that specifies how its parts are decomposed into individual functional components and how they interact with each other. The decomposition of the enterprise, the definition of those parts, and the orchestration of the interaction among those parts constitutes the enterprise architecture (Iyer, 2004).

2.1 Zachman Framework

Zachman proposed the Information Systems Architecture (ISA) a framework for enterprise architectures that has been widely used since (Zachman, 1987)

The ISA framework represented a new way of addressing concepts, different from the vision of software architecture (IEEE, 1998) more concerned how the system is built internally. However, the main reasons for framework acceptance was its simplicity and a translation between concepts used in building into concepts of Information Systems (IS) (Zachman, 1992). This mapping, which constitutes the "perspective" dimension, corresponds to five rows in the ISA framework.

	What (Data)	How (Function)	Where (Locations)	Who (People)	When (Time)	Why (Motivation)
Scope (contextual) Planner	List of things important to the business	List of processes that the business performs	List of locations in which the business operates	List of organizations important to the business	List of events/ cycles important to the business	List of business goals/strategies
Enterprise Model (conceptual) Business Owner	e.g. Semantic Model	e.g. Business Process Model	e.g. Business Logistics System	e.g. Workflow Model	e.g. Master Schedule	e.g. Business Plan
System Model (logical) Designer	e.g. Logical Data Model	e.g. Application Architecture	e.g. Distributed System Architecture	e.g. Human Interface Architecture	e.g. Process Structure	e.g. Business Rule Model
Technology Model (physical) Implementer	e.g. Physical Data Model	e.g. System Design	e.g. Technology Architecture	e.g. Presentation Architecture	e.g. Control Structure	e.g. Rule Design
Detailed Representation (out-of-context) Subcontractor	e.g. Data Definition	e.g. Program	e.g. Network Architecture	e.g. Security Architecture	e.g. Timing Definition	e.g. Rule Definition
Functioning System	e.g. Data	e.g. Function	e.g. Network	e.g. Organization	e.g. Schedule	e.g. Strategy

Figure 1 – Zachman Framework (www.enterpriseunifiedprocess.com).

Several authors and institutions adapted and enhanced the original Zachman Framework and the methodology based on the framework – the Enterprise Architecture Planning (Spewak, 1992) – to suit their needs. Some examples of those efforts are the Federal Enterprise Architecture Framework (FEAF, 1999) by the American Federal Government, the Joint Technical Architecture (DoD, 2002), the Treasury Enterprise Architecture Framework (TEAF, 2002), a framework for ISA design and evaluation by The Open Group Architectural Framework (TOGAF, 2002) and the CEO Framework (Vasconcelos, 2001; Vasconcelos, 2003).

2.2 Drill–Down of Architecture

Nowadays, enterprise architecture serves the following purposes:
- Divides the vast amount of information content into manageable parts;
- Provides a navigation map for other levels of abstraction or perspectives;
- Provides a contextual perspective focusing on selected aspects of the enterprise;
- Prevents the isolation of a problem in one cell from the other cells by providing a relation map between the cells.

From the business perspective, the enterprise architecture is a tool that helps to understand all aspects of the business (processes, information, people, etc.) and their relationships, helping to align IT with business strategies.

The enterprise architecture is usually split into a few others architectures, which could roughly correspond to some of the views of the Zachman Framework, for instance (Vasconcelos, 2003b):
- Informational Architecture – fundamental data that support the business;
- Application Architecture – applications for data management and business support;
- Technological Architecture – the technological infrastructure used for applications implementation and deployment.

However, different authors have proposed different architectures (e.g. Business Architecture, Information Architecture and Technical Architecture) each of one could be the composition of sub–architectures (Martin, 2005) or domains (Hoogervorst, 2004). For instance, the Business Architecture could be embodied by developing specific architectures for products and services, processes and organizational structures (Martin, 2005) or alternatively domains deemed relevant such as Mission, Strategy, Market, Competitors, Products/Services, Key Resources, Operating Method, Economic and Revenue Model, Customers, Stakeholders and Environment (Hoogervorst, 2004).

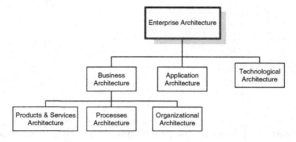

Figure 2 – Hierarchy of Architectures.

Each one of the architectures would be distributed by one of main layers, and each layer can contain several architectures. An example of architecture layers is presented in (Jonkers, 2004) and includes the Business layer, Application layer and Technology layer. Different perspectives (or models) of each architecture are denoted as sub–layers within a layer. The architectures in a layer are consumers as well as provider of services, from/to cross–layers or within the same layer.

The layers and sub–layers are characterized by perspectives, which mean levels of abstraction or types of presentation, customized to the needs of different stakeholders, and providing them with insights of a particular level of detail in a specific domain. Perspectives also facilitate understanding of cross–domain interrelationship, as well as provide a way to visualize and perform impact analysis of intended enterprise's developments and changes (Jonkers, 2004).

Several types of elements (and relationships) are relevant to the realization of the model's layers. Schedule events and constraints through business rules could also enrich the model.

Figure 3 presents the meta–model of existing enterprise architecture frameworks.

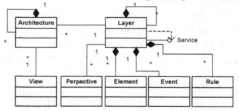

Figure 3 – Meta–Model of Enterprise Architecture Frameworks.

It is worth mentioning the difference between the concepts of service and integration. Integration, as addressed in (Vasconcelos, 2004), does not arise at the business layer and is only a way to support services provisioning. One service can be implemented by several integrated components and one component could provide support for several services.

Services could be seen therefore, as a way of joining architectural components, to give them coherence, and simultaneously a way of obtain flexibility in the operation of those components, achieving agility facing environmental changes.

3. THE LACK OF SERVICE'S REPRESENTATION

With the increasing competitiveness and market's globalization, most organizations are concentrating on activities that are their core business and, as a result, activities with less value have been contracted out to partners. This has resulted in networked organizations exchanging services with their suppliers, customers, and partners, namely by outsourcing. Therefore, for a growing network of services exchanged, there is an increasing difficulty to precise the boundaries of enterprise architecture components.

Furthermore, competitiveness turns difficult to archive a correct balance between coherence and agility of organization's enterprise architecture. Architecture is coherent if it is able to adapt its components to respond to the current enterprise activities. Architecture is agile if it is able to react to threats and opportunities noticeable in the environment, maintaining at the end of the process, its coherence (Martin, 2005).

If an organization puts more weight in agility, costs of its products and services will tend to rise due to inefficiency. Information transfer with stakeholders will probably be hard to provide. As a consequence it will be more difficult to introduce competitive products and services into the market.

If coherence is organization's primary concern, it runs the risk of creating the best products and services, but making them available to the market too late. The customer either no longer needs the product or has already chosen from one of the competitors. It is precisely in finding the correct balance between coherence and agility of enterprise architecture, that the concept of services could help, namely through evaluation of its effectiveness and efficiency.

However the service's notion has a difficulty: its several semantic meanings and levels of abstractions which claim for a previous ontological work.

For instance, the business model perspective (Gordijn, 2000), is more business oriented and the objects with it deals with (services) have a low level of granularity, and are analyzed from the point of view of its value and origin.

Those business services could be implemented with support of IT systems, based in a plethora of packages – such as ERP, CRM, and SRM –, as well as customized software solutions that gravitate around those standards solutions, filling out the gaps in functionality. Achieving the right balance between coherence and agility of business services in the aforementioned scenario, requires another kind of services (technical services), called integration services.

Service Oriented Architecture (SOA) and Web Services are within technologies currently used as integration enablers. SOA, as architectural style, has the goal of establishing the interaction between software agents in a loose coupling way (Krafzig, 2004). The interaction between providers and consumers for service exchanging could be implemented by Web Services. In this context, a service is perceived as a unit of work done by a service provider to achieve desired end results for a service consumer. Both provider and consumer are roles played by software agents on behalf of their software systems.

Other examples illustrate the usage of the service's concept with different meanings. The outsourcing of business support processes and IT infrastructure, protected by service level agreements, or the acquisition of services by "pay-as-you-go" – provided by some vendors, where the customer choose the hardware and services needed and pays for them as utilities like electricity –, are another examples of new forms of services that are reshaping the technological architecture and hence impact the enterprise architecture.

The way workers carry out some support activities (Porter, 1985) – based on collaborative tools accessible from anywhere such as mail, instant messaging or office tools delivered by providers with new business models (e.g. Google) – as well as primary activities such as marketing and sales provided by a virtual services such as CRM (e.g. Salesforce.com), illustrate also how new ways of using services are blurring the boundaries of application architecture.

Therefore, the importance and dynamics of services within and outside the organization must also be captured in the enterprise architecture (McGovern, 2003). This should be accomplished as a consistent set of models and rules that guide the definition, design and implementation of new services – with support of shared processes, organizational structures, information flows, and the technical infrastructure (Martin, 2005) –, as well as with tools (e.g. impact analysis, simulation tools) which be able to assess the consequences for the organization, of breakdown of services or any strategic or operational change requested by management.

That's why we claim that there is a lack of representation of services in the Zachman's framework – which can only be implicitly, devised by the composition with the others elements of the framework (data, processes, locations, etc.) – so our proposal to start modeling services explicitly in the framework using a new column.

4. MODELING SERVICES

Our proposal is therefore to extend the Zachman's framework in a way that we could map the available sources of internal and external services and specify their different perspectives, or levels of abstraction, according to the rows of the framework. We propose to use the question word "whence" to entitle the column since we want to be able to know from what origin or source the service comes, requested by whom, and how it is modelled in different views of the framework (see figure 4).

	Data "what"	Functions "how"	Network "where"	People "who"	Time "when"	Motivation "why"	Service "whence"
Planner							
Owner							
Designer							
Builder							
Subcontractor							

Figure 4 – Service's column in Zachman's framework.

As appears in the original version of the framework, we make no claims about priority of the service's view over the others views. The service's view just represents a different insight about the same enterprise reality.

The concept of service has its own autonomy from other elements depicted in the framework. A service encapsulates data, is deployed by processes, on different physical and virtual locations, by actors or units; its availability is constrained by time; and it is provided by a business or technical motivation.

It must be noted that the service concept we are dealing here is different from the other one linked to the process view. Our service notion describe what is being offered (which service), rather than how the service is being offered (process perspective) (Obelix, 2001).

Because each perspective reflects different sets of constraints, the meaning of service will change from row to row. Therefore, as we navigate from lower to top rows, and top models become coarse grained when compared to the bottom models, each cell suggests different semantic for services (see Table 1):

- Subcontractor – guarantees the service availability of each part of the technological components.
- Builder – deals with the technological conditions of service's availability namely by systems integration;
- Designer perspective – deals with customization of services to stakeholders, namely for each market segment;
- Owner perspective – at business level the main concerns are with the services requested from suppliers, planned with partners and provided to consumers;
- Planner perspective – deals with the strategic definition of the enterprise's business model and organization's mission (Gordijn, 2000).

Table 1 – The "whence" column.

Row	Perspective	Cell Example	Prov./Cons.	Service
1	Planner	Strategic definition of core business	Industry	Business Model
2	Owner	Definition of core services	Major Suppliers, Partners, and Customers	Business Outsourcing, Partnership Contracts with SLA
3	Designer	Market Segmentation	B2B, B2C, B2E	Customization
4	Builder	System Integration	CRM, ERP, SRM, Brokers	Information availability (accomplished by SOAP, Web Services, XML, ebXML, ...)
5	Subcontractor	"pay–as–you–go", IT Outsourcing	Soft. / Hard. Constructors	Support and maintenance

As an example of this extension of the Zachman's framework, suppose that an enterprise envision an opportunity to launch a new concept of product in the market. The services needed to develop and delivery the concept should be framed by the enterprise's business model. This also will be the driver for definition of main supplier's services and the particular products/services to deliver to the market. We could drill-down and assess the customization of services to its different segments, assess available internal services, and eventually the organization needs to increase and/or adapt some of them, such as the production capacity, human resources, applications and server's capacity to achieve the main purposes established at strategic level of the organization.

5. CONCLUSION

We emphasize the importance of modelling services in addition to other elements modelled in the Zachman's framework. A rigorous and extensible map of the internal and external services managed and operated in the organization will allow a greater insight about the coherence and agility of its architectural parts.

Future work will be driven by the following three issues. First, we intend to build an ontology of services, i.e., a model that represents services on enterprise and could be used to reason about them and their interrelationships. This model will allow a unified view of service's column, so we can consistently navigate, upward or downward on the column's cells. Second, we will use formal methods for the specification, development and verification of systems based on service's view. Finally, we will extend the enterprise architecture methodologies (e.g. Spewak's EAP) in a way that could explicitly cover the view of services, and its implementation in the enterprise.

6. REFERENCES

1. Department of Defense Joint Technical Architecture. July 2002.
2. Federal Enterprise Architecture Framework, version 1.1. September 1999.
3. Gordijn J, Akkermans H, Vliet H. Business Modelling is not Process Modelling. 2000.
4. Hoogervorst J. Enterprise Architecture Enabling Integration, Agility and Change Agility and Change. International Journal of Cooperative Information Systems, Vol. 13, No. 3 (2004) 213–233. 2004.
5. IEEE, Architecture Working Group, Recommended Practice for Architecture Description – Draft IEEE standard P1471/D4.1, IEEE, December 1998.
6. Iyer B, Gottlieb R. The Four–Domain Architecture: An approach to support enterprise architecture design. IBM Systems Journal, Vol. 43, No 3. 2004.
7. Jacobson I, Booch G, Rumbaugh J. The Unified Software Development Process. Adisson Wesley. 1999.
8. Jonkers H. et al. Concepts For Modelling Enterprise Architectures, in International Journal of Cooperative Information Systems, Vol. 13, No. 3 (2004) 257–287, 2004.
9. Martin van den Berg et al. Dynamic Enterprise Architecture: How to Make it Work. John Wiley & Sons, Inc. 2005.
10. McGovern J, Ambler SW, Stevens ME., Linn J, Jo EK, Sharan V. Agile Enterprise Architecture – Techniques for Successful Evolutionary/Agile Database Development. Prentice Hall PTR. November 15, 2003.
11. Krafzig D, Banke K, Slama D. Enterprise SOA: Service–Oriented Architecture Best Practices (The Coad Series). Prentice Hall PTR. 2004.
12. Kurose JF, Ross KW. Computer Networking: A Top–Down Approach Featuring the Internet, 3/E, Addison–Wesley, 2005.
13. Mira da Silva M. Information Systems Integration (In Portuguese). FCA. 2003.
14. OBELIX. Service Ontology IST Project IST–2001–33144. 2001
15. Open Group. The Open Group Architectural Framework (TOGAF) – Version 8.1. November 2002.
16. Porter, Michael. Competitive Advantage. 1985.
17. Spewak S, Hill S. Enterprise Architecture Planning: Developing a Blueprint for Data, Applications and Technology. Wiley–QED. ISBN 0–471–599859. 1992.
18. Treasury Enterprise Architecture Framework, July 2002.
19. Vasconcelos A, Caetano A, Neves J, Sinogas P, Mendes R, Tribolet J. A Framework for Modelling Strategy, Business Processes and Information Systems. Proceedings of 5th International Enterprise Distributed Object Computing Conference EDOC, Seatle, USA. September 2001.
20. Vasconcelos A, Sousa P, Tribolet J. Information System Architectures: Representation, Planning and Evaluation. Proceedings of International Conference on Computer, Communication and Control Technologies Orlando, U.S.A. July 2003.
21. Vasconcelos A, Sousa P, Tribolet J. "Information System Architectures". "Business Excellence '03 Proceedings, First International Conference on Performance Measures, Benchmarking and Best Practices in New Economy, Universidade do Minho, Guimarães, Portugal. June 2003.
22. Vasconcelos, A., M. Mira da Silva, A., and J. Tribolet, An Information System Architectural Framework for Enterprise Application Integration. 2004
23. Zachman JA. A Framework for Information Systems Architecture, IBM Systems Journal 26, No 3, 276–292. 1987.
24. Zachman JA. Sowa JF. Extending and formalizing the framework for information systems architecture. IBM Systems Journal 31, No. 3 590–616. 1992.

AUTOMATIC PARTITIONING OF PROBLEMS THROUGH SUBMODEL DECOMPOSITION A PROMISING TECHNIQUE OF DIGITAL ENTERPRISE TECHNOLOGY

Zsolt János Viharos, László Monostori and Zsolt Kemény
Computer and Automation Institute, Hungarian Academy of Sciences, Hungary
{viharos,monostor,kemeny}@sztaki.hu

This paper presents two main groups of results in the field of process modeling; first, highlighting complexity-related properties shared by several, if not all, levels of production; second, a family of methods set up to handle problems resulting from the aforementioned properties. The presented algorithms lead up to a submodel decomposition method combining generalized feature selection and artificial neural networks. Aside from theoretical presentation, practical results in various levels of actual industrial production demonstrate the feasibility of the methods, suggesting that they can cope with complexity-related problems of different production levels in a uniform way.

1. INTRODUCTION

Reliable process models are of key importance in computer integrated manufacturing (Merchant 1998) as model-based solutions can make difficult problems of production control tractable. Models facilitate elaborating new algorithms, supporting decisions, decreasing investment risks and coping with changes and disturbances.

However, modeling manufacturing processes may bear difficulties: the diversity of operations, their multidimensional, nonlinear and stochastic nature, partially understood relations, unreliable or incomplete data sets etc. Often, the only feasible approach is the decomposition of the model to several smaller interconnected submodels—though not equal to problem decomposition but a first step towards it.

In modeling complex systems, it is common practice to highlight relevant variables in measurement information, e.g. through feature selection. From the selected parameters, process models are often obtained and maintained through learning (Viharos and Monostori 2001). This can be achieved e.g. through artificial neural networks (ANNs)—general, multivariable, nonlinear estimators which can be trained to represent a given model.

In the first part of this paper (Section 2), common characteristics of various production levels are addressed, along with the idea of applying a method elaborated for one production level to other layers of the hierarchy. Section 3 presents a submodel decomposition method combining feature selection and ANN training, meant to handle complexity-related problems of various production levels. Finally, Section 4 gives practical application examples in various levels of production.

2. SIMILARITIES BETWEEN PRODUCTION CONTROL LEVELS WITH RESPECT TO MODELING AND ASSIGNMENT TASKS

2.1 Hierarchic levels of production systems

No single prevailing scheme identifying production levels exists, yet all share some fundamental principles. A general overview of noteworthy stratification schemes can be found e.g. in Horváth and Markos (1995), Tóth (1998), Luttervelt *et al.* (1998) and T. Tóth (1989). The examination of production levels, independently of the specific scheme used, shows one general phenomenon: various forms of complexity, as detailed in the next subsection, appear throughout all layers of the hierarchy.

2.2 Similarities between levels of production systems

As many other domains, all levels of production systems exhibit high complexity and uncertainty, requiring efficient methods for learning the system's properties and dependencies and depositing them in a reconfigurable form to suit various interpretations. Though all levels of production bear specific inherent difficulties, the following characteristics are shared by all systems and levels in general:

A high number of parameters. For systems consisting of many components, such as production lines, biochemical processes etc., a large number of parameters is required for description, and the control and modeling experts' efforts to work with simplified models may fail. For manufacturing processes, a variety of approaches exists for simplification (Tóth 1998), but even using those leave a large number of variables.

A high number of dependencies. Production systems are composed of several components, each of which may have its own complex set of relations. Combining these components in a large system, the number of relevant dependencies quickly increases, even if some of the less relevant inherent relations of the components are omitted.

Nonlinear dependencies. Though some "conventional" methods can also handle nonlinear models, in most cases their success depends on a-priori information about the general nature of the nonlinearity—which is rarely given to a proper degree in unknown complex systems, especially in the field of production.

Uncertainty of measurement data. Gathering knowledge about physical systems through measurement introduces noise and data uncertainty. This calls for robust methods to handle uncertain parameters within the corresponding tolerance limits.

Incomplete information. Related to uncertainty is the partial availability of information, meaning that some elements of measurement data vectors are missing (either due to sensor malfunction or because at the given point of the process, the data element has no sensible meaning) or invalid. Discarding these incomplete vectors can often be unpracticable as they are a substantial part of all data. Therefore, a method is needed to handle incomplete data sets (Viharos *et al.* 2002, Zhang and Rong 2005).

Unknown input/output character of parameters. The input/output nature of relevant parameters may change—either depending of the problem to be solved or the given point of view of modeling (and may thus be different for another problem), or it may be entirely unknown if a-priori knowledge about the system is sparse—this is typical for ANN application cases (Viharos and Monostori 1999c).

Numerous methods can master one or a few of the above challenges, yet few can address all of them simultaneously—this may give the latter approaches an outstanding role in future production control. It is of key importance to develop methods that address generic system properties in the fundamental structure of the methodology, while the algorithms applied can be exchanged for others in a "plugin-like" manner. This—just as the fact that all production levels share the above features—encourages researchers to apply one method, elaborated for one given level of production, to solve problems of other layers of the hierarchy as well, promising a versatile problem solving technology. This paper presents such a method, submodel decomposition, which is able to cope with the aforementioned challenges and was, in a number of industrial application and test cases, successfully used in various levels of production.

3. INTRODUCTION TO SUBMODEL DECOMPOSITION

3.1 Description of the submodel decomposition method

Now, let us present the submodel decomposition method in detail. The procedure we propose combines generalized feature selection and improved ANN training in a dynamic way. Generalized feature selection proposes a set of assumed submodels which are individually validated by ANN training, either to be accepted or to be rejected.

3.1.1 Generalized feature selection. Let us assume that submodels have to be extracted from a list of n parameters whose input/output nature is not known in advance. Feature selection proposes n possible submodels, each having another output variable, and a list of further parameters in the order of their potential impact on the output.

The original feature selection algorithm by Devijver and Kittler (1982) assumes a pure classification task with the goal of reducing the number of inputs needed for one single output. As a generalization, continuous output parameters can be mapped onto the discrete classification scheme with an appropriate heuristics. The first step selects the output and its values encountered in the training data set are grouped into the highest possible number of clusters (i.e. intervals of equal length), so that at least one element is contained in each interval (this, in itself, being the first heuristic decision).

Ranking remaining variables using suitable heuristics (Devijver and Kittler 1982) with respect to a given "measure of distinction" delivers a list of variables and corresponding measure values. Taking more and more of them for input, the separability measure of the corresponding output deteriorates, and a further heuristic decision can determine how many of the best-ranked variables should be taken. These variables, together with the selected output, form one possible submodel, ignoring whether they were selected for input or output during feature selection. This is repeated with all parameters of the system selected as outputs, resulting in as many proposed submodels as the total number of parameters. Continuing the same with recursive partitioning of all submodels already created, the possible submodels form a multilevel decision tree.

 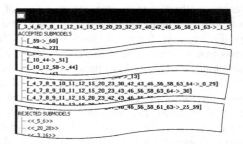

Figure 1 – Two cases of submodel decomposition.

In the example to the left, the net of accepted submodels consists of five main relations (in brackets), partitioning a system containing eleven description parameters. The fourth row in the window, e.g. shows that the algorithm identified a submodel with parameters 2, 3 and 6 as inputs for the estimation of output 5. The four identified submodels have common parameters, e.g. parameter 6 is estimated by the submodel shown in the second row, but it is to be found among the input variables of the next two submodels, too. Thus, a structure of interconnected submodels can be recognized additionally to the identification of its individual parts. To the right, the result of submodel decomposition in an industrial example with a large number of system parameters is shown.

3.1.2 ANN training. The three heuristic decision steps taken to obtain the candidate submodels makes them only assumptions, to be either verified or rejected by ANN training. To overcome difficulties of "classical" ANN application, a generic, reusable ANN-based model should compiled—such a strategy is introduced in the approach of Viharos and Monostori (1999c). Supplying the algorithm with a sufficiently large set of training patterns and corresponding tolerances, the best input/output configuration for learning the dependencies of the training vectors will be found automatically. The successful completion of the latter is equal to a proof of the assumed submodel as it is practically realized by the ANN. Does this not succeed; the model is rejected and will be avoided in subsequent steps.

3.1.3 Dynamic submodel decomposition. While the separate application of preparing training data by feature selection and subsequent ANN learning already reduces the computational costs of modeling the entire system, the flexibility of the method is most exploited if feature selection and ANN training are executed as complements in alternating steps. Here, feature selection first selects only one submodel candidate for validation by ANN training involving only the variables of the proposed submodel. Is the ANN training successful, the submodel is accepted and removed from the free pool of unidentified submodels, and the rest of the learning parameters is processed again by a feature selection procedure, delivering a modified submodel candidate set which is again tested by a corresponding ANN training.

3.1.4 The user's perspective. For practical application, by non-expert users as well, a software package was developed which, upon supplying measurement data in a suitable form, automatically determines and learns the net of submodels of a complex system. As a prerequisite, the user has to provide the following:

i   A sufficiently large data set, e.g. a database table, columns meaning the system variables and each row standing for these variables recorded at a given time.

ii   Since in subsequent parts of the algorithm, an ANN is employed to test whether a given variable can be estimated using other parameters, a maximal tolerable error has to be assigned to each variable when estimating it with an ANN model.

Is a data set supplied in the above form, the submodel decomposition algorithm can be started, which delivers the following results:

i   A set of valid submodels, with as many of the parameters labeled as output as the ANN algorithm could find.

ii   A set of rejected submodels judged invalid by the ANN algorithm. Storing these is useful for an early pruning of submodel candidates bound to fail. Also, this list can be used to reject hypotheses concerning the analysed system.

iii Since valid submodels were spotted as ANN's were learning their dependencies, this knowledge is readily accessible as a network separate neural nets, each of them representing one submodel.

Figure 1 shows a screenshot of an actual industrial application in a rather low level of manufacturing where a part of a production line is modeled using more than sixty parameters.

3.2 The place of submodel decomposition among related and preceding methods

Having presented our proposed submodel decomposition technique, let us examine which classes it belongs to and which are some of its forerunners and related methods.

• As for modeling, submodel decomposition relies on ANNs, more specifically, multilayer perceptrons (MLPs). A modified form of the accelerated back-propagation method SuperSAB (see Tollenare 1990) is used for training the MLPs.

• The model building method can be looked upon as a special case of learning algorithms as well. The fact that no predetermined layout of input and output parameters is required, classifies it as an unsupervised learning algorithm. This is a noteworthy achievement as here, feed-forward ANN structures are created with unsupervised learning. Moreover, the resulting networks can be tuned with both supervised and unsupervised learning later on.

• Modeling of many-valued mapping is solved by the introduced algorithm as well. Brouwer and Pedrycz (2003) addressed a similar problem with a totally different approach before aiming at handling incomplete data sets—similarly, by coincidence, to the authors of the submodel finding method presented here (Viharos *et al.* 2002).

- Several approaches are known in literature which, also for the case of MLPs, can alter the structure of the networks to improve them, usually adding or deleting neurons whenever needed for further training (Yasui 1997). The network of (interconnected) networks arrangement built in submodel decomposition is actually the result of a process of this kind, and can be considered a special result of a structure determination process of ANNs, as well as the product of a specific class of combined pruning-learning methods.
- The application of ANNs is often preceded by some kind of preprocessing of raw learning data. This consists, especially in manufacturing (Viharos and Monostori 1999c, Erdélyi and Hornyák 2003), in picking out parameters that "are worth learning," i.e. in feature selection. This is also practiced in our submodel decomposition method, however, as opposed to the traditional separation of feature selection and subsequent ANN training (Egmont-Petersen *et al.* 1998), the submodel identification approach presented here combines feature selection and ANN training in alternating steps, resulting in a hybrid technique.

4. APPLICATION IN HIGH AND LOWLEVELS OF PRODUCTION CONTROL

Submodel decomposition, as well as the fixed-topology ANNs applied therein, found application in various levels of industrial production. The following examples show application cases of the techniques that led up to submodel decomposition—ranging from feed-forward ANN application over ANN-model-based problem solving and optimization to submodel decomposition. These cases show the versatile applicability of the techniques in various levels of manufacturing which may open a broad scope of research to transfer these—and related—techniques to other levels of production.

4.1 Low level application examples

Classical modeling. Application of "plain" modeling with fixed-topology ANNs in lower levels of production is shown by Viharos *et al.* (2003) for simulating chip formation in turning and milling processes and for modeling surface quality properties of a cutting process depending on various technical parameters whose choice may change from task to task.

Problem solving. The ANNs obtained through input/output search, without the decomposition to submodels, can be used to solve a variety of estimation problems. Numerous practical application examples for low levels of production (metal cutting again, as in the examples mentioned before) are given by Viharos and Monostori (1999c). Another application example for lower levels of manufacturing, Viharos *et al.* (2002b) shows another case for multiple solutions of a non-invertible relation. In Viharos *et al.* (2002b), the influence of the simultaneous selection of several requirements is examined from the point of view of estimation accuracy.

Optimization. With the help of the ANNs, a solution can also be found using iterative optimization. An application example of multipurpose optimization with constraints is shown by Viharos and Monostori (2001) where simulated annealing is used to obtain a set of valid solutions to manufacturing problems.

Submodel decomposition. Figure 1 shows a screenshot of an actual industrial application in a rather low level of manufacturing where a production line is modeled using more than sixty parameters.

4.2 High level application examples

Classical modeling. Application of ANNs for modeling higher levels of production was proposed by Monostori *et al.* (2001), where an improved ANN modeling concept is extended to process chains and entire production plants.

Problem solving. An example for the use of the generic ANN model in higher levels of production is given by Viharos and Monostori (2001) where various problems related to efficiency improvement had to be solved in manufacturing processes of multilayer printed circuit boards.

Optimization. Constrained optimization techniques initially applied to only one production step are extended by Viharos and Monostori (2001) to a higher level of production: The block-oriented ProcessManager framework presented by Viharos and Monostori (2001) can deal with an entire process chain where the result of an earlier step may influence all subsequent steps. Even higher levels of production are handled by Monostori *et al.* (2001) where a hybrid optimization technique (supported by AI, machine learning (ML) and simulation) is used to optimize the arrangement of manufacturing processes within a production plant. A substantial gain in optimization time (acceleration by a factor of 6000) is reached by substituting discrete event simulation with ANNs trained by results of earlier simulation runs. Submodel decomposition. The identification of submodels in a complex system was also applied in an intermediate level of production (Viharos *et al.* 2003b).

5. FURTHER RESEARCH

Currently ongoing research activities are aimed at extending submodel decomposition towards an agent-based framework where knowledge specific to an agent is mapped onto a given submodel. The feasibility of this generalization is assumed because of remarkable analogies between ANN-based submodels and agents: the fact of decomposability, the existence of localized knowledge with strongly limited connections beyond a given neighborhood, a network architecture, learning or adaptive behavior and estimation or prediction abilities. Additionally to the submodel principle, the automatic decomposition approach itself is expected to be applicable to autonomous agents as well; moreover, agents could be dynamically set up, grouped or split up according to various efficiency criteria, such as learning ability or skills of predicting relevant events. It is envisaged that such a multi-agent system can be erected as a higher level envelope for lower level production control to determine an efficient initial layout of entire production plants or provide decision support for their reorganization.

6. CONCLUSION

The first part of this paper highlighted fundamental phenomena equally shared by higher and lower levels of manufacturing (complexity due to a dense network of interdependencies, and a large number of relevant system parameters). To handle these, a submodel decomposition method, integrating generalized feature selection and ANN training, was presented in the second part of the paper. The versatility of the method was demonstrated by examples of practical use for various levels of manufacturing systems. The results obtained so far suggest that the approach, if proven successful for one production level, can be modified for use in other levels, such new experience possibly bringing mutual improvement in all domains of application. Finally, as a concluding remark to the method, future research plans of combining submodel decomposition with a flexible multi-agent system were outlined.

7. ACKNOWLEDGEMENT

The research work presented in this paper is in part financed through the EU 6th Framework project No. NMP2-CT-2004-507487 VRL-KCiP—Virtual Research Lab for Knowledge Communities in Production—network of excellence (with respect to knowledge handling) and Multisens (with respect to production feedback) under contract No. 512668, as well as the Hungarian National Research Fund under grant Nos. OTKA T 043547, OTKA T 049481, and NKFP 2/010/2004 (with respect to production control and submodel extraction).

8. REFERENCES

1. Brouwer, R.K., Pedrycz, W., Training a feed-forward network with incomplete data due to missing input variables. Applied Soft Computing vol. 3, 2003 23–36
2. Devijver, P.A., Kittler, J., eds.: Pattern recognition, a statistical approach. Prentice-Hall International Inc, England, London, 1982
3. Egmont-Petersen, M., Talmon, J.L., Hasman, A., Ambergen, A.W., Assessing the importance of features for multi-layer perceptrons. Neural Networks vol. 11, 1998 623–635
4. Erdélyi, F., Hornyák, O.: Advanced simulation of nc turning operations. In: Production Systems and Information Engineering. Miskolc University Press, 2003, 41–53
5. Ghiassi, M., Saidane, H., A dynamic architecture for artificial neural networks. Neurocomputing, vol. 63, 397–413
6. Horváth, M., Markos, S., Gépgyártástechnológia. Univ. lecture notes, Technical University of Budapest, 1995
7. Luttervelt, C.A., Childs, T.H.C., Jawahir, I.S., Klocke, F., Venuvinod, P.K., Present situation and future trends in modelling of machining operations. In: Progress report of the CIRP working group "Modelling of Machining Operations", CIRP STC cutting keynote paper, 1998 1–47
8. Merchant, M.E., An interpretive look at 20th century research on modelling of machining (inagural address). Proc. of the CIRP International Workshop on Modelling of Machining Operations, 1998, 27–31
9. Monostori, L., Viharos, Zs.J., Markos, S., Satisfying various requirements in different levels and stages of machining using one general ANN-based process model. In: Proc. of the 15th International Conference on Computer-Aided Production Engineering, CAPE'99, 1999 477–484
10. Monostori, L., Márkus, A., Brussel, H.V., Westkämper, E., Machine learning approaches to manufacturing. CIRP Annals vol. 45, 1996, 675–712

11. Monostori, L., Viharos, Zs.J.: Hybrid, AI- and simulation-supported optimisation of process chains and production plants. CIRP Annals vol. 50, 2001, 353–356
12. Tollenare, T.: SuperSAB: fast adaptive backpropagation with good scaling properties. Neural Networks vol. 3, 1990, 561–573
13. Tóth, T., Tervezési elvek, modellek és módszerek a számítógéppel integrált gyártásban. Univ. lecture notes, Publishing House of the University of Miskolc, 1998
14. T. Tóth, I.D., On a new theoretical approach of integration. In: Information Control Problems in Manufacturing Technology, INCOM89, 1989, 273–279
15. Viharos, Zs.J., Monostori, L., Markos, S., A framework for modelling, monitoring and optimisation of manufacturing processes and process chains by using machine learning and search algorithms. In: Proceedings of the 9th IMEKO TC-10 International Conference on Technical Diagnostics, 1999, 249–254
16. Viharos, Zs.J., Monostori, L.: Automatic input-output configuration of ANN-based process models and its application in machining. In: Lecture Notes of Artificial Intelligence—Multiple Approaches to Intelligent Systems, Conference, Cairo, Egypt. (1999) 659–668
17. Viharos, Zs.J., Monostori, L., Optimisation of process chains and production plants using hybrid, AI- and simulation based general process models. The Fourteenth International Conference on Industrial & Engineering Applications of Artificial Intelligence & Expert Systems, Book: Lecture Notes of Artificial Intelligence, Springer Computer Science Book, Springer-Verlag Heidelberg, 2001, 827–835
18. Viharos, Zs.J., Monostori, L., Vincze, T., Training and application of artificial neural networks with incomplete data. In: Proc. of the 15th International Conference on Industrial & Engineering Application of Artificial Intelligence & Expert Systems, 2002 649–659
19. Viharos, Zs.J., Novák, K., Tóth, G., Markos, S., Modelling of different aspects of the cutting process by using ANNs. In: Proceedings of the XIII. Workshop on Supervising and Diagnostics of Machining Systems . Open and global manufacturing design (CIRP), 2002, 241–249
20. Viharos, Zs.J., Markos, S., Szekeres, C., ANN-based chip-form classification in turning. In: Proceedings of the XVII. IMEKO World Congress—Metrology in the 3rd Millennium, 2003, 1469–1473
21. Viharos, Zs.J., Monostori, L., Novák, K., Tóth, G., Csongrádi, Z., Kenderesy, T., Sólymosi, T., Lõrincz, Á.., Koródi, T., Monitoring of complex production systems, in view of digital factories. In: Proceedings of the XVII. IMEKO World Congress—Metrology in the 3rd Millennium, 2003, 1463–1468
22. Viharos, Zs.J.: Automatic generation of a net of models for high and low levels of production. In: Proc. of the 16th IFAC World Congress, 2005 Reg. No. 05127
23. Yasui, S., Convergence suppression and divergence facilitation: Minimum and joint use of hidden units by multiple outputs. Neural Networks vol. 10, 1997 353–367
24. Zhang, Q., Rong, G., Industrial application of data reconciliation for hybrid systems. In: Proc. of the 16th IFAC World Congress, 2005, Reg. Nr. 01903

SESSION 2

DISTRIBUTED AND COLLABORATIVE DESIGN

IMPLEMENTING DIGITAL ENTERPRISE TECHNOLOGIES FOR AGILE DESIGN IN THE VIRTUAL ENTERPRISE

C. D. W. Lomas[1], P. G. Maropoulos[2] and P. C. Matthews[1]
[1]Durham University, School of Engineering, UK
c.d.w.lomas@durham.ac.uk, p.c.matthews@durham.ac.uk
[2]University of Bath, Mechanical Engineering Department, UK
p.g.maropoulos@bath.ac.uk

Digital Enterprise Technology (DET) is defined as a synthesis of digital and physical systems across the product lifecycle which can be exploited for two main benefits: risk mitigation through consistent and seamless data standards; and reduction in product development times through improved access to the most accurate project data at any time, from anywhere, by anyone. Agility is defined as responsiveness to unpredictability, particularly unpredictable events in the environment external to a process. The general need for agile response in turbulent environments is well documented and has been analyzed at the manufacture phase.

This paper introduces a framework for an agile response to these turbulent environments during the design stages of product development. The Agile Design Framework is based on the founding principles described as DET, with the added benefit of reduced reaction time and therefore greater agility in the face of unpredicted external events. A 4 level classification scheme for event impact is discussed and a common toolbox of Digital Enterprise Technologies (Core Tools) for agile design is introduced. The paper proposes the implementation of the DET-based Core Tools during a meta-design stage, for maximum benefit from the synergies of the many systems.

1. INTRODUCTION

The benefits of agility in the manufacture of products is well documented. (Jiang et al, 2003, Kara et al, 2001) Recent research has also explored the application of agile methodologies from the manufacturing process to other aspects of the product development cycle (Matthews et al, 2005). This paper builds on the Agile Design Framework (Armoutis et al, 2003), an extension of the Digital Enterprise Technology methodology, previously defined by the authors to propose a meta-design stage of the design process, during which the Core Tools of the Agile Design Framework are defined and configured. This meta-design stage is undertaken once the initial requirements gathering has been completed and the collaborative design team begins to come together, usually under the direction of a prime contractor or system integrator.

The remainder of this paper is structured as follows: Section 2 describes the background research activities of the team in the area of agile design, and introduces the Agile Design Framework in the context of Digital Enterprise Technologies. Section 3 presents the Core Tools of the Agile Design Framework while Section 4 presents the arguments for a meta-design stage and the proposed benefits of introducing an additional stage in to the design process, with a view to reducing the overall process time. Section 5 discusses the findings with regard to the theoretical benefits of Digital Enterprise Technologies for Agile Design while Section 6 concludes the paper and proposes the next steps in Agile Design research.

2. BACKGROUND

In order to concentrate on unique core competences, there is a trend towards multiple smaller companies collaborating on a short-term basis to acquire all the necessary competencies to complete a project, without having to each maintain the excess competences during projects for which they are not required (Lomas et al, 2005). This allows *Virtual Enterprises* to have the knowledge of a large organisation without the overheads associated with one. Companies are selected on the basis of their expertise (Lomas et al, 2005). The Virtual Enterprise forms the basis of the Agile Design Framework, which seeks to define what happens when a design project, decomposed into multiple distributed components, is interrupted by an Unpredictable External Event (UEE).

The level of impact of a UEE has been categorised into 4 levels of severity (Maropoulos, 2003), and each can be dealt with in a different manner. *Trivial* events can be resolved completely at the local level, incurring a small penalty, represented as time. This could be a requirements change due to government legislation, but crucially, the existing agent is still able to satisfy the requirements and deliver its part of the design. *Minor* events require the agent to seek external assistance, or redeploy a part of the work to another partner. For example specialist knowledge in a particular field will now be needed, so another partner with the necessary competence is brought into the project team to assist. A *major* UEE cannot be resolved by the agent or another member of the virtual enterprise. The redeployment of work to a new team member and initiation of the new member to the project incurs a serious time penalty. Finally a *fatal* UEE cannot be resolved by the agent, and there exists no external agent that can provide support. Effectively, the design is fundamentally flawed and is not realisable.

Each UEE has an impact (normally negative) on the percentage of work remaining for that stage, which can be translated into a time penalty. If the task is on the critical path, then the time penalty is transferred to a global time penalty for the project.

The goal of an agile system, in this case a design process, is to have the ability to respond quickly to unpredicted changes in the environment. The nature of the events have been discussed here, in terms of there causes and the level of impact they impose on a project. In order to respond to these events, the Digital Enterprise Technology (DET) Framework (Maropoulos, 2003) presents an initial template on which we can build a set of *Core Tools* comprising the Agile Design Framework.

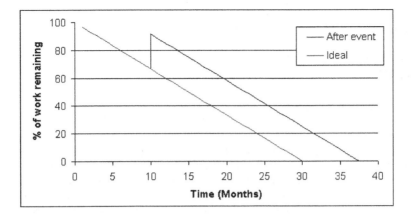

Figure 1 - Time penalty caused by a UEE.

The Agile Design framework is aligned to the DET framework (figure 2) through a common distributed and collaborative environment. Agile Design builds on the 4 cornerstones of DET to identify specific Digital and associated tools. The main focus of exploiting the synthesis between digital tools across the product lifecycle has been risk mitigation through eliminating conversions between partners and software systems, and to allow more seamless access to data across the Product Lifecycle.

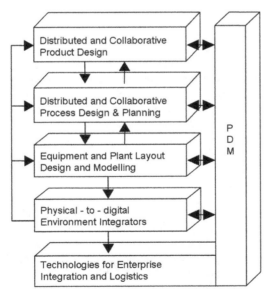

Figure 2 - The 4 cornerstones of Digital Enterprise Technology.

The aim of the Agile Design Framework is to develop this methodology in order to reduce not only the conventional product development time, but also use the

Digital environment and the physical to digital integrators to reduce the penalty (time, economic or quality) caused by unpredictable external events.

3. CORE TOOLS FOR AGILE DESIGN

3.1 Competence Profiling

In the event of a minor or major level of UEE, there exists a requirement for external intervention, either in assisting an existing agent of the project, or in replacing a failed agent. This process of identifying alternative agents has been shown to delay projects' progress, due to a lack of direction in the search for new agents and a lack of information about their capabilities and competencies being available (Lomas et al, 2005). During this process no direct work is completed on the project and a time penalty can be incurred. Competence Profiling is one tool which can be used to respond more rapidly when a new agent is needed. Companies complete an on-line form relating to their core competences, as well as other information such as geographical locations, international awards obtained and current customers. This database can then be searched for one or more competences in a single search, and a company or group of companies will be scored and recommended based on their performance against the search criteria. The Competence Profiling system then provides a full company report on any companies that could be investigated further to meet the requirements. In this way, the process of finding companies to assist or replace existing agents is greatly speeded up.

3.2 Design for Assembly

In the cases of minor and major events, where external companies are brought into a project part-way through, it is important that they can be integrated as easily as possible in order to minimize the delay caused by their inexperience with the project. Design for manufacture principles such as the use of early defined and standard interfaces between components/sub-assemblies, can help this. This principle is also referred to as de-coupling tasks (Ulrich et al, 2005) and Modular Architecture (Gu et al, 2004).

3.3 International Standards

International Standards such as SI units and terminology can play a vital role in how seamlessly a company can integrate into a project part way through. While some standards may be obvious, such as SI units, it is important to stipulate from the outset the standards, languages and terminology that will be used for a collaborative project. One example of the importance of this is the use of CAD data. In a distributed and collaborative project where the same CAD packages are used, there appears no need to use neutral file formats such as STEP for the exchange of data between partners. However, if an unexpected event requires that a new agent must be introduced to the project, then it is important that their CAD package does not become an obstacle and cause further delay, because they cannot easily share files with other agents. The trial carried out by Durham and Oregon State Universities clearly showed the negative impact of using different CAD systems for a distributed collaborative design project (Arnold et al, 2004).

3.4 Web-based Product Data Management

Product Data Management (PDM) systems have been around for a number of years, and recently have migrated to web-based systems. The benefits of this development to an agile design process are significant, and related to the previous two tools. Once a UEE occurs during a project and the level of that UEE has been identified, there may exist a need to introduce new partners to the project. Without the use of a web-based PDM system, the process of integrating that new partner or partners becomes more complex. PDM systems do not only offer access to the majority, if not all, of the information a new agent would need, but also the project history through discussion boards and document revision control. This insight into the progress of the project so far, the reasons behind decisions made and importantly, any failures which might have caused their involvement, will mean that any new agent can more quickly become effective within the project than if they were entering 'blind'. The web-based nature of modern PDM systems can allow a new agent to gain access to this information simply with a username and password, rather than having to speak to each of the other affected agents individually. There is also a guarantee that the new agents obtain the most up-to-date information.

Although there exist many other tools which could further increase the agility of the response to unpredictable events, these tools have been identified by the authors as Core Tools, that is they can have significant effect on the response time, and are readily available.

4. META-DESIGN

The Agile Design Framework described in the previous section builds on the DET framework to define a set of Core Tools to enhance the benefits into dealing with UEEs, therefore creating an agile process.

As discussed, the way in which product development projects are carried out has changed over the last ten to twenty years, and now adopts a more collaborative, distributed model. However there is little evidence of the product development process changing to reflect this trend.

Meta-Design is proposed as 'designing the design process'. In order to maximize the benefits of the core tools it is proposed that all members of the virtual enterprise must be familiar with them and committed to their use. Therefore, the introduction of these tools must be well planned in order to maximize the cumulative benefit.

The traditional product development process follows a staged process as shown in figure 3.

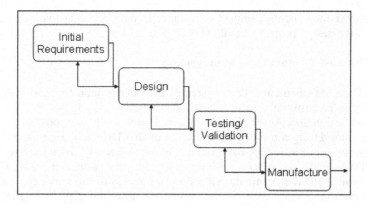

Figure 3 - Traditional Staged Product Development Process.

Through the introduction of a meta-design stage the virtual enterprise is preparing itself for the design process. Therefore, the impact of an Unexpected External Event can be limited through the use of procedures and tools already introduced and agreed.

One example might be the development of a new technology which means that welding airplane wings is possible, rather than the traditional riveting. The Agile Design Framework proposes Competence Profiling as a method of identifying specialist collaborators who could be introduced to the virtual enterprise to assist with this particular change in requirements and reduce the impact of the UEE. If, during a meta-design stage, the existing partners have agreed on Competence Profiling via a particular system, then the process of identifying new partners is greatly reduced because training has already taken place on a tool which has been agreed and tested. Furthermore, Web-based Product Data Management is a Core Tool of the Agile Design Framework. By introducing the web-based PDM during a meta-design stage and training administrators, a new company such as that discussed could easily be added to the PDM system and gain access to the relevant project data more quickly.

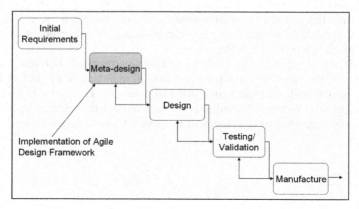

Figure 4 - Meta-design stage for definition of Core Tools.

The meta-design stage is best placed in-between Initial Requirements gathering and Design to allow the overall integrators of the project to identify the make-up of the virtual enterprise. Competence Profiling may be used to match the initial requirements to interested companies to form the project team. Preliminary discussions will then allow an initial team to form the virtual enterprise, whose first task should be to develop the customer requirements into concepts. At this stage of design concepts the issues of data sharing procedures, international standards, software standards for sharing digital files and many more become relevant. Therefore meta-design, for defining these processes and standards before they become problems, must precede the conceptual design work, and therefore sits well between requirements gathering and design.

The meta-design should be lead by the integrator or manager of the project, and all participating collaborators should be in agreement. At this stage it may be appropriate for training to take place.

It is also proposed that a part of the meta-design process, in addition to the agreement of procedures and tools, should include scenarios to allow partners to appreciate the benefits of the Core Tools and procedures, and also enhance understanding of the way in which they may be used to limit the negative impact of any UEEs. This use of scenarios can help to overcome the cultural resistances to operating in such an open and collaborative environment.

Essentially the Meta-Design process facilitates three purposes:
- Definition of Core Tools
    - Web-based PDM
    - Competence Profiling
    - International Standards
    - Design for Assembly/Manufacture
- Training
- Scenario Planning

5. DISCUSSION

The Agile Design Framework discussed relates specifically to collaborative design projects in a virtual enterprise. The main focus of research in this area has been on tools which may be of benefit to the collaborative effort through improved data-sharing. The proposed meta-design stage of the product development process allows a virtual enterprise the opportunity to use these and other tools (the Core Tools) for maximum agility. This is achieved through the definition of tools and procedures, and appropriate training, prior to any design work being undertaken, as soon as the initial partners of the team are identified.

6. CONCLUSIONS

This paper has introduced the Agile Design Framework as a development of the Digital Enterprise Technology methodology for product lifecycle management. The

Agile Design Framework seeks to exploit the synergies between digital technologies in collaborating and distributed organisations to not only mitigate risk, but to enhance their ability to respond to Unpredictable External Events. This is achieved in a number of ways: Definition of a set of Core Tools used across the virtual enterprise for identifying new partners and managing communications within the project team; Early definition of the Core Tools during a meta-design stage which is lead by the project integrator and defines the tools and procedures for use throughout the project by all members; The use of scenarios to illustrate the benefits of the Core Tools and overcome any resistance. In this way the Digital Technologies employed will be more effective because of early definition and planning, enabling a faster response to Unexpected Events and a reduced product development cycle.

Future work will include lab-based experiments to demonstrate the benefits of early implementation of the Agile Design Framework. This will be followed by retrospective industrial case analysis and implementation of this methodology in industry.

7. ACKNOWLEDGEMENTS

The authors would like to thank The Virtual Research Laboratory for a Knowledge Community in Production (VRL-KCiP) for their support in funding this research.

8. REFERENCES

1. Armoutis, N.D and J Bal. Building the Knowledge Economy: Issues, Applications, and Case Studies, chapter E-Business through Competence Profiling, pages 474-482. IOS Press, 2003.
2. Forrest Arnold, Nathan Moody, William Reiter, Cary Maunder, Brian Rogers, Paul Baguley, Peter Chapman, Chris Lomas, Defen Zhang, Paul Maropoulos. An Extended Virtual Enterprise SMARTEAM Engineering Project. Proceedings of the 2nd International Conference on DET. Seattle, USA, 2004.
3. Gu, P, Hashiemian, M, Nee A.Y.C, Adaptable Design. Annals of the CIRP 53/2/2004.
4. Jiang, Z and R.Y.K Fung. An adaptive agile manufacturing control infrastructure based on TOPNs-CS modelling. International Journal of Advanced Manufacturing Technology, 22:191-215, 2003.
5. Kara, S. Kayis, B. and Kaebernick, H. Concurrent Resource Allocation (CRA): A Heuristic for Multi-Project Scheduling with Resource Constraints in Concurrent Engineering. International Journal of Concurrent Engineering: Research and Applications, 9(1), 64-73, 2001.
6. Lomas, C.D.W, Matthews, P.C, Armoutis, N.D, Maropoulos, P.G, Verification of event impact levels for an Agile Design framework. Proceedings of ICMEN, Greece. 5-7th Oct 2005.
7. Lou P, Zhou Z.D, Chen Y.P, Ai W. Study on multi-agent-based agile supply chain management. International Journal of Advanced Manufacturing Technology 23 (3-4): 197-203. Feb 2004.
8. Maropoulos, P.G, Digital Enterprise Technology – defining perspectives and research priorities. International Journal of Computer Integrated Manufacture. Vol. 16, 7-8, pages 467-478. 2003
9. Matthews, P.C, Lomas, C.D.W, Armoutis, N.D, Maropoulos, P.G. Foundations of an Agile Design Methodology. Proceedings of the International Conference on Agility. Helsinki, Finland. 27-28th Jul 2005.
10. Ulrich, Karl T. and Eppinger, Steven D. Product Design and Development. McGraw-Hill 1995.

DYNAMICS OF STATE-PROBLEMS AND DESIGN INTERMEDIATE OBJECTS IN DISTRIBUTED AND COLLABORATIVE DESIGN PROCESS

Reza Movahed khah, Egon Ostrosi and Olivier Garro
Laboratoire de recherche Mécatronique3M, Université de Technologie de Belfort-Montbéliard, France
{Reza.Movahedkhah; Egon.Ostrosi; Olivier.Garro}@utbm.fr

The implementation of multi-agents systems aided collaborative and distributed design requires a deeper understanding of the real interactions between actors, inside multidisciplinary teams. In this view, the implementation of these systems requires to observe, to model and to analyze this process with finer granularities levels. This paper presents an approach of collaborative and distributed design process analysis based on the modeling of interactions between actors during this process. The approach consists in discerning, from the real interactions, the relationship between the state-problems and the dynamics of design intermediate objects (DIO) in the computer mediated collaborative and distributed design process. The analysis of state-problems, in a real design process experience shows that the dynamics of the state problems has the influence on dynamics of DIOs.

1. INTRODUCTION

The implementation of multi-agents systems aided collaborative and distributed design requires a deeper understanding of the real interactions between actors, inside multidisciplinary teams. In this view, the implementation of these systems requires to observe, to model and to analyze this process with finer granularities levels. Indeed, the collaborative and distributed design is a complex process (Chiu, 2002, Ostrosi, 2003 and Ostergaard, 2003). This complexity results from the conjugation of a great number of heterogeneous data (domains, actors, organizations, methods) that are interacting between them (Garro, 1995). Moreover, the variety of the points of view results in multiple goals to carry on during the design process. The interaction between the actors, during the collaborative and distributed design process, shows that this one is a key variable. In the majority of the cases, the results issued from the interactions must be consensual in order to be accepted. Under these conditions, the final solution of the design process can result only from the reached consensus on the different elements of this solution. The comprehension of convergence towards an acceptable solution, as a whole, requires a modelling of variables intervening for the period of the interactions between the different actors (Coiera, 2002), the aims and the relations which they maintain during the design process.

In this context, during design process, the designers spend most clearly of their time to create, to discuss, to interpret, to evaluate, to transform, etc, the texts, the graphs, the computing results, the different product representations of the product (under the form of various diagrams, drawings or numerical models). These objects are called Design Intermediate Object (DIO) (Boujut, 2000, Mer, 1995, (Gregory, 1997 and Sanchis, 2001). According to *Jeantet and Al,* the ***intermediate objects*** are the produced or used objects, the traces and the supports of the action to be conceived (in relation to the tools, procedures and actors) during the design process. The concept of DIO corporate an effective means of reading of the activity of real design. We will thus be interested in the analysis of a process of collaborative design remotely through of DIOs.

If designers spend, on the one hand, 80% of the time generating and retrieving their data (Baya, 1995), and on the other hand, 93% of the time assessing information on a non-quantitative level of abstraction, then information tools should offer external memory aids to retrieve these data (Dong, 1997). Inside the design teams, as the designers must communicate their thoughts between them, the verbal communication offers a fairly direct path to the state of the design process and its related problem, which we call ***state-problem***.

In this paper, we propose an approach that, beginning with the real interactions and the concepts emergence, consists, on the one hand, in discerning the different state-problems and their dynamics characterizing the collaborative and distributed design process, and on the other hand, in searching the history of DIOs and the causes of the dynamics of DIOs.

In the second section, we present the dynamics of state-problems. Here, their identification and evolutions in time permits deepened understanding of the dynamics of the problems that occur during the collaborative and distributed design process. The developed approach is demonstrated by a distributed and collaborative design experience of the GRACC group (***GRACC:*** *Groupe de **R**echerche sur l'Activité de Conception Coopérative*). In the third section, we propose a data analysis between the design intermediate objects and the emerged state-problems during their emergences as a public (in synchronous and shared representations). Finally, we summarize the important results of our approach.

2. DYNAMICS OF STATE-PROBLEMS IN DISTRIBUTED AND COLLABORATIVE DESIGN PROCESS

Modelling of interactions. During the collaborative and distributed design process, each domain is represented by an actor, which has specific responsibilities in the design process. Thus, each actor is authorized to be an expert on certain fields of knowledge called *registers of reference*. We note q the number of actors and A_k ($k=1... q$) the actor k corresponding to the register of reference k. During the design process, the actors interact. For example, an actor A_k proposes, at the moment t, a conjecture related to a problem. It is about a potential solution, candidate to become an entire solution. An actor A_l representing the domain l, reacts to this proposition. He advances, for example, a criterion of evaluation of the proposed conjecture. We note Int_i, $i=1..., n$, the ith interaction, with n the number of interactions. In the most elementary form, an interaction Int_i of an actor A_k, at the moment t, is characterized by one or several transmitted messages. Thus, we consider a message as being a form of representation of *the knowledge domain*. It can be characterized by a *syntactic element* (for example, verb or noun), with a *specific semantic* to a knowledge domain. We call these elements, ***entities of analysis*** and we note e_j, where $j=1,..., m$.

Then, for analyzing the collaborative and distributed design process, each interaction is filtered with the aide of the entities of analysis. The filtered interaction ***Int_j*** is called *enriched interaction*. It is noted ***Int'_i***. Then, the relationship between the enriched interactions ***Int'_i*** and the entities of analysis ***e_j*** is given by the matrix ***C[c_ij]***, where $i=1..., n; j=1..., m$. If the enriched interaction ***Int'_i***, contains the entities of analysis e_j, then ***C_ij=1***, otherwise ***C_ij=0***.

For example, a collaborative and distributed design is done within the GRACC. Four research laboratories (CRAN-Nancy, IRCCyN-Nantes, M3M-Belfort and 3S-Grenoble) have participated in this experience. The problem is the design of a children's trailer. A group of work with four actors was constituted with a *project manager*, a *form designer*, a *frame designer* and a *link designer*. The design experiences that we have carried out are mainly *remote design experiences* which implement computer means and software of the market (CAD, MS-Office, video conference, sharing of applications...). There were four meetings overall. The total duration of each synchronous meeting is two hours and their corresponding corpus contains approximately 750 interventions. We analyzed the first synchronous meeting of the experience of collaborative design (*GRACC*). For this design experience, the matrix ***C[c_ij]*** (see Figure 1), corresponding to an extract of the corpus, represents the relation between the enriched interactions ***Int'_i*** and the entities of analysis e_j.

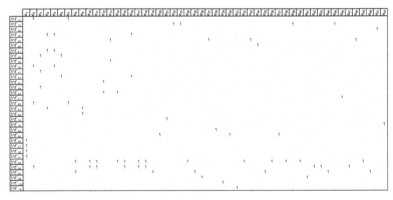

Figure 1 – Matrix ***C[c_ij]***.

Identification of state-problems and their dynamics. In the case when a family of enriched interactions corresponds to a family of entities of analysis, the matrix ***C[c_ij]***, $i=1..., n; j=1..., m$ takes a particular form. Here, the partition of the set of the enriched interactions and the partition of the set of the entities of analysis are carried out so that each part of the enriched interactions corresponds to a part of the entities of analysis. Ideally, the search of these correspondences allows the decomposition of the matrix ***C[c_ij]***, in sub-matrix C(Diagonal) and C(Out-Diagonal) where sub–matrices C(Diagonal) are filled only with "1", and sub-matrix C(Out-Diagonal) are filled with "0". In practice, it is not always the case. During the interaction, it is necessary to have confrontation and the negotiation in order to reach to finally a consensus. Mathematically, the search of the families of enriched interactions and the families of entities of analysis is a search problem of simultaneous partitions in the two sets, the *enriched interactions* and the *entities of analysis*, in correspondences or quasi-correspondences, class of partition to class of partition. Then, the basic idea consists in carrying out permutations of lines and columns of the matrix $C[c_{ij}]$ such as to find the structure of the correspondence on the crossing of these two sets (Marcotorchino, 1987).

The structure of the matrix $C[c_{ij}]$ makes possible to identify the families of entities of analysis. The sequence of these *entities of analysis* in a family is called *concept* (Movahed-Khah, 2005). Emergence here means that a concept, as a group of entities of analysis, was not previously represented, but can be represented because it has been constructed now (Gero, 1998). Moreover, the correspondences per block permit to characterize a family of interventions by the corresponding concepts. Each concept offers a fairly idea to a state of the design process and the related design problem, which we called state-problem. Thus, a family of enriched interactions allows identifying the *state-problem* of the collaborative and distributed design process.

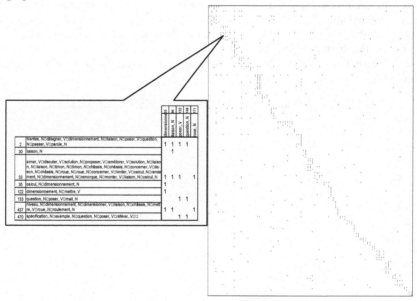

Figure 2 – Partition of matrix $C[c_{ij}]$ for a meeting.

For example, the "Figure 2" shows the partition of enriched interactions-entities of analysis matrix $C[c_{ij}]$ for the considered design experience. It shows the identification of the 33 families of entities of analysis corresponding to 33 *state-problems*.

The relationship between the interventions and state-problems permit to note their continue evolution. Then, the design process, as a dynamics system, is represented as a change of qualitative states. A state can be considered as attractor in a dynamics system. It is represented then, as a state which drew up the other neighbour's states. The representation of the state-problems in time allows to note the dynamics of the problems in relation to the design process organization, as well as in relation to the evolution and/or the emergence of the solutions. For example, the dynamics of 33 state-problems in "Figure 2" is represented in "Figure 3" for a synchronous meeting of 500 interventions (two hours). The analysis of these state-problems shows that this dynamics is characterized rather by many irregular leaps. These leaps, probably unforeseeable, show that the design process, on a micro scale, is far from being harmonious. In fact, these leaps depend strongly as much on the structural causes, such as the auto-organization (or self-organizing) inside of the team (Stempfle, 2002), the human action, such as the creative characteristic of the design (Movahed-Khah, 2006 and Movahed-Khah, 2004).

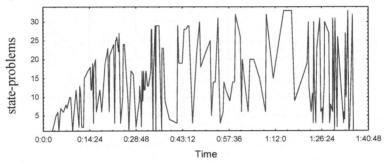

Figure 3 – Dynamics of state-problems in a synchronous meeting.

3. RELATIONSHIP BETWEEN DIOS AND STATE-PROBLEMS

The relationship between Design Intermediate objects (DIOs) and State-Problems (SPs) can be represented by a matrix which consists in crossing a set of DIOs with of a set of state-problems and to look what occurs in the cells from crossing. We note v number of DIOs and O_K, $k=1..., v$, the kth emerged DIO at the moment t. During the design process, the actors interact while discussing on DIOs. For example, an actor puts, at the moment t, the O_K in public (shared space in synchronous situation). This emergence of O_K in public gives the opportunities of a discussion on this object and influence the exchanges (interactions) between the actors. Table 1 shows some emerged DIOs in design process experience.

Table 1– Represented DIOs in a meeting of distributed and collaborative design.

Software	SolidWork 2001	MS-Excel 2000	Ansys	MS-Photo Editor	NetMeeting
Object	3D model	Table sheet	FEM result	Image	Sketch

These interactions are marked by the various acts which are transcribed, initially in the corpus, and afterwards by our means of analysis, in the form of concepts emergence (which are related to the state-problems). We note $P_l(t)$, $l=1..., w$ with w the total number of the state-problems, the emerged state-problem l, at the moment t.

Then, the relation between the state-problem $P_l(t)$ and the DIO O_k is given by the matrix $Y[y_{kl}(t)]$, $k=1..., v$ $l=1..., w$. If the emerged DIO in public O_k is simultaneous with the emerged state-problems $P_l(t)$ then we have $y_{kl}(t)=1$, otherwise $y_{kl}(t)=0$. The matrix $Y[y_{kl}(t)]$ represents the relation between DIOs (rows) and the state-problems according to time (columns) (see Figure 4).

For representation the number of occurrences x_{kl} of the O_k in the state-problem P_l, we transform the first matrix $Y[y_{kl}(t)]$ into a quantitative matrix $X[x_{kl}]$, $k=1..., q$ $l=1..., n$ (see Figure 5).

$$Y[y_{kl}(t)] = \begin{array}{c|cccccc} & P_a(t_I) & P_b(t_{II}) & P_c(t_{III}) & P_d(t_{IV}) & ... & P_w(t_t) \\ O_1 & y_{1a}(t_I) & y_{1b}(t_{II}) & y_{1c}(t_{III}) & y_{1d}(t_{IV}) & ... & y_{1w}(t_t) \\ O_2 & y_{2a}(t_I) & y_{2b}(t_{II}) & y_{2c}(t_{III}) & y_{2d}(t_{IV}) & ... & y_{2w}(t_t) \\ O_3 & y_{3a}(t_I) & y_{3b}(t_{II}) & y_{3c}(t_{III}) & y_{3d}(t_{IV}) & ... & y_{3w}(t_t) \\ O_4 & y_{4a}(t_I) & y_{4b}(t_{II}) & y_{4c}(t_{III}) & y_{4d}(t_{IV}) & ... & y_{4w}(t_t) \\ ... & ... & ... & ... & ... & ... & ... \\ O_v & y_{va}(t_I) & y_{vb}(t_{II}) & y_{vc}(t_{III}) & y_{vd}(t_{IV}) & ... & y_{vw}(t_t) \end{array}$$

$$X[x_{kl}] = \begin{array}{c|cccccc} & P_a & P_b & P_c & P_d & ... & P_w \\ O_1 & x_{1a} & x_{1b} & x_{1c} & x_{1d} & ... & x_{1w} \\ O_2 & x_{2a} & x_{2b} & x_{2c} & x_{2d} & ... & x_{2w} \\ O_3 & x_{3a} & x_{3b} & x_{3c} & x_{3d} & ... & x_{3w} \\ O_4 & x_{4a} & x_{4b} & x_{4c} & x_{4d} & ... & x_{4w} \\ ... & ... & ... & ... & ... & ... & ... \\ O_v & x_{va} & x_{vb} & x_{vc} & x_{vd} & ... & x_{vw} \end{array}$$

Figure 4 – Crossed matrice $Y[y_{kl}(t)]$.   Figure 5 – Quantitative matrix $X[x_{kl}]$.

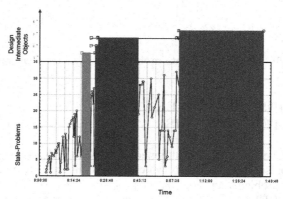

Figure 6 – Overlapping of state-problems and DIOs.

Structuring of the matrix $X[x_{kl}]$ permits to identify the families of the emerged state-problems during emergence of the families of O_k. If a family of DIOs corresponds to a family of state-problems, then sub-matrices corresponding to the diagonal blocs of the matrix $X[x_{kl}]$ represent the strong relationship between DIOs and SPs. For example, the matrix $X[x_{kl}]$ (see Figure 7) represents the relation between the four DIOs and the 33 emerged state-problems in an experience meeting (see the example of overlapping represented by different colours in "Figure 6"). "Figure 8" presents the structuring of matrix $X[x_{kl}]$. The result of structuring helps us to identify the emerged state-problems in family of SPs in relation with each family of DIO.

	P₁	P₂	P₃	P₄	P₅	P₆	P₇	P₈	P₉	P₁₀	P₁₁	P₁₂	P₁₃	P₁₄	P₁₅	P₁₆	P₁₇	P₁₈	P₁₉	P₂₀	P₂₁	P₂₂	P₂₃	P₂₄	P₂₅	P₂₆	P₂₇	P₂₈	P₂₉	P₃₀	P₃₁	P₃₂	P₃₃
O₁	0	1	1	0	0	1	0	0	0	0	0	3	0	0	1	1	1	2	1	1	0	0	0	0	0	0	0	0	0	0	0	0	0
O₂	0	0	0	0	0	0	0	0	0	0	0	0	0	0	0	0	0	0	0	1	0	1	0	0	0	0	0	0	0	0	0	0	0
O₃	4	2	2	0	0	2	0	1	4	1	1	4	3	1	1	2	6	0	1	0	2	3	3	2	1	1	2	5	0	0	0	0	0
O₄	4	2	5	2	0	6	1	1	2	2	1	2	2	4	4	0	0	0	1	4	0	0	2	0	0	2	2	0	0	3	3	3	3

Figure 7 – Quantitative matrix $X[x_{kl}]$.

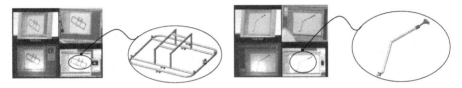

		A											B	C											D								
		P_5	P_7	P_8	P_1	P_{19}	P_{28}	P_{29}	P_{31}	P_{32}	P_{33}	P_6		P_2	P_9	P_{12}	P_{13}	P_{16}	P_{17}	P_{21}	P_{22}	P_{23}	P_{24}	P_{25}	P_3	P_4	P_6	P_{10}	P_{14}	P_{15}	P_{20}	P_{26}	P_{27}	P_{30}
A	O_2																																	
B	O_1												1				1																	
C	O_3													1	1	1	1	1	1	1	1	1	1	1	1		1							
D	O_4													1	1	1	1	1				1			1	1	1	1	1	1	1	1	1	1

Figure 8 – Partition of matrix *X[xₖᵢ]* (threshold >= 33%).

Initially, the chaining of (the set of) these state-problems enables us to describe the concepts relating to the contents of DIOs. For example, O_3 and O_4 (see Figure 9) are respectively related with the family of SPs $\{P_1,P_2,P_3,P_6,P_9,P_{12},P_{13},P_{16},P_1,P_{21},P_{22}, P_{23},P_{24},P_{25}\}$ and the family of SPs $\{P_1,P_2,P_9,P_{12},P_{13},P_{23},P_3,P_4,P_6,P_{10},P_{14},P_{15},P_{20},P_{26}, P_{27},P_{30}\}$.

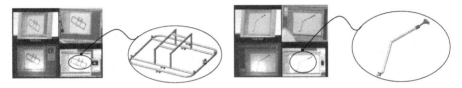

Figure 9 – The 3rd and 4th DIOs in synchronous representation.

The search for the entities of analysis relating to SPs, permit to understand and describe the simultaneous emergence of the corresponding of the DIOs. For example, some entities of analysis in the family of state-problems corresponding to the simultaneous emergence of the *3rd* DIO, are the following:

P_2= {**dimensionnement, .N** ; **liaison, .N** ; poser, .V ; question, .N ; **roue, .N**} ;
P_3= {attendre, .V ; **châssis, .N** ; commencer, .V } ;
P_{12}= {homme, .N ; **main, .N**, humain, .N} ;
P_{24}= {accrocher, .V ; dessous, .N} ;
P_{25}= {regarder, .V ; **dimension, .N**, dessus, .N} ;

The interpretation of these relative data concerning the O_3 enables us to enter to the implicit contents of DIO via the verbalization of the thoughts. Hence, we note that the interactions of the actors in the presence of O_3 are focused on the problems of configuration (orientation) of the product components, the computing from mechanics of materials (strength of materials) and the ergonomic aspect.

4. CONCLUSION

The implementation of collaborative and distributed multi-agent systems requires to observe, to model and to analyze the design process with finer granularities levels. In this paper, a framework for understanding the relationship between state-problems and simultaneous emergence of DIOs in the collaborative and distributed design is proposed. The interaction between actors in the presence of DIOs and during this design process shows that the dynamics of DIOs is an influential variable on the management of the meetings. The analysis of the state–problems and their relationship with DIOs, in a real experience of distributed and collaborative design, shows that theirs dynamics is the result of the interactions of actors with DIOs in the public space (shared space). Moreover, these dynamics, apparently instantaneous, show that this process strongly depends on the relationship between the emergence of DIOs and the state-problems. Based on the proposed approach, we are currently working on the development of a multi-agents systems for discovering the influence of the DIOs on the state-problems in the computer mediated distributed and collaborative design process.

5. REFERENCES

1. Baya V. and Leifer L. Understanding design information handling behaviour using time and information measure. Proceedings of the 1995 Design Engineering Technical Conferences, ed. A. C. Ward, ASME DE- 1995, Vol. 83, Vol. 2: 555-562.
2. Boujut J.F. and Blanco E. Intermediary objects as a means to foster cooperation in engineering design. Int. Workshop on the role of objects in design cooperation, COOP'2000, Sophia Antipolis, mai 2000.
3. Chiu M. An organizational view of design communication in design collaboration. Design Studies, 2002, Vol. 23, Issue 2: 187-210.
4. Coiera E. Interaction design theory. International Journal of Medical Information 00, 2002: 1-18.
5. Dong A. and Agogino A.M. Text analysis for constructing design representations. Artificial Intelligence in Engineering, April 1997, Volume 11, Issue 2: 65-75.
6. Garro O., Salau I. and Martin P. Distributed Design Theory and Methodology. Int. J. of Concurrent Engineering: Research and Application (CERA), 1995, 3(3): pp 43-54.
7. Gero J. Concept formation in design. Knowledge-based systems, 1998, Vol. 11: 429-435. Mer S., Tichkiewitch S. and Jeantet A. Les Objets Intermédiaires de la Conception: Modélisation, et Communication, dans J Caelen et K Zreik « La communicationnel pour concevoir », EUROPIA, ISBN: 2-909285-04-9, 1995: 21-41.
8. Gregory N., Blanco E., Brassac C. et Garro O. Analyse de la distribution en conception par la dynamique des objets intermédiares, dans les actes de design, Les objets en conception, coordinateurs Trousse B. et Zreik K., Editions Europia, 1997: 135-155.
9. Marcotorchino F. A Unified Approach of the Block-Seriation Problems. Journal of Applied Stochastic Models and Data Analysis, 1987, 3(2): pp 1-13.
10. Movahed-Khah R., Ostrosi E. and Garro O. Analyse des processus de conception mécanique distribuée à l'aide d'émergence des concepts. CFM (17 ème Congrès Français de Mécanique), Université de technologie de Troyes du 29 août au 2 septembre 2005.
11. Movahed-Khah R., Ostrosi E. and Garro O. An approach based on the communicative traces for the collaborative design process analysis. Scenario-Based Design of Cooperative Systems, COOP'04 (6th International Conference on the Design of Cooperative system), May 11-14 2004: pp 31-39, Hyères, France.
12. Movahed-Khah R., Ostrosi E. and Garro O. A Cluster Based Approach for Collaborative Design Process Analysis. In "Advances in Design", Published by Springer-Verlag UK, Edited by H.A. ElMaraghy and W.H. Elmaraghy, ISBN: 1846280044, Jan 2006.
13. Ostergaard D. and Summers D. A taxonomic classification of collaborative design. ICED03, Stockholm, August 19-21, 2003.
14. Ostrosi E., Ferney M. and Garro O. A Fractal Approach for Concurrent Engineering. Int. J. of Concurrent Engineering: Research and Application (CERA), 2003: 11(4): 249-265.
15. Sanchis E., Pan Z.Y. and Selves J-L. Emerging Solutions, Software Agents and New Product Development. in CE 2001.
16. Stempfle J. and Badke-Schaub P. Thinking in design teams- an analysis of team communication. Design studies 23: 2002: 473-496.

AN INTEGRATED DESIGN SYSTEM FOR MOLDED INTERCONNECT DEVICES (3D-MID)

Yong Zhuo, Christian Alvarez and Klaus Feldmann
University Erlangen-Nuremberg, Germany
{zhuo, alvarez, feldmann}@faps.uni-erlangen.de

In this paper, MIDCAD, an integrated design system for Molded Interconnect Devices, is presented and some important techniques for the development of this design system are discussed. A series of MID-related special functions and an integrated MID product model, which are not supported by conventional MCAD und ECAD systems, were developed in MIDCAD. Based on the product model, the simulation of the injection molding process is successfully integrated into MIDCAD. A module supporting the connection of MID-specific automatic placement equipment is also being developed in MIDCAD in order to be able to accomplish a manufacturing-oriented optimization and to guarantee the manufacturability of MID products.

1. INTRODUCTION

One of the fundamental and trend-setting innovations in the field of mechatronics is the direct integration of mechanical and electronic functions using Molded Interconnect Devices (3D-MID technology).

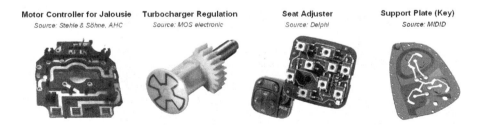

Figure 1 – Current applications of the MID technology.

Some current products using MID technology are shown in Figure 1. One can easily see that these products do not contain conventional 2D circuit board but circuits running directly on the surfaces of the 3D circuit carrier. The enhanced design freedom and the integration of electronic as well as mechanical functions in a single injection-molded part allow a substantial miniaturization. They provide

enormous technical and economic potential and offer a remarkably improved ecological behavior compared to conventional circuit boards (Feldmann, 1998).

Currently, the common MID-design process uses the coupling of 2D electronic
CAD (ECAD) and 3D mechanical CAD (MCAD). The MCAD system does e.g. not
know what electrical connectivity is, and on the other way an ECAD system ignores
any requirements of 3D circuit carriers because of its two-dimensional nature. Such
a design process slows down the application of MID technology to a considerable
degree.

The difference between MIDs and conventional mechatronic products is the
mutual dependency between the geometry and the electronics. That makes it
impossible to independently design one aspect without considering the other one in
the system integration design stage (VDI 2206, 2004). Consequently, the efficient
design of complex MID-products requires a special design tool which should
consider the mechanical structure and electronic function of MIDs in a 3D
environment at the same time. It has to provide design functions especially fitted to
the needs of MIDs by combining functions of ECAD and MCAD systems. Existing
tools like EM-Designer (Zuken, 2006) and NEXTRA (Mecadtron, 2006) only
provide a rather limited support for an efficient design of complex MID-products
(Zhuo, 2005).

2. FRAMEWORK OF THE INTEGRATED MIDCAD SYSTEM

A prototype-like MIDCAD system has been developed to provide designers with an
integrated environment for design and analysis of MID products. An overview of the
system architecture is shown in Figure 2.

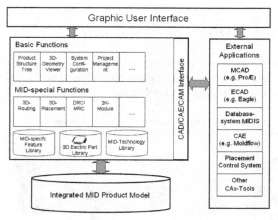

Figure 2 – Architecture of the integrated MIDCAD system.

MIDCAD was developed under the condition to ensure a large freedom of
geometrical modelling while at the same time providing an integration of electronic
and mechanic functions in one system. The system is based on the commercial 3D-
MCAD system Pro/ENGINEER and was developed using Pro/TOOLKIT, which
is a full C++ application program interface (API) that allows MIDCAD to

communicate directly with Pro/E at the code level. The choice of a 3D-MCAD system as foundation has the advantage that the system can directly use the basic modelling functions and geometrical processing algorithms to build up an integrated design environment for MID products.

The basic functions provide the user with an overview of the product structure in order to facilitate the development of a complex product. By integrating MID-specific functions, the MID design is supported more effectively in MIDCAD than in other CAD systems. Among these special functions, 3D-placement and 3D-routing are essential for MID design. There are different libraries, for example a 3D electronic part library, an MID-specific feature library, an MID technology library and an MID material library available in the system. External applications refer to independent CAx-tools, which are used during the MID design process. These CAx-tools are usually mono-disciplinary and lack the ability to communicate with each other directly. In order to realize an integrated design environment, two conditions have to be fulfilled: integrated modelling for MID products and integration of independent CAx-tools. In MIDCAD, a CAD/CAE/CAM interface to realize the data exchange between MIDCAD and these CAx-tools is developed. MIDCAD also contains an integrated product model in which design- and analysis-related data are stored.

3. THE INTEGRATED MID PRODUCT MODEL

3.1 Conception of an integrated MID product model

Designing products based on MID technology is a complex process and involves interactions between different engineering domains. In this case, the product model has to contain information from the electronics domain such as the data of the circuit diagram as well as information from the mechanics domain, e.g. the geometry model of the circuit carrier. Within the individual domains specialized CAx-systems are often used. In this case, apart from the horizontal integration of the information from different domains (here: MCAD and ECAD), the product model must also vertically integrate the information from the different product development phases (here: CAD and CAE). The concept of the integrated MID product model is shown in Figure 3.

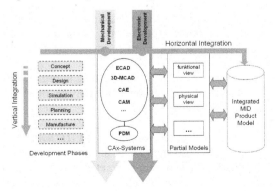

Figure 3 – Concept of an integrated MID product model.

3.2 Horizontal integration of electronic and mechanical information

In order to realize the horizontal integration of electronic and mechanical data, the product model must be composed of two partial models: one for describing the electric circuit and another one for the 3D geometry of the circuit carrier.

For the description of the ECAD and MCAD partial models, the multi-view technology is used to define a physical and a functional view. In the functional model, the data regarding electric circuits, e.g. part list, net list and electronic-referred aspects can be described abstractly. Every physical model can be connected to one functional model; the physical model describes the geometric structure information. This schema and methodology, which is similar to STEP-AP210 (Electronic Assembly, Interconnect and Packaging Design, ISO, 2001), is applied to horizontal integration and forms the basis of the whole integrated product model. In MIDCAD, the application objects of AP210 are used to describe horizontal integration and to create an electromechanical data model.

3.3 Vertical integration of CAD/CAE information

In order to realize the vertical integration of data from different product development phases, the feature technology is applied in MIDCAD. That way, analysis-related data, e.g. material data or boundary condition etc., can be assigned to the corresponding features, and later be used to create a simulation model for the injection molding process.

Definition and type of features for MID products
As the majority of MID products are thin-walled thermoplastic parts, the general feature types can be hierarchically defined (Al-Ashaab, 2003; Deng, 2002), such as wall, hole, boss, rib, round, etc. Wall features form the basis of a plastic part. Hole, rib and boss features belong to the development features, which are developed from wall features. The treatment features include chamfers, rounds and fillets which are used for the treatment of other features.

Furthermore, MID-specific features have been defined to represent some special construction elements that have additional electronic functions coming from the direct electromechanical integration. These specific features behave like electronic components, but they are only geometric structures belonging to the circuit carrier. Therefore, these special features such as vias, connectors, battery holders etc. belong to the component features. Some types of specific features are shown in Figure 4. The specific feature type "via" e.g. consists of a hole through which the electric current can run from one surface to another.

These general and specific features are created and organized using an additional feature tree. The geometry of the features can easily be modified afterwards due to the use of a parametric modelling method.

Application of features for the integration of CAD-CAE data
The features not only contain geometric but also non-geometric information which are called feature attributes. The non-geometric information can be electronic-related data as well as analysis- and manufacturing-related data (Figure 4).

In order to support the simulation of the injection molding process, the feature attribute must contain information needed for later analysis. The part feature contains the analysis-related attributes such as material, constraints, analysis type and the relevant boundary condition and processing condition data.

Once the geometry of the carrier has been created, the general features can be defined by assigning the desired geometry to them, and the geometry of the special features can be automatically created and defined by using the developed feature functions. After the geometry has been defined, non-geometric information relating to these features can also be specified by using the provided user interface. With all the features created or defined and their relevant information specified, the features will be automatically merged into the integrated product model.

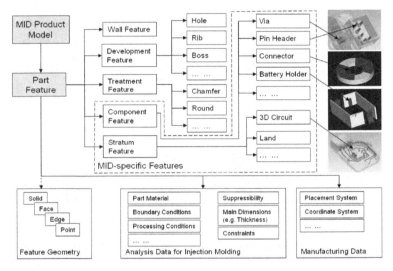

Figure 4 – Types of MID features and integration of CAD-CAE data.

4. MID-RELATED SPECIAL FUNCTIONS

The development and realization of special functions in MIDCAD can greatly facilitate the design process of MID products (Figure 5).

The most important MID design task lies in the placement of the electronic components and the routing of circuits on and/or within the circuit carrier. Therefore, the core functions 3D-routing and 3D-placement in MIDCAD are developed as a substitute for 2D-layout functions in traditional 2D-ECAD systems.

The 3D-placement function has been developed based on the Pro/E-assembly functions and had to be enhanced for the application to MIDs by performing design- and manufacturing rule checks (DRC/MRC) during placement.

Autorouting on traditional 2D multilayer Printed Circuit Boards (PCB) has been well developed since the 70s, but there are still few solutions for 3D automatic routing. Compared to traditional routing, MID-routing has to deal with a more complex geometry. For MIDCAD, new 3D autorouting algorithms (Feldmann, 2003, 2005) were developed and integrated, so that the routing on the surfaces of the circuit carrier will be completed automatically while at the same time the design rules regarding conductor and insulator width are satisfied. Due to the complexity of the 3D MID-design, manual routing, ripup and re-route functions can be used afterwards in order to improve the result.

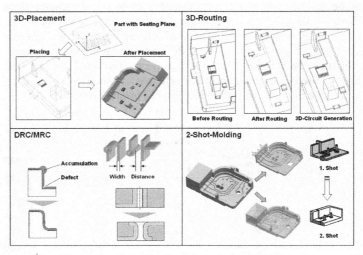

Figure 5 – Specific functions in MIDCAD.

Among the various MID manufacturing processes, 2-shot-molding offers the greatest geometric freedom of design. The term 2-shot-molding refers to the molding of two plastic materials on top of each other (3-D MID, 2004). The 2K-Module is a special function to support the MID-design using 2-shot-molding. Different types of 2-shot-molding can be selected and the cross section of circuits can be defined. Based on the geometry model of the carrier and the routing result of the 3D circuit, the geometry model of the first and the second shot for the mold design are created automatically.

The basic function of the DRC/MRC module is to check the minimum 3D-distance between the electronic components and special features such as tracks, pads, vias etc. According to the selected design or manufacturing rules, DRC/MRCs run automatically by extracting the corresponding data and relationships from the product model.

5. INTEGRATION OF THE SIMULATION OF THE INJECTION MOLDING PROCESS

As most circuit carriers of MID products are thermoplastic, either one- or two-shot-molding is used for manufacturing. By simulating the molding process, moldability and measures of quality can be assured in an early development phase.

To perform the simulation, a special analysis model has to be built from the integrated product model. After the analysis-related information is defined and vertically integrated into the product model, the simulation model can be abstracted.

This involves the derivation of a simplified geometric model and the abstraction of non-geometric analysis-related information, such as gate location etc. Simplifying the geometric model is realized by suppressing non-significant features.

In order to provide an integrated environment for MID product design, the CAE-system "Moldflow Plastics Insight (MPI)" is to be directly connected to MIDCAD. Even though Pro/E already has an integrated module called "Pro/PlasticAdvisor" to simulate the molding process, designers still need to manually generate an analysis model and to specify the analysis-related information. Both systems are in fact connected on a relatively low level. The application programming interface (API) of MPI makes MPI functionality available to external applications like MIDCAD. A special interface is developed based on the API of MPI so that MIDCAD can automatically activate the analysis routines in MPI to run an injection molding simulation. The simulation model with the geometric and non-geometric information can be used directly without extra data or file exchange.

6. CONNECTION TO MID PLACEMENT EQUIPMENT

The development of suitable placement equipment and assembly systems for MID products is mainly affected by the complex geometry of the circuit carrier and the positions of electronic parts. Two alternative specific placement equipments were developed and realized at the author's institute (Krimi, 2001).

The number of electronic components to be placed on the circuit carrier is usually so large that a manual input of the assembly-relevant data would be far too time consuming and too expensive. An automatic generation of manufacturing data and connection to the placement equipment are therefore very important to improve design efficiency and product quality.

Hence, in the 3D part library of MIDCAD the location of the sucking point and a corresponding coordinate system must be defined for every part. Apart from the coordinate system, the seating plane and geometric information of the individual part are also necessary. Based on the 3D-placement the part placement position with respect to the coordinate system of the circuit carrier and placement machine is to be calculated. Then the static collision checking must be carried out to identify potential problems during placement.

After the first static collision check in MIDCAD, the collision-free instruction list from the design view can be provided with the help of the interface between MIDCAD and the control system of the placement machine. Afterwards, the control system processes the part-relevant data together with other machine-relevant data, e.g. mapping file, feeder position etc. Before creating the final collision-free instruction list, a kinematics simulation for dynamic collision checking during assembly can be applied.

7. CONCLUSION

Designing products based on MID technology is a complex process and involves interactions between many engineering domains: electronic circuit, mechanic geometry etc. The design automation and optimization level for MID-products is much less advanced than for many other high-tech products. In order to improve MID design, MIDCAD, an integrated design system for Molded Interconnect Devices is presented and some important techniques for the development of this design system are discussed. MIDCAD contains a series of MID-related special functions, which are not supported by MCAD and ECAD systems now. Apart from these special functions, the development of an integrated product model in MIDCAD is a key task. The integrated product model has been developed based on multiple views, feature modeling and STEP techniques to support not only mechanical and electronic integrated design but also other product development phases. For the design of MID-products, the simulation of the injection molding process is a vital prerequisite to ensure moldability and measures of quality. Based on the product model and developed interface the simulation of the injection molding process could be integrated successfully into MIDCAD to support the concept of design for moldability. A module supporting the connection of MID-specific automatic placement equipment is also developed in MIDCAD in order to be able to accomplish a manufacturing-oriented optimization and to guarantee the manufacturability of MID-products according to the concept of design for manufacturing.

8. REFERENCES

1. Al-Ashaab A, Rodriguez K, Molina A, Aca M.C, Saeed M, Abdalla H. Internet-based Collaborative Design for an Injection-moulding System. In: Concurrent Engineering: Research and Application. 2003. 11: 289-297.
2. Deng YM, Britton GA, Lam YC, Tor SB, MA YS. Feature-based CAD-CAE integration model for injection-moulded product design. In: International Journal of Production Research. 2002. 40: 3737-3750.
3. 3-D MID e.V. Technologie 3D-MID, Räumliche elektronische Baugruppen. Carl Hanser Verlag, 2004.
4. Feldmann K. Introduction: MID – Entering Markets by Products and Technologies. In: Proc. of the 3rd International Congress on Molded Interconnect Devices. Erlangen, 1998. 5-17.
5. Feldmann K, Shi YP, Zhuo Y. Three-Dimensional Automatic Routing in Design of Molded Interconnect Devices (MID). In: Production Engineering. 2003. X-1: 65-68.
6. Feldmann K, Zhuo Y, Alvarez C. 3D gridless routing for the design of molded interconnect devices (MID). In: Production Engineering. 2005. XII-2: 89-94.
7. ISO 10303-210, 2001, Industrial automation systems and integration – Product data representation and exchange – Part 210: Application protocol: Electronic assembly, interconnection, and packaging design, International Organization for Standardization, Geneva, Switzerland.
8. Krimi S. Analyse und Optimierung von Montagesystemen in der Elektronikproduktion, Dissertation, FAPS, Universität Erlangen-Nürnberg, 2001.
9. MECADTRON GmbH. http://www.mecadtron.de/produkte/nextra.php.de (Date: 04.2006).
10. N.N. VDI-Richtlinie 2206 Entwicklungsmethodik für mechatronische Systeme. VDI-Verlag, Düsseldorf, 2004.
11. Zhuo Y, Alvarez C, Feldmann K. MIDCAD – Ein rechnergestütztes System für den Entwurf räumlicher spritzgegossener Schaltungsträger. In: VDI-Berichte 1892.2. VDI Verlag 2005, 1117-1135.
12. ZUKEN GmbH. http://www.zuken.com/electromechanical/em_designer.asp (Date: 04.2006).

A NOVEL KNOWLEDGE MANAGEMENT METHODOLOGY TO SUPPORT COLLABORATIVE PRODUCT DEVELOPMENT

Wai M Cheung and Paul G Maropoulos
University of Bath, UK
w.m.cheung@bath.ac.uk, p.g.maropoulos@bath.ac.uk

This paper discusses the theoretical aspects and applications of a novel methodology for exploiting a knowledge management editor tool to structure organizational knowledge. An organizational knowledge framework for capturing and representing design and manufacturing know-how has been defined using an ontological approach. The key business benefit of adopting such an approach arises from the closer integration between the key technical and business activities taking place during early design. In particular the effectiveness of decision making is increased.

1. INTRODUCTION

Ontology's are increasingly becoming important in the fields of intelligent searching on the web, knowledge sharing and reuse, and knowledge management (Hausser 2000). Ontology's have been used to share and reuse knowledge and information, predominately in the field of medical informatics. The main reason ontology's have become so popular is the fact that they provide a shared and common understanding of a domain that can be communicated between people and application systems (Davies *et al.* 2002). Lately, there have been an increasing number of research projects applying ontological techniques in the context of product development (Ciocoiu *et al.* 2001, Duineveld *et al.* 2000, Lin and Harding 2003). However, none of these projects directly address the issues of utilizing ontology technique to share manufacturing knowledge during product development in a collaborative and distributed manner.

The aim of this paper is to discuss a methodology of creating an axiom-controlled ontology for use in an "organizational knowledge" framework. An axiom is a statement that defines or constrains some aspects of the knowledge model and is intended to control or influence the behaviour of the model (Ontoprise 2004). In addition, this paper describes a manufacturing know-how data structure which has been constructed as part of an "organizational knowledge" framework using an ontological approach. The term organizational knowledge is defined as "a collective wisdom of a firm which may be explicit, in the form of databases or documents, or tacit, expressed by action" (Rich and Duchessi 2001). An ontological approach can be used to elaborate the organizational knowledge by defining the semantics to capture the meaning of the terms and axioms (to define a set of rules if applicable). This is used to enhance and encapsulate the way of reusing the knowledge-based system in a collaborative manner within a production network.

2. KNOWLEDGE-BASED SYSTEMS AND ONTOLOGY

2.1 Introduction to Ontology

In information technology terms, an ontology is the working model of entities and interactions in some particular domain of knowledge or practices, such as electronic commerce or the activity of planning (Davies *et al.* 2002). In Artificial Intelligence (AI) terms, according to specialists at Stanford University (Noy and Klein 2004), ontology's can be used to express "a set of concepts such as things, events and relations that are specified in some way in order to create an agreed vocabulary for exchanging information, in particular over the World-Wide-Web". Apart from providing a common understanding, Valarakos *et al.* (2004) also state that ontology's can be used to facilitate dissemination and reuse of information and knowledge. The main technologies used to create ontology's are the Process Specification Language (PSL) (Schlenoff *et al.* 2000) and Web-based technologies. The standard of Web-based technologies utilised in creating ontology's are the eXtensible Markup Language (XML), the Resource Description Framework (RDF), the Web Ontology Language (OWL) (W3 2005) and the XML Metadata Interchange Format (XMI) (OMG 2005).

2.2 Using Ontology's in Knowledge Based-Systems

Given that ontology has the potential to improve knowledge capturing, organization, sharing and re-use, it was chosen in this research to create a knowledge-based system to support the organization knowledge framework. Furthermore, using ontology's in the knowledge framework can provide the following advantages:
▪   Sharing knowledge domains across the Webs.
▪   Not relying on a set of rule-based techniques.
▪   Capable of handling complex and disparate information from different domains.
    However, modelling organizational knowledge is a very complex task, often requiring a combination of different types of ontology-derived techniques. To support the organizational knowledge-based system, the following ontology techniques are considered as being important:
▪   *Domain ontology*, which organizes concepts, relations and instances that occur, as well the activities that take place, into a domain (Van Heijst *et al.* 1997).
▪   *Top-level/generic/upper-level ontology*, which organizes generic domain independent concepts and relations, explicating important semantic distinctions (Sowa 1995).
▪   *Application ontology*, which consists of the knowledge of a particular application domain (Van Heijst et al., 1997).

3. THE ORGANISATIONAL KNOWLEDGE FRAMEWORK

Figure 1, depicts the organizational knowledge framework which is an ontology-based environment that has been created specifically to manage the capture of qualitative and quantitative knowledge statements related to manufacturing and assembly processes for complex products. These knowledge statements are generated by a distributed team as shown in figure 1. The data exchange format used within the framework is the industrial standard XML. A Java-based XML Parser has been implemented for extracting the knowledge to be reused by a process planning system. The resulting process plans, which contain an evaluation of the likely quality cost and delivery performance, can be stored into an information management system as illustrated. The implementation of this framework is flexible, as the specific information systems must be adapted to the needs of the enterprise. For example, knowledge may be distributed via either a centralised PDM system or a decentralised Peer-to-Peer (P2P) network (Penserini *et al.* 2003). The research at this stage, however, has adopted the PDM system approach for knowledge management and distribution. This has been combined with a system that applies Web-based technologies to the captured knowledge statements. The captured knowledge is converted into an XML-formatted file and shared within a web-centric PDM system to support the collaborative product development process.

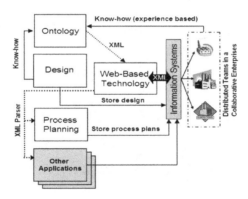

Figure 1 - The Organizational Knowledge Framework.

3.1 The General Structure of Organizational Knowledge

There are four kinds of knowledge that are generally recognized as being important in a knowledge-based economy (ITAG 1999). The first, *'Know-what'* is knowledge about facts. The second is *'Know-why'* and refers to scientific knowledge and understanding, for instance, the principles of why things happen. This also encompasses the skills often found in research laboratories or generated as a result of collaborative research between organizations. The third type of knowledge is *'Know-how'* which refers to skills and capabilities, for example, the ability to use a particular machine or skills gained through practice and experience. In industry, *'know-how'* is often used interchangeably with the term knowledge management from design to manufacturing, whether its context is described explicitly or implicitly. The final component is *'Know-who'*, which describes where in the enterprise knowledge is stored. Capturing *'Know-who'* requires a deep understanding of the expertise within an organization. In this particular application *'Know-who'* is only used to record the name of the knowledge owner, it has been implemented as an attribute of *'Know-how'* class. In future versions of the work it may be possible to make a separate module, so that meta-information about confidence in the judgement of a person may be recorded for example.

3.2 The Main Organizational Knowledge Ontology

Figure 2 shows a class taxonomy of the organizational knowledge ontology which is specifically constructed to model manufacturing knowledge for this research. According to Jenz & Partner (2003), an ontology is based on a taxonomy which represents a class hierarchy in the object-oriented world. The organizational knowledge ontology consists of three major modules, namely Organization Knowledge *'Know-how'*, *'Know-what'* and *'Know-why'*, which are defined as *is_a_kind_of* organizational knowledge. The modules are imposed with *constraints* namely *Probability, LargerTheBetter, SmallerTheBetter, NominalTheBest, Factor-Target* and *FactorBenchmark*. The research work at this stage is mainly focused on applying *Probability* to define a constraint related to the instances captured within the ontology.

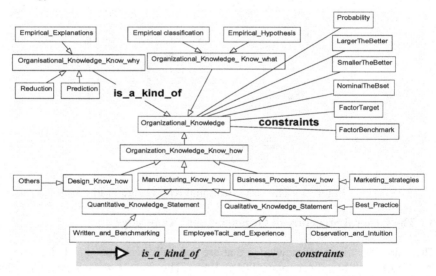

Figure 2 - The Structure of Organizational Knowledge Ontology.

Organization Knowledge *Know-how* is further broken down into different sub-levels. The *'Business_Process_Know_how'* module defines marketing strategies, purchasing, supply chains and costing data. *'Design_Know_how'* represents the information on product design and standards, and customization such as bespoke customer designs. *Manufacturing_Know_how* forms an integral part of the framework and consists of quantitative and qualitative knowledge statements related to the production processes and equipment. It captures production skills, process best practice and experience-based information. The *'Organisation_Know_what'* module is used to define empirical knowledge based upon facts and hypotheses. Finally, *'Organisation_Know_why'* defines principles of why things happen.

The organizational knowledge ontology have been developed using the knowledge building system Protégé2000 (Protégé 2000, 2004). The class diagram, shown in figure 2, was initially constructed to model the domain using the Unified Modeling Language (UML). The UML class diagram was imported into the Protégé2000 KBS Editor, via (XML Metadata Interchange Format) XMI to create the ontology. XMI is an open industry standard for applying XML to abstract systems such as UML. The intention of XMI is to propose a way to standardize XML for users to exchange information about Metadata in distributed and heterogeneous environments (OMG 2005). XML bridges part of the gap by providing the building blocks for "serializing" UML data textually. XMI is required for complex ontology-based systems, because it can capture and express the *relationships* that can be expressed using UML class diagrams (Laird 2001).

3.3 The activities to design the knowledge-based system

To design a knowledge based-system using the ontology technique is a complex task. The approach in this work proposes a way of constructing a knowledge model which involves four activities as illustrated in Figure 3:

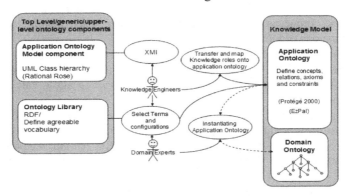

Figure 3 - Activities in the design of an ontology-based knowledge system.

a) The first activity in KBS construction is to form a UML (Unified Modelling Language) representation of the ontology and define the relations among the classes.
b) Transfer the UML class taxonomy onto the application ontology using XMI (XML Metadata Interchange) and subsequently mappings the roles and the concepts in the ontology.
c) Select and configure appropriate ontology's. This activity involves the construction of an application-specific ontology. In general, ontology construction is a difficult

process that requires the expertise of knowledge engineers and domain experts. A library of reusable ontological theories can ease this process. The knowledge engineers and domain experts work as a team to select the reusable theories and, if necessary, tune them and define agreeable vocabulary to meet the demands of the application.

d) Instantiate the application ontology with domain knowledge. While the application ontology defines which concepts are used in the domain, the application knowledge describes the actual instances of these concepts. Hence, this requires the domain experts to gather all necessary knowledge to instantiate the domain ontology.

3.3.2 The application of axioms and constraints within the Ontology

It is important to be able to define axioms and constraints within an ontology. The axioms and constraints are used to define a specific value or condition in relation to a specific knowledge statement. In terms of implementation of axioms and constraints with in the ontology, there are several plug-ins available within the Protégé 2000. The EZPal tab (Hou *et al.* 2002) is designed to facilitate the acquisition of Protégé Axiom Language (PAL) based constraints without the need to understand the language itself. The plug-in uses a library of templates based on reusable patterns of previously encoded axioms. The interface allows users to compose constraints using a 'fill-in-the-blanks' approach. The EZPal tab makes use of a Protégé-2000 ontology to store three major categories of information which is classified as *Property, Template* and *Pattern* as shown in figure 4 (a).

*   A *property* is an abstract description for the common features of a group of *templates*. Properties are not mutually exclusive: each *template* may satisfy more than one property.
*   Each *template* describes a set of frequently used axiom design *patterns* based on their semantic and structural similarities. It stores the relevant 'variation' information to allow retrieval of a specific *pattern* to allow value entries for axiom generations.
*   A *pattern* is defined as a logical sentence derived from a group of axioms that are structurally identical except for specific references. Individual *patterns* are not stored explicitly in the library but further generalized into *templates*.

For example, in the *Organisational_Knowledge* ontology, *Probability* has been declared as one of the *superclasses* used to define a constraint related to the instances captured within the ontology. In order to set the axiom constraint in the *Probability* class, there were three stages that must be executed as shown in figure 4 (a). First, the ontology builder must select which description under *(property)* is suitable to describe the constraint. In this case, the description "*Values of a slot contain slot values for related instances*" has been used. Under *(template)* there were several modes to be selected to describe the values of a slot, in this case "*At least one instances of class (name) contains (value) in slot (name)*" was the appropriate mode to be used to declare the values within the multiple slots. *Pattern* is the final stage for the ontology builder to fill in the actual values of the slots. As the selection processes are based on skill and experience, the above process may have to undergo a number of iterations in order to obtain the optimum solution.

Figure 4 (b) illustrates an example of the constraints declared in the organizational knowledge ontology as a result of using the EZPal tab. The constraints were built upon the syntax of the axioms statements, descriptions and range. The syntax describes the *Probability* factor which contains the probability values shown as direct instances in the *Probability* class. The direct instances were then selected (*instances used by*) to form an association with a specific knowledge statement.

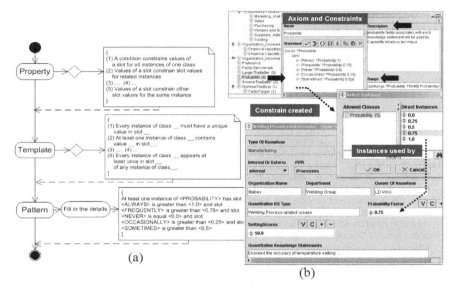

Figure 4 - (a) Method of defining constraints; (b) Example of using constraints.

4. CONCLUSION

In this paper, an Organizational Knowledge Framework using web-based technologies and information management systems for the collaboration of distributed teams in product development has been defined. The novelty of this part of the work is the development of a know-how data structure which has been constructed as part of an Organizational Knowledge Framework using an ontological approach towards capturing and reusing design and manufacturing knowledge.

This paper has also discussed the implementation of capturing and reusing manufacturing know-how using various ontological activities and the application of axioms and constraints. With the development of user-friendly ontology editing software and automatic data exchange functions, the application of ontological approaches to exchange information across the Webs is most likely to be an essential aspect of the next generation of global knowledge management tools.

5. ACKNOWLEDGMENTS

The authors would like to acknowledge the financial support of the UK's Engineering and Physical Sciences Research Council (EPSRC), for the project Grants GR/R26757/01. We are also grateful for the support of the industrial collaborators ArvinMeritor, LSC Group, Mabey & Johnson and PTC.

6. REFERENCES

1. Ciocoiu, M., Gruninger, M., Nau, D.S., "Ontologies for Integrating Engineering Applications", Journal of Computing and Information Science in Engineering, 2001, 1(1), 12-22.
2. Davies, J., Fensel, D., and van Harmelen, F., On-To-Knowledge: Semantic Web enabled Knowledge Management, John Wiley and Sons Ltd, ISBN: 2002, 0470848677.
3. Duineveld, A.J., Stoter, R., Weiden, M.R., Kenepa, B., and Benjamins, V.R., "WonderTools? - A comparative study of ontological engineering tools", International Journal of Human-Computer Studies, 2000, 52, 1111-1133.
4. Hausser, R., "The Four Basic Ontologies of Semantic Interpretation", The Tenth European – Japanese Conference on Information Modelling and Knowledge Bases, Finland, 2000, pp. 21-40.
5. Hou, C.S.J., Noy, N.F., Musen, M.A., "A Template-Based Approach Toward Acquisition of Logical Sentences", *Intelligent Information Processing 2002, World Computer Congress*, Montreal, Canada, 2002, pp. 77-89 5.
6. ITAG, "The Knowledge Economy", A submission to the New Zealand Government by the Minister for Information Technology's IT Advisory Group, August, ISBN 0-478-23435-X, http://www. med.govt.nz/pbt/infotech/knowledge_economy/. 1999.
7. Jenz & Partner, "Document of Frequently ask Questions in Ontology", Jenz & Partner GmbH, 2003, http://www.jenzundpartner.de/FAQ_Ontology.pdf
8. Laird, C., 2001, "XMI and UML Combine to Drive Product Development", Vice president, Phaseit Inc., http://www-106.ibm.com/developerworks/xml/library/x-xmi/
9. Lin, H.K. and Harding, J.A., "An Ontology Driven Manufacturing System Engineering Moderator for Global Virtual Enterprise Teams", Proceedings of the 1st International Conference on Manufacturing Research (ICMR), Glasgow, UK, 2003, pp. 365-370.
10. Noy, N.F. and Klein, M.C.A., "Ontology Evolution: Not the Same as Schema Evolution", Knowledge and Information Systems, Publisher: Springer-Verlag London Ltd, ISSN: 0219-1377 (Paper) 0219-3116, 2004, 6(4), 428 - 440.
11. OMG., 2005, http://www.omg.org
12. Ontoprise, 2004, http://www.ontoprise.de/products/ontobroker_en, Last access on 4th March 2004.
13. Penserini, L., Liu, L., Mylopoulos J., Panti M., Spalazzi L., "Cooperation Strategies for Agent-Based P2P Systems", International Journal of Web Intelligence and Agent System, 2003, 1 (1) 3-21.
14. Protégé2000, "Knowledge-Based System Development Tools", http://protege. stanford.edu/ last accessed, 3rd January 2004.
15. Rich, E. and Duchessi, P., "Models for Understanding the Dynamics of Organizational Knowledge in Consulting Firms", Proceedings of the 34th Hawaii International Conference on System Sciences, Maui, Hawaii, (HICSS-34) 3, 2001, pp. 3007-3014.
16. Schlenoff, C., Gruninger, M., Tissot, F., Valois, J., Lubell, J., and Lee, J., "The Process Specification Language (PSL) Overview and Version 1.0 Specification," National Institute of Standards and Technology, NISTIR 6459, Gaithersburg, MD, 2000.
17. Sowa, J.F., "Top-level Ontological Categories", International Journal of Human Computer Studies, 1995, 43, 669-685.
18. Van Heijst G., Schreiber A.T., and Wielinga B.J.,"Using Explicit Ontologies in Knowledge-based Systems Development", International Journal of Human-Computer Studies (IJHCS), 1997, 46, 183-291.

KNOWLEDGE ENGINEERING SYSTEMS FOR DIGITAL ENTERPRISE PERFORMANCE IMPROVEMENT

Alain Bernard, Samar Ammar-Khodja, Alexandre Candlot and Nicolas Perry

IRCCyN, Ecole Centrale de Nantes, France
{Alain.Bernard, Alexandre.Candlot, Samar.Ammar-Khodja,
Nicolas.Perry}@irccyn.ec-antes.fr

This contribution is related to the proposition of some fundamental key elements related to knowledge engineering methods applied to digital enterprise performance improvement. To face the new over unstructured information world, engineers have re-thought their ways of collaborating, taking the best of the NTIC. Knowledge structuring has a key role for an efficient actor exchange and innovation creation. A proposition of some extension points from MOKA methodology illustrates these benefits.

1. INTRODUCTION

Engineers have to face new knowledge challenges. On the one hand knowledge references are moving continuously and quickly. On the other hand, domain interest networks arise from delocalised actors from extended or different enterprises. These new virtual organizations become the knowledge expert references and knowledge exchange areas. In order to be sure if the most shared references must be believed, and if they will be able to ease the innovating process, context and expert knowledge needs have to be refined and pre-structured. To adapt the concurrent engineering approaches to this evolving environment, new innovating procedures and information flow management must be set up. Some technologies tend to support knowledge objects capitalization/use. These technologies have to integrate the dynamic aspect of the information sharing. Moreover, the user needs are different and will change. The agility of the technology should make re-structuring concepts possible depending on the expert viewpoint presentation. We aim to address this problem in this paper and to propose an intermediary state in order to propose an ideal auto-adaptive solution. The first part deals with the expertise evolution and with the organizational adaptation to the increasing potential information flow, and their impact on concurrent engineering to improve enhancement innovation. The second part illustrates this tendency. It presents a case study based on the integration of manufacturing expertise in a CAD-CAM system. The knowledge-structuring proposal is here tackled using a modified MOKA methodology that will be characterized. This case study emphasises the necessity of agile formalization and will look at the proposed approach.

2. HOW EXPERTISE FITS WITH THE IMPACT OF NEW TECHNOLOGIES IN THE PRODUCT LIFE CYCLE

Knowledge Engineering (KE) is an emerging activity area that meets new economic and industrial criteria. When classical economic models reach their limits (Perry et al., 2006) (Process costing, ABC, Job order), it contributes to the shift from an economic capital to intellectual capital driven models. Nowadays, new time lines impose PLC to anticipate customer needs and to manage day-to-day innovation. Besides, design becomes a sensitive spot where decisions are linked to all other expertise. In this section, concepts are introduced to detail this transition. First of all we shall show the different enterprise-management generations that lead to the need of a new vision of design and PLC. Then a brief epistemology of the representation concept is proposed to introduce the main model dilemma, concerning its dependency on objectives. Then, as the representation of knowledge is still being discussed among concerned groups, a model is proposed, adapted to describe design expertise. Finally the main categories of knowledge management methods are compared in order to highlight their strengths and weakness and to identify the key issues that need to be addressed to ensure the actual transition to knowledge driven organizations.

2.1 A new enterprise-management generation

These considerations are driven by the enterprise-management generation introduced by Savage (Savage, 1991) and Amidon (Amidon, 1997). To improve our understanding of the generations in the context of new technologies and KE, the levels of CMM, "Capability Maturity Model", formalized in ISO 15504 as a model for evaluation and evolution of software development capacity, has been aligned in the next Column (see Table 1). In the two last columns, a synthesis is then built, benefiting from the decision-making steps as level transitions. Horizontally, the first enterprise generation is managed directly by the *product (build)*. The main objectives are to multiply the manpower through industrialization. A given product can be produced *reproducibly* in a given situation but the global structure struggles to adapt to contextual changes. This optimisation race leads to a need for modelling in order to understand how to define concrete projects to stabilize the production cycles. When computerization first appeared in enterprises and after its first calculating use, computers assisted this optimisation and help to share personal views. The second generation associates process, product and modelling in this new dimension. Quickly understood, the next step consists in spreading project tactical advantage throughout the whole enterprise and in generalizing the use of this new dimension. The expertise becomes interrelated through a common enterprise management, with concepts like ERP or PLC. This level is characterized by the importance of collaboration and by a human-to-computer-to-human link. At this level, there is a shift from a focus on domain expertise to organizational expertise. As products and processes have been optimized with the help of modelling, this enterprise organizational level can also be optimized in the same way by a generalization of best practices. Finally, circumstances of globalisation and new technologies open the trade boundaries of enterprises and countries. Design is submitted to a higher amount of constraints. The causes of this increase can be seen in the following new requirements: quick reactivity to markets, continuously shortened life cycles, more knowledge-intensive production means, smaller batches, shift of the cost sharing in favour of the variable part, sustainable development that implies having a better estimation of real costs. The design outputs become key resources, a centre of several kinds of strategies: benchmarking (align level of expertise), lean enterprise (sharing of expertise impact), co-design (sharing of the cost of the expertise and synergy between specialties), externalisation (withdrawal of a given expertise) and relocation (driving instead of using a part of the expertise). These strategies point out a new kind of economy organized into networks.

Table 1 – Evolution of enterprise management maturity.

Enterprise Generations [Amidon]	Capability Maturity Model	Synthesis	Project Decision-Making Dimension
	Level 1 « initial »	"Fire Fighting"	
		CRAFT	
1st - Asset: Produit (unpredictable change)	Level 2 « reproductible »	"hand made"	
		INFORMATICS: Human - Computer	Operational
2nd - Asset: Project (Interdependance)	Level 3 « define »	Procedures, PC, Software Tools	
		INFORMATICS: Human - Computer - Human	Tactical
3rd - Asset: Enterprise (Technology & Systematic Management)	Level 4 « master »	Interoperability, local network, PLC integration	
		INFORMATICS: Human - Computer - Groupe	Strategic
4th - Asset: Client (global change, experience feedback)	Level 5 « optimise »	Behaviour, mystake anticipation	
		INFORMATICS: "Knowledge Workers"	
5th - Asset: Knowledge (participative innovation, symbiotic network)		autonomous learning, global network, synergy throughout fences (country, enterprise...)	

This paper aims to highlight the influences of this new generation on design and to help enrichment of actual best practices in order to produce a system taking the benefits from both and helping the transition. As representation mechanisms seem to have a deep importance in the progression through enterprise generation, the next point comes back to an epistemological construction of "representation" and proposes a simplified view of its mechanism. Based on this analysis, a positioning of knowledge and associated concepts enables the identification of a general model of value adding in design through the classical V cycle.

2.2 A need to understand and master representation

A model is a representation of ideas, concepts or knowledge that has recognized similarities with these elements (*http://w3.granddictionnaire.com*). The representation mechanism gives a first understanding of what models are able to produce and how they behave. To clarify this representation mechanism, the German discussion of Kant and Frege raises a four-step representation process (Cassin, 2004). Representation is articulated as follows: Vorstellung: Mental state of a perceived idea, Gedanken: Act to present to oneself ideas in order to handle them intellectually, Vertretung: Act to transcript an idea on a support. Repräsentierung: Vehicle supporting an idea. If we consider the classical inclusion of data in information and then in knowledge (Gardoni, 1999) (Labrousse, 2004) a KLC emerges from these four steps. Table 2 presents classical knowledge life cycles (Nonaka, 1994) (Grundstein, 1994) (Ermine *et al.,* 1996) in the context of the four-step representation mechanism. Business Process Modelling (BPM) or Generalized Enterprise Reference Architecture and Methodology (GERAM) also keep up with this articulation. So the global approaches of four classical examples of BPM and GERAM are added to Table 2.

The main lesson from the analysis of "representation" and the comparison of these different approaches is that a model is objective-dependant. A representation, and by consequence, its efficiency has to fit with the expected use. But the reuse is still very difficult and most real industrial experiments start from scratch (Bachimont, 1996). The new design constraints described above require flexibility of resources, through notably the concept of a "platform". This efficiency of reuse is specifically important for design expertise. Design requires knowledge adapted to a given situation by expert decision. The value of the design phase lies in these decisions. It transforms the investment cost in core enterprise competencies, into artifacts negotiated through a price to the customer. To facilitate design, a capitalization methodology should be deployed. The following point summarizes KE methods through the transformation of knowledge (K) into knowledge bases (KB) to be finally exploited through knowledge-based systems (KBS). These systems assist the decision makers. Compared to research on ontology and the emergence of social networks, this progression K $\rightarrow$ KB $\rightarrow$ KBS constitutes the backbone of a global methodological research to help design to optimize its decisions impacting the PLC.

Table 2 – Knowledge representation mechanism compared to SoA KLC.

		ENRICHMENT		DEGRADATION		
		Perception (DATA)	Mental Act (INFORMATION)	Action (KNOWLEDGE / INFORMATION)	Vehicle (DATA)	Point of view
Philosophy	Kant / Frege	Vorstellung	Gedanken	Vertretung	Repräsentierung	German Epistemology
	Approximative Translation	Sensation	Thought	Proxy	Representation	
Consolidated KM Meanings for "Representation"		Perception	Mental Act	Action	Vehicle	Point of view
KM (Knowledge Management)	Nonaka SECI Model	Internalization	Combination	Externalization	Socialization	Social aspect
	Ermine Marguerite Model	Learning	Creation	Capitalisation	Sharing	Continuous improvment
	Grundstein GAMETH Model	Identify	Actualise	Preserve	Valorise	KLC maintenance
BPM (Business Process Modelling) & GERAM (Generalised Enterprise Reference Architecture Model)	PERA	Identify	Analyse	Build	Operate + Kill	Life Cycle
	CIMOSA BPM 4 Objectives	acquire explicit knowledge about the business processes	support the decision making activities	exploit this knowledge in BPR projects	ease interoperability	Standardisation / interoperability
	GRAI	Model	Diagnose	Conceive	Set Up	Decision Flow
	PMI (Muench) Representative Software Development	Identify	Design	Construct	Evaluate	Project Management

2.3 Design evolution in accordance with the whole PLC

In design engineering, these KBS tools are called KBE tools. This distinction is due to the large amount of geometrical data involved and the highly recursive behaviour of engineering. Several methodologies have already proposed some solutions for expertise modelling in order to build assisting tools.

- Pre-structured methods (MASK, KADS, MOKA): Top down. It helps to map the interpretation aspect of a precise expertise. This straightforward clarification and appliance of existing models facilitate the development of a given solution, but limits the capacity to reuse materials. Some of these methods try to separate the organization of knowledge in models using natural language (K to KB) from a later phase of formalization for integration (KB to KBS) (e.g. MOKA detailed in the next section). But even so, a KB is difficult to maintain and reuse. It is sometimes difficult to handle by new users.

- Ontology framework. Should be Bottom Up, but most works propose to first build structures in which the system should behave and then force the organisation of upcoming elements. The objectivity of the organizing structure always depends on the subjectivity shared by the modeller and user groups. This structure helps small structures to converge efficiently if they are accepted by partners. In this case it can help to obtain a clear KB. But the bigger the group is, the more difficult and expensive it is to maintain coherency. The level of expertise and of involvement of users is critical.

- Expertise networks. (Inspired from social web emergence through tools such as Blogs, RSS feeds or Wiki networks). It helps to map the application aspect of knowledge for general expertise because context explanation can be easily added between users. Auto assessed by the users, these systems constitute a reference that is not a unique point of view but a sum of the compared ideas. It is still difficult to deploy such systems for determined industrial objectives. It helps to transfer K to KB dynamically, but the integration in KBS is difficult because of the lack of formalism.

From these three families, global enterprise architecture emerges to help design take the maximum benefits from enterprise knowledge. Continuously feeding in informal knowledge, a KB constitutes a global base for enterprise core competencies. The integration of the advantages of the three previous families consists in a KB including both product and process models and organizational knowledge. It should be open and flexible enough to let people from the whole life cycle give their feedback and to have some personal benefits in navigating it. It should be structured enough to help the constitution of KBS to assist notably design experts on high-level decisions. To help the transition to the new generation management, several methodological locks have to be solved. Based on KE backgrounds and experiments, the following points constitute these methodological locks and are addressed in the following sections: what are the best practices of the classical KBS approaches? To answer this question, an example of KBE tool deployment with MOKA is studied. This tool facilitates the links between design and production with semi-automatic process planning.

3. ARTICULATION BETWEEN DESIGN AND PRODUCTION

During design phase, engineering problem-solving typically involves large groups of people from different engineering disciplines. Engineers who must set up new product cycles deal with important information flows that make decision-making difficult. To face these difficulties, a KE process is necessary to structure the information and its rush. This KE process deals with the design of data processing solutions in order to automate the design of routine tasks. The solutions are in three important phases:
- capitalize relevant knowledge, often called raw knowledge,
- structure the acquired knowledge using models,
- design KB to help the definition of development specifications for KBS.

The traditional practice of storing engineering knowledge has taken many forms, such as workbooks, drawings, reports and information embedded in software application tools, but none of these forms of representation enables the use of computational tools to assist collaboration between engineers. The knowledge held within KBE systems is the same knowledge as that held in traditional knowledge storage systems. The only difference being that all the knowledge has been entered into a software KB that enables collaboration between engineers through a set of rules. The following sections introduce an example of a KE process deployment in a way of building a KB to help different actors to work collaboratively. Our goal is to propose one referential view of the domain, the context and the objectives assuming that it will help them regarding better decision making, during product and process design phases.

3.1 A case study: The USIQUICK Project

The work presented here is part of the output from a project called USIQUICK (*http://www.usiquick.com*) financed by the French Ministry of Industry. The project was started with the aim of producing a knowledge-based engineering system to help experts to define the process planning for mechanical parts. It focuses on the definition of milling process plans in aircraft manufacturing with a high amount of re-engineering. Because of the sizes of batches induced by frequent re-engineering; this activity must be fast and flexible. This specificity of the problem made the theoretical solutions compete with the integration reality. The difficulty is then to identify the knowledge elements that have to be kept customisable and that have to be definitively validated and integrated. Concepts have to be firstly identified and extracted, secondly structured and formalized and then refined to an accurate level of maturity (Du Preez *et al.*, 2005). The project involved eight partners:

- an aircraft manufacturer who was in charge of specifying the expected results. He also proposed his expertise on complex part design and on process planning,
- a CAD/CAM development leader who planned the industrialization of outputs in its software solution,
- five laboratories which were responsible for ensuring the scientific coherence of the project and proposing innovative solutions to solve strategic locks,
- a French-government institute analysed the possible use in other fields and proposed extra test cases and tool databases.

The partners started working together in a same setting with different cultures, contexts, goals and backgrounds. Furthermore, they used different jargons and terminologies sometimes diverging or overlapping, thus generating confusion. Our role was to propose solutions to enable these partners to effectively cooperate on the same objective despite the above-mentioned differences. To make this cooperation possible we are going to have put at their disposal contextualised and structured information, in the form of knowledge, to help them to have a shared understanding of the domain, the contexts and the goals. Knowledge capitalization (KC) is our proposal to reach collaboration between experts. The capitalization consists in a set of activities of knowledge identification, extraction, analysis and structuring. The identification step is a preliminary domain investigation and analysis that aims to recognize the knowledge objects that must be acquired. In our context, the input specifications consist of texts, tables, and images in MS Word format. To analyse these specifications and define knowledge object types, the ontology proposed in the MOKA Methodology has been used and updated to our specific needs, related to process design.

3.2 Knowledge capitalization: adaptation of MOKA methodology and project

MOKA for Methodology and tools Oriented to Knowledge Engineering Applications (MOKA, 2001) describes in terms of rules, process, modelling techniques and definitions the necessary stages for the specification of KBE systems. It provides a framework, both for representing and for storing Knowledge, which works at two levels: an informal level and a formal level. The first one is relatively simple and oriented to represent and formalize knowledge in language that can be understood by experts without being specialist in formalization languages. The second level is more formal and aims to represent and store knowledge in an encoding form in order to plug it into computers. A knowledge extraction tool, Pc-Pack, helps the methodology deployment (*http://www.epistemics.co.uk/*). To analyse the project's domain MOKA proposes a set of knowledge object types to help its description. Relations among these objects are also defined as well as their use constraints. The types of these objects are: illustrations representing comments, past experiences, specific cases and complex explanations, constraints describing the products' or its components' limitations, activities to describe problem resolution stages, rules to describe knowledge that directs the choices of the activities, entities to represent knowledge elements that describe the product, its components, its assemblies, parts and features. An entity can be structural or functional. These types were proposed regarding the product and its design process. However within the USIQUICK context the final product is a process planning which is a process. The types of the objects then become not reusable as proposed. For example, if we consider the structural entity it describes a physical component of the product but within our context the product is not a set of physical components but a set of activities that consist in geometry recognition, manufacturing mode identification, manufacturing operation definition and organization. Starting from the MOKA ontology a first reading of the specifications led us to the identification of the following types: illustration, constraints, activities with the distinction between domain and process activities, resources that can be utilized by one or several activities, rules, entities to represent the manufacturing features, functions to describe the role of specific features or design process activities. At this stage the knowledge to be kept has been identified and the extraction step can be done. It consists of recognizing a subset of knowledge objects and their relationships. The eventual output of extraction can be in plain text, in XML, or in Excel form, depending on the application of the supported software. In this example the output is in plain text. Once the knowledge has been extracted it must be analysed. This analysis has two objectives: its structuring and its evaluation. The structuring will be achieved using trees and diagrams according to the MOKA approach. Knowledge objects having the same type are linked using trees with "Is a" and/or "Composed of" relation types. Knowledge objects of different types are linked using diagrams. For diagram building the relations are defined according to the objects they link. It can be "Has a rule", "Has a constraint", "Has function", etc. The evaluation consists in analysing the knowledge according to criteria: completeness and feasibility. The completeness indicates if, as transmitted by the expert in the specifications, the knowledge is enough to define a process plan. This criterion highlights the additional knowledge to capture or to explain more than has already been done. Each one knows that a gap exists between the real world and the computer world. The analysis of the feasibility aims to point out the knowledge that cannot be coded as specified by the expert and the knowledge that requires the development of additional algorithms to make its automation possible.

4. CONCLUSION

This paper shows the major aspects that have to be considered in order to favour the efficiency of KM, for improved use during design phase. Our experience is based on a new concurrent engineering working methodology that has enabled us to identify that the evolution of the knowledge referential and the expert's community borders force new ways of collaboration. Furthermore, the information flows have to be mastered if engineers hope to benefit from it. A structuring approach is compulsory. As an example of this knowledge/information structure, the case study highlighted the necessity of adapting to a specific problem. A second feedback comes from the difficulty of ensuring the completeness of the structured knowledge. The situation will change due to expert know-how improvements or user needs. The evolution of concurrent engineering, emphasised by the NTIC and worldwide globalisation, force all actors, and at all life-cycle levels (product, enterprise, technologies), to rethink working methodologies, and even more, the value chain created during the product life cycle. Agile knowledge structure within the numerical chain seems to have great potential for design improvement.

5. REFERENCES

1. Perry N., Mauchand M., Bernard A., 2006, Integration of Cost Models in Design and Manufacturing, "Advances in Design", Springer Series in Advanced Manufacturing, ElMaraghy H.A. & ElMaraghy W.H. (Eds.) ISBN: 1-84628-004-4, p. 315-325.
2. Savage C., 1991, Fifth Generation Management, Co-creating through Virtual Enterprising, Dynamic Teaming and Knowledge Networking, Butterworth Heinemann, ISBN 0-7506-9701-6.
3. Amidon D.M., 1997, In: Innovation Strategy for the Knowledge Economy- The Ken Awakening, Butterworth Heinemann, ISBN: 0750698411.
4. Cassin B., 2004, Vocabulaire Européen des Philosophies, 2004, ISBN 2-85-036-580-7, ISBN 2-02-030730.
5. Gardoni M., 1999, Maîtrise de l'information non structurée et capitalisation de savoir et savoir-faire en Ingénierie Intégrée. Cas d'étude Aérospatiale, Thèse de Doctorat de l'Université de Metz.
6. Labrousse M., 2004, Proposition d'un Modèle Conceptuel Unifie pour la Gestion Dynamique des Connaissances d'entreprise, Thèse de Doctorat de l'École Centrale de Nantes et l'Université de Nantes.
7. Nonaka I., 1994, A Dynamic Theory of Organizational Knowledge Creation, Organization Science, Vol. 5, No. 1, 1994, pp. 14-37.
8. Grundstein M., 1994, Développer un système à base de connaissance: un effort de cooperation pour construire en commun un objet inconnu, Actes de la journée Innovation pour le travail en groupe, CP2I.
9. Ermine J-L., Chaillot M., Bigeon P., Charreton B., Malavieille D., 1996, MKSM, méthode pour la gestion des connaissances, Ingénierie des Systèmes d'Information, AFCET-Hermès, Vol. 4, n° 4, pp. 541-575.
10. Bachimont B., 1996, Herméneutique matérielle et Artéfacture : des machines qui pensent aux machines qui donnent à penser, Thèse de Doctorat de l'Ecole Polytechnique.
11. Du Preez N., Perry N., Candlot A., Bernard A., Uys W. and Louw L, 2005, Customised high-value document generation, CIRP Annals, Vol. 54/1/2005, Edition Colibri Publishers, ISBN 3-905 277-43-3, pp.123-126.
12. MOKA, Managing Engineering Knowledge, MOKA: Methodology for Knowledge Based Engineering Application, Edited by Melody Stokes for the MOKA Consortium, 2001.

COLLABORATIVE DESIGN
IN THE ASSEMBLY SYSTEMS

Gordana Ostojic, Vukica Jovanovic, Branislav Stevanov,
Stevan Stankovski and Ilija Cosic
Faculty of Technical Sciences Novi Sad, Serbia,
{goca, vukica, stevan, findean @uns.ns.ac.yu}@uns.ns.ac.yu,
branisha@gmail.com

Today companies are specialized for partial technology processes. Hundreds, sometimes even thousands, of collaborative processes depend on workers' interaction and communication in product assembly and disassembly phases. Close coordination accompanies all manufacturing phases of designing a product, whereby the technology documentation is produced in digital form on a CAx workstation. Product Lifecycle Management can be achieved by using specialized software solutions. Some of the Product Lifecycle Management solutions offer an integrated portfolio for engineering design and realization of products and services, which enables companies to create their own digital e-business projects. In this paper are presented modern solutions for collaborative design and examples of using these solutions in the industry.

1. INTRODUCTION

Contemporary production conditions demand the application of distributed production concept, because there is an enormous pressure on the manufacturers to comply with market changes and continuous shortening of the product life cycle. Changes on the factory floor are taking place on a daily basis. Many manufacturing companies are in search for the ways of coping with this problem by creating virtual enterprises, refining their supply chain or implementing eManufacturing principles into their plants. Besides, the expansion of enterprises through geographically distributed factory plants, administrative facilities, and sales offices has created the concept of distributed production systems.

In this paper, an approach is suggested concerning some ideas of the development of collaborative design in assembly systems. The objective was to meet the technology challenges present in the trend of changing relationships between the different parts of a company (dislocated project manager, dislocated designers and information gathered from the factory floor).

2. COLLABORATIVE DESIGN

2.1 Basic Concepts

Complex products, consisting of a number of parts, components, and modules are finally assembled in one functional unit of a company, but all of them may not be manufactured in one place. Huge factories and production complexes that existed in Serbia in the past comprised all the phases of the product life cycle, from the development of a concept solution to assembly. The technology of the product manufacturing, resource logistics, quality control, product testing and the verification of product characteristics, were the activities performed by specified departments. Design and technology documentation were created on the basis of information given by these departments.

Nowadays, companies are specialized for partial technology processes. Hundreds, and sometimes thousands, of collaborative processes depend on the workers' interaction and communication in the product assembly phase. Close coordination is involved in all the product manufacturing phases, whereby the technology documentation is produced in digital form on a CAx workstation. Product Lifecycle Management can be achieved by using specialized software solutions. Some of the solutions for Product Lifecycle Management offer an integrated portfolio for engineering design and realization of products and services, which enables companies to create their own e-business projects.

Recent trends in computing environments and engineering methodologies indicate that the future engineering infrastructure will be distributed and collaborative, where designers, process planners, manufacturers, clients, and other related domain personnel communicate and coordinate their activities using a global web-like network. The designers use heterogeneous systems, data structures, or information models, whose form and content may not be the same across all domains. Hence, appropriate standard exchange mechanisms are needed to realize the full potential of sharing information models.

The various applications are coordinated by a work flow management system, which acts as a project manager. They are connected one to another through a design network, which provides the infrastructure for high bandwidth communications. These applications retrieve design data and knowledge from a distributed design repositories and the evolving design (or designs) is stored in a database. This database provides various snapshots of the evolving design, with design artifacts and associated design rationale stored at various levels of abstraction. Finally, design applications communicate with other manufacturing applications through various networks, such as the production, process planning, and user networks (Fleig, 1998.).

2.2 DVCDGIE System Architecture

Collaborative web design can be either a client-server based suite of tools to facilitate design activities and capture design rationale or e.g. the use of the VRML as a communication and visualization medium for evaluation of detailed design (Baudin, 2000.).

Some of the problems that can arise in the application of distributed collaborative design are related to the heterogeneity, trust, awareness, interaction, overloads management, determination of access rights, system maintenance, and mutual understanding.

The concept presented in this work is a starting point of a future research project conceived at the Institute for Industrial Systems in Novi Sad (Serbia). Dynamic Virtual Collaborative Designing and Gathering Information Environment (DVCDGIE, see figure 1) is an idea of collaborative design in the process of the product development and assembly phase.

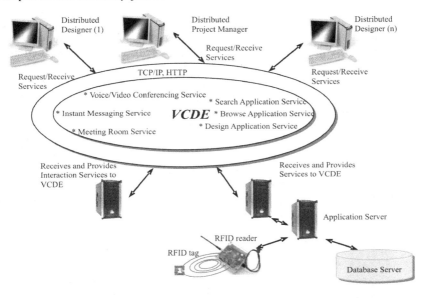

Figure 1 - DVCDGIE System architecture.

The DVCDGIE is a core of an information system that provides the data structure for dislocated project manager and dislocated designers. There are many different ways of sharing information. It can be either through instant messaging service, meeting room service or voice/video conferencing service. It is very important to enable the manager and the designers to share the data accurately and in real time. Any change in the product design, production of parts, and assembly/disassembly process, can lead to a completely different working procedure. The server, which receives and provides interaction services to the VCDE, must be able to support communication even if the manager and the designers are on different locations, or they are work in different operational systems or have different connection speeds.

The other part of the VCDE provides the application services. These services are meant to function as a search application service, browse application service, and design application service. The Application Server has to operate both with the RFID reader and the Database Server. The RFID reader obtains data from a RFID tag placed on the product and the application server should make an inquiry to the database server. The database server stores all the information needed for product disassembly.

2.3. Collaborative Design in Assembly Systems

Manufacturing of complex products, like cars, aircrafts, etc., is nowadays performed in a number of dislocated companies, steered on the principles of distributed production. In these circumstances, it is necessary to accomplish real-time communication between the participants in all manufacturing processes and during the whole product life cycle.

In the car industry, changes in product design are very frequent. The product is readjusted to the demands specified by the customer (colour, air conditioner, seats, etc.), so that each product is unique. Designs, management of production and assembly, being very complex processes, have to be supported by modern in-formational technology solutions, in order to meet the demanded quality, costs and delivery deadline. As the production is done in distributed companies, it is necessary to achieve communication between the designers, implemented at the production control level of communication in the company.

The application of distributed design in the car industry will be shown on the example of the communication between the dislocated project manager and dislocated designers in charge for the car subassembly. The project manager has a higher authority and is authorized to assign inquiry for the changes in assembly parts geometry to the designer. The example of subassembly, named Distributor, which consists of seven parts, is shown in figure 2.

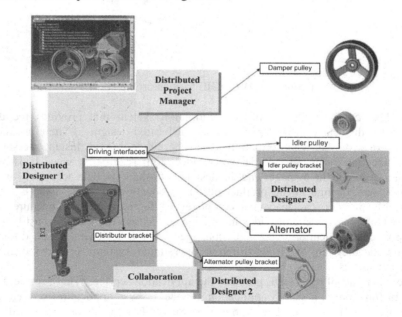

Figure 2 - Communication between the project manager and the designers.

Geometry of assembly parts depends on the geometry of the other subassembly components which are at the same assembly level or in the same assembly. The project manager is authorized to access and change every assembly constraint or the assembly itself. The position of a part, designed by an engineer, is defined by the reference axes, planes and points. The design of each part depends of the position of the four defined axes which exist in a subassembly.

In this case, it is necessary to change position of one of the four axes, and only the project manager is being authorized to do it. Assembly parts are designed by an engineer located in the distributed company. A first step in applying the required change is made by the project manager who approves the changes for parts that are supposed to be the same, by "locking" model geometries of those parts. Afterwards, the designer changes axes position on a certain solid model (see figure 3), define the parts which are affected by this change, record the changed model and declares it as a current revision. The current revision is now shown by visual representation, with the parts relationships affected by this change. The designer accesses the model geometry current revision, searches for the applied changes in the axes positions, and then makes the changes in the model geometry of subassemblies for what he/she has been authorized to do. In the same manner, the geometry of other parts, subassemblies and assemblies can be changed.

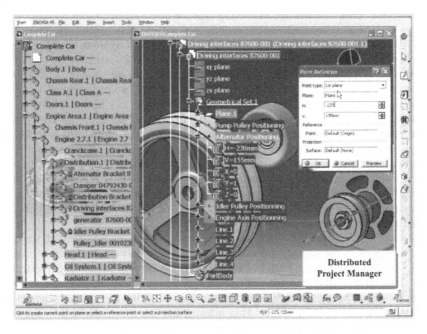

Figure 3 - Change of the axes positions on the solid model.

2.4 RFID Technology

One of the most important things in assembly/disassembly is the graphical presentation of the exploded state of a product. The other is the assembly process itself, the sequence of assembly operations and tasks needed to make a product from the base parts. Sometimes the necessary information is not available, so that the product has to be disassembled to its subassemblies. Nowadays, when a sustainable development is getting more and more important, every company must take care of its products at the end of its lifecycle. It is very difficult to create a disassembly system for any kind of a product. It would be better if every company could trace its products and find out where they are at the end of their life cycle, and gather them at the own collection centers, to disassemble them. Later, the company can also reuse these assembly items as spare parts or as recycle materials. The exploded state and assembly sequence can be stored in the server database and, using RFID technology, obtain the data needed for the disassembly management.

Automatic identification technologies improve the data accuracy and acquisition of real-time information. Bearing in mind that the RFID systems enable automatic and contactless identification of the objects, the possibility of their application as an integral part of the production automation and logistics systems is a research subject of increasing importance.

RFID systems comprise two main components - RFID tags and an RFID reader. The RFID tags can be either passive or active. Passive tags are energized only when they are in the reader's RF transmission field, while active tags are battery-operated and constantly emit an RF signal. The operation of an RFID data transmission is basically the same irrespective of the tag type. When energized, the RFID tag emits signals several hundred times per second. When they pass within the range of an RFID reader, the tag information is received by the host system. The host system then filters the multiple signals and begins processing the information.

With the readers strategically placed throughout a warehouse, a distribution center or an assembly system, the tag with its respective product or item is followed along its journey through the supply chain. RFID tags can be read-only or read-writable. Read-writable tags allow the information stored on and emitted by the tag to be modified or rewritten during the use. Passive read-only tags are the most affordable tag option available. They are also most limiting, because their signal reach and data use are constrained. An important variant of RFID tags is the Auto-ID tag, which is encoded with an electronic product code (EPC), a 96-bit unique naming scheme that can provide vast product details. The EPC is currently the most common encoding scheme for warehouse and distribution applications. EPC tags can be active or passive, read-only or read-writable.

Most of RFID data are simple. Unless a system is using sophisticated, expensive tags, all it gets is the item serial number, time, and location. RFID tags (transponders) - affixed to the cases, pallets, cartons, products or their parts - begin to transmit RF signals when in the read zone of a stationary or mobile reader (interrogator). The reader picks up the signal and decodes the unique EPC that identifies the name, class and serial number of the product. This information is then matched with the record data in the host computer system and database application (see figure 4).

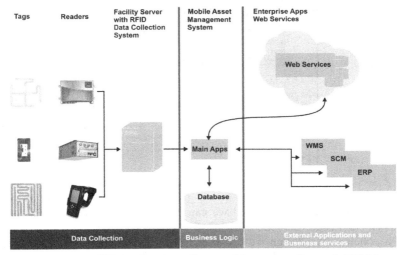

Figure 4 - RFID readers in a disassembly system (Junwei, 2004.).

2.5 Product Database for Disassembly

To establish the data source for collaborative design we have to create a database. Since this is a simple database we can use Microsoft Access.

When planning a database, the first thing is to see which data we need for the process of collaborative design. These data can be organized in more tables and connected via primary keys. For every part we need to know: EPC, Part code, Material, Is the part base or not, Assembly sequence, Constraints – Align, Mate, or Insert, Part life cycle, Manufacturing date, Manufacturer.

For the materials we need information about the ID of the material and its name. For the manufacturer of a part we can use information about its name, address, phone number, email address and contact person.

Following the previously made plan about the needed data, we have to construct three tables in Microsoft Access: Table of Parts, Table of Materials, and Table of Manufacturers (see figure 5, 6 and 7, respectively).

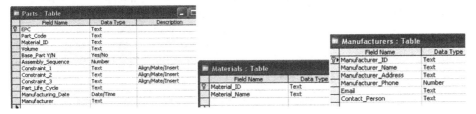

Figure 5 - Parts.　　　Figure 6 - Materials.　　Figure 7 - Manufacturers.

Foreign keys in the Table of Parts are Manufacturer and Material. We use them to create relationships between the tables (see figure 8).

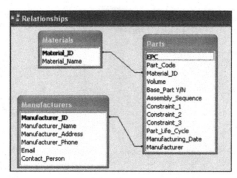

Figure 8 – Relationships between the tables.

Once the database is constructed we can use it over the web via Macromedia Cold Fusion Application server.

For a collaborative design we can use data by developing Cold Fusion application, which can access the database server and use data from the existing database. Cold Fusion application collects the data from database server or any other data source (in our case an RFID reader) and sends it to the web server as an HTML document, which is then presented to the dislocated manager, who originally made the request for the data.

To do this we configure our database as a data source for a Cold Fusion application. For a Microsoft Access database we can use either ODBC, or OLE/DB drivers, to make connection.

3. CONCLUSION

Modern means of production management are crucially dependent on the information technology and more than ever they rely on the web usage. Collaborative web enabled environment can be used on a daily basis for communication between product designers and engineers in the assembly/disassembly process. This is getting more and more important because of the frequent changes in the global market. RFID technologies can be really helpful in terms of sustainable development, regarding disassembly, recycling and reuse. According to the WEEE Directive, certain measures must be undertaken in order to prevent waste, e.g. electrical and electronic equipment. All manufacturers should take care of the recycling of such equipment and of reuse of its components by applying the RFID technology to trace the products in all phases of its life cycle.

4. REFERENCES

1. Baudin, M., Rao, A.: RFID Applications in Manufacturing, MMTI – Manufacturing Management & Technology Institute, 2000.
2. Fleig, J., Schneider, R.: The Link to the 'Real World': Information, Knowledge and Experience for Decision Making, in Shop Floor Control – A Systems Perspective, From Deterministic Models towards Agile Operations Management, edited by Scherer E., Springer, Cirih, 1998.
3. Junwei, C.: Lightweight RFID framework, DeveloperWorks, November 2004, Shanghai.

FUZZY PRODUCT CONFIGURATION IN ADVANCED CAD SYSTEMS

E. Ostrosi and M. Ferney
Laboratoire de Recherche Mecatronique 3M
Université de Technologie de Belfort-Montbéliard, France
{egon.ostrosi, michel.ferney}@utbm.fr

Today, configuring the mechanical systems and their components correctly so that they meet their functions efficiently and can be easily manufactured and assembled is crucial to effective product design. However, currently there exists no systematic and effective method for designing configurations. This paper proposes and develops a formal representation for supporting the computer-aided design approach for configuration. Two interrelated questions are taken into account: 1. What are configuration features? (Configuration feature concept); 2. How can be constructed the design procedures capable to configure the product? (Computer-aided design approach for configuration). This approach, under the guide of the proposed formal representation, has been implemented in computers by using the functions of current CAD software.

1. INTRODUCTION

The design process is the series of activities by which the information known and recorded about the design product is added to, refined, modified, or made more or less certain. There have been many attempts to draw up models of the design process in systematic steps (French 1971, Pahl and Beitz 1984, Suh 1990, Albano and Suh, 1992).

In engineering design, to configure a mechanical system means to arrange the relative positions of its functional components and to determine what the functional components are to be (Dixon and Poli, 1995). The task of a system configuration is to select or determine what functional components the system will poses and how these functional components are to be arranged and connected in order to satisfy a set of requirements and a set of constraints imposed on the product (Tiihonen et al. 1996, Sabin and Weigel 1998, Brown 1998). Similarly, the task of part configuration is to select or determine what configuration features the part will posses and how those configuration features are to be arranged and connected.

When a mechanical system is decomposed into its components and associated couplings are specified, engineers are in effect determining and arranging its elements; that is, they are configuring the mechanical system. From the engineering point of view, the *system-component-feature* relationships are appropriate means for a general product representation. Since such means are recursive, any proper granularity level of representation must be introduced to assess design possibility.

Many attempts have been made for modeling the configurable products (Snavely and Papalambros 1993, Männistö et al. 2001, Siddique and Rosen 2001). However in CAD systems there are not the formal representation for supporting the designing configurations. Often, designers will generate only one alternative configuration, evaluate it subjectively, and then redesign by revising. The lack of trial configurations, missing of some creative or less obvious configurations, incomplete evaluations are some difficulties with a single alternative configuration process.

This paper proposes a formal representation for supporting the design for configuration. In the second part of the paper, an approach for basic configuration searching is presented. To solve the closer cases to real–world situations, it is proposed to enrich the part–configuration features and configuration features–configuration features relation with fuzzy logic. An example illustrates the proposed approach. Lastly, conclusions are presented.

2. BASIC CONFIGURATION SEARCHING

2.1 Configuration features

Configuration feature: concept for the representation of systems. Engineers do need concepts to represent their way of reasoning on the systems to be designed. This inevitable role is played by the configuration features.

Configuration feature: ontological concept. The selection of a set of configuration features indicates that engineers are not interested in other features. This consequence is inevitable because engineers have the opportunity to focus the attention on those aspects of the system that they believe relevant. The selection of an ontology in spite of the others can produce different views of the system to be designed.

Configuration feature: concept for the intelligent reasoning. This role is obvious because the initial design of configuration features is typically justified by how engineers can reason intelligently to configure. The intelligent reasoning, often implicit, can become explicit while examining the question of inference that configuration features propose and recommend.

Configuration feature: concept of computing. From a purely mechanic point of view, the reasoning is a process of calculus. Features offer ideas concerning the way to organize the knowledge that facilitate inferences. The content of the knowledge that they carry and the way of which this knowledge is represented, defines the efficiency of the computing. If one ignore the considerations of computing, then the knowledge represented by configuration features are inadequate for a real use.

Configuration feature: concept of communication. Finally, a configuration feature is a means of expression and communication. The relation between the possibility of a language based on configuration features and his utility, also the relation between the language utility and the facility of the utilization are some problems that surround the concept of configuration features.

2.2 Approach for basic product configuration

Engineering design can be considered as a process of reducing the uncertainty with each design alternatives is described. During the design process, the designer deals with some distinct forms of uncertainty: imprecision, randomness, fuzziness, ambiguity and incomplete (Deciu et al. 2005). The fuzzy set approach is particularly suitable for handling uncertain information by providing a set of solutions with different degrees of preference (Zadeh 1965, Bellman et al. 1970, Antonsson and Otto 1995, Kaufmann and Gupta 1988, Bahrami and Dagli 1993, Zimmermann 1996,). In this research, considering the fuzziness of handling uncertain design information, an approach for basic product configuration is proposed. This approach includes the three phases. The first phase, called configuration features based part model, consists of CAD parts representation based on the configuration features. The second phase, called configuration feature-configuration feature model, consists in representing the relationship between configuration features. The third phase, called basic configuration of product, consists in searching a preliminary configuration of product. The schematic chart of figure 1 shows the architecture of this approach.

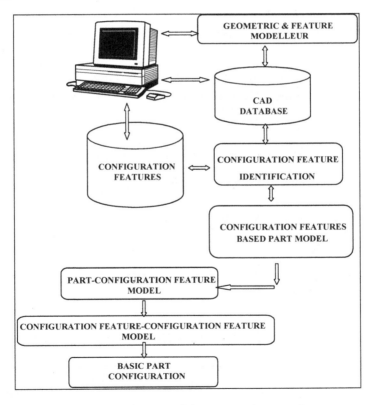

Figure 1 - Structure of the proposed approach.

Configuration Features Part based Model. The most direct way to express the relationship between elements of two sets is to use ordered pairs made up of two related elements.

Let $P = \{p_1, p_2, \ldots p_i \ldots p_n\}$ be the set of parts in a database, and let be $X = \{x_1, x_2, \ldots x_j \ldots x_n\}$ be the set of features. Let R_l be the relation that consists of those pairs (p_i, x_j), where p is a part containing the feature f. For instance, if the part "shaft" contains the feature "hole" then (shaft, hole) belong to R_l, otherwise (shaft, hole) is not in R_l. The relation between the sets $P = \{p_1, p_2, \ldots p_i \ldots p_n\}$ and $P = \{p_1, p_2, \ldots p_i \ldots p_n\}$ can be represented using a zero-one matrix. The relation R_l can be represented by the matrix $A = |a_{ij}|$ where $a_{ij} = 1$, if (p_i, x_j) belong to R_l, otherwise $a_{ij} = 0$. However, in the case of the mechanical design, a finite set of manufacturing features can produce an unlimited number of configurations of manufacturing features in interaction. The information of feature membership to a part implies an uncertainty. This uncertainty means the existence of a fuzzy relationship $\tilde{R}_l$ between the set of parts P and subset of manufacturing features X, and therefore, between the set of parts P and the set of features X. This fuzzy relationship, noted $\tilde{R}_l$, is a subset of the Cartesian product $P \times X$ with the membership function $\mu_{R_l} \in [0,1]$ and it can be noted: $p_i \tilde{R}_l x_k$ $p_i \in P, i = 1, 2, \cdots n;$ $x_k \in X, k = 1, 2, \cdots p$. The graph which represents the fuzzy relationship $p_i \tilde{R}_l x_k$ is called the fuzzy part – operational feature graph, and the corresponding matrix is called the fuzzy part –feature matrix (figure 2).

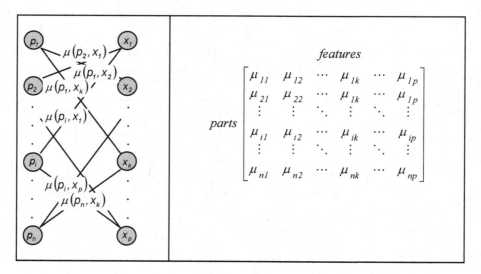

Figure 2 - Fuzzy part-operational feature graph and its corresponding matrix.

Configuration Feature-Configuration Feature based Model. Relation from the set $X = \{x_1, x_2, \ldots x_j \ldots x_n\}$ to itself is of special interest. Consider a simple example of the relationship between the features.

Let us consider the part p1 and its relationship with the set of features $X = \{x_1, x_2, \ldots x_j \ldots x_n\}$. The fuzzy relation between the features in $X = \{x_1, x_2, \ldots x_j \ldots x_n\}$, $x_i \tilde{R}_2 x_j$ $x_k \in X, k = 1,2, \cdots p$ for the part p_1, is given by the fuzzy matrix $B_1 = \left[b_{ij}^1 \right]$ where $\left[b_{ij}^1 \right]$ is defined as minimum of pairs (p_1, x_i) and (p_1, x_j).

$$\text{features}$$

$$\left[B_1 (x_i \, \tilde{R}_2 \, x_j) \right] = \begin{bmatrix} \mu_{11} & \mu_{12} & \cdots & \mu_{1k} & \cdots & \mu_{1p} \\ \mu_{21} & \mu_{22} & \cdots & \mu_{1k} & \cdots & \mu_{1p} \\ \vdots & \vdots & \ddots & \vdots & \ddots & \vdots \\ \mu_{i1} & \mu_{i2} & \cdots & \mu_{ik} & \cdots & \mu_{ip} \\ \vdots & \vdots & \ddots & \vdots & \ddots & \vdots \\ \mu_{n1} & \mu_{n2} & \cdots & \mu_{nk} & \cdots & \mu_{np} \end{bmatrix} \text{features}$$

In this way, one can process for each part p_i in the set P. Then, the fuzzy relation between the features in X, for the set of parts P, can be given by the fuzzy matrix $B = \left[b_{ij} \right]$, where b_{ij} is defined as the maximum value for all parts $b_{ij} = max\left(b_{ij}^{p1}, b_{ij}^{p2} \ldots b_{ij}^{pn} \right)$. This is a max-min operation. For example, the fuzzy relation between the features in X, for the set of parts P, is given by the fuzzy feature-feature matrix $B = \left[b_{ij} \right]$.

$$\text{features}$$

$$\left[B (x_i \, \tilde{R}_2 \, x_j) \right] = \begin{bmatrix} \mu_{11} & \mu_{12} & \cdots & \mu_{1k} & \cdots & \mu_{1p} \\ \mu_{21} & \mu_{22} & \cdots & \mu_{1k} & \cdots & \mu_{1p} \\ \vdots & \vdots & \ddots & \vdots & \ddots & \vdots \\ \mu_{i1} & \mu_{i2} & \cdots & \mu_{ik} & \cdots & \mu_{ip} \\ \vdots & \vdots & \ddots & \vdots & \ddots & \vdots \\ \mu_{n1} & \mu_{n2} & \cdots & \mu_{nk} & \cdots & \mu_{np} \end{bmatrix} \text{features}$$

The matrix is symmetric and reflexive. This fuzzy relation is transformed into a similarity relation, which satisfies the transitivity. To define the consistent membership function between a pair of features, the maximum value for all possible routes can be taken. This is also a max-min operation.

Basic part configuration. The basic configuration of a part represents a maximal sub similarity relation. In this case, a parameter alpha can be used to indicate the strength of association between features to configure a part. The decomposition of the similarity relation into maximal similarities subrelations is based on the Boolean algebra.

Boolean algebra provides the operations and the rules for working with the set $B = \{0,1\}$. The variable is called a Boolean variable if it assumes values only from B. A function from B_n, the set $\{(x_1, x_2, ..., x_n) \mid x_i \in B, \ 1 \le i \le n\}$, to B is called a Boolean function of degree n. Boolean functions can be represented using expressions made up from the variables and Boolean operations. A Boolean algebra is a set B with two binary operations Boolean sum, denoted by (+), and Boolean product, denoted by ($\cdot$), and a unary operation ($^{-}$) such that the following properties hold for all x, y and z in B:

$$x + y = x \qquad\qquad \text{Identity laws}$$
$$x \cdot 1 = x$$
$$x + \overline{x} = 1 \qquad\qquad \text{Dominance laws}$$
$$x \cdot \overline{x} = 0$$
$$x + y = y + x \qquad\qquad \text{Commutative laws}$$
$$x \cdot y = y \cdot x$$
$$x + (y + z) = (x + y) + z \qquad \text{Associative laws}$$
$$x \cdot (y \cdot z) = (x \cdot y) \cdot z$$
$$x + y \cdot z = (x + y) \cdot (x + z) \qquad \text{Distributive laws}$$
$$x \cdot (y + z) = x \cdot y + x \cdot z$$

Given the similarity relation and the value of the parameter alpha, used to indicate the strength of association between features, how can a Boolean expression that represents the maximal similarities subrelation can be found? This problem is solved knowing that any Boolean function may be represented by a Boolean function may be represented by a Boolean sum of Boolean products of the variables and their complements. For searching the maximal similarities subrelation, the following algorithm is used (Pichat, 1969):

Step 1: Consider the first row.
Step 2: Consider all zeros in the considered row.
Step 3: For every zero, considering the elements corresponding to columns as Boolean variables, form:
> Boolean Product (.) between the corresponding elements of columns where the zeros are;
> Sum booléienne (+) between the element, which denote the considered row, and the Boolean product. If not zero is in the row, the sum is equal to 1.

Step 4: Repeat the steps 2-4, until all the rows are considered
Step 5: Form the product of results. A Boolean function is obtained.
Step 6: Take complements of every term. The maximal subrelations of similarities are found.

3. APPLICATION

Let us consider a representative subset CAD parts and a set of pertinent features $\{a,b,c,d,e,f\}$. After the recognition process of features, the feature-feature model is given in the figure 3.

	a	b	c	d	e	f
a	1	0.72	0.8	0.9	0.12	0.84
b		1	0.24	0.84	0.32	0.94
c			1	0.9	0.24	0.32
d				1	0.18	0.91
e					1	0.88
f						1

Figure 3 - Feature –Feature matrix.

Using a threshold value ($\alpha \geq 0.5$), the Feature-Feature matrix is transformed into a binary matrix (figure 4).

	a	b	c	d	e	f	
a	1	1	1	1	0	1	a+e
b		1	0	1	0	1	b+ce
c			1	1	0	0	c+ef
d				1	0	1	d+e
e					1	1	1
f						1	1

Figure 4 - Feature –Feature matrix ($\alpha \geq 0.5$).

Applying the algorithm, the results from the step 1 to the step 4, are given on the left of the figure 2. The following Boolean function results in the step 5:

$$S = (a+e) \cdot (b+ce) \cdot (c+ef) \cdot (d+e) \cdot 1 \cdot 1$$

After applying the properties of Boolean algebra, this function is reduced into:
$S = abcd + ce + bef$

The complements of every terms, give the maximal sub relation of similarities:
$S' = ef + abdf + acd$

Here, the terms *ef, abdf,* and *acd* represent the basic configuration for three maximal parts in term of the strength ($\alpha \geq 0.5$) between their respective features. The first maxima part is composed by the features e and f; the second maximal part by the features a,b,d,f; and the third maximal parts by the features a,c,d.

4. CONCLUSIONS

Currently there exist no systematic and effective methods for designing configurations. The lack of trial configurations, missing of some creative or less obvious configurations, incomplete evaluations are some difficulties with the one alternative configuration process. This paper proposes and develops a formal approach for supporting the computer-aided design approach for configuration based on the concept of configuration features and the fuzziness. The characteristics of design for configuration are described by resorting the structural relationships between configuration features, which are very strong in design. The fuzzy configuration feature-part and relation are used to compose the fuzzy configuration feature-feature configuration, which is represented by the corresponding matrix. After fuzzy configuration feature-configuration feature matrix decomposition, the maximal sub relations of similarities. They correspond to the initial product configuration. Configuration features and fuzziness provide a means to include the flexibility in designing the basic configuration. This flexibility depends on the chosen threshold value. The subsequent CAD modelling is implemented in computers by using the functions of current CAD software.

5. REFERENCES

1. Albano, L.D., Suh, N.P., 1992, Axiomatic Approach to Structural Design. Research in Engineering Design, 4, 171-183.
2. Antonsson, E.K., Otto, K.N., 1995, Imprecision in Engineering Design. ASME Journal of Mechanical Design, 117B, 25-32.
3. Bahrami, A., Dagli, C.H., 1993, From Fuzzy Input Requirements to Crisp Design. International Journal of Advanced Manufacturing Technology, 8, 52-60.
4. Bellman, R.E., Zadeh, L.A., 1970, Decision-Making in a Fuzzy Environment. Management Science, 17B, 141-164.
5. Brown, D.C., 1998, Defining configuring. Artificial Intelligence for Engineering Design, Analysis and Manufacturing. 12, 301-305.
6. Deciu, E.R., Ostrosi, E., Ferney, M., and Gheorghe, M., 2005, Configurable product design using multiple fuzzy models. Journal of Engineering Design, 16(2), 209-235.
7. Dixon J.R. and Poli C., "Engineering Design and Design for Manufacturing a structured approach", Field Stone Publishers, Conway, Massachusetts, USA, 1995.
8. French, M.J., 1971, Engineering design: the conceptual stage (London: Heinemann Educational Books Ltd).
9. Kaufmann, A. and Gupta, M., 1988, Fuzzy mathematical models in Engineering and Management Science (New York: North-Holland).
10. Männistö, T., Soininen, T., and Sulonen, R., 2001, Modelling Configurable Products and Software Product Families. Presented at the IJCAI'01 Workshop on Configuration, Seattle.
11. Pahl, G., Beitz, W., 1984, Engineering Design: A Systematic Approach (London: The Design Council), (original German text, Springer-Verlag, 1977).
12. Pichat, E., 1969, Algorithm for finding the maximal elements of finite universal algebra, Inform. Processing 69 (Amsterdam: North Holland).
13. Sabin, D., Weigel, R., 1998, Product Configuration Frameworks – A survey. IEEE Intelligent Systems, 13(4), 32-85.
14. Siddique, Z. and Rosen, D.W., 2001, On combinatorial design spaces for the configuration design of product families. Artificial Intelligence for Engineering Design, Analysis and Manufacturing, Vol. 15(2), pp. 91-108.
15. Snavely, G.L. and Papalambros, P.Y., 1993, Abstraction as a configuration design methodology. Advances in Design Automation, (New York: ASME) DE-Vol. 65-1, 297-305.
16. Suh, N., 1990, Principles of Design (New York: Oxford University Press).
17. Tiihonen, J., et al., 1996, State of 10 cases in the Finnish industry. In Knowledge Intensive CAD, edited by Tomiyama, T., Mäntylä, M., and Finger, S. (London: Chapman & Hall), pp. 95-114.
18. Zadeh, L.A., 1965, Fuzzy Sets. Information and Control, 8, 338-353.
19. Zimmermann, H.J., 1996, Fuzzy set theory and its applications, 3rd edition (Boston: Kluwer Academics Publishers).

AN ADAPTIVE TOLERANCE MODEL
FOR COLLABORATIVE DESIGN

Alex Ballu, Jérome Dufaure and Denis Teissandier
Bordeaux 1 University, France
{alex.ballu, jerome.dufaure, denis.teissandier}@u-bordeaux1.fr

To ensure the robustness of geometric tolerance in collaborative design, a multi-view tolerance data representation is needed as well as a multi-level representation. The goal of multi-level representation is to detail tolerances as knowledge of the product evolves during its development.

After a brief discussion, IPPOP product model and GeoSpelling tolerance model are chosen as basis of definition and implementation of an adaptive tolerance model. In this model, the multi-level and multi-view capabilities are permitted by level and view adaptations. Level and view adaptations consist of an evolution of the viewable tolerance data according to the step of design and to the actors.

These adaptations are presented and applied on a part of an automated cutting machine for fabrics.

1. INTRODUCTION

In the global product development process, geometrical tolerance should take a major role. In fact, geometrical tolerance, as geometrical modeling, is an important way of collaboration between the actors of the lifecycle of the product. Tolerancing leads to many data from the expression of the functional requirements to maintenance, including conceptual design, embodiment design, detail design, manufacturing and control. However, most of the commercial tolerance tools are not able to share data with other expertises such as functional analysis, manufacturing and metrology.

In the context of digital enterprise:

- the tolerance expression must be formalized to be integrated in a product model,
- the tolerance expression must be adapted to conceptual design until detail design (multi-level),
- the tolerance expression must be adapted to each activity of the enterprise such as design, manufacturing, metrology, control, maintenance (multi-view).

For that, a global framework is stated by the choice of a product model and of a tolerance model. Then, the paper develops how the integration of the tolerance model chosen allows adaptation during the product development.

2. PRODUCT MODEL FOR TOLERANCING

2.1 Context

In digital enterprise context, a data structure is necessary to ensure the management of the product lifecycle, including the management of tolerance. Several product models have been developed to take up this challenge (Summers, 2001). One major consequence is that the kernel of a product model can not be a geometric model traditionally used by the commercial CAD systems (Noel, 2004).

Current product models are dedicated either to generic product description along its design cycle or to a specific expertise. On one hand, the entities used in generic product model have semantics which can ease the dialog between the actors of the design cycle, nevertheless, the semantic of these entities is too poor to ensure the robustness of the knowledge of a particular expertise (Krause, 1993) (Yoshikawa, 1994) (Tichkiewitch, 1996). On the other hand, a product model specific to one expertise (Salomons, 1996) (Johannesson, 2000) can not be used in digital enterprise context. In consequence we propose the use IPPOP product model in this paper.

The authors have participated in the IPPOP project (Integration of Product, Process and Organization for Performance Enhancement in engineering) which goals are to develop and set up an appropriate environment for collaborative design including management and coordination (Girard, 2004).

The product model developed for IPPOP (Noel, 2004) formalizes the techno-logical knowledge about product (function, structure, behavior, expert view, etc.). Particularly, IPPOP product model supports the product description all along the design cycle with various expert points of view. For that, the semantic of IPPOP entities can evolve during the design. The implementation in object oriented language facilitates this evolution. Dufaure and Teissandier have presented an application of IPPOP product model in the tolerance context (Dufaure, 2004).

2.2 IPPOP product model

To ease the use of computer aided design tools in a collaborative context, IPPOP product model is based on three main objects: component, interface and function (In figure 1, the shape of the three objects are distinguished for a better understanding of the next figures). These three objects allow to support both functional and structural descriptions of products.

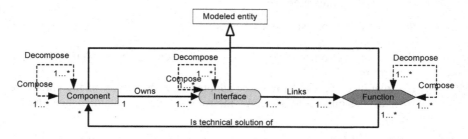

Figure 1 – Objects and relationships of IPPOP product model.

Component instances describe the product in terms of assemblies, sub-assemblies and parts. Each component can be decomposed into several ones to contribute to the description of the product structure.

Interface instances allow to describe the geometric elements of a component which are in relation with the external medium. The links between component and interface instances signifies that one component owns one or several interfaces. Component and interface instances represent the structural decomposition of the product at one particular stage.

Function instances describe the relation between interfaces. A function represents a functional requirement on the product or a contact condition between interfaces. The semantic of these relationships is that a function instance links together one or several interface instances. The decomposition related to a function instance allows to describe the functional description of the product.

The relationships between structural and functional descriptions of a product are realized by the relationships between interfaces and function instances of the product.

2.3 Tolerancing as a function

Compared to current product models, the tolerances are not simple attributes of geometrical instances or specific objects, but are considered at the same level as functional or technical requirements of the product. Geometrical tolerances are particular specifications among all the product requirements.

For IPPOP product model, the requirements link interfaces and are classified in the functions. In consequence, as geometrical tolerances are requirements, they link also interfaces. A location of a plane, with respect to a cylinder, is defined as a function instance in relation with the plane interface and the cylinder interface.

The advantage of merging requirements and tolerances is that a functional requirement in conceptual design or a geometric specification in detail design are described by the same type of object. As the object is unique, the management of the instances and the traceability of the functional data during the design cycle are easier.

3. TOLERANCE REPRESENTATION

As the product model is defined, the tolerance representation has to be discussed; the existing tolerance models and their particularities are briefly presented, then the adaptive model is developed.

As Salomons et al wrote, representation and specification of the tolerances can be clearly distinguished (Salomons, 1996). The presented paper develops the tolerance representation in the enterprise context.

One of the earlier important research paper on tolerance representation is due to Requicha (Requicha, 1983). In his approach, a tolerance zone is described as a global offset zone. Since this work, a significant amount of research has been devoted to the development of specification models distinguished between:

- parametric models (Turner, 1990) (Wirtz, 1991) (Gaunet, 1993),
- boundary models (Jayaraman, 1989) (Robinson, 1998).

Standards have also greatly evolved during this period (ISO GPS). Mathematical expressions of the standardized tolerances have been developed (ASME Y14.5.1M, 1994). More recently ISO (ISO/TS 17450-1, 2005) gave a more general framework based on the GeoSpelling model. The GeoSpelling model attempts to formalize the tolerance representation and to answer to the needs of tolerance expressions in the enterprise (Mathieu, 2003). GeoSpelling model introduces a tolerance semantic (for standardized tolerance or not), ensuring quite all the current needs. In GeoSpelling, a specification is defined as a characteristic on features defined by operations.

Sudarsan et al. (Sudarsan 2005) suggested to integrate ISO standards in a general product model. Some CAD systems begin to integrate the specification syntax (Functional Tolerancing and Annotation, FTA in CATIA), and STEP standard defines an exchange language between CAD systems (ISO 10303-47, 1997), nevertheless, the semantic leaves fairly poor. In this work, a more reach syntax is integrated in IPPOP product model on the basis of the GeoSpelling concepts.

4. ADAPTIVE TOLERANCE MODEL

4.1 Principles

To adapt tolerances according to the evolution of the product during its lifecycle, the tolerances are defined with different levels of detail. In some cases, at the beginning of product development, top level details can be sufficient. If an expert needs more information, the tolerances may be detailed. According to the evolution of the product during its lifecycle, tolerance may be more or less detailed; it is named **detail adaptation** (figure 2).

To adapt tolerances according to the activities, a tolerance may be seen according to different views. For example, a tolerance can be shared distinguishing the nature of the toleranced features (integral or extracted), the criteria of association of a datum feature (minimax or least-squares). The adaptation to different views is assumed by the multi-view system integrated in IPPOP model, it is named **view adaptation** (figure 2).

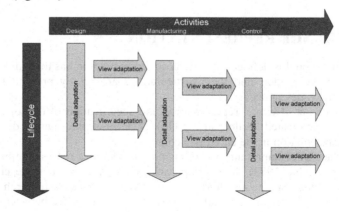

Figure 2 – Detail and view adaptations.

In the following, an example illustrates these adaptations. We must pay attention to the fact that three models of the tolerances are used: the product model, the nominal model and the geometrical model with defaults. In the **product model**, the tolerance is presented under the form of instances of the model, which corresponds to records in the database. In the **nominal model**, the tolerance is presented as symbols on nominal geometry, which is what the designer can see in the CAD viewer. In the **geometrical model with defaults**, the semantic of the tolerance is explained by a drawing representing the defaults of the geometry, which represents what the designer has to imagine when he writes or reads a tolerance in the CAD viewer. These three models are represented respectively by a diagram and two drawings.

4.2 Detail adaptation

Let us consider a support of the cutting head of an automated cutting machine for fabrics; the designer knows that the axis of the cutting head has to be parallel to a contact plane, at a distance of 32mm.

At this stage, a parallelism tolerance and a location tolerance are defined. *Plane1* and *axis2* are interfaces of the *Support* component, and the *Parallelism1* tolerance links the interfaces (figure 3.a). The interfaces may be represented as a skeleton in the CAD system, with a non–standardized tolerance (figure 3.b). In the CAD system, the skeleton consists in a plane and an axis respecting the constraints of parallelism and distance.

Until now, the type and dimensions of the surfaces of the part are unknown; the tolerances are parametric tolerances on the ideal features of the skeleton (figure 3.c). The tolerance data may be extracted by an API toward a tolerance analysis software permitting to already quantify the tolerance values.

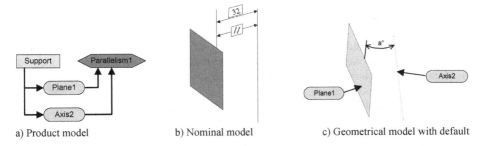

a) Product model   b) Nominal model   c) Geometrical model with default

Figure 3 – Tolerance on skeleton.

When the technical solutions are known, surfaces may be defined. Here, the axis is materialized by two bearings. At this stage, the tolerances may be detailed, the *Parallelism1.1* concerns the contact plane and the group made up of the two cylinders, corresponding to the housings of the ball bearings. *Parallelism1.1*, *Plane1.1*, *Cylinder2.1* and *Cylinder2.2* are decomposed instances, respectively from *Parallelism1*, *Plane1* and *Axis2*. This is the first step of detail adaptation, *Parallelism1*, *Plane1* and *Axis2* are detailed trough this decomposition.

The geometrical and tolerance data may be accessed by the manufacturer to start the definition of the process planning and the verification of the feasibility of the tolerances.

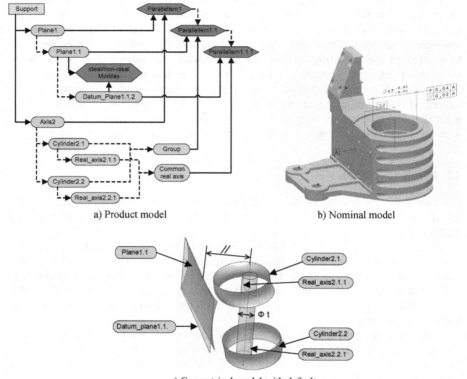

a) Product model   b) Nominal model

c) Geometrical model with default

Figure 4 – ISO GPS tolerance.

In a last step, the part is completely defined in the CAD system and the final tolerances are defined by ISO GPS tolerances (figure 4.b). The meaning of the tolerances can be completely defined as in figure 4.c. The product model is adapted by detailing the toleranced features and the datum features. In the example (figure 4.a), the toleranced feature is made up of the composition of two real axes, *Real_axis2.1.1* and *Real_axis2.2.1*, and the datum feature *Datum_plane1.1.2* is an ideal plane tangent to *Plane1.1* (non-ideal plane). The contact is represented by a function instance *Ideal/non ideal* (figure 4.a) which links the two surfaces, attributes of this function instance may detail the criteria of association. It points out the fact that function instances are used generally to make a relation between interfaces as requirement, tolerance, joint, datum association.

The different instances are specialized by attributes. These attributes allow to define type and band width of filters, association criteria. As design is evolving, adaptive tolerance model permits to integrate more and more details.

4.3 View adaptation

The second type of adaptation is view adaptation. IPPOP product model allows to specialize a modelled instance (component, interface or function) in different views.

Multi-view is particularly efficient for collaborative activities, and tolerances are used in different activities, principally in design, manufacturing and control.

To control the parallelism in coordinate metrology, the first difference with design is that the controlled tolerance is based on measured points. *Plane1.1* is measured in a finite number of points. This set of points is a particular view of the plane, denoted extracted plane, *Extracted_plane1.1.2*. To detail *Extracted_plane1.1.2*, attributes may define sampling strategy, number of points, and density of points. Similarly, the real axis cannot be measured; only points on sections may be measured, providing centers of sections. In the same manner, attributes may define how the measured points are chosen and how the section centers are computed.

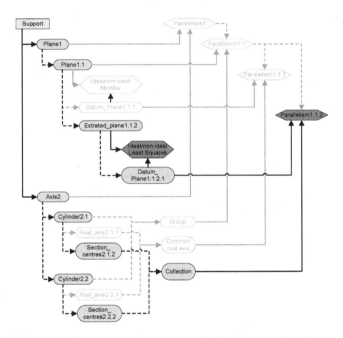

Figure 5 – Control tolerance view (design view is in pale grey).

The second difference is the dependence with the metrology software used. Indeed, the metrology software do not furnish every geometrical operations defined by the GPS standards. In this case, another operation must be used, the "nearest" operation. As example, for the association of a datum plane, the minimax criterion does not exist in every software, instead of it; the least squares criterion is used.

Figure 5 represents the control view of the parallelism and the design view is represented in pale grey. IPPOP product model permits to define these views and to pick a particular view.

5. CONCLUSION

The tolerances are among the most often shared data between the activities all along the lifecycle. They must be adaptive in detail to follow project development and must be adaptive in view to be shared between activities. The proposed model integrated in IPPOP product model allows these adaptations. One expert can detail a tolerance representation all along his activity, and another one can specialize a shared tolerance representation to adapt it to his own point of view. This adaptive model facilitates the traceability of the tolerances.

For an easy understanding of the paper, the example concerns a single part, but the concepts presented allow to take into account assemblies, even if ISO tolerances do not yet include assembly tolerances.

IPPOP project is a national project and it is encouraged by French industry and research ministry in the framework of RNTL program. More information is available on the website http://ippop.laps.u-bordeaux1.fr.

6 REFERENCES

1. ASME Y14.5.1M. Math. Definition of Dimensioning and Tolerancing Principles, ASME, 1994.
2. Dufaure D, Teissandier D, Debarbouille G. Product model dedicated to collaborative design: A geometric tolerancing point of view. IDMME (Bath, UK) 2004: In cdrom
3. Gaunet D. Vectorial tolerancing model. 3rd CIRP CAT (Cachan, France) 1993 : 25-49.
4. Girard P, Eynard B. Integration of Product-Process-Organisation for Advanced Engineering Design. Perspectives from Europe and Asia on Engineering Design and Manufacture. Kluwer Academic Publishers 2004; ISBN 1-4020-2211-5.
5. ISO 10303-47, Industrial automation systems and integration - Product data representation and exchange - Part 47: Integrated generic resource: Shape variation tolerances, ISO, 1997.
6. ISO/TS 17450-1, Geometrical Product Specifications (GPS) - General concepts - Part 1: General concepts for geometrical specification and verification, ISO, 2005.
7. Jayaraman R, Srinivasan V. Geometric tolerancing: I. Virtual boundary requirements. IBM Journal of Research and Development 1989; Vol. 33/2: 90-104.
8. Johannesson H, Söderberg R. Structure and Matrix Models for Tolerance Analysis from Configuration to Detail Design, Research In Engineering Design 2000; 12: 112-125.
9. Krause FL, Kimura F, Kjelberg T, Lu S. Product modeling. Annals of the CIRP 1993; 42/2: 149-152.
10. Mathieu L, Ballu A. GeoSpelling: a common language for geometric product specification and verification to express method uncertainty. 8th CIRP CAT (Charlotte, NC, USA) 2003: 70-79.
11. Noel F, Roucoules L, Teissandier D. Specification of product modelling concepts dedicated to information sharing in a collaborative design context. IDMME (Bath, UK) 2004: In cdrom
12. Requicha AAG. Toward a theory of geometric tolerancing. International Journal of Robotics Research 1983; Vol.2, n°4, pp. 45-60.
13. Robinson D M, "Geometric tolerancing for assembly", PhD thesis, Cornell University, May 1998.
14. Roy U, Sudarsan R, Sriram RD, Lyons KW, Duffey MR. Information architecture for design tolerancing: from conceptual to the detail design, DETC/DAC-8704 (Las Vegas), 1999: In cdrom
15. Salomons OW, Jonge Poerink HJ, Haalboom FJ, Van Slooten F, Van Houten FJAM, Kals H.JJ. A computer aided tolerancing Tool I: Tolerance specification. Comp. in ind. 1996; Vol. 31: 161-174.
16. Sudarsan R, Fenves SJ, Sriram RD, Wang D. A product information modeling framework for product lifecycle management. Computer Aided Design 2005; Vol. 37: 1399-1411.
17. Summers JD, Vargas-Hernandez N, Zhao Z, Shah JJ, Lacroix Z. Comparative study of representation structures for modeling function and behavior of mechanical devices. ASME DETC01/CIE 2001.
18. Turner JU. The M_space Theory of Tolerances. Advanced in Design Automation, ASME 1990; Vol. 23/1: 217-226.
19. Tichkiewitch S. Specifications on integrated design methodology using a multi-view product model. ASME Third Biennal Joint Conf. on Eng. Systems Design & Analysis 1996; PD-Vol. 80: 101-108.
20. Wirtz A. Vectorial tolerancing for production quality control and functional analysis in design. 2nd CIRP CAT (Pennstate, USA) 1991: 77-84.
21. Yoshikawa H, Tomiyama T, Kiriyama T, Umeda Y. An integrated modelling environment using the metamodel. Annals of the CIRP 1994; Vol. 43/1: 121-124.

SESSION 3

PROCESS MODELING AND PROCESS PLANNING

COST ESTIMATION AND CONCEPTUAL PROCESS PLANNING

P. Martin, J.-Y. Dantan and A. Siadat
Laboratoire de Génie Industriel et de Production Mécanique
Ecole Nationale Supérieure d'Arts et Métiers (ENSAM), France
{patrick.martin, jean-yves.dantan, ali.siadat}@metz.ensam.fr

Engineering cost estimation is now compulsory from the very first stages of design. The later a cost issue will be detected, the more it will cost. This paper tends to show how to define which information is needed to allow this estimation to be done. A taxonomy that builds a structure in this information has been created. Using this taxonomy, we designed a method to calculate manufacturing costs thanks to an expert system. The cost is determined by considering Cost Entities using pertinent inductors and parametric calculation methods.

1. INTRODUCTION

Cost considerations are nowadays critical in the engineering field. We know how tiny the liberty of action and decision for companies is. We also know how to evaluate the costs engagement during a project. During the conceptual design stage, the decisions we make engage a lot of money for the following stages of the future. This is the stage where most of the choices that imply a cost are made. However, it is also the stage where changing the decisions is the cheapest. When a company has to bring modifications on the design while in the industrialisation stage, it is very costly because all the design process has to be done again.

Therefore it is necessary to bring to designers as much information as possible so that they can take the accurate decisions. In this context, letting designers to have

In the very first stages of design a tool to evaluate the costs can be very attractive. It can prevent an inaccurate design that would go to the industrialisation department, which would send it back to designers because it is too expensive to manufacture.

We will then try to define a tool that could handle these tasks.

2. CONCEPTUAL PROCESS PLANNING/CONCEPTUAL DESIGN

This chapter is based on research by Shaw C. Feng research (Feng, 2000). It deals with the means to determine a Conceptual process design from the conceptual design.

To evaluate the manufacturing costs, it seems obvious that we need to know exactly what processes will be used to manufacture the part. However, in the conceptual design stage, we have no idea of what the processes will be. The aim of this chapter is to show how we can define a conceptual process design in the very first stages of a project.

2.1 Link between Conceptual Design and Conceptual Process Planning

Conceptual design refers to a stage in the design procedure. This stage is the one where designers define rough part characteristics based on the part requirements. Information such as the material, the general part shape and main geometrical data is provided during this stage. However, data are still rough and do not allow to define extensively the manufacturing processes.

Conceptual process design is a first estimation of what the process plan could be. Manufacturing operations are not very detailed but it allows engineers to have an idea of processes and attached resources. These data make a first cost evaluation possible. These results will allow designers to adapt their decisions regarding the costs, which is something they can not do for the time being.

Now the problem remains how to define the conceptual process plan from the conceptual design. Figure 1 shows how the two stages can be performed simultaneously.

After this stage, the project will continue with a detailed design stage. The interest in the method is to start the detailed design stage with a validated conceptual design. This will prevent the detailed design stage to be done several times.

Shaw C. Feng proposed a method to generate the Conceptual Process Planning from the Conceptual Design data. Three main steps can be found in this method. All of them are critical in the cost evaluation process.

2.2 Manufacturing processes selection (Boothroyd et al., 1994)

This activity can be divided in four activities. Its aim is to select processes that are compatible with the data we have obtained from the Conceptual Design stage. The different activities are the following:

- Determine compatible processes based on materials
- Determine compatible processes based on quantity
- Determine compatible processes based on product shape
- Determine compatible processes based on tolerances.

For this selection process, we will consider as potential processes the total range of processes. Then the material will prevent some of these processes. So the outcome will be a narrowed range of compatible processes. For example, we know we will not propose to forge a plastic part. Thanks to these four steps in a row, we will come out with a reduced range of processes that will be proposed for the Conceptual Process Plan.

Once these compatible processes are selected, we could rank them in terms of relative cost and finally let the user choose those he will consider for the upcoming stages.

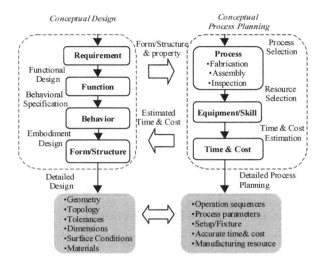

Figure 1 - Interaction between Conceptual Design and
Conceptual Process Planning (Feng, 2000).

Processes are now considered known. If we want to evaluate the induced cost, we also need to determine what will be the used resources: type of machines, toolings, tool, fixtures and labour skills.

2.3 Manufacturing cost estimation

Once the manufacturing processes and the manufacturing resources have been selected, we have the information to evaluate the cost. We have to keep in mind that this calculated cost will be a rough evaluation. The purpose is not to determine the actual manufacturing cost but to assess manufacturability and cost in the early design stage. For this estimation stage, we propose another method than Shaw C. Feng's one. This method will be developed in part 3.

3. COST ESTIMATION

3.1 Cost evaluation methods

There are several methods that exist for calculating costs. Table 1 presents the main techniques. Accordingly with this table, in the conceptual design stage, the best methods to apply are analogical or parametric. Indeed, we do not have much information on the product yet and an analytical method would be inappropriate. However, these methods might give too rough estimation to allow the designer checking the validity of the product he has started to design. These methods may not help the designer very much in his tasks.

Therefore, we will adapt an analytical method to the conceptual design stage. As we have already shown above, we can determine what processes and what resources can be used. This means that from the Conceptual Design stage, we have deduced some information usually provided in the detailed design stage. Yet, the information is still not accurate enough to allow an usual analytical method.

Table 1- Main cost estimation techniques (Creese & Moore, 1990).

	Description	Best applicable for	Accuracy
Intuition method	Evaluation of cost regarding personal knowledge and intuition.	Preliminary stage	from -30% to 50%
Comparison	Evaluation using similar parts	Preliminary stage	from -30% to 50%
Analogical method	Case-based evaluation, definition of main parameters for comparison with previous cases	Conceptual design	from -14% to 30%
Parametric method	One or several parameters are chosen to be critical. They are used along with coefficients to evaluate the cost	Conceptual design	from -14% to 30%
Analytical method	Direct and indirect costs are considered. Each cost is calculated and then they are all summed to get the product cost	Detailed design	from -5% to 15%

3.2 Adapted cost entity method

The cost entity method was created by H'Mida (H'Mida et al., 2006). It is an evolution of the well-known ABC method. These methods are analytical methods.

The cost entity method separates the company in several activities. To each activity corresponds a cost entity, figure 2 represents how this cost entity is defined.

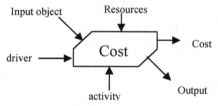

Figure 2 - Cost entity model (H'Mida et al, 2006).

Each cost entity is calculated by using equation 1. We can note that there is homogeneity between all the activities which is one of the advantages of the method. All activities can be considered identically in terms of cost contribution form.

Cost entity = d x Σ (a_r x IR_R)
  d: Unique driver chosen for the Cost Entity
  α_r: Resource R consumption coefficient
  IR_r: Resource R imputation rate

To adapt this method to conceptual design, we will simplify the formula by selecting one driver and one linked coefficient for the whole cost entity. The coefficient can be a property of a machine or a material for example. As these coefficients may be difficult to evaluate, the company may use old cost estimations to determine them. Then the used formula reduces to the following equation:

Cost entity (€) = Driver (type) x Imputation rate (€ / type) + fixed cost (€)

Roughly speaking, this method results in using the structure of a cost entity model with a parametric method. However here the parametric method is not applied to the part but to the cost entity.

3.3 Considered cost entities

To represent all the costs we will consider in our evaluation, we use a taxonomy. This representation details what are the components of the Part Cost Entity and what they are composed of. This drawing is presented in figure 3.

This scheme shows that we consider both direct costs and indirect costs with the same importance. Thanks to this cost entity, we will be able to evaluate the overall cost of the product while we are just in the conceptual design stage.

The table 2 shows examples of cost entities expressions. Yet the table is not exhaustive and some additional research has to be done to determine every cost entity expression

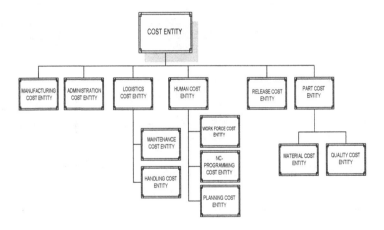

Figure 3 - Cost Entity Taxonomy.

4. SYSTEM IMPLEMENTATION

If we can go through the two stages we have shown so far, we would be able to evaluate with a good accuracy the cost part in the early design stage. These two stages are the conceptual process planning and the cost entity model calculation.

However, these steps are difficult steps to go through. In this chapter, we will show how an expert system can help with the process implementation.

Table 2 - Cost entities examples.

	driver	description	depends on
Rough material cost	part volume	$\square$ material density (kg/m^3)	material
		Vb rough part volume (m^3)	part
	formula	Cunit material unit cost per kilo (€/kg)	material
	Cmaterial = Ir x Vb x ρ x Cunit	Ir : filling index (<1)	part
Launching per machine cost	Entity complexity index	CM : machine cost rate (€ / h)	machine
		A : configuration time coefficient (h / Ie)	machine
	formula	Ie : entity complexity index	part
	Csetup=Ie x A x CM	Depends on topology, tolerances....	
Quality per tolerance cost	tolerance	IT : tolerance (mm)	part
	formula	b : coefficient (€.mm)	machine
	Ctol=a+b/IT	a : coefficient (€)	machine
Administrative cost per batch	production size	Q : production size (qty)	part
	formula	k : coefficient (€/qty)	administrative operation
	Cadmin = Q x k + F	F : fixed cost coefficient (€)	administrative operation
Material handling cost per material	Transfer amount	Q : production size (qty)	part
	formula	S : part projected surface (m^2)	part
	Chandling={(QxS)/ Strans]xB	Strans : transportation surface (of truck) (m^2)	handling facility
		B : coefficient (€/transfer)	handling facility

4.1 Ontology and taxonomy

Before implementing the estimation process with an expert system, we have to structure the information. This can be made thanks to an ontology and a taxonomy.

The ontology is used to represent the vocabulary linked to part manufacturing field. It contains object classes such as Tools or people or concepts such as Costs. It also contains the different attributes that can be added to these classes (description, size, velocity) and the relations between objects (a Machining Operation can be linked to a Machine by the relation "is made by"). To structure it, we will use a taxonomy. This graphic representation exposes clearly the hierarchy and class instances.

4.2 Application to conceptual process planning

The data we will deal with in conceptual process planning can be classified in three main categories. First will be data related to the entity (general information on the product), then data related to the processes and finally data related to the resources.

A detailed version of the "Operation" branch is presented on figure 4. We will not develop here the other branches because it will not be of a great importance in the presentation. This hierarchy is taken from Marty and Linares work upon manufacturing processes (Marty & Linares, 1994).

Thus, while selecting the processes thanks to the previously viewed method, we will look for processes among these. We consider it is not necessary to continue with a finest description of processes ("Drilling" can be "Short drilling" or "Deep drilling" for example) because we will not have the information to satisfy such a level of detail. Besides, the described precision will be accurate enough to have a general view upon manufacturing costs.

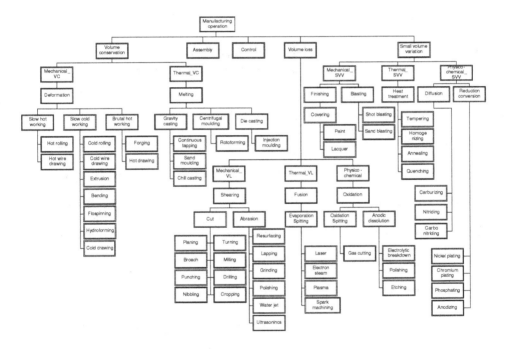

Figure 4 - Operation branch (Marty & Linares, 1994).

4.3 Expert system development

To implement the system, we chose to use the "C Language Integrated Production System" (CLIPS) (http://www.ghg.net/clips/CLIPS.html). This system was created by the NASA. CLIPS provides a complete environment for the construction of rule and/or object based expert systems.

Here is an example of a selection rule translated in CLIPS.

- *(defrule material_aluminium (declare(salience 100))*
  ?o<-(object(is-a ALUMINIUM_ALLOY)) =>
  (make-instance slow_cold of PROCESS_MATERIAL (name slow_cold))
  (make-instance slow_hot of PROCESS_MATERIAL (name slow_hot))
  (make-instance by_gravity of PROCESS_MATERIAL (name by_gravity))

This rule can be translated as follows: IF the class «ALUMINUM ALLOY» contains an element (which means the used material is an aluminium alloy), THEN create objects «slow_cold», «slow_hot», «by_gravity» in the list "PROCESS_MATERIAL". This means that this list will contain all the processes that can be applied to aluminium alloys.

So by entering all these rules in the expert system, we will be able to select what are the compatible processes. Afterwards the user will be asked for the one he wants to use and we will then know the process and will be able to evaluate the cost.

5. CONCLUSION

We presented in this paper how we can evaluate parts costs from the early design stage. This activity would be very attractive for manufacturers and may make companies save time and money.

This evaluation process implies a conceptual process planning. We have described how we can link conceptual design to conceptual process planning.

However, the implemented program deals only with the processes selection. The program is not achieved as resources selection and cost calculation are lacking. Nevertheless the theory has been shown.

We have also described the method we may apply to calculate the costs. This method would allow considering the global package of costs that could be linked to the part manufacturing. It means not only direct and manufacturing costs are taken into account but also indirect costs such as handling. However, this method needs to have a high number of coefficients and a good knowledge of costs is necessary to allow these coefficients calculation.

6. REFERENCES

1. Boothroyd G., Dewhurst P., Knight W., Product design for manufacture and assembly, Textbook, Edition Marcel Dekker Inc, University of Rhode Island, 1994.
2. Creese R.C. & L.T. Moore "Cost Modelling for concurrent engineering", Cost engineering, Vol. 32, 1990.
3. Feng Shaw C., Conceptual Process Planning, a Definition anf Functionnal Decomposition, Manufacturing Science in Engineering, V10 in the proceedings of the international mechanical engineering congress and exposition, 2000.
4. H'Mida F., Martin P., Vernadat F., Cost estimation in mechanical production: the cost entity approach applied to integrated product engineering, International journal of production economics Volume 103, Issue 1, September 2006.
5. http://www.ghg.net/clips/CLIPS.html
6. Marty C., Linares M., procédés de fabrication, Vol. 3, Industrialisation des produits mécaniques, édition Paris hermés, 1999.

SEMI-GENERATIVE MACRO-PROCESS PLANNING FOR RECONFIGURABLE MANUFACTURING

Ahmed Azab, Giulio Perusi, Hoda ElMaraghy and Jill Urbanic

Intelligent Manufacturing Systems (IMS) Centre, University of Windsor, Canada
{azab, perusi, hae, urbanic}@uwindsor.ca

Global competition and frequent market changes are challenges facing manufacturing enterprises at present. Manufacturers are faced with new unpredicted modifications at the part design level, which require increased functionality at the system design level. Reconfigurable Manufacturing Systems (RMS) addresses this situation by providing the exact capacity needed when needed. Process planning concepts and methods should be developed to support this new manufacturing environment. Variant process planning systems with their rigid definition of the boundaries of part families do not satisfactorily support Reconfigurable Manufacturing Systems. A semi-generative macro process planning system has been developed and is reported in this paper. Precedence graphs, which depict the precedence relationships between features/operations, are reconfigured by adding and removing nodes. The problem of generating optimal macro-level process plans is combinatorial in nature and proven NP-hard. Hence, a random-based heuristic based on Simulated Annealing is tailored for this problem. Finally, a realistic case study is presented to illustrate the proposed methodology. A family of single-cylinder front covers is used. The proposed method produced good quality optimal solutions and is proven efficient in terms of computation time as demonstrated by the obtained results.

1. INTRODUCTION

Mass customization and agile manufacturing are paradigms that have emerged quite recently to face the new challenges of the twenty-first century. Manufacturers are faced day after day with varying product mixes. They are required to machine parts, which are not strictly defined within the boundaries of their respective families of parts. Considerations of product variety and new product introductions at the fundamental design stage for a dedicated manufacturing system are ignored. A Flexible Manufacturing System (FMS) on the other hand overcomes this challenge by having all the needed functionality built-in from day one; however this results in high initial capital investments as well as relatively lower utilization. In order to stay competitive, new types of manufacturing systems that are more responsive must be developed (ElMaraghy, 2006). Reconfigurability, an engineering technology that deals with cost-effective, quick reaction to market changes, is needed (Koren *et al.*, 1999). Reconfigurable Manufacturing Systems (RMS) is created by incorporating basic process modules that can be rearranged or replaced quickly and reliably (Mehrabi *et al.*, 2000).

Process planning has two distinguished levels, Macro- and Micro-level planning (ElMaraghy, 1993). At the Macro-level, planning is concerned with identifying the main tasks and their best sequence and the type of manufacturing processes. Micro-level planning details process parameters, required tools and setups, process time and resources. Process planning can also be classified into variant and generative. Retrieval-based process planning techniques, based on a master template of a composite part, lend themselves to RMS predicated on a defined part family. However, this approach results in less than optimum process plans because of the lack of specificity, precision, refinement and optimization possible at this high level of abstraction. Generative process planning is better able to handle products variety by generating process plans from scratch using rule- and knowledge-based systems, heuristics and problem specific algorithms. Pure generic generative systems are not yet a reality. Hence, a practical macro-level system, which is variant in nature, but yet also able to generate process plans for new parts that are not members of the original part family's master plan, is proposed for RMS.

Hetem (2003) discussed research, development and deployment of concepts and technologies to develop variant process planning systems for RMS. Bley and Zenner (2005) proposed another variant concept - an integrated management concept that allows meeting requirements of different markets and changing needs by generating a generalized product model. Both papers presented a strictly retrieval type system, which did not support introduction of new features into the part family caused by changing demands. There is a dearth of literature that offers generative process planning solutions for RMS.

The following papers implemented simulated annealing in process planning. Lee *et al.* (2001) proposed four simulated annealing algorithms to solve the operation sequencing problem. Ma *et al.* (2000) reported a simulated annealing algorithm for operations selection and sequencing. Li *et al.* (2002) developed a hybrid genetic algorithm-simulated annealing approach to optimize process plans by concurrently considering machine assignment, selection of setup plans and sequencing. Brown *et al.* (1997) proposed a generative simulated annealing algorithm. Ma *et al.* (2002) presented the development of a computer-aided process planning (CAPP) system based on genetic algorithm and simulated annealing. In this paper, a heuristic based on simulated annealing, tailored to meet the need of hybrid process planning, generates optimal operation sequences for reconfigured parts with features beyond the pre-defined boundaries of the original part families.

2. METHODOLOGY

2.1 Knowledge Representation and Manipulation

The basic input to process planning is the part CAD description including the part's form features attributes, the working Geometric Dimensions and Tolerances (GD&T) and surface finish specifications. The large number of interactions that exists between the different form features constituting the part complicates the problem. A Feature Precedence Graph (FPG), which is a tree-like structure graph, is adopted where machining features are mapped onto nodes. Arcs between nodes represent features precedence. Each arc carries a cost, which approximates the number of tasks to be performed. The FPG is manipulated by adding and removing nodes to accommodate additional as well as missing machining features in the new parts. An FPG is translated into an Operations Precedence Graph (OPG), where each feature corresponds to one or more machining operation (figure 2).

2.2 Developed Heuristic

The objective is to sequence a global set of machining operations of a given part subject to a number of precedence constraints in order to minimize the total idle time spent mainly in repositioning the workpiece or fixture and tool changes. This problem has already been proven to be NP-hard. Hence, a search heuristic based on Simulated Annealing is developed. Simulated Annealing is a hill-climbing search method suitable for solving combinatorial problems as well as continuous problems with multi-modal objective functions (Vidal, 1993). The proposed algorithm is comprised of two nested loops, an outer loop where the annealing temperature (T) decreases and an inner one, which iterates a number of loops that decrease with T. In the inner loop new moves to neighboring solutions are accepted if they are of better quality to allow for hill climbing. Lower quality solutions are also accepted with an exponential probability distribution. An algorithm is developed to validate the generated relaxed sequences against the precedence constraints and, then as needed, repair them if no valid feasible solutions are generated after a certain number of moves. The reason behind this validation process is that the solution space before the application of the constraints is factorial in size. It is also believed that the size of this part of the solution space is exponential in nature, which renders the search infeasible after applying the constraints. Therefore, it would be inefficient to wait until a feasible solution is generated randomly since the probability of its generation proved to be very low. Therefore, a shuffling operator is applied at the end of each outer loop to increase the chances of exploring more parts of the feasible solution space. The best solution found is always stored and updated.

3. CASE STUDY

3.1 The Front Cover Part Family

A single cylinder, air cooled, overhead valve engine front cover family of parts is used as an example to demonstrate the developed method. The aluminum front covers are die cast to the near net shape; finish machining is required for precision features and the tapped holes. The family's composite part is shown in figure 1. A sample of features, their labels, corresponding operation information, the Tool Access Direction (TAD) and the number of each feature type are shown in Table 1. A three axis horizontal Reconfigurable Machine Tool (RMT) is assumed to be used; hence, three setups are required to produce the part in order to access the features on the front and back faces (–Z, +Z) and the side face (+X). The ratio of the time required to position the workpiece on a different fixture (composed of unloading the workpiece, cleaning the setup, and loading the workpiece) to the tool changeover time is assumed 2:1. The FPG shown in figure 2 can be easily translated to an OPG using the operations information found in Table 1. The type of precedence is shown on the FPG by having the arrows carry a symbol denoting its type. S stands for precedence due to fixture or setup datum points; and d for dimensional precedence. If it is a dimensioning datum constraint, the appropriate GD&T symbol is then used. Some feature labels in the FPG are suffixed by an r or f; this indicates that both roughing and finishing operations are required for these specific features. The precedence constraints that must be satisfied are: 1. The features must be accessible by the tool; 2. The logical sequence of operations; 3. The dimensional and geometrical precedences are considered; 4. The non-destructive constraint; 5. The precedence due to machined setup datum points; and 6. Good machining practice. The roughing and finishing operations may be separated by some other features to satisfy the non-destructive precedence. This constraint, for example, influences the feature precedence of features f2 and f3 on the cover.

Table 1 - Features, operations, tools and TAD for the composite part.

Features	Operation description	Operations	Tool ID	Tools	TAD	# of features
f1	Drilling	1	T1	Step drill Ø7mm	z	2
	Boring	2	T2	Bore Ø7.5mm		
	Finish boring	3	T3	Bore Ø8mm		
f2	Drilling	4	T4	Core drill Ø7mm	-z	1
	Boring	5	T2	Bore Ø7.5mm		
	Finish boring	6	T3	Bore Ø8mm		
f3	Rough milling	7	T5	End mill	z	1
	Finish milling	8	T6	Face mill		
f4	Finish milling	9	T6	Face mill	-z	1
f5	Rough boring	10	T7	Special rough boring tool	z	1
	Boring	11	T8	Special boring tool		
	Finish boring	12	T9	Special finish boring tool		
f6	Drilling	13	T4	Core drill Ø7mm	z	8
f7	Milling	14	T5	End mill	-z	1
f8	Drill's spot face	15	T10	Spot face and tap drill	x	1
	Tapping	16	T11	M20-1.5 tap		
f9	Tapping	17	T12	M10-1.5 tap	-z	4
f10	Rough boring	18	T13	Bore Ø16.25mm	z	1
	Boring	19	T14	Bore Ø17.25mm		
	Finish boring	20	T15	Bore Ø18mm		
f11	Drilling	21	T1	Step drill Ø7mm	-z	6
	Tapping	22	T16	Special 9/32 (inch) tap		
f12	Drilling	23	T1	Step drill Ø7mm	z	1
f13	Drilling	24	T1	Step drill Ø7mm	z	1
f14	Finish milling	25	T6	Face mill	-z	1
f15	Finish milling	26	T6	Face mill	z	1
f16	Drilling	27	T4	Core drill Ø7mm	-z	1
	Boring	28	T2	Bore Ø7.5mm		
	Finish boring	29	T3	Bore Ø8mm		
	Drilling	30	T17	Special drill Ø4.5mm		

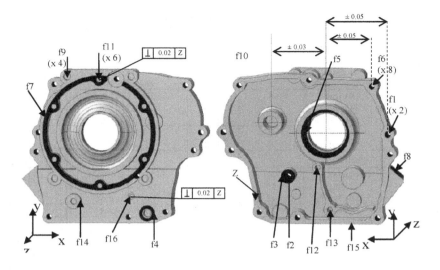

Figure 1 - The composite cylinder front cover.

A new member of the front cover extended family, illustrated in figure 3, is introduced. It contains 8 features in common with the existing composite part (highlighted in black in both figures 1 and 3), but it also has 7 new features, which do not exist in the original part family's composite part. Details of the features are shown in Table 2. The original three-axis horizontal configuration of the RMT is not sufficient for producing the new part; an extra dedicated setup or two special angle head tools would be required to machine feature f17, for example. Hence, the machine tool is reconfigured by adding an appropriate rotational axis of motion onto the spindle or table, i.e. the RMT becomes a 4-axis horizontal machining center.

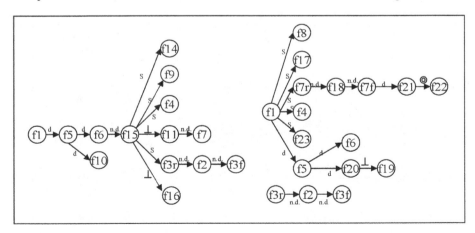

Figure 2 - Feature precedence graph (FPG) of the original composite and the new cylinder front cover.

Table 2 - Features, operations, tools and TADs for the new cylinder front cover.

Features	Operation description	Operations	Tool ID	Tools	TAD	# of features
f1	Drilling	1	T18	Drill Ø7mm	z	2
	Boring	2	T19	Bore Ø7.5mm		
	Finish boring	3	T20	Bore Ø8mm		
f2	Drilling	4	T18	Drill Ø7mm	-z	1
	Boring	5	T19	Bore Ø7.5mm		
	Finish boring	6	T20	Bore Ø8mm		
f3	Rough milling	7	T21	End mill	z	1
	Finish milling	8	T22	Face mill		
f4	Finish milling	9	T22	Face mill	-z	1
f5	Rough boring	10	T23	Step drill Ø49mm	z	1
	Boring	11	T24	Bore Ø51mm		
	Finish boring	12	T25	Bore Ø52mm		
f6	Drilling	13	T18	Drill Ø7mm	-z	8
f7	Rough milling	14	T21	End mill	-z	1
	Finish milling	15	T26	Face mill b		
f8	Surface finish	16	T27	Spot face and tap drill	x‡	1
	Tapping	17	T28	M18-1.5 tap		
f17	Surface finish	31	T27	Spot face and tap drill	x‡	1
	Tapping	32	T28	M18-1.5 tap		
f18	Tapping	33	T29	Tap drill Ø7mm	-z	8
f19	Rough boring	34	T30	Bore Ø19mm	-z	1
	Boring	35	T31	Bore Ø20.5mm		
	Finish boring	36	T32	Bore Ø21.5mm		
f20	Rough boring	37	T23	Step drill Ø49mm	z	1
	Boring	38	T24	Bore Ø51mm		
	Finish boring	39	T25	Bore Ø52mm		
f21	Boring	40	T33	Bore Ø14mm	-z	1
	Boring	41	T34	Bore Ø16mm		
	Groove	42	T35	Special bore Ø5mm		
	Finish milling	43	T26	Face mill b		
f22	Drilling	44	T18	Drill Ø7mm	-z	1
f23	Milling	45	T21	End mill	-z	1

‡ *f8 & f17 TAD is different; however reconfiguring the RMT, adding a 4th axis, eliminated this distinction.*

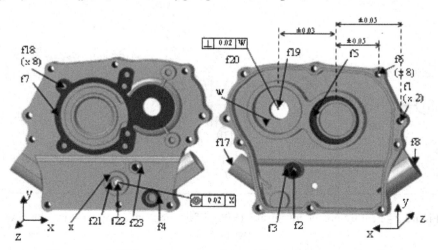

Figure 3 - Additional new part of the cylinder front cover family.

3.2 Results

Ten runs were performed for each engine front cover, the composite as well as the additional new part of the front cover family. The best near optimal operation sequences are given in Tables 3-4. For the composite part, the mean and standard deviation of the objective function values are 32.4 and 0.52 respectively. As for the additional new part the mean and standard deviation are 40 and 0.94 respectively. It can be concluded from the close difference between the best objective function values obtained and the averages, and also the small values of the standard deviation that the results obtained were consistent and of very close quality. In many cases, even more than one solution is obtained with the same objective function value. The search algorithm parameters were tested to arrive at the best working ranges.

Table 3- Results for the composite part.

Near-optimal sequence of operations	O
24 1 2 3 10 11 12 13 26 16 27 28 29 4 30 5 21 22 14 17 6 9 25 7 18 8 15 19 23 20	
1 2 3 23 24 10 11 12 13 26 4 27 28 29 30 21 17 9 15 22 25 14 5 6 16 18 19 7 20 8	
1 23 2 3 24 10 11 12 13 15 26 16 18 19 20 7 8 27 25 21 9 17 28 4 22 5 6 29 30 14	32
1 24 2 3 10 23 11 12 13 26 4 27 28 5 17 21 6 29 25 16 22 9 7 30 14 15 18 19 8 20	
15 16 1 2 3 10 11 12 13 24 26 23 25 9 21 27 22 17 14 4 5 6 7 18 19 20 8 28 29 30	
1 2 3 10 11 12 13 23 26 27 28 29 30 17 9 25 21 22 14 4 15 16 5 6 7 8 18 19 24 20	

O = Objective function value.

Table 4 - Results for the member part.

Near-optimal sequence of operations	O
1 2 3 7 10 11 12 37 38 39 34 9 14 45 35 4 33 5 15 40 8 41 42 6 43 36 13 44 31 32 16 17	
1 2 3 10 11 12 7 37 38 39 9 34 14 35 36 33 15 40 41 8 4 13 45 5 6 42 43 44 31 16 17 32	39
1 2 3 10 11 12 37 38 7 39 34 45 14 4 33 15 40 5 41 6 42 35 31 16 17 36 43 13 44 32 9 8	

O = Objective function value.

4. CONCLUDING REMARKS

A practical semi-generative process planning approach suitable for the reconfiguration of both the products and manufacturing systems has been developed. The macro-level process plan is formulated as a sequence of operations corresponding to a set of features in the part. The interactions between the part's different features/operations are modeled using Features/Operations Precedence Graphs (FPG/OPG). The FPG/OPG graphs of a part family's composite part are edited to account for the missing as well as the added features. A random-based heuristic is developed to obtain optimal or near-optimal operation sequences. A validation scheme is developed and used to maintain the specified precedence relationships.

An optimal single operations sequence can easily become less optimal in a changeable production environment; hence the importance of adapting to the changes and producing alternate optimal operations sequences for the changed parts becomes obvious.

The proposed method is applied to an industrial example of single-cylinder family of front covers defined by a composite cover and a corresponding master process plan. A new macro-level process plan is generated for a new cover, the features of which differ (new, missing and modified) from those that exist in the original family's composite part. The manufacturing system machines had to be reconfigured accordingly to be capable of producing the new features in the introduced front cover. Although this re-planning is normally done off-line, the developed heuristic has the advantage of being fast (10 minutes on average per run on a Pentium 4 with 1 GB RAM); hence, multiple runs are possible to arrive at alternate solutions efficiently. Moreover, converting the code deployed on MATLAB™ (an interpreter) into an executable could further reduce the algorithm execution time. For future work, a hybrid heuristic with Genetic Algorithms may be developed to transform the point search into a population search, and hence more than one sub-optimal solution could be obtained from a single run.

5. REFERENCES

1. Bley, H and Zenner, C. Feature-based planning of reconfigurable manufacturing systems by a variant management approach. CIRP 3rd International Conference on Reconfigurable Manufacturing 2005.
2. Brown, KN and Cagan, J. Optimized process planning by generative simulated annealing. Artificial intelligence for engineering design, analysis and manufacturing 1997; 11 3: 219-235.
3. ElMaraghy, HA. Flexible and Reconfigurable Manufacturing Systems Paradigms, Special Issue of the International Journal of Manufacturing Systems (IJMS), In Press, 2006.
4. ElMaraghy, HA. Evolution and future perspectives of CAPP, CIRP Annals, 1993; V. 1, 42 2: 739-751.
5. Halevi, G and Weill, RD. Principles of process planning. Chapman & Hall, 1995.
6. Hetem, V. Variant process planning, a basis for reconfigurable manufacturing systems. CIRP 2nd International Conference on Reconfigurable Manufacturing 2003.
7. Koren, Y, Heisel, U, Jovane, F, Moriwaki, T, Pritschow, G, Ulsoy, G and Van Brussel, H. Reconfigurable manufacturing systems. CIRP Annals- Manufacturing Technology 1999; 48 2: 527-540.
8. Lee, D-O, Kiritsis, D and Xirouchakis, P. Search heuristics for operation sequencing in process planning. International journal of production research 2001; 39 16: 3771-3788.
9. Li, WD, Ong, SK and Nee, AYC. Hybrid genetic algorithm and simulated annealing approach for the optimization of process plans for prismatic parts. International journal of production research 2002; 40 8: 1899-1922.
10. Ma, GH, Zhang, YF and Nee AYC. A simulated annealing-based optimization algorithm for process planning. International journal of production research 2000; 38 12: 2671-2687.
11. Ma, GH, Zhang, YF and Nee AYC. An automated process planning system based on genetic algorithm and simulated annealing. Proceedings of the ASME Design Engineering Technical Conference 2002; 3: 57-63.
12. Mehrabi, MG, Ulsoy, AG and Koren Y. Reconfigurable manufacturing systems: key to future manufacturing. Journal of Intelligent Manufacturing 2000; 11 4: 403-19.
13. Vidal, R. Applied simulated annealing. Springer-Verlag, 1993.

MODELING MANUFACTURING CELLS USING PRINCIPLES OF REENGINEERING AND COMPONENT CLUSTERS

Rafael d'Ávila
Federal University of Rio Grande do Sul (UFRGS), Brazil
rafaeld@ieee.org

This paper presents a framework to support the analysis of manufacturing processes, providing the correct understanding concerning information and material flows. In addition, this analysis is combined with design structure matrixes based on components to consider better arrangements to the manufacturing process in cells, intending to provide high performance capabilities. To demonstrate the framework an example has been carried out in modeling the manufacturing of a control pack unit, which is a part of an airplane climate control system.

1. INTRODUCTION

Considering the benefits of modular products, many manufacturing companies are undertaking critical analysis and redesign of their productive process and manufacturing organization.

Understanding a product architecture as the arrangement of functional elements into physical chunks that compose the building blocks for a product, studies have shown that innovations in this subject represent a source of competitive advantage for product research and development enterprises (Ulrich; Eppinger, 2000 and Henderson; Clark, 1990).

The modularity of product architecture is inversely proportional to the modules interaction, and can be adopted with strategically interests. The development of modular products requires full identification of highly interactive groups of elements and clustering them into product modules or productive cells.

This paper presents a robust framework to identify, model, optimize and analyze component clusters, intending to provide correct understanding about relationships between product components and optimized arrangements to the manufacturing process in cells based in component clusters. This is demonstrated with an applied study analyzing a control pack unit, a subsystem of an airplane air conditioning system.

2. PROCESS MODELING USING IDEF0

The IDEF (Integration Definition for Function Modeling) pattern its provided to design, to model and to understand the set of activities that compose a specific process, as well as data that support connectivity between these activities (Colquhoun, 1993). The IDEF was derived from a well-established graphical language know as the Structured Analysis and Design Technique (SADT). The literature about IDEF reports sixteen methods, which provide a high visibility of manufacturing and business process (Aguilar-Savén, 2003).

In this paper the IDEF0 is used, which represents hierarchically process decomposed in activities or functions, through ICOM (Input, Control, Output, Mechanism) diagrams using a simple and efficient notation, as shown in figure 1.

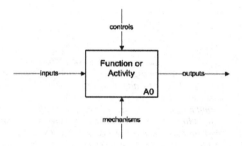

Figure 1 – ICOM Model (Aguilar-Savén, 2003).

As can be observed in figure 1, each function or activity is described by a rectangular box that can be decomposed in many levels of hierarchy. The arrows defining "Controls" refer to all necessary conditions to the activity or function operation, generating expected outputs after processing the inputs. On the other hand, the arrows defining "Mechanisms" indicate the executor of the activity, which can be persons, machines, equipments, or even other organizations.

Thus, IDEF0 provides powerful means of analysis and development for the manufacturing enterprise, establishing the scope of analysis either for a particular functional analysis or for future analyses from another system's perspective. As an analytical tool, IDEF0 assists the modeller in identifying the performed functions and what is needed to perform them.

3. DESIGN STRUCTURE MATRIX (DSM)

3.1 General

The design structure matrix (DSM) is a popular analysis tool for system modeling and representation, especially for purposes of integration and decomposition (Browning, 2001). A DSM displays the relationships established between components of a system in a compact and visual format.

Based on information extracted from IDEF0 modeling, it's possible to decompose data in a graph that represents precedence and connectivity relations between different mapped activities, through information flows. An information flow (t_{ij}) is represented by an arc and an activity by a node on graph, as shown in figure 2.

Figure 2 – Information flow.

Thus, the activity t_i represents the operation time required by activity i, what indicates that each information flow t_{ij} is defined by an activity pair (i,j). The graph originated from relations between activities can be expressed as $P(V, A)$, where V is the set of activities and A the set of information flows in the graph.

Considering K as a graph with a vertex-set $\{v_1, v_2, v_3, v_4,...,v_n\}$, then the adjacency matrix of K is the $n \times n$ matrix $G(K) = (g_{ij})$, where g_{ij} is the number of edges joining g_i and g_j. There are various other matrixes associated with K. For example, if the edges of K are $\{e_1, e_2, e_3, e_4,...,e_m\}$, then the binary incidence matrix of K is the $n \times m$ matrix $A(K) = (a_{ij})$ (GOULD, 1988).

Given a binary activity-to-activity matrix $A(K) = \lfloor a_{ij} \rfloor_{n \times m}$, where

$$a_{ij} = \begin{Bmatrix} 1 \\ 0 \end{Bmatrix}, \text{ adopting 1 if activity } i \text{ is used to process activity } j \text{ and 0 otherwise}, \quad (1)$$

the most desired decomposition of matrix A would be into mutually separable matrices $A_1, A_2, A_3, A_4,..., A_t$. Some algorithms are used to transform an initial matrix (1) into a more structured form by the permutation of rows and columns, aiming to rearrange the rows and columns of the matrix in order to place the non-zero elements in sub-matrices, associated with a cluster. An example of a DSM is showed in figure 3.

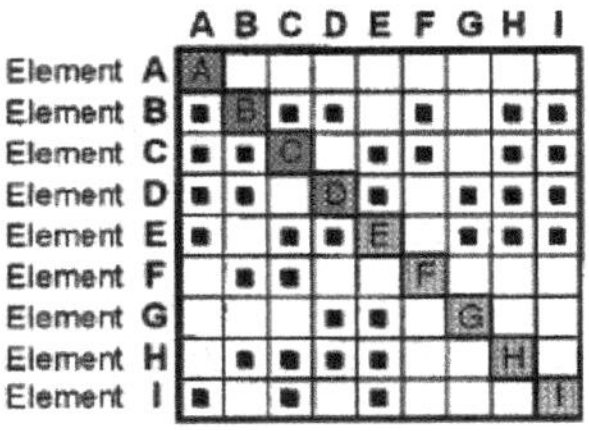

Figure 3 – Example DSM (Browning, 2001).

Summarizing, an off-diagonal mark in a DSM signifies the dependency of one element on another. Reading across a row reveals what other elements the element in that row provides to (output sinks); otherwise, scanning down a column reveals what other elements the element in that column depends on (input sources). (Browning, 2001).

3.2 Component-based DSM

The component-based DSM is a static representation of system elements existing simultaneously, such as components of a given product architecture or groups in an organization. Product architecture is the arrangement of functional elements into physical chunks that compose the building blocks for a product or a family of products (Ulrich; Eppinger, 2000). Many studies have shown that innovative product architectures represent a source of competitive advantage for product research and development enterprises (Henderson; Clark, 1990).

An essential prerequisite for innovation is understanding, which can be developed and increased through the use of models that highlight the interfaces or interactions between system elements. A DSM can represent a product architecture in terms of the relationships between its constituent components. In general, the system engineering exercise to obtain a correct understanding involves the following three steps:

a)   decompose the system into elements;
b)   document and understand all interactions or integrations between the elements;
c)   analyze potential reintegration of the elements into clusters;

Integration analysis by clustering off-diagonal elements and reordering rows and columns of the DSM can provide new insights into system integration and decomposition. However, clustering requires some considerations. The foremost objective of clustering is to maximize interactions between elements within clusters while minimizing interactions between different clusters (Sanchez; Mahoney, 1997). It has also been suggested to minimize the size of the clusters (Altus; Kroo; Gages, 1995). Also it may be useful to allow for some overlapping of clusters, for example, recognizing certain elements in more than one cluster.

Clusters algorithms are very helpful in integration analysis. By reordering rows and columns, a clustering algorithm seeks a DSM configuration that optimizes an objective function. Several algorithms and heuristics have been offered (Fernandez, 1998). After clustering analysis, any exogenous interactions to the cluster should be noticed as interfaces, requiring special attention and verification. No single clustering approach is the best solution, but visual inspection and manipulation are often adequate for small or sparse matrices.

4. PURPOSED MODEL

The purposed model and its tools provides a complete framework to identify, model, optimize and analyze component clusters, originated after a process reengineering project team has identified and modelled the manufacturing process. This paper is concerned about the use of IDEF0 methods to identify components, the DSM to model, clustering algorithms to optimize data and qualitative analysis to evaluate results obtained using the framework. The purposed model is shown in figure 4.

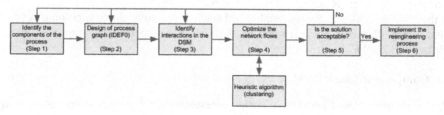

Figure 4 – Purposed Model.

In the first step the team must to identify core components of the process in a manufacturing enterprise. This information can be frequently revised and involves data about time, cost and information flows. In the step two is designed all the activities using an IDEF0 model and linked one to each other that have some relationship. After designed the IDEF0 model, in step three this model is transposed to a DSM and all relationships between the elements are marked in the matrix. After this, in step four a heuristic clustering algorithm is applied in the DSM to optimize the arrangement of information flows between elements previously marked in the structure. Finally, is necessary to evaluate if the obtained solution is considered acceptable, in step five. If the solution is not acceptable, is recommended to avail the enter parameters since the first step and to execute various simulations. Else, if solution is considered usable, the team may implement the reengineering process analyzed.

The clustering algorithm used in step four of this purposed model is based on the work of Fernandez (1998), where a coordination cost function can be developed to evaluate different clustering arrangements within the DSM. For each team in the DSM the algorithm calculates a coordination cost. Then, the sum of all coordination costs for each team gives a total coordination cost. Equations 2 and 3 show the coordination cost from a team i.

If both teams i and j are in any cluster k, then

$$Coordination\ Cost(team_i) = \sum_{j=1}^{size} \left(DSM(i,j) + DSM(j,i)\right) * \sum_{k=1}^{Cl} cl\_size(k)^{pow\_cc}, \quad (2)$$

else, (if no k cluster contains both i and j, the entire DSM acts as a cluster)

$$Coordination\ Cost(team_i) = \sum_{j=1}^{size} \left(DSM(i,j) + DSM(j,i)\right) * size^{pow\_cc}, \quad (3)$$

where

size	is the size (or the number of teams) of the DSM
DSM(i,j)	is the value of the interaction or dependency between teams i and j, noting that when i=j, DSM(i,j)=0 and DSM(j,i)=0, because the diagonal entries in the DSM don't list interactions.
Cl	is the maximum number of clusters or system teams that the algorithm explores. In the algorithm Cl is equal to *size*.
cl_size(k)	is the number of teams contained in cluster k.
pow_cc	is a parameter that controls the type of penalty assigned to the size of the cluster in the coordination cost.

Equation 4 is the expression for the total coordination cost and is the objective function that the algorithm attempts to minimize.

$$Total\ Coordination\ Cost = \sum_{i=1}^{size} Coordination\ Cost(team_i). \quad (4)$$

The algorithm proceeds as follows. Initially, there are as many clusters as there are DSM elements. Then, the algorithm randomly selects an element and calculates a bid from clusters. The highest bid is chosen, and if there is an improvement in the total coordination cost, the task is added to the bidding cluster. This process continues until, after several attempts, there is no further improvement in the coordination cost (Fernandez, 1998).

5. APPLYING THE PURPOSED MODEL: A STUDY CASE

5.1 General

Intending to demonstrate the operation and to validate the purposed model was used for analysis a control pack unit, a subsystem of an airplane conditioning system (ACS). This control pack unit is composed by many different components that were enumerated, to attend the first step of the framework. After this, as recommended in second step, were identified the relationship flows by each one with others and designed an IDEF0 model, as shown in figure 5.

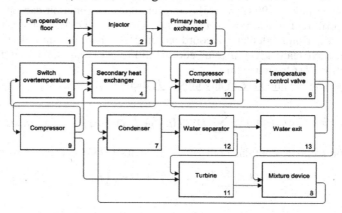

Figure 5 – IDEF0 model for a control pack unit of an airplane ACS.

This IDEF0 model was used to transpose all the identified relationships between components into a DSM matrix, as described in the third step of the purposed model. This transcription of IDEF0 into a DSM is shown in figure 6.

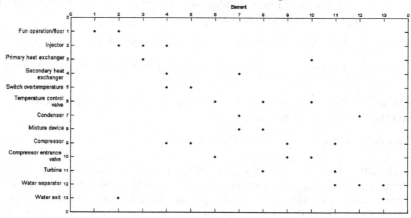

Figure 6 – DSM Matrix identifying dependencies between elements.

The clustering algorithm purposed by Fernandez (1998) and described in section 4 was applied to the generated DSM, intending to optimize and rearrange components through the measurement of coordination costs. The algorithm was applied using a MATLAB toolbox written by Thebeau (2001) and the clustered version of the DSM is shown in figure 7.

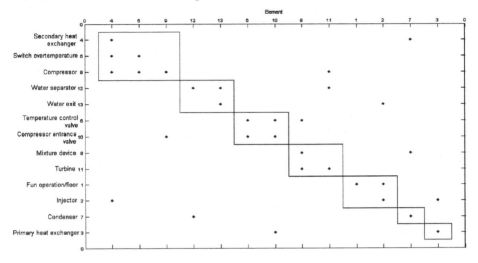

Figure 7 – Clustered DSM Matrix.

The obtained results were acceptable and reasonable, considering that elements with strong interactions, demonstrated by relationships designed in IDEF0 and after identified in DSM, were put together in the same clusters. To reach this solution, a total coordination cost was calculated and when, after several attempts, there was no further improvement in the coordination cost, the solution was considered optimal, as shown in figure 8.

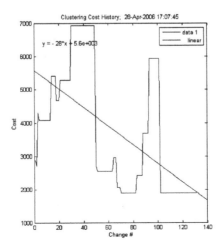

Figure 8 – Clustering cost history.

6. CONCLUSIONS

This paper started by reviewing the IDEF0 modeling tool and DSM literature related to clustering and product modularity. Then, was presented a framework to support the identifying, modeling and optimization of manufacturing processes. Providing the correct understanding about information and material flows, the identified process is converted in a component design structure matrix, intending to obtain better arrangements to the manufacturing process in cells.

To demonstrate the framework an example using a real-world problem has been carried out in modeling the manufacturing of a control pack unit, a subsystem of an airplane climate control system. The DSM is a powerful tool for representing product architectures, allowing for the analysis and development of modular products, by clustering the DSM.

As can be observed, decomposition of a product manufacturing into clusters of components can reduce the complexity of the process, decrease the size of the design product team and may have a real impact on its performance. As a result of decomposition, the design product cycle can be reduced and there is a simplification of scheduling and management of manufacturing process.

7. REFERENCES

1. Aguilar-Savén R, "Business process modeling: review and framework", International Journal of Production Economics, vol. 90, pp. 129–149, 2003.
2. Altus SS, Kroo IM, Gage PJ, "A genetic algorithm for scheduling and decomposition of multidisciplinary design problems," in Proc. 21st ASME Design Automation Conf., Boston, MA, 1995.
3. Fernandez CIG, "Integration analysis of product architecture to support effective team co-location", Master Thesis, Massachusetts Institute of Technology, 1998.
4. Henderson RM, Clark KB, "Architectural innovation: The reconfiguration of existing product technologies and the failure of established firms," Administ. Sci. Quart., vol. 35, pp. 9–30, 1990.
5. Sanchez R, Mahoney JT, "Modularity, flexibility, and knowledge management in product and organization design," IEEE Eng. Manage. Rev., pp. 50–61, 1997.
6. Thebeau, RE, "Knowledge Management of System Interfaces and Interactions for Product Development Processes", MIT Masters Thesis, System Design & Management Program, Feb. 2001.
7. Ulrich KT, Eppinger SD, Product Design and Development, 2nd ed. New York: McGraw-Hill, 2000.

CONSTRAINT PROGRAMMING APPROACH TO DESIGNING CONFLICT-FREE SCHEDULES FOR REPETITIVE MANUFACTURING PROCESSES

Robert Wójcik

The Institute of Computer Engineering, Control and Robotics
Wrocław University of Technology, Poland
robert.wojcik@pwr.wroc.pl

A problem of designing conflict-free schedules for concurrent repetitive manufacturing processes using resources in mutual exclusion is considered. Processes that share resources can wait for resources (machines) required to complete successive operations in their production routes. Systems of processes sharing only one resource are considered. A problem of finding operation times and starting times of the processes for which a schedule exists, with no process waiting for access to the shared resource has been solved using the constraint programming (CP) approach. The necessary and sufficient conditions for existence of conflict-free schedules have been implemented in the Oz/Mozart constraint programming system used to find the schedules.

1. INTRODUCTION

Planning of production flow in modern enterprises often requires solving a problem of finding a schedule defining an order of the operations executed by concurrent repetitive manufacturing processes using common resources in mutual exclusion, which in turn requires solving a problem of resource conflicts resolution (Alpan, 1997). A solution of this problem is the best schedule taking into account some constraints imposed on manufacturing operations as well as other objectives, e.g. producing parts according to just-in-time philosophy (Kanban, 1989), ensuring deadlock-free execution of processes (Banaszak, 1990), or robustness of processes (Wójcik, 2001).

In the repetitive manufacturing processes the same components are produced over and over again according to given production routes, defining a sequence of operations required for completion of the final product (Kanban, 1989), (Wójcik, 2004). Each operation in the route is using one resource (machine, buffer) for a certain amount of time defined by the operation time. Assuming that the next component may be started when the previous one has been produced a repetitive manufacturing process is created with a cycle time equal to the sum of the operation times specified in the executed production route. In case when several orders are processed at the same time the production system can be seen as a system of concurrent, repetitive manufacturing processes sharing resources in mutual exclusion (Alpan, 1997), (Wójcik, 2001).

The increased requirements concerning the time necessary to design a production plan implies a need to apply methods and tools which can be used for rapid prototyping of alternative ways of manufacturing processes execution (Banaszak, 1990), (Alpan, 1998). The method presented in this paper is based on the constraint programming (CP) (Saraswat, 1994). This approach allows finding of a feasible manufacturing schedule, which satisfies constraints imposed on the processes execution, e.g. constraints ensuring that no process will ever wait for resource allocation (Wójcik, 2001). It can be seen as an attractive alternative for methods based on computer simulation or operations research.

2. PROBLEM FORMULATION

Consider a system composed of n repetitive manufacturing processes, which are sharing a single resource, i.e. the n-process. For given domains of the operation times, assuming the processes are being repeated forever (a number of parts produced according to a production route can be infinite), the problem considered consists in finding the operation times and the starting times of the processes for which a feasible schedule exists with no process waiting for access to the shared resource. The conflict-free schedule must fulfil all constraints imposed on the processes' execution by the precedence relations and by the resources availability.

3. DEFINING SYSTEM OF REPETITIVE PROCESSES

In a manufacturing system shown in Fig. 1 three types of parts P_1, P_2, P_3 are produced using machines R, O_1, O_2, O_3. Assuming the infinite number of parts for each type, the production of the parts creates three cyclic manufacturing processes, repeated forever, and sharing resource R in mutual exclusion, i.e. the 3-process.

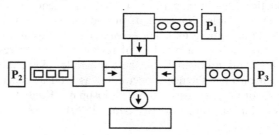

Figure 1 – A manufacturing system producing three types of parts P_1, P_2, P_3.

The n-process system $(P_1,...,P_i,...,P_j,...,P_n)$ consists of n repetitive manufacturing processes sharing a single resource R, e.g. the 3-process system (P_1,P_2,P_3). Each process P_i executes periodically a sequence of operations using resources defined by $Z_i = (R, O_i)$, where R denotes a shared resource used by the processes, O_i represents the non-shared resources used by process P_i, and $i=1,2,...,n$. The operation times $ZT_i = (r_i, o_i)$, corresponding to the route Z_i, belong to certain domains $r_i \in DR_i$,

$DR_i=\{r_{i1},r_{i2},\ldots,r_{ij},\ldots,r_{iw}\}$, and $o_i\in DO_i$, $DO_i=\{o_{i1},o_{i2},\ldots,o_{ij},\ldots,o_{iv}\}$, where r_{ij}, $o_{ij}\in N$. A cycle time of P_i is defined by relation $c_i=r_i+o_i$.

It has been shown (Wójcik, 2001) that the behaviour of the n-process system depends on the operation times and starting times (phases) of the component 2-process subsystems. In the following conditions for existence of a waiting-free schedule for n-process system will be given (Wójcik, 2004).

4. THE ALGEBRAIC MODEL OF THE SYSTEM

A natural model describing dynamics of repetitive manufacturing processes sharing a resource is modulus algebra (Schroder, 1997), (Wójcik, 2001). To avoid resource conflicts it is enough to exclude situations when a process is requesting shared resource while other process is using it. Taking into account the properties of the modulus algebra it is possible to design recurrent modulus equations that define times of any process resource request in relation to a chosen process request and to find conditions ensuring waiting-free execution of the n-process system.

4.1 Local Starting Times

Consider a system of cyclic processes $(P_1,\ldots,P_i,\ldots,P_j,\ldots,P_n)$ sharing a single resource (Fig. 1). Let $x_i(k)\in N\cup\{0\}$ for $k=0,1,2,\ldots$, denote times at which a process P_i, where $i\in\{1,2,\ldots,n\}$, requests access to the shared resource R and $a_i(k)\in N\cup\{0\}$ times at which it receives access to the resource (Fig. 2). There is $0\le x_i(k)\le a_i(k)$ and it is assumed that a starting time of a chosen process P_i is given and equal to $x_i(0)=0$. A starting time of any other process P_j, where $j\ne i$ is such that $x_j(0)\ge 0$. The times $x_i(k)$, $a_i(k)$, $i=1,2,\ldots,n$, and $k=0,1,2,\ldots$, define a schedule of the processes.

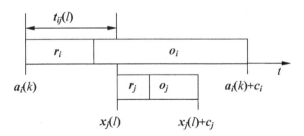

Figure 2 – Local resource requesting time $t_{ij}(l)$ for processes (P_i,P_j).

Assuming that only one process P_j is executed in the system (no resource sharing) subsequent resource requesting times $x_i(k)$ are equal to the allocation times $a_i(k)$ and can be calculated according to the equation $x_i(k+1)=a_i(k+1)=a_i(k)+c_i$ (Fig. 2). Therefore, $x_i(k)=a_i(k)=a_i(0)+k*c_i$. In the case of concurrent execution of the processes the relevant formula has to take into account a waiting time $w_i(k)$ of the process P_i, i.e. $a_i(k+1)=x_i(k+1)+w_i(k)=a_i(k)+c_i+w_i(k)$. A parameter $t_{ij}(l)\in N$ & $t_{ij}(l)\in[0,c_i)$, $l=0,1,2,\ldots$ (Fig.2), defines distance between a resource request time $x_j(l)$ of process P_j and the nearest resource allocation time $a_i(k)\le x_j(l)$ of process P_i.

The shift $t_{ij}(l)$ can be used as a local starting time of P_j in relation to the nearest, previous resource allocation time of P_i.

For any 2-process subsystem (P_i,P_j) of the n-process system, where $i \neq j$ & $i,j \in \{1,2,...,n\}$, it is possible to derive (Wójcik, 2004) values $t_{ij}(l)$, $l=0,1,2,...$, using recurrent modulus equations. It can be proven that in the case of no resource conflicts, resource request times of process P_j, calculated in relation to resource allocation times of process P_i, can occur only at times $t_{ij}(l) \in [0,c_i)$ given by

$$t_{ij}(l) = x_j(l) \bmod c_i = a_j(l) \bmod c_i = f_{ij}(l)D_{ij} + y_{ij}(l) \ \& \ l=0,1,2,... \qquad (1)$$

$a_j(0), j \in \{1,2,...,n\}$ – starting times of the processes,
$D_{ij}=D_{ji}=g.c.d.(c_i,c_j)$ & $c_i=D_{ij}m_{ij}$ & $c_j=D_{ji}m_{ji}$ & $g.c.d.(m_{ij},m_{ji})=1$ & $m_{ij},m_{ji}\in N$ &
& $f_{ij}(l)=[f_{ij}(0)+lm_{ji}] \bmod m_{ij}$ & $y_{ij}(l)=y_{ij}(0)$ &
& $t_{ij}(0)=a_j(0) \bmod c_i$ & $f_{ij}(0)=t_{ij}(0) \operatorname{div} D_{ij}$ &
& $y_{ij}(0)=t_{ij}(0) \bmod D_{ij}$ & $0 \leq f_{ij}(0) < m_{ij}$ & $0 \leq y_{ij}(0) < D_{ij}$
& $g.c.d.$ - the greatest common divisor.

By the symmetry of (P_i,P_j) and (P_j,P_i) a starting time $t_{ji}(l) \in [0,c_j)$ can be defined.

4.2 The Conditions for the Conflict-Free Processes Execution

To avoid resource conflicts between the processes it is enough to avoid requesting of the shared resource by P_j at time intervals $[a_i(k), a_i(k)+r_i]$, and analogously, requesting it by P_i at time intervals $[a_j(l), a_j(l)+r_j]$. The necessary and sufficient condition for the existence of a conflict-free schedule for n-process system has been given in (Wójcik, 2001), (Wójcik, 2004).

Theorem 1. A conflict-free (waiting-free) schedule exists for n-process system if and only if for each 2-process subsystem (P_i,P_j), where $i<j$ & $i,j \in \{1,2,...,n\}$, exists a local starting time $t_{ij}(0) \in [0,c_i)$, where $t_{ij}(0)= f_{ij}(0)D_{ij} + y_{ij}(0)$ (1), or a local time $t_{ji}(0) \in [0,c_j)$, where $t_{ji}(0)=f_{ji}(0)D_{ji} + y_{ji}(0)$ (1), such that

$$(r_i \leq y_{ij}(0) \leq D_{ij} - r_j) \ \vee \ (r_j \leq y_{ji}(0) \leq D_{ji} - r_i) \qquad (2)$$

When the condition (2) holds for each $i<j$ & $i,j \in \{1,2, ...,n\}$ then a cycle time of a conflict-free n-process system is equal to $T = l.c.m.(c_1,...,c_i,...c_j,...,c_n)$; $l.c.m.$ - the least common multiple.

Since the conflict-free (waiting-free) n-process system has a cyclic, steady-state with a period $T=l.c.m.(c_1,...,c_i,...c_j,...,c_n)$ it is enough to consider starting times $a_i(0)$, $i=1,2,...,n$, of the processes such that

$$0 \leq a_i(0) < T \ \& \ T = l.c.m.(c_1,...,c_i,...c_j,...,c_n) \qquad (3)$$

5. THE CONFLICT-FREE SCHEDULES DESIGN

The problem of designing a conflict-free schedule for the considered n-process system can be formulated as follows: Given are domains of the operation times $DR_i=\{r_{i1},r_{i2}, ...,r_{ij},...,r_{iw}\}$ – admissible values for operation time r_i, and $DO_i=\{o_{i1},o_{i2},...,o_{ij},..., o_{iv}\}$ – admissible values for operation time o_i, $i=1,2,...,n$. Find values of the operation times $r_i \in DR_i$, $o_i \in DO_i$, and starting times $a_i(0)$, $i=1,2,...,n$, of the processes for which a conflict-free steady-state schedule exists. Assuming $r_i \in DR_i$, $o_i \in DO_i$, and $c_i = r_i + o_i$ the considered constraint satisfaction problem (CSP) consists of finding times $a_i(0)$ (3) for which constraints (1) and (2) hold.

The problem will be solved using CP method and CP Oz/Mozart tool (Saraswat, 1994). In this approach the model defining variables and constraints of the problem can be implemented in a declarative way (without implementing an algorithm for solving the problem), using predefined abstractions of the CP language Oz. This creates an attractive alternative for currently available, decision support systems used for manufacturing processes design, based on computer simulation or conventional operations research techniques.

5.1 The Constraint Programming Method

Two basic techniques of constraint programming are constraint propagation and constraint distribution (Saraswat, 1994).

The constraint propagation is an efficient inference mechanism designed to narrow the variable domains. It is based on a logical analysis of the constraints to derive the new constraints, which define a smaller space of the admissible solutions. The constraint propagation reduces size of a search space.

The constraint distribution splits a problem into complementary cases once the constraint propagation cannot advance further. Usually, a distribution strategy is defined with a sequence of variables x_1, x_2, ..., x_k used in a model of a problem. When a distribution step is necessary, the strategy selects (according to the standard strategy or user defined heuristics) a not yet determined variable in the sequence and distributes on this variable, i.e. the search space can be distributed into disjoint spaces by substitution $x_1=u$ and $x_1 \neq u$, where an integer u belongs to variable's x_1 domain. The art of constraint programming consists in designing a model for a problem and a distribution strategy that yield the smallest search tree.

5.2 The Constraint-Based Model

Let us consider starting times $a_i(0) \in [0,T)$ (3) of the processes, $i=1,2,...,n$. Behaviour of the n-process system can be analysed in any time interval $B_k=[a_k(0), a_k(0)+c)$ such that $0 \leq a_k(0) < a_k(0)+c < T$, and $k \in \{1,2,...,n\}$, $c \in N$. It can be noticed that for $c=cmax=\max(c_1,...,c_n)$, i.e. $cmax$ is a cycle time of the slowest process, the interval B_k is the smallest one for which each process P_i in a waiting-free system receives access to the shared resource at least once. Therefore, it is enough to consider starting resource allocation times $a_i(0) \in [a_k(0), a_k(0)+cmax)$. In particular, it is possible to choose $a_k(0)$ equal to a starting time of the slowest process P_k and to assume that the observation zone starts at $a_k(0)=0$. Hence, for $cmax=c_k$, domains of variables $a_i(0)$ are defined by the following constraints:

$$a_k(0)=0 \ \& \ 0 \leq a_i(0) < c_k \ \& \ c_k=\max(c_1,...,c_n) \qquad (4)$$

In order to solve the problem considered, all values $a_i(0)$ (4) for which local starting times $t_{ij}(0) \in [0,c_i)$ (1) and $t_{ji}(0) \in [0,c_j)$ (1) fulfilling constraints (2) exist, have to be found, where $i<j$ & $i,j \in \{1,2,...,n\}$. By introducing variables s_{ij}, s_{ji}, which denote a

distance between any two starting times of the processes, it is possible to derive the new constraints integrating constraints given by (2) and (4).

$$s_{ij} = a_j(0) - a_i(0) \ \& \ a_j(0) \geq a_i(0)$$
$$s_{ji} = a_i(0) - a_j(0) \ \& \ a_i(0) \geq a_j(0) \tag{5}$$

From (4) $a_i(0), a_j(0) \in [0, c_k)$, hence also $s_{ij}, s_{ji} \in [0, c_k)$, where $c_k = \max(c_1, ..., c_n)$ & $i < j$ & $i, j \in \{1, 2, ..., n\} / \{k\}$. According to (5) $s_{kj} = a_j(0) - a_k(0) = a_j(0)$ and $s_{ki} = a_i(0) - a_k(0) = a_i(0)$. Hence, taking into account (5) $s_{ki}, s_{kj} \in [0, c_k)$. The following conditions hold:

$$s_{ij} = s_{kj} - s_{ki} \ \& \ s_{kj} \geq s_{ki} \ \& \ s_{ji} = s_{ki} - s_{kj} \ \& \ s_{ki} \geq s_{kj}$$
$$s_{ij}, s_{ji}, s_{ki}, s_{kj} \in [0, c_k) \ \& \ c_k = \max(c_1, ..., c_n) \tag{6}$$

Local starting times $t_{ij}(0) \in [0, c_i)$ (1) and $t_{ji}(0) \in [0, c_j)$ (1) can be derived using formulas $t_{ij}(0) = s_{ij} \bmod c_i$, and $t_{ji}(0) = s_{ji} \bmod c_j$.

Let $u_{ij} = (s_{ij} \ \text{div} \ c_i)$, $u_{ij} \in N \cup \{0\}$. There is $s_{ij} = (s_{ij} \ \text{div} \ c_i)c_i + (s_{ij} \bmod c_i) = (u_{ij})c_i + t_{ij}(0)$. Hence, using (1) $s_{ij} = (u_{ij})D_{ij}m_{ij} + f_{ij}(0)D_{ij} + y_{ij}(0) = [u_{ij}m_{ij} + f_{ij}(0)]D_{ij} + y_{ij}(0) = v_{ij}D_{ij} + y_{ij}(0)$, where $v_{ij} = [u_{ij}m_{ij} + f_{ij}(0)]$. Finally, taking into account constraint for u_{ij} and $m_{ij}, f_{ij}(0)$ (1) there are $s_{ij} = v_{ij}D_{ij} + y_{ij}(0)$ and $v_{ij} \in N \cup \{0\}$. A domain of variable v_{ij} can be reduced. For $s_{ij} \in [0, c_k)$ (6) there is $0 \leq v_{ij}D_{ij} + y_{ij}(0) < c_k$ & $y_{ij}(0) \in [0, D_{ij})$ (1), hence, $0 \leq v_{ij} < c_k / D_{ij}$. Taking into account (2) and denoting $y_{ij} = y_{ij}(0)$ the following formulas hold, based on necessary and sufficient conditions, defining a distance between starting time of the process P_j and starting time of the process P_i in a conflict-free schedule:

$$s_{ij} = v_{ij}D_{ij} + y_{ij} \ \& \ v_{ij} \in [0, c_k / D_{ij}) \ \& \ y_{ij} \in [r_i, D_{ij} - r_j] \tag{7}$$

Formula defining $s_{ji} \in [0, c_k)$ can be given analogously, by changing i, j.

The model presented defines the following CP problem: Let P_k be the slowest cyclic process. Find $s_{ki} \in [0, c_k)$ for $i \in \{1, 2, ..., n\} / \{k\}$, and $s_{ij}, s_{ji} \in [0, c_k)$ for $i < j$ & $i, j \in \{1, 2, ..., n\} / \{k\}$, such that constraints (6) and (7) hold. This problem will be solved using CP programming tool Mozart (Saraswat, 1994).

5.3 Computational Example

For a 3-process system shown in Fig.1, all possible conflict-free schedules will be derived using the constraint-based model presented. A standard *first fail* (*ff*) distribution strategy available in the Oz language is selected to distribute the constraints on the variables (Saraswat, 1994).

Let us consider a system $S_3 = (P_1, P_2, P_3)$ with the following parameters: $r_1 \in [1, 1]$, $o_1 \in [16, 17]$, $ZT_1 = (r_1, o_1)$; $r_2 \in [1, 1]$, $o_2 \in [10, 11]$, $ZT_2 = (r_2, o_2)$; $r_3 \in [4, 4]$, $o_3 \in [2, 3]$, $ZT_3 = (r_3, o_3)$. Analysis of all possible values from the domains of the operation times leads to the following eight cases defined by vectors $(r_1, o_1, c_1; r_2, o_2, c_2; r_3, o_3, c_3)$: (1,16,17; 1,10,11; 4,2,6), (1,16,17; 1,10,11; 4,3,7), (1,16,17; 1,11,12; 4,2,6), (1,16,17; 1,11,12; 4,3,7), and (1,17,18; 1,10,11; 4,2,6), (1,17,18; 1,10,11; 4,3,7), (1,17,18; 1,11,12; 4,2,6), (1,17,18; 1,11,12; 4,3,7).

In all cases P_1 is the slowest process, i.e. $c_k = \max(c_1, c_2, c_3) = c_1$, and $k=1$. Hence, starting times s_{12}, s_{13} (6) of the processes P_2, P_3 are defined in relation to time $a_1(0) = 0$, i.e. $s_{12}, s_{13} \in [0, c_1)$. Time shifts $s_{23}, s_{32} \in [0, c_1)$ can be calculated using s_{12}, s_{13} defined by (6). According to (7), the following constraints hold for the variables s_{12}, $s_{13} \in [0, c_1)$, and $s_{23}, s_{32} \in [0, c_1)$:

$$s_{12}=v_{12}D_{12}+y_{12} \ \& \ v_{12}\in[0, c_1/D_{12}) \ \& \ y_{12}\in[r_1, D_{12}-r_2]; \tag{8}$$
$$s_{13}=v_{13}D_{13}+y_{13} \ \& \ v_{13}\in[0, c_1/D_{13}) \ \& \ y_{13}\in[r_1, D_{13}-r_3];$$
$$s_{23}=s_{13}-s_{12} \ \& \ s_{13}\geq s_{12} \ \& \ s_{23}=v_{23}D_{23}+y_{23} \ \& \ v_{23}\in[0, c_1/D_{23}) \ \& \ y_{23}\in[r_2, D_{23}-r_3];$$
$$s_{32}=s_{12}-s_{13} \ \& \ s_{12}\geq s_{13} \ \& \ s_{32}=v_{32}D_{32}+y_{32} \ \& \ v_{32}\in[0, c_1/D_{32}) \ \& \ y_{32}\in[r_3, D_{32}-r_2].$$

These constraints define the CP problem with the following solution vectors: $(s_{12}, s_{13}, s_{23}, y_{12}, y_{13}, y_{23})$ and $(s_{12}, s_{13}, s_{32}, y_{12}, y_{13}, y_{32})$. Assuming values for $(r_1,o_1,c_1; r_2,o_2,c_2; r_3,o_3,c_3)$ it is possible to solve the problem using predefined abstractions available in the Oz language – a programming tool of the Mozart system.

It can be shown that solutions of the problem exist only for case (1,17,18; 1,11,12; 4,2,6). In this case: $D_{12}=D_{21}= g.c.d.(c_1,c_2)=6$, and $D_{13}=D_{31}=g.c.d.(c_1,c_3)=6$, and $D_{23}=D_{32}=g.c.d.(c_2,c_3)=6$. Since, $c_1 = \max(c_1,c_2,c_3) = 18$, hence process $P_{k,}$, where $k=1$, is the slowest one. According to (7), (8) the following constraints hold: $s_{12}, s_{13}, s_{23}, s_{32}\in[0,18)$; $v_{12}\in[0,3)$, $y_{12}\in[1,5]$; $v_{13}\in[0,3)$, $y_{13}\in[1,2]$; $v_{23},v_{32}\in[0,3)$, $y_{23}\in[1,2]$, $y_{32}\in[4,5]$. The executable script given below can find solution vectors defined by $(s_{12}, s_{13}, s_{ij}, y_{12}, y_{13}, y_{ij})$, where $i\neq j$ & $i,j\in\{2,3\}$. The following program generates solutions for $(s_{12}, s_{13}, s_{32}, y_{12}, y_{13}, y_{32})$.

```
                                              local Find in
                                                proc {Find Root}
                    S12 S13 S32 Y12 Y13 Y32 V12 V13 V32 D12 D13 D32 in
                    Root=sol(s12:S12 s13:S13 s32:S32 y12:Y12 y13:Y13 y32:Y32)
                                                              %variable domains
            S12::0#17 S13::0#17 S32::0#17   D12::6#6  D13::6#6  D32::6#6
                                  V12::0#2  V13::0#2  V32::0#2
                    Y12::1#5  Y13::1#2  Y32::4#5   %for Y23 change into 1#2
                                                    %constraints for the variables
                            S32=:S12-S13 S12>=:S13
            S12=:V12*D12+Y12 S13=:V13*D13+Y13 S32=:V32*D32+Y32
                                      %start propagation and distribution
                                        {FD.distribute ff Root}
                                                                           end
                          {Browse {SearchAll Find}}   %find all solutions
                                                                           end
```

In the case considered 9 solutions have been found. Solutions with the same values of (y_{12}, y_{13}, y_{32}) define starting times, which belong to the same conflict-free schedule. Two different schedules exist for the 3-process system considered. Starting times of the processes corresponding to a schedule shown in Fig. 3:

sol(s_{12}:**5** s_{13}:1 s_{32}:**4** y_{12}:5 y_{13}:1 y_{32}:4); sol(s_{12}:**11** s_{13}:1 s_{32}:**10** y_{12}:5 y_{13}:1 y_{32}:4);
sol(s_{12}:11 s_{13}:7 s_{32}:4 y_{12}:5 y_{13}:1 y_{32}:4); sol(s_{12}:17 s_{13}:1 s_{32}:16 y_{12}:5 y_{13}:1 y_{32}:4);
sol(s_{12}:17 s_{13}:7 s_{32}:10 y_{12}:5 y_{13}:1 y_{32}:4); sol(s_{12}:17 s_{13}:13 s_{32}:4 y_{12}:5 y_{13}:1 y_{23}:4).

In the case $(s_{12}, s_{13}, s_{23}, y_{12}, y_{13}, y_{23})$ a number of solutions is the same. All derived vectors define states belonging to the waiting-free schedules, which have been found for the case $(s_{12}, s_{13}, s_{32}, y_{12}, y_{13}, y_{32})$.

```
····0··································36¶
····|·····························|······¶
·P1·|R0000000000000000000R000000000000000000|R00000000¶
····|··5··································|¶
·P2·|-----R000000000000R0000000000000R000000|00000R00¶
····|1···································|¶
·P3·|-RRRR00RRRR00RRRR00RRRR00RRRR00RRRR00RRRR0|0RRRR00R¶
····|··············T·=·36··············|¶
```

Figure 3 – A conflict-free schedule. Letter R denotes a time unit of using shared resource and letter O a time unit of using non-shared resource.

6. CONCLUSIONS

The constraint programming approach to designing of conflict-free schedules for repetitive manufacturing processes using common resources in mutual exclusion has been presented. For a system with n processes sharing single resource a constraint-based model has been derived and then implemented into a searching procedure used to find the operation times and starting times of the processes for which waiting-free schedules exist. The procedure has been programmed with the aid of the Oz/Mozart language and tested in the case of a 3-process system. The example is simple, however, the more complex systems can be considered since they can be seen as a composition of n-process subsystems.

The method presented can be used to answer several interesting questions. What are the operation times and starting times of the processes ensuring their conflict-free execution? What is the number of different waiting-free schedules for a given system? How many parts is it possible to produce in a given planning horizon? Is it possible to load new parts into the system without disturbing the other parts?

Therefore, this method creates an attractive alternative for classical design approaches based on computer simulation and the operations research techniques.

7. REFERENCES

1. Alpan G., Jafari M.A. Dynamic analysis of timed Petri nets: a case of two processes and a shared resource. IEEE Trans. on Robotics and Automation 1997; Vol.13, No.3: 338-346.
2. Alpan G., Jafari M.A. Synthesis of sequential controller in the presence of conflicts and free choices. IEEE Trans. on Robotics and Automation 1998; Vol.14, No.3: 488-492.
3. Banaszak Z., Krogh B. Deadlock avoidance in flexible manufacturing systems with concurrently competing process flows. IEEE Trans. on Robotics and Automation 1990; Vol.6, No.6: 724-734.
4. Kanban Just-In-Time at Toyota: Management Begins at the Workplace. Japan Mgmt Assoc (ed.), Productivity Press, 1989.
5. Saraswat V. Concurrent Constraint Programming. MIT Press, 1994.
6. Schroder M.R. Number Theory in Science and Communications. Springer-Verlag, Berlin, Heidelberg, 1997.
7. Wójcik R., Banaszak Z., Polak M. A state space decomposition approach to dynamics analysis of chain-like coupled repetitive manufacturing processes. Proc. of the 10th IEEE Int. Conf. on Methods and Models in Automatics and Robotics, MMAR 2004, Międzyzdroje, Poland, eds. S. Domek, R. Kaszyński 2004; Vol. 2: 1267-1272.
8. Wójcik R. Towards strong stability of concurrent repetitive processes sharing resources. Systems Science 2001; Vol.27, No.2: 37-47.

THE RELEVANCE OF LEAN MANUFACTURING PRINCIPLES IN DIVERSE APPLICATIONS AND DIGITAL ENTERPRISES

Stephen Davies, Tim Coole and David Osypiw
Buckingham Chilterns University College, UK
{rdavie01, tcoole01, Dosypi01}@bcuc.ac.uk

The lean manufacturing model through the elimination of waste creates customer value and efficient manufacturing work flows matched to customer demand. Promoters of the lean model contend that lean manufacturing will become the global manufacturing standard across the totality of industrial applications for the 21st century. This assertion is assessed across a variety of industrial sectors and the relevance of the lean model is considered within a Digital Enterprise Technology Environment, a construct that serves to manage product life-cycles on a global scale.

1. INTRODUCTION

The Lean Manufacturing Model emerged from research conducted through the International Motor Vehicle Program at the Massachusetts Institute of Technology during the latter half of the 1980's. The research was presented to a wider audience through a seminal work, 'The Machine That Changed the World' (Womack et al, 1990) The authors observation of the Toyota Production System (Monden, 1998) with its ruthless focus of eliminating waste, spurned the creation of what became Lean Manufacturing. The authors present a compelling case for the implementation of Lean Manufacturing compared to the Mass Production methods of the time, showing a 2:1 differential in favour of lean manufacturing across a number of dimensions. In a further work, 'Lean Thinking' (Womack and Jones, 1996) the authors present the Lean Model as a construct consisting of five related principles:

1. Value: Defined in terms of the final customer.
2. The Value Stream: Create a stream of activities geared toward delivering customer value through the elimination of non-value added activities.
3. Flow: Introduce working methods that allow the value added activities to flow.
4. Pull: Ensure that all value added activities are synchronised to the customer demand.
5. Perfection: Create a culture of continuous improvement that creates greater customer perceived value and removes successive layers of waste.

The authors contend that the implementation of the first four principles leads to new sources of value, waste and reveal impediments to flow and pull production. Within the lean model, therefore, there exists a continuous cycle of improvement of each of the principles creating a 'virtuous circle' implying a never ending pursuit of perfection. A significant conclusion from the 'Machine That Changed the World' is that the Lean Manufacturing Model will become the standard global production system of the 21st century in all areas of industrial endeavour.

This is a bold assertion and implies that each of the defined principles is directly applicable to any given manufacturing scenario and that the model is universally relevant. The universal relevance of Lean Manufacturing is considered through lean applications across diverse industrial sectors particularly the Aircraft and Building Construction Industries.

The concept of Digital Enterprise Technology (DET) is presented as a holistic framework combining product design; manufacturing and logistical process within an integrated information technology environment to manage product life cycles within a global context and the relevance of the Lean Model is assessed within a DET environment.

2. APPLICATIONS OF LEAN MANUFACTURING

The literature describing lean applications across diverse industrial and other applications is prevalent. In the Shipbuilding industry, examples of lean influences are given by Koenig et al (2002) Storch and Lim (1999) and the in the United States, the 'Lean Ship Building Initiative' exists as an industry link to implement lean practises, (NSPR, 2006). In more diverse applications, for example, the healthcare profession, working concepts developed through the Toyota Production System are beginning to influence the management of patient care (McCarthy, 2006 and Spear 2005). Also, The Scottish Office commissioned a report to evaluate the application of lean principles to the business management of the public sector (Scottish Executive, 2006). The application of the lean model is assessed below in more detail in the Aircraft and Building Construction Industries.

2.1 Aircraft Industry

Two factors emerged in the early part of the 1990's that were instrumental in the take up of lean principles within the aerospace industry (Ward, 2003). Firstly, the end of the cold war resulted in far-reaching reductions in defence procurement budgets due to reduced military markets and secondly, the aftermath of the first Gulf War saw a fall in demand of passenger traffic forcing airlines to cancel or postpone civil aircraft orders.

The response in America to this unfolding situation was the creation of 'The Lean Aerospace Initiative (LAI)' in 1993. The LAI was founded at the Massachusetts Institute of Technology (MIT) through a consortium of leaders from the U.S. Air Force, MIT, labour unions, defence aerospace businesses and civil aircraft manufacturers that formed an 'evolving learning and research' community implementing lean practices throughout the American aerospace industry to counter diminishing defence budgets and rising production and development costs. A similar initiative emerged in 1998 in the United Kingdom through collaboration between the "The Society of British Aerospace Companies" (SBAC) and the University of Warwick. Both initiatives attempt to accelerate lean deployment through identified best practice, shared communication, common goals and strategic implementation tools gained through the collaboration of consortium members.

Typical of the success of the work of the LAI in the United States is witnessed in the deployment of lean practices in the maintenance programme for the C5 Galaxy, a four engine cargo and troop carrier (Barrett and Fraile, 2005). Maintenance turn around time was reduced by one third (340 down to 225) freeing capacity to return work outsourced to private contractors.

Independently of the LAI, applications of lean principles within the USA Aerospace Industry are reported. For example, Venables et al (2006) describe working practices based on the Toyota Production System at the Boeing Aircraft Company and Smiths Aerospace during the introduction of lean working practices. Boeing through principally hiring retired Toyota personnel and Smiths through studying the latest lean literature and introducing training courses for its senior managers. Similarly, a successful implementation of lean principles in the aircraft industry is provided by Northrop Grumman in the USA who applies the principles to both its aircraft manufacturing and ship building divisions. Their lean programme has resulted in success in reducing the manufacturing cycle time of aircraft as much as 30%, (Northrop Grumman, 2005).

In the United Kingdom, the SBAC initiative reports the application of lean principles to the 'New Product Introduction (NPI)' programmes at Rolls Royce Aero Engines, Weston Aerospace and Smiths Industries (Haque, 2001). The principles are applied at Rolls Royce to streamline their generic design process by removing wasteful and non-value adding activities. At Weston Aerospace, lean principles are applied to introduce 'single piece flow' to their NPI project management activities to reduce project lead time through a focus of 'Value Stream Analysis' by eliminating the then current method of batching and queuing of project activities. Smiths Industries through lean deployment, introduced a system of 'off line' product development. In this process, 'product elements' are designed, tested and produc-tionised and become available for later customisation and integration into product applications. Due to the diversity of their product range, Smiths Industries are able to gain benefit through the availability of common sub-assemblies enabling a reduction in time from customer selection to product delivery.

Independently of the SBAC initiative, at the operational level, Parry and Turner (2006) describe the application of 'Visual Process Management Tools' based on Lean Principles, at Airbus (UK), Weston Aerospace and Rolls Royce Civil Aerospace. Airbus introduced visual aids to communicate the output of value stream mapping that focused on delivery to customer, the effective use of resources, identification of bottlenecks and work in progress and the display of relevant measures for continuous improvement. Weston Aerospace has developed a lean manufacturing facility and use a single visual management board to drive business processes across the whole of their activities. Rolls Royce communicate their ERP generated production schedules via a 'Visual Control Board' that enables process ownership at the operator level providing a focus toward continuous improvement.

2.2 Building Construction Industry

Green and May (2005) suggest that though the concept of 'Lean Construction' attracted academic interest since the early 1990's, the dissemination of lean principles within the United Kingdom Construction Industry gained prominence with the publication of the British government sponsored 'Egan' Report - *"Rethinking Construction: The Report of the Construction Task Force"*, (Egan,

1998). The report recommended that the adoption of lean principles would return similar improvements that had been experienced in the automotive industry from which the lean concept originated. A subsequent report, "Accelerating Change", (Egan, 2002) reports on the improvements within the UK Construction Industry since the adoption of Egan report indicating improvements recorded across 12 key performance Indicators. Some examples include Client Product Satisfaction (16%), Client Service Satisfaction (23%) and a reduction of 50% of reported accidents per 100 employees. Other improvements include:

- Significant improvement in predictability and timing of construction projects
- Enhanced quality and reduction in defects
- Construction projects are safer and healthier
- Greater client satisfaction
- More repeat business.

However, Green and May (2005), while recognising the influence of the Egan report, suggest that the understanding of the application of Lean Principles amongst practitioners within the construction industry is a 'vague construct'. Green (1999) observes that the report emphasises the more advantageous aspects of the lean model and ignores an observation that the success of the Japanese automotive industry is due in part to Japan's protected home market that allowed the lean model to mature. Conversely, the Egan Report, Green states does not consider the possibility of protecting the UK construction industry form foreign competition to allow lean construction to mature.

Negative aspects aside, the lean construction literature provides example of successful lean implementations. In the United States, Garnett et al (1998), illustrates the improvements achieved in the American Construction Industry by implementing lean principles. Similarly in the United States, Arbulu et al (2003), discuss define the application of Value Stream Mapping to improving the Supply Chain for delivery of pipe supports for use in power plants that highlighted some 96% of the time in the original supply chain was non-value added. Naim and Barlow (2003) discuss a supply chain strategy for customised housing in the United Kingdom that combines lean methods of eliminating waste with an 'agile' production approach using market knowledge to exploit profitable opportunities in a volatile market place.

3. DIGITAL ENTERPRISE TECHNOLOGY

Digital Enterprise Technology (DET) is a holistic framework that combines product design, manufacturing and logistical process within an integrated information technology environment. Maropoulos (2003) defines DET as:

"The collection of systems and methods for the digital modelling of the global product development and realisation process, in the context of life-cycle management"

Through this '*collection*', Maropoulos constructs a DET Framework, replicated in Figure 1, as a synthesis of technologies and systems from five main technical areas. In a further work, Maropoulos et al (2004) define the purpose of DET is to 'shorten product development and realisation, by estimating and therefore controlling quality, cost and delivery factors for products at an early stage in their lifecycle'.

The framework is not necessarily a theoretical construct and for example, provides the basis of work by Monostori et al (2003 (i) and 2003 (ii)) in introducing the Digital Enterprise concept in Hungary.

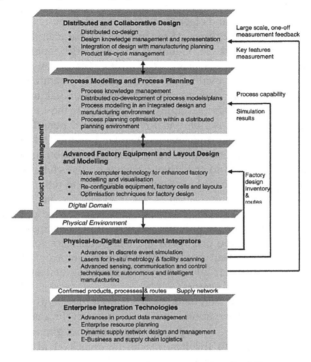

Figure 1 - DET Framework, Maropoulos (2003).

3.1 The Relationship between DET and the Lean Model

A theme that emerges from Lean Thinking, (Womack and Jones, 1996), is that the logical destination for a company embarking on a lean implementation is the enterprise (and extended enterprise) wide dissemination of the lean model. Similarly, Hines and Rich (1997) create a 'Value Stream Mapping' construct based on lean principles that can be applied across the extended enterprise. Essentially, therefore, the lean model is a holistic approach of eliminating waste and providing customer value throughout the extended enterprise. The 'holistic' concept is similarly shared between the lean model and the DET approach. But beyond this shared holistic philosophy, is there a more definitive relationship between the Lean Model and DET? Moreover, is it essential that for a Digital Enterprise to be lean for the Enterprise to be successful?

The preceding section demonstrated the diverse applications of the lean model. In creating the DET Framework, Maropoulos (2003), classifies manufacturing activity into four categories:

1. **High Value/complexity product integrators:** Examples include satellites, aerospace, shipbuilding.
2. **Smaller Scale, heavy engineering products:** Examples include land transport systems, articulated trucks, excavators.

3. **Automotive and high precision products:** Examples include products and components for the defence, aerospace and automotive industries.

4. **Lower complexity/higher volume products and electronics:** Examples include home appliances, mass produced light weight products for domestic or industrial use and electronic components manufacture.

For each of these categories, 'Key Industrial Characteristics' and 'Technology Requirements' are defined. For example, characteristics include, life cycle duration and management, and supply chain capabilities. Technology requirements include the importance of early evaluation of designs for manufacture, modelling and analysis for manufacture and assembly using 3D digital modelling. Maropoulos suggests that the conditions that apply to category 1, the key characteristics being 'unit of one, high customisation and life-cycle based manufacture' will over time prevail over most manufacturing sectors. The DET framework introducing computer modelling, graphic visualisation and disrupted information management will according to Maropoulos serve to 'positively impact on the global product development and realisation under increased mass customisation and reduced product life cycles' with the benefit of the 'minimisation of risk in global product realization'.

Across each of the industry categories defined by Maropoulos, the lean model can be shown to apply. The previous section illustrated applications in aerospace and shipbuilding while the origins of the lean model are found in the automotive industry. A survey of lean implementation programmes 'Lessons in Lean' (The Manufacturing Foundation, 2004) provides examples of lean applications in both category 2 and 4 industrial sectors.

While it is clear that DET and the lean model are applicable across the same industrial sectors, the observation is not a coincidence. Product life-cycles are either short or reducing. The concept of concurrent engineering and design for manufacture are central to the lean model (Womack et al 1990, Henderson and Larco, 2003), enabling products to productionise quicker than previous sequential methods of introducing product designs into manufacturing. The 'Distributed and Collaborative Design' construct of the DET Framework enhances the capability of realising product designs. The examples in the previous section relating to lean principles applied to managing 'New Product Introduction' serve to support further the design function. The 'Process Modelling and Process Planning' construct has a lean analogy in the 'Value Stream' concept, such that this DET construct can be applied to create value in terms of customer needs. The DET construct of 'Advanced Factory Equipment and Layout Design and Modelling' can be applied to create production flow and minimise inventory. In the Physical Environment of the DET Framework, the Physical-to-Digital Environment Integrators provide the basis for continuous improvement, particularly from the ability for recording production performance through real-time shop floor monitoring systems. Finally, the DET construct of 'Enterprise Integration Technologies' provide the basis for lean shop floor operations and supply chain management.

Though it is possible to establish a relationship between DET and lean princeples, the available literature discussing lean concepts within a DET environment is sparse. However, Ranky (2003 (i)) attempts to define the network requirements for a distributed lean manufacturing system in digital environment that consists of individuals or teams of operators working in front of multimedia workstations or machines and robots within a real-time network that interact witheach other. In a second publication, Ranky (2003 (ii)), discusses the architecture requirements for a lean flexible, just-in-time controlled manufacturing system operating in cells or modules dealing with a high level of distributed data processing and automated material flow. Ranky suggests that without the appropriate 'lean infrastructure architecture' combining lean, flexible, market driven just-in-time principles coupled with advanced networking, production and quality control methodologies within a seamlessly integrated digital factory, even the best and leanest manufacturing system will not be able to produce to its full potential on the shop floor.

5. CONCLUSIONS

Clearly, the lean manufacturing principles replicated in the introduction from *Lean Thinking*, (Womack and Jones, 1996) are applicable across diverse industrial applications and the principles are influencing the management of less obvious endeavours such as health care and local government management. Constructs such as creating value, reducing waste and continuous improvement are becoming a '*mind set*' across all areas of industrial, commercial and public activity. However, the application of lean principles is more embedded in some industries than others. Within the Aircraft Industry, particularly through the influence of the LAI consortiums both in the UK and the USA, lean principles are maturing. In the Building Industry, lean concepts are not necessarily understood even though the application of lean principles are returning benefits. However, within the Building Industry, the lean model is a relatively new construct, and through a combination of further training, consultancy and academic partnership (as observed in the LAI consortiums) will over time embed more thoroughly lean principles within the Building Industry.

The DET construct is shown to apply across a range of industrial sectors each of which it is possible to apply lean principles. The DET and lean approaches share a holistic philosophy of enterprise wide application. Moreover, each element of the DET Model is shown to have a synergy with a lean principle. However, this relationship is inferred rather than proved. The literature discussing lean and DET relationships or applications is sparse, though Ranky (2003 (ii)) concludes that within a DET environment, matching the system architecture with the needs of the lean system provide the greatest benefit to an organisation. That there is a definitive relationship between the lean model and DET is likely and that for DET to be effective, the underlying business model should be lean.

6. REFERENCES

1. Arbulu R.J., Tommelein I.D., Walsh K.D., and Hershauer J.C. "Value stream analysis of a re-engineered construction supply chain", Building Research and Information 31 (2) pp 161 – 171, 2003.
2. Barret B. and Fraile L. "Lean at the C-5 Galaxy Depot: Essential Elements of Success". Available at http://lean.mit.edu. 2005.
3. Egan J. "Rethinking Construction: The report of the Construction Task Force to the Deputy Prime Minister, John Prescott, on the scope for improving the quality and efficiency of UK construction", Department of Trade and Industry, 1998.
4. Egan J. "Accelerating Change: A Report by the Strategic Forum for Construction chaired by Sir John Egan", Department of Trade and Industry, 2002.
5. Garnett N., Jones T.J., and Murray S. "Strategic Application of Lean Thinking", Proceedings of 6th Ann.Conf.Itnl. Group for Lean Construction, Guaruja Brazil, Aug 13-15, 1998.

6. Green S.D. and May S.C. "Lean Construction: arenas of enactment, models of diffusion and the meaning of 'leanness'". Building Research and Information. 33(6). 2005.
7. Green S.D. "The Missing Argument of Lean Construction". Construction Management and Economics, 17, 1999.
8. Haque B. "Case Studies in Lean Production". Available at http://sbac.cu.uk 2001.
9. Henderson B.A. and Larco J.L. "Lean Transformation. How to Change Your Business into a Lean Enterprise". The Oaklea Press Richmond Virginia, 1999.
10. Hines P., Rich N., and Esain A. "Value stream mapping. A distribution Industry example". Benchmarking: An International Journal. Vol. 6, No.1, pp 60 – 77, 1999.
11. Koenig P.C, Narita H., and Baba K. "Lean Production in the Japanese Shipbuilding Industry", Journal of Ship Production, Vol. 18. No.3, pp 167 – 174, 2002.
12. McCarthy M. Can Car Manufacturing Techniques Reform Health Care. The Lancet Vol. 367 January 28, 2006.
13. Maropoulos P.G. "Digital enterprise technology – defining perspectives and research priorities". International journal of Computer Integrated Manufacturing. Vol. 16 No. 7 – 8, pp 467 – 478, 2003.
14. Maropoulos P.G., Bramall D.G., Chapman P., Cheung W.M., McKay, K.R., and Rogers B.C. "Digital enterprise technology in production networks. Advances in e-Engineering and Digital Enterprise Technology" - Proceedings of the Fourth International Conference on e-Engineering and Digital Enterprise Technology, 2004.
15. Monden Y. "Toyota Production System – An integrated Approach to Just-in –Time (3rd Ed)". Chapman and Hall. 1998.
16. Monostori L., Váncza J., Márkus A., Kádár B., and Viharos Zs.J. "Towards the Realization of Digital Enterprises". Proceedings of the 36th International Seminar on manufacturing systems. Progress in Virtual Manufacturing Systems. Saarbucken Germany pp 99 – 106, June 3-5 2003.
17. Monostori L., Váncza J., Márkus A., Kádár B, and Viharos Zs.J. "Digital Enterprises: First Results of a national R&D project". IEEE/RSJ International Conference on Intelligent Robots and Systems Las Vegas Nevada USA. October 27-31, 2003.
18. Naim M. and Barlow J. "An innovative supply chain strategy for customized housing". Construction Management and Economics 21 September 2003.
19. NSPR: National Shipbuilding Research Program. http://www.nsrp.org 2006.
20. Northrop Grumman: "Breaking Down the Walls. Vice President Lean Manufacturing Presentation" available at http://www.northropgrumman.com. 2005.
21. Parry G.C. and Turner C.E. "Application of Lean Visual Process Management Tools". Production Planning and Control. Vol. 17, No. 1, January 2006.
22. Ranky P.G. "Network simulation models of lean manufacturing systems in digital factories and an intranet server balancing algorithm". International journal of Computer Integrated Manufacturing. Vol. 16, No. 4 – 5, pp 267 – 282, 2003.
23. Ranky P.G. "Designing a Lean Infrastructure". Manufacturing Engineer February 2003.
24. Scottish Executive. "Evaluation of the Lean Approach to Business Management and its Use in the Public Sector". Scottish Social Research. 2006.
25. Spear S.J. "Fixing healthcare from the Inside Today". Harvard Business Review. September 2005.
26. Storch R.L. and Lim S. "Improving flow to achieve lean manufacturing in shipbuilding". Production Planning and Control, Vol. 10, No. 2, pp 127 – 137, 1999.
27. The Manufacturing Foundation. "Lessons in Lean: A research report on support for lean manufacturing". The Manufacturing Foundation, Wolverhampton, England. Available at Http://www.manufacturingfoundation.org.uk. 2004.
28. Thomas H.R., Horman M.J., Minchin R.E., and Chen D. "Improving Labour Flow reliability for better Productivity as Lean Construction Principle". Journal of Construction Engineering and Management. May/June 2003.
29. Venables M., Walters M., and Bevan J. "Boeing Flies the Toyota way". Strategic Direction Vol. 22, No. 8, pp 14 – 16, 2006.
30. Ward Y. "Lean in Aerospace: The Changing Global Aerospace Environment". Available at http://sbac.co.uk 2003.
31. Womack J.P., Jones D.T., and Roos D. "The Machine That Changed the World: The Story of Lean Production". Harper Business. 1990.
32. Womack J.P. and Jones D.T. "Lean Thinking, Banish Waste and Create Wealth in your Corporation". Simon and Schuster UK Ltd. 1996.

ONTOLOGY SUPPORTED ADAPTIVE USER INTERFACES FOR STRUCTURAL CAD DESIGN

Carlos Toro[1], Maite Termenón[1], Jorge Posada[1],
Joaquín Oyarzun[2] and Juanjo Falcón[3]
[1]VICOMTech Research Centre, Spain
{ctoro, mtermenon, jposada} @ vicomtech.es
[2] LANIK S.A, Spain.
joyarzun@lanik.com
[3]SOME S.L., Spain
jfalcon@somesi.com

In the early stages of the Steel Detailing Design process (Structural Design), most of the activities are focused in the designer. Nowadays Detailing CAD packages offer a wide range of options that in some cases exceeds the ones needed to fulfill a specific task. Sometimes having such a wide range span can be self-defeating for a smooth process evolution as the designer has to browse repetitively in the user interface for a particular tool. In this paper we present a Knowledge based approach for the exploitation of semantic aspects (e.g. user intentions and tasks) for the real time automatic generation of graphical user interfaces on a Steel Detailing CAD software. We base our approach in international standards (CIS/2) for the specific domain and as test case we present a system implementation of the proposed schema.

1. INTRODUCTION

In the Steel Detailing process (Structural Design), most of the early activities are focused in the designer (CIS/2, 2006). Actual Computer Aided Design tools (CAD) represent a time saving aid as they help in the 3D design process while, in the meantime, the contained information in the model can be used in other stages of the structure's life cycle. Today's Steel Detailing CAD software packages offer a wide span of options in order to perform myriads of manipulations on the elements contained in the model. In a sense, it can be said that the amount of options offered to a CAD user nowadays is as huge as the capabilities of the program itself.

It is common that the user has to navigate through the menus searching for a specific tool, slowing the design process and therefore falling into a situation where the cost of the design stage increases.

In this paper, we present a Knowledge based approach for the exploitation of semantic aspects (e.g. user intentions and tasks) for the real time automatic generation of graphical User Interfaces (UI) on a Steel Detailing CAD software. We base our approach in international standards (CIS/2) for the specific domain and, as test case; we present a system implementation of the proposed schema.

This paper is organized as follows: In chapter two, we present a brief state of the art, mentioning some approaches relevant to our work. In chapter three we explain our methodology for the real time automatic generation of UI based on semantic technologies and we show, in chapter four, a test case based in our methodology, applied in the domain of Structural Design. Lastly, in chapter five we present some conclusions derived from the paper and future work.

2. RELATED WORK

In recent times, the problem of producing a good UI has been a constant topic in research papers and conferences. To highlight some approaches, we can mention the work by Furtado (Furtado, 2001) who presented an ontology based methodology to produce UI where multiple users carry out multiple tasks in a universal context. In this approach, they divided the UI design in three layers: a conceptual layer where a domain expert defines an ontology of concepts, relationships and attributes of the domain; a logical layer where a designer specifies multiple models based on the ontology and a physical layer where a developer derives multiple user interfaces from the previously specified models with alternatives. The mentioned approach is not fully automatic as it needs a developer to take care of the alternatives programmatically. The interface development is focused in the modeling of the user which is opposite to our approach where we intend to model a manufacturing process of a specific-well known and standardized domain (Steel Detailing design).

Puerta (Puerta, 1997) based his approach on a model ontology, showing a UI development environment and system implementation with both, static and dynamic behaviors. In this approach, the domain model allowed the creation of interfaces for medical applications. In our approach, we model the user as the executioner of a design task, meaning that the design process is, in fact, divided in stages where the user takes actions that need tools in order to fulfill. Hovestadt (Hovestadt, 1995) presented a prototypical implementation of a graphical UI intended for the architectural design process. In this approach, the interface integrates CAD-like object manipulation and navigation through large data sets oriented to help the user in the process of shifting directly from construction tasks to navigation tasks. In this approach, the main focus is to change the representation of the menus from the traditional pull down distribution to a hyperbolic shape.

In a non UI approach related to the exploitation of semantics in a CAD program, Ekholm (Ekholm, 2001) presented a work where, by means of the modelling of a sociotechnical system, the user, his role and design activities are specified. His approach claims to enhance the functionality of a building design software in the problem definition and analysis phases of the design.

Igarashi (Igarashi, 2000) presented a methodology to design UIs focused on visual thinking activities (creativity design). The basic idea is to make transparent interfaces so that the user can directly interact with the target visual representations without using menus and buttons in a sort of predictive approach. For the structural design problem, it would be difficult to predict tools as the process itself is engineering based although some creativity is allowed.

3. SEMANTIC BASED GENERATION OF USER INTERFACES

We define a CAD tool as the means whereby some act for design, drafting, display or modify entities in a computer graphically oriented environment is accomplished. In the field of steel detailing design, the structure life cycle can be viewed from a product point of view, where the object being designed passes through a series of stages where transformations can be distinguished. Our approach for the UI generation starts with the prerogative that every stage of a structure life cycle can be divided in sub processes. In figure 1 (Right) a design sub process schema is presented. In each sub process, a set of CAD tools can be applied by the user. Any CAD tool can be placed in more than one sub processes.

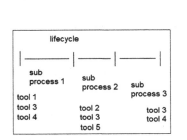 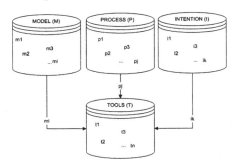

Figure 1 – (Right) Sub processes View, (Left) Model-Process-Intention View.

We argue that an efficient UI should contain only the needed tools for a given sub process, model type and user intention. Upon the spectrum of techniques that can be used in order to model a process based application (e.g. relational databases, taxonomies, Petri Nets, etc), we choose to use an ontology approach in order to take advantage of the semantics inherited by the process modeling. To model the process ontology that allows the recommendation of the set of CAD tools via a query engine, we have used an international standardization effort (CIS/2) in order to name the classes and relations. The process ontology has a set of allowed tools (AT) with an object type property that allows the connection between them and the rest of the ontology. The set of tools is composed by actual tools belonging to the CAD system itself (e.g. element generation, primitives, queries, manipulators, etc), applets or extensions to the base system and even external calls to programs in the user's computer. For a given Model m_i, Process p_j and User Intention i_k, the goal will be to produce a set of recommended tools extracted from a set of Tools T (figure 1, Left).

In order to formalize the problem, we must define an injective relation $\Re$ that assigns every triple (m_i, p_j, i_k) to one or more tools t_n belonging to the set of tools **T**. That can be formally expressed as:

$$\Re \subseteq X \times T,$$
$$\text{where } X := M \times P \times I = \{(m_i, p_j, i_k): m_i \in M, p_j \in P, i_k \in I \}$$

Where the restriction **R** will map to a subset of the available tools **T** as shown in the following expression:

$$R_{(m_i, p_j, i_k)} = t_i \cup t_j \cup \dots \cup t_r$$

The allowed tool set (**AT**) is then described by the following expression:

$$\mathbf{AT}_{(mi,\,pj,\,ik)} = \overline{(\mathbf{T} \cap \mathbf{R}_{(mi,\,pj,\,ik)})}$$

4. STEEL DETAILING CAD INTERFACE GENERATION

In this section, we present a sample application based in our approach introduced in chapter 3. Depending on the sub process (process stage), model and user intention we semantically generate a structural CAD User Interface containing the recommended tools. In order to generate the UI, we use process ontology whose classes and relations are modeled according to an international standard for the specific domain (CIS/2).

4.1 Modeling of the Process ontology according to CIS/2 standard

The structural steelwork lifecycle supported by CIS/2 is shown in figure 2. This is a high level overview of the process model. CIS/2 describes three major stages needed to design a structural steel frame for a building: (i) Analysis, (ii) Design and (iii) Fabrication. Each phase has its own data model that serves for information exchange between each other and possible external applications. The three different models of a steel structure are called "Views" (Geogiatech CIS/2, 2006). These views served as the initial source for our process ontology implementation where they are used as a simplified model of the structural design process (this process ontology will be extended in a future work to reflect a more explicit representation).

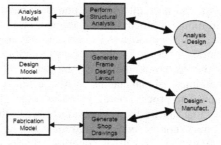

Figure 2 – Simplified process model identifying the various CIS/2 views and major exchanges, supported by high-level conformance classes (CIS/2, 2006).

4.2 Knowledge representation using Ontologies – The OWL approach

The existence of tools for ontology definition, querying and reasoning gives interesting possibilities to several application domains, including the engineering domain (Posada, 2005). An ontology is the explicit specification of a conceptualization (Gruber, 2006). In simple terms, it is a description of the concepts and relations in a domain for the purpose of enabling knowledge sharing and reuse. A body of formally represented knowledge is based on a conceptualization: the objects, concepts and other entities that are assumed to exist in some area of interest and the relations that hold among them (Gruber, 2006). A widely used ontology language is OWL, which is a semantic mark-up language for publishing and sharing ontology's on the World Wide Web. OWL is developed as a vocabulary extension of RDF (the Resource Description Framework) and it is derived from the DAML+OIL Web Ontology Language allowing more expressiveness than RDF depending on the OWL flavour used (Knublauch, 20003). There exist several OWL API's to handle computationally an ontology, between the most known ones, we can mention the Protégé OWL API (Knublauch, 20003), KAON2 (KAON2, 2006) and the WonderWeb OWL API (WonderWeb 2006).

Our Process Ontology implementation is divided in two main classes: Available Semantic Tools and Tasks. The first contains the available tools and the second, the overall actions, as composition of a Model type (steel or wood), sub Process (analysis, design or fabrication) and User Intention (assembly, detailing or review). In order to simplify our implementation, our set of tools contains as a proof of concept three plug-ins developed within the framework of a research project. Our test tools are: (i) a Virtual Reality (VR) visualizer that provides a 3D enhanced visualization of a large data set, (ii) a Dimensioning Tool (DIM) which dimensions special beams for workshop manufacturing and (iii) an Element Generation Tool (GEN) which generates structural CAD objects automatically. In figure 3, a detail of the ontology modeling (with some OWL restrictions) is shown.

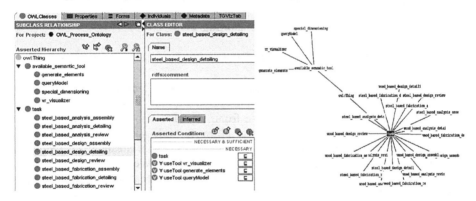

Figure 3 – Detail of the Process Ontology based on CIS/2.

4.3 Modeling of the restrictions for tool selection in OWL

As stated before, a combination of model type, process stage and user intention produces a set of available tools. To implement 𝕽 (the injective relation) in the ontology, the open world assumption and OWL description logics are used in order to relate both parts of the ontology via a restrictions. Description Logics are a family of knowledge representation languages which can be used to represent the terminological knowledge of an application domain in a structured and formally well-understood way. The ontology implementation of a logic for the description of such combination usually requires the use of a reasoner like Pellet or RACER (Knublauch, 2003).

We simplify the problem by creating a sub class of the Task class for each element in the combinatory set (figure 4). This means, for example, that for a modelled subclass inside the ontology (e.g.): *steel_based-analysis-detailing*, a table with relations can be constructed in where a simple map to the allowed tools can be modelled. For the example case *(steel_based-analysis-detailing)*, the allowed tools set will contain the Virtual Reality (VR) visualizer and the Element Generation Tools (GEN). In figure 4 part of the test relations table used in our example is presented.

model_type	process_stage	for	user_intention	useTool	VR	DIM	GEN
steel_based	design		assembly				
steel_based	fabrication		assembly				
steel_based	analysis		assembly				
steel_based	design		detailing				
steel_based	fabrication		detailing				
steel_based	analysis		detailing				
steel_ba:	desien						

Figure 4 – Detail of the relations table.

In order to model the mapping from the Available Tools (**AT**) subclass of the ontology and the task class, we restrict an object type property using OWL DL (description logics) restrictions. The restriction for this specific case is:

$$\textbf{R = Dimensioning Tool}$$

$$\textbf{T = Visualization Tool} \cup \textbf{Element Generation Tool} \cup \textbf{Dimensioning Tool}$$

$$\textbf{AT} = \overline{(\textbf{T} \cap \textbf{R})} = \textbf{Visualization Tool} \cup \textbf{Element Generation Tool}$$

Apart from the three tools to choose from, we have also implemented a fourth tool that will be presented in every set of allowing tools (and hence in every UI). This tool is called "Query Tool" and provides the user with means to semantically interrogate the geometries contained in the CAD model. We generate also a menu operations tool called "options" in order to perform maintenance operations like for example, destroy a semantically generated UI in the case that the user wants to create a new one.

For the implementation of the prototype, we used AutoCAD 2006 running Pro Steel V17, which is a commercial software that runs as an add-in to the base CAD extending the capabilities of the system from the structures design point of view. For the modeling of the CIS/2 ontology, we used Protégé interfacing with the ontology with the provided OWL API. In the figure 5 a screenshot of a test CAD with a generated semantic UI for the example is shown.

For testing the prototype, the presented schema was implemented as a part of a research project called MiroView where the ontology supported UI is being used for the recommendation of CAD tools in an actual steel detailing company. At present time, tests are still in an ongoing stage therefore the results will presented in a future work.

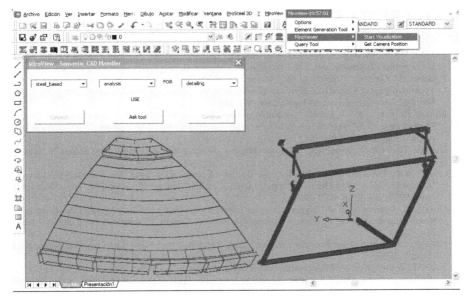

Figure 5 – A Semantically generated UI.

5. CONCLUSIONS AND FUTURE WORK

In this paper, we presented a Knowledge based approach for the exploitation of semantic aspects (e.g. user intentions and tasks) for the real time automatic generation of graphical user interfaces on a structural CAD software. This approach deals directly with the structural design process in order to suggest the user with the most appropriate tools for every stage of the design. The presented schema was modeled using an ontology that allows the semantic interrogation of the different parameters needed to produce the menu. As test tool, we presented an example based in the methodology with three test tools and a simplified process division. As future work we will extend the presented results in order to use more tools. We will extend in a future work the process ontology in order to have a more precise stage division, allowing a better tools recommendation. Also as future work, the different tests in a real environment will be analyzed in order to check the efficiency of the methodology.

5.1 Acknowledgments

We want to thank the Basque Government for the partial financing of the MiroView Project (INTEK-4140/2004). A special mention is given to our Steel Detailer partner LANIK S.A, who served as test users, providing key points in their design workflow to apply the techniques presented in this paper. We also thank SOME for their participation in this research project.

6. REFERENCES

1. CIS/2 – CIMSteel Integration Standard, WebPage: http://www.cis2.org/ Last access 26 January 2006.
2. Ekholm: "Activity objects in CAD-programs for building design". In: Proceedings of the Ninth International Conference on ComputerAided Architectural Design Futures Eindhoven, 2001, 61-74.
3. Fridman, McGuinnes: "Ontology Development 101: A Guide to Creating Your First Ontology" Technical Report KSL-01-05 and Stanford Medical Informatics Technical Report SMI-2001-0880, Stanford Knowledge Systems Laboratory, Mar 2001.
4. Furtado E, Furtado J, Silva, et al: "An ontology-based method for universal design of user interfaces", Proceedings of Workshop on Multiple User Interfaces over the Internet: Engineering and Applications Trends, Lille, 2001.
5. Georgia Tech CIS/2 HomePage, WebPage: http://www.coa.gatech.edu/~aisc/ Last access 26 January 2006.
6. Gruber TR: "Toward principles for the design of ontologies used for knowledge sharing". International Journal of Human-Computer Studies. 1995. Volume 43, Issue 5-6 Nov./Dec. 1995. Pages: 907-928. ISSN 1071-5819.
7. Hovestadt, Gramberg, et al. "Hyperbolic User Interfaces for Computer Aided Architectural Design", Conference on Human Factors in Computing Systems Denver, Colorado, United States , 1995, 304-305.
8. Igarashi. "Supportive Interfaces for Creative Visual Thinking" Collective Creativity Workshop, Nara (Japan), 2000.
9. KAON2, WebPage: http://kaon2.semanticweb.org/ Last access 26 January 2006.
10. Knublauch, Musen, Noy. Tutorial: Creating Semantic Web (OWL) Ontologies with Protégé. International Semantic Web Conference (ISWC2003).
11. WonderWeb OWL API HomePage, WebPage: http://owl.man.ac.uk/api.shtml/ Last access 26 January 2006.
12. Posada J, Toro CA, Wundrak S, Stork A: Ontology Supported Semantic simplification of Large Data Sets of industrial plant CAD models for design review visualization. In LNCS - Lecture Notes in Computer Science/Artificial Intelligence (Selected papers from KES05). Springer Verlag GmbH. 184-194.
13. Puerta, Eriksson, Gennari: "Model-Based Automated Generation of User Interfaces" International Conference on Intelligent User Interfaces. San Francisco, California, United States, 1997, 65-72.

RAPID DESIGN OF MODEL-BASED PROCESS CHAINS – A GRAPH BASED APPROACH

Christian Wagenknecht and Jan C. Aurich
Institute for Manufacturing Engineering and Production Management (FBK)
University of Kaiserslautern, Germany
{wagenknecht, aurich}@cck.uni-kl.de

Process chains in manufacturing and order processing increasingly depend on the successful usage of information systems. However, available approaches typically lack the opportunity to evaluate the expecting process chain and modeling quality or rely on a system driven in-depth analysis. The presented easy-to-use graphical approach overcomes existing drawbacks and integrates the domains of manufacturing and order processing at the same time.

1. INTRODUCTION

The proper design of manufacturing and corresponding order processes represents one of the major core competencies of discrete parts manufacturers. In addition, the enterprise must consider appropriate information systems to support the design and implementation of the processes. Due to increasing process and process chain complexity, the usage of information systems is almost inevitable. Hence, model-based process chains are a synonym for information system supported process chains stress the corresponding foundation in particular, i.e. process models.

The individual user, however, faces an increasing variety of alternative information systems. It becomes more and more difficult to choose the adequate information system and to evaluate its usability (Monostori, 2003; Wagenknecht, 2005). Due to the information system driven perspective of the software suppliers, information systems are very often brought into the market without deeper concepts of suitable manufacturing and order processes. Generic information systems standards (Chen, 2004; Mertins, 2005; Schekkerman, 2004) often lack individual industrial applicability due to the high level of abstraction.

The process modeling must cover the needs of a successful process design, the integration of information systems and relevant design interactions. The design process is usually divided into the domains of factory planning and order processing using different information systems leading to a broad variety of process models, notations and database locations. Order processing is typically observed as the end of a consecutive design chain with no feedback loops. As a result, it must cope with fixed design decisions without taking account of relevant interdependencies. Moreover, the aspect of continuous process improvement must be considered.

In most cases, available process design concepts (e.g. Kuhn, 1995; SCOR, 2005; Schönsleben, 2004; Sepet, 1998, VDI, 2000) either focus on strategic aspects in process design or rely on a highly detailed in-depth process modeling. Additionally, only very few approaches (Haats, 2000; Kuhn, 1999) transfer the findings of process modeling (Booch, 1992; Chen, 2004; Dangelmaier, 2001) to the domain of manufacturing as well as order processing and consider relevant design interactions.

2. DESIGN CONCEPT

The following paper intends to fill the described gap as it presents a basic concept for the rapid design of model-based process chains. Due to the conceptual nature and the usage of information systems for the design and implementation of both manufacturing as well as order processing, process design is interpreted under the perspective of process modeling. The graph-based approach particularly takes the needs of a fast and efficient design of process alternatives during the early design stages into account. Accordingly, for the sake of simplicity, the concept follows an inductive design principle (Schäfer, 2003) deriving general findings out of individual and empirical data from selective industrial use cases.

The consideration of design as modeling poses the opportunity to derive a more detailed view of the design process. Following the findings for a successful modeling methodology (Booch, 1992; Dangelmaier, 2001), the design concept comprises four elements: design constructs and rules, a design notation and a design methodology. The proposed design concept can be seen as an umbrella for the variety of existing design concepts (e.g. factory planning, production planning and control) particularly taking modeling aspects in process design into account. This explicit consideration of the modeling aspects allows supporting and depicting the original process designs.

The usage of process modules as basic design constructs, design rules (e.g. configuration, segmentation, linkage), which describe valid directional and undirected (constraint) relations between these constructs, as well as a suitable design methodology has been already described in previous work (Wagenknecht, 2005). Process design is considered as a two-step modeling course, which comprises the initial design of the manufacturing processes and the subsequent design of the model-based order processing processes linked via hierarchical control loops. For example, if a proper design of an information system supported order processing is not possible, modifications of the manufacturing processes must be considered.

The particular aspect of choosing a proper process notation, which covers both static as well as dynamic process aspects, is addressed in the following. The adequate modeling of static aspects allows visualizing relevant process elements, relations and functions in process chains

3. STATIC ASPECTS IN PROCESS MODELING

3.1 Process notation

Based on an appropriate symbolism, the process notation depicts all relevant process modeling information. The proposed easy-to-use process notation is hereby understood as a support notion that is not intended to replace original commercial and standard notations (e.g. Bernus, 2006; Chen, 2004), which are mostly more detailed. Having the role of a mediator and communicator, the process notation is rather intended to render the different worlds of process modeling comparable.

The proposed process notation allows depicting and interconnecting process modeling both in factory planning as well as order processing. Factory planning and order processing are typically separated, however highly interrelated. The primary models of factory planning are usually stored in tools of the digital factory (e.g. Technomatix). Models of order processing are stored mostly in ERP-systems (e.g. bill of materials, process plan, inspection plan). Both worlds are only rarely integrated (e.g. SyteAPS/AIM). A shared notation allows expressing and communicating knowledge of different domains in a common and agreed language.

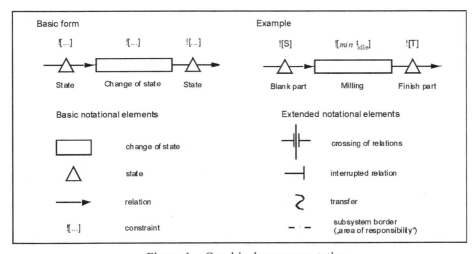

Figure 1 – Graphical process notation.

Enhancing existing approaches (Dangelmaier, 1993; Felser, 1996), the proposed graphical process notation uses elementary nodes and arcs (see figure 1). The systematically representation of manufacturing and order processing, corresponding system elements, their states and relations as well as relevant constraints (e.g. model consistency, stock, idle time, due date) addresses both sufficient modeling performance as well as simplicity. As a mediator notation for the domains of factory planning und order processing, the notation allows anticipating expectable modeling and corresponding process quality. Some of the very basic graphical design elements can be already found in commercial information systems (e.g. Technomatix) or can be easily depicted using standard visualization software (e.g. MS Powerpoint).

3.2 Model consistency

In the case of using information systems (e.g. digital factory, advanced planning & scheduling), model based activities should not call for a subsequent human trouble shooting in order to provide feasible solutions.

Model consistency secures an appropriate fit between model-based order processing and manufacturing process. Due to the usage of manufacturing process models, the success of order processing is tightly bound to the accuracy of the provided models in the information system. The consistency condition implies that the processing results are actually feasible. The appropriateness of model-based order processing is analyzed based on the explication of the applied manufacturing model using the same notation as applied in the design and modeling of the manufacturing processes (see figure 2).

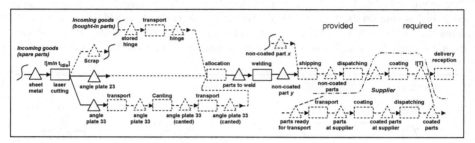

Figure 2 – Model consistency of medium to short-term planning (abridged).

The process notation clearly depicts the successful or missing modeling support by the used information systems. The provided and required modeling support is denoted with a solid ("———") and dotted ("- - - -") line respectively.

In case of order processing, modeling is only appropriate in case the provided model perspective fits the manufacturing processes. Deviations between the provided and required modeling perspective are a direct result of using information systems with limited applicability. Fortunately, based on the provided graphical notation, the need for additional concepts, e.g. the integration of additional human planners, can be derived directly from the missing gaps in the sketch of the required manufacturing process chain.

3.3 Use case

To illustrate the applicability of the proposed design concept, a design example from a medium sized automotive and construction industry supplier is given. The introduced new order processing system both extends as well as substitutes the current information systems. However, due to the complexity of IT-structure and functions, it has been difficult to clearly elaborate and evaluate the order processing quality to be expected, necessary modifications of the order processing system and the required integration of organization, material structure and information systems.

In this situation, the proposed process design concept appeared to be a helpful approach. For example, following the initial mapping of the existing manufacturing processes, a closer view upon medium to short term planning revealed that the new information system strongly supports the planning of machining processes considering the required resources and planning objectives (see figure 3). However, transport, storage and inspection as well as external coating processes remained unsupported or are processed by legacy systems. That is, to achieve proper order processing results, the new information system must be highly integrated into the information structure while the shop floor worker must support the adherence to delivery dates. Moreover, excess part storage must be abandoned leading to a modified material flow while external coating needs a clearly fixed lead-time.

Additionally, to meet the individual process design task, the process modeling of provided and missing information system support has been extended for different color codes to represent the different information systems.

4. DYNAMIC ASPECTS IN PROCESS MODELING

So far, the proposed process design concept supports the static modeling of process structures and functions. In the following, it is shown that the concept can be extended to cover dynamic aspects in process modeling for manufacturing, i.e. process parameters.

4.1 Process states

In general, the number of relevant n parameters of a process can be represented in the form of n-dimensional state space (Westkämper, 1994). The graphical representation of the state space can however be difficult if many specific properties and their corresponding parameters must be taken into account.

Considering a manufacturing process from the point of view of the material flow, the properties of time, quantity and location are sufficient to clearly define the state of a part. However, as the detailed definition of the location leads to a three-dimensional parameter, a 5-dimensional state space with limited possibilities for graphical representation would be the result. Fortunately, the aspect of distance is usually sufficient to characterize the individual state of a process. The aspect of location can therefore be reduced to the aspect of distance. Correspondingly, the concept of a three-dimensional state space of manufacturing processes representing the relevant states of time, quantity and distance is proposed (figure 3).

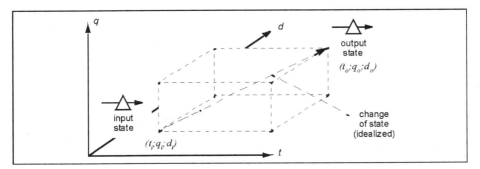

Figure 3 – State space of a manufacturing process.

The proposed static nation of a process can be transferred into the three dimensional state space. Every node representing the specific state of a process can be located within the state space based on the specific values of the parameters of time, quantity and distance. The change in state of a process corresponds to the state space between subsequent process states. The idealized linear change in state of a process with each one input and output state is given in figure 3.

The concept of a state space cannot only be used to represent processes but process chains as well. Figure 4 depicts a simple example of a process chain, which consists of two manufacturing processes. The individual processes are depicted using the process modules "transport" and "packaging" (for more details see Wagenknecht, 2005). The overall change in state for the part corresponds to a change in distance (transport) and a decrease of quantity due to the aggregation of several transport units to one packaging unit (packaging).

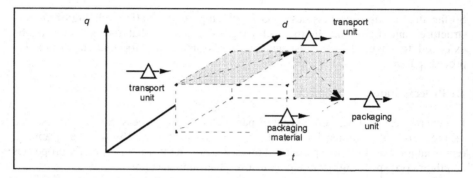

Figure 4 – Process modules in the state space diagram.

The given process chain is characterized by the introduction of an intermediate state for the processing of the input state into the output state. The process module packaging requires introduction of an additional state representing the packaging material. Additionally, figure 4 depicts that the necessary linkage characteristics, i.e. the identity of output and input states of subsequent processes, is given.

4.2 Tolerance specification

In practice, each manufacturing process within a process chain is not only characterized by different setting parameters but state deviations as well (denoted as Δ). Out of the perspective of the material flow, such deviations can affect all the three dimensions of time t, quantity q and distance d and can reach both positive ($+\Delta$) as well as negative ($-\Delta$) values. Reasons are the planned collating (aggregation) respectively decollating (desegregation) of process elements as well as inevitable disturbances of a manufacturing process. As a direct result, manufacturing processes must be considered as rather inhomogeneous. Positive and negative deviations lead to a specific range of tolerances with upper and lower limits.

The individual modeling of each parameters deviation can be combined to a three-dimensional state space as well. To do so, every given state of a process element within a manufacturing process, while considering relevant deviations, can be depicted by a three-dimensional state space (see figure 5).

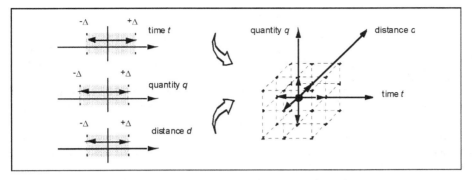

Figure 5 – Combination of tolerances of a manufacturing process state.

The consideration of relevant deviations extends the state modeling of system elements of a manufacturing process. The individual deviations of the values of the different nodes must be integrated into the concept of a state space (see figure 6).

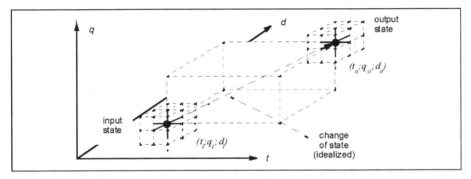

Figure 6 – State space of a process module with tolerances.

A model-based order processing must both properly depict as well as manage possible deviations in manufacturing. The specific range of tolerances must cover the specific characteristics of a manufacturing process (e.g. lot size, scraped parts, variable machining times, delivery locations). The final tolerance requirements are usually defined directly and indirectly by the customer specifications. Initial tolerance specifications are the responsibility of the supplier. Tolerance specifications of the intermediate manufacturing processes are the direct result of values and interrelations of operation, resource and part characteristics, i.e. the manufacturing technology itself. As a result, the dimensions of the individual processes must be gradually brought up to the required specification.

In order to maintain the linkage condition of subsequent processes, the output tolerance of a process must correspond to the input tolerance of the subsequent process. Following the concept of a tolerance channel (Westkämper, 1994) to visualize single parameter tolerances, manufacturing in terms of time, quantity and distance can be described as a tolerance tube through which the manufacture is to be successfully led.

5. SUMMARY AND OUTLOOK

The proposed concept strongly supports the graph based design of process chains in manufacturing and order processing taking particular care of the information system characteristics, deficits and limitations. Results of industrial use cases prove the usability and applicability. Major benefits include both the individual design of processes in manufacturing and model-based order processing as well as the simplicity to rapidly synthesize and analyze alternative process solutions. Future work is required to development a modeling support for the dynamic process aspects as the modeling of static process aspects can be easily done via visualization tools (e.g. MS Visio) or customized in Digital factory or ERP-software.

6. REFERENCES

1. Bernus P. Handbook on architectures of information systems. 2. ed. Springer, Berlin, 2006.
2. Booch G. Object oriented design. 7. ed. Redwood City, Calif: Benjamin/Cummings, 1992.
3. Chen D, Vernadat F. Standards on enterprise integration and engineering - state of the art. Journal of Computer Integrated Manufacturing 2004, 17 (3): 235-253.
4. Dangelmaier W, Wiedenmann H. Modell der Fertigungssteuerung. Berlin: Beuth, 1993.
5. Dangelmaier W. Fertigungsplanung. 2. ed. Springer: Berlin, 2001.
6. Felser W. Eine Methode zur Erstellung von Fertigungssteuerungsverfahren aus Bausteinen, HNI-Verlagsschriftenreihe, vol. 17. Paderborn: HNI, 1996.
7. Haats C. Produktionsplanung und -steuerung für Unternehmen mit linearen Prozessketten. Heimsheim: Jost-Jetter, 2000.
8. Kuhn A. Prozessketten in der Logistik. Dortmund: Praxiswissen, 1995.
9. Kuhn A. Referenzmodelle für Produktionsprozesse zur Untersuchung und Gestaltung von PPS-Aufgaben, HNI-Verlagsschriftenreihe, vol. 52. Paderborn: HNI, 1999.
10. Monostori L, Váncza J, Márkus A, Kádár B, Viharos ZsJ. "Towards the realization of digital enterprises". In Progress in virtual manufacturing systems, Proceedings 36th CIRP ISMS, H. Bley, ed. Saarbrücken: Univ., 2003: 99-106.
11. Mertins K, Jochem R. Architectures, methods and tools for enterprise engineering. International Journal of Production Economics 2005, 98 (2): 179-188.
12. Schäfer L. Analyse und Gestaltung fertigungstechnischer Prozessketten, FBK Produktionstechnische Berichte, vol. 45. Kaiserslautern: Univ., 2003.
13. Schekkerman J. How to survive in the jungle of enterprise architecture frameworks - creating or choosing an enterprise architecture framework. 2. ed. Victoria, B.C., Trafford, 2004.
14. Schönsleben P. Integral logistics management. 2. ed. Boca Raton, FL: St. Lucie Press, 2004.
15. Sepet N, Warnecke G. "Controlling of scheduled production processes. In Networked manufacturing, Proceedings 31st CIRP ISMS, Berkeley, 1998: 189-194.
16. Supply Chain Council. Supply Chain Operations Reference Model, SCOR Version 7.0. Url: www.supply-chain.org, 2005.
17. VDI. VDI-Guideline 4400, Part 1 – 3: Logistic indicators. Düsseldorf: Beuth, 2000.
18. Wagenknecht C, Aurich JC. Design of modular planning processes using model-based predictive control. CIRP Journal of Manufacturing Systems 2005; 34 (4): 363-371.
19. Westkämper E. Zero-Defect Manufacturing by means of learning supervision of process chains. Annals of the CIRP 1994; 43 (1): 405-408.

AN APPLICATION OF ISO-GUM IN THE METHOD FOR ESTIMATING THE DIMENSIONAL ERRORS OF BENT PARTS

T. H. M. Nguyen[1], J. R. Duflou[2] and J.-P. Kruth[2]

[1] *Hanoi University of Technology, Vietnam*
NguyenThiHongMinh@mail.hut.edu.vn
[2] *Katholieke Universiteit Leuven, Belgium*
{joost.duflou, jean-pierre.kruth}@mech.kuleuven.be

The current study addresses the accuracy of bend elements and global dimensions with tolerances based on an analytical method, where each deviation in part dimension is represented by type A and type B errors, as instructed by ISO-GUM. Meanwhile, a generic formula is presented to estimate the deviations in the global dimensions of interest in bent parts based on the deviations in the participating bend elements. The deviations in the bend elements formed in each operation are in turn estimated through an analytical simulation model. Therefore, the error propagation in consecutive bending operations using a specified process plan is simulated. Using such a top-down analytical approach, the errors of the global dimensions with tolerances were represented and estimated through the errors encountered for each operation. Finally, a procedure for estimating dimensional errors in bent parts is suggested and illustrated with an example to show the applicability of the method.

1. INTRODUCTION

Forming using sheet bending introduces straight bend lines into flat patterns cut out from metal sheets in order to form three-dimensional parts with various bend features for a wide range of part complexity and weight. Workpiece preparation for the process includes modelling the part, calculating and cutting out the corresponding flat pattern. Geometric approximations and material behaviour assumptions are applied in both modelling and calculation. Due to the discrepancies between the model and reality, there exists an error in the calculation of the unfolding (Streppel, 1993). The subsequent cutting step may also provide various dimensional imprecision, depending on the selected cutting process. During the forming process afterwards, the workpiece is positioned against a backgauge of the machine before being bent linearly by a punch penetrating into the die cavity. The accuracy of the resulting dimensions therefore depends on the repeatability of the gauging system, the gauging method, the estimation of the location of the gauging edge according to the process plan (de Vin, 1996), the material handling method (Nguyen, 2005), the accuracy of the punch positioning (Singh, 2004).

Considering the accuracy aspects for global dimensions of bent sheet metal parts, studies employing deterministic approaches (de Vin, 1996) and Monte-Carlo simulations (Hagenah, 2003) have been conducted. The relationships between the causes and the effects of the inaccuracies have been investigated in order to estimate the achievable dimensional accuracy. A deterministic view of the tolerances (de Vin, 1996) allows a fast estimation of the achievable tolerance zones, but the stochastic characteristics of the process cannot be taken into account. In contrast, Monte-Carlo simulation incorporates this aspect, with the computation time sacrificed.

2. ERROR ANALYSIS MODEL

According to studies reported in (de Vin, 1996), (Hagenah, 2003), (Nguyen, 2005), (Singh, 2004) and (Streppel, 1993), the dimensions achieved from bending operations suffer from various sources of errors. As instructed by (ISO, 1997), once a quantity Q is expressed by a function of n normally distributed variables in such form as expressed in Formula (1), then the deviation ΔQ of the quantity Q from the nominal value Q^0 can be expressed through a combination of the influencing errors, as expressed in Formula (2).

$$Q = f_Q\left(X_0, ..., X_k, ..., X_n\right) \tag{1}$$

$$\Delta Q = \Delta(Q) \pm k_p \times u_c(f_Q) \tag{2}$$

Where

$\Delta(Q)$ is the correctible systematic error of Q, representing errors that are known and can be compensated for, as classified by (ISO, 1997). According also to (ISO, 1997), the value of ΔQ is estimated through the errors ΔX_k of the influencing factors k by Formula (3).

$$\Delta(Q) = \sum_{k=0}^{2n_t+1} \Delta(Q_k) = \sum_{k=0}^{2n_t+1} c_{Q,k} \times \Delta X_k \tag{3}$$

k_p is the coverage factor to obtain a confidence interval having level of confidence p, assuming a normal distribution of Q. According to (ISO, 1997), k_p takes a value of 2 for $p = 95.45\%$.

$u_c(f_Q)$ is the combined uncertainty of quantity Q, covering all the uncertainties introduced by the unknown systematic errors and the random errors of the influencing factors. The value of $u_c(f_Q)$ is estimated through the standard uncertainty $u(X_k)$ of the influencing factors k by Formula (4).

$$u_C^2(f_Q) = \sum_{k=0}^{2n_t+1} u_k^2(f_Q) = \sum_{k=1}^{2n_t+1} c_{Q,k}^2 \times u^2(X_k) \tag{4}$$

The standard uncertainty $u(X_k)$, or deviation, of random errors are generally estimated by statistical analysis. Meanwhile, the unknown systematic errors are generally estimated using 'expert knowledge' by assuming a range for the corresponding errors and the most likely statistical distribution, from which a standard deviation is estimated.

$c_{Q,k}$ is the sensitivity coefficient of element k in function f_Q, calculated by (5).

$$c_{Q,k} = \partial f_Q / \partial X_k \tag{5}$$

Therefore, when the errors of the participating elements and the sensitivity of function f_Q for each element k are known, the error of quantity Q, which is expressed through a relationship function as expressed in Formula (1), can be estimated by Formula (2). Hence, in order to estimate the errors expected for the dimensions of bent parts using this model, there are two tasks to be carried out: The first task is to find the expression of the bent dimensions through the influencing factors, and the second task is to find the errors of the influencing factors. These aspects are dealt with in the following sections.

3. MODELLING OF ERROR PROPAGATION

In (Nguyen, 2005), the influence of the various uncertainties on the angular and linear bend elements resulting from a bending operation has been quantified. Besides, according to (de Vin, 1996) and (Shpitalni, 1999), dimensional errors of bent parts propagate in the bending process from one bending operation to the others. Meanwhile, the error expected for a global dimension is influenced by the dimensions participating in the dimension chain. In order to investigate these phenomena, this study divides the dimensions of bent parts into two groups:
1. Simple dimensions are the dimensions specified for a single bend element, such as the angle between two adjacent flanges, or the length of a bend leg between two adjacent bend lines.
2. Complex or global dimensions are the dimensions specified for a *partition* that consists of a group of adjacent bend elements.

The following subsections provide the modelling of error propagation and stack-up in bent parts through two models: The first model in Section 3.1 provides the geometric functions of the global dimensions of a partition through its participating elements. Applying the error analysis model presented in Section 2 for such functions, the errors expected for the global dimensions can be calculated through the errors of the participating elements. Meanwhile, in Section 3.2, the second model investigates the propagation of the errors through the consecutive bending opera-tions. By using the second model, the errors expected for each bend elements can be calculated to provide the data for the first model.

3.1. Error stack up on a global dimension

Among the various types of complex dimensions that can be specified for a bent part, the models for the two most common types are explained:
- The linear distance from a point to a flange, and
- The angle between two non-adjacent flanges.
The modelling discussed below for these types of dimensions uses the following assumptions:
1. All bend lines involved in a partition with tolerances are parallel to one another and the dimensions with tolerances are specified in cross sections perpendicular to the bend lines;
2. Bend radius and sheet thickness are not taken into account, as extended foil models (Duflou, 2005) are used to represent bent parts; and
3. The base points of dimensional tolerances are defined on the edges of bend flanges.

Linear distance between a point and a flange

Take a partition of n_t bend lines, as illustrated in figure 1, where a linear distance $H_{nt+1,0}$ is specified between a point on the edge $(n_t + 1)$ and the first flange L_0.

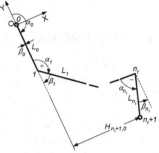

Figure 1 - Linear dimension between a point and a flange.

In the coordinate system fixed to flange L_0, as seen in figure 1, the projections L_i^x and L_i^y of each linear bend element L_i are calculated as in Formula (6):

$$L_i^x = L_i \sin\left(\sum_{j=0}^{i} \alpha_j - i\pi \right) \text{ and } L_i^y = L_i \cos\left(\sum_{j=0}^{i} \alpha_j - i\pi \right) \tag{6}$$

Where

i is the index of the edges of the flanges participating in the partition. Note that in this system, i's with value from 1 to n_t correspond to the bend lines in the partition, while $i = 0$ or $n_t + 1$ correspond to the outer edges of the partition;

α_i is the angle formed at bend line i;

L_i is the bend length of flange i, which lies between edge i and $i+1$;

α_0 is the angle between the vertical axis (+Oy) of the current coordinate system and the flange L_0

By selecting the coordinate system so that $Oy \equiv L_0$ (i.e. $\alpha_0 = \pi$), distance $H_{nt+1,0}$ is calculated through the bend elements participating in the dimension according to Formula (7).

$$H_{nt+1,0} = \sum_{i=0}^{n_t} L_i \sin\left(\sum_{j=0}^{i} \alpha_j - i\pi \right) \tag{7}$$

Complex angular dimensions

A complex angular dimension $\varphi_{n_t,0}$ is defined by the angle formed between two non-adjacent flanges L_{n_t} and L_0. The dimension represents the change in the direction vectors $\vec{L_0}$ and $\vec{L_{n_t}}$ between the two flanges, as shown in figure 2.

From the figure, it can be seen that:

$$\varphi_{n_t,0} = \beta_{n_t} - \beta_0 \tag{8}$$

where $\beta_0 = (\pi - \alpha_0)$

and $\beta_i = \beta_{i-1} + (\pi - \alpha_i)$ (9)

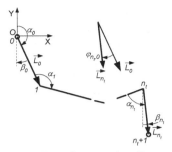

Figure 2 - Complex angular dimension.

Thus $\varphi_{n_t,0} = n_t \times \pi - \sum_{i=1}^{n_t} \alpha_i$ (10)

Formula (10) expresses the angular dimension as a function of angular bend elements locating between the flanges defining the dimension. Therefore, once the angular bend elements are known, the complex angular dimension can be calculated. Note that the angular dimension is not influenced by any linear bend element.

3.2 Error propagation in the bending process

The errors are propagated in the process through the sequence in which the bend lines of the part are made, the intermediate part shapes and the selection of the gauging options. For each operation, placing a workpiece against backgauge(s) positions the bend line to be bent at the designated position. The edge of the part that contacts with the backgauge is referred to as *the gauging edge*. Considering the relative position of the gauging edge to the position of the current bending line recognises two possible gauging options:

1. Direct gauging: no performed bend line between the gauging edge and the current bending line, as shown in figure 3.a.
2. Indirect gauging: the gauging edge is connected to the current bending line through at least one performed bend line, as illustrated in figure 3.b.

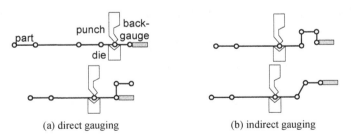

(a) direct gauging   (b) indirect gauging

Figure 3 - Examples of gauging option.

When compared to the direct gauging situation, indirect gauging induces extra gauging errors to the bending operation. As illustrated in figure 4, for each bend step s where bend i is performed by gauging to a line g, the error starts to propagate from the gauging line g towards the bend line i and finally stops at edge k, with k being the nearest bend line to i which is already bent at the operator side (OS). Therefore, the errors introduced into the operation influence only the actual unfolded length, locating between two edges k and j, where j the nearest bend line to i which is already bent at the machine side (MS). The errors do not have an impact on the *backgauge partition* $G_{j,g}$ standing between edges j and g, or the partition between the free edge at the OS and edge k. Meanwhile, the cumulative error on the backgauge partition contributes to the total gauging error introduced to the bend lengths produced by the bending operation.

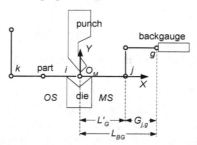

Figure 4 - A complex model with indirect gauging.

From figure 4, the length of the bend leg before bending at the MS is calculated by Formula (11). Note that, since the gauging movement occurs in the X direction of the machine coordinate system (MCS), only the error component in X direction actually influences the gauging accuracy.

$$L'_G = L_{BG} - G^x_{j,g} \tag{11}$$

Where, L_{BG} is the distance between the current bend line and the actual backgauge and $G^x_{j,g}$ is the length of the projection in X direction of the gauging partition. Meanwhile, gauging against edge g introduces an intrinsic error ΔL^0_G to the nominal value L^0_{BG} of distance L_{BG}, as expressed in Formula (12).

$$L_{BG} = L^0_{BG} + \Delta L^0_G \tag{12}$$

Similarly, an intrinsic error ΔL^0_R is also introduced to the residual length at the operator side. Both ΔL^0_G and ΔL^0_R suffer from the unavoidable uncertainties participating in the process such as the material handling method, the machine factor, the bend allowance and the punch displacement, as reported in (Nguyen, 2005). Therefore, for step s, the total gauging error due to the combined effect of the intrinsic error and the additional error due to gauging is calculated through:

$$\Delta L_{G|s} = \Delta L^0_G - \Delta G^x_{j,g} \text{ and } \Delta L_{R|s} = \Delta L_{U|s} + \Delta L^0_R + \Delta G^x_{j,g} \tag{13}$$

$\Delta L_{G|s}$ and $\Delta L_{R|s}$ are the errors expected for linear bend elements at the MS and OS,

ΔL^0_G and ΔL^0_R are the intrinsic errors encountered at the MS and OS for direct gauging,

$\Delta L_{U|s}$ is the error in the unfolded length $L_{j,k}$ due to cutting process, as for the first bending operation, or due to previous bending operations.

$\Delta G^x_{j,g}$ is the additional error due to indirect gauging, which is the X component of the error expected for $G_{j,g}$. According to Section 3.1, the global dimensions of this partition can be estimated through its participating elements. Therefore, according to Section 2, the error $\Delta G^x_{j,g}$ can be calculated through those of the bend elements of the backgauge partition.

Thus, after step s is executed, the resulting linear bend elements at the machine side and the operator side are estimated as expressed in Formula (14).

$$L_{G|s} = L^0_{G|s} + \Delta L_{G|s} \text{ and } L_{R|s} = L^0_{R|s} + \Delta L_{R|s} \tag{14}$$

Where

$L_{G|s}$ is the linear bend element formed between the current bend line i and edge j, the nominal value of which is $L^0_{G|s}$.

$L_{R|s}$ is the linear bend element formed between the current bend line i and edge k, the nominal value of which is $L^0_{R|s}$.

Note that for each production condition, the intrinsic errors as well as the errors of the initial unfolded length can be measured in advance. By repeated use of Formulas (13) and (14) from the unfolded state till the completely folded state of the part, the formation of all the linear bend elements is simulated. For any step with indirect gauging option, the additional gauging error is calculated through the errors attached to the bend elements participating in the gauging partition. Therefore, all the final bend elements can be calculated with their expected errors, providing a set of data to estimate the errors for any global dimension specified for the part.

4. PROCEDURE FOR ERROR ESTIMATION

The previous sections have provided the theoretical background to estimate the error for a dimension imposed with tolerance in a bent part. Complementary to the theory, the following paragraphs illustrate the procedure for such estimation through a real case.

4.1. Representation of the part using a foil model

A part with complex dimensions is given with the bend sequence as shown in figure 5. In order to make use of the models presented in the previous sections, the part is converted into a foil model using the mid-planes of the original flanges. Two complex dimensions D_3 and φ_2 are selected to demonstrate the procedure.

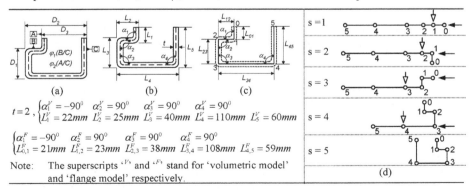

$$t = 2, \begin{cases} \alpha^V_1 = -90^0 & \alpha^V_2 = 90^0 & \alpha^V_3 = 90^0 & \alpha^V_4 = 90^0 \\ L^V_1 = 22mm & L^V_2 = 25mm & L^V_3 = 40mm & L^V_4 = 110mm & L^V_5 = 60mm \end{cases}$$

$$\begin{cases} \alpha^F_1 = -90^0 & \alpha^F_2 = 90^0 & \alpha^F_3 = 90^0 & \alpha^F_4 = 90^0 \\ L^F_{0,1} = 21mm & L^F_{1,2} = 23mm & L^F_{2,3} = 38mm & L^F_{3,4} = 108mm & L^F_{4,5} = 59mm \end{cases}$$

Note: The superscripts 'V' and 'F' stand for 'volumetric model' and 'flange model' respectively.

Figure 5 - Original part description (a) with dimensions of interest, (b) part representations in volumetric model, (c) foil model and (d) the selected bend sequence and gauging edges for each bending step: white arrows indicate bending edges, while black arrows indicate gauging edges.

4.2. Estimation of all bend elements and the corresponding errors

For estimating the errors expected for all the bend elements, the formation of the bend elements through all the bending steps is simulated according to the bend sequence. The simulation starts with the intrinsic errors and the error of the unfolded length measured for 6 series produced on 6 machines, coded M1 to M6, as shown in Table 1. Among all the bend steps, only step 3 has indirect gauging, where an additional gauging error is calculated through the errors estimated for the previously formed bend elements. As result, Table 2 shows the errors estimated for each bend element through two components: the standard deviation and the average value shift.

Table 1 - The intrinsic errors measured for 6 series of parts produced on 6 machines.

Error type	$\Delta\alpha$ [deg]		$\Delta L_{U|0}$ [mm]		ΔL_G^0 [mm]		ΔL_R^0 [mm]	
Machine	stdev	avg	stdev	avg	stdev	avg	stdev	avg
M1	0.510	0.366	0.021	- 0.088	0.166	0.147	0.160	- 0.672
M2	0.095	0.422	0.032	- 0.080	0.042	- 0.006	0.102	0.766
M3	0.123	0.328	0.022	- 0.090	0.029	0.033	0.046	0.185
M4	0.161	0.586	0.023	- 0.058	0.029	- 0.029	0.035	0.078
M5	0.110	0.314	0.019	- 0.080	0.039	0.051	0.044	- 0.006
M6	0.096	0.102	0.027	- 0.083	0.022	0.046	0.030	0.201

Table 2 - Simulation result - estimating the errors of the bend elements.

bend step	s = 1		s = 2		s = 3				s = 4		s = 5	
element	L_{01}		L_{12}		G_{20}		L_{23}		L_{34}		L_{45}	
machine	stdev	avg	stdev	avg	stdev	avg	stdev	avg	stdev	avg	stdev	avg
M1	0.093	0.147	0.093	0.147	0.112	0.281	0.145	-0.134	0.093	0.147	0.222	-2.494
M2	0.051	-0.006	0.051	-0.006	0.073	0.149	0.089	-0.155	0.051	-0.006	0.145	3.133
M3	0.025	0.033	0.025	0.033	0.061	0.153	0.066	-0.120	0.025	0.033	0.093	0.805
M4	0.057	-0.029	0.057	-0.029	0.078	0.186	0.097	-0.215	0.057	-0.029	0.148	0.438
M5	0.065	0.051	0.065	0.051	0.084	0.166	0.106	-0.115	0.065	0.051	0.160	0.060
M6	0.022	0.046	0.022	0.046	0.056	0.083	0.061	-0.037	0.022	0.046	0.093	0.802

4.3. Estimation of the error for the global dimensions

Investigating the foil model allowed expressing the complex dimensions of interest, namely D_3 and φ_2, through their participating bend elements as follows:

- D_3 is a complex linear dimension defined from point 0 to point 5 in the coordinate system of the reference flange $L_{4,5}$. Therefore, according to (7),

$$\begin{cases} D_3 = D_{0,5}^x = & L_{4,5} \times \sin(\alpha_0) + L_{3,4} \times \sin(\alpha_0 + \alpha_4 - \pi) + L_{2,3} \times \sin(\alpha_0 + \alpha_4 + \alpha_3 - 2\pi) + \\ & L_{1,2} \times \sin(\alpha_0 + \alpha_4 + \alpha_3 + \alpha_2 - 3\pi) + L_{0,1} \times \sin(\alpha_0 + \alpha_4 + \alpha_3 + \alpha_2 - \alpha_1 - 4\pi) \end{cases} \quad (15)$$

- φ_2 is a complex angular dimension between flange $L_{0,1}$ and $L_{4,5}$. Therefore according to Formula 10, φ_2 is calculated by Formula 16:

$$\varphi_2 = \varphi_{L_{0,1},L_{4,5}} = 4 \times \pi - \alpha_1 - \alpha_2 - \alpha_3 - \alpha_4 \quad (16)$$

In order to apply the error analysis model discussed in Section 2, the sensitivity coefficients $c_{Q,k}$ are calculated for each pair of quantity Q, being either D_3 or φ_2, and the influencing factor, being any of the variables in the functions expressed by Formulas (15) or (16). Plugging the errors of the participating bend elements from the simulation result, shown in Table 2, and the sensitivity coefficients calculated from Formulas (15) and (16) into Formulas (3) and (4) allowed estimating both components of the errors expected for the global dimensions of interest.

In order to validate the result, these dimensions have been measured on the real parts and the corresponding ranges of deviations have been calculated for each series. Figure 6 illustrates the comparison between the estimated and the measured values of the errors expressed by the error ranges calculated for $\pm2\sigma$.

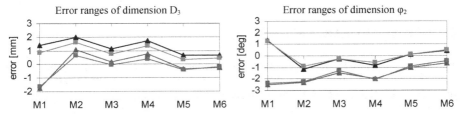

Figure 6 - Graphical comparison of the $\pm2\sigma$ error ranges for the dimensions of interest between the measured values (-■-: max, -■-: min) and the values estimated (-▲-: max, -▲-: min).

It can be seen from the graphs that the ranges of the estimated and measured errors have good agreement in most cases. Furthermore, it has been observed from the result, which has been used to plot these graphs, that the uncertainty component of the linear dimensions shown by the standard deviations has been predicted with an absolute error ranging between 0.01 to 0.06 mm. Occasionally, the estimation error can reach a very high value, e.g. 0.17 mm for machine M1, or a very low value, e.g. 0.01mm for machine M2. The average estimation error over all machines is 0.05 mm. The standard deviations of the angular dimensions have been predicted with an absolute error ranging mainly between 0.03 to 0.05 degrees. The estimation errors can seldom reach values as high as 0.08 degrees for machine M4, or as low as 0.03 degrees for machine M5. The average estimation error over all machines is 0.05 degrees. On the other hand, the average offsets of the linear dimensions are predicted with an average error of 0.26 mm. Most of the prediction errors for the average offset range between 0.20 to 0.30 mm. This prediction error is occasionally low, i.e. with a value of 0.08 mm, for machine M6. For the angular dimensions, the average offsets are predicted with an average error of 0.08 degrees. For most of the cases, the prediction errors range between 0.02 to 0.07 degrees.

5. CONCLUSION

The study has established a method for estimating the dimensional errors for bent parts. Making use of the GUM method, it has been shown that such task can be tackled by two subtasks: the first step is establishing an analytical expression for the dimensions of interest through the participating bend elements, while the second subtask is to calculate the errors expected for these elements. The subtasks are correspondingly resolved by two mathematical models. Finally, the different pieces of the puzzle are fixed together through a procedure for estimating dimensional errors illustrated for an example. Validating the data achieved from the procedure against the measured data from real production has shown promising results for various series of parts produced by different machines. In brief, the study has shown the possibility to use simple analytical models in combination with experimental data to predict the dimensional errors in low time complexity yet with a useful level of accuracy. Such a prediction can be applied in automatic process planning systems to judge the compatibility of the alternative process plans against the tolerance imposed for bent parts.

6. ACKNOWLEDGEMENT

The authors acknowledge the co-operations of the EMAP centre of the XIOS High School Limburg, financially supported by the Institute for the Promotion of Innovation by Science and Technology in Flanders through contract HOBU/20110, in providing the experimental data for this study. The authors also gratefully acknowledge the receipt of a grant from the Flemish Interuniversity Council for University Development cooperation (VLIR UOS) which enabled them to carry out this work.

7. REFERENCES

1. de Vin, L.J., Streppel, A.H. and Kals, H.J.J., "The accuracy aspect in set-up determination for sheet bending", in: *Int.l J. of Advanced Manufacturing Technology,* 11, 1996, 179–185.
2. Duflou, J.R., Vancza, J. and Aerens, R., "Computer aided process planning for sheet metal bending: A state of the art", in: *Computers in Industry,* 56/7, 2005, 747-771.
3. Hagenah, H., "Simulation based Evaluation of the Accuracy for Sheet Metal Bending caused by the Bending Stage Plan", in: *Proc. 36th CIRP Int. Seminar on Manufacturing Systems,* Jun. 2003, Saarland University, Saarbrücken, Germany
4. ISO standard, "Technical drawings - Geometrical tolerancing - Tolerancing of form, orientation, location and run-out - Generalities, definitions, symbols, indications on drawings", in: *ISO 1101 1983 (E),* 57-69.
5. ISO standard, "Guide to the expression of uncertainty in measurement", in: *ISO/TC 213/WG 4 N 65 ISO/DTR 14253-2:1997(E)*
6. Nguyen, T.H.M., Duflou, J.R., Kruth, J.-P., Stouten, I., Van Hecke, J., and Van Bael, A., "Tolerance Verification for Sheet Metal Bending: Factors Influencing Dimensional Accuracy of Bent Parts", in: *Proc. 9th Int.l Seminar on Computer Aided Tolerancing,* Tempe, USA, Apr. 2005.
7. Shpitalni, M. and Radin, B., "Critical Tolerance Oriented Process Planning in Sheet Metal Bending", in: *Trans. of ASME Journal of Mechanical Design,* 121, Mar. 1999, pp. 136-144.
8. Singh, U.P., Maiti, S.K., Date, P.P. and Narasimhan, K., "Numerical simulation of the influence of air bending tool geometry on product quality", in: *J. Materials Processing Technology,* 14/35, Feb. 2004, 269-275.
9. Stouten I., Van Hecke J., and Van Bael A., "Tolerance control of complex bent parts", *Project report for contract HOBU/20110,* XIOS Hogeschool Limburg, Belgium, 2004.
10. Streppel, A.H., de Vin, L.J., Brinkman, J. and Kals, H.J.J., "Suitability of sheet bending modelling techniques in CAPP applications", in: *Journal of Materials Processing Technology,* 36/3, Mar. 1993, pp. 339-356.

SIMULATION-BASED PRODUCTION PLANNING BASED ON LOGISTIC MONITORING AND RISK MANAGEMENT ASPECTS

Steffen Reinsch, Karim Ouali and Jens Stürmann
IPH - Institut für Integrierte Produktion Hannover gGmbH, Germany
{reinsch, stuermann}@iph-hannover.de

For companies which are part of complex supply chains structures, risk management is getting increasingly important. This development is the result of actual trends that can be observed, especially in the automotive industry.
Companies reduce their work in progress to cut down the cost level of stock; certainly the delivery performance is expected to be excellent. However, the reduction of work in progress frequently results in missing parts or raw material. Moreover, the logistic environment is continuously getting more turbulent by continuously fluctuating demands and in some cases - like steel for example - increased delivery times for raw materials. Combined with the mentioned reduction of work in progress, achieving the agreed logistic performance is not ensured without a significant additional effort.
An approach, developed by IPH, is the use of discrete-event simulation tools for the combination of production planning and control methods with logistic monitoring tools. Based on the periodic analyses of the logistic supply chain performance and the simulation of different alternative scenarios, the relevant planning parameters are identified and adopted to the planning processes.
For this feedback loop, logistic risk management aspects need to be considered as well. By identifying potential risks and developing counter measures, the logistic performance is increased tremendously and consequently the performance of the complete supply chain is improved.
In this paper, the specific challenges of forging companies that are part of an automotive supply chain are described and lined out. The forging industry is subject to the implementation of new forging technologies for being able to battle the competition from low cost countries. Those new technologies are not only beneficial; they bear a lot of risks for the companies as well. For some technologies, the tool life cannot be forecasted accurately; hence the lot sizes are only estimated roughly and not calculated with a well proofed algorithm.

1. PRODUCTIOIN PLANNING AND CONTROL IN THE CONTEXT OF CUMULATIVE QUANTITY

Cumulative quantity is a method to record and describe cumulated actual and target data over defined time periods. The method is usually applied for material movements of sourcing products or in-house products as well as assemblies or completed, finished products.

In the context of the Collaborative Research Centre 489 – control and planning of flexible supply chains for the manufacturing of precision forged high performance components – methods are developed for an adaptive production planning and control system. Forging companies are frequently integrated in automotive supply chains. The importance of using risk management methods – as a part of the logistic monitoring – has continuously increased for forging companies. Identifying potential risks and using the opportunity to react in time helps to reduce negative impacts to the company performance significantly.

The main field of application of the cumulative quantity method is found in companies with serial production of standard product with high diversity (Wiendahl, 1997; Heinemeyer, 1988). Cumulative quantity is appropriate to the high volume production of forging companies. It is well adapted to the coordination of the production program planning in supply chains and contributes importantly for the containment of the bullwhip-effect (Lödding, 2005).

Within the scope of cumulative quantity methods were developed for program planning, quantity planning and scheduling. The calculation models and methods for the forecast of the customer and the supplier behaviour have been developed and integrated in an instrument for production planning. Furthermore planning methods have been developed based on the cumulative quantity method which can be parameterised depending on the situation of the order spectrum in the predefined planning period. The developed methods use dynamic instead of static planning parameters. For an efficient calibration of the parameters, the planning methods have been linked to a monitoring instrument. This instrument enables the measurement of turbulences as well as the analyses of logistic performance and logistic costs. Furthermore, a control tool for stock levels has been developed as a support to the production planning and control processes. In the following section, the elaborated methods are described in more detail. A specific and methodical adaptation for forging companies is shown in this context.

Program planning

The production programs are continuously "rolling" over a constant period of time. Due to the planning complexity the generation of the production programs occurs in regular intervals. Periods between four or six weeks are typical. In most instances, basic agreements are negotiated between forging companies and their customers. On basis of those agreements delivery schedules are ordered. These orders can take place weekly for example and include upcoming and committed demands as well as an updated forecast of future demands. The forecasts in these orders are the basis of the program planning.

In a first step, the planning horizon is supposed to be defined by the production planner of a company. The advance planning process is expected to determine production orders well in advance and release them in time.

Afterwards the forecast of the customers demand is arranged according to the different products. To represent the demand curve, the forecast of the planning time horizon for every single customer is cumulated. A fundamental advantage of this method is the early consideration of expected events which do influence the supply chain and moreover the possibility to consider this information in the sales planning of forging companies.

The result of a survey, accomplished by IPH, demonstrated, that the forecasted quantity differs from the committed order quantity for different reasons. The indicator "forecast performance" was defined to evaluate these circumstances. This indicator is used for production planning processes. The forecast performance of every customer is expected to be calculated. This results in a value between 0 and 100% whereas 100% characterizes a "perfect forecast". The difference between the perfect and the real forecast performance is represented by a vector for the adaptation of the customer demand curve (for example: the difference of 12% equals a forecast performance of 88%). Having a "forecast performance" below 100% requires the establishment of a safety stock to compensate forecast uncertainties. Afterwards the demand curves adapted by the forecast uncertainties are deferred by a customer-specific transport vector. Different transport times for every customer result in different customer specific transport vectors.

Logistic monitoring
Cumulative quantity diagrams are also used for measuring and visualizing the logistic performance (Reinsch, 2003). As a result of the monitoring the logistic specifications of the process chain are provided. The target criteria for the process chain which apply for the individual process elements are a high utilisation, short lead times, short throughput times, minimum stocks level and a high delivery performance. By means of cumulative quantity diagrams the actual values of the logistic targets as well as the deviations of the actual values and the target values are determined. A fundamental advantage of the cumulative quantity is the simplified inventory level control. By analysing the difference between consecutive actual values of the cumulative quantity, the actual stock levels in all process elements are supposed to be determined at any given time. Furthermore the order throughput time can be calculated by means of cumulative quantity. It equals the sum of all throughput times related to the actual resources, even in chopped process chains. By comparing the target and the actual values at the finished product stock the delivery reliability is evaluated (Ouali, 2004a).

The logistic induced costs are assigned by adopting the activity-based costing model to measure the logistic efficiency. Based on the research work of Kerner (Kerner, 2002), a cost model is configured which links the emerging costs of the forging sub-processes to the individual forging process elements (Ouali, 2004b).

Simulation based production planning and control
The lined out considerations and calculation approaches were consolidated to a method for the planning and control as well as the monitoring of forging processes. Then the method has been implemented in object-oriented software modules for planning and monitoring. A modular built discrete-event simulation model was developed for the validation of the method. The model is composed of three modules: supplier, manufacturer and customer. The modules are combined by an MS-Access data base and integrated to a simulation based system for the monitoring and the planning as well as control of supply chains (Wiendahl, 2005).

Because of long reaction times in combination with the bullwhip-effect it is required for the forging industry to act actively and not to react to market changes. For this purpose an approach is developed, which helps to identify the logistic risks in the forging processes and derives corrective measures for the risk control. This approach – the operative risk management – is implemented as an add-on to the monitoring tool. The interface with the production planning and control is the feedback data of the manufacturing simulation. This is the input of the monitoring module, which converts them into logistic key figures, such as the mean throughput time and mean work-in-progress. According to the resulting key figures, the system user can finally adapt the planning parameters in the ERP system (Wiendahl, 2005).

Operative risk management

The term "risk" has different meanings in a lot of disciplines. In everyday life the term risk is reduced to the possibility or the increased feasibility of the admittance of a negative rated incident (Dahmen, 2002). In general the term risk is defined as the statistical spread about an expected issue. Accordingly, positive issues (chances) are considered as well as negative issues (dangers). The main challenge of risk management is the methodical identification and embankment of risks for a successful realisation of the business objectives. Thereby chances and risks need to be systematically identified and rated regarding their incidence rate and their potential influence on the given business objectives. The intention is to prevent or reduce negative impacts and to increase chances. Risk management has a strategic and an operative dimension. Strategic risk management represents the basis of the whole risk management (Romeike, 2002). In form of a policy towards risks, the objectives of the risk management are configured. At this juncture the positioning in the area of a conflict between chances and risks is the main aspect. The intention is to solely develop methods for the operative risk management. Therefore strategic risk management is not yet researched in appropriate detail. Operative risk management contains risk-identification, risk-analysis and rating as well as risk-control and monitoring.

Risk-Identification

Risk-identification is the key for a successful realisation of a comprehensive risk management. At this stage potential logistic risks for forging companies are identified. The supply chain of forging companies can be classified in three business processes: sourcing, manufacturing and distribution. Accordingly the forging relevant risks are assigned to these three categories. Well-established actual approaches of risk management do mainly classify risks in two categories, namely external risks and business risks. External risks do primarily result from fiscal influences as, environmental impacts and social or political risks (Diederichs, 2004). Risks resulting from the production processes, e.g. sourcing or manufacturing risks are hardly regarded, but definitely need to be considered. Hence, those technological risks and their potential interactions to logistic objectives and operative logistic risks are identified which put the whole supply chain of forging companies at risk. All identified risks are stored in a data base and are legitimated continuously while applying the data base. Figure 1 shows examples of risks that are expected to endanger the accomplishment of the given logistic objectives of the considered companies. Consequently, in-house risks and risks caused by the supply chain (external risks), need to be distinguished.

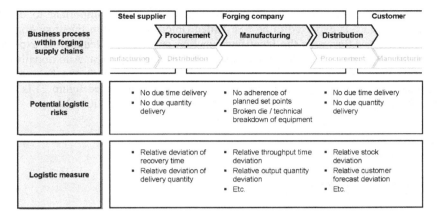

Figure 1 - Logistic risks in supply chains of forging companies.

Risk- analysis and rating

The next step is to analyse the risk and to rate it. Therefore the actual risk value needs to be calculated for prioritising the identified risks. The first step for calculating the incidence rate of a given risk is to identify potential trends based on historical data. For this purpose, corresponding data of the data base is extracted and simultaneously written on (hardware or software) logistic control charts which base on "quality control charts". The range of tolerance is supposed to be defined within an upper and a lower action control limit. In contradiction to the quality inspection, the limits are not calculated mathematically but drained off the logistic operation curves (Wiendahl, 2004). After calculating the logistic key figures and plotting them in the logistic control chart, an iteration function w(t) is determined (see figure 2). Herewith statements for the future risk-development are possible.

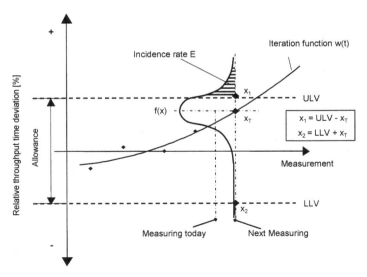

Figure 2 - Calculation of the risk incidence rate.

Before actually determining and selecting the function it is important to decide which procedure is expected to be best-suited (interpolation, non-linear smoothing, Newton, etc.). Afterwards the identified function enables to calculate the expected risk value ($x_T = w(T)$). T is the time of the following measurement. Additionally, the standard deviation σ of the historical data is calculated. With the help of the parameters x_T and σ^2 a Gauss-distribution-shaped curve f(x) (see figure 2) is lined out. The curve represents the resulting probability density (Equation 1).

$$f(x) = \frac{1}{\sqrt{2\Pi\sigma^2}} e^{-\frac{(x-x_T)^2}{2\sigma^2}}$$ (1)

with:
X_T expectancy value
σ standard deviation
σ^2 variance

The incidence rate IR of the risk results from the probability that x is either bigger than the upper limit or smaller than the lower limit of the predefined target area. Based on equation 2, IR is calculated as follows (see figure 2):

$$IR = \int_{-\infty}^{x_2} f(x)dx + \int_{x_1}^{+\infty} f(x)dx$$ (2)

with:
IR   risk incidence rate

Based on the probability, the economical dimension of the risk can be determined. As shown in figure 3, the logistic operation curve can be used as a basis for this determination.

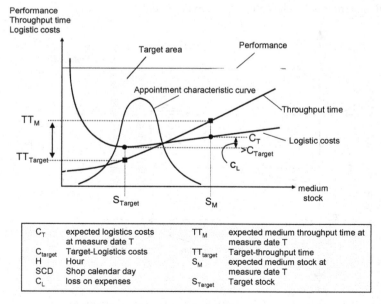

Figure 3 - Derivation of the loss on expenses out of the logistic operation curve.

The above determined value for the risk value x_T is able to display the relative throughput time deviation. Based on this value, the expected target values can be derived. In the sample case, it is derived for the expected mean throughput time TT_M for the following reference (measurement) point T. The loss on expenses C_L is subsequently derived from the logistic operation curve. It results from the difference between the target costs C_{Target} and the expected costs C_T. The relative loss on expenses is determined by comparing different risk values. It quantifies the economic dimension and is calculated by equation (3):

$$V = \frac{C_T - C_{T\arg et}}{C_{T\arg et}} * 100 \qquad (3)$$

with:
V   relative economic dimension [%]
C_T expected costs at point T [€]
C_{Target} target costs [€]

This task of the operative risk management is completed with the calculation of the risk value RV (equation 4):

$$RV = IR * V \qquad (4)$$

with:
RV   risk value
IR   risk incidence rate
V   relative economic dimension of the risk

Risk control and monitoring
The aim of the risk control and monitoring step is to prepare arrangements for influencing the risk situation of a company. This happens either by avoiding potential risks, consequently to reduce the risk incidence rate or to reduce the financial risk. Generally the option exists to accept specified risks without operational discharge of arrangements. The identified potential risks of the risk analysis are inscribed in a so called risk portfolio which is characterised by 3 category groups which correspond to 3 different risk classes. Class A risks have high risk values, class B risks have medium risk values and class C risks have low risk values. The limit values between the classes are defined by the risk strategy of the company. Generally, the objective of the risk control is to avoid class A risks, to reduce class B risks and to accept class C risks. Established methods of the quality management (e.g. cause and effect diagrams) are used to identify the risk causes for the risk control. Thereafter risk control scenarios are established. The compiled control scenarios are checked up on their efficiency by the described simulation tool before seizing required arrangements.

2. CONCLUSION

Recently logistic risk management becomes increasingly more important. Particularly for forging companies which are mainly integrated in supply chains of the automotive supply industry, the requirement to manage potential risk has obviously intensified. Forging companies have to face a turbulent logistic environment caused by fluctuating customer demands and long delivery times of steel suppliers. The dilemma of an efficient reaction to unreliable and fluctuating customer demands with the focus of reducing the stocks requires a methodical approach for the risk management. This is especially important for forging companies with high set-up times and large batch sizes. On this account, a production planning and control system for forging companies has been developed. This system is able to identify technological (forging) and logistic relevant risks at an early stage in the process chain of high precision performing and to evaluate the consequences of these risks belonging to the achievement of the logistic aims. For these purposes methods for the forecast of the risk incidence rate and their organisational and monetary consequences were developed. Based on this, a risk portfolio was implemented which classifies risks in three different risk classes. Thereafter risk control scenarios were established and validated by an in-house programmed simulation tool.

3. ACKNOWLEDGEMENT

The presented work is performed within the framework of the collaborative research center 489 "Process chain for the manufacturing of precision forged high performance components", in the part project C4 – "design and control of flexible supply chains for the production of precision forged components". The project is funded by the DFG - Deutsche Forschungsgemeinschaft (German Research Community).

4. REFERENCES

1. Dahmen, J. Prozessorientiertes Risikomanagement zur Handhabung von Produktrisiken. Dissertation Universität Aachen, Shaker Verlag 2002
2. Diederichs, M.: Risikomanagement und Risikocontrolling. Verlag Vahlen, München 2004
3. Heinemeyer, W.: Produktionsplanung und -steuerung mit Fortschrittszahlen für interdependente Fertigungs- und Montageprozesse. RKW-Handbuch Logistik, HLO, 14. Lieferung XII/88. Berlin: Erich Schmidt Verlag 1998
4. Kerner, A.: Modellbasierte Beurteilung der Logistikleistung von Prozessketten. Dissertation, Universität Hannover 2002
5. Lödding, H.: Verfahren der Fertigungssteuerung. Berlin, Heidelberg: Springer Verlag 2005
6. Ouali, K.; Reinsch, S.: Logistic Performance Controlling – Assessment and Continuous Improvement of Processes Applied on an Example of a Forging Process. In: Proceedings of the International Conference on Competitive Manufacturing COMA '04, Progress in Innovative Manufacturing, 04-06. Februar, Stellenbosch, Südafrika, 2004a, ISBN 0-7972-1018-0
7. Ouali, K.; Nofen, D.; Reinsch, S.: Simulation von Lieferketten – ungenutzte Potenziale. In: phi – Produktionstechnik Hannover informiert, Jahrgang 5 (2004b) 3, S.6-7
8. Reinsch, S.; V. Gleich, C. F.; Ouali, K.: Logistic oriented Supply Chain Monitoring. In: Proceedings of the 36th CIRP International Seminar on Manufacturing Systems, Saarbrücken 03-05. Juni 2003, ISBN 3-930429-58-6
9. Romeike, F.: Risiko Management als Grundlage einer wertorientierten Unternehmenssteuerung. In RATING aktuell, 02/2002, S.12-17
10. Wiendahl, H.-P.; Reinsch, S.; Ouali, K.: Simulationsgestützte Planung und Steuerung von Lieferketten. In: wt Werkstattstechnik online, Jahrgang 95 (2005) H.4, S. 242-247

SIMULATION BASED ORGANIZATIONAL CHANGE IN MULTIPLE PRODUCT ASSEMBLY SYSTEMS

Aysin Rahimifard and Richard Weston
Wolfson School of Mechanical and Manufacturing Engineering
Loughborough University, UK
{A.Rahimifard, R.H.Weston}@lboro.ac.uk

During the last few decades, Manufacturing Enterprises (ME) have been facing increasingly volatile market conditions due to changes such as globalization, reduced product lifetimes and increased competition. Simulation modeling (SM) has been widely deployed to help MEs optimize their operations by assessing uncertainties and possible future organizational behaviours. This paper reports ongoing research study which is developing and testing the use of a unified set of SM concepts within the context of Enterprise Modelling (EM) to facilitate process oriented organizational change related to the planning and control of ME's operations. Case study research findings are described which focus on optimizing multi-product flows through assembly shop resources available to a furniture making SME based in UK.

1. INTRODUCTION

Typically, Manufacturing Enterprises (MEs) change and improve their processes continuously during their lifetime in order to remain competitive in a highly volatile market. The ways in which MEs operate and add value to process inputs including material, information and knowledge can be defined in the form of 'a process network' (Weston 2004). Process network change can take the form of: (1) modifications to the order of activities within one or more process threads (2) modifications to the resource assignment made available to one or more segments of process threads (human and technical systems) and (3) modifications to product variety, volumes and mixes that flow through process threads. Enterprise modelling (EM) facilitates (collective and individual) reasoning about the multi-perspective aspects of process oriented organisation design and change by providing a systematic approach and suitable mechanisms for modelling business processes.

The authors recognise that current EM approaches focus on encoding relatively enduring entities, and structures linking entities. However as the complexity of enterprise models (EMs) must remain within manageable bounds, generally they do not provide sufficient support for capturing dynamic characteristics of process networks and this has limited business improvement projects. In addition EMs do not facilitate solution generation in the sense that they lack necessary mechanism for future prediction by visualisation and relative quantification of possible alternative ME designs; such as by exercising differently configured resource systems when they are subjected to changing workloads. The research emphasis in this paper concerns a generalised attempt to develop a set of concepts for realising synergistic use of EM and simulation modelling (SM) techniques. The research concepts developed have been applied and tested within a number of small and large MEs. This paper considers the combined use of EM and SM to achieve improvements to the process network of a furniture making SME based in UK. The initial findings related to 'machining processes' of the case study organisation are previously reported in the literature (Rahimifard and Weston, 2006). This paper complements the original paper, and describes follow-on research related to another part of the case study process network, namely downstream 'assembly processes'.

2. BACKGROUND

Manufacturing enterprises in general comprise extremely complex systems of processes and resource systems that need to be 'loaded' by product flows that vary over time. Simulation modelling provides modellers with capability to replicate ME's product flows and related causal and temporal relationships between process, resource and product variables lead to a replication of real behaviours. In general alternative product (volume and mix) flows can directly be input into models of 'as is' processes used by the ME, in order to verify that the models behave as the real ME behaves. However, it is known that in order for SM to be practical modelling abstraction needs to be suitably limited given the scope of the problem tackled; so as to overcome the modelling complexity without compromising the model validity.

The authors observe that EM can provide an explicit and holistic description of 'elemental building blocks' and in-depth understandings of ME and its environmental context. Consequently EMs can define a context for building feasible simulation models so that in principle the additional modelling complexity generated when developing any SM can be reduced by focusing on self-contained meaningful process segments defined by the EM. Therefore, the authors argue that a combined use of EMs and SMs can significantly improve modelling in support of process oriented organisational change through replicating and predicting the reality well. Within this combined use of EM and SM the modeller can encode possible 'could be' or future 'to be' product flows and other modified dynamic aspects by achieving a systematic reuse of SM fragments informed by the EM so that the impact of alternate business (and manufacturing) strategies, policies, rules and dependencies can be predicted prior to the need for expensive and time-consuming real changes. This provides the modeller with an approach to creating simulation models (SMs) more rapidly and effectively. It will also enhance change recommendations as the specific context in which the organisation needs to operate can be fully incorporated in the simulation experiments and subsequent analysis of simulation results.

This paper reports on findings from ongoing EPSRC funded research entitled "Study of the Interplay between Role Dynamics and Organisational Performance". In this research project, a methodology has been being developed to systematically decompose relatively enduring aspects of ME's processes and resource systems into a specific set of interoperating processes and resource systems using best-in-class EM techniques. It is also aimed at facilitating detailed specification and design of the needed changes to ME process and resource systems, by re-encoding selected segments of static ME models into dynamic models so as to understand their time-based behaviours, via the adoption of suitable performance measures within the specific context described by the static models (i.e. EMs). Subsequently selected structures and parameters encoded by the static and dynamic models can be transformed into a tertiary model form which can be enacted by best-in-class workflow management technology in order to facilitate improved specification, design and implementation of planning and control structures within specific MEs. The remainder of this paper reports on a systematic reuse of fragments of an enterprise model in such a way that simulation models help structure decision making about organisation change within a case study company.

3. STATIC MODEL GENERATION

The case study company (referred to by the pseudonym 'Woodlands') in which the research concepts applied is a UK based pine wood furniture manufacturing SME with 50 employees. The Woodlands Company's product portfolio includes over 300 different designs of tables, cabinets, wardrobes, beds and other miscellaneous furniture items and its customers are the furniture retailers. The production processes involve complex routings of cutting and shaping operations of furniture parts in the machine shop, assembling of furniture parts in two 'specialist' assembly areas corresponding to different product families, and spraying and painting the furniture items with the desired colour and finish as defined by the customer order specification. The company operates in a make-to-order fashion. Over the last few years, the production lead time has increased significantly from 4 weeks to 8 weeks between the receipt of order and customer delivery due to the recent withdrawal of a major competitor from the market. Thus, Woodlands management decided to investigate organisational change, so as to cater for the increased demand without making significant investments in new human and technical production resources.

Following a detailed discussions with directors and other senior managers, Woodlands' enterprise modelling techniques were used to decompose, document and understand the company's current process network. The baseline EM technique selected was Computer Integrated Manufacturing Open Systems Architecture (CIMOSA) (ESPIRIT-CIMOSA Standards 1993) since previous experience of the authors and their colleagues and the literature review had shown this to be a powerful yet fairly easy-to-interpret (by non-modellers) public domain EM approach. Four types of CIMOSA diagramming templates, namely 'context diagrams', 'interaction diagrams', 'structure diagrams' and 'activity diagrams' were utilised to capture coherent sets of static models that collectively represent the process network (Rahimifard and Weston, 2006).

Following discussion with knowledge holders in the company, the Woodlands' process network was decomposed into three main end-to-end process threads namely 'Strategy Making and Realising Process', 'New Product Engineering Process', 'Make and Deliver Furniture to (aggregated) Order Process'. This high level process decomposition was also determined with reference to the general ME process classification published by Salvendy (1992). This paper focuses on results of modelling part of the 'make and deliver furniture to (aggregated) order' process thread in WOODLANDS which has two primary process segments, namely so called 'business management' and 'produce and deliver furniture' processes: which loosely correspond to the 'obtain an order' and 'fulfil an order' process types defined by Pandya *et al.* (1997). The part of the ongoing research that is reported in the remainder of this paper concerns the produce and delivers furniture process. The produce and deliver furniture process is defined as the collection of manufacturing activities that starts with the receipt of a production order and realised all needed furniture parts and final assembled items, until finished furniture is delivered to customers. It was observed that this process thread was one of the main contributors of 'as is' lead time of 8 weeks. Hence because the objective of the organisational improvement and change consideration was to reduce lead times, improvement in the make-span of this segment was expected to directly reduce the overall lead time.

The main business processes (BPs) of Woodlands produce and deliver furniture process comprised *make furniture to order, spraying and finishing, package and delivery, support production and finally manage and maintain production process segments*. Relationships between these process segments were shown in figure 1 using a CIMOSA 'Structure Diagram'. Each of these business processes were detailed with knowledge elicited from relevant Woodlands personnel and by populating a number of CIMOSA activity diagram templates of the type presented in (Rahimifard and Weston, 2006) with that knowledge. This documented relevant transformations of inputs into outputs using necessary resources. Therefore, activity diagrams were found to be of particular significance in establishing a link between static models and simulation models.

The EM exercise was proven to be effective by allowing key aspects of the company's current processes and their structural dependencies to be formally documented; thereby collating and externalising key knowledge collectively possessed by various knowledge holder employees of the Woodlands Company. The approach also enabled both the modeller and the company personnel with the development of new understandings about the scope and focus of the company's current approach to making furniture. However, it was observed that, in order to specify process improvement opportunities, additional knowledge is also needed about related (temporal) dynamic properties of processes such as time dependent flows of control, material, product, value addition and cost.

4. MODELLING OF DYNAMIC ASPECTS

In general, a large numbers of instances of interactions occur between product elements, process elements and their underpinning resource elements within the process network of any ME. These system dynamics can be modelled using existing simulation techniques and tools, and the build up of queues, stochastic events, breakdowns or absences of resource can be replicated and uncertainties can be assessed. Complexity inherited within the context of the process network used by

MEs makes it practical to explicitly visualise and specify necessary changes to improve ME processes. Thus, SM provides a better understanding about 'as-is' system behaviours that can lead to more effective 'to-be' design alternatives for ME change by visualising the whole process within a given period of time.

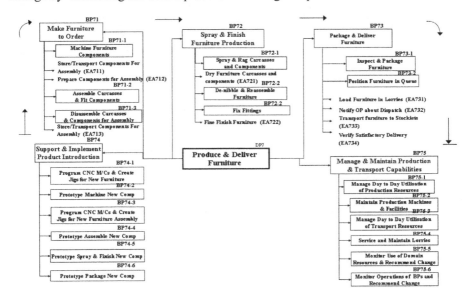

Figure 1 - Structure Diagram for Produce and Deliver Furniture Process.

Bearing this in mind, selected segments of the static models of Woodland's process network were transformed into simulation models to facilitate ME change specification. The SM study reported in the remainder of this paper is based on the assumption that by systematically following a decomposition process, in this case informed by static models defined by EM, essentially separable process segments can be described which then can be usefully modelled in greater detail. A discrete event simulation tool, namely 'Simul8' (Simul8 Cooperation 2000) was used to encode both relatively enduring and dynamic characteristics of the assembly process segment some properties of which had already been identified through EM. The main purpose of SM was to investigate lead time improvement opportunities by placing alternative product loads on the assembly process segment.

The static CIMOSA enterprise models were found to partly capture data required for building the simulation model. The EM was found to naturally encode the sequence of activities required for processing and aspects of material and information flows. Additional data collection for more specific and/or time related information was also organised by deploying the framework provided by the static models. The resulting user interface to the simulation model for Woodlands' assembly process is illustrated by figure 2. Following model validation, tests were conducted to understand in detail the 'as-is' behaviour of assembly processes of Woodlands. As indicated earlier, twice weekly production order list is released to the Assembly Shop. Each production order list defines the types and quantities of furniture items which need to be assembled during a given run which on average needs to be 2-5 working days. Item types and quantities are largely determined by chance because each run comprises those items randomly ordered in a given 4 weeks time slice by a specific group of customers who share a UK location to which a delivery van will travel. Once a particular production order has been determined and released, shop supervisors seek to maximise work throughput by assigning the assembly jobs to appropriate operators in appropriate batches. This 'as-is' approach to scheduling and dispatching workloads has proven effective but is known to give rise to significant variations in throughput for different assembly runs. Consequent swings occur in assembly shop behaviours from near state of panic to slow paced working.

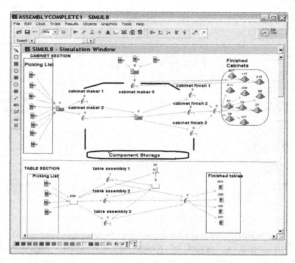

Figure 2 - Simulation model of Woodlands' assembly process in Simul8.

To enable replication of 'as-is' assembly shop behaviours historical patterns of work load were studied. Determining historical work patterns proved to be a non-trivial exercise because that data was not easily manipulated into the form required as input to the 'as-is' assembly shop simulation model. It was found to be necessary because of the very large number of furniture items and parts involved to simplify matters by consolidating items and parts into a similar product groups. figure 3 illustrates the example 'as-is' simulation results and very significant variations in lead times of different job runs. This tallied closely with the actual variations within that shop. These 'as-is' behaviours were subsequently used as a benchmark against which alternative assembly work organization policies could be compared. An intended use of the simulation model created was to suggest possible alternative policies and rules for creating production order list and particularly to observe the impact of suggested changes on process lead times. The as-is simulation model not only formed benchmark behaviours but also provided tactical insights to the modeller to devise alternative product loads by indicating the bottleneck resources and alternative routes. Furthermore, it enabled visualisation of possible outcomes arising from the suggested changes in the way the production order list is generated and released. For example one interesting line of enquiry centred on the assumption that the delivery van constraint on production scheduling could be released. Here, for example, it was assumed that some or all customer deliveries could be outsourced to a competent external agency. By releasing this constraint, rather than waiting for up to 4 weeks to define and release each production order list various alternative scheduling rules could be applied to (1) release production order lists earlier and (2) seek to optimize the design of each production order list from the viewpoint of minimizing processing lead time.

	group 1	group 2	group 3	group 4	group 5	group 6	group 7
min	27.6	48.4	73.3	83.2	68.6	75.8	69.2
max	198.4	240.4	267.1	247.0	666.4	560.3	589.2
average	67.2	90.0	93.5	107.9	241.1	225.7	226.3

Figure 3 - Lead time (in mins) of product groups based upon a set of historical production runs.

With these kinds of opportunities in mind, the authors are currently quantifying the benefits and costs of various possible future scheduling and releasing policies that Woodlands could adopt. Figure 4 illustrates some early results when seeking to group historical patterns of ordered furniture items over one and two week periods with a view to minimize set up times. By comparing figure 3 and 4 it is evident that for all product types significant lead-time savings could be realized without any need for additional investment in (human or technical) assembly system resources.

	group 1	group 2	group 3	group 4	group 5	group 6	group 7
min	27.6	48.4	73.3	83.2	68.6	75.8	69.2
max	104.6	127.4	145.3	103.6	177.9	162.7	154.0
average	28.8	49.9	74.6	84.2	79.8	91.0	82.8

Figure 4 - Lead time (in mins) of product groups based upon a set of reorganised production runs.

5. OBSERVATIONS AND DISCUSSIONS

This paper describes early results of a part of an ongoing industry-based case study research that is seeking ways to facilitate rapid, effective and systemic design and change in complex organisations by gaining synergy from an integrated use of enterprise modelling and simulation modelling techniques.

The CIMOSA diagramming templates implemented a process-oriented, hierarchical decomposition technique to create a rich knowledge base about the current ME and its environment prior to decision making about future organisation design and change. However, it was observed that because the resultant models were static in nature it was not possible to replicate or predict the possible outcomes of the proposed changes to the design of the ME. Initial investigations using simulation modelling related to possible organisational changes in Woodlands aimed at reduction in manufacturing lead time. Different manufacturing policies were incorporated into separate simulation models of well decoupled process segments comprising Woodlands' 'Produce and Deliver Furniture' process. The company is currently considering alternative ways of organising workflows and resources in respect of both individual and collective process segments. For example, supported by the authors EM and SM studies, they are investigating use of a new set of production strategies. At present, the authors and their colleagues are investigating means of realising interoperability between the assembly simulation model with SM of other process segments that are also being modelled by the authors' colleagues. As Woodlands operate a make-to-order policy, before they can realise significant benefits from increased throughput and lead time improvements in one production shop the company must achieve similar throughput improvements in other related shops. The 'as-is' activity diagrams of Woodlands encoded by the EM provide some key details of the various activity flows and their relatively enduring dependencies for consolidated product groups. This provides a big picture of how the performance of one process segment can impact on other process segments. To develop the use of this picture from a dynamic systems (temporal) viewpoint the causal impacts of one production shop on the other production shops was modelled using causal loops. The collective understandings documented by the EM and the casual loops have fed into the authors' current thinking and combined SM experimentation with a view to selecting improved schedules and workflow control policies that balance the future throughput as defined by the new forms of production order list through Woodlands' machining, assembly, painting and finishing shops. Early results indicate that significant savings predicted in the assembly shop need not be compromised by other shops. Thereby in principle the use of the combined SMs predicts that by making policy changes as opposed to cost investments in resources, Woodlands can increase its competitiveness significantly.

In conclusion, the integrated use of EM and simulation modelling shows great promise in providing ways of facilitating a holistic static and dynamic picture to facilitate organisational change. The use of EM provides simulation modeller with broad based company understandings that bear in mind the specific context in which the organisation will need to operate. It has been found that collectively EM and SM provides a sound basis for managing and enacting change through structuring decision making about organisation change, analysing the impact of alternative change scenarios and presenting a better visualisation of the possible competitive futures.

6. REFERENCES

1. ESPIRIT-CIMOSA Standards, 1993, CIMOSA: Open System Architecture for CIM (Spinger-Verlag, Berlin).
2. Pandya, K.V., Karlsson, A., Sega, S., Carrie, A., 1997, Towards the manufacturing enterprises of the future, International Journal of Operations and Production Management, 17(5), 502-521.
3. Rahimifard, A. and Weston, R.H. 2006, The Enhanced Use of Enterprise Modelling Based Techniques to Support Factory Changeability, Accepted to be published in International Journal of Computer Integrated Manufacturing.
4. Salvendy, G. (ed), 1992, Handbook of industrial engineering, 2(1), 2780.
5. Simul8 Corporation, 2000, Simul8 User's Manual, ISBN: 0-97081-100-4.
6. Weston, R.H., 2004, Coherent Models of Processes and Human Systems. International Conference on Enterprise Integration and Modelling Technology (ICEIMT'04), Toronto, Canada 9-11 Oct 2004.

WEB BASED MULTI AGENT PLATFORM FOR COLLABORATIVE MANUFACTURING

Manish Bachlaus[1], Manoj K Tiwari[1], Sanjeev Kumar[2], Aydin Nassehi[2]
and Stephen T Newman[2]

[1]National Institute of Foundry and Forge technology (NIFFT) Ranchi, India
manish_bachlaus@yahoo.co.in, mkt09@hotmail.com
[2]Department of Mechanical Engineering, University of Bath, UK
{S.Kumar, A.Nassehi, S.T.Newman}@bath.ac.uk

*The incessant pressure of meeting customer demands at a decreasing cost across the globe is forcing the modern day manufacturers to adopt a paradigm shift from the traditional way of manufacturing. This includes the utilization of digitalized manufacturing information flow in the form of agents to facilitate the collaborative product development and manufacturing across different geographical locations. To meet these growing needs and fierce competition in the current manufacturing arena, the authors in this paper have presented an "**iManufacturing**"-an intelligent manufacturing based on internet, intranet, web and agents. The architecture utilizes the distributive and autonomous behavior of the functional agents, CORBA, XML, Java and web.*

1. INTRODUCTION

Modern day manufacturers have been challenged by global competition and growing customer expectations for quick product delivery at competitive prices. This has caused a paradigm shift in traditional methods of manufacturing and businesses, resulting in a shift from legacy information systems to internet-based environments. The pressure over these industries is greater than ever beforethus to achieve success in this situation organizations are relying on distributive technologies and cooperative partnerships with other organizations (Choo, Detor, and Turnbull, 2000). Digital manufacturing has emerged as a promising solution to support responsive manufacturing that aims to *"create, validate, monitor and control agile, distributed manufacturing production systems geared towards build to order and lean production"* (Brown, 2000). In order to do away with ambiguities of tacit knowledge and fulfill aforementioned targets, digital manufacturing hinges on tangible knowledge convertible to digital values (Seino et al., 2001).

Recent research in this field has emphasized the need to have a collaborative product development (CPD) system which has been defined as: "an Internet based computational architecture that supports sharing and transfer of knowledge and information of the product life cycle among geographically distributed companies to aid taking right engineering decisions in a collaborative environment (Rodriguez and Al-Ashaab, 2002). The present paper utilizes the communication and control aspects of machining units in a web based architecture which is the essence of digital manufacturing. An industrial survey carried out by Rodriguez and Al-Ashaab (Rodriguez and Al-Ashaab, 2005) clearly indicates the need for collaborative product development i.e. distributed manufacturing. This has been portrayed in figure 1.

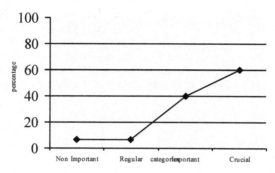

Figure 1 - Comparative study supporting product development (adapted from (Rodriguez and Al-Ashaab, 2005)).

The on-going research in this area has proved to be successful in developing technologies that support collaborative product development but has been mainly concentrated sharing product data and providing collaborative tools integrating multidisciplinary systems. There are still issues such as the sharing of know-how of the geographically distributed partners which need further investigation. The authors perceive the distributed manufacturing system to be spread all across the globe and the information such as design, manufacturing knowledge, process planning, and product models, which exist at different locations, are to be shared and coordinated through the web to facilitate manufacturing at diverse locations as portrayed in figure 2.

Based on this distributive manufacturing concept, *iManufacturing*- an intelligent distributive manufacturing system based on the Internet, intranet, agents and web has been introduced in this paper. This architecture utilizes the communication, coordination and autonomous behavior of agents and aims to integrate collaborative product design and development. In order to achieve better global competitiveness and enhanced communication, communication and coordination among diverse geographical locations, the web based architecture is governed by the attributes of digital information exchange that help in alleviating the prevailing ambiguity and impreciseness.

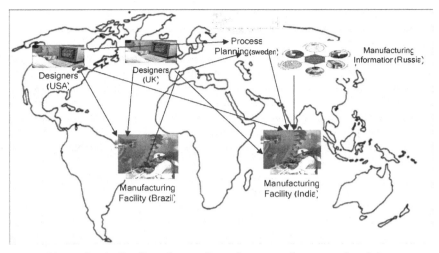

Figure 2 - A distributed manufacturing scenario across the globe.

This architecture works on the basis of coordination and information exchange among the process planning agents which work under centralized web based control and are guided on the principles of random search algorithms. The focus of the paper is to present the *iManufacturing* architecture that helps in avoiding the ambiguities of the information exchange with the utilization of the digitized information which helps in easing the information data flow among the different agents, to ensure seamless data and information transfer within the manufacturing system.

The rest of the paper is organized as follows: Section 2 discusses a number of web based architectures with the proposed *iManufacturing* architecture being described in section 3. The intelligent search engine is described in section 4 and a range of implementation issues are discussed in section 5. The final section of the paper provides a number of conclusions.

2. WEB BASED MANUFACTURING SYSTEMS

The Web has become one of the most important internet tools providing a platform independent way for sharing, disseminating and retrieving information. This environment has made it possible for the design models to be dynamically shared, updated, accessed and manipulated remotely. Chen and Liang (Chen and Liang, 2000) have presented a web-based system that integrates and shares engineering information for facilitating design and manufacturing activities in the form of a domain investigation, together system design and modelling. A platform-independent real-time monitoring system has been proposed by Ong and Sun (Ong and Sun, 2003) which utilizes mobile agents within a web-based distributed architecture. A web-based system based on the Java Applet programming named as CyberCut has been developed (Smith and Wright, 1996) in the University of California at Berkeley. This system includes mainly three modules, a Web-based feature-based design tool, a new geometric representation for information exchange between design and process planning modules, and an automated process planning and machining systems. Xiao et al. (Xiao et al., 2001) effectively demonstrated an organized workflow for the design process which can be altered by users through assembling components with the help a Web-DPR system. A web based fixture design system has been presented (Mervyn et al., 2003) which uses an XML format for transferring information and knowledge between functional modules in the distributive environment. Choi et al. (Choi et al., 2003) have shown the utilities of web based architectures in establishing a new generation of distributed design and manufacturing platform. Amidst all these research developments in web based systems, some research issues (Li, 2005) still need further investigated which are summarized as follows:

(i)   *There is a need for the adaptable wrapping mechanism for effective web based applications.*

(ii)   *An intelligent manufacturing system based on the web still needs to be developed that integrates visualization based systems and remote application services to facilitate product design and manufacturing on the web.*

Keeping with the current research trends, an architecture based on the web and agents for intelligent manufacturing is presented in next section.

3. *iMANUFACTURING* FRAMEWORK

The framework entitled as *"iManufacturing"* has been proposed to support a range of manufacturing facilities in the distributed manufacturing environment. These facilities are considered as shop floor manufacturing workstations with CNC controllers such as Siemens, Faunc, and Mazak to carry out the manufacturing tasks. The present framework has been proposed to realize a plug-and-play operational environment to support these facilities which are distributed throughout the world. The major aim of the present framework is to provide distributed intelligence in the form of digitized information to perform manufacturing operations starting from the point of accepting product design information from a number of remote locations. The operability of the system depends on several vital factors such as data exchange, data sharing, communication protocol and architecture. The framework is presented in figure 3, and makes use of the three agent's type design agent's, process planning agents, and manufacturing execution agents, in addition with product and process databases. Design, process planning and execution of the manufacturing tasks are carried out by distributed cooperative agents. The autonomous behavior of the agents plays a vital role in the decision making in the distributive environment which requires a high level of autonomy in utilizing the resources. The agents are proposed to be implemented using the Common Object request broacher architecture (CORBA) (Rosenberg, 1998) objects with Interface Definition Language (IDL) (CORBA, 2003), that provides the application-independent specifications to the client i.e. web servers in the various facilities at different locations. Since CORBA is platform independent and language independent, it is useful in distributed communi-cations in manufacturing. The function of the agents is based on a communication layer that depends knowledge Query Modeling Language (KQML)/XML message representation along with a user interface. The agents function according to the needs of the manufacturing execution environment that help in collaborative product development. The design activities are supported by the design agent that initiates queries to other agents regarding the manufacturability of the design. The process planning agents provide the process plan on the basis of process database to carryout the manufacturing operations. The manufacturing execution agent is responsible for performing manufacturing operations. These facilities contain different CNC machining workstations which are integrated via the Intranet and are controlled at a facility level by Java-based terminals (Cheng, Pan, and Harrison, 2001). At this facility level these terminals enable adaptability of manufacture between each of the CNC workstations. The manufacturing execution agent which resides inside each of the CNC's are connected through these Java –based terminals to coordinate with other agents and carry out the manufacturing tasks. The different functional elements of the architecture are described as follows:

(i) Product database: class features model the generic product libraries and are distributed at different locations. Class features are mainly composed of element-features, attributes, and relation among features and attributes. These class features are distributed remotely and are gathered using web links. The product database is created using class features which are created at one location and accessed at different locations using web-browsers. A VRML browser is used for extracting modelling product geometry.

(ii) Design Agent: The product data base provides the part feature related information in the form of the Extendable Stylesheet Language transformation (XSLT), which is processed by a design agent. A message is generated by the design agent that includes the part information and machining features which is sent to the manufacturing execution agent based in the different facilities to check the corresponding manufacturing feasibility. This is sent in the form of a XML file to the manufacturing execution agent who in turn sends back the information regarding the preferred processes and resources. This is further sent to the process planning agent to carry out the process planning operation. The web accessibility of the product database with different classes helps in the possible design improvements at an early stage of manufacturing that helps in maintaining the product quality and also in reducing the manufacturing cost.

(iii) Process database: This contains the different machining data, material data and tooling data which is accessed by the process planning agent.

(iv) Process Planning Agent: All the relevant features and process data is made available to this agent through XML parser (2004) which means processing of information carried out by the design agent. The process planning agent employs intelligent algorithms such as the Genetic Algorithm (GA), Simulated Annealing (SA), Tabu Search (TS), Artificial Immune System (AIS), based search engine that performs process planning for a feature-based part. These optimization tools help in reducing the machining time which reduces the cost. The message from this agent is communicated to the manufacturing execution agent at the CNC manufacturing workstation to carry out the necessary sequencing of the machining operations. This agent also works as the decision agent and allows the interpretation of the process plan for the specific workstation using the process database to provide a specific manufacturing plan for an individual CNC workstation.

(v) Manufacturing Execution Agent: This agent is responsible for processing the manufacturing of parts and generates the manufacturing codes for the operations

from the controllers to the different machines. In addition it provides feedback for communication with the design agent and process planning agent and reports the required process control information for the corresponding design and process planning.

(vi)

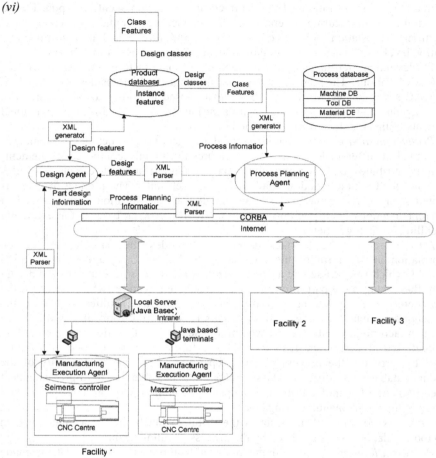

Figure 3 - *iManufacturing* framework.

4. INTELLIGENT SEARCH ENGINE

The process planning agent incorporates an intelligent search engine that carries out the process planning for the part features with the use of intelligent algorithms such as GA, SA, AIS, TS etc. The functionality of the process planning agent is shown in the following figure 4.

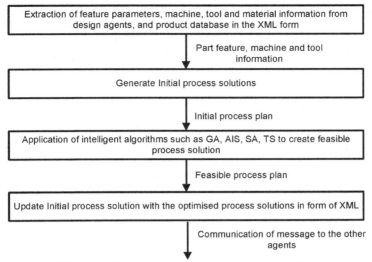

Figure 4 - Process planning agent functionality.

The intelligent engine utilizes the random search algorithms ability to search through all possible alternatives and generate the feasible and optimised solutions. This agent initially extracts the design features, tooling, material, machines in XML form which is later being optimised using the intelligent search algorithms to generate the optimised process solutions. The optimization is to be carried out based on certain optimization models that aim to minimize machining cost, tooling cost, machining time, set-up costs with relative various constraints such as machining, designing, feature interactions. A form of the XML file has been represented in the following figure 5.

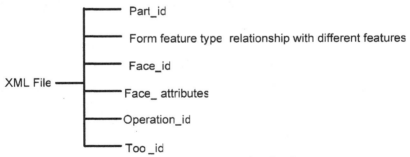

Figure 5 - XML file representation for the part.

5. IMPLEMENTATION ISSUES

There are certain important implementation issues such as security, privacy and system reliability that can affect the performance of these systems over different facilities throughout the world. One of the important issues in the collaborative manufacturing is related to the privacy of proprietary information in the form of competitive manufacturing information related with order and cost details related to particular facility. Majority of systems are implemented on the intranet behind a firewall, there is still communication across different intranets and internet. However the agents are autonomous, the communication among the agents should be reliable to ensure the stability and reliability of the manufacturing systems.

6. CONCLUSIONS

A framework composed of agents such as design, process planning, and manufacturing execution agent shows significant potential for supporting collaborative manufacturing. The framework provides a seamless integration of different agents communicating messages regarding the part design, planning information with the different CNC controllers in the various facilities across the web. The proposed web based system consists of an intelligent search engine within process planning agent that aims to obtain optimized process plans which help in reducing machining, tooling and setup costs.

7. REFERENCES

1. Brown R.G., "Driving Digital Manufacturing to Reality", *Proceedings of the 2000 Winter Simulation conference,* 2000, 224-228.
2. Chen Y. M., Liang M. W., Design and Implementation of a collaborative engineering information system for allied concurrent engineering, International Journal of Computer Integrated Manufacturing, 13(1), 2000, 11-30.
3. Cheng K., Pan P. Y., and Harrison D. K., Web-based design and manufacturing support systems: implementation perspectives, International Journal of Computer Integrated Manufacturing, 2001(1), 14-27.
4. Choi H. J., Panchal J., Allen J. K., Rosen D., and Mistree F., in: Proceedings of ASME 2003 Design Engineering Technical Conferences, Chicago, IL, USA, DETC03/CIE-48279, Towards a standardised engineering framework for distributed, collaborative product realization 2003.
5. Choo W. C., Detlor B., Turnbull D., Web Work: Information Seeking and Knowledge Work on the World Wide Web, Kluwer Academic Publishers, The Netherlands, 2000.
6. Li W. D., A Web-based service for distributed process planning optimization, Computers in Industry, 56(2005), 272-288.
7. Mervyn F., Senthil Kumar A., Bok S. H., Nee A. Y. C., Development of an Internet-enabled interactive fixture design system, Computer-Aided Design, 35(2003), 945-957.
8. OMG CORBA (2003) http://www.omg.org/corba. 20th November 2003.
9. Ong S. K., and Sun W. W., Application of mobile agents in a web-based real-time monitoring system, International Journal of Advance Manufacturing Technology, 2003, 22, 33-40.
10. Rodriguez K., Al-Ashaab A., A review of internet based collaborative product development systems, in: Proceedings of the International Conference on Concurrent Engineering: Research and Applications, Cranfield, UK, 2002.
11. Rodriguez K., Al-Ashaab A., Knowledge web-based system architecture for collaborative product development, Computers in Industry 56(2005), 125-140.
12. Rosenberg J. (1998), In: Wikert JB(ed) Sam's teach yourself CORBA in 14 days, 1st edn. Sams publishing, ISBN, 0-672-31208-5.
13. Seino T., Ikeda, Y., Kinoshita, M., Suzulu, T., Atsumi, K., "The Impact of "Digital Manufacturing" on Technology Management", *Management of Engineering and Technology, 2001. PICMET '01. Portland International Conference,* 2001, 1, 31-32.
14. Smith C. and Wright, P. K. CyberCut: A World Wide Web based Design to Fabrication Tool, Journal of Manufacturing Systems, 1996, 15(6), 432-442.
15. Xiao A., Choi H-J., Kulkarni R., Allen J., Rosen D., Mistree F., and Feng S. C., A web-based distributed product realization environment , ASME 2001 Design Engineering Technical Conference and computers and information in Engineering Conference, PA, 9-12 sep. 2001.
16. XML parser for JAVA (2004) http://www.alphaworks.ibm.com/tech/xml4j-6th January

CONTRACT NEGOTIATION WIZARD FOR VO CREATION

Luís M. Camarinha-Matos[1] and Ana Inês Oliveira[2]
[1]New University of Lisbon, Portugal, cam@uninova.pt
[2]UNINOVA, Portugal, aio@uninova.pt

The establishment of collaboration commitments, represented by contracts or agreements, is a crucial step in a virtual organization (VO) creation process. The contract negotiation shall proceed in parallel with the other phases of the VO creation process, namely preparatory planning, consortia formation, and VO launching. In each step specific elements for the contract / agreement are collected as a result of a focused negotiation processes. The specifications for a contract negotiation wizard in this context are proposed.

1. INTRODUCTION

VO creation context. The possibility of rapidly forming a virtual organization (VO), triggered by a business opportunity and specially tailored to the requirements of that opportunity, gives enterprises an expression of agility and survival mechanism in face of market turbulence.

However, finding the right partners and establishing necessary conditions for starting the collaboration process has proved to be costly in terms of time and effort, and therefore an inhibitor of the aimed agility. Among others, obstacles include lack of information (e.g. non-availability of catalogs with normalized and updated profiles of organizations, non-availability of past performance in collaborative processes), lack of common collaboration infrastructure, and above all lack of preparedness of organizations to join the collaborative process. Overcoming mismatches resulted from heterogeneity of potential partners (e.g. in ICT infrastructures, corporate culture, methods of work, and business practices) requires considerable investment; furthermore, building trust, that is a pre-requisite for any effective collaboration, is not straight forward and requires time.

It is also important to note that partners' selection is not simply an "optimization" problem. In addition to a matching process based on potential and abilities (e.g. competencies and capacities), many other factors, some of them of subjective nature (e.g. personal preferences and established trust based on previous experience) suggest that fully automated processes are not at all a realistic approach for VO creation. It is rather preferable to conceive a computer-assisted framework to help the human planner in making decisions.

An approach to overcome the mentioned difficulties is to consider the VO creation process to happen in the context of a VO Breeding Environment (VBE) (Camarinha-Matos & Afsarmanesh, 2003; Camarinha-Matos, Afsarmanesh et al., 2005b; Rabelo et al., 2000). A VBE can be defined (Afsarmanesh & Camarinha-Matos, 2005; Camarinha-Matos, Afsarmanesh et al., 2005a) as: an association of organizations and their related supporting institutions, adhering to a base long term cooperation agreement, and adoption of common operating principles and infrastructures, with the main goal of increasing both their chances and their preparedness towards collaboration in potential VOs. This long term collaborative association is composed of organizations that are prepared to collaborate and thus rapidly respond to a collaboration opportunity.

A VBE is created as a long term "controlled border" association and its members are recruited from the "open universe" of organizations according to the criteria defined by the VBE creators or administrators. A VO is a temporary organization triggered by a specific business/collaboration opportunity. Its partners are primarily selected from the VBE members. In case there is a lack of skills or capacity inside the VBE, organizations can be recruited from outside. For difficulties of prepared-ness, trust, etc, this last category will, of course, be the last resort.

In this context and in order to better identify the necessary support functionality, a number of steps (Figure 1) have been suggested for the VO creation process (Camarinha-Matos, Silveri et al., 2005).

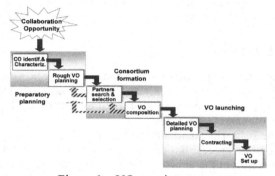

Figure 1 – VO creation process.

The role of contracts and negotiation. An important process that runs across and embedded in the steps shown in Figure 1 is the negotiation and contract establish-ment. Similarly to the traditional business relationships, the virtual organization also relies on the notion of contract and collaboration agreement among its members. Standard paper contracting is often slow and requires involvement of human actors in all contracting phases. In order to enable a fast contracting process an electronic representation of contracts is required (Grefen & Angelov, 2002). To (Rocha et al., 2004) an electronic contract describes the rights and duties of all virtual organization partners, as well as penalties to apply to those that do not satisfy the agreement. Computer assisted negotiation and e-contracting is expected to provide a faster and cheaper solution than standard contracting.

In this paper a contribution to the characterization of the negotiation and contracting processes in the context of VO creation is presented and the functionalities for a contract negotiation wizard being developed in the ECOLEAD project are outlined.

2. RELATED WORK

Contracts and the way they are established are being challenged by new technology, such as: communication channels, artificial intelligence, intellectual property rights, electronic legal entities, etc. The negotiation process can follow various paradigms: auctions, game theory, intelligent agent mechanisms, etc (Rocha & Oliveira, 1999). Nevertheless, and according to (Angelov & Grefen, 2002), the efforts in this direction did not yet produce any context-independent solution.

Although much work is still necessary in this area, several approaches and initiatives are being carried out in order to solve (or at least reduce) the difficulties faced in the contracting process by enterprises that want to work together. Some of these concepts and techniques will be described bellow and the most relevant milestones related to e-contracting research are summarized in the time line of the Figure 2.

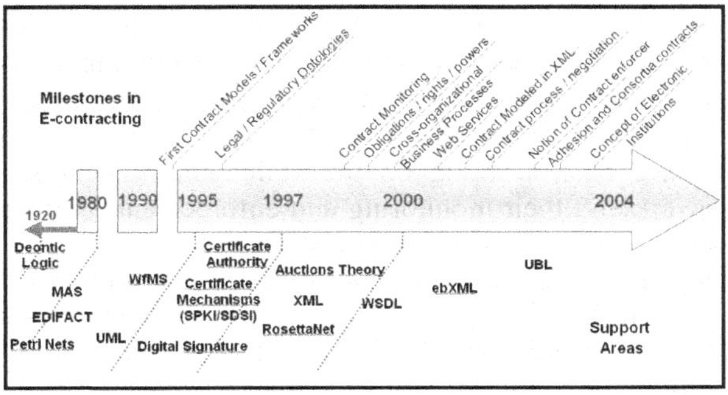

Figure 2 – e-Contracting development through time.

Some related and relevant current research topics are listed below.

Contract representation. Deontic Logic is being tried to describe contract models specifying obligations, permissions, and forbiddances for a specified business process which works in an extremely ideal process. Some works in this area can be found in (Quirchmayr et al., 2002), as well as (Xu, 2004) that make use of deontic logic for the representation of the contract clauses.

Trust. (Dimitrakos et al., 2004) through the TrusCom European Project, among other objectives, tried to focus on the provision of trust services to support the management of electronic contracts, the incorporation of guarantees to facilitate trustworthy collaboration, and performance assessment at the enactment of electronic contracts.

Legal Issues. Legal issues, especially about VO legal personality and contract with third part (B2C e-contract), have been studied mainly in the **ALIVE** project.

According to (Shelbourn et al., 2002), a VO needs a legal personality that will allow it to be seen as a legally independent entity in the country in which the contract has been incorporated. This requirement is however a subject of controversy as many definitions of VO claim that it does not have a legal entity. In the eLegal European Project (Carter et al., 2001) the main goal was to develop solutions to legal issues related to VEs in the area of construction. These solutions would result in a framework for specifying legal conditions and contracts to enable admissible use of ICT in project business. Nevertheless, this framework would be prepared specifically for each project. Furthermore, (Shelbourn et al., 2005), describe the legal and contractual issues associated with each of these contracts/ agreements, concentrating on the ICT perspective.

Electronic Signatures. Electronic signatures are methods to authenticate digital information using cryptography techniques. The directive 1999/93/EC of the European Parliament and of the Council on a Community framework for Electronic signatures provides clarification regarding its use.

Electronic institutions. An electronic Institution is a framework that enables through a communication network, automatic transactions between parties, according to sets of explicit institutional norms and rules. Thereby, the Electronic Institution ensures the trust and confidence needed in any electronic transaction (Rocha et al., 2004). In (Rocha & Oliveira, 1999) this area is combined with a multi-criteria negotiation protocol based on a multi-agent system. It consists on the traditional architecture representing enterprises by agents and introducing into the community a market agent that plays the role of coordinator in the electronic market and its main goal is the virtual enterprise formation when a consumer's needs are identified. The negotiation protocol is through the MAS paradigm. Also on this topic (Cardoso & Oliveira, 2004) have been working on the validation of contracts according to normative framework and their monitoring and enforcement. Further developments in various projects try to establish the notion of e-notary.

Contract Clauses. Clauses defined in an ICT contract often overlaps with those of the business contract (Shelbourn et al., 2002; Shelbourn et al., 2005). More specific clauses on electronic data exchanged, the use of objects; ownership of electronic data/information; and the use of software agents, is included in the ICT contract. The ownership of electronic data/information is an important issue that needs to be addressed in the ICT contract. Clauses should state who owns the information, which has access rights to the data/information to read, write, or delete data and information. In the work of (Xu, 2004) it is pointed out that a Business Contract Architecture should have: Contract repository; Notary; Legal rules repository; Contract validator; Contract negotiator; Contract arbitrator; Contract monitor; and Contract enforcer.

Supportive Frameworks. For the support of those contracts and negotiation some tools have been suggested such as "Contract wizards" that contains a clause library, contract editor and Virtual Negotiation Room. A Clause Library is the knowledge base of the Wizard (Shelbourn et al., 2002), the contract editor uses this knowledge base to electronically produce contracts and the Virtual Negotiation Room (VNR) that could be used by the different parties to collaborate, choose the different terms of the contracts and download the last version of the contract. However, in terms of implementation such concepts are at a very primitive stage.

(Andreoli & Castellani, 2001), have developed a framework based on multi-agent systems to permit partners to engage into flexible negotiation. The negotiation mechanisms is an extension to the Contract Net protocol and it exploits the coordination mechanisms provided by CLF/Mekano, that consists in a middleware platform designed to integrate negotiation and transaction aspects in distributed systems. The framework is based on unidirectional "announce/collect/decide" paradigm, but intends to go towards a multi-directional "announce/refine/decide" paradigm allowing flexible refinement of the negotiation terms.

3. CONTRACT MODELING

The purpose of establishing contracts in this context is to regulate the internal behaviour of the VO to be created in a VBE environment. It shall be noted that in a VBE context, all possible (or most) partners for the VO are members of the VBE and take advantage of all the infrastructures provided.

Classes of Contracts. The major classes of contracts that can be related to VOs are: The ones associated to the number of parties involved, such as Bilateral contract that is an agreement in which both parties to the contract makes a promise or promises to the each other; or Multi-party or multi-lateral contract that is an agreement in which it is required information from all participating sides. On the other hand, contracts can also be classified by the promises implicated, where an Adhesion contract is a standardized contract form that in general is offered to consumers of goods and services without affording them a realistic opportunity to bargain and under such conditions that they cannot obtain the desired product or service except by accepting all the contract terms; an Internal contract does not include supply to third parties (although the members goal's might include it); and an External contract represents the "joint" activity to third parties.

In the considered context, where the VOs are created in the VBE environment, the most suitable application for these types of contracts would be: the adhesion contract for the members to enroll the VBE; the internal contract as the agreements that will regulate the internal behaviour of the consortium; and the external contract to represent the commitment of the VO to the client.

Structure of Contracts. When dealing specifically with VOs, there are two different types of contracts that should be considered: the consortium internal contract/agreement and the contract established with the client. The first one regulates the behaviour of the VO typically through a multi-party contract; whereas the second establishes the actual contract with the client.

For instance, in the case of the explicit consortium (Figure 3), the collaboration is regulated by a joint contract with the customer and a consortium agreement; in this case, the client has all the information about who is part of the consortium. In the internal consortium structure (Figure 4) there is a contract between one representative of the consortium and the client. Here, the client does not necessarily know about the way the consortium is organized. Only the representative of the consortium holds the contract with the client, whereas the other partners are committed to the one that signs the contract.

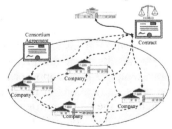 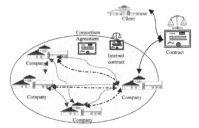

Figure 3 – Explicit Consortium structure.   Figure 4 – Internal Consortium structure.

Life-cycle of Contracts. The contract life-cycle includes several phases between the intention of establishing a contract and its actual enactment. The contract establishment process is the process of finding suitable contracting parties and negotiating a contract with them. Contract enactment is the fulfilment of the promised obligations of the parties involved and the correspondent benefits. The contract management process starts before the contract establishment process, runs in parallel with contract establishment and enactment and ends after the completion of the contract enactment process.

In this work, the focus of the addressed research is the contract establishment, whereas the contract enactment is out of the scope of this paper.

4. CONTRACT ESTABLISHMENT

At the current stage the focus of the negotiation wizard being developed in the ECOLEAD project is put on the negotiation of the internal consortium contract/ agreement, rather than on the contract with the client. Therefore, the use of the term "contract" or "agreement" (here used indistinctly) shall be understood as the result or synthesis of all agreements established among the participants of the VO being created and that will regulate their collaboration.

Taking into account the phases of the VO creation shown in Figure 1 (Camarinha-Matos & Oliveira, 2005), a suitable approach would be to have a contract negotiation wizard that would be capable of helping the right users to construct the VO contract in each phase of the VO creation, resulting in a multi-step iterative process. The elements for the contract are incrementally collected along the various steps of the VO creation process.

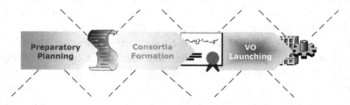

Figure 5 – Steps for VO internal Contract establishment.

There are other works that try to accomplish results for establishing contracts, namely in the area of the multi-agent systems (especially when dealing with e-commerce). Such approaches try to reach a solution that is as fully-automated as possible, while in the present work, the goal is not to have a fully-automated, but a semi-automated process to help in human decision making. For instance, taking the simplified view of Figure 5 at a certain stage, the results from the preparatory planning phase can lead to the selection of a contract template that is appropriate for the collaboration opportunity (CO) (depending on the specifications of the requirements identified in the preparatory planning that includes the CO identification and characterization and subsequent draft of the VO plan) and some fields of this template can be filled in with the results of this initial planning. More intensive negotiation steps will then take place during the consortium formation (selection of partners) and detailed VO planning. The results of all partial agreements will then be integrated into a single document, the "contract", or the VO internal agreement.

Table 1 illustrates the VO creation phases and the activities towards a contract negotiation wizard, as well as the actors involved and the situation of the contract in each phase.

Negotiation "focus". At a macroscopic level two important stages of the negotiation steps lead to different negotiation "focus":
- The negotiation towards the selection of partners to compose the VO;
- The negotiation of the details of the VO (negotiation objects) among the selected partners once the consortium is defined.

Nevertheless it is expected that at an abstract level the negotiation support mechanisms will be basically the same.

Table 1 – Approach to contract negotiation wizard.

VO Creation Phases	Sub-phases	Description	Actors Involved	Contract situation
Preparatory planning	*CO identification & characterization*	From a repository/library of contract templates, a part of the contract could be filled, namely the one related to type of CO and consequently the needed VO requirements, like: structure, topology, etc.	Opportunity Broker Client	➡ Contract type specification and general definitions
	Rough VO planning		Opportunity Broker VO Planner	
Consortia Formation	*Partners search and suggestion*	After the suggestion of potential partners, a negotiation round takes place in order to obtain the most suitable combination of partners and agreements among them. This stage will lead to the VO Composition.	VO Planner VBE Member	➡ Contract under negotiation ➡Agreed and in progress negotiation objects
	VO Composition			
VO Finalization	*Detailed VO planning*	In this phase, the VO constitution is nearly finalized so, after having a refinement of the VO plan, it is possible to further fill the VO contract in terms of its members, obligations, sanctions, etc.	VO Planner VBE Member	➡ Signed agreements / assembled contract
	Contracting		VO Planner VBE Member VO Coordinator	
	VO Launching		VO Coordinator VBE Member VBE Administrator	

A Scenario. Considering the characteristics of the needed human interaction, a support environment offering typical functionalities of a CSCW system can be foreseen. The full negotiation process involves a number of elementary negotiations, i.e. reaching agreements on a number of "negotiation objects". A "negotiation object" (e.g. definition of the schedule and location for delivery of a prototype), once agreed by all involved parties, will become part of the global contract.

The initiator of the negotiation process (VO planner) shall have mechanisms to create new negotiation objects and "open" a kind of "virtual negotiation room" or "negotiation channel" for each negotiation object. One (in a bilateral negotiation) or more (in a multi-party negotiation) participants will then be invited to join the "room". Using standard collaboration tools (e.g. chat, forum, notification, file sharing) the discussion over the "negotiation object" will proceed, driven by the human negotiators, until the process ends. Possible outcomes include:
- *Agreement reached* – in which case the "negotiation object" can be stored in a dedicated "agreed negotiation objects" folder for later integration in the contract.

- *Negotiation failed* – in which case the "negotiation object" is discarded.
- *Re-negotiation needed* – in which case a new "negotiation object" might be created, although some data from the previous one might be re-used.

The full negotiation process may be guided by a "contract template" composed of a number of sections. When a "negotiation object" is created it is associated to a specific section of the contract where a link to the object can be kept (Figure 6). After all negotiation objects are agreed, the final contract is built by a kind of "compilation" or integration of these objects.

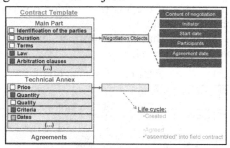

Figure 6 – Negotiation objects.

The processes described in this scenario are quite hard to structure in terms of well defined workflows/protocols as several flows depend of the decisions made by the human negotiators and also their individual timing (mostly asynchronous regarding each other).

However some "organizational/operational support" can be envisaged, namely in terms of:
- Specialized CSCW-like environment: document management and sharing, versions management, access rights definition and control, interaction mechanisms (chat, forum, notification, invitation, etc.).
- Specialized data structures and ontology's, and some minimal data-driven flow control (keeping track of the negotiation status, reached agreements, etc.).

From this simplified scenario it can also be inferred that there is a need for a close interaction between the Negotiation Wizard and other tools supporting the VO creation framework as they provide the main inputs of the wizard. On the other hand, the results of the negotiation steps influence or even determine the actual selection of partners for the VO being built. Therefore, it is not enough to design a loosely coupled architecture but rather it is necessary to invest more on the understanding of the inner interactions of the various sub-processes illustrated on Figure 1.

Functional Specifications. As previously mentioned, the focus of this wizard is not intended to reach a fully-automated tool for the contract establishment, but a semi-automatic tool to enable and facilitate human-based negotiation and decision-making. The reason for this is that the contract establishment involves a large complexity as well as huge risks; consequently the wizard will play the role of an auxiliary system in human decision making.

The planned negotiation wizard is designed to have two main layers. The first layer of the architecture consists of an extension/adaptation of the functionalities already provided by CSCW tools, such as:

−Logging including functionalities for identifying users and their properties;
−Administration with qualifications for calendar administration, generation of Gantt diagrams etc;
−Communication with possible usability of chats, forums, email, etc;
−Projects where commitments can be specified and where events for partners can be generated, as well as the inclusion of to-dos. There is also the possibility for file storage with versioning; and
−Export Objects, namely files in several formats, like pdf, xml, xls, doc, html, etc.

The second layer of the architecture is designed to facilitate and regulate the negotiation of the VO internal agreement/contract. Main components to include in this layer are:
−Contract templates repository (CTR), is a collection of contract templates and negotiation objects templates to support the contract creation,
−Contract editor, uses the repository to produce contracts,
−Virtual negotiation room (VNR) supporting the human interactions in a negotiation process, and
−Facilities for contract signing, notifications and notary.

From the wizard point of view, the other tools being developed for the VO creation framework can be considered as a third layer of the architecture, as they will all interact with the contract negotiation wizard tool.

The following table summarizes the functionality and outputs of the contract negotiation wizard:

Table 2 – Functionalities of contract negotiation wizard.

Functionality	Description	Outputs	Actors
Contract Templates repository (CTR)	Collection of contract and negotiation objects templates to support the contract creation	"skeleton" of contracts	VO Planner
Contract Editor (CE)	uses the CTR and agreed negotiation objects to add new clauses to contracts	contracts	VO Planner
Virtual negotiation room (VNR)	Virtual "place" where the negotiation participants can access the various negotiation objects and can "discuss" in order to reach agreements	Agreed negotiation objects	VO Planner and all possible partners
Support for agreement establishment (SAE)	With facilities for contract signing and notification to relevant parties, and repository/archive for its storage	"notary" with signed contracts	VO Planner and all partners involved

5. CONCLUSIONS

It is unrealistic to assume that the complexity of generic contract and contracting process can be fully automated. But what makes e-contracting so appealing is that it provides a way to decrease costs and time to reasonable values. Also the idea of having a virtual space that allows negotiation for all parties involved seems very promising. What should not be ignored is that there are a large number of organizations and SMEs that will still have to catch up with the ICT e-contracting requirements.

Some open issues that still have to be considered are: the legal implications of data exchange, both for the provider of the information and for the recipient; relation of past collaboration between organizations with "levels" of success; how should metrics and weights be assigned for the products parts and then for the partners; etc.

Acknowledgements. This work was supported in part by the ECOLEAD project funded by the European Commission. The authors also thank the contributions from their partners in the ECOLEAD Consortium.

6. REFERENCES

1. Afsarmanesh, H., & Camarinha-Matos, L. M. (2005, 26-28 September). *A Framework for Management of Virtual Organization Breeding Environments.* Paper presented at the 6th IFIP Working Conference on Virtual Enterprises, Valencia.
2. Andreoli, J. M., & Castellani, S. (2001, 5 September). *Towards a Flexible Middleware Negotiation Facility for Distributed Components.* Paper presented at the DEXA'2001 - Workshop on E-Negotiation, Munich, Germany.
3. Angelov, S., & Grefen, P. (2002). An Approach to the Construction of Flexible B2B E-Contracting Processes. University of Twente, Computer Science Dept., The Netherlands.
4. Camarinha-Matos, L. M., & Afsarmanesh, H. (2003). Elements of a base VE infrastructure. *J. Computers in Industry, Vol. 51*(Issue 2), pp. 139-163.
5. Camarinha-Matos, L. M., Afsarmanesh, H., & Ollus, M. (2005a, 26-28 September). *ECOLEAD: A Holistic Approach to Creation and Management of Dynamic Virtual Organizations.* Paper presented at the 6th IFIP Working Conference on Virtual Enterprises, Valencia.
6. Camarinha-Matos, L. M., Afsarmanesh, H., & Ollus, M. (2005b). *Virtual Organizations: Systems and Practices.* Boston: Springer.
7. Camarinha-Matos, L. M., & Oliveira, A. I. (2005). *Requirements and mechanisms for VO planning and launching.* (ECOLEAD Deliverable, IP 506958).
8. Camarinha-Matos, L. M., Silveri, I., Afsarmanesh, H., & Oliveira, A. I. (2005, 26-28 September). *Towards a Framework for Creation of Dynamic Virtual Organizations.* Paper presented at the 6th IFIP Working Conference on Virtual Enterprises, Valencia.
9. Cardoso, H. L., & Oliveira, E. (2004). *Virtual Enterprise Normative Framework within Electronic Institutions.* Paper presented at the ESAW'04.
10. Carter, C., Hassan, T., Mertz, M., & White, E. (2001). The eLegal project: specifying legal terms of contract in ICT environment (Special Issue - Information and Communication Technology Advances in the European Construction Industry ed., Vol. ITcon Vol. 6, pp. 163-174).
11. Dimitrakos, T., Golby, D., & Kearney, P. (2004). Towards a Trust and Contract Management Framework for dynamic Virtual Organisations: eChallenges Workshop.
12. Grefen, P., & Angelov, S. (2002). *On t-, u-, p-, and e-contracting.* Paper presented at the CAiSE Workshop on Web Services, e-Business, and the Semantic Web (WES2002), Toronto, Canada.
13. Quirchmayr, G., Milosevic, Z., Tagg, R., Cole, J., & Kulkarni, S. (2002). Establishment of Virtual Enterprise Contracts. In R. Cicchetti & e. al. (Eds.), *DEXA 2002* (pp. 236-248): Springer-Verlag.
14. Rabelo, R. J., Camarinha-Matos, L. M., & Vallejos, R. V. (2000). Agent-based Brokerage for Virtual Enterprise Creation in the Moulds Industry, *E-business and Virtual Enterprises* (pp. 281-290): Kluwer Academic Publishers.
15. Rocha, A. P., Cardoso, H. L., & Oliveira, E. (2004). *Contributions to an electronic Institution supporting Virtual Enterprises' life cycle.* Paper presented at the Virtual Enterprise Integration: Technological and Organizational Perspectives.
16. Rocha, A. P., & Oliveira, E. (1999). An Electronic Market Architecture for the Formation of Virtual Enterprises, *Infrastructures for Virtual Enterprises.* Boston: Kluwer.
17. Shelbourn, M., Hassan, T., & Carter, C. (2002). *Legal and Contractual Framework for the VO* (IST-1999-20570): eLegal Project.
18. Shelbourn, M., Hassan, T., & Carter, C. (2005). Legal and Contractual Framework for the VO. In L. M. Camarinha-Matos & H. Afsarmanesh & M. Ollus (Eds.), *Virtual Organization Systems and Practices*: Springer.
19. Xu, L. (2004). *Monitoring Multi-Party Contracts for e-Business.* Unpublished PhD., Faculty of Economics and Business Administration of Tilburg University, Tilburg.

A PROBABILITY-REACTIVE ORDER PROCESSING METHOD BASED ON THE LOOR FOR MAINTENANCE OF CAPITAL INTENSIVE GOODS

B. Scholz-Reiter and J. Piotrowski
BIBA-IPS, University of Bremen, Germany
{bsr, pio}@biba.uni-bremen.de

The maintenance of complex capital goods wins more and more in importance. This article will describe a method to raise a condition prognostication of modules and spare parts and the corresponding order probabilities of spare parts during the tear down process. It will give an overview how uncertainty can be represented by the use of probabilities. The consideration of different factors of influence, for example external effects such as the operation period of a product, causal relationships and influence of damaged spare parts, can be represented by the use of Bayesian Networks.

1. INTRODUCTION

Maintenance processes are known in practice as so-called "MRO processes" (MRO - Maintenance, Repair and Overhaul). The customer-supplier relations are indicated by the demand for short downtimes and a high schedulability of the maintenance of the capital goods (Schaffitzel, 1995).

Low reaction time and process stability of the supplier can be measured by the customer on logistic target figures like delivery time and delivering faithfulness during the complete product life time.

MRO processes are threads of the maintenance of complex capital goods e.g. of aircraft jet engines. In the industrial practice, special MRO-service-providers deal with the maintenance of such aggregates. The service providers go back to competences and capacities of suppliers which execute the real MRO-processes.

The maintenance of complex capital goods, for example the maintenance of aircraft jet engines, represents a special challenge to maintenance supporters due to product complexity and customer requirements. On the one hand, challenges result from the usually unknown product condition, on the other hand from very cost-intensive spare parts. Generally it is difficult to classify expert knowledge, mostly incomplete statistic data of a product and uncertain product conditions in order to forecast the expected maintenance line capacity and part requirements.

1.1 Separation of terms

To develop a better appreciation of the difficulties of the maintenance, at first the terms MRO are separated from each other. The tasks "inspection", "servicing" and "repair/overhauling" are partial tasks of the maintenance as shown in figure 1. During the "inspection", the condition of an aggregate is established; the servicing has to protect a specified condition during maintenance. The processes Repair (R), Overhaul (O) and Replace (P) are integrated into the task "repair/overhauling". The range and duration of these processes are hardly to forecast, due to the fact that the condition of the aggregate is unknown until the inspection process.

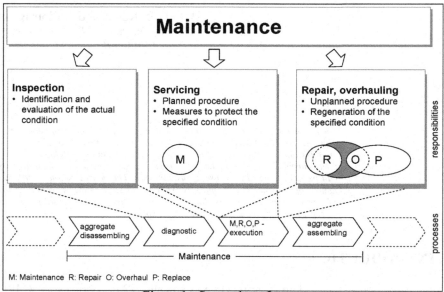

Figure 1 - Separation of terms.

2. MODELLING ON BASIS OF BAYESIAN NETWORKS

2.1 Product structure

The product structure is based on the parts list. To the German Institute for Standardization (DIN199, 2003; DIN31051, 2003) the product structure forms the order plan after which the drawing and parts list of the product are constructed.

Figure 2 represents a possibility of the diagrammatic representation of a product structure.

On the bases of the product structure, the construction of a multi-level product B_1 can be reproduced. The structure steps appear from the fact that modules or spare parts of a lower level are contained in the higher group.

The representation of the product structure model and calculation of the order probabilities are realized with the help of Bayesian Networks. New is the development of a method to transfer a product structure, as shown in figure 2, into a

Bayesian Network and the calculation of the order probabilities resulting from the Network.

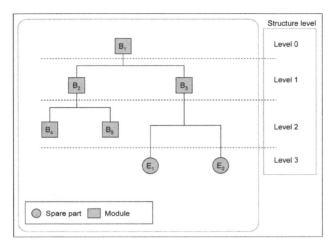

Figure 2 - Diagrammatic representation of a product structure.

The Bayesian Network is a directed acyclic graph with a set of variables (nodes) and a set of directed edges between the variables. To each variable a table is attached, which contains conditional probabilities of causal relationships (Jensen, 2002). Figure 3 represents an exemplary Bayesian Network.

The respective conditional probabilities between variables can be established for example from appropriate statistic data of past orders or empirical values. The probability of an event or a condition B is called P(B).

P(B) represents a real number in the interval I = [0, 1].

The condition of a situation in which A is true, thus $P(A_{true})$, under the condition that B is true is marked with $A_{true}|B_{true}$. The conditional probability can be calculated by using the Bayes' theorem:

$$P(A \mid B) = \frac{P(A) * P(B \mid A)}{P(B)}$$

Using the beginning probabilities, which are represented as rectangles in figure 3 of the exemplary Bayesian Network, some probability calculations can be executed. Assuming that the index "true", thus B_{true} represents a faultless module, the probability that the module B and the spare parts A and C are also faultless, can be calculated by the Bayes' theorem (Koch, 2000; Sander, 1991):

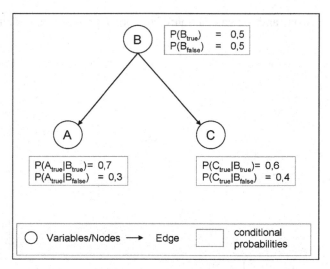

Figure 3 - Graphical representation of an example for a Baysian Network.

$$P(B_{true} \cap A_{true} \cap C_{true}) = P(B_{true}) * P(A_{true} \mid B_{true}) * P(C_{true} \mid B_{true})$$
$$P(B_{true} \cap A_{true} \cap C_{true}) = 0,5 * 0,7 * 0,6 = 0,21$$

The probability for the condition mentioned above in this example amounts to 21%.

A Bayesian Network to calculate the order probabilities can be derived directly from the product structure of the considered product as followed:

- Modules and spare parts are represented as variables or nodes
- Edges arise from the structural product construction
- The probability distribution is determined from appropriate statistic data of past orders

The Bayesian Network modelled in this way also offers the possibility to involve internal and external factors of influence. Internal factors of influence consider the dependences and the mutual influencing between the spare parts of foreign modules or other spare parts (Scholz-Reiter, 1996, 2003).

External factors of influence for example modules- and spare part age, operating time or points of use have an effect on modules or spare parts from the outside. External factors of influence mostly arise from the application profile of the considered product.

A Bayesian Network serves to represent the common probability distribution of all involved modules and spare parts in a compact way under utilization of known conditional dependences which arise from appropriate statistic data (Weibel, 1978).

The condition and therefore the order probability for a module or spare part can be calculated with the help of the Bayes' theorem under consideration of the internal and external factors of influence as mentioned above.

With the placing of order to the maintenance of an aggregate, the Bayesian Network is initialized with all available information including external factors of influence. As a first result, the Bayesian Network will deliver order probabilities. These order probabilities can be used to calculate the needed capacity, for example man power to execute the maintenance or number of needed replacement parts.

3. REPRESENTATION OF UNCERTAINTY

The parts list and the pertinent probability tables of the aggregate are converted in a file format which can be read directly in the software module SMILE (Structural Modelling, Inference, and Learning Engine) (Smile, 2006). With the help of the software module SMILE, Bayesian Networks can be represented and calculated. The choice of the software module SMILE to the representation of Bayesian Networks and calculation of order probabilities as founded by the free use and availability of the source code.

Figure 4 shows the transfer of the product structure (figure 1) in a Bayesian Network. The rectangular nodes represented in figure 4 represent in each case a module (B_x), a spare part (E_x) or external factors of influence.

External factors of influence, as for example part age, operating time or points of use are ordered in the lower row of figure 4. In the illustrated example the modules and spare parts can accept the following conditions:

- R = Reliable: Spare part is faultless.
- I = In-house: In-house maintenance
- O = Outsource: Outsourced maintenance
- P = Replace: Replacement of a spare part
- M = Missing: Spare part is missing

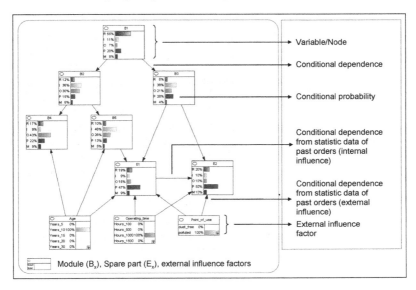

Figure 4 - Transfer of the product structure from figure 2 in a Bayesian Network.

The order probabilities can be read directly in the respective nodes. Considering the spare part "E1" in figure 4, the probability amounts to 47% that this spare part must be replaced.

4. PROBABILITY-REACTIVE ORDER MANAGEMENT

In the previous section a method for the modelling of uncertainties spare part conditions was introduced.

In the course of the tear-down process, new information about the condition of the already disassembled modules or spare parts are won, which are directed back as a new additional knowledge basis to the Bayesian Network. The Bayesian Network will calculate much sharper probabilities about the condition of the other remaining modules and spare parts.

As already mentioned, probabilities are used to represent the uncertainties about the condition of modules or spare parts.

These probabilities are not static, each aggregate, even identical in construction, has different initial properties caused by the external influence factors.

In addition, not all required informations are available to describe the complete properties of an aggregate. This means that the knowledge about the aggregate condition has to be sharpened during the tear-down process.

These probabilities and information about the spare part condition can be immediately passed to the order release. Considering to the 'Load-oriented order release' (LOOR) (Wiendahl, 1995) that influences throughput times on a shop floor by controlling the amount of jobs released and, thus, the input to the production system, the load limit LL for a work station is calculated as followed:

$$LL(WS) = PSL(WS) + PDL(WS)$$

The variables are defined as:
- WS   = work station
- LL(WS)   = load limit
- PSL(WS)   = average planned stock level
- PDL(WS)   = average planned dispatch level

According to LOOR the planned processing times of the n-th work station within the planning period are discounted by using the loading percentage, LOAP which is calculated as followed:

$$LOAP(WS) = \frac{LL(WS)}{PDL(WS)} \times 100\%$$

To pass the calculated probabilities to the order release the processing time for maintenance of a spare part has to be multiplied with the calculated probabilities.

The probability oriented work station capacity is calculated according to the following formula:

$$C(A) = P(A) \times T(A)$$

The variables are defined as:
- $P(A)$ = probability
- $T(A)$ = processing time
- $C(A)$ = probability oriented work station capacity

Relating to the example in figure 4 and looking at the module B_5, the probability for in-house maintenance is 46%. Assuming that the processing time for this module is 100 hours, the needed capacity can be planned with 46 hours.

According to the fact the calculated probabilities will change during the tear-down process, the needed work station capacity will change. To handle the variability of the probabilities it is necessary to set the LOAP higher as calculated above. The future work will determine the factor to raise the LOAP by the use of a simulation model.

A further advantage using probabilities calculated by the Bayesian Network is the reduction of disassembling steps. The tear-down order usually arises from the product structure, disassembling steps can be left out in case that the contained modules or spare parts are faultless.

5. CONCLUSIONS AN FUTURE WORK

This paper described a method to raise a condition prognosis of modules and spare parts and the corresponding order probabilities of spare parts during the tear-down process. It is based on a product specific Bayesian Network, which contains information about the condition of spare parts.

Different uncertainties resulting from different influence factors and the possibility to trace back new information during the tear-down process can be represented by Bayesian Networks.

It was shown that the method produces adequate surroundings for predicative and reactive planning.

The next step will be the implementation of a software prototype, which allows a simple creation of Bayesian Networks based on a product structure.

6. ACKNOWLEDGMENT

This research is funded by the German Federation of Industrial Research Associations "Otto von Guericke" (AiF) and Bundesvereinigung Logistik e.V (BVL). The authors also wish to acknowledge the valuable input from the project members of the research project "RAsant" and the "Institut für Fabrikanlagen und Logistik" at the University of Hannover.

7. REFERENCES

1. DIN 199, Technical product documentation - CAD-Models, drawings and items lists - Part 1, Vocabulary, Beuth Verlag GmbH, Berlin, 2003
2. DIN 31051, Fundamentals of maintenance, Beuth Verlag GmbH, Berlin, 2003
3. Jensen F., Bayesian Networks an Dicision Graphs, Springer Verlag, New York/Berlin/Heidelberg, 2002
4. Koch K-R., Einführung in die Bayes-Statistik, Springer Verlag, New York/Berlin/Heidelberg, 2000
5. Sander P., Badoux R., Bayesian Methods in Reliability, Kluwe Academic Publishers, Dordrecht, 1991
6. Schaffitzel E., Navel H.-Chr., Optimierungs-ansätze innerhalb der Ersatzteilversorgung - Ebenenübergreifende und sortimentsbezogene Möglichkeiten zur Rationalisierung innerhalb der Vertriebslogistik, VDI Berichte Nr. 1206, 1995: 22
7. Scholz-Reiter B., Höhns, H., Wissensbasierte Auftragskoordination im Supply Chain Management mit Agentensystemen: Aspekte des Knowledge Engineering zur Entwicklung agentenbasierter dezentraler PPS-Funktionalitäten, Industrie Management Nr. 19, GITO-Verlag, Berlin, 2003: 26-29
8. Scholz-Reiter B., Zussmann E., Schnarke H., Planung in reaktiven Demontageprozessen, Industrie Management Nr. 12, GITO-Verlag, Berlin, 1996: 16-21
9. SMILE (Structural Modeling, Inference, and Learning Engine), Decision Systems Laboratory, http://genie.sis.pitt.edu, 2006
10. Weibel B., Bayes'sche Entscheidungstheorie, Verlag Paul Haupt, Bern, 1978
11. Wiendahl H.-P., Load-Oriented Manufacturing Control, Berlin et al., Springer, 1995

TOWARDS INTERACTIVE CLP – BASED AND PROJECT DRIVEN ORIENTED DSS DESIGN

Robert Wójcik[1], Izabela Tomczuk-Piróg[2] and Zbigniew Banaszak[3]

[1] *Institute of Computer Engineering, Control and Robotics,*
Wrocław University of Technology, Poland,
robert.wojcik@pwr.wroc.pl
[2] *Department of Management and Production Engineering,*
Technical University of Opole,, Poland,
itomczuk@po.opole.pl
[3] *Department of Computer Science and Management,*
Technical University of Koszalin, Poland,
banaszak@tu.koszalin.pl

A *unified framework standing behind of a methodology aimed at object oriented decision support system (DSS) design is considered. First of all the consistency of the assumed knowledge bases describing an object (enterprise) and requests (standard options supporting a decision maker), respectively are examined. Then the knowledge base representation is transformed into representation of so called constraint satisfaction problem (CSP). Possible ways of the CSP decomposition as well as possibility of different programming languages application lead then to a problem aimed at searching for a distribution strategy allowing one to interact in an on-line model. The results obtained are implemented in a software package supporting production flow planning in the SMEs. Illustrative example of the ILOG-based software application is provided. Experiments carried out by means of the package have been executed in Archimedes S.A., a hydraulic and pneumatic equipment manufacturer.*

1. INTRODUCTION

Decision taking supported by task-oriented software tools plays a pivotal role in modern enterprises. Managers need to be able to utilize a modern decision support tools as to undertake optimal business decisions in further strategic perspective of enterprise operation. Often repeating requests regard the questions such as: Can the consumer's requirements be fulfilled within the assumed extended enterprise structure? Does the assumed set of SMEs guarantee a resultant extended enterprise to accomplish a given production order? In other words, it enables finding an answer to the most important question whether a given production order (treated as a new project) can be accepted to be processed in the manufacturing system at hand (treated as a multi-project environment), i.e. whether its completion time, batch size, and its delivery period satisfy the customer requirements while satisfying constraints imposed by the enterprise set up and the process of manufacturing of other products.

Respond to the questions usually involve many different aspects and contexts, e.g. money flow, personnel and/or resources allocation, tasks scheduling, workflows planning, and so on. In that context, the Constraint Programming/Constraint Logic Programming (*CP/CLP*) languages by employing the constraints propagation concept and by providing unified constraints specification can be considered as a well-suited framework for development of decision taking software aimed the small and medium sized enterprises (*SMEs*) (Banaszak, Zaremba, 2005). Because of their declarative nature, for a use that is enough to state *what* has to be solved instead *how* to solve it (Banaszak, Józefczyk, 2005) the approach seems to be very friendly for modelling of a company real-life and day-to-day decision-making. In that context our objective is to provide a constraint programming based methodology aimed at designing of task oriented decision support systems (DSS). In other words, the framework we are looking for should be able to cope with a problem defined in terms of finding of a feasible schedule that satisfies the constraints imposed by the duration of production order processing, the cost assumed, and the time-constrained resources availability.

2. PROBLEM STATEMENT

Consider a manufacturing system providing a given production capability while processing some other production orders. Therefore, only a part of the production capability (specified by the time-constrained resource availability) is available in the system. A given production order is represented by an activity-on-node network, and determined by project duration deadline, which is equivalent to a presumed completion time (the production order cycle) as well as a total project cost constraint. Each activity may be executed in one of the resources system set. An activity may not be pre-empted and a resource once selected may not be changed.

The problem consists in finding a makespan-feasible schedule that fulfils the constraints imposed by the precedence relations and by the time-constrained resources availability as well as assumed duration deadline. Production flow planning requires solving many different subproblems (e.g. batching, routing and scheduling) simultaneously (Brucker, 1999). Considered problems complex nature implies the necessity to apply respective methods and tools to improve these processes.

The requirement for planning simultaneous multi sort production processes, which characterizes SME, is not met by the computer systems available on the market (Tomczuk, Bzdyra, 2005). Commercially available software packages employing the methods based on local search meta-heuristics such as simulated annealing, tabu search, genetic algorithm, are quite costly and require skilful and well trained personnel. Decision makers face the problem of making optimal decision in uncertain situation under given constraints with various sources of knowledge (often semi-structured or ill structured). Moreover, they are not able to integrate such different tasks as production and transportation routings, production and batch sizing as well as tasks scheduling. This fact increases the demand for decision support systems (DSS) for this class of enterprises (i.e. packages which are easy to use, do not require highly qualified staff). Such system should facilitate generating a solution in a possible short time (feasible schedule on-line).

Decision support systems based on CLP approach could constitute an attractive alternative (in solving combinatorial problems) for the currently available systems of computer-integrated management (Ilog, 1995), (Tomczuk, Muszyński, 2005).

3. CSP-BASED MODEL OF DSS

Concurrent execution of several projects is interrelated with the necessity to evaluate the time and cost potential of the every new production order execution (a group of production orders). A company should therefore provide an answer to a few questions, e.g. *whether the company production capacity is sufficient for the execution of a production order in accordance with the customer's requirements, and especially what the planned production order execution deadline and cost are.*

3.1 Modelling

In order to balance the producer's abilities with the customer's requirements the CSP-based model of DSS is proposed. The model is developed especially for the needs of small and medium enterprises. The model includes parameters, which determine the enterprise capacity and production order (Fig. 1). It is necessary to answer the following question: does it answer all questions asked? If not, which of the questions could be answered? To answer the questions the analyzed decision problem can be formulated as a Constraint Satisfaction Problem (CSP), for which many Constraint Programming (CP) languages (especially Constraint Logic Programming (CLP)) were developed (Wallace, 2000).

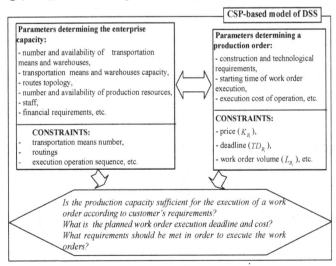

Figure 1 – CSP-based model of DSS for SME.

Consider the CSP that consists of a set of variables $X = \{x_1, x_2, \ldots, x_n\}$, their domains $D = \{D_i \mid D_i = [d_{i1}, d_{i2}, \ldots, d_{ij}, \ldots, d_{im}], i = 1..n\}$, and a set of constraints $C = \{C_i \mid i = 1..L\}$. A solution is such an assignment of the variables that all the constraints are satisfied.

CSP is based on a description of specific problem as a set of constraints, which specify some of its features. Solution of the problem is based on searching the so-called decision tree in order to find its branches, which reflect the X variable value, meeting all the set C constraints. Formulating a problem in a form of CSP facilitates analysis of all potential (unconstrained by possibilities, applied programming systems in CLP languages) ways of problem solving.

The decision problem is to answer the question: are there such constraints in the set of constraints, which are contradictory to the remaining, assumed ones? In other words, there is a contradiction if there is no combination of decision variables, which meet the constraints. The solution of the problem is a feasible solution (a set of solutions), which meets a set of constraints linking decision variables describing a producer's capabilities as well as variables, which characterize the conditions for the execution of a production order. The CSP-based model constraints are, e.g.: production order execution cost, deadline, resource availability periods, and production order volume (Baptiste, 1998). Assumptions of the CSP-based model of DSS:

1) Every resource, in a given time unit can execute at most one operation
Allocation of operation A_j to a resource Z_l takes the value zero or one

$$P_{A_j,t,z_l} = \begin{cases} 1 - \textit{if an } A_j \text{ operation is allocated to} \\ \quad \text{a resource } Z_l \text{ in a time unit } t \in N \\ 0 - \text{otherwise} \end{cases}$$

$$\underset{t,z_l \in N}{\forall} \sum_{j=1}^{m} P_{A_j,t,z_l} \le 1 \tag{1}$$

2) The operations cannot be pre-empted, the time of their execution is:

$$T_{A_j,z_l} = tk_{A_j} - tp_{A_j} \tag{2}$$

where: tk_{A_j}, tp_{A_j} - signify, subsequently the time of finishing and commencement of operation A_j, on the resource Z_l.

3) A resource once chosen cannot be changed

$$\underset{\substack{j \in (1,m) \\ l \in (1,n)}}{\forall} \sum_{tp_{A_j}}^{tk_{A_j}} P_{A_j,t,z_l} = T_{A_j,z_l} \tag{3}$$

4) Every operation can be executed by at least one of the system resources

$$\underset{t,j}{\forall} \sum_{l=1}^{n} P_{A_j,t,z_l} \ge 1 \tag{4}$$

3.2 Reference Model of Constraint Satisfaction Problem Decomposition

The following CSP notation is applied: CSP = ((X,D),C), where $c \in C$ is a constraint specified by a predicate $P[x_k, x_l, \ldots, x_h]$ defined on a subset of the X set. In general case the CSP problem may be decomposed into a set of subproblems.

For the purpose of illustration lets us consider the following problem example: given a CSP = ((X,D),C), where X = $\{x_1, x_2, ..., x_{12}\}$, D = $\{D_1, D_2, ..., D_{12}\}$, C = $\{c_1, c_2, ..., c_8\}$, where: $c_1 = P_1[x_1, x_2, x_3]$, $c_2 = P_2[x_2, x_4, x_5]$, $c_3 = P_3[x_4, x_6]$, $c_4 = P_4[x_7, x_8]$, $c_5 = P_5[x_4, x_7]$, $c_6 = P_6[x_9, x_{10}]$, $c_7 = P_7[x_8, x_9]$, and $c_8 = P_8[x_{11}, x_{12}]$. The feasible decompositions (arbitrary chosen) of the CSP considered are shown in figure 2. The subproblems that cannot be decomposed are so called the elementary problems.

a)

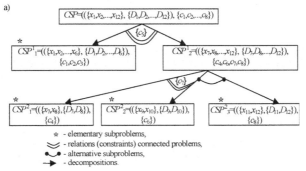

* - elementary subproblems,
≋ - relations (constraints) connected problems,
•—• - alternative subproblems,
→ - decompositions.

Figure 2 – The CSP feasible decompositions.

In a situation when we have a given set of specifications $Z = \{z_1, z_2, ..., z_i\}$, their decompositions $W = \{w_{11}, w_{12}, ..., w_{21}, w_{22}, ..., w_{i1}, w_{i2}, ..., w_{ij}\}$ and solution strategies $S = \{s_{1,1,1}, s_{1,1,2}, ..., s_{ijl}\}$ where i – specification number, j – decomposition number, l – solution strategy number, we are searching for an answer to the question: Which solution searching strategy (and of which decomposition) is the best one (i.e. it allows for the fastest obtained decision, (Barták, 2004))?

In order to estimate which decomposition, or corresponding searching strategy is the best one a *number of potential backtrackings* (Nw) is proposed as an evaluating criterion:

$$\text{Nw} = \sum_{i=1}^{LP} \left(\prod_{k=1}^{i} ZD_{k,i} - 1 \right) \qquad (5)$$

where: LP – a number of subproblems; $ZD_{k,i}$ – a number of potential assignments of the i-th decision variable of the subproblem in the k-th sequence defining an order of solving the subproblems (e.g. for two subproblems $A = ((\{x_1\}, \{f_1, f_2, f_3, f_4, f_5\}), c_1)$ and $B = ((\{x_2\}, \{p_1, p_2, p_3\}), c_2)$ there is: $LP = 2$, $ZD^A = 5$ (five assignments for x_1), and $ZD^B = 3$ (three assignments for x_2); two search strategies are possible (A,B) and (B,A); for the sequence (A,B): $Nw = (ZD_{1,1} - 1) + (ZD_{1,2} \cdot ZD_{2,2} - 1) = (5-1) + (5 \cdot 3 - 1) = 18$; for the sequence (B,A): $Nw = (ZD_{1,1} - 1) + (ZD_{1,2} \cdot ZD_{2,2} - 1) = (3-1) + (3 \cdot 5 - 1) = 16$; hence, the last searching strategy for a possible solution is characterized by a lower number of potential backtrackings and in light of this criterion it is accounted as optimum strategies).

The reference model facilitated a series of experiments, which helped specifying (before implementation) what kind of searching leads (in a possibly short time) to a solution, which would meet all constraints. The model helps evaluating specific feasible solutions (within different searching strategies) according to a chosen criterion.

4. ILLUSTRATIVE EXAMPLE

Application of CLP techniques from the point of view of the SMEs implies a possibility of development of cheap, and need oriented, decision support systems. The possibilities shall deal with the construction of a user interface based on the common programming languages (as e.g. OPL for Ilog system, or Oz for the Mozart system). A software package – Production Order Verification System – a POVS (developed by means of Ilog) is an example of this kind of system. The system allows automating the process of production order taking and analysis, in conditions of determined production system resource constraints.

The POVS has been applied at a SME producing the hydraulic and pneumatic equipment. In order to illustrate its application let us consider the following example regarding of three production orders (B_1, B_2, B_3) planned for the execution (Tab. 1).

Table 1 – Specification of production orders

Work orders	Name	Number of operations in a process	Production size (pcs.)	Suggested price (cost units)	Execution time (time units)
B_1	Filter set	10	100	1000	3500
B_2	Main body	27	120	1500	5500
B_3	Valve	7	50	1200	4200

After the introduction of data included in Tab. 1 user/operator can introduce the production process of a given production order. The process can be chosen from the system database or can be defined by the user. For example, Tab. 2 covers subsequent production operations and their execution times, which make the execution of the production order B_1. The filter set consists of two parts: filter and connector.

After completion of each production operation a transportation operation to the next position of a given technological production route is executed. The transportation means, their capacity, transportation routings and the duration times are defined. The following sequence of execution of the set production orders B_2, B_1, B_3 is considered.

Table 2 – Specification of the operations and their duration time in work order B_1

Operation name	Production operation number	Execution time (time unit/pcs.)	tpz_{A_j}	Resources	Operation name	Number of the subsequent production operation	Execution time of an operation (time units/pcs.)	tpz_{A_j}	Resources
Execution of the filter					Execution of the connector				
Cutting	A_1	1	50	R_8	Cutting	A_4	1	20	R_{12}
Washing	A_2	1	120	R_2	Turning	A_5	1	90	R_{13}
Control	A_3	3	20	R_{19}	Washing	A_6	1	60	R_2
					Turning	A_7	2	110	R_{27}
					Hand treatment	A_8	1	50	R_7
					Washing	A_9	1	60	R_{31}
					Blacking	A_{10}	2	60	R_{17}

Legend: A_j – j-th operation, $j = 1,...,10$; R_i – i-th production resource, $i = 1,...,32$; Tpz_A – preparation-finishing time.

Input data introduction facilitates commencement of the verification of single production order (group of production orders).

Due to the system's capability following from the currently realized production plan, all the introduced production orders cannot be taken for production. So, the production order B_1 cannot be processed, however, the remaining production orders can be taken for execution.

In case if a production order is rejected (i.e. a negative verification was obtained), POVS allows changing the priority of the planned production orders. It facilitates a next on-line verification, which leads to their "over planning". This gives another chance for a positive verification of the set of production orders introduced to the system. In other words, production orders that can use up the possibility of introduction of subsequent production orders (e.g. they engage too many resources or have a long operation time) are considered at the end.

In order to check a different opportunity to execute production orders, their priorities are changed as follows: B_1, B_2, B_3. The corresponding verification facilitates acceptance of all orders for their execution. It means the production orders B_1, B_2, and B_3 may be finally taken for execution. The plan obtained provides the time of starting the production order B_1 at 1 time unit, the production order B_2 at 151 time unit, and B_3 at 1 time unit (Fig. 3).

The solution takes into account the possibility of execution of a production order due to the technological sequence of operations, transportation routings among resources and the production volume, capacity of buffers and their allocation. Moreover, knowing the resources availability the cost of the production order execution can be easily estimated as well.

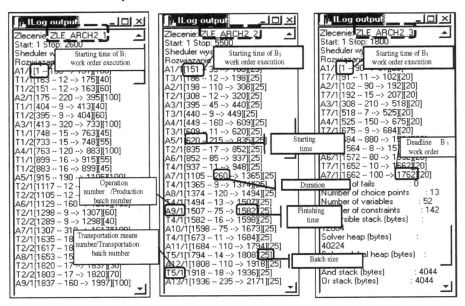

Figure 3 – Obtained solution.

The system presented constitutes an attractive possibility of on-line work, which is an alternative for the current available solutions in computer integrated management. It includes the requirements of small and medium size enterprises, which deal with frequent decision taking resulting from the execution of many projects.

5. CONCLUDING REMARKS

Most of SME work in a multi-project environment, with a necessity to coordinate many simultaneous production orders at different stages. Growing market competition imposes a need for making decisions solving resource conflicts of production orders under execution as well as taking new production orders (which engage free production capacities).

The presented production flow organization is based on the division of a production order into production and transportation batches, taking into account resource, logistic and cost constraints.

Application of the CLP techniques in solving production flow planning problems facilitate choosing solutions in the searching space, which meet the amount constraints (related with the evaluation of the solution according to time, financial constraints etc.), and the quality constraints (i.e. without deadlock or breaks).

6. REFERENCES

1. Banaszak Z., Zaremba M., Muszyński W. CP-based decision making for SME. Preprints of the 16th IFAC World Congres, 3 – 8 July, 2005, Prague, Czech Republic, Eds P. Horacek, M. Simandl, P. Zitek 2005; DVD.
2. Banaszak Z., Józefczyk J. Towards CLP-based task oriented DSS for SME, Applied Computer Science and Production Management 2005; Vol. 1, No.1: 161-180.
3. Barták R. Incomplete Depth-First Search Techniques: A Short Survey, Proceedings of the 6th Workshop on Constraint Programming for Decision and Control, Ed. Figwer J., 2004; 7-14.
4. Baptiste P., Le Pape C., Peridy L. Global constraints for partial CSPs: a case-study of resource and due date constraints. In Proc. 4th Int. Conf. on Principles and Practice of Constraint Programming (CP98). Springer-Verlag, LNCS 1520, 1998.
5. Brucker O. Resource-constrained project scheduling: Notation, classification, models, and methods, European Journal of Operational Research 112, 1999; 3-41.
6. Ilog Solver, Object oriented constraint programming, Ilog S.A., 12, Av. Raspail, BP 7, 94251 Gentilly cedex, France, 1995.
7. Tomczuk I., Muszyński W., Banaszak Z. Production flow planning based on CLP approach, Proc. of the 10th IEEE Int. Conf. on Emerging Technologies and Factory Automation, 2005, Italy, L.L. Bell, T. Sauter Eds.; Vol. 2: 637-642.
8. Tomczuk I., Bzdyra K., Banaszak Z. Decision support system based on CP approach, Proceedings of the Workshop on Constraint Programming for Decision and Control, CPDC, Gliwice, 2005: 7-45.
9. Van Hentenryck P., Perron L., Puget J. Search and Strategies in OPL, ACM Transactions on Computational Logic; Vol. 1, No. 2, 2000: 1-36.
10. Wallace M. Constraint Logic Programming, Ed. Kakas A.C., Sadri F., Computat. Logic, LNAI 2407, Springer-Verlag, Berlin, Heidelberg 2000; 512-532.

APPLYING THE ZACHMAN FRAMEWORK DIMENSIONS TO SUPPORT BUSINESS PROCESS MODELING

Pedro Sousa[123], Carla Pereira[3], Rute Vendeirinho[4], Artur Caetano[12] and JoséTribolet[12]

[1] Department of Information Systems and Computer Engineering, Instituto Superior Técnico, Technical University of Lisbon, Portugal
[2] Organizational Engineering Center, INESC INOV, Lisboa, Portugal
[3] Link Consulting, S.A , Lisboa, Portugal
{pedro.sousa, carla.pereira}@link.pt, {artur.caetano, jose.tribolet}@inov.pt
[4] Sogrupo SI, Grupo CGD, Lisboa, Portugal
rute.felix@cgd.pt

Business process models assist business and information technology managers while adapting, reengineering and optimizing the organizational processes through analysis, visualization and simulation. Despite the number of notations and techniques to support business process modeling, there is no agreement on the modeling criteria to be used by different organizational stakeholders. This paper describes a method to infer business activities in order to facilitate the consistent representation of business processes, thus facilitating their sharing, dissemination and analysis. The method relies on using a number of properties derived from the dimensions of the Zachman framework.

1. INTRODUCTION

Process blueprints are fundamental to document, analyze and sustain organizational change, as documented by multiple works related to business process management (Davenport, 1990; Davenport, 1994; Hammer, 1990; Hammer, 2001; Grover, 1995; Labovitz, 1997). Process blueprints are developed according to specific goals as well as to the modeller's perspective. This means conflicting specifications may exist for the same process. However, and despite a number of notations and techniques assisting the modelling task, there is no agreement on the modelling criteria that can be used by different stakeholders. Organizations are then faced with disparate blueprints for the same process and no formal procedures to sort out their relevance. In fact, these models are probably accurate while representing the actual organization but from the modeller's view of that particular process. Given that business processes often cross multiple organizational units, they are often shared among different stakeholders and represented from multiple perspectives, such as quality, auditing, information technology and security. As a result, process blueprints must be able to address the different stakeholder's perspectives and interests (Towers, 2005) and their management and sharing may be simplified if they are handled by a process repository (Malone, 2003).

To tackle these issues, this paper proposes using a set of modeling criteria derived from the Zachman framework to model business processes activities. The proposal plays an important role in the Distributed and Collaborative Process Design and Planning cornerstone of the Digital Enterprise Technology framework, since it details how multiple and independent stakeholders can design a consistent process blueprint. The Digital Enterprise Technology framework consists of the collection of systems and methods for the digital modeling of the global product development and realization process, in the context of lifecycle management (Maropoulos, 2002). It comprises five main areas that correspond to the design of product, process, factory and technology for ensuring the conformance of the digital with the real environment as well as enterprise design and logistics.

The outline of the paper is as follows: Section 2 presents the fundamental concepts used in the paper related to business process modeling. Sections 3 and 4 describe a number of criteria for business process modeling derived from the Zachman framework, exemplified in Section 5. Section 6 introduces guidelines to design a business process repository to manage process blueprints. Finally, we draw some conclusions and describe ongoing research.

2. BUSINESS PROCESSES AND ACTIVITIES

Multiple definitions of business process coexist in current literature such as:
4   A process is a course of action, a series of operations, or a series of changes (Simpson, 1989).
5   Processes represent the flow of work and information throughout the business (OMG, 2005).
6   A business process is a collection of activities that take one or more inputs and creates an output that is of value to the customer (Hammer, 2001).
7   Every organization exists to accomplish value-adding work. The work is accomplished through a network of processes. Every process has inputs, and the outputs are the results of the process (ISO, 1995).
8   A kind of process that supports and/or is relevant to business organizational structure and policy for the purpose of achieving business objectives. This includes manual and/or workflow processes (W3C, 2002).
9   Business process is the manner in which work is organized, coordinated, and focused to produce a valuable product or service (Laudon, 2000).
Based on these definitions, a business process can be inferred as a set of connected activities with inputs and outputs, which interact with people, contribute to achieving business goals, take place in a specific location and occur during a period of time. It is important to notice that while we refer to a process as a set of activities, both concepts are actually interchangeable. Such view implies a recurring usage of these terms but with similar means. The use of the different terms simply reflects the hierarchical relationship between them, being an activity part of a process. However, some major questions arise when modelling business processes:
10   How to identify top level business process?
11   How to establish business process hierarchy?
12   How to link activities into business processes?
13   How to identify activities?

The first three issues are fundamental to process modelling but are out of the scope of this paper, although they have been widely discussed in the literature (Hammer, 1990; Porter, 1985). However, approaches to tackle the last issue seem oversimplified, since the task is usually left to the modeller's discretion, which often results in disparate results (Coelho, 2005). This paper focus on how to consistently identify activities, particularly on how to specify when an activity should be further decomposed. Having a consistent decomposition mechanism ensures a sound representation of the same process across different perspectives.

Activities comprise a number of atomic tasks, and it is up to the modeller to decide how to aggregate them into activities. This means different modellers can compose tasks into activities differently, leading to different representations of the same process. As an example, consider the design of the "Requirements Definition" process to support the development of an information system. If both the client manager and IT quality manager are asked to design such process, two different results will probably emerge: while the client manager is focused on documenting the information entities related to the process, the quality manager is concerned with the activities that allow controlling the overall process (v. Figure 1).

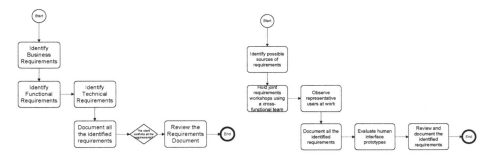

Figure 1 - Quality Manager's Perspective (left); Client Manager's
Perspective (right).

3. THE ZACHMAN FRAMEWORK

The Zachman framework for enterprise architecture proposes a matrix-like structure for classifying and organizing the representations of an enterprise (Sowa, 1992; Zachman, 1987). The rows consider six different *perspectives* on the enterprise, representing its major stakeholders: visionary, executive leader, architect, engineer, implementer and the organization worker. The columns specify six contextual *dimensions* summarized in Table 1.

In the context of process modeling, two out of the six basic properties of the Zachman framework apply (Pereira, 2004; Pereira, 2005; Sousa, 2004; Spewak, 1992; Sowa, 1992; Zachman, 1987). First, the framework is recurrent in the sense it can be used to further specify the contents of each cell. Second, each cell must be described with the sufficient level of detail so that it accomplishes its purpose.

Therefore processes must be defined in this cell since business processes are defined in the second row and second column (how/executive leader).

Table 1 - Dimensions of the Zachman framework

Dimension	Focus	Purpose
What	Data	The enterprise's data and how it is used.
How	Function	The process of translating the mission of the organization into its business and into successive definitions of its operations.
Where	Network	The geographical distribution of the organization's activities and artifacts.
Who	People	Who is related with the major artifacts of the organization: business processes, information and IT. Higher level cells refer to organizational units; lower level refers to system users.
When	Time	How each artifact relates and evolves with timeline.
Why	Motivation	The translation of goals into actions and objectives.

4. CRITERIA FOR ACTIVITY DECOMPOSITION

A rule for identifying business process activities can be proposed by analysis of the six Zachman framework dimensions. This rule specifies that an activity α can be decomposed into two or more distinct discrete activities if and only if one of the conditions stated in Table 2 is satisfied.

Table 2 - Criteria for activity decomposition

Dimension	Criteria
What	α is composed by two or more activities which receive/create different data entities.
How	α is composed by two or more activities which are processed using different applications.
Where	α is composed by two or more activities which occur in different locations.
Who	α is composed by two or more activities which are managed by different business actors.
When	α is composed by two or more activities which are performed in distinct periods of time.
Why	α is composed by two or more activities which exist to satisfy different purposes.

Several observations can be formulated from these rules. For example, when activities α and β are supported by different information systems, it normally corresponds to a change in the "how" column, since it expresses how the business is done. Other case is when α and β have different security levels, meaning there is a relationship between the "what", "who", and "how" columns. The proposed rule can then facilitate different business actors to model the same process with a minimum of differences as exemplified in Figure 2.

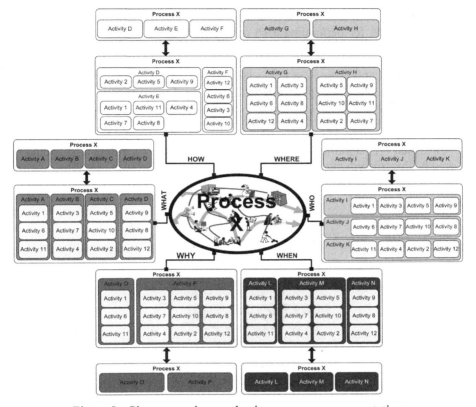

Figure 2 - Six perspectives on business process representation.

5. EXAMPLE

This section describes the application of the decomposition rule to the requirements definition process previously introduced. Figure 2 represents the representation of the process reached by the multiple stakeholders according to the following scenario.

Case 1: What?

The information entities needed to be managed during the Requirements Definition, since there are different classes of software requirements used in existing specification structures. This leads to different activities related with Requirement Identification that create different type of data entities, namely List of Business Requirements, List of Functional Requirements and List of Technical Requirements.

Case 2: How?

The modeller is concerned with the specific activities that are performed in a distinct way creating value to the overall process.

Case 3: Where?

The modeller is concerned with the location where each activity is performed; meaning activities performed in different locations must be disjoint.

Case 4: Who?

Actor responsible for performing each activity within the process must be clearly identified.

Case 5: When?

The modeller is also concerned with representing the sequence of activities of the process that take place in a specific period.

Case 6: Why?

The modeller is concerned with the motivation behind each activity.

The result is exemplified in Figure 3, which depicts the six different perspectives shared by the different modellers.

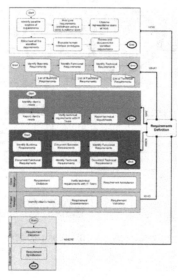

Figure 3 - Generic representation of the process.

This example shows the different process blueprints that each approach may leads to using the framework's six dimensions as the only rule for activity decomposition. In a real scenario, the problem is far more complex because intuitively people take decisions based on combinations of two or more of such basic dimensions, some of which that may even be meaningless.

We have analysed some real cases where different blueprints were produced for the same business process and concluded that the modellers have considered different priorities in what concerns to these six dimensions. The initial problem was defining basic criteria so that different teams observing the same process would produce similar blueprints. We argue that most of the differences can be perceived by observation of the Zachman framework's six dimensions, and if process modelling criteria is defined over these dimensions, then similar blueprints can be produced.

6. USING PROCESS LAYERS IN REPOSITORIES

A business process repository is an enterprise-wide tool that supports the management and sharing of process blueprint. However, most business process repositories[1] have limited query capabilities. One of the missing concepts is that of *layering*. Layers can be attached to each repository object so that users are able to filter objects according to the layers they belong to.

We propose defining six basic layers, each corresponding to each one of the six dimensions. For example, the Human Resource Department could view the "who" layer to have a perspective of how human resources were being involved in the process.

7. CONCLUSIONS AND FUTURE WORK

If no criteria for specifying activities are defined or even if the dimensions of the Zachman framework are applied without guidelines, the result will most probably be a number of different blueprints even if the actual business process is unique. To overcome this issue, we have proposed rules to specify how to compose business process activities regardless of the stakeholder's perspective, thus facilitating the task of having different actors consistently modelling the same process. The rule's conditions are based on the six dimensions defined in the Zachman framework.

We are currently evaluating this approach in real organizations using teams that are aware of the framework structure and who have agreed on the rules for activity decomposition. These results will be reported in the near future. Our ongoing work also includes understanding the relationships between the Zachman framework's rows and columns as well as the joint criteria that can be obtained from them. It is also important to analyse the correct sequencing of the criteria in order to define a business process modelling method within a given context.

8. REFERENCES

1. Coelho J. Taking a Business Object View of a Business Process, Business Process Management Conference Europe, 2005.
2. Davenport TH, Short JE. "The New Industrial Engineering: Information Technology and Business Process Redesign," Sloan Management Review, Summer 1990, 11-27.
3. Davenport TH. "Reengineering: Business Change of Mythic Proportions?" MIS Quarterly, July, 1994; 121-127.
4. Grover V, Jeong SR, Kettinger WJ, Teng JTC. "The Implementation of Business Process Reengineering," Journal of Management Information Systems, 1995; 12(1), 109-144.
5. Hammer M. "Reengineering Work: Don't Automate, Obliterate," Harvard Business Review, July-August, 1990, 104-112.

---

[1] ASG-Rochade (www.asg.com); planningIT (www.alfabet.de); System Architect (www.telelogic.com)

6. Hammer M, Champy J. Reengineering the Corporation: A Manifesto for Business Revolution. London: Nicholas Brealey Publishing, 2001: 38-42.
7. ISO. ISO/IEC 10746 ODP Reference Model.: International Standards Organization, 1995.
8. Labovitz G, Rosansky V. Power of Alignment: How Great Companies Stay Centered and Accomplish Extraordinary Things. New York: John Wiley & Sons Inc, 1997: 52-55.
9. Laudon K, Laudon J. Management Information Systems. New Jersey: Prentice Hall, 2000: 78-79.
10. Malone TW, Crowston K, Herman GA. Organizing Business Knowledge: The MIT Process Handbook. Cambridge, MA: MIT Press, 2003.
11. Maropoulos, PG. Digital Enterprise Technology – Defining Perspectives and Research Priorities, Proceedings of the 1st CIRP International Seminar on Digital Enterprise Technology, Durham, UK, 16-17, September 2002, 3-12.
12. OMG. Unified Modeling Language: Superstructure, version 2.0.: Object Management Group. 2005: Retrieved December, 15 2005, from http://www.omg.org/cgi-bin/doc?ptc/2004-10-02.
13. Simpson, JA. The Oxford English Dictionary, Second Edition. Oxford University Press, USA; 2 edition, 1989.
14. Pereira C, Sousa P. A Method to Define an Enterprise Architecture using the Zachman Framework. In Haddad, H., Omicini, A., Wainwright, R. & Liebrock, L. (Eds.): Proceedings of the 2004 ACM Symposium on Applied Computing (SAC), (pp. 1366-1371). Nicosia, Cyprus, 2004.
15. Pereira C, Sousa P. Enterprise architecture: business and IT alignment. In Haddad, H., Liebrock, L., Omicini, A. & Wainwright, R. (Eds.): Proceedings of the 2005 ACM Symposium on Applied Computing, (pp. 1344-1345). Santa Fe, New Mexico, USA, 2005.
16. Porter ME, Miller, VE. 'How information gives you competitive advantage', Harvard Business Review, 1985, 63 (4), 149–160.
17. Sousa P, Pereira C, Marques J. Enterprise Architecture Alignment Heuristics. Microsoft Architects Journal, 2004; 4, 34-39
18. Sowa J, Zachman J. Extending and formalizing the framework for information systems architecture. IBM Systems Journal, 1992: 31, 590-616.
19. Spewak S, Hill S. Enterprise Architecture Planning: Developing a Blueprint for Data, Applications and Technology. New Jersey: Wiley-QED Publication, 1992:85-112.
20. Towers S, Burlton R. In Search Of BPM Excellence: Straight From The Thought Leaders. Meghan Kiffer Pr, 2005: 119-130.
21. W3C. Web Services: World Wide Web Consortium. 2002: Retrieved December, 15 2005, from http://www.w3.org/2002/ws/
22. Zachman J. A Framework for Information Systems Architecture. IBM Systems Journal, 1987: 26(3), 276-292.

SESSION 4

ENTERPRISE INTEGRATION TECHNOLOGIES

A FRAMEWORK TO INTEGRATE MANUFACTURING INFORMATION SYSTEMS

Li Kuang and James Gao
School of Engineering, UK
l_kuang@hotmail.com, james.gao@cranfield.ac.uk

Information systems play a critical role in today's manufacturing business, and the need for enterprise-wide integrated information system has grown rapidly. Although there are different integration approaches reported in the published literature, in today's industrial practice, most of the information system integration projects are still done on a trial-and-error basis owing to the lack of practical and feasible integration methodologies. This research proposed an integration framework which provides a logical and structured methodology to tackle information systems integration problems in real-world manufacturing environments. The framework is driven by the corporate strategy of manufacturing enterprises. The 'Decomposing-and-Mapping' method, normally used in the engineering axiomatic design approach, has been utilised here in a novel setting to design an integrated manufacturing information system.

1. INTRODUCTION

Information systems play a critical role in today's manufacturing business, and the need for enterprise-wide integrated information system has grown rapidly, as isolated information systems represent inadequate business solutions. In order to successfully and profitably operate in rapidly changing markets, we need to integrate different information systems such as enterprise resource planning system (ERP), supply chain management (SCM), and customer relationship management (CRM) in a company (Chang, 2000). The current interests in manufacturing industry focus heavily on integrating isolated computer-based systems into a unified system, which handles and transforms information among these systems to facilitate a smooth production environment (Aldakhilallah and Ramesh, 2003).

This paper proposed an integration framework which provides a logical and structured methodology to tackle information systems integration problems in real-world manufacturing environments.These rules should be followed in order to guarantee the consistency in the proceedings book.

2. MAIN ISSUES FOR THE DESIGN OF INTEGRATED INFORMATION SYSTEM

Although manufacturing companies have benefited from integrated information systems, some disappointing results from the heavy investment in the large information systems are an obvious signal to the companies to suggest there lacks a sound framework to align business strategy, information flow, and the design of integrated information systems.

Four types of integration in the Enterprise Integration have been identified (Vernadat, 1996), i.e., Presentation integration, Data integration, Functional integration and Process integration. Presentation integration aims to provide a uniform look and feel for user interfaces of different programs. Data integration is the system integration to which application tools are able to share common data and information. Functional integration is the system integration to which applications are able to interact with each other by requesting and providing functional services. Application tools communicate by means of events or requests. Process integration concerns the ability to embed function of different applications in one process. Integration can also be classified as internal and external integration. Within enterprise information system, there are different sub-systems which provide different functions to organisations. External integration, such as integration between ERP system and CAD, even NC machines, bridges the information system with other applications. The benefits of such external integration are greater, however, they are difficult to achieve. An integrated information system should enable various functions within an organisation to obtain the right information in real-time thereby enabling the company to gain competitive edge over competitors.

Another main issue identified by international researchers is the alignment of manufacturing strategy with integration process of information systems (Grant, 2003). Ellis (1999) pointed out that the implementation of an integrated manufacturing information system formed part of the strategic approach to satisfy the corporate objectives. There is a general weakness in the current manufacturing integration approaches, i.e., it lacks specific guidance or techniques to help the manufacturing companies to integrate their information systems, especially in linking their manufacturing strategy to the integration project. Manufacturing strategy is the set of co-ordinated tasks and decisions in manufacturing environment which need to be taken in order to achieve the company's required competitive performance objectives. Therefore, the information system and other systems should be integrated and serve the purpose defined the manufacturing strategy. The manufacturing strategy needs to be converted into a set of detailed and achievable targets for information system implementation.

3. DESIGN OF THE PROPOSED FRAMEWORK

This section explains the underlying principles of the proposed framework for information system integration. The proposed framework is divided into five stages with fifteen steps to give a step-by-step procedure for the analysis and implementation. The stages should be followed sequentially, as each stage requires the information and analysis input from the preceding stage, as shown in figure 1.

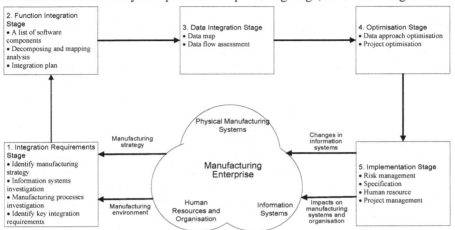

Figure 1 - The Proposed Framework for Information System Integration.

3.1 Integration Requirements

The first stage of the proposed framework is integration requirement stage. This stage focuses on the identifying manufacturing strategy, investigation of information systems and manufacturing environments, and captures the key integration requirements. This allows the manufacturing information system designers to formalize and increase their understanding of the vision of the business, manufacturing functions and information systems and to provide a record of the state of the enterprise when the objectives of integrating manufacturing information systems was proposed, and the integrated systems was designed. The key integration requirements are then captured.

Manufacturing strategy is about a set of co-ordinated tasks and decisions in manufacturing environment which need to be taken in order to achieve the company's required competitive performance objectives. During the integration process, the manufacturing strategy needs to be converted into a set of key integration requirements which are detailed and achievable targets for information system development and implementation. They are highest level functional requirements that cover different systems or different sub-systems within information system. Integration between the systems is a crucial task in the system development.

The key integration requirements should also be made with the knowledge of the limitations and the functional attributes that manufacturing information systems are able to achieve, after the investigation of manufacturing information system.

3.2 Function Integration

Once manufacturing strategy and key integration requirements have been identified, the information system integration plan can be developed based on the requirements. Integration plan will be produced against each key integration requirements at the end of this stage. Upon obtaining the information about manufacturing functions and information systems, a 'decomposing-and-mapping' methodology has been utilised to design an integrated manufacturing information system.

Suh (1990) defined design as the creation of synthesised solutions in the form of products, processes or systems that satisfy perceived needs through the proper mapping of the functional requirements (FR) in functional space with the design parameters (DP) of the physical space, as shown in figure 2. A decomposition process named zig-zagging is used. Only after the higher level requirement is satisfied, can the lower level functional requirements be decomposed. Since new information about the functional requirements and the design parameters have to be updated in order to be processed with synthesis, neither functional requirements nor design parameters can be decomposed independently. Two important techniques used in this design methodology are decomposition and mapping. More importantly, the definition of functional requirements and the selection of design parameters are governed by the two design axioms, i.e.,

- **Axiom 1: The Independence Axiom, which maintains the independence of functional requirements (FRs); and**
- **Axiom 2: The Information Axiom, which minimises the information content of the design.**

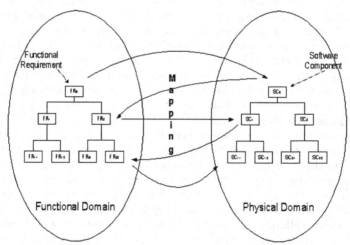

Figure 2 - Decomposing and Mapping in Suh's Axiomatic Design Theory.

This methodology is used not only in product design (Suh, 1990, Jiao and Tseng, 1999) but also in manufacturing system design (Suh, 1990).

The following points should be noted in the design of the integrated information system, i.e.:

- The hierarchical structure of the functional and physical domains can be decomposed and prioritised;

- There is a correspondence between each level of the functional and the physical hierarchies; and
- It becomes meaningless if FRs at the i level is decomposed into the next level without proper mapping onto the physical domain and then develops a solution that satisfies the i level FRs with all the corresponding DPs.

In this stage, the functions in the information system need to be decomposed into more detailed sub-functions further down the structure hierarchy in this stage. The higher-level function describes the main purpose of the subject system and the lower-level function blocks describe the supporting sub-systems which exist to serve the upper levels. At the uppermost level, it is the key integration requirement derived from manufacturing strategy. Data and function are considered together. An integration plan will be generated at the end of this stage. A structured procedure which subdivides the key integration requirement into further processes can help in practice to solve the difficulties in developing the integration plan.

3.3 Data Integration

The third stage of this framework is data integration using data analysis techniques. The main tasks are to investigate information flow in the integration plan, and identify any information flow bottleneck.

The first step of this stage intends to model the high level information flows within the manufacturing organization. It intended to give system integration designers a detail level of the manufacturing information systems from data point of view. In this step, it employed standard methods such as Data Flow Diagram to specify its functionality, and the Logic Data Model to define its data and data flow structure among manufacturing processes and software components. At the end of this step, it might be possible to find that there are no information flow between manufacturing functions, or the data entities links are insufficient to pass information needed by from one manufacturing function another one, further investigation on the proposed integration plan are needed.

The second step of this stage intends to identify any data flow bottleneck in the proposed integration plan, and to determine the best integration solution by utilizing data measure techniques to access the information flow between the software components of information systems. This constitutes two levels of data flow assessment, i.e., Simple data measurement and Comprehensive data measurement. Simple data measurement is a technique which only measures the data flow within the software system. It focuses on the software program and related data entities. Software metrics or software measurement is suggested to be most appropriate method for measuring data flow if it only considers the data flow within software system. Comprehensive data measurement is a technique to measure the data flow from different angle in order to provide a comprehensive view of the data flow. In the real life situation, measuring data flow could be much complicated than just investigating software system. Not only software system, but also the volume of data, computer network and user interface affect the data flow. This research considers six integration criteria, i.e., currency, content, quality, flexibility, importance and scalability, to provide a comprehensive view to evaluate the data flow within information systems of manufacturing organizations.

3.4 Integration Optimization

In this research, various tools are used to optimize the resource allocation in achieving the strategic goals. One of the difficulties in the integration process is how to balance the different contributions of individual software components and the investment. The Goal Programming techniques are used to produce the best solution according to a set of criteria. Whilst appreciating this difference, the proposed method considered all software components and their inter-dependencies to propose an optimal solution relative to the business objectives.

This stage starts with the optimization of the software and related resource allocation using the results from data map. There is a relationship between the software size and data density/data flow. A high count for data input and output in software means a large or complex task for the software. Therefore it costs more time and labour in an integration project comparing with others. If the total number of days is already allocated to an integration project, the number of days for each software component can be computed according to the data entities. It is intended to give optimization solution for a single project in this step.

3.5 Integration Implementation

The final stage of the framework consists of planning and performing the actual implementation of the integration project, including risk management, specification, human resource management, and the progress of the implementation.

Risk management is a tool to help users to identify the potential risk in the integration project, and to understand what investment and work might be at risk if the integration is abandoned and what delays might result if potential, identified events come. Specification, human resource management, and project management specify the needs for controlling the implementation project, which will help to convert the integration plan into a working system.

Integration specification is a comprehensive document describing the integrated system. All user requirements and functions should be considered for their relevance to the system being designed, and all the required data are included. Based upon the analysis done in previous steps, a new system design is already confirmed. At this step the requirements are expanded to give detail necessary to build the system. A typical specification should at least include hardware, software, database, networking, interface, schedule of the implementation and the cost.

Implementing integrated information systems is not a matter of changing software systems; rather it is a matter of repositioning the company and transforming the business practices. Due to enormous impact on the competitive advantage of the company, top management must show its commitment before embarking on the project. The project management tool should be used to ensure the integration project finish on time and on budget. The project control assumes that the overall integration project has been signed off, and has been decided that complete project is going to start. At the outset, a blueprint needs to be produced for the project. This will give the whole project a purpose, with appropriate benchmarking at strategic project landmarks. The formulation of the implementation plan should revolve around the key integration requirements, by taking each in turn and identifying the requirements needed to satisfy them.

4. APPLICATION DEVELOPMENT OF THE FRAMEWORK

The framework discussed in the previous section has been implemented within an Enterprise Resource Planning (ERP) system. User interface is Graphical User Interface. The main part of the implemented framework, or the prototype system, was developed based upon a Baan ERP environment which is installed on the Unix server. Some parts of the prototype system were located in a Microsoft Window server, and can be accessed through the main interface. Users can access the prototype system through the Local Area Network (LAN). The five modules of the prototype system are Integration Requirements Module, Function Integration Design Module, Data Integration Module, Optimization Module, and Implementation Module, as shown in figure 3.

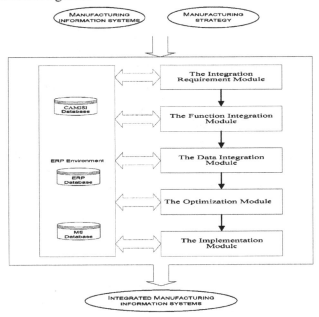

Figure 3 - The Structure of the Application System.

An application has been carried out and tested in an UK rail transportation company. The company intends to offer customers a complete range of attractive, modular rolling stock, support services, signaling and total rail systems. Its mission is to be in a position to be the single source providing fast, efficient and reliable solutions for rail transport needs. An integration project in the sales and marketing department of the company has been used to demonstrate how to use the framework and prototype system. The sales and marketing department of the company plays a pivotal role in the business. Integrating the parts tendering process in the information systems is the main goal of this project. The parts tendering is the most difficult job in the sales and marketing department. There are five people employed in the department to handle this process, including the customer enquiries, purchasing and scheduling of the production order. And even that, occasionally there were mistakes in the order scheduling and parts purchasing due to the human error. The management hoped that an integrated information system would improve the quality of the parts, reduce human error, and reduce the costs. This eventually leads to high quality products and services. On successful implementing the integrated information system, the staff on controlling Parts Tendering had been reduced from 5 to 3. The company also found error made during the process has been reduced significantly. Customer order delivery on-time has been improved to new high level.

5. CONCLUSIONS

This project proposed, implemented and tested a novel framework for enterprise information system integration. At the centre of the framework, is the manufacturing strategy which drives the information system integration process. This approach considers information systems in a holistic manner and emphasises the importance of the corporate strategy in the whole process of integration. The developed framework provides practical guidelines for industrial implementation and a software tool which can be used to go through the five stages and fifteen steps to give users a comprehensive solution. The proposed framework enables a company to assess its own business problems and the availability of its resources so that it is able to establish a realistic integration plan. The use of example application of the prototype software suggests that the proposed framework is valid and can bring real benefits to business. The framework includes a 'decomposing-and-mapping' methodology based on the axiomatic design approach, which is a technique so far used for physical product design. This project proves, for the first time, that this technique can also be used for information system integration design.

6. REFERENCES

1. Aldakhilallah, K. A. and Ramesh, R., 2003. "Computer techniques and applications of automated process planning in manufacturing systems" In: by Leondes, C. (Ed.), Computer aided and integrated manufacturing systems, World Scientific, New Jersey, USA.
2. Chang, H. H., (2000), "The Implementation and Integration of Information Systems for Production Management in Manufacturing: an Empirical Study", Int. Journal of computer Integrated Manufacturing, Vol. 13, pp. 369 – 387.
3. Coronado Mondragon, A. E., 2002. "Determining information systems contribution to manufacturing agility for SME's in dynamic business environments," PhD Thesis, Brunel University, UK.
4. Ellis, R. R., 1999. "Strategically-driven analysis and implementation of an integrated manufacturing information system," PhD Thesis, Cranfield University, Cranfield, UK.
5. Grant, G. G., 2003. "Strategic alignment and enterprise systems implementation: the case of Metalco," Journal of Information Technology, Vol. 18, No. 3, pp. 159 – 175.
6. Jiao, J., Tseng, M.M. (1999) A requirement management database system for product definition, Integrated Manufacturing Systems, Vol. 10, No. 3, 146 –153.
7. Kusiak, A., 2000. "Computational intelligence in design and manufacturing," John Wiley & Sons Inc, New York, USA.
8. Suh, N.P., 1990. "The principles of design." Oxford University Press, New York, USA.

IMPLEMENTATION OF COLLABORATION MODEL WITHIN SME'S

Adrian Guniš, Ján Šišlák and Štefan Valčuha
Slovak University of Techologie, Slovac Republic
{adrian.gunis jan.sislak, stefan.valcuha}@stuba.sk

World globalization affects customers and push toward rapid products replacement. Companies compete to get their product on the market first. Continual reduction of product life cycle and in product development time results in perpetual change of processes. This puts enormous pressure on engineering activities (design, production, logistics, etc.) to be performed with higher quality and in shorter time. In this paper is presented the research project "Research and Implementation of the Virtual Enterprise Model - RIVEM" which deals with co-operation among SME's. Its aim is to implement collaboration tools within companies to be able to perform activities electronically connected with product development and production to cooperate with other participating partners. In this research project manufacturing companies geographically spread cooperate. Although the paradigm of Virtual Enterprise itself is exploited on reasonable level, the technical and technological solutions that allow companies to work in qualitative new environment, have only begun to be implemented in the SME's. The groundwork of this project is focused on homogenous and holistic solutions to make the virtual enterprise operational.

1. INTRODUCTION

Nowadays the environment where companies compete is under significant change. Setting processes within small and medium enterprises (SME's) to sustain competitiveness is being crucial for facing new challenges. Companies have to deal with more exacting requirements within more complex projects. It is difficult to handle the cooperation and coordination among geographically distributed partners, and what is more this becomes the order of the day.

Continual time reduction of product life cycle and product development results in perpetual change of processes. This puts on engineering activities (design, planning, production, logistics, etc.) enormous pressure that have to be performed with higher quality and in shorter time. These increasing pressures are driving organizations to work in ways that overlap the traditional approach.

2. VIRTUAL ENTERPRISES

2.1 Concepts of Virtual Enterprise

The virtual enterprise can be understood as an organization structure unit, a strategy of the company to handle constant scenario or a way to manage processes in single company or among all cooperating companies.

A large number of research publications focus on the benefits brought by virtual enterprises (VE)/virtual organizations (VO). The idea of highly dynamic organizations forms according to the needs and opportunities of the market, as well as remaining operational as long as these opportunities persist (Camarinha-Matos, L. M., Afsarmanesh, H., 2003).

Enterprise interconnection allows companies to share resources. Cooperation of companies enables to accomplish more complex projects.

Contributing entities are added to the network when they can add value and are disengaged as their competencies as long as they are no longer required. This poses a specific set of requirements on the capabilities and resources of organizations that take part or want to take part in a virtual organization (Saabeel, W. et al., 2002).

The main contributions of the VE paradigm:

- Growing complexity of projects
- Shortening of product life cycle
- Increasing the productivity
- Flexibility and agility
- Cost reduction
- Sharing resources (knowledge, information …)

The concept of VE is supported by the newest Information and Communication Technology (ICT) and enables enterprise to cope with processes exacting cooperation and engineering issues.

1.2.   Collaboration in Virtual Enterprise

It is usual that between development centers and production facilities are quite big distances. The development of complex product brings together large number different mutually independent companies figure 1. This creation of efficient cooperation entities leads to intricate organizational unit.

Figure 1 - Virtual Enterprise – cooperating enterprises.

Research publications concerning the VE collaboration address the general processes that have to be done (set up and break up). The area of implementation research of specific process operation to the VE environment is rare. However, this appears as the limiting factor in real enterprise operation as well.

The implementation and configuration of a supporting ICT infrastructure requires considerable engineering effort. This is still an obstacle to dynamic VE's (Hannus, M. et al., 2004).

During the product design and its production it is necessary to handle large number of processes. To deal with this, it is necessary to bring the final solution, which consists of combination of many independent support tools. Therefore, the interconnections are inevitable among supporting systems. This leads to continual work process with respect to design, development, testing and production.

From this viewpoint can be differentiated support tools for engineering activities as followed:

- CAx systems (CAD, CAM, CAQ, CAE, …)
- PLx systems (PDM, ERP, CRM, SCM,…)

The next category could comprise of collaboration tools. But in this could arise a polemic if this should be not included in the PLx systems category. The set of collaboration tools:

- Communication systems (MSN Messenger, Sametime, NetMeeting, Skype, ICQ, …)
- CAD viewers (DWG Viewer, Autodesk DWF Viewer, SolidWorks 2005 Viewer, VoloView Express, WHIP, PS-Exchange, Bentley View, DWF Composer, eDrawings)
- Design Collaboration Modules (ProE –PTC, Catia V5 - Dessault Systems) with communication backbone (Groove, Netmeeting)

- Project management tools (MainsGate, Flypaper Enterprise Collaboration Platform, TeamSpace, eRoom Collaboration, Groove Workspace, PH Projekt, TUTOS, TeamCrossing, IBM LOTUS Team Workspace, IBM Lotus Quickplace, eProject, ePeople)

2. PRODUCTION ENVIRONMENT IN SME'S

Impact of the virtual enterprise paradigm, its relatively open and easily reconfigurable structure, affects the way of work. In general, companies focus on their core competencies and the missing elements are outsourced. The companies define the specifications and submit them to potential suppliers. In this point appears that the key factor for SME's is the ability to prepare detailed project proposals in a very short time. This becomes a barrier in context of project proposal complexity. Handling of this important issue and to place the order, relies on the processes within the company.

During the preparation period, from the order acceptation to the final proposal presentation, is maintained the majority of groundwork procedures needed for the real production process. But in fact the manufacturing company haven't had signed the contract and the whole proposal was made without any assurance that the order will be approved by customer figure 2.

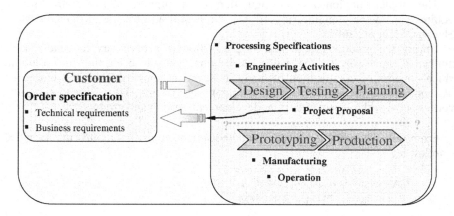

Figure 2 - Procedure of project proposal and ongoing production.

From the company point of view appear two approaches for the collaboration. Firstly, collaboration process is between the customer and company. Secondly, the next collaboration process could be focused on collaboration among teams within the single company. In fact it is going here about almost the same processes; if it is not taken on account the different software equipment in companies.

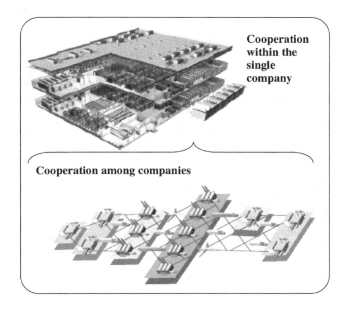

Figure 3 - Cooperation in a single and among manufacturing companies.

Processes provided within single company, have to be operated also in terms of enterprise collaboration.

The development and operations of Extended Manufacturing Enterprises often suffer from insufficient co-operation within the manufacturing company (Higgins, P. et al., 2005). This pushes companies to standardize their processes, which are already partly enforced by big companies during the supplier selection.

In the past, the implementation of team collaboration tools was mainly oriented to designing teams. This implementation leaked also to the manufacturing area, where the designed part comes to real environment. Assembly, its process stability as the final points verified the whole design. The need of modification has to be operated with assistance of process engineers.

It is the reason why engineers call for efficient collaboration tools not only in product development but also in production areas. For them, it is essential to work together and to bring the concept to real a product (Šišlák, J. and Valčuha, Š., 2005).

Within a complex project as a car surely is, may appear problems during the assembly of series prototype with component supply of different suppliers. Here the problem emerges because of different design versions. At the end during the assembly of series prototype are different versions of components assembled. Therefore, next very necessary requirement is to implement project collaboration tools. It should be considered the collaboration at lowest levels of company structure as well.

3. RESEARCH FOCUS

The research project "Research and Implementation of the Virtual Enterprise Model - RIVEM" deals with co-operation among SME's. Its aim is to implement collaboration tools within companies to be able perform electronically activities connected with product development and production to cooperate with other participating partners.

Inside this research project cooperate geographically distributed manufacturing companies. Although the own paradigm of Virtual Enterprise is exploited on sufficient level, the technical and technological solutions which allows companies to work in qualitative new environment, only start to be implemented in the SME's.

Groundwork of this project is focused on homogenous and holistic solution for operation the virtual enterprise.

Within this project was created preliminary model of Information system and model of project collaboration.

4. COLLABORATION MODEL

The very first step of implementation process of the collaboration model was the intimate analyze of conditions in manufacturing companies. Introduction of VE paradigm for companies brought overview which resulted to specification the expectation of companies. As well were analyzed tools to integrate the virtual and physical work of companies. From this analyze was concluded the cooperation structure figure 4. The role of central coordinator is playing Dept. of Manufacturing Systems.

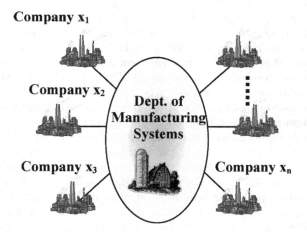

Figure 4 - Structure of cooperation model.

During the collaboration with Slovak companies was examined that the internal collaboration activities within the company have big gaps. Therefore, the research project is firstly focused on the internal processes which results can be exploited also in the outward processes.

The collaboration model of the project considers data sharing and processing with respect to the exploitation of manufacturing potential (human resources, machines, tools, fixtures...). It takes on account as well tools that involve support for communication and online product consultations in native design environment.

The preliminary model consists of tools focused on collaboration support:

- Communication system - MSN Messenger
- CAD viewer - eDrawings
- Design Collaboration Module of Catia V5 with communication backbone Netmeeting
- Project management tool (not specified yet)

This model is a starting point for future enlargement. In present time is the work orientated toward the information system and project collaboration.

5. DISCUSSION

Recent way of cooperation puts high demands on social factor in system. This includes communication, coordination, sharing information and applications among geographically distributed partners. Technical requirements which arise together with collaboration strategy of VE consist especially in new processes operation.

There is however the need for a more holistic understanding of the area, namely in terms of the emerging collaborative teams, and the optimization of the support infrastructure and tools. It is also important to reach harmonization of models and approaches in order to achieve inter-operability.

During online product consultations engineers call for support that involves effective communication. The video conferences together with prepared presentations do not offer possibility to discuss effectively detailed technical issues (design modifications and associated simulations...) (Somora, et al., 2005). From this point of view prepared presentations create boundaries due to of ad hoc solutions.

These increasing pressures are driving engineers to work in ways that challenge traditional information and collaboration systems.

6. CONCLUSION

Even though the systems for VE support are partly implemented in companies their mutual cooperation is lacking. Therefore, it is the need for an integrated approach leading to truly joint of work of different areas.

It is important to mention also the legal and trust issues which appear as a hold back factor. These issues arise together with setting up the partner cooperation.

7. ACKNOWLEDGMENTS

This paper has been written within the project "RIVEM - Research and Implementation of Virtual Enterprise Model" granted by Slovak Grant Agency for Science, under project identification. number VTP AV/1014/2003.

8. REFERENCES

1. Hannus, M., Anastasiou, M., Bifulco, A., Findeisen, P., Karvonen, I., Löh, H., Plüss, A., Ollus, M., Weidemann, M., 2004, Guidelines for Virtual Organizations, pp. 1-32, VTT Technical Research Centre of Finland, Espoo.
2. Higgins, P., Eschenbächer, J., Strandhagen, J. O.,   Horten, A., 2005, "An Operations Model for the Extended Manufacturing Enterprise", in Integrated Engineering of Products, Services and Organizations, ed. by Pawar, K. S., Weber, F., Thoben, K. D., Katzy, B., Munich
3. Camarinha-Matos, L. M., Afsarmanesh, H., 2003, "Elements of a base VE infrastructure", Computers in Industry, Vol. 51, pp. 139-163
4. Somora, D., Šišlák J., Tolnay, M., Valčuha, Š., 2005, Model of Cooperation among Small and Medium Enterprises within Virtual Enterprise, in the Networked Enterprise: a challenge for a sustainable development, Fisciano
5. Šišlák, J., Valčuha, Š., 2005, "Model of Small and Medium Enterprises within Virtual Enterprises", in Computers Integrated Manufacturing, ed. by Skolud Gliwice, pp. 254-257
6. Saabeel, W., Verduijn, T.M., Hagdorn , L., Kumar, K., 2002, "A Model of Virtual organization: A Structure and Process Perspective", Electronic Journal of Organizational Virtualness, Vol. 4, No. 1, pp. 1-16
7. Zhou, M., Nemes, L., Shimonome, M., Hasimoto, H., Fuse, A., Bernus, P., Uppington, G., 1998, "A framework for design a virtual manufacturing enterprise and its implementation as a workbench", Information Infrastructure Systems for Manufacturing II, pp.1-22

FRAMEWORK FOR A KNOWLEDGE SUPPORT SYSTEM FOR DISTRIBUTED COLLABORATIVE DESIGN PROJECTS

Aurelie Vacher and Daniel Brissaud
3S Laboratory, Grenoble, France
{aurelie.vacher, daniel.brissaud}@hmg.inpg.fr

Engineering design projects are more and more often developed in network of R&D services of several companies. It is particularly the case of projects developed in the context of European Network of Excellence (NoE). Such a research network is characterized by assignments. One of them is new knowledge creation; it represents the core of the network assignments. In this paper, we aim to characterize the process of new knowledge creation in collaborative and distributed scientific research context. Then we suggest some specifications and a framework for a system to support the creation of new knowledge in a context of distributed collaborative project of engineering design.

1. INTRODUCTION

Nowadays, worldwide economy and competition often lead companies to set up temporary alliances with other companies. These alliances enable product or service development within a short period by making the best use of all the available resources (people, data, hardware, software). This distributed structure is called Virtual Enterprise (VE) (Harwick, 1997) and is supported by an interconnected information network. This computing environment is mandatory for the virtual enterprise to exist. Indeed, it enables collaboration between all the participants wherever they are located in the world. Our interest in this paper is focused on the early stages of a research and development (R&D) project in a virtual enterprise. We aim to analyze how new knowledge is created in such a context and how it is or it should be supported.

In section 2, we try to characterize a R&D project in a virtual enterprise by identifying its assignments and the existing tools that can support each of those assignments. Section 3 deals with the activity of knowledge production in such a context. We identify the requirements to support this activity. To finish, we suggest, in section 4, a framework for a system supporting knowledge creation in virtual enterprises R&D projects.

2. R&D PROJECT CHARACTERIZATION IN A VIRTUAL ENTERPRISE

2.1 Assignments of R&D

R&D consists in "discovering new knowledge about products, processes and services, and then applying that knowledge to create new and improved products, processes and services that fill market needs"[1]. This definition highlights the two main sides of R&D: on the one hand, new knowledge production implied by research and, on the other hand, the reuse of this new knowledge in order to develop new applications.

In this paper, we focus on the early stages of a R&D project, that is to say new knowledge production. However, we have to keep in mind that this new knowledge is to be reused afterwards.

2.2 Distributed R&D project and virtual teams

A R&D project is composed of a team of people and a common objective (developing a new product or service, improving a production process, etc.). The companies people work in are also involved. But in virtual enterprise, the team of people is not a traditional working group: in this context, teams are virtual teams. Thus, what does make a virtual team different from a traditional working group?

The main differential factor lies certainly in face to face situation (Coat, 1998). Indeed, in a traditional working group, people are often brought together in order to work. In a virtual team, people are geographically distributed, consequently face to face situations become scarce. Due to this difference, virtual teams need a technological support for team members to be able to work together. They need an informational environment by way of place (for information sharing) and a technological infrastructure by way of time (for asynchronous communication). To sum up, virtual teams require technological means to free themselves from place and time constraints. Nevertheless, technology does not solve all the problems, it brings new difficulties too. Moreover as explained afterwards, time constraints cannot be always avoided due to activities that require synchronous work.

2.3 Tools for supporting collaborative work

Some of the tools for supporting collaborative work already exist. On what concerns information sharing, there exist file sharing applications, collaborative word processors, collaborative portals (such as wiki[2] websites), group calendars, etc. or applications that gather all those functionalities. Regarding communication tools, emails and forums enable asynchronous communication whereas chat, videoconference, telephone, voice IP enable synchronous communication. In this category, there also exist software for application sharing.

---

[1] From the online dictionary http://www.investorwords.com.
[2] A wiki is a piece of server software that allows users to freely create and edit Web page content using any Web browser.

All those tools can support communication and collaborative documents gathering or building but none of them can really support knowledge production as defined in next section.

3. KNOWLEDGE PRODUCTION IN SUCH A CONTEXT

Knowledge production consists in series of tasks. Once the team is constituted and the common objective and individual roles are clarified, a research project often begins with grouping literature about existing knowledge of the concerned domain. Then a synthesis is written in form of state of the art. Then, a brain storming task is launched in order to catch all the new ideas of all the participants, followed by a selection task in order to collect the adoptable solutions. Among those tasks, it is possible to identify two categories: opening tasks and closing tasks (Coat, 1998).

Brain storming and grouping literature are *opening tasks*. That is to say that all the individual contributions are additive. It is an accumulation of documents and ideas. This task can be a synchronous or an asynchronous task. It can be modeled by an opening funnel (see figure 1). On the contrary, synthesis and especially selection tasks are *closing tasks*. The team has a group of ideas, data and information that has to be reduced. The addition of all the individual contributions cannot constitute the solution of the group. It can be modeled by a closing funnel (see figure 1). Thus, for closing tasks, negotiation between the team members is necessary to find the group solution. As a consequence, it has to be a synchronous task so as to enable discussion.

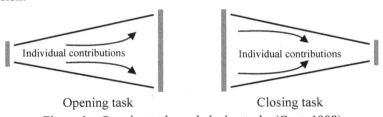

Opening task   Closing task

Figure 1 – Opening tasks and closing tasks (Coat, 1998).

For opening tasks, ideas can be stored in documents and collected with a file sharing system so that every team member can consult all the documents. Distant meetings (videoconferences) can be organized for each member to present his ideas to the whole team. The problem is that all the ideas are embedded in the documents (often text documents). The accumulation of documents does not provide a big picture of all the suggestions and then the selection task is very difficult. Thus, knowledge production requires a specific support in order to facilitate the emergence of new solutions, therefore new knowledge.

4. FRAMEWORK PROPOSAL FOR A SYSTEM SUPPORTING KNOWLEDGE PRODUCTION IN DISTRIBUTED R&D PROJECTS

4.1 Requirements for supporting knowledge production

As we explained in the previous section, what we need here is a support for the knowledge production stage. As a consequence, this support has to enable knowledge representation. Moreover, in our collaborative context, this support has to enable discussion between individuals and negotiation around existing knowledge and emerging knowledge (especially for the closed tasks we have introduced above).

Those two specifications lead us to the concept maps (or conceptual maps). A concept map is a tool that is used to represent knowledge in a visual way. As we said in section 3, knowledge is usually embedded in documents and mainly in textual documents. The difficulty with such documents is that knowledge (concepts, ideas...) is drowned in the text. It is always more difficult to discuss about a text than about a diagram, a draw or a schema. Thus visual representation makes discussion be much easier.

Our idea here is to use concept maps in order to represent existing knowledge and new ideas extracted from different documents and to merge everything into one visual representation. Thus, it would be simpler to discuss and determine what is connected to what and to build new knowledge on this basis.

4.2 Concept maps

Concept maps are diagrams that represent organized knowledge (Novak & Gowin, 1984). Coffey and al (Coffey, 2003) identify four main characteristics concerning concept maps: First, concept maps are composed of concepts and relationships between them. *Concepts* are defined as "a perceived regularity in events or objects, or a record of events or objects, designated by a label". They constitute the nodes of the graph, they are often represented by a labeled box or circle. *Relationships*, the arcs of the graph, are represented by connecting lines that link two concepts together. Those connecting lines include a label, word that specifies the relationship. A triple concept-link-concept is called a *proposition*, which is a meaningful statement (often called a semantic unit). The second characteristic of a concept map is that concepts are organized in a hierarchical way: the most general concepts are at the top of the diagram while more specific concepts are arranged below. The third point deals with *cross-links*. Cross-links are relationships between concepts of different regions or domains within the concept map. This point is very significant for knowledge creation because that kind of link often represents creative leaps for the knowledge producer. The last characteristic is the possibility to include examples or specific objects in order to make the meaning of a concept clearer.

Thus, this kind graph seems to be very interesting to represent knowledge and support knowledge creation in our context. Indeed, this tool is a semi formal graph that is flexible enough to make the visual representation of every kind of knowledge possible, it includes semantic, it allows knowledge creation by facilitating the identification of new relationships between concepts and, to finish, it makes it possible to add specific objects (instantiations of concepts) to support meaning. Next section provides an example of technical knowledge representation through concept map.

4.3 Example: technical knowledge representation

In order to illustrate and validate our ideas, our first trial consists in translating an article about vibratory drilling (Peigne, 2005) into a concept map. We chose this paper because it stems from a very technical work, the kind of work that could presumably be lead in a R&D project. Furthermore, this paper is very rich concerning existing and new knowledge. It is thus interesting to test whether concept maps are suitable for structuring and representing such an amount of knowledge.

The concept map that stems from this paper is shown in figure 2. Hatched boxes represent the mostbom dia general concepts of the map. White boxes are the existing concepts and grey boxes are the new concepts introduced in the article. This figure gives a rough idea of the complexity of the whole map: it is composed of 39 concepts and more than 40 links. Yet, this map is not complete. It indeed represents only a small part of the knowledge embedded in the paper, details are missing. We decided to stop building this concept map because it became unreadable and unusable. Yet, the analysis of this concept map gave us good results.

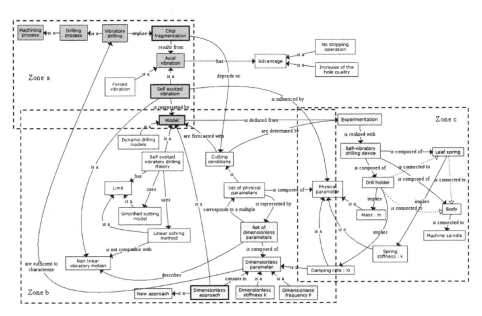

Figure 2 – Conceptual map representing knowledge extracted from (Peigne, 2005)[3].

---

[3] This concept map has been drawn with MotPlus, software edited by the LICEF research center : http://www.licef.teluq.uquebec.ca.

In figure 2, the map is divided into three zones to facilitate the analysis. Zone a gathers the most general concepts. Those concepts enable the reader to fix the context of the knowledge represented in the map. In the example, we know that knowledge is about a machining process and more precisely a drilling process: vibratory drilling, which causes chip fragmentation, etc. We can imagine that those general concepts could permit to connect this conceptual map to a domain ontology in the context of a knowledge management system.

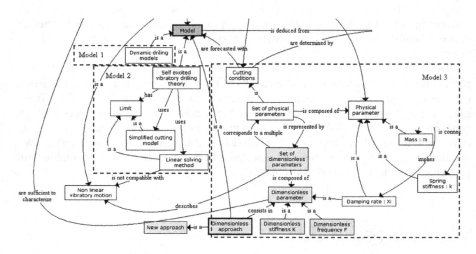

Figure 3 – Zone b: Conceptual representation of the models presented in the paper.

Zone b gathers the representations of the different models presented in the (Peigne, 2005)[4]. They are not represented the same way, depending on the level of details given in the text. Three models are presented: dynamic drilling model, self excited vibratory drilling theory and the dimensionless approach. The latter model is the core of the paper. Those three models are differently represented and we could say that there exist as many possible representations as concept map designers. A consequence is that this kind of representation does not make knowledge easily reusable afterwards. The problem is that the concept entity is a too small unit and people can organize them differently in concept maps even if the represented knowledge is the same. The case is the same for zone c, which gathers all the concepts used to represent knowledge about the experiments presented in (Peigne, 2005). However it is possible to identify permanent features in knowledge representation about models or experiments that leads us to the concept of *brick*.

---

[4] The models are not complete as we said before, because of the complexity of the map. In this instance, equations, hypothesis, etc. are not included in the map.

4.4 The "brick" concept

As we said above, by analyzing the paper about vibratory drilling in details, it is possible to identify permanent features in models or experiments representations. For example, a model can be represented with the following structure: a physical model based on a simplification of reality (schematic representation), on hypothesis and defined on a validity domain; the mathematical model (that stems from the physical model), which is composed of governing equations, which made of mathematical parameters and variables and those mathematical parameters and variables correspond to physical parameters. Thus it is possible to build an entity with a set of pre-structured concepts in order to represent a physical model (see figure 4). A similar analysis leads to the same kind of structure for knowledge representation about experiments (see figure 5). Thus, what we call *bricks* are boxes with pre-structured concepts inside. Moreover, those bricks are not independent; they are connected to each other. For example, we identified that the model brick and the experiment brick are connected to each other with the physical parameters.

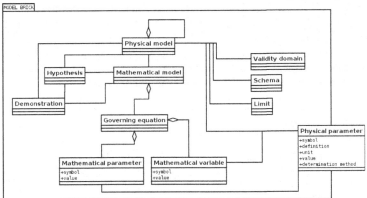

Figure 4 – UML schema of the Model brick.

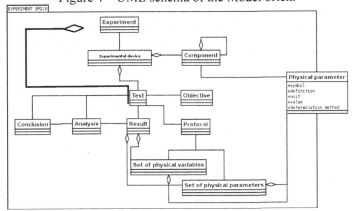

Figure 5 – UML schema of the Experiment brick.

5. CONCLUSION

In this paper, we identified the need of a specific tool that could support knowledge production. Concept map is a known means for representing knowledge. As a graphical tool, it seems to us that this tool is a good basis to support knowledge production by it capacity to give a big picture of the domain showing how everything is or should be related. We have experimented concept map in order to represent highly technical scientific knowledge. This led us to a concept map that was far too complex to be readable or reusable afterwards. Thus, we found a means to enhance concept maps with sets of pre-structured concepts in order to represent specific kinds of knowledge (knowledge about experiments or physical models) in a systematic way that makes it reusable afterwards. Those bricks can be connected to each other and to the most general concepts of the concept map that fix the context.

To conclude, in this paper we started from knowledge representation to finally merely focus on the framework of the system, that is to say how knowledge can be stored and not really represented. Indeed, the bricks are only structures, not real representations of knowledge. We now have to identify and build other bricks that represent knowledge about simulation or empirical laws for example and see how those bricks are connected to each other. Then we have to build a user friendly GUI (Graphical User Interface) that will enable a readable and usable view of the represented knowledge. Indeed, we have to keep in mind that this tool is a support that has to "help" people creating knowledge collaboratively.

6. REFERENCES

1. Coffey JW, Carnot MJ, Feltovich PJ, Feltovich J, Hoffman RR, Cañas AJ, Novak JD. A Summary of Literature Pertaining to the Use of Concept Mapping Techniques and Technologies for Education and Performance Support. Technical Report submitted to the Chief of Naval Education and Training, Pensacola, FL, 2003.
2. Coat F, Courbon JC, Trahand J. Le travail en groupe à l'âge des réseaux. Marc Favier edition, Economica, 1998.
3. Harwick M, Bolton R. The industrial virtual enterprise. Communications of ACM; 40: 59-60, 1997.
4. Novak JD, Gowin DB. Learning how to learn. New York: Cambridge University Press, 1984.
5. Peigne G, Kamnev E, Brissaud D, Gouskov A. Self-excited vibratory drilling: a dimensionless parameter approach for guiding experiments. IMechE 2005; 219: 73-85, 2005.

A CONCEPT FOR THE CONFIGURATION OF VALUE ADDED NETWORKS BASED ON QUALITY CAPABILITIES DURING RAMP-UP

Gisela Lanza and Jörg Ude

Institute of Production Science (wbk), University of Karlsruhe (TH), Germany
{lanza, ude}@wbk.uka.de

The ubiquitous globalization, which opens up new markets with their specific local conditions and labor costs, as well as the increasing pressure regarding time, costs and flexibility lead to the decentralization of the value added. The resulting global value added networks, consisting of company-owned and external sites as well as logistic partners, have to be configured, operated and optimized. An important criterion for these networks is their ability to a fast and efficient ramp-up. This article presents a concept to assess and select potential value added network's nodes (sites or external partners) according to their ramp-up performance to achieve an optimal configuration of the network.

1. INTRODUCTION

Due to shorter product lifecycles the number of production ramp-ups of more and more variable and customer specific products (mass customization) is increasing. The economic pressure to shorter time to market as well as shorter time to customer forces these production ramp-ups to be planned and conducted fast and in shorter intervals (Schuh, 2004; Terwiesch, 1998). Hence production ramp-ups become a major step within the entire product lifecycle which determine the economic success as with the introduction of new products higher product prices can be achieved. The production ramp-up is generally defined as the period between finished product development and the achievement of full production capacity (Terwiesch, 1998).

Due to these shorter product lifecycles and the relatively low quantities, competitive advantages (e.g. through economies of scale) can only be achieved by specializing and concentrating on the companies' core competences (Höbig, 2002). This leads to the decentralization of the value added and in relation to the tendency of increasing globalization to the creation of global value added networks (Wiendahl, 2003; Eversheim, 2000). Value added networks are meant as value adding systems independently from company boundaries, which integrate the intra-organizational view (e.g. sites, cost or profit centers within a company) and the cross company view (inter-organizational, e.g. suppliers).

The objective of these value added networks is a flexible and cost-optimized distribution of the value added, both at company-owned sites as well as at external partners (Fleischer, 2004). For the configuration of these networks not only the conditions of a stable running network have to be taken into account. Due to the economic relevance especially the ramp-up phase has to be considered. For this, the potential value added network's nodes (sites or partners) have to be assessed and selected according to their performance for a fast and cost-efficient ramp-up to achieve an optimal configuration of the value added network.

Production ramp-ups are characterized by their effectiveness and their efficiency (compare figure 1). As the performance of production ramp-ups with given capacities especially depends on the quality of the processes, it is necessary to evaluate the quality capabilities of the different value added activities.

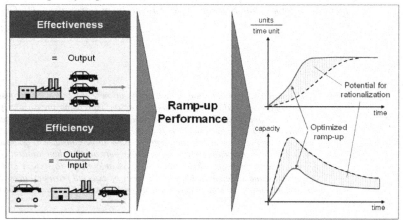

Figure 1 – Potential for rationalization regarding efficiency and effectiveness.

The following approach allows the configuration of value added networks with special consideration of ramp-up costs. It is developed within a research project funded by the Landesstiftung Baden-Württemberg's support program for young scientists. The approach enables producing companies to distribute the value added which is necessary for the production of their products among their sites and partners in a global surrounding. It also allows them to guarantee highest ramp-up performance at optimal quality and costs.

In the following, the basic concepts for the configuration of value added networks and for the evaluation of quality capabilities are described. Based on these concepts the approach of the quality development during ramp-up within the configuration of value added networks and the therefore needed working steps will be presented.

2. CONFIGURATION OF VALUE ADDED NETWORKS BASED ON BUSINESS CAPABILITIES

Within a former research project at the Institute of Production Science (wbk), a method for the configuration of global value added networks was developed

(Fleischer, 2005a). It bases on a model which defines an enterprise's capabilities (Business Capabilities) and the decomposition of value added into Value Added Modules. A Business Capability (BC) is defined as a special ability or characteristic to achieve a specific aim (Curtis, 2002) and describes the value added independent of used technologies and resources. A valid combination of a Business Capability, technologies and resources is called Value Added Module (VAM). By using these resources and technologies Value Added Modules cause the costs of goods and services.

The method bases on the allocation of required Business Capabilities to possible nodes of the value added network (own sites or partners) (compare figure 2) and includes the following steps (Fleischer, 2005b):

- Defining requirements of the planned value added
- Deriving BCs from the determined requirements
- Aligning required BCs with existent BCs at nodes of the network
- Deriving VAMs by combining BCs, technologies and resources
- Balancing the capacities at each node
- Evaluating configuration alternatives using rating functions
- Selecting and implementing the best configuration alternative

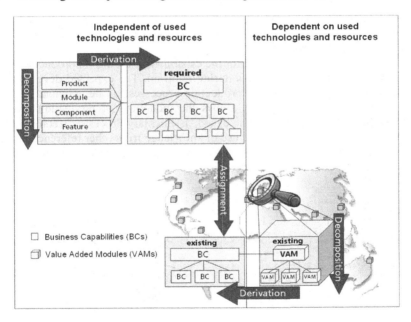

Figure 2 – Approach for configuration of value added networks.

The high complexity due to the number of involved nodes within the configuration process can be reduced by using "Business Capability Maps" (Sternemann, 2005). A Business Capability Map structurally displays the capabilities of enterprises, sites and partners as well as the necessary invest to build up new capabilities.

By reducing the target system including time, quality and costs to a target cost function, which calculates the costs of a stable running network, it is possible to find the best configuration. The method leads to a greater transparency combined with a decrease in risk of wrong decisions and simultaneously to the acceleration of the configuration process.

3. QUALITY DEVELOPMENT DURING RAMP-UP

Whereas the Business Capability concept focuses on the configuration of value added networks consisting of several nodes the approach presented in this chapter concentrates on the production system of one specific node. The approach allows the description, structuring and evaluation of a production system, especially in the unstable condition during production ramp-up and not only for the stable running system (Lanza, 2004).

Controlling the quality capabilities of the production processes is most relevant for a successful production ramp-up. The quality capability is defined as the ability of a production process to meet the required tolerances of the parts' quality criteria (Hering, 1993). In practice, production processes are statistically evaluated only after the start of production. These processes are improved until the capability can be seen as a constant parameter of the process. But during ramp-up, the quality capability cannot be presumed as a constant parameter as quality relevant factors such as people, machines, materials and processes are influenced by various disturbing factors (Englert, 1996).

The approach allows a forecast for the capability of the whole production system and the variable needs of resources during ramp-up. The expected development of the quality capabilities of instable production processes can be anticipated. Core of the approach is a simulation that allows the modelling of production processes, using standardized basic modules, so called "Elementary Processes" (compare figure 3). On the one hand, they allow the use of knowledge from other reference processes (for the use of standardization). On the other hand, a simple way of modelling the company specific processes with predefined basic modules is available.

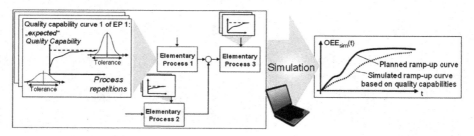

Figure 3 – Simulation of ramp-up curves.

The elementary processes are characterized by their specific quality capabilities. They define the suitability of the process to meet the required output quality. That means, the quality capability guarantees that the demanded quality parameters, which are influenced by the elementary process, are within specific tolerances. The quality capability of an elementary process is modelled by various graphs. These "Quality Capability Curves" forecast the actual ability of a parameter to match its requirements at different times (expressed in process repetitions). Each critical quality parameter, which is influenced by the elementary process, is represented by a quality capability curve.

Based on the modeled quality capability curves of the several elementary processes, the approach allows a conclusion about the capability of the whole production system. Therefore, the simulation serves to anticipate the entire output of the system in a classical ramp-up curve (compare effectiveness of ramp-up in figure 1). Additionally, the needed effort in terms of variable resources due to malfunctions of quality as well as reworking and rejections is being determined and the efficiency of the ramp-up (compare figure 1) is calculated. Finally this represents the base for calculation the costs of the production ramp-up.

4. CONSIDERATION OF QUALITY DEVELOPMENT DURING RAMP-UP WITHIN THE CONFIGURATION OF VALUE ADDED NETWORKS

The objective of the presented project is the development of a method for the configuration of value added networks with consideration of the ramp-up costs (compare figure 4). A configuration which is only based on the costs of a stable running network seems to be more and more suboptimal due to the relevance of the ramp-up period. The consideration of ramp-up costs enables the comparison of the value added network with forecasted sales figures and it also enables a conclusion about the quality of the configuration.

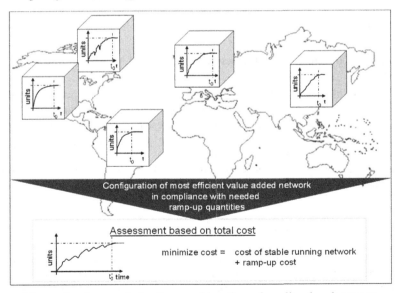

Figure 4 – Approach for the consideration of quality development.

Besides a shorter time to volume and a shorter time to customer which result from well coordinated start-up periods of the several Value Added Modules (nodes of the value added network, e.g. sites, partners etc.) also cost reduction potentials through an optimized application of resources can be observed. In compliance with given sales figures (effectiveness of the ramp-up), the ramp-up costs are determined by the efficiency in terms of input of resources. As mentioned before, this ramp-up efficiency depends on the quality capability of the unstable production processes and is time-variant (Lanza, 2004). Therefore, the presented approach is based on the development of the quality capabilities of several Value Added Modules. The necessary working steps to achieve the mentioned objectives are presented in the following.

4.1 Definition of Value Added Modules based on quality capabilities

Based on the developed concept of Business Capabilities (see chapter 2), an extended concept will be developed, which considers the varying capabilities over time. Therefore, especially the ramp-up phase has to be analyzed, which has not yet been considered in the Business Capability concept. Relevant criteria have to be determined and have to be included in the concept.

By assigning the predefined Business Capabilities with technologies and resources, the Value Added Modules will be deduced. These combinations of technologies and resources are responsible for low output ratios, lost output due to malfunctions, additionally needed effort and hence for an uneconomic production result during ramp-up. In consequence the effectiveness and the efficiency during ramp-up are determined by these combinations. This ramp-up capability is implemented as quality capabilities of the Value Added Modules. Each quality capability is developing over time and leads to a time-variant function. Derived from the quality capabilities of production processes (compare chapter 3), it is necessary to define a quality capability of Value Added Modules in the next step.

4.2 Modeling of quality capabilities of Value Added Modules

The defined Value Added Modules have to be allocated with quality capabilities. Thereby, it is necessary to break up the classical understanding of production processes and their quality capabilities (see research work of business process capabilities (Gerboth, 2002)). A representation of the quality capabilities across all hierarchical levels of Value Added Modules has to be achieved. The results are representative quality capability curves for each Value Added Module, which have to be classified for following configurations. This allows the transferability for Value Added Modules with similar combinations of technologies and resources.

4.3 Deduction of ramp-up costs for Value Added Modules

In this step the costs, which are created in a Value Added Module during ramp-up, have to be derived for later evaluation. Ramp-up costs are defined as a loss of maximum ramp-up performance corresponding to the TPM (Total Productive Maintenance)-concept. TPM is based on the idea, that every system has an ideal working potential, which is reduced by losses of the system (Nakajima, 1989). This approach has to be assigned to Value Added Modules and furthermore to the whole value added network.

First, the maximum ramp-up performance is determined as the resulting part of the ideal working potential. The essential losses of this maximum ramp-up performance are the quality capabilities of the Value Added Modules. Furthermore, loss of availability and performance due to malfunctions etc. has to be considered as well.

To determine the ramp-up performance data of each Value Added Module is necessary. Normally, this data is only available for the company's own sites. If this data is unknown, an estimation of the ramp-up performance has to be given. This is made by using characteristic values which have to be defined.

In the next step, the ramp-up performance has to be transformed into ramp-up costs. While the curves of the ramp-up performance show the best achievable performance, the so called capacity limit, the costs have to be calculable depending on the quantities. As a result, the costs per unit over time as well as the cumulated costs of the whole ramp-up period can be calculated.

4.4 Configuration of value added network alternatives with evaluation and decision based on total costs

Knowing the ramp-up costs of each Value Added Module a configuration method is developed to define valid value added network alternatives. The first step of the configuration is the definition of the required Business Capabilities for the planned value added. The method provides only these combinations of the possible nodes, which meet the required quantities (effectiveness).

To determine this effectiveness in form of the defined ramp-up curve the developed ramp-up simulation is adapted and used (Lanza, 2004). Thereby it is possible, that different Value Added Modules deliver the entire capacity in the sense of scaling. In the next step this combinations will be evaluated by their efficiency.

For the economical assessment of value added networks with special consideration of the ramp-up an objective function will be developed. Parts of this function are the identified ramp-up costs as well as the costs for operating the network in stable conditions. The result will be costs per unit as function of time. On this basis the average costs per unit and the total costs of the value added network configuration can be determined. Particularly with regard to the fulfillment of target costs, the function allows the assessment of the value added network configuration and the selection of the most efficient alternative for the planned value added.

5. CONCLUSION AND OUTLOOK

The scheduled result of the project is a method for the configuration of value added networks, which achieves a given production ramp-up (time and sales guidelines) across all included Value Added Modules at optimal costs. The presented research work is funded by the Landesstiftung Baden-Württemberg within the support program for young scientists. The project is running from January 2006 until the end of 2007.

The outcome of this research project will be a support in the production planning, which allows a transparent decision about the question, which part of the value added should be realized at which site or from which external partner. The responsible persons are able to get an optimized configuration of the value added network considering the ramp-up capabilities of the several Value Added Modules.

6. REFERENCES

1. Bergholz M et al. Die Fabrik von Morgen. In: Wettbewerbsfaktor Produktionstechnik. AWK – Aachener Werkzeugmaschinen-Kolloquium 2002. Aachen: Shaker-Verlag, 2002.
2. Curtis B, Hefley WE, Miller SA. The People Capability Maturity Model: Guidelines for improving the workforce (SEI Series). New York: Addison Wesley, 2002.
3. Englert E. Qualitätsgerechte Auslegung flexibler Produktionssysteme mit Hilfe von Simulation. Fakultät Konstruktions- und Fertigungstechnik, Universität Stuttgart, 1996.
4. Eversheim W, Schellberg O, Terhaag O. Gestaltung und Betrieb von Produktionsnetzwerken. In: Produktions- und Logistikmanagement in virtuellen Unternehmen und Unternehmensnetzwerken, Kaluza B, Blecker T ed. Berlin: Springer-Verlag, 2000.
5. Fleischer J, Herm M, Schell MO. Wertschöpfung in Netzwerken – Integrierte Planungsmethodik zur Konfiguration von globalen Wertschöpfungsnetzwerken. ZWF 99 (2004), H. 9, 2004.
6. Fleischer J, Herm M. A Method to configure Value Added Networks based on Business Capabilities. In: 38th ISMS International Seminar on Manufacturing Systems, Florianopolis, Brazil, 2005a.
7. Fleischer J, Herm M, Peter K, Sternemann KH. A Concept for the Configuration and Optimization of Global Value Added Networks Based on Business Capabilities. In: 1st CARV International Conference on Changeable, Agile, Reconfigurable and Virtual Production, München, Germany, 2005b.
8. Gerboth T. Statistische Prozessregelung bei administrativen Prozessen im Rahmen eines ganzheitlichen Prozesscontrollings. In: Fraunhofer-Institut für Produktionsanlagen und Konstruktionstechnik, Institut für Werkzeugmaschinen und Fabrikbetrieb, Technische Universität Berlin, Berlin, 2002.
9. Hering E, Triemel J, Blank HP. Qualitätssicherung für Ingenieure. Düsseldorf: VDI-Verlag, 1993.
10. Big M. Modellgestützte Bewertung der Kooperationsfähigkeit produzierender Unternehmen. VDI-Fortschrittsberichte, Reihe 16, Nr. 140. Düsseldorf: VDI-Verlag, 2002.
11. Lanza G. Simulationsbasierte Anlaufunterstützung auf Basis von Qualitätsfähigkeiten von Produktionsprozessen. Forschungsberichte aus dem Institut für Produktionstechnik (wbk), Universität Karlsruhe (TH), 2004.
12. Nakajima S. TPM Development Program. Cambridge: Productivity Press, 1989.
13. NN. Consortium-AMICE, CIM Open System Architecture (CIMOSA). Heidelberg: Springer-Verlag, 1993.
14. Schuh G, Geissbauer R. Global Footprint Design: Die Spielregeln der internationalen Wertschöpfung beherrschen. München: Roland Berger Strategy Consultants, 2004.
15. Sternemann KH, Homann U: Global Manufacturing in Networks. In: 16th IFAC World Congress, Prague, Czech Republic, 2005.
16. Terwiesch C, Chea KS, Bohn RE. Learning and Process Improvement during Production Ramp-Up. San Diego: The Information Storage Industry Centre, University of California, 1998.
17. Wiendahl HP. Wandel auch in der Fabrikplanung. wt Werkstattstechnik online 93 (2003), Nr. 4, S. 226, www.werkstattstechnik.de. Düsseldorf: Springer-VDI-Verlag, 2003.

DYNAMIC PERFORMANCE MANAGEMENT IN BUSINESS NETWORKS ENVIRONMENT

Américo Azevedo and Roberto da Piedade Francisco
Faculdade de Engenharia da Universidade do Porto and Inesc Porto,Portugal
{ala, roberto.piedade}@fe.up.pt

This paper underlines the necessity of developing a framework supported by methodologies and concepts that make it possible to provide instances of the network's global performance management system in collaborative networks, and to simultaneously lead to the necessary alignment of all participants. We propose a way to identify and suggest the requirements to develop a framework that can support a dynamic Performance Management System efficiently through a conceptual schema that enables the implementation.

1. INTRODUCTION

A dynamic transformation in the business environment intensified the collaboration among different and geographically distributed entities that effectively combine the most suitable set of skills and resources temporarily in order to achieve a common goal, generating so-called collaborative networks (Chituc & Azevedo, 2005). The subject is at present an important trend assumed and recognized by the scientific community and the practitioners because it is co-related with the need to improve competitiveness.

Reaching competitiveness, world-excellence and agility in the severe conditions imposed by markets makes it interesting to act in collaborative networks (CN). This implies complying with requirements like common strategies and goals, level of mutual trust, interoperable process and infrastructures and policies for business practices in collaborative networks. The integration and agility of a CN is possible if these challenging base conditions are achieved (Camarinha-Matos, Afsarmanesh & Ollus, 2005).

To manage this new model, inter-organizational performance must be dealt with more intensely. A performance management system (PMS) can help organizations improve performance, but the CNs are dependent on the individual knowledge of its participants (Evans, Roth & Sturm, 2004). Defining, setting up and implementing an effective PMS for a dynamic CN are challenges to be achieved in order to contribute to the support of the CN decision-makers. The paper is organized as follows: the next section presents some issues on collaborative networks and their performance aspects. The third section briefly presents the main approaches to performance management, strategic alignment and technological support. Then, the next section addresses the main ideas towards dynamic performance management and, finally, the last section contains the conclusions.

2. BUSINESS NETWORKS

2.1 Collaborative Networks

The collaborative business environment can be seen as an interaction between enterprises that want to cooperate in order to achieve common goals. To easily adapt to the dynamics of the market, the temporary networks seem to match better to the typical short duration of business opportunities while long-term organizations are more worried about investments in common infrastructures and practices and with the trust building process (Camarinha-Matos, Afsarmanesh & Ollus, 2005).

Many topologies of CN are proposed and researched. Some are chosen by types of enterprises, others by the interaction mechanisms adopted and the rest by other criteria. To find a classification for dynamic markets, the choice of time related aspects would be the most suitable. Afsarmanesh, Marik & Camarinha-Matos (2004) considered three different CN types: 1) long-term partnership of SMEs with one dominant partner, 2) dynamic project-based partnership without a dominant partner, and 3) temporary partnerships intended by one organization to explore short-term market opportunities.

A dynamic CN is supposed to have intensive care because its performance is developing in a short period. Its life-cycles are increasingly shorter and it is crucial to understand which parameters or indicators must be used in a PMS and if they will be useful and bring back solutions that will allow us to deal with strategies and respective operations performance. The life-cycle can be presented in the following phases:

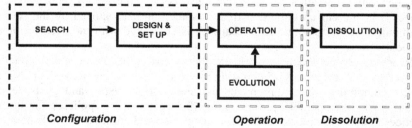

Figure 1 – Life-cycle of a collaborative network's main phases.

In order to verify if a dynamic CN is effective, it is necessary to find mature management skills seen in experience in strategy formulation. If this is found, there will be adjusted and effective PMS to manage the performance and solve problems or inclusively reconfigure the CN. The absence of meaningful goals and the use of wrong measures can lead organizations in the wrong direction.

2.2 Collaborative Network Performance

Indeed, the emerging models of business collaboration, namely the ones in the context of business networking, require adequate technologies and supporting infrastructures, proper management tools and performance measurement solutions that can guarantee technological, strategic and business goal alignment among business partners in a collaborative networked business environment.

Then, it is extremely important that the CN develops a structured form to design their PMS. It is a prudence way to reach proper management tools and performance measurement solutions with adequate technologies and supporting infrastructures.

Busi & Bititci (2006) present some questions that can be used to point important considerations such as: 1) Which performance measures should be collaboratively selected? 2) How can multiple individual measures be aggregated to give an overall picture of the collaborative enterprise performance? 3) How can a company that belongs in more than one collaborative enterprise have one single measurement system? 4) How can conflicting measures and objectives be managed in a collaborative enterprise?

Those are very pertinent questions to build a PMS in order to obtain a consistent system but more specific questions can also be raised:

- What CN topology must exist?
- What is the most appropriate framework to be used?
- How to make it possible to reach the alignment?
- How to manage problems, solutions and to make reconfiguration with the PMS outputs data?

At least those questions must guide the design of the PMS and they can be treated during the design of the network itself as well. A repository contains data on the past performance of all participants in CN which is an adjusted way to know their potentials and competencies. It will also help answer that question above in order to support the Search and Design & Set Up phases.

3. PERFORMANCE MANAGEMENT AND ALIGNMENT

3.1 Performance Measurement and Management

According to Busi & Bititci (2006), the "integrated performance management in collaborative enterprises is the process of using inter-organizational systems to collaboratively measure performance of collaborative enterprise processes and use the measurement to enable decision-makers to proactively and strategically manage the collaborative enterprise itself". These authors referred that five "actors" can be identified: (1) the collaborative enterprise; (2) the collaborative operational processes; (3) the collaborative process of measuring and managing performance; (4) the inter-organizational systems; and (5) the decision makers. Those concerns have brought a change from the measurement view to a management view in order to necessarily obtain information through indicators that make support configure, re-configure or dissolute the collaborative network. According to Evans, Roth & Sturm (2004) today, a performance measurement system is a subset of a PMS.

A PMS can continuously show if the investments are amortizing (effectivity), if the external and internal processes are obtaining the expected results (effectiveness) and also if the operational activities are functioning within controlled and defined parameters (efficiency). When measuring the real-time performance we can encounter the static and dynamic indicators that must be searched and defined because some (static) are mentioned to regular operations and other (dynamic) to actions that solve problems.

Kaplan and Norton (1992) stand out the need for measurement saying that: "if the companies wish to survive and to prosper in the age of the information, they must use systems of management and measurement of performance derived from its strategies and capabilities".

Many performance management models can be encountered and applied to practitioners and after this, adapted to each application such as Balanced Scorecard System (Kaplan & Norton, 1992), Performance Prism model (Neely, Adams & Kenerly, 2002), GPM-SME (Alba et al., 2004), PMS-EVE (Saiz, Rodríguez & Bas, 2005), SCOR (Cabral et al., 2005) and also the business excellence models that combine results, for instance the individual organizational performance related to a specific market or territory. The Malcom Baldridge Price (MBA) in USA, and Deming Price in Japan, and EFQM Excellence Award in Europe are good examples. Every model consists in congregating some concepts to build a framework that can aim for specific purposes and support the decision-makers. However it is essential that the chosen one enables a consistent integration.

But it can also be a chance to review the functionality of the organizational structure. Trivial organizations can choose between two basic forms of structure for its management: functional or procedural. In a procedural structure, a horizontal vision of the organization is applied. This enables the adoption of process-oriented management, it focuses on the value aggregation chain and also on the concept of internal customer-supplier, clearly identifying the used resources and permanently searching for the external customer satisfaction (Varvakis et al., 1998). The contribution of this approach to the alignment of the CN partners can be considered.

Francisco & Machado (2005) alert to the effect caused by changes seen in the organization when it implements new strategies, structures and technologies which may induce internal resistances. It is also necessary to have change management knowledge.

3.2 Strategic Alignment

A framework must be developed to address the need for performance measurement and management, applied mainly on Operation and Evolution phases. Maybe it is more important to reach alignment among participants of a CN than to define the framework.

According to Kaplan & Norton (1992), the balanced scorecard approach intends to make sure it is possible to align individual, organizational and inter-departmental initiatives to identify new processes or tools meant to meet the clients' demands and stakeholders' objectives. The main principle is to integrate the goals with strategies and thus reach a better definition of the process, their performance and their relationship with the internal and external clients. It encourages a state of synergy.

The term 'synergy' is the point to be considered. The "synergy is the interaction of two or more agents or forces so that their combined effect is greater than the sum of their individual effects, or also a cooperative interaction among groups, especially among the acquired subsidiaries or merged parts of a corporation, that creates an enhanced combined effect" (dictionary.com). It is the perceived vision.

To Saiz, Rodríguez & Bas (2005), the cooperative interaction maximizes the combined capacities to reach the strategic objectives through integrated solutions to provide efficiency and effectiveness in the operations meant to take care of customers' needs. The integration between scorecards makes it possible to manage the collaborative service units and the decentralized business units as a unique entity (Kaplan & Norton, 2001). It intends to build an interactive performance management system that can be a tool capable of turning strategies into actions if alignment exists on all relevant and critical activities (Chituc & Azevedo, 2005). The alignment brings sustainable gains allowed in an effective interaction.

Furthermore, a CN needs to have their inter-organizational processes duly defined, established and kept. Divergences in the objectives can also occur as well as some gaps, more or less expressive, in terms of competencies on organizational and technological management among partners. This implies a management system which depends on the vocation and abilities of the CN in its business environment. However, the difficulty in developing a collaborative culture and appropriate performance measures has been identified as an obstacle to the successful implementation of collaborative PMS overall in a dynamic environment (Busi & Bititci, 2006).

A dynamic performance management intends to build an interactive and aligned structure to quickly and consistently support performance-based decisions in networks existing for a specific life-cycle mainly on these in which the time for reconfiguration is short and limited and where there is neither time to test and optimize collaboration between participants, nor to improve processes by trial-and-error procedures (Graser et al., 2005). Let us not forget that the "actors" cited by Busi & Bititci (2006) must be based on the aligned structures perfectly explored in Operation, Evolution and Dissolution phases of the life-cycle.

3.3 Technological Support

The CN is growing also due to many improvements on information and communication technologies (ICT) which is a contribution to the continuous application of new approaches, solutions and conceptual schemas.

Furthermore, the aim is to address the different requirements of technological supports systems that can support a dynamic performance management system tailored for business networking environment. In this context, one of the main objectives is to search for technological supports applications and explore features that give priority to PMS and its respective framework during the Design & Set Up phase of CN implementation project. Thus, some questions must be answered, such as: what kind of technological support can be used?

There are some interesting management models that can contribute to manage the CN through management technologies that brings new dedicated approaches to improve the operations performance, promote agility and stimulate the use of many available tools that enable the increase the competencies.

4. TOWARDS A DYNAMIC PERFORMANCE MANAGEMENT

We propose a way to identify and suggest the requirements to develop a framework that can efficiently support a dynamic PMS through a conceptual schema that enables the implementation naturally.

The framework is based on two main layers: data and information layer and functionality layer. The first layer comprises several services related to data acquiring and repository management. The second layer comprises three main performance functionalities: network performance management to support mainly the Design & Start-up phase, real-time performance measurement and management to measure the outputs, solve emergent problems and formulate improvements on Operation and Evolution phases, and performance analysis to know and understand the performance and knowledge reached during the life-cycle (figure 2).

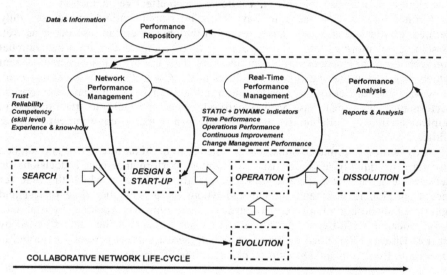

Figure 2 – Performance Management Framework.

The view of a performance repository of partners on CN intends to provide trustworthy information about trust, reliability, competency (skill level), experience and know-how. A time gain can be reached in the Search phase as well as in the Design phase.

To appropriately manage the CN Operation phase, there is a set of indicators in a specific chosen PMS framework through static and dynamic indicators that enables the improvement of time factor (agility), operations performance and provides sustainability to continuous improvement and change management. It has also an implication on Evolution phase.

An explanatory case study research can be used to find such interesting approaches based on a scientific method. It is convenient to look at the real environment and understand the issues that can be important to measure and manage the systems and explore them.

Finally, a performance analysis must be carried out in order to understand if the CN has reached its goals and to obtain a memory about their performance enabling a state of learning and proper knowledge of itself. It is mandatory on Dissolution phase.

Specifically on the PMS framework, some concerns must be viewed (figure 3). The main functionality is the interaction among the CN partners from their own local performance management system (LPMS) as well as the interaction among each one of them and the global network performance management system (GNPMS).

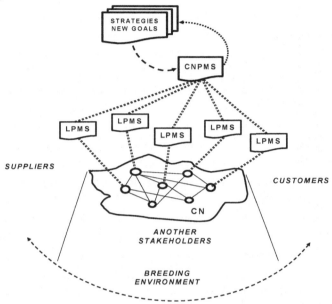

Figure 3 – Towards to a dynamic performance management.

First, a LPMS in every significant partner must be found or developed, and the partner should use an adequate framework and consider the alignment of that local system with the strategies and common global goals.

Another important requirement is the ICT interoperability process and their infrastructures. Also the computer programs and languages must be integrated or adapted to obtain consistent data.

The action of a broker for the NC management has an important role to play in the integration and alignment. On the other hand, its inexistence in mature CN with effective PMS can be replaced by the individual enterprise competencies.

5. CONCLUSIONS

In general, the aim of setting up new innovative forms of organization, such as collaborative networks, is the reduction of uncertainty concerning challenges market environment, the exploitation of new business opportunities as well as the increase of competitiveness levels on target domains. In this context, the use of a suitable performance management system, supporting all life-cycles of collaborative business networks, intends to build an interactive and aligned structure to quickly and consistently support performance-based decisions.

The growing importance of this subject justifies further work. Therefore, authors intend to explore this line of research, namely in understanding the mechanisms for the support of the design and set-up of performance management frameworks for business networking environment.

6. REFERENCES

1. Afsarmanesh H, Marik V, Camarinha-Matos LM. "Challenges of Collaborative Networks in Europe". In A Research Agenda for Emerging Business Models. Norwel: Kluwer, 2004.
2. Alba M, Diez L, Olmos E, Rodríguez R. "Global Performance Management for Small and Medium-Sized Enterprises (GMP_SME)". In Collaborative Networks and their Breeding Environments. New York: Springer, 2005.
3. Busi M, Bititci US. "Collaborative Performance Management: Present Gaps and Future Research". In International Journal of Productivity and Performance Management 2006; Vol. 55 No. 1: 7-25.
4. Cabral R, Doumeingts G, Li M-S, Popplewell K. "Supply-Chain Operations Reference-Model: SCOR version 7 Overview". In Enterprise Interoperability Research Roadmap, V2.0. Information Society Technology, 2005.
5. Camarinha-Matos LM, Afsarmanesh H, Ollus M. "Ecolead: a Holistic Approach to Creation and Management of Dynamic Virtual Organizations". In Collaborative Networks and their Breeding Environments. New York: Springer, 2005.
6. Chituc CM, Azevedo AL. "Multi-Perspective Challenges on Collaborative Networks Business Environment". In Collaborative Networks and their Breeding Environments. New York: Springer, 2005.
7. Dictionary.com. http://dictionary.reference.com/
8. Evans S, Roth N & Sturm F. "Performance Measurement and Added Value of Networks". In A Research Agenda for Emerging Business Models. Norwel: Kluwer, 2004.
9. Francisco RP, Machado RL. "Mudança eficaz: usando metodologias para auxiliar a liderança na implementação de novas visões ou estratégias". In Anais do XXV ENEGEP - Encontro Nacional de Engenharia e Produção. Porto Alegre: XXV Enegep, 2005.
10. Graser F, Jansson K, Eschenbächer J, Westphal I, Negretto U. "Towards Performance Measurement in Virtual Organizations – Potentials, Needs, and Research Challenges". In Collaborative Networks and their Breeding Environments. New York: Springer, 2005.
11. Kaplan RS, Norton DP. Organização Orientada para a Estratégia: como as empresas que adotam o balanced scorecard prosperam no novo ambiente de negócios. 2. ed. Rio de Janeiro: Campus, 2001.
12. Kaplan RS, Norton DP. The Balanced Scorecard – Measures that Drive Performance. In Harvard Business Review, January-February, p. 71-79, 1992.
13. Neely A, Adams C, Kenerly M. The Performance Prism: the Scorecard for Measuring and Managing Business Success. London: Prentice Hall/Pearson Education, 2002.
14. Saiz JJA, Rodríguez RR, Bas AO. "A Performance Measurement System for Virtual and Extended Enterprises". In Collaborative Networks and their Breeding Environments. New York: Springer, 2005.
15. Varvakis GJ et al. Gerenciamento de processos. Florianópolis: PPGEP-UFSC, 1998.

A QUANTIFIED APPROACH TO TACIT KNOWLEDGE MANAGEMENT IN R&D-ENVIRONMENTS THROUGH THE USE OF DOCUMENT-BASED USER PROFILES

Joris Vertommen and Joost Duflou
Centre for Industrial Management, Katholieke Universiteit Leuven, Belgium
{joris.vertommen, joost.duflou}@cib.kuleuven.be

Few corporate activities result in the density of knowledge generation that Research and Development activities do. This knowledge comes at high cost and should be managed as an high-value asset.. Of paramount importance in the knowledge management process, is the knowledge availability for (re-)use within the enterprise.
This paper discusses a quantified approach to the management of tacit knowledge through the creation of user profiles that capture the expertise of an employee. Once constructed, these profiles can be used to make tacit knowledge searchable, as well as to bring together experts and those in search of expertise.

1. INTRODUCTION

Knowledge management is becoming one of the key processes in many enterprises, due to the increasing awareness of the knowledge value. Products and money are not the only assets that a company generates; knowledge even exceeds these in importance. Besides successful product and project outcomes, previous failures and trials are stored in the entire body of knowledge that resides with company employees. The difficult part is keeping that knowledge with these and future employees. Several situations that bring about the disappearance of knowledge can be identified, the most common being (1) inaccessibility of previously acquired knowledge to employees, (2) insufficient communication between novices and experts, and (3) experts leaving the company. A 2004 survey by Delphi Research indicates that professionals, including R&D engineers, spend 20% of their time looking for information, representing a runaway expense item in many organizations (Delphi, 2004).

Knowledge is generally differentiated into two kinds (Nonaka, 1995). Explicit knowledge is written down in documents, such as product manuals or research papers. Tacit knowledge is obtained through experience and more difficult to grasp. It is stored in the heads of employees, and cannot simply be written down.

Supporting the knowledge management process are the knowledge management systems (KMS). These software systems automate parts of the process, and offer extra functionalities such as a document search on the company servers, thereby making it easier to gather knowledge that has already been made explicit.

A wide range of methods and techniques for knowledge management have been published during the last few years (e.g. Dalkir, 2005; Rao, 2005 and Wiig, 2004), some of them more applicable in reality then others, and several of these are gaining popularity in industry. One example of such a technique is the "community of practice" (CoP) (Wenger, 1999), and will be discussed further in the course of this paper.

The goal of the research discussed in this paper is to enable the inclusion of tacit knowledge in a knowledge management system, thereby making this knowledge searchable as well as supporting functionalities such as the CoP's mentioned above. For this purpose, user profiles are developed capturing the knowledge of an employee. The focus lies on R&D environments, as the activities in such departments are very knowledge-intensive.

2. USER PROFILES

The goal of the user profile is to offer a good representation of the available tacit knowledge. The profile will serve as a handle on the expertise of a specific employee. An important characteristic of a user profile in the context of a KMS is that the construction and maintenance of the profile should require little effort from the end-user, because users are less likely to tolerate a system that requires heavy interaction. If however, the KMS is perceived as a useful, stand-alone tool, the user will be more willing to supply correct information in the case such information is needed.

2.1 Input

The proposed method for the construction of a profile is based on a collection of documents that are written or read by the user. As mentioned before, documents contain explicit knowledge. However, they are also reflective of their author's tacit knowledge even though they do not completely contain it. Furthermore, documents that are read by a user indicate a (growing) interest, if not expertise, in a certain subject.

The selection of documents can happen in several ways. The KMS could, e.g. monitor which file is inserted into the system by whom, assuming the inserter is the author. Another possibility is to use a dropbox system, in which the user inserts documents that he considers to be indicative of his expertise.

2.2 Construction

In order to construct the user's profile, the documents should be converted into a workable format, i.e. a computer should be able to identify the contents of a document and compare documents with each other. A widely used technique is to convert each document into a multidimensional vector, where each dimension is represented by a word contained in the vocabulary of the document. The entire vocabulary of the document corpus defines a vector-space; hence this technique is called the Vector Space Model (VSM) (Salton, 1989 and Baeza-Yates, 1999). The representation of documents in the VSM is often referred to as a "bag-of-words".

2.2.1 Stemming

Each word in a document is reduced to its most basic form. E.g. each of the following words is reduced to the stem "connect":

- connect
- connecting
- connection
- connected

The stemming algorithm to be used is dependent on the language of the document (Porter, 1980).

The two main reasons to perform this stemming are (1) each of these words basically has the same meaning and (2) the vocabulary that is used throughout the document collection is reduced with approximately 33%. The latter is important for computational reasons. The former is important when comparing different texts with each other. For instance, "the telephone connection" and "the cable connecting telephones" share a certain meaning that is not apparent when comparing the words used in both phrases (at least not to a computer). Stemming the phrases would result in "the telephone connect" and "the cable connect telephone". Now both sentences share three words and can be identified by a computer as being similar. The same holds for entire documents.

2.2.2 Term Weighting

After the stemming process, each document has been reduced to a list of stems. In order for a computer to grasp the content of a document, a weight will be given to each stem that appears in the list. The height of the weight indicates the importance of the stem in reflecting the document's content. Stems that are part of the corpus vocabulary, but don't appear in a particular document, are added to that document's representation with a weight of 0. These results in a series of vectors, one for each document, that are all represented in the same dimensions, i.e. the entire corpus vocabulary.

There are several approaches to determine the weight of a stem in a specific document vector (Salton, 1989 and Baeza-Yates, 1999). The easiest is to simply count the number of occurrences of the stem in the document. This is called the Term Frequency (TF). The more a stem occurs, the higher its importance in describing the document contents. Because such a weighting scheme assigns a large weight to stopwords, the TF-factor is often counter-balanced by the Inverse Document Frequency (IDF). IDF is defined as the total number of documents, divided by the number of documents the stem occurs in. TF and IDF are combined in the popular TF-IDF weighting scheme as

$$w_{ij} = tf_{ij} * \log\left(\frac{N}{n_i}\right)$$

where w_{ij} is the weight of stem i in document j, N is the total number of documents and n_i is the amount of documents stem i occurs in.

This formula assigns a large weight to those stems that appear frequently in a document, but rarely in other documents. This approach makes sense intuitively, and has proven it's effectiveness in the research domain of Information Retrieval.

2.2.3 Vector Space
Now that each document is defined in function of the same collection of stems, they can be manipulated in the vector space using Linear Algebra techniques. The most important of these in the course of this paper, is the definition of a distance measure between vectors, and, consequently, between documents. A good measure to use is the cosine distance between vectors, i.e. the complement of the angle between two document vectors as seen from the vector space origin.

2.2.4 The Profile
To build the eventual profile, the documents that are assigned to a user are combined by making a normalized, linear combination of their respective document-vectors. The result will be a new vector, defined in the same vector space as the document vectors.

Combining all document vectors into a single profile vector poses some problems however. Since the profile vector is a combination of several document vectors, the high-weighted dimensions of the profile vector will be a combination of the highweighted dimensions in the individual documents. As long as these documents cover a similar topic, this is not an issue. However, when a user has multiple expertises, and with most employees in an R&D environment this is the case, stems from these different expertise domains will mingle, resulting in a vector that offers no clear interpretation. As far as the authors are aware, all currently available KMS's that provide user profiling, employ a single vector solution.

To solve this problem, this paper proposes to assign a user profile several vectors, each covering an expertise domain. The individual vectors are based on the documents that can be linked to the domain they cover. However, it is not necessary to ask the end-user to define these domains; it suffices to detect their presence. This is done by applying a clustering algorithm on the document vectors that are linked to a user (Jain, 1988). Depending on the algorithm used, documents that are similar to each other will be grouped together into clusters. Similarity is defined by the cosine measure, as described in 2.2.3. If the number of documents in a cluster is sufficiently large, the assigned document vectors are combined into a profile vector, and the user profile is defined as this collection of profile vectors. A further distinction can be made between profile vectors that reflect "expertise", and those that reflect "interest". This distinction can be based on the number of documents in the cluster, or the density of the cluster.

2.3 Maintenance

Since expertise evolves over time, this evolution should be reflected in the user profile. Using the profiles described above, no extra effort is required from the user to update his profile. Assuming that the user keeps on providing the KMS with new documents, as can be expected in a working environment, the KMS should regularly rerun the profiling algorithm. Document clusters that were previously too small to qualify as an expertise domain, might have evolved to a more mature state. Clusters that have had little or no documents added to them over a certain period of time can be labelled as "old" knowledge and eventually discarded.

3. TACIT KM FUNCTIONALITIES

3.1 Expert Search

Expert search is a functionality that is geared directly towards the location of experts within a company. Much like well-known web search engines, such as Google and Yahoo, expert search is a matter of typing in keywords that relate to the desired expertise. The KMS will return a list of employee names as well as contact information. Such a direct link to expertise can significantly accelerate the problem solving process.

The expert search functionality is already enabled through the construction of the user profiles as described in section 2. Each individual vector profile is a linear combination of document vectors and resides in the same vector space. To a computer, there is no difference between documents and user profiles, and the same techniques that are used to search for documents in an Information Retrieval system can be applied here for the detection of user profiles. The collection of query terms entered by the user of the system is treated as a vector itself. The individual terms are stemmed and each is assigned an equal weight. This query vector is then compared with the profile vectors by calculating the cosine distances between them. Employees that have a profile vector that lies sufficiently close to the query vector in the vector space will be returned as the "results" to the query.

3.2 Communities of Practice

The goal of a CoP is to bring together experts and novices into a network, providing them with the opportunity to discuss and learn from each other. Typically, each CoP is organized around a specific topic, and this topic is the subject of discussion. Usually, the company provides the CoP with an IT-platform to conduct their discussions, such as a message board.

The major difficulty with organizing a CoP is identifying experts and novices that could potentially benefit from such a network. Especially in large companies, where the knowledge management problem is very pronounced, a multitude of employees are trying to solve similar problems. Even worse, these problems have often already been solved by others.

The initiation of expertise networks can be supported by user profiles. As mentioned above, all user profiles consist of vectors in the same vector space. Just like clustering is applied in the construction of these vectors, a clustering algorithm can be applied to the profiles themselves, thus resulting in groups of similar profile vectors. If such groups can be identified, they indicate that a certain amount of tacit knowledge is shared between the contributors of a group.

Given below is a small example of how this technique works. Profiles have been made of 12 academic researchers within the department of Mechanical Engineering. Some of them have a single profile vector, some have multiple, and several of them share a research interest. The profiles are based on academic papers published by the involved test persons; none of these has been used for more than one profile however. Table 1 gives an overview of the researchers and their interests.

Table 1 - Researchers and their expertise

User	Research topic	User	Research topic
A	- Selective laser sintering (SLS)	G	- Lifecycle engineering - Sheet metal bend sequencing - Laser cutting
B	- Selective laser sintering (SLS) - Electrical discharge machining (EDM) - Coordinate measuring machines (CMM)	H	- Laser cutting
C	- Electrical discharge machining	I	- Operations research (OR) -pooling
D	- Coordinate measuring machines	J	- Operations research (OR) - routing
E	- Lifecycle engineering	K	- Operations research (OR) - routing
F	- Sheet metal bend sequencing	L	- Operations research (OR) - pooling - Operations research (OR) - routing

For each of these researchers, papers were collected and used to construct a user profile. Subsequently, the profiles were used as input for a hierarchical clustering algorithm, resulting in the dendrogram shown in figure 1. This dendrogram depicts the gradual construction of clusters, starting with one cluster per profile vector at the origin of the X-axis, and the eventual evolution to one large cluster containing all vector profiles. The clustering process can be stopped at any point between these two extremes.

Potential CoP's are indicated with grey rectangles and assigned a label. Researchers A and B, for instance, have a shared interest in SLS. Broadening this topic to "Lasers" in general, would result in a larger group of interested researchers, containing G and H as well.

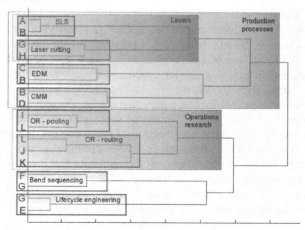

Figure 1 - Identification of CoP's based on the hierarchical clustertree.

3.3 Enhanced Document Search

User profiles can also provide added value to the typical document search functionality. A drawback of common search engines is that they do not know the user. Hence, a query entered by person A will provide the same results as the query entered by person B, irrespective of their respective backgrounds which may be entirely different. E.g., when a researcher is looking for information on a company product, his needs are presumably quite different from those of an accountant looking for the same product.

By adding user profiles to the document search process, the background of an end-user can be taken into account. When this user enters a query into the system, the query vector is combined with a profile vector. This combined vector is then compared with the document corpus, and results are returned. The function of the profile here is to divert the query vector away from uninteresting documents, in the context of the profile content, towards more interesting documents. The choice of profile vector can be determined by the user, automatically chosen by the system based on proximity to the query vector, or the KMS can return a list of results per profile.

Recently, an experiment on the effectiveness of several search functionalities was conducted by the authors at a large European engineering company. Part of this experiment involved the enhanced document search described here. 20 Engineers participated, several of them testing their profile in combination with document search. A total of 27 queries were performed with a profile in the background. The users were free to choose which profile to apply. After processing, two result lists were returned, one using the profile as background, the other without using the profile. The participants were then asked to rate the documents that were added to the result list when applying the profile, and those that were removed. They rated on a scale of 1 to 5 with 1 being "not relevant to my query" and 5 being "very relevant to my query". The documents that were added had a mean score of 3.29; those that were filtered out had a mean score of 1.44. This indicates that search results are improved when using the profile.

4. CONCLUSIONS

Tacit knowledge is difficult to manage, but through the construction of user profiles, a quantified approach to this problem is offered. The bases of these profiles are documents that were written or read by an employee, imposing the restriction that the employee actually has to read and write as part of his function. Because the research described in this paper is primarily oriented towards R&D-environments, this should not pose a problem. The profiles are constructed with minimal effort from the user, and can be applied in several functionalities, including expert identification and refined document retrieval.

5. ACKNOWLEDGEMENTS

The authors would like to recognise the financial support from IWT-Vlaanderen (Instituut voor de Aanmoediging van Innovatie door Wetenschap en Technologie).

6. REFERENCES

1. Baeza-Yates R. and Ribeiro-Neto R., Modern Information Retrieval, Addison-Wesley, 1999, ISBN 020139829X
2. Dalkir K., Knowledge Management in Theory and Practice, Elsevier, 2005, ISBN 075067864X
3. Delphi Group, Information Intelligence: Content Classification and the Enterprise Taxonomy Practice, white paper, 2004
4. Jain A.K. and Dubes R.C., Algorithms for Clustering Data. Prentice Hall, 1988, ISBN 013022278X
5. Nonaka I. and Takeuchi H., The Knowledge Creating Company. Oxford Press, 1995, ISBN 0195092694
6. Porter M.F., "An Algorithm for Suffix Stripping". Program, 14(3):130-137, 1980
7. Rao M., Knowledge Management Tools and Techniques: Practitioners and Experts Evaluate KM Solutions. Elsevier, 2005, ISBN 0750678186
8. Salton G, Automatic Text Processing. Addison-Wesley, 1989, ISBN 0201122278
9. Wenger E., Communities of Practice: Learning, Meaning and Identity. Cambridge University Press, 1999, ISBN 0521663636
10. Wiig K., People-Focused Knowledge Management: How Effective Decision Making Leads to Corporate Success, Elsevier 2004, ISBN 0750677775

INNOVATION SCORECARD: A BALANCED SCORECARD FOR MEASURING THE VALUE ADDED BY INNOVATION

Nelson Gama[1], Miguel Mira da Silva[1] and José Ataíde[2]

[1]*Instituto Superior Técnico, Portugal*
nfpg@mega.ist.utl.pt, mms@tagus.ist.utl.pt
[2]*Grupo Portucel Soporcel, Portugal*
jose.ataide@portucelsoporcel.com

In the last few years, organizations were compelled to innovate just to stay competitive. However, the value added by that innovation is rarely measured. At the same time, the Balanced Scorecard (BSC) became popular as a tool to measure business performance. Unfortunately, the traditional BSC is not appropriate to measure the value added by innovation.
In this paper we propose an Innovation Scorecard based on innovation metrics and the traditional BSC in order to measure the value added by innovation and also guarantee the alignment with the organization strategic objectives. We are currently developing a pilot for a large industrial company that demonstrates how the proposal can be applied in practice.

1. INTRODUCTION

Organizations currently operate in markets characterized by globalization, geo-political instability, strong competition, ever smaller market segments, emergent technologies, substitute products, shorter product life cycles and bargain power of consumer's power. On the other hand, shareholders put an increasing pressure for reducing costs and optimizing investments.

There are two well-known approaches to increase profits and create a sustainable competitive advantage: a short-term one via operational cost reduction and a longer-term one by making a difference being innovative. Usually, especially in periods of economic recession, organizations follow the cost reduction approach even though the results typically disappear after two or three years (Kubinski, 2002). That leaves innovation as the only source of sustainable competitive advantage.

Innovative organizations create more value to shareholders in the long-term (Hamel, 1997). Without innovation, an organization's value proposition can be easily imitated, leading to competition based solely on price for its now commoditized products and services. In some industries (e.g. pharmaceutical and semiconductors) innovative capability is a prerequisite to even participate in the market.

Despite the value of innovation as a growth force, most organizations do not estimate the benefits created by their innovation projects. Many of them do not have internal structures to measure innovation, and do not pay attention to the process of innovation management. Others fail to obtain senior management support, take too long to produce a tangible output, or even work in an organizational vacuum (Kaplan, 1998; Muller et al, 2005; Hamel, 2006).

Appropriately managed innovation creates long-lasting advantages when that innovation is based on something novel or creates something new, in a systemic and systematic way, encompassing a range of processes and methods, ultimately bringing new products or services to market. Well managed innovation is an integral part of an organization's strategy and activities, and even creates new business strategies (Wong, 2001; Hamel, 2006; Kaplan, 2003; Milbergs & Vonortas, 2005).

Although the importance of innovation is recognized, innovation has been seen as a "black box" in which management tools cannot be applied. Sometimes the problem is not a lack of innovation, and even less of innovation spending, but in a lack of measured and managed innovation. However, innovation projects (like any other projects) can and should be aligned with the strategic objectives, create value to the organization, and support internal procedures (Kaplan, 2003; Taylor 2006).

In this paper we propose an Innovation Scorecard based on the traditional Balanced Scorecard (BSC) that not only measures the value created by innovation projects but also guarantees those projects are aligned with the organization strategy. Our proposal is based on innovation metrics defined before the project is evaluated (and then eventually approved) in order to help the project create the intended benefits. When the project is implemented, the chosen metrics are used to measure the value added by that innovation project to the organization's overall value.

That means the Innovation Scorecard can be used not only to measure the value added by innovation projects that are implemented but also, and perhaps even most importantly, as a general management tool that can be used to select which innovation projects should be implemented and later to put pressure on those projects to deliver the promised benefits.

We are currently developing a pilot based on the Innovation Scorecard for a large industrial company and this pilot, including the metrics and objectives used for implementing the BSC, will also be briefly presented in the paper.

2. BALANCED SCORECARD (BSC)

The BSC has been used by many organizations as a management tool to measure their business performance, especially when compared against the strategy. The BSC is also useful for integrating strategic management and communicating to employees the innovation expectations in measurable terms (Magalhães, 2004).

However, we claim that the traditional BSC cannot properly measure the value added by innovation. Innovation projects typically create much more intangible (e.g. an increase in the customer satisfaction level) than tangible value, and intangible value cannot be calculated using traditional financial methods. In addition, many innovation projects are difficult to justify because the ROI depends on tangible value and, as a result, organizations waste lots of money in opportunity costs.

But innovation has been part of the BSC from the beginning, in particular as part of the "innovation and learning perspective" that addresses the organization ability to innovate, improve and learn (Kaplan, 1992). Later on, the BSC authors realized that innovation was a critical internal process (Kaplan & Norton, 1996) and innovation is currently treated in the traditional BSC as a strategic theme inside the "internal business processes perspective" (Kaplan & Norton, 2004).

We believe that innovation is much more than a strategic theme. Innovation is a strategic objective, a way to create a sustainable competitive advantage in which the goal cannot be only to increase the profit level.

Although the focus of each perspective is different, there is a common thread of causality that provides a universal linkage between the four perspectives of the BSC. If an organization invests in learning and growth to improve employee skills and know-how, then those results will be translated into improved internal business processes by leveraging best practices and change management programs such as Six Sigma, Just-in-Time and TQM. These activities will then result in superior quality products and services for the customer, which in turn will drive increased sales and finally an improved profit. However, if an organization innovates in their business model, the impact will be seen in all perspectives. That means innovation must be treated in all perspectives, not only in one perspective.

In the BSC, innovation is perceived as new products or services. But innovation may also allow changes in management, business model, marketing, organizational structure, processes, products, services, supply chain or strategic objectives (Hamel, 2006). Also, performance measurement is usually operationally driven and based on hard numbers, not strategic or intangible.

The BSC translates the organization mission and strategic objectives into operational measures that everyone in the organizations should follow in order to align customer relationships with market segments and increase the financial results.

We align innovation initiatives with strategic objectives by using innovation metrics thus unifying strategic planning and operational innovation processes. Our proposal uses a BSC to integrate innovation with strategy by integrating innovation metrics with projects implemented throughout the organization.

3. INNOVATION METRICS

We start by citing an author that says "the life expectancy of competitive strategies based on customer and business process indicators has become so short that future-oriented indicators (i.e. development and innovation) are rapidly becoming the most important in terms of management control" (Magalhães, 2004) a statement aligned with "disruptive innovation" (Christensen, 1997).

Innovation is a multidimensional and complex activity that cannot be measured by only one metric. In addition, a list of metrics to measure the various aspects of innovation is also insufficient because the evaluation methodologies are based only in financial parameters, i.e. tangible values. However, there are a few examples of metrics used in organizations that allow informed decisions and benchmark with competitors (Picoito & Caetano, 2006; Milbergs & Vonortas, 2005).

Metrics for innovation are important for at least three reasons. Firstly, such metrics demonstrate the value of innovation and can be used to justify investments in this type of fundamental, long-run, but very risky projects, supporting better investment decisions based on hard data. Secondly, good innovation metrics enable organizations to evaluate employees, objectives, programs and projects in order to allocate resources more effectively. Thirdly, metrics affect human behavior and support a common language resulting in better communication throughout the organization.

However, wrong metrics may lead to narrow, short-term, and risk-avoiding decisions and actions (Muller et al, 2005; Hauser & Zettelmeyer, 1996; NetQoS, 2005). Thus, selecting the right metrics for each innovation project is fundamental. Organizations cannot obtain the highest value from each project, nor get the correct alignment between strategic objectives and innovation projects, if the same metrics are applied to all innovation projects in the entire organization. Bad metrics may lead to incorrect diagnoses that create non-intended orientations with unpredictable consequences (Milbergs & Vonortas, 2005; Hauser & Zettelmeyer, 1996).

As a result, innovation metrics must be chosen by each organization depending on their strategic objectives. However, many generic metrics will be similar within a given industry; for instance, most retailers will use the same (or at least similar) innovation metrics, such as increase in sales by square foot.

Traditionally, innovation metrics measure "outcomes" such as increased sales, satisfaction levels, or incremental profit. For example, one popular innovation metric is the profit generated by new products divided by the amount spent on innovation. When used alone, these metrics increase profits in the short-term but sacrifice the future (Hauser & Zettelmeyer, 1996).

Risk aversion and short-term preferences – such as those evident in the metric exemplified above – lead to something called "false rejection" because short-term projects with tangible results are always favored when compared to projects that create much higher value to the firm in the long-term (Hauser & Zettelmeyer, 1996). The only way to avoid this "false rejection" is to place a lower weight on financial metrics relative to other intangible metrics that must be used as well.

Despite the problems in using financial based innovation metrics, they cannot be rejected entirely because they are critical to ensure good results for the organization in the short term. Moreover, employees feel safe and secure when grounded in financial metrics and objectives they always used (Rae, 2006).

On the other hand, many organizations only use innovation metrics based on traditional R&D and product development, such as number of registered patents and investment on R&D as a percentage of sales (Muller et al, 2005). Even leading edge organizations use innovation metrics based on traditional costing systems and financial variance reporting (Kaplan, 1998). Besides their importance, these innovation metrics can only offer a limited view of the value created by innovation, with an excessive emphasis in technological development when compared to other types of innovation, such as changes to business processes.

Many innovation metrics are based on sales percentages and thus assume that innovation is basically a fixed cost (Koch, 2006). This assumption is particularly dangerous during a recession when the opportunities created by innovation are typically even more important than usual. Investments in information systems projects, most of them genuine process innovations, are typically measured as a percentage of sales.

Finally, using innovation metrics by itself can also be considered an organizational and management innovation because these metrics help allocate internal resources inside organizations and reflect a reorientation in the governance model (Picoito & Caetano, 2006).

We can manage innovation only if we can measure innovation – this is why good innovation metrics are important. Without metrics, innovation management can only be based on common sense, personal feelings and/or political interests. Thus innovation metrics should be combined with a BSC not only to measure the value added by innovation but also to align innovation projects with strategic objectives.

Note: we have already collected a large list of innovation metrics that are omitted here for reasons of space. Please contact the authors if you are interested on them.

4. INNOVATION SCORECARD

We propose that organizations should use the BSC together with innovation metrics to measure and manage innovation as well as to provide the alignment between innovation projects and strategic objectives. In order to facilitate, we call Innovation Scorecard to this proposal.

In order for investments in innovation to actually deliver results, we must have a systematic approach to managing innovation with a cause and effect relationship and a broad and clear definition of innovation for the entire organization. Otherwise, investments on innovation may be wasted and the organization does not even know. The Innovation Scorecard supports both the definition and the relationship.

Furthermore, innovation can be divided into two perspectives: as part of the organization strategy or as complement to the organization strategy (Henderson & Venkatraman, 1999; Wong, 2001). The traditional BSC does not support the simultaneous focus, but the Innovation Scorecard also supports these two perspectives because different metrics can be used for each perspective.

The Innovation Scorecard forces organizations to identify and define a coherent portfolio of innovation metrics directly associated to their strategy, such as number of ideas generated, time consumed in innovation, growth of market share, ROI of new products, and so on. The specific metrics chosen by each organization depend on how senior management intend to use innovation in that organization, for example, to increase results from innovation, to align innovation to strategy, as part or complement to strategy, and so on.

As the Innovation Scorecard is based on the traditional BSC, strategic objectives can be linked in a cause-effect relationship to innovation projects throughout the entire organization, going all the way down to individual quantitative and qualitative indicators that can be used to evaluate employees and departments as far as innovation is concerned. Just this pressure to become more innovative is probably enough to justify the Innovation Scorecard in most organizations!

Senior managers typically take decisions based on the past (e.g. using financial records), the present (e.g. using customer and process indicators) and the future (e.g. using development and innovation indicators). The Innovation Scorecard can also support the decision process at the top level because the BSC already uses both lagging indicators and leading indicators.

In summary, based on the proven traditional BSC and innovation metrics, we propose that the Innovation Scorecard can be used by organizations to:

- Communicate the organization strategy, as well as the benefits expected by innovation projects, to everybody in the organization;
- Evaluate the potential value that will be created by innovation projects;
- Align innovation projects to the strategic objectives of the organization;
- Map a cause-effect relationship to identify the sources of intangible benefits;
- Measure the value created by innovation projects after implementation;
- Provide a framework to manage innovation projects;
- Identify the most innovative employees and departments;
- Put pressure on employees to become more innovative.

In the following section we describe how the Innovation Scorecard has been used to manage innovation in a real case study.

5. CASE STUDY

We are currently developing an Innovation Scorecard for Grupo Portucel Soporcel, a large paper company with a vision to become a global supplier of uncoated wood-free paper and leader in two segments: office paper and offset paper for the printing industry (Grupo Portucel Soporcel, 2005). Their mission is to have available products with distinctive quality made from eucalyptus fibber produced with high environmental concerns and the best available technology, increasing the perceived value to the customers and the value for shareholders.

The strategic goals (needed to identify the innovation metrics) are reduce the costs, increase the productivity, focus on quality, differentiate the products, consolidate the international markets, reinforce the competitive position, and strengthen vertical integration over the entire value chain.

Grupo Portucel Soporcel is committed to innovation and received in 2005 a high-recognition prize "Best of European Business" awarded by Roland Berger Strategy Consultants in partnership with the Financial Times (Roland Berger, 2005).

In 2006, Grupo Portucel Soporcel created an internal area dedicated to innovation management and wants to further improve the management of innovation projects, in particular evaluating better which projects must be approved first and keeping the alignment with strategic objectives. The Innovation Scorecard is being developed at Grupo Portucel Soporcel as part of this commitment to innovation.

Figure 1 presents the strategic objectives for the Innovation Scorecard. Although these objectives are based on the 2005 annual report and many other sources, they do not represent any official strategy of the Grupo Portucel Soporcel and should be considered examples for illustration purposes only.

For example, the objective "Processes improvement" is connected (in a cause-effect relationship) to/from other objectives. This objective is calculated from two indicators "Business process time" and "Process quality" that are themselves calculated from two innovation metrics "Customer processes average time" and "Amount of waste" with targets (a percentage that should be decreased this year) of 5% and 10% respectively.

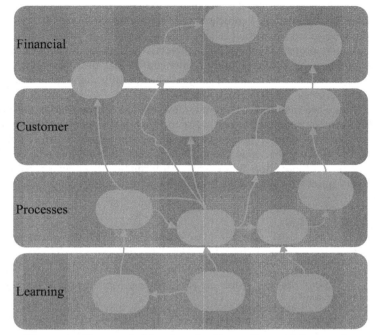

Figure 1 – Proposed objectives for Grupo Portucel Soporcel.

Furthermore, the same objectives, indicators and innovation metrics should be used when analyzing proposals for innovation projects in order to decide whether they should be implemented. In order to achieve this goal, a software prototype we are also developing helps to assign a set of innovation metrics (and their targets) to proposals in order to demonstrate how much that innovation project will contribute to the organization strategic objectives.

6. CONCLUSION

The Innovation Scorecard proposed in this paper combines the traditional BSC with innovation metrics not only to measure the value added by innovation but also to align innovation projects with strategic objectives.

Management depends on metrics. Without metrics, investment decisions are based on intuition, nobody knows the value created by innovation, employees cannot be recognized, and top management never know why their excellent strategies are not being implemented in practice.

The Innovation Scorecard can be used to communicate the strategy, evaluate investment proposals, align projects to strategy, understand the sources of value, measure the value created by projects, and identify the most innovative employees. As a result, the Innovation Scorecard is much more than a simple decision support system for managers; the Innovation Scorecard is a comprehensive management tool for measuring and managing many different aspects of innovation.

Our experience developing the proposal in the context of a real-world case study shows that the Innovation Scorecard can be implemented easily provided the innovation metrics are identified. (Interestingly enough, an organization can only align innovation projects with strategic objectives if those objectives are clearly defined) Furthermore, the case study demonstrated that the Innovation Scorecard can be used to measure all types of innovation, not only innovation based on new products and services.

In the future we plan to conclude the development of the Innovation Scorecard for Grupo Portucel Soporcel, in particular to finish a software application (already started) to analyze project proposals based on innovation metrics and another application to measure the value created by projects after implementation. We also plan to adapt the Innovation Scorecard to Information Systems projects that are typically very innovative and suffer from the same difficulties.

7. REFERENCES

1. Christensen C.M., 1997, "The Innovator's Dilemma: When New Technologies Cause Great Firms to Fail". Harvard Business School Press.
2. Grupo Portucel Soporcel. Annual Report, 2005.
3. Hamel, Gary, 2006, "The Why, What, and How of Management Innovation". Harvard Business Review, February.
4. Hamel, Gary, 1997, "Killer Strategies That Make Shareholders Rich". Fortune, pages 70-88, June 23.
5. Hauser J.R., Zettelmeyer F. "Metrics to Evaluate R, D & E". Research Technology Management, November 1996.
6. Henderson J.C., 1999, Venkatraman N. "Strategic Alignment: Leveraging Information Technology for Transforming Organizations". IBM Systems Journal, Vol. 38, Nos 2$3.
7. Kaplan Robert S., 2004, Norton D.P. "Strategy Maps: Converting Intangible Assets into Tangible Outcomes". Harvard Business Scholl Press.
8. Kaplan, Robert S., 1998, "Innovation Action Research: Creating New Management Theory and Practice". Journal of Management Accounting Research.
9. Kaplan, Robert S., 2003, "Managing Innovation". Harvard Business Review.
10. Kaplan, Robert S., 1992, "The Balanced Scorecard – Measures That Drive Performance". Harvard Business Review.
11. Kaplan Robert S., 1996, Norton D.P. "The Balanced Scorecard: Translating Strategy Into Action". HBS Press.
12. Koch, Christopher, 2006, "The Metrics Trap... And How to Avoid It". CIO Magazine, 1 April. Available online at http://www.cio.com/archive/040106/metrics.html.
13. Kubinski, Ron, 2002 "Building a Culture of Innovation". The Conference Board, Executive Action N. º 40, December.
14. Magalhães, Rodrigo, 2004, "Organizational Knowledge and Technology: An Action-oriented Perspective on Organization and Information Systems". Edward Elgar.
15. Milbergs E, Vonortas N., 2005, "Innovation Metrics: Measurement to Insight". White Paper of National Innovation Initiative, 21st Century Innovation Working Group. IBM Corporation.
16. Muller A, Välikangas L, 2005, Merlyn P. "Metrics for Innovation: Guidelines for Developing a Customized Suite of Innovation Metrics". Strategy and Leadership. Available online at http://www.strategos.com/articles/InnovationMetrics/InnovationMetrics.pdf.
17. NetQoS, 2005, "Show Me The Metrics! Increase Your ROI with Metrics that Matter". White Paper, NetQoS, Inc. Available online at http://www.technology-reports.com/report.asp?id=214.
18. Picoito J, Caetano I., 2006, "Como fazer empresas saudáveis e inteligentes", Público, 20 March.
19. Rae, Jeneanne, 2006, "Closing the Gap on Innovation Metrics". BusinessWeek, April 28.
20. Roland Berger, 2005, Best of European Business.
21. Taylor, William C., 2006, "Here's an Idea: Let Everyone Have Ideas". New York Times, 26 March.
22. Wong, Amy. 2001, "The Metrics of Innovation". Virtual Strategist. Journal of Strategy & Business Transformation, Issue 1, Spring.

THE EMERGING TECHNOLOGIES AND STANDARDS ON BPM AND THE SOCIO-TECHNICAL APPROACHES: CONTRIBUTIONS TO COLLABORATIVE ENVIRONMENTS

Cláudio Sapateiro and Patrícia Macedo
Escola Superior de Tecnologia, Instituto Politécnico de Setúbal, Portugal
{csapateiro, pmacedo}@est.ips.pt

In the last 15 years, initiatives aiming to improve Business Process Management (BPM) have increased significantly. Agility, distribution and interoperability are BPM requirements for the emergent new organizational forms, which have an important role in providing distributed shared process management. In collaborative activities, it is extremely relevant the interactions between several actors for the process success. In order to develop information system that efficiently support collaborative activities this interactions should be contemplated during system specification. The recently emerged/adopted socio-technical approaches to systems development have contributed with theories and methods which allow contemplating the social environment lived in organization(s), in systems specification.
This paper analyze how the current BMP initiatives and social-technical approaches can contribute to the digital information systems development process, in order to address the main characteristics of a collaborative environment

1. INTRODUCTION

Based on the continuous technological evolution different architectures of information systems had emerged, each one supported by different approaches concerning the new challenges that arise.

Systems have evolved from the old day's data centric models to systems developed with a business processes perspective (Smith, 2004) (Jablonski, 2001), based on service oriented architectures (SOA) (Bea, 2005) (Avantys, 2005) with organization integration in mind (Smith, 2002) (Srinivasan, 2005).

This perspective has origined the recent Business Processes Management Systems (BPMS), whose had contributions from the Workflow Management Hollingsworth, 2004) (Chebbi, 2004), SOA (Tibco, 2005) and Enterprise Application Integration (EAI) (Smith, 2002) disciplines.

The new BPMS aims an agile and flexible description of business processes in order to face the current market dynamics and demands. In fact, the emergence of new organizational forms as Networked Production, Clusters and Virtual Organizations, Professional Virtual Communities, where several organizational entities have to share the management of distributed processes, brings several additional challenges to business process management. Considering the example of Collaborative Product Design, it is extremely relevant the interactions between several actors for the process success. In this kind of process a set of informal contacts are usually established.

Nevertheless, most of the focus, of the actual BPMS is in service composition and automation and less in human activities, in particular the informal ones. Informal activities are those who weren't capture in system requirements/design and by so, operate at outside the developed system which doesn't support them.

So, are the currently used methodologies with the wrong focus on systems requirement capture/gathering?

In opposition to the traditional structured approaches such as UML/UP (Silva, 2001) we have, nowadays, agile methodologies for project development, like XP and SCRUM (Schwaber, 2004). Although these methodologies present agile/flexible process for systems development, the end product often lacks on agility/flexibility itself, because the focus/perspective in the system analysis and requirements gather and specification do not capture de social and cultural environment presented in the organization, and in which the business processes are executed. Usually they gather and describe functionalities, rigid procedures/tasks for actors that lead, for example, to the necessity of exception handling in many workflow systems.

In (Charette, 2005) are presented failure cases of systems development and implementation. In spite of several studies identify frequent problems and their consequences in systems development, the failure cases continue.

Some of the causes that lead to projects failure pointed by (Charette, 2005) are:

- Non realistic or not articulated objectives
- Badly driven requirements capture
- Problems in dealing with project complexity

These causes often lead to:

- Missing important systems requirements/functionalities
- Lack of usability

Socio-technical approaches to systems development have emerged recently, in order to address the issues described above. These approaches aims to contemplate in systems specification the social environment lived in organization(s).

As collaborative environments present intensive interactions between actors, digital technologies and modeling techniques should address this as a requirement.

The goal of this paper is to analyze how the current BMP initiatives and social-technical approaches can contribute to the digital information systems development process, in order to address the main characteristics of a collaborative environment.

In section 2 we describe the current BPM initiatives. Section 3 present socio-technique approaches and in section 4 we propose a methodology based on the discussion of the contributions of both approaches to information systems development. Section 5 presents conclusions from this work and future research agenda on the topic.

2. BPM INITIATIVES

As stated in the previous section, there are currently three main contribution areas for Business Process Management Systems (BPMS): Workflow Management, Enterprise Application Integration (EAI) and Service Oriented Architectures (SOA).

The workflow line of thought sees organizations structured as associated roles and responsibilities, it consider both human and systems as resources (Hollingsworth, 2004). Processes are sequence of activities (or in some cases sequences of other processes) governed by business rules in which each have a responsibility role associated as well as resources.

Workflow systems tend to be centralized and hard coded and typically present limited connectivity to other Workflow Management Systems (WfMS) or BPMS. So, they are becoming not as suitable for dynamic business processes as required in collaborative environments.

The Inter-Organizational branch of workflow, addresses some issues related with relationships between partners in collaborative processes, (Chebbi, 2004) (Chebbi, 2004a) like public and private views of the shared processes, but still misses flexibility in processes and local autonomy of participants.

Enterprise Applications Integrations (EAI) addresses a key requirement of Distributed Business Process Management Systems (DBPMS): interoperability (Smith, 2004) however the EAI approach focuses on technical issues in order to achieve activities/processes automation which is not particularly adequate in the human involvement/interactions characterization.

Respecting to Service Oriented Architectures (SOA), a process can be composed by a set of exposed services on the network that can be executed in a highly distributed manner (BEA, 2005). SOA aims increasing business agility (Srinivasan, 2005) by enabling IT departments to reuse services that have known scalability and quality of service characteristics. Such reuse can help reduce time to market as well as development costs. SOA may be implemented in different technologies but the most popular (and supported by standards) is Web Services (WS) based (Papazolou, 2004) (Oracle, 2004). SOA addresses the lack of connectivity experienced in the workflow systems and the lack of management services in EAI.

Concluding, actual BPMS use a unified vision of the SOA and Workflow process definition, this process centric approach aims to formally describe processes in order to translate them to a level of direct execution in process execution engines.

3. SOCIO-TECHNICAL SYSTEMS

The emergence of the socio-technical approaches to systems development aims to capture and specify systems requirements considering the social environment and organizational culture lived in the context of business processes execution.

As stated, before informal activities often affect the execution and performance of business processes. These activities are hardly modelled in traditional approaches/methodologies. This issue has been addressed by initiatives like Genre Analysis (Spinuzi, 2003) (Yates and Orliskowski, 1992)(Yates and Orliskowski, 2002)(Saunders and Chiasson, 2005); Thinklets, representing collaboration patterns

(Briggs et al, 2003)(Gwendolyn et al, 2004); Contexts (Zacarias et al, 2005)(Elst et al, 2001)(Bouqet et al, 2002); Actor Network and Social Actors Networks theories (Pinho and Soares, 2005)(Pereira and Soares, 2005)(Anklam, 2005)(Groth, 2002)(Martinez et al, 2004).

Genre Analysis is particularly adopted to study communication patterns of non formal communications and ad-hoc work structures (Antunes et al, 2006). A genre may be defined as a taxonomic collection of speech or written text types showing the systematic use of genre elements (which describes the kind of element based on form or content properties) (Lacey, 2000).

Another viewpoint considers communicative purpose as a fundamental property of genres (Yates and Orlikowski, 2002). Here, a genre is a template for action enacted within a community to accomplish a socially recognized purpose.

Thinklets constitute elementary units of intellectual capital to create and repeat patterns in collaboration processes among people with a common objective. The thinklets may be categorized accordingly collaboration patterns and may constitute the building blocks in the specification of informal activities (Gwendolyn et al, 2004).

Thinklets are in the genesis of a new research area called collaboration engineering. Thinklets were suggested in first place to document and reuse collaboration patterns in group support systems (GSS) e.g. electronic meeting systems (EMS). Here we propose the extension of the thinklet concept to collaboration within business processes execution context.

In the Contexts research it is emphasized the concern of modelling information needs of actors during their tasks execution attending the context they are in (Zacarias et al, 2005). This line of thought explores the context notion in organizational models based in the contributions of the classical engineering and social approaches to context.

Approaches based on Actor Network and Social Actor Network theories focuses on identifying the existing relations between actors during their participation in business processes execution. These approaches suggest a network of inter-relations representation and provide some parameters (centrality, collaboration potential, maximal flow, etc.) to assess/characterize this relation (Pereira and Soares, 2005).

In fact some of these initiatives aren't yet in a mature state to embrace professional/practical projects (e.g. contexts, thinklets) others like Genre Analysis and SAN presents very specific applications like in (Antunes et al, 2006)(Pereira and Soares, 2005) but they lack of holistic approach in relation with organizational architecture.

4. PROPOSED METHODOLOGY

In this work we consider an information system development process divided in five main phases: requirements capture and specification, modelling, design, development and deployment. These phases compose an iterative and incremental process in which, one of our main objectives, is that it could be flexible and agile due the focus/description adopted in our modelling approach.

Attending the design and development phases of an information system project, the BPM initiatives contribute to develop agile/modular systems operation and promote existing services reuse.

Nevertheless, the modelling and systems requirements capture, specification and also design phases, should consider the social-technical approaches in order to embrace the informal activities that may be part of business processes execution. At these phases it's essential to understand interaction among participants in order to:

- achieve a real/effective processes structure,
- identify vital people and activities in processes executions,
- and perceive knowledge flows and path ways.

Questions like: *"How often a participant receive information from each of the others that he need to do to his work?"*, *"How well a participant understands the knowledge, skills, and experience of each of the other people?"*, should be answered to achieve the social network representation. With a social network representation we can visualize/identify relations that help or constrain collaboration and information sharing processes. It also allows the identification of actors, who perform main roles or isolated ones, bottlenecks in information flow and communication (formal and informal) channels. As stated in section 2, social networks have several variables available that helps analyze the network in order to infer about the mentioned issues.

Figure 1 represents in a graphical way, the mapping between system development phases and contributions from social-technical approaches and BPMS initiatives.

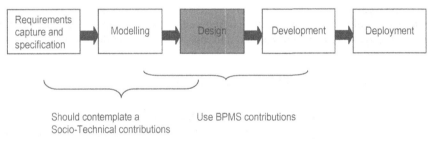

Figure1 – Map between development phases and different contributions.

One discipline that can contribute to gather needed information in order to achieve an effective social network representation is Genre Analysis (GA). GA claims that the work structures (including informal ones) may be inferred by inquiring about communicative actions. The observed communicative actions, materialized through: memos, reports, emails, phone calls, etc. are analysed/related (Yates and Orlikowski, 2002; Yoshioka, et al, 2001) and aggregated in a genre system trying to explain work patterns (Antunes et al, 2006). This can be done by several techniques e.g. document analysis, interviews, contextual inquiry, etc. (Beyer and Holtzblatt, 1998).

Once identified, informal activities, work structures and relations, across functional and organizational boundaries, we should focus on:

- Evaluate their impact in BP performance
- Consider them in BP management (in a agile manner)
- Represent the organizational knowledge/culture/social environment
- Define the needs of information in a contextualized manner at operational level (in order to increase productivity and responsiveness)
- Contemplate procedures and information needs in the ICT infra-structure

By adopting the proposed methodology we embrace an additional task in the project development which is the translation of the model which considers the social environment to the model for services description that will provide the operational execution support of the business processes. Thinklets may be a form to represent the bridge between these two models.

The identified activities, work structures, communications and relations may be represented as a choreographed set of thinklets. This set may include existing (mature) thinklets and new developed ones (representing/documenting this way in a structured manner the identified patterns).

In the field of research of collaboration engineering, the concept of thinklets have evolved from a more technological proximity, to a superior abstraction/ technological independence level (Gwendolyn et al, 2004). We propose that each thinklet constitute a guide to form a set of choreographed (available or new) services that implements the thinklet.

If service orientation architecture is used it have the advantage of being an architecture already prepared to choreograph services, deal with internal and external resources (including human) and integration in a modular manner.

5. CONCLUSIONS AND FUTURE WORK

One of the goals of this work is to show that in the development of information systems requirements gather and specification, as well as, design phases, must move its concerns to the social relations between participants and their informal activities. Social informal interactions exist and in order to be manageable, measured and their impact on business processes performance evaluated, they should be contemplated in system modelling.

In this paper we have discuss the recent business process management systems initiatives and had concluded that these initiatives play an important role in design and development phases to achieve agile, distributed and interoperable systems. Nevertheless, related to system modelling this initiatives lacks in concerning informal activities.

In the methodology proposed we aim to guide the system development process, first by modelling based on social-technical approaches and then developing in an agile, flexible, service oriented way recurring to BPMS initiatives. To link this to paradigms, we suggest the use of thinklets that at lower level could be implemented as a service composition and at a higher level could be (re)used to represent collaborative patterns.

As a future research agenda we suggest that it is also necessary to evaluate the models proposed in psycho-sociology discipline (Ferreira et al, 2001) they may contribute to systems specification/representation with its models of work satisfaction/motivation, productivity, leadership and team work. In these theories the complementarities and interdependence of social and technical subsystems, as well as, individual vs collective and organization vs environment, are well documented.

When one consider relations (informal or not) we must support the knowledge generation, representation and sharing needs, so in future, we should also consider contributions from semantic web (Sure et al, 2002) and ontology's development areas to knowledge representation.

6. REFERENCES

1. Advantys white paper. Workflow and Service Oriented Architecture (SOA). March 2005.
2. Anklam P., Social Network Analysis, http://www.byeday.net/sna/index.html. 2005.
3. Antunes P, Costa C. J, Pino J. A. From genre analysis to the design of electronic meeting systems. 2006.
4. BEA, (2005) Domain Model For SOA Realizing the Business Benefit of Service-Oriented Architecture, BEA white paper.
5. Beyer H. and Holtzblatt K. Contextual design: Define custumer-centered systems. San Francisco, CA: Morgan Kaufmann. 1998.
6. Bouquet P., Ghidini C., Giunchiglia F., Blanzieri E., Theories and Uses of Context in Knowledge Representation and Reasoning, Journal of pragmatics - Special issue on context 35(3): 455-484, 2002.
7. Briggs R. O, Vreede Gert-Jan, Nunamaker Jr J. F. Collaboration Engineering with ThinkLets to Pursue Sustained Success with Group Support Systems. Journal of Management Information Systems/Spring 2003, Vol. 19, No. 4, pp. 31–64.
8. Business Process Execution Language for Web Services (specs), Version 1.1
9. Chang J. The current state of BPM Technologies. BPM.com. 2005.
10. Charette R. N, Why software Fails. IEEE Spectrum, September 2005.
11. Chebbi I. Samir Tata, Schahram Dustdar Cooperation policies for inter organisational workflow. 2004
12. Chebbi I., Samir Tata, Schahram Dustdar. The view based approach to dynamic inter organisational workflow cooperation.
13. Ferreira J.M.C, Neves J, Caetano A. Manual de psicossociologia das organizações. McGraw Hill 2001.
14. Green, Richard Available BPEL runtime environments, evaluation criteria and evaluation results, Deliverable D-D1, RepoMMan Project.
15. Groth K., "Using Social Networks for Knowledge Management", Department of Numerical Analysis and Computing Science, Royal Institute of Technology, Sweden, (2002).
16 Gwendolyn L. Kolfschoten, Briggs R. O, Jaco H. Appelman, Vreede Gert-Jan. ThinkLets as Building Blocks for Collaboration Processes: A Further Conceptualization. CRIWG 2004: 137-152.
17. Hollingsworth, David. The Workflow Reference 10 Years On. Fujitsu Services, United Kingdom Chair, Technical Committee, WfMC. 2004.
18. Jablonski S., Horn S., Schlundt M., Process Oriented Knowledge Management, 1. Konferenz Professionelles Wissensmanagement: Erfahrungen und Visionen, 2001.
19. Ken Schwaber. Agile Project managment with SCRUM. Microsoft Press 2004.
20. Lacey N. Narrative genre: Key concepts in media studies. New york: St. Martins Press. 2000.
21. Marsh, R. Guidelines for Adapting web services for system Integration", Business Integration Journal. 2005.
22. Martínez A., Dimitriadis, Y., Tardajos, J., Velloso, O., Villacorta, M. B., "Integration of SNA in a mixed evaluation approach of the study of participatory aspects of collaboration", (2004).
23. Naidoo T, Michael zur Muehlen. The State of Standards and their Practical Application, (member of the board of directors of BPMI.org, AIIM Conference May 2005.
24. Oracle BPEL: Building Standards-Based Business Processes with Web Services. 2004.
25. Papazolou, Michael P., Jean-jacques Dubray. A survey of web service technologies. 2004.

26. Pereira C. S, Soares A. L. Tecnologias de colaboração em organizações de I&D: Uma abordagem por redes sociais. 6ª CAPSI, 26-28de Outubro de 2005, Bragança, Portugal.
27. Pinho A, Soares A. L. Teoria Actor-Network na análise de requisitos de sistemas de informação. 6ª CAPSI, 26-28de Outubro de 2005, Bragança, Portugal.
28. Saunders C, Chiasson M. Using Genre Systems to Investigate the Interplay Between Technology-in-Practice and the Knowledge Management Practices of Lawyers. Proceedings of the 38th Hawaii International Conference on System Sciences, 2005.
29. Shapiro R. A Comparison of XPDL, BPML and BPEL4WS. 2002.
30. Silva A, Videira C. UML, Metodologias e Ferramentas Case. Centro Atlântico. 2001.
31. Smith H. and Peter Fingar. Business Process Fusion Is Inevitable. 2004.
32. Smith H. A Systems Integrator's Perspective on Business Process Management", Workflow and EAI, Infoconomy Agile Business conference. 2002.
33. Spinuzi C. Tracing genres through organizations: A sociocultural approach to information design. Cambridge: The MIT Press, 2003.
34. Srinivasan M., Dave Shaffer. Agile IT Through SOA requires new technology. 2005.
35. Sure Y, Erdmann M, Angele J, Staab S, Studer R, Wenke D. OntoEdit: Collaborative Ontology Development for the SemanticWeb. pp. 221-235. ISCW Berlin 2002.
36. Talbot, Steve R. Web Services choreography and Process Algebra. 2004.
37. TIBCO white paper. BPM on SOA foundation, a unified framework for process design and deployment. November 2005.
38. Van Elst L., Abecker A., Maus H., Exploiting User and Process Context for Knowledge Management Systems. Workshop on User-Modeling for Context Aware Applications at the 8th International Conference on User Modeling, 2001.
39. Yates J, Orlikowski W. Genre systems Structuring interaction through communicative norms. Journal of Business Communication 39, no. 1, 13-35, 2002.
40. Yates J, Orliskowski W. Genres of organizational communications: A structurational approach to studying communication and media. Academy of management Review 17, no. 2, pp. 299-326, 1992
41. Zacarias M., Caetano A, Pinto H, Tribolet J. Modelling contexts for business process oriented knowledge support. WM, Kaiserslautern, Germany. 2005.

ENTROPY AS A MEASUREMENT FOR THE QUALITY OF DEMAND FORECASTING

Bernd Scholz-Reiter, Jan Topi Tervo and Uwe Hinrichs
Department of Planning and Control of Production Systems,
University of Bremen, Germany
{bsr, ter, hin}@biba.uni-bremen.de

Production planning and control is a highly complex process influenced by many factors. An important part of this broad task is demand forecasting, for which many methods already have been developed. But due to the occurring dynamics in the used data, the prediction may differ strongly from the optimum and thus errors leading to rising costs are inevitable. In this paper we will propose the entropy as a measurement for the quality of order forecasting respectively as relative estimation for the forecasting error. In general, entropy is a measurement for disorder and thus also for information content. Since lack of information leads to inaccuracy of forecasting, the entropy can be identified with the quality of order prediction. First results on the basis of time-series obtained from mathematical functions, discrete-event simulations of a production network scenario and a real shop-floor system will show the successful transfer of this method.

1. INTRODUCTION

Nowadays, production planning and control is a challenging task due to changing market conditions and increasing dynamics in global network organizations. Its primary objective is to schedule and realize the ongoing production plan efficiently (Eversheim et al., 1996). To do so, the production capacities and the needed amount of resources have to be regarded.

While the number of machines is constant in general, the demand for any kind of resource or material has to be forecasted and ordered with respect to the planned output in a defined time-period. Incorrect or invalid forecasts can lead to severe consequences: ordering too much material will result in higher stocks with rising costs for stock-holding and materials. When ordering less than the needed amount the risk of production downtimes arises. Therefore, exact and secure methods for the important process of demand forecasting are needed.

This becomes clearer when looking at the several factors or sources of information which influence the planned demand for materials in a defined period of time. First of all, exact numbers from the sales market are needed, which determine the production plan. Here, seasonal fluctuations can occur depending on the kind of produced goods. Furthermore, increasing dynamics in present markets have been observed and nonlinear effects in production systems or production networks have been verified (Scholz-Reiter et al., 2003), (Wiendahl et al., 2000). Regarding all these factors and the possible economic results, it is obvious that adaptive and trustful methods have to be used when forecasting the demand.

Until now several approaches for demand forecasting based on statistical and mathematical techniques are used. The future demand is forecasted by using a time-series consisting of former values (Granger, 1989). Although these methods were tested and show a strong reliability, there are still no means to measure the quality of the calculated result. But since order forecasting techniques basically depend on preceding information; a measurement for the prediction quality should be based on the available information content. Hence, we propose the entropy to characterize the quality of order forecasting respectively the relative estimation for the forecasting error, as entropy is a measurement for disorder and, thus, also for information content.

In the following, several forecasting methods as well as the entropy in general are presented. The next step is to apply these techniques to different time-series showing demand values and compare the measured forecasting error with the calculated entropy. Therefore, several time-series taken from different mathematical functions, discrete-event simulations of a production network scenario and a real shop-floor system were used.

2. FORECASTING METHODS

In recent publications many forecasting methods have been proposed for a broad variation of different settings (Makridakis et al., 1998). But since the focus of this paper is rather on the quality of the forecasting than on the method itself, we will concentrate on two different basic techniques, which will be presented briefly here.

The first is the moving average approach, which is best suitable for simple time-series with identifiable fluctuations around a mean value and without cycles. Thereby, not all available data from a time-series is used, but only the last n values. The demand in the future period λ_{i+1} is then determined by the averaged demand $\lambda_i(n)$ of the considered past period (Granger, 1989):

$$\lambda_{i+1} = \lambda_i(n) = \tfrac{1}{n} \sum_{j=i-n}^{i} \lambda_j. \tag{1}$$

The number of values given by n allows looking at a limited time segment and thereby shows a high flexibility. But also, n influences the reaction to changes: a large value of n neglects rapid changes, while a smaller value of n follows fast dynamics.

The other applied method is exponential smoothing or exponentially weighted moving average (Granger, 1989). Here the future demand λ_{i+1} is calculated from the weighted average of the measured demand λ_i and the forecasted demand $\lambda_i(\alpha)$ of the past period:

$$\lambda_{i+1}(\alpha) = \alpha\lambda_i + (1-\alpha)\lambda_i(\alpha) \text{ with } 0 < \alpha < 1. \tag{2}$$

When including the n past values, this leads to the weighted average of the data:

$$\lambda_{i+1}(\alpha) = \alpha \sum_{j=i-n}^{i} (1-\alpha)^{i-j} \lambda_j. \tag{3}$$

The factor $(1-\alpha)^{i-j}$ causes an exponential decrease of the influence of the past values on the average. If α is near one, the decay is strong, i.e., the effect of the past values is weak. In contrast, when α is near zero, the decay is weaker and past values are taken into account more strongly. The challenge is to find a suitable value for α. Until now there is no objective way to define this factor.

3. ENTROPY

Commonly, the word entropy is associated with disorder, uncertainty or ignorance. It originates from two different domains of science, namely physics and information theory. Both derivations have similarities, but require knowledge in each domain.

Entropy as a measure with physical meaning was introduced by Clausius (1865) and later precised by Boltzmann (1880). In thermodynamics, a macroscopic state is described by the microscopic behaviour of all its N particles. These are defined by their positions and their impulses, which span a $6N$-dimensional phase space. Entropy then gives a measurement for the quantity of different possible microstates of that thermodynamical system or the volume of phase space occupied by it. In other words, it describes the internal disorder within a system. Since entropy in statistical physics gives a probabilistic treatment to a system's thermal fluctuations, higher entropy also means a greater lack of information on the exact configuration of the system. Hence, it has many similarities with entropy derived in information theory. This definition is principally based on Shannon (Shannon, 1948) and in this sense it is a measure for the amount of randomness hidden in an information sequence. This means that a sequence with redundancies or statistical regularities exhibits small values of entropy and in contrast, a uniform distribution of sequence symbols, e.g., white noise, leads to the highest entropy value. As a consequence, history and future of that sequence are completely uncorrelated. Since this paper is focussed on time-series analysis, the information theoretical definition of entropy will be considered.

3.1 Symbolic dynamics

In order to calculate a value for entropy, a sequence of symbols is needed. In time series with discrete values, e.g., buffer levels, this condition is granted. But for a continuous variable, the values have to be transformed into an adequate sequence. Nevertheless, the number of discrete values may also be reduced by such a transformation. In physics, this method is well known as 'symbolic dynamics' (Hao, 1988).

Apparently, when transforming a time-series into a symbol sequence, a large amount of detailed information is lost, but some invariant and robust characteristics such as periodicity, symmetry and chaos can be conserved. But this strongly depends on the choice of the transformation. Due to the reduction of details, the analyses of symbol sequences are less vulnerable to noise (Daw et al., 2003) and, consequently, conclusions drawn from these sequences are more precise.

Before calculating the entropy, the first choice to make is the alphabet size $|A|=l$, i.e., the number of symbols used to transform the original time-series into a sequence of symbols. This variable determines how much of the original information is conserved. The simplest case is a binary alphabet with $l=2$ and $A=\{0,1\}$. The next step is to decide about the transformation itself. There are two elementary different ways: static and dynamic transformations (for illustration see figure 1). The static transformation is realized by choosing one (in the binary case) or more thresholds and the different symbols are then assigned to the intervals between them. There are diverse rules to calculate those thresholds, e.g., data mean or median value (Daw et al., 2003). The dynamic transformation is preferred when the dynamics are more important than the absolute values. Thereby, step-to-step differences in the sequence are taken into account and, in the binary case for example, a positive difference leads to one and a negative to the other symbol. Of course it is possible to make a bad choice for the transformation, hence all or at least the relevant information is lost.

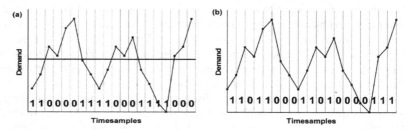

Figure 1 - Illustration of symbol sequence generation. In (a) a binary static and in (b) a binary dynamical transformation is shown.

3.2 Calculation of entropy

In order to calculate the Shannon-Entropy symbol sequence statistics have to be performed. More precisely, a histogram of repeating sequences of length L has to be obtained. Therefore, L consecutively following symbols s are combined to a word s^L and every word is uniquely coded to a decimal number (see figure 2) to avoid the handling of long symbol sequences.

```
1 1 0 1 1 0 0 0 1 1 0 1 0 0 0 0 1 1 1
1 1 0
  1 0 1
    0 1 1
      .....
6 5 3 6 4 0 1 3 6 5 2 4 0 0 1 3 7
```

Figure 2 - The code sequence (lower row) is produced by a window of length $L=3$ being slid over the symbol sequence (upper row).

Figuratively, one can think of a window of size L being slid from the beginning to the end of the sequence and at every position a word of length L is found. Then, a histogram of the relative word frequencies $p(s^L)$ can be obtained and with

$$H_S = -\sum_{s^L \in A^L} p(s^L)\log_l p(s^L) \qquad (4)$$

the Shannon-Entropy can be calculated as the sum over all possible words of length L. Since the value of the entropy is strongly dependent on the word length L, a standardisation with the maximally possible entropy is required:

$$H = \frac{H_S}{H_{MAX}} \in [0, 1] \tag{5}$$

This maximum value is obtained for a uniform distribution of the word frequencies

$$p(s^L) = \frac{1}{L^l}, \forall s^L \tag{6}$$

and thus $H_{MAX} = L$. This leads to a zero entropy for constant sequences of symbols and to $H=1$ for a completely random symbol sequence.

4. MEASUREMENT FOR QUALITY OF DEMAND FORECASTING

The entropy as a reliable measurement for order forecasting quality is evaluated by comparing the forecasted demand with the real demand value of the next time step. Then the correlation between forecasting error and calculated entropy is identified. But previously, the parameters l (alphabet size), L (word length), n (time horizon) and α (smoothing factor) in Equations (1)-(5) have to be determined.

The maximum possible word length strongly depends on the alphabet size and the length of the time-series: The larger the alphabet and the shorter the time-series, the smaller is the possible word length (and vice versa) (Daw et al., 2003). Since real time-series are in general rather short, we use a binary alphabet to be able to get a word length up to $L=5$. The data mean was used as a threshold for a static transformation, except for the real shop-floor system where additionally a dynamical transformation was applied. Also, for the shop-floor system it was unfortunately only possible to calculate the entropy up to a word length $L=4$ due to the shortness of the time-series of only 360 samples. To be as realistic as possible, the time horizon is chosen to be half a year, i.e., with one time sample per day. This leads to $n=150$ time samples and additionally, the smoothing parameter was found to produce in average best results for $\alpha=0.76$.

4.1 Simple examples

To depict the properties of the entropy, its value for three simple time-series generated from a constant, a sine and a uniformly distributed random function (see figure 3) is used.

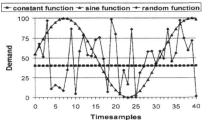

Figure 3 - Extract from the constant, sinusoidal and random function, respectively the generated time-series (denoted as points), used for entropy calculation and forecasting.

The calculated values are enlisted in Table 1. As stated above, a constant function leads to a single peak in the distribution of generated words and thus zero entropy will follow. The computational calculation for different word lengths confirms this result. As a consequence, forecasting without error is possible. Contrarily, a time-series of random values leads to a uniform distribution of generated words and hence to a maximum entropy of value one; an exact forecasting is impossible. The sine function produces for increasing word lengths decreasing entropy values (cf. Table 1) with a mean of approximately 0.5, because a longer word implies more information and a better predictability.

Table 1 - Entropy values of different word lengths for the three
different time-series generated by a constant, sine and random function.

Word length	Entropy		
	constant	sine	random
3	0.00	0.56	1.00
4	0.00	0.50	1.00
5	0.00	0.47	1.00

The forecasting of a constant time-series is trivial. Both methods (gliding average and exponential smoothing) will deliver exact results of future demand without any error. This coincides with the entropy value of zero. Similarly, the forecasting error for the random function corresponds to the calculated entropy. Here, the forecasting method has no significance, since the past values do not correlate at all with future values. This is shown by the forecasted values (calculated with gliding average method) varying only a little around 50 and their error to the real demand, fluctuating between 0 and 100. Table 3 enlists these values for three randomly picked points in time of the time-series. The prediction of the demand for the sine function is in average better with the exponential smoothing than with the gliding average method.

For the forecasting error it is of major importance at which time step a prediction is made. Around the minimum and maximum values of the function good values can be obtained, while rather large errors occur when the slope is large. This reflects the entropy value of about 0.5 calculated in Table 1.

4.2 Simulation time-series

To generate more application-oriented time-series a discrete event simulation model of a supply chain of three enterprises with external customer driving (Scholz-Reiter et al., 2005) was used. The customer demand was realized by a discrete sinusoidal and a uniformly distributed random function (cf. figure 4). The entropy values calculated for both time-series are comparable to those calculated in Section 4.1.

Table 2 - Entropy values of different word lengths for the two different time-series generated by the DES model with a sinusoidal and random customer demand and entropy values of different word lengths for the time-series of the real shop-floor system created with static and dynamical transformation.

Word length	Entropy			
	Simulation Data		Real Data	
	Sine	Random	Dynamical	Static
2	-	-	0.95	0.90
3	0.61	1.00	0.93	0.90
4	0.56	1.00	0.92	0.90
5	0.52	1.00	-	-

The random demand leads to a random fluctuation in the time-series and so an entropy value of one follows. On the other hand, the sinusoidal demand causes a deterministic structure similar to the sine function and accordingly an entropy value of about 0.57 is calculated (cf. Table 2). These values correspond to the forecasting errors. As shown in Table 3 the sine function can be forecasted well because the used forecasting methods deliver best results when only marginal dynamics are present. Again a comparison for randomly picked points in time of the time-series were done (see Table 3).

4.3 Real data

The last time-series to be analysed is taken from the demand of a real shop-floor system (cf. figure 5). Here, the entropy is calculated with static and dynamical transformations to constitute the differences between them for this time-series. As shown in Table 2 the values differ only slightly with values of 0.9 and 0.93 respectively. Again, the entropy value corresponds to the predictability of the time-series: It shows an almost random behaviour with only little determinism. This is confirmed by the calculated forecasting values compared with real demand (cf. Table 3).

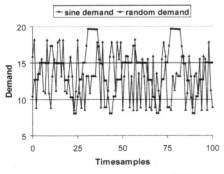

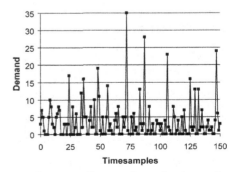

Figure 4 – Extract from two different time-series generated by the DES model with a sinusoidal and random.

Figure 5 – Extract form the demand time-series of a real shop-floor system.

5. SUMMARY

The entropy can be calculated quickly and easily for rather short word length (up to $L=8$) and realistic demand time-series of a length of max. 10000 time steps. Since it is a measurement for uncertainty it corresponds to the predictability of time-series. Therefore, no absolute forecasting error can be obtained, but a graduation between 0 (perfectly predictable) and 1 (not predictable at all) is very well possible.

The presented results show that this property of the entropy can be successfully transferred to relatively measure the reliability of demand forecasting. But for a promising application in order forecasting methods further research has to be done, which will deal with the evaluation of the several parameters and concrete recommended actions especially.

Table 3 - Forecasted and real demand values for all mentioned time-series for randomly picked points in time, respectively their relative error.

Time-Series	Forecasted value	Real Value	Relative Error
sine function	29.1	18.7	55.6%
	84.9	92.4	8.1%
	1.6	1.4	14.3%
random function	53.9	60.9	11.5%
	53.3	77.9	31.6%
	53.1	18.5	187.0%
sinusoidal demand	15.1	12.59	19.9%
	15.03	14.99	0.3%
	10.88	10.31	5.5%
random demand	13.33	18.38	27.5%
	13.55	10.85	24.9%
	13.41	11.35	15.4%
Real data	3.01	3	24.0%
	3.05	1	205.0%
	3.42	11	68.9%

6. REFERENCES

1. Daw, C. S.; Finney, C. E. A.; Tracy, E. R., 2003, A review of symbolic analysis of experimental data, Review of Scientific Instruments 74, 915-930.
2. Eversheim, W.; Schuh, G., 1996, Produktion und Management Bd. 2, Springer.
3. Granger, C. W. J., 1989, Forecasting in Business and Economics, Academic Press, London.
4. Hao, B.-L., 1988, Elementary Symbolic Dynamics and Chaos in Dissipative Systems, World Scientific.
5. Makridakis, S; Wheelwright, S. C.; Hyndman, R. J., 1998, Forecasting, Wiley and Sons.
6. Scholz-Reiter, B.; Freitag, M., 2003, On the Dynamics of Manufacturing Systems – A State Space Perspective, Proceedings of the 36th CIRP-International Seminar on Manufacturing Systems, pp. 455-462.
7. Scholz-Reiter, B.; Hinrichs, U.; Delhoum, S., 2005, Analyse auftretender Instabilitäten in dynamischen Produktions- und Logistiknetzwerken, Industrie Management 21 (2005) 5, S. 25-28.
8. Shannon, C. E., 1948, A mathematical theory of communication, The Bell System Technical Journal, 27, 379-423 and 623-656.
9. Wiendahl, H.-P.; Worbs, J., 2000, Simulation based analysis of complex production systems with methods of nonlinear dynamics. IMCC'2000 International Manufacturing Conference in China.

KNOWLEDGE–BASED AND CP–DRIVEN METHODOLOGY FOR DEDICATED DSS DESIGN

Zbigniew Banaszak[1], Izabela Tomczuk-Piróg[2] and Paweł Sitek[3]

[1]*Technical University of Koszalin, Department of Computer Science and Management, Poland*
banaszak@tu.koszalin.pl
[2]*Opole University of Technology, Department of Management and Production Engineering, Poland*
itomczuk@po.opole.pl
[3]*Technical University of Kielce, Department of Electrical and Computer Engineering, Poland*
sitek@tu.kielce.pl

An analysis of unified framework standing behind a methodology in object oriented decision support system design has been analysed. First of all the consistency of the assumed knowledge bases describing an object (enterprise) and requests (standard options supporting a decision maker), respectively are examined. Then the knowledge base representation is transformed into representation of so called constraint satisfaction problem (CSP). Possible ways of the CSP decomposition as well as possibility of different programming languages application lead to a problem of searching for a distribution strategy which gives possibility to interact in an on-line mode.

1. INTRODUCTION

Decision making supported by task-oriented software tools plays a pivotal role in modern enterprises; the commercially available ERP systems are not able to make a decision in an interactive on-line/real-time mode. A new generation of DSS (Decision Support Systems) that enables fast prototyping of production flow in multi-project environment as well as an integrated approach to a layout planning, production routing, batch-sizing and scheduling problems is required. In that context, the constraint logic programming (CLP) techniques which allow declarative representation of a decision making problem provide quite an attractive alternative [6,7]. The paper includes modelling of decision making and searching strategies development.

2. PROBLEM STATEMENT

We analyse knowledge-based representation of small and medium size enterprises and knowledge-based representation of context-oriented queries. The *SME's* specification includes parameters describing the number of resources available, their efficiency, capacity; time constrained resources availability etc., as well as relations linking particular workstations, pallets, tools, manpower etc. Due to the prevailing unique character of work orders in *SME's,* it is necessary to be able to evaluate quickly and precisely the possibility to balance the production capacity of a company with the requirements set in agreement with the customer [1]. Solution to a makespan-feasible problem opens a possibility to investigate the effect of a new work order impact on the performance of a manufacturing system. The queries encompassing standard options of *SME* management are, in turn, specified by data relevant to a production order requirements and the enterprise capacities. The objective is to find a *DSS* to respond to any questions related to the *SME* considered in an interactive mode. The problem we are facing deals with a question, whether there is a way which enables evaluating a possibility of relevant *DSS* design for the commercially available programming languages. The graphic illustration of the considered problem has been presented in Fig. 1.

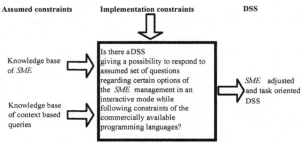

Figure 1 - Illustration of the problem statement.

3. KNOWLEDGE-BASED REPRESENTATION

It is assumed that any system can be specified in terms of knowledge base composed of facts and rules determining the system's respective properties and relations linking them. Formally, RW knowledge base is defined as a pair: $RW = < \alpha, F(\alpha)>$, where, $\alpha = (\alpha_1, \alpha_2, \dots, \alpha_N)$ – is a sequence of elementary formulas specifying system's properties; α_i – *is the i-th assertion (specified in terms of binary logic), and* $a_i = w(\alpha_i) \in \{0,1\}$ is a logic value of the assertion α_i

$F(\alpha) = \{F_1(\alpha), F_2(\alpha), \dots, F_K(\alpha)\}$ – is a sequence of facts specifying relations between properties (in terms of logic operators: conjunction, disjunction, negation, and implication); $F_j(a)$ – refers to a binary value of $F_i(\alpha)$.

So $a = (a_1, a_2, \dots, a_m)$ corresponds to any $\alpha = (\alpha_1, \alpha_2, \dots, \alpha_N)$. Consequently $(a_1, a_2, \dots, a_m)$ refers to a sequence of values associated with $w(\alpha)$.

In any system description, the following categories can be distinguished:

$\alpha_x = \{\alpha_{x1}, \alpha_{x2}, \dots, \alpha_{xk}\}$ – a set of elementary formulas specifying the so called input system variables, $\alpha_{xu} \in \{\alpha_1, \alpha_2 \dots, \alpha_N\}$,

$\alpha_y = \{\alpha_{y1}, \alpha_{y2}, \dots, \alpha_{yp}\}$ – a set of elementary formulas specifying the so called output system variables, $\alpha_{yu} \in \{\alpha_1, \alpha_2, \dots, \alpha_N\}$,

$\alpha_w = \{\alpha_{x1}, \alpha_{x2}, \dots, \alpha_{xr}\}$ – a set of auxiliary elementary formulas specifying the system functioning, $\alpha_{wu} \in \{\alpha_1, \alpha_2, \dots, \alpha_N\}$.

Of course, $\alpha_x \cup \alpha_y \cup \alpha_w = \alpha$, $\alpha_x \cap \alpha_y = \varnothing$, $\alpha_x \cap \alpha_w = \varnothing$, $\alpha_y \cap \alpha_w = \varnothing$, *and* $a_x = \{a_{x1}, a_{x2}, \dots, a_{xk}\}$, $a_y = \{a_{y1}, a_{y2}, \dots, a_{yp}\}$, $a_w = \{a_{x1}, a_{x2}, \dots, a_{xr}\}$, *so* $a = (a_{x1}, a_{x2}, \dots, a_{xk}) \wedge (a_{y1}, a_{y2}, \dots, a_{yp}) \wedge (a_{x1}, a_{x2}, \dots, a_{xr})$ *corresponds to* $\alpha = (\alpha_{x1}, \alpha_{x2}, \dots, \alpha_{xk}) \wedge (\alpha_{y1}, \alpha_{y2}, \dots, \alpha_{yp}) \wedge (\alpha_{x1}, \alpha_{x2}, \dots, \alpha_{xr})$.

$F_x(\alpha_x) = \{F_{x1}(\alpha_x), F_{x2}(\alpha_x), \dots, F_{xp}(\alpha_x)\}$ – a set of input facts, i.e. assertions describing properties of system input,

$F_y(\alpha_y) = \{F_{y1}(\alpha_y), F_{y2}(\alpha_y), \dots, F_{yR}(\alpha_y)\}$ – set of output facts, i.e. assertions describing properties of the system output.

Of course, besides the real objects such as SMEs the above representation can be applied to any other objects, e.g., constraints, specifications, etc.

4. CONSTRAINT SATISFACTION PROBLEM REPRESENTATION

The declarative character of Constraint Programming languages and a high efficiency in solving combinatorial problems constitutes an attractive alternative for the available systems (applying operation research techniques) of computer-integrated management [2]. The Constraint Satisfaction Problem $CSP = ((X,D,),C)$ consists of a set of variables $X = \{x_1, x_2, \dots, x_n\}$, their domains $D = \{D_i \,|D_i = [d_{i1}, d_{i2}, \dots, d_{ij}, \dots, d_{im}], i = \{1, \dots, n\}\}$, and a set of constraints $C = \{C_i \,|i = \{1, \dots, L\}\}$. A solution to be obtained is such an assignment of the variable values in which all the constraints are satisfied.

As the general *CSP* is NP-complete, constraint propagation is usually incomplete. This means that some but not all the consequences in the set of constraints are deducted. In particular, constraint propagation can not detect all inconsistencies. Consequently, we need to find out whether the *CSP* instance at hand has a solution or not. The solution to that problem can be the proper knowledge-based representation and decomposition of *CSP*. The *CSP* problem decomposes in a natural way into subproblems, in particular to elementary subproblems, which are not decomposed further. The elementary problems can be seen as problems encompassed by constraints.

In the above considerations it should be noted that a $CSP = ((X,D),C)$ can be decomposed into a set of: elementary subproblems, loosely coupled subproblems, dependent subproblems of strongly coupled problems.

In general case any *CSP* may be decomposed (Fig. 2), either into a set of loosely coupled problems or into a set of strongly coupled problems. Possible ways of *CSP* decomposition give a possibility to take into account the real life constraints following from: a way of a problem specification (i.e., a set of elementary problems recognized); a programming language implemented (some structures of dependent problems may or may not be accepted by *CP/CCP/CLP* packages); a way of a *CSP* resolution (e.g., the loosely coupled subproblems can be computed independently within a multiprocessor environment); a searching strategy applied (the order of subproblems resolution results in a *CSP* makespan).

The above observation leads to a reference model concept of a *CSP* decomposition, [3]. So, since each subproblem corresponds to a standard constraint problem structure: *(({a set of decision variables}, {a set of variable domains}), {a set of constraints})*, hence some AND/OR – like graph representation can be used both in the analysis of the *CSP* programming and its resolution. It should be noted that any knowledge base can be represented in terms of $CSP = ((a,D), \{F(a)=1\})$, where $D = \{D_i \mid D_i = \{0,1\}, i = 1..N\}$, $F(a)=1$ a sequence of facts: $(F_1(a)=1, F_2(a)=1, ... , F_K(a)=1)$.

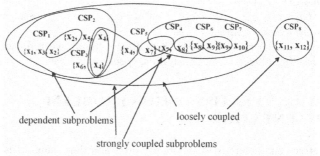

Figure 2 - $CSP = ((X,D),C)$ decomposition into loosely and strongly coupled as well as into dependent subproblems.

5. FEASIBLE SOLUTIONS

The question considered regards $F_x(\alpha_x)$ the following implication: $F_x(\alpha_x) \Rightarrow F_y(\alpha_y)$. In other words, the question is: What are α_x and $F_x(\alpha_x)$, if either, ensuring the system property $F_y(\alpha_y)$. Consider the knowledge base $RW'=<\alpha',F'(\alpha)>$ corresponding to a system considered and the knowledge base stating a question $RW'' = <\alpha'',F''(\alpha)>$, e.g. regarding a given system's property. The resultant knowledge base $RW = <\alpha,F(\alpha)>$ (see Fig. 3) provides a framework for the considered problem statement: Is there an $F_x(\alpha_x)$, ensuring $F_y(\alpha_y)$? More precisely, in order to determine the feature $F_x(\alpha_x)$ a set of facts following feature $F_y(\alpha_y)$ while do not following $\neg F_y(\alpha_y)$ have to be determined. The scheme of the searching procedure is shown in Fig. 3. It means the knowledge base *RW1* including the conditions implying $F_y(\alpha_y)$ as well as the knowledge base *RW2* not including the conditions implying $F_y(\alpha_y)$ are refined from the knowledge base considered *RW*. The knowledge bases obtained enable to determine the final knowledge base *RW3*, i.e. modified *RW1* (not including elementary formulas and facts included in *RW2*). In order to implement the above procedure in terms of logic-algebraic method the sets of binary values S_a, S_x, and S_y following a, a_x, and a_y, (while corresponding to $F(\alpha)$, $F_x(\alpha_x)$, and $F_y(\alpha_y)$) have to be defined due to formulas: $S_a = \{a: F(a) = 1\}$, $S_x = \{a_x: F_x(a_x) = 1\}$, $S_y = \{a_y: F_y(a_y) = 1\}$.

Assumption that all the *RW* facts are true implies that among α sequences, there are also sequences for which $F(a) = 1$ holds, see $S_a = \{a: F(a)=1\}$. The associated set S_a guaranteeing the facts describing the system are true can be treaded as *RW*. Searching for the set S_x representing $F_x(\alpha_x)$ which can be treated as *RW3* requires two subsets, i.e. S_{x1} corresponding to *RW1* while following $F_y(a_y)=1$, and S_{x2} corresponding to *RW2* while following $F_y(a_y)=0$.

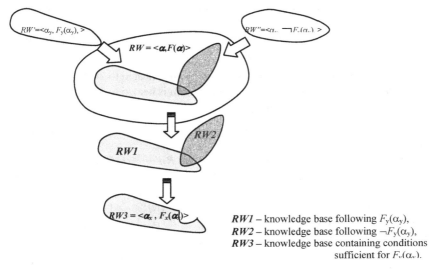

$RW' = <\alpha_y, F_y(\alpha_y), >$

$RW = <\alpha, F(\alpha)>$

$RW'' = <\alpha .. \neg F.(\alpha.) >$

$RW2$

$RW1$

$RW3 = <\alpha_x , F_x(\alpha)>$

RW1 – knowledge base following $F_y(\alpha_y)$,
RW2 – knowledge base following $\neg F_y(\alpha_y)$,
RW3 – knowledge base containing conditions
sufficient for $F_x(\alpha_x)$.

Figure 3 - Sufficient conditions refinement.

Finally, $S_x = S_{x1} \setminus S_{x2}$, where S_{x1}, and S_{x2} are determined for a_x from equations:

$$\text{for } S_{x1}: \begin{cases} F(a) = 1 \\ F_y(a_y) = 1 \end{cases}$$

$$(1)$$

$$\text{for } S_{x2}: \begin{cases} F(a) = 1 \\ F_y(a_y) = 0 \end{cases}$$

$$(2)$$

where: $F(a)=1$ stands for the set of facts: $\{F_1(a)=1, F_2(a)=1,..., F_K(a)=1\}$

6. METHODOLOGY FOR INTERACTIVE DEDICATED DECISION SUPPORT SYSTEM DESIGN

The proposed methodology consists of two stages (see figure 5). According to the first one, the CLP_L including the sufficient conditions (i.e. guaranteeing a solution exists) is provided. As the input data - the SME based knowledge base KB_{SME} and the request based knowledge base KB_R are considered. Of course, the different request based knowledge bases may result in different sets of sufficient conditions. This observation provides a way of the sufficient conditions refinement, i.e. a way of DSS adjustment. The CLP_L extended for other kinds of variables and constraints (so called algebraic ones) results in CLP problem. So, as a consequence of the second stage, programming languages as well as decision variables substitution strategy guaranteeing interactive usage of the DSS design is provided (Banaszak et al., 2005). Both stages are based on the $CP/CCP/CLP$ languages. The key point of the methodology proposed regards the procedure for CSP_L design. In order to illustrate this procedure partially introduced in the Section 5, let us consider the following example.

Consider a controller composed of two switches P_1 and P_2. The room temperature is controlled by relevant set up switches

- If P_1 is turned on and P_2 is turned off, then the room is heated to 20 ^{0}C.
- If P_1 is turned off and P_2 is turned on, then the room is heated to 30 ^{0}C.
- If both P_1 and P_2 are turned on, then the room is heated to 40 ^{0}C.

The question is: What switches set up leads to obtaining the room temperature between 20 and 40 ^{0}C?

The controller's knowledge base representation is: $RW = <\alpha, F(\alpha)>$:

$\alpha = (\alpha_1, \alpha_2, \alpha_3, \alpha_4, \alpha_5)$, where: $F(\alpha) = (F_1(\alpha), F_2(\alpha), F_3(\alpha), F_4(\alpha))$,

where:

α_1: "switch P_1 is turned on", $F_1(\alpha)$: $\alpha_1 \wedge (\neg\alpha_2) \Leftrightarrow \alpha_3$

α_2: "switch P_2 is turned off", $F_2(\alpha)$: $(\neg\alpha_1) \wedge \alpha_2 \Leftrightarrow \alpha_4$

α_3: "the room is heated to 20 ^{0}C", $F_3(\alpha)$: $\alpha_1 \wedge \alpha_2 \Leftrightarrow \alpha_5$

α_4: "the room is heated to 30 ^{0}C", $F_4(\alpha)$: $(\neg\alpha_1) \wedge (\neg\alpha_2) \Leftrightarrow \alpha_6$

α_5: "the room is heated to 40 ^{0}C"

α_6: "the room is not heated"

Elementary input and output formulas are: $\alpha_x = (\alpha_1, \alpha_2,)$, $\alpha_y = (\alpha_3, \alpha_4, \alpha_5, \alpha_6)$

Required output property is: $F_Y(\alpha_y) = \alpha_4 \vee \alpha_5$

The Fig. 4 illustrates the logic-algebraic method based procedure for the CSP_L design. Note that the procedure follows the scheme of sufficient conditions refinement shown in Fig. 3.

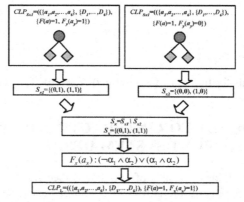

Legend:

$a_i = w(\alpha_i)$ – decision variable determining logic value of the formulae α_i,

$D_i = \{0, 1\}$ – binary domain of the variable a_i,

$F(a)=1$ – the constraint guaranteeing all facts F_i hold: $(F_1(\alpha)=1, F_2(\alpha)=1, F_3(\alpha)=1, F_4(\alpha)=1)$,

$F_y(a_y)=1$ – the constraint guaranteeing, the output fact is true,

$F_y(a_y)=0$ – the constraint guaranteeing, the output fact is false,

$F_x(a_x)$ – the input fact, i.e. resultant sufficient condition.

Figure 4 - Illustration of the logic-algebraic method procedure for the CSP_L design.

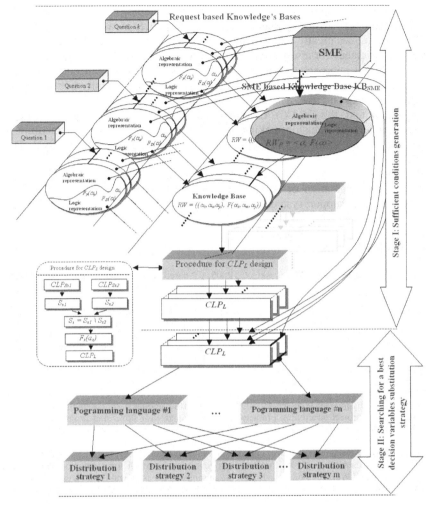

Figure 5 - Methodology for interactive dedicated decision support systems design.

7. CONCLUSIONS

A *CP/CCP/CLP* – based modelling framework driven by the logic-algebraic method provides a good platform for development of the task oriented *DSS*. The discussion provided has shown the versatility of *CP/CCP/CLP* paradigm for the decision making problems. Possible applications of logic-algebraic method to the examination of sufficient conditions ensuring assumed system's properties as well as the consistency checking techniques greatly reducing the search space and supported by *CP/CCP/CLP* prove their efficiency for resolution of the project-driven manufacturing tasks.

The proposed approach can therefore be considered as a contribution to design automation of interactive and task oriented *DSS*. That is especially important in the context of a cheap and user-friendly decision support for the *SME's*.

In that context, the *CP/CCP/CLP* can be considered as a well-suited framework for development of decision-making software supporting small and medium size enterprises at the stage of production process planning (Van Hentenryck et al., 2000).

Further research focuses on the development of the task oriented searching strategies, implementation of which could interface a decision maker with a user-friendly intelligent support system.

8. REFERENCES

1. Banaszak Z., Zaremba, M., Muszyński, W., 2005, CP-based decision making for SME. Preprints of the 16th IFAC World Congres, 3 – 8 July, 2005, Prague, Czech Republic, Eds P. Horacek, M. Simandl, P. Zitek, DVD.
2. Banaszak Z., Zaremba, M., 2004, CLP-based project-driven manufacturing. Prep. of the 7th IFAC Symposium on Cost Oriented Automation, June 6-9, 2004, Gatineau, Quebec, Canada, pp. 269-274.
3. Banaszak Z., Józefczyk, J., 2005, Towards CLP-based task oriented DSS for SME, Applied Computer Science and Production Management, Vol.1, No.1: 161-180.
4. Barták R., 2003, Constraint-based scheduling: An introduction for newcomers, Preprints of the 7th IFAC Workshop on Intelligent Manufacturing Systems, 6-8 April, 2003, Budapest, Hungary, pp. 75-80.
5. Mika M., Waligóra G., Węglarz J., 2003, Metaheuristic approach to the multi-mode resource-constrained project scheduling problem with discounted cash flows and progress payment. In: Project-Driven Manufacturing. Banaszak Z., Józefowska J. Eds., WNT, Warsaw, pp. 34-47.
6. Rossi F., 2000, Constraint (Logic) programming: A Survey on Research and Applications, K.R. Apt et al. (Eds.), New Trends in Constraints, LNAI 1865, Springer-Verlag, Berlin, pp. 40-74.
7. Tomczuk I., Banaszak Z., 2004, Constraint programming approach for production flow planning, Proc. of the 6th Workshop on Constraint Programming for Decision and Control, pp. 47-54.
8. Van Hentenryck P., Perron L., Puget J., 2000, Search and Strategies in OPL, ACM Transactions on Computational Logic, Vol. 1, No. 2, pp. 1-36.
9. Van Hentenryck, P., 1991, Constraint Logic Programming, Knowledge Engineering Review, Vol. 6, pp. 151–194.
10. Wallace M., 2000, Constraint Logic Programming, Ed. Kakas A.C., Sadri F., Computat. Logic, LNAI 2407, Springer-Verlag, Berlin, Heidelberg, pp. 512-532.
11. Wallace M., 1996, Practical applications of constraint programming, Constraints Journal, Vol. 1(1), pp. 139-168.

PERSPECTIVES OF MOULD MAKING INDUSTRY FOR DIGITAL GLOBAL MANUFACTURING

Elsa Henriques [1], Paulo Peças [1] and Pedro F. Cunha [2]

[1] Instituto Superior Técnico, Portugal
elsa.h@ist.utl.pt; ppecas@ist.utl.pt
[2] Instituto Politécnico de Setúbal, Portugal
pcunha@est.ips.pt

In production engineering radical changes are taking place supported in new manufacturing paradigms and in technological developments. The increasing demand for meeting customer requirements and technological innovations have influenced the degree of flexibility built in the manufacturing system and its ability to respond in terms of cost, volume and time delivery. Taking the example of Portuguese mould making industry, this paper will analysed the main changes that have occurred in this industry and its ability to adapt to the availability of higher level of digital technologies and how they support new business models, extending their value adding chain.

1. INTRODUCTION

During the past years significant changes have taken place in the industrial world. Mould making companies have to face an increasing pressure to improve quality and to meet stricter delivery times. Competition is marked with a strong pressure on price reduction to satisfy tailored orders, volatile and global demand, shorter product life cycles, increased product customisation and reduced time to market (Henriques, 2004). To meet these challenges, companies are moving away from traditional organisations and structures into simultaneous engineering activities where product and processes are designed and developed in a more integrated manner. (Sohlenius, 1992) describes very clearly how concurrent or simultaneous engineering could be viewed as an approach to increase the competitiveness by decreasing the lead-time and still improving quality and cost, supported in the technology developed to promote it. These trends and drivers, as well the new approaches to product and process engineering have had a profound impact in mould manufacturing companies.

As an industrial sector, mould making industry has a particular relevance in Portuguese economy and many companies have emerged, showing a good level of competitiveness. These companies have a common ability to adopt organizational and technological changes, acting as important contributors in the supply chain of several OEMs, from different industrial sectors (e.g household appliances, electric/electronic and automotive sector). These companies are mainly small and medium enterprises (SMEs) with a strong investment in technical skills and manufacturing technologies and with high quality based culture. The dependence on technical tacit knowledge, acquired within long experience years, has been felt as a critical factor in most mould-makers (Henriques, 2005).

The objective of this paper is to present a discussion regarding the use of digital technologies in the mould making industry, based on our own perspective about the challenges and opportunities foreseen for Portuguese mould making companies.

Taking into account the companies' size and the global market the authors discuss the strategy that should be designed, competences that should be developed and, finally, what should be the role of digital technologies, as a differentiation factor for their competition in global market.

2. THE PRESENCE OF DIGITAL TECHNOLOGIES IN MOULDMAKING: ACTUAL STATE AND EVOLUTION

In the global mould making industry *quality*, *cost* and *delivery-time* form the essential basis of competition. For many OEMs time is the winning criteria, however in order to compete on time (i.e. lead time) and cost, mould making companies must have a clear technology strategy, based on the most modern generation of processing machines and deploy work, from the mould design to its delivery and in-production setting-up, in an around the clock concept.

As far as moulds manufacturing chain is typified by one-of-a-kind production systems, being each mould a unique device involving specific and tailored solutions, the engineering knowledge and manufacturing skills had and will maintain a central role in the business (Henriques, 2004, 2005). As illustrated in figure 1 the diversity of technologies used in mould manufacturing has increased significantly over the last decades.

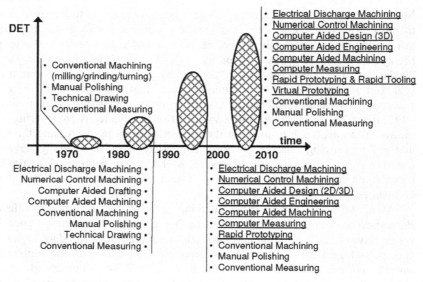

Figure 1 – Time evolution of most relevant moulds manufacturing technologies.
(The technologies based on DET are underlined).

After the 90's, most of the introduced manufacturing technologies are deeply based on microprocessors or digital technologies able to support the programming and control tasks. Thus, nowadays it is difficult or even impossible to detach mould design & manufacturing technologies from DET. The computer plays a central role in this sector at different individual and interrelated tasks. Digital based technologies can be found from the design to the manufacturing processes, where five-axis machining, coordinate measuring or rapid prototyping are only few examples. Automation has shifted the focus of technological expertise from shop-floor to the office, e.g. mould design, process and production planning, and CNC part programming.

Taking the example of evolution observed in the EDM process, it can be considered as a paradigm of the impact of DET in the performance improvement of the manufacturing technology. In the early days, it was slow and difficult to control machining process. Currently it is a highly reliable manufacturing process incorporating the most advanced DET found among the mould manufacturing technologies. The impact of sinking EDM on mould making industry, with all its developments, has been especially profound and vice-versa: more than 40% of sinking EDM equipment is set up in moulds & dies companies. The first equipments launched in 1950s were based in a simple resistance-capacitance power supply and were used in simple sinking operations on difficult-to-machine metals. A single electronic circuit promoted the discharge and actuated the servo system clutched to the electrode. The effort pursued during the following decade originated the innovation seeds at the automation level: the electrode orbital movement, the improvement of the discharging process through more sophisticated electronic circuits based on transistor and capacitors and the piloting of the spark generator. In the 1980s, the advent of computer numerical control (CNC) brought tremendous advances in the efficiency of the EDM machining operations. CNC facilitated an automatic and unattended machining, from inserting the electrodes in the tool changer to a finished polished cavity or cavities, and allow a complete integration with CAD/CAM systems. The interactive communication between the operator and the machine was possible, the programming became a real computer assistant task and the tool changer device allowed the management of multiple electrodes for unattended operation.

The spread of artificial intelligence took place during the 1990s and the EDM technology was improved. Predictive learning systems, adaptive process control and optimisation, intelligent lift-off movements, constant monitoring of all machine operations, intelligent adaptation of the machining current to the electrode area, automatic eliminations of abnormal discharges and the use of "expert-programs" that optimize programs for specific application are examples of developments which contribute for inexperienced operators to use the machine at (or at least near) full capacity.

In this century, the connectivity era for EDM, the equipments start to include complementary communication devices, allowing their integration in intranet/ internet networks, the remote monitoring and even the remote control. These EDM systems can be programmed to send SMS messages to facilitate a 24 hour usage. The inclusion of webcams is becoming a standard for remote maintenance and problem solving assistance. The current software in EDM equipment offers a total package for managing and producing specific data for EDM machining. Increased process security can be achieved through the implementation of a chip-based identification system, ensuring that jobs consistently run with the correct CNC program, electrode off-set values and magazine position.

The EDM technology has a history of being "ahead of the curve" in adopting innovative concepts in metalworking technology. The concept of *autonomatisation* is a more recent approach in which the equipment can be fully automated, for the performance of consecutive jobs, and the process can be fully autonomous with artificial intelligent-based adaptive control systems supporting the operation without human assistance. If assistance is need the equipment can call the operator by SMS/email/etc. The development of *autonomatisation* concept was only possible due to a strong presence of advanced DET.

Besides its importance in the manufacturing processes, digital technologies were fundamental to allow the communication among entities and individuals all along the mould making value chain. It is clear the importance of a continuous interaction with the clients, to create the trustfulness foundations for responsive and long-term partnerships on a world wide basis. During the last 25 years 80% to 90% (depending on the years) of the Portuguese moulds production has been delivered to foreign countries. Thus, digital technologies were and are the means to overcome the physical (and even cultural) barriers and to continuously communicate and exchange different types of data. The recent advances in digital communication infrastructures and tools (figure 2) culminates in the virtual facilities, such as meeting rooms where work-teams at distance can meet in a virtual space, performing engineering colla-borative work supported in video, voice and even software applications which allow the sharing of data in real time.

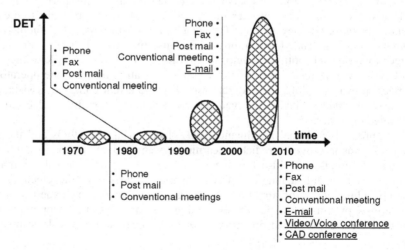

Figure 2 – Evolution of communication technologies in mould making companies.
(technologies based on DET are underlined).

As it happens world wide, the Portuguese mould making companies are typically small and family owned firms with a high ability to manage technological changes. This capacity is recognized as the source for the observed innovations in the sector and the main driver for changing operational principles and for the development of new business strategies. As regards digital technologies they should support more consistent and effective work and promote the cooperation with clients which, according to Tang (2004), is still reduced to mere information exchange. The successful moulds factory will need to be agile and to extend their activity upstream and downstream in mould value chain. Beside this, the value perceived by clients will no longer be based strictly on moulds, but instead will derive from the capacity to provide integrated services along the value chain.

3. DET AS COMPETITIVE ENABLERS

DET have until now reinforced the current ways of working and strengthened the current sources of competitive advantage (deliver of cost effective moulds conforming to part/production specifications, in a reduced timeframe). Considering the companies' small size and the global market, the role of DET as competitive enablers to face the major expected (and even occurring) changes in the business strategies can be discussed.

In exploring new market opportunities, mould making companies have just started looking for an effective management of mould life cycle. Mould life cycle management can be considered as a holistic approach to mould development considering all aspects from its preliminary design to its retirement, involving the simultaneous engagement of cross functional teams and multi-disciplinary competences. It requires the integration of all the steps within the mould life cycle from part and mould design, in a design for manufacturing approach, moulds manufacturing and trail out, to mould in-production support (maintenance, repair, modifications in accordance to product updates) and finally to its dismantling or its recycling/reuse. Furthermore the success of such an embracement relies on companies' ability to evolve upstream and downstream in the mould value chain (figure 3).

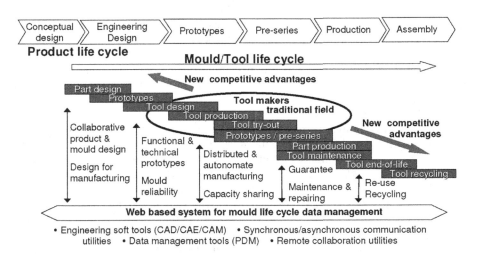

Figure 3 – Moulds life cycle management based on DET.

Going upstream means the involvement of mould makers in new product development process. Early interaction between mould makers and product developers encompasses mutual benefits. The latter incorporates process expertise within design decision making and the former gets involved in high value engineering tasks, valuing their competences through an economic service providing. To implement concurrently the product and mould design requires collaborative engineering abilities, targeting a distributed but improved streamlined value generation from the market perspective. Mould engineers depend on CAD/CAE/CAM software applications for drafting, design and manufacturing their moulds. Distributed engineering and manufacturing concepts include design, process and production planning, shop-floor control and numerical control manufacturing in disperse geographical locations. The advance of manufacturing technology, collaboration and communication tools, as well as in the infrastructure utilities, has driven to a manufacture framework in which a product designed in one side of the world has their moulds designed and produced simultaneously in the other side and is produced and assembled somewhere else. Future CAD/CAM/CAE systems will be fully integrated with real knowledge based engineering systems becoming highly effective tools to drive and assist the mould engineers in their decision making processes. Within a web based environment, they will become more collaborative, with applications integrating asynchronous and synchronous communication tools (voice/video conference, CAD conference with 3D geometry manipulation and sketch annotations facilities), data share and internet based Product Data Management and work management tools to support an effective distributed design and manufacturing environment. Engineering services can be developed, emphasizing client driven innovation in a globalize business environment.

The upstream evolution to develop competences in product development is also pushing mould makers to dominate and explore the prototyping opportunities, particularly as regards functional and technical prototypes. The selection of the best prototyping process and parameters, and an effective control of each process performance is a difficult task since it requires a very wide technological background. The developed software applications, based eventually in artificial intelligence, will assure the success of prototyping process selection and parameter setting. Moreover, as far as the prototype field is in a fast evolution, in which technologies proliferate with specific application domains, the penetration of mould makers in this field as service providers must be supported in a well established network to guarantee the near to real time access to the most appropriate technologies, wherever they physically are based.

Besides contributing to the focus on core competences, distributed manufacturing in mould making also facilitates the resolution of one significant problem: a rigid capacity in a highly variable demand context. As far as distributed manufacturing promotes the capacity sharing each company can enlarge their market assuming, through distribution, a flexible capacity. The correct use of digital technologies applied to manufacturing processes (e.g in process simulation and control) is becoming an advantage to be used by mould makers. Data gathering and treatment during mould manufacturing will allow mould makers to structure and explicit their tacit knowledge, facilitating its dissemination among collaborators. The overall process will be more efficient, less time consuming and more reliable. The widespread of the *autonomation* concept (i.e. autonomy + automation), the incorporation of the remote process/production monitoring, automated/computer-assisted process planning and virtual simulation into the mould manufacturing processes will improve their robustness and will contribute to the fully implementation of the internet-based manufacturing.

The life cycle costs of a mould remain a major penalty factor in any moulding process. Nevertheless, a subjective approach has been historically taken to measure mould life and mould reliability and in the definition of the mould end of life. If a mould is a production mean and represents a significant investment effort, its overall efficiency and its guarantee during a specified in-production phase must be considered as a mould design variable and should be presented as a marketing argument. Failure modes and reliability engineering of the mould are complex subjects, depending on design solutions and operative and maintenance conditions at client (mould user) site. Any analysis on that level requires data, which only can be retrieved from the mould in-production phase. The monitoring of the mould operative conditions (number of shots, cycle time, injection pressure, temperatures, clamping forces,...) allows the feedback of life data regarding mould performance to support reliability and failure mode analysis, the data collection for preventive maintenance and the certification used in accordance to the design specifications. The latter is indeed a necessary condition to put into practice the mould guarantee as a quality differentiation attribute. In this context, monitoring devices with the capability to process and archive digital signals in a secure way (mould digital black box concept) can be perceived as an innovative evolution to support the next step in mould business: to supply moulds guaranteeing its overall efficiency (involving the concepts of reliability, availability, and maintainability and performance) during a life time. If a guarantee service is foreseen, assistance, maintenance and repair services at a client site must be provided. In fact, and as mentioned by Cunha (2004), although a lot of effort is devoted to enhancing reliability and maintainability in the design phase, occurrences of malfunctions during the in-production phase are almost inevitable. At that level the distance issue between mould shop and client site is a geographical barrier that again can be overcome with remote engineering collaboration and communication utilities and portable diagnosis, maintenance and repair technologies. Digital technologies will be crucial for the development of a guarantee-based strategy as regards their definition and implementation, as well as to manage effectively the mould data and the knowledge generated along the mould life cycle.

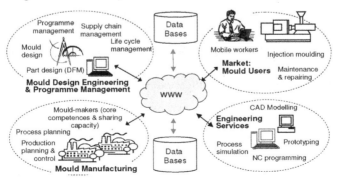

Figure 4 – Future DET-based mould making company.

In the near future mould making companies will become real Internet based virtual companies, concerned with the entire mould life cycle assurance, from the cooperative part and mould design engineering and distributed manufacturing to the mould programmes management involving supply chain resources planning and mould in-production monitoring at user site providing maintenance and repairing services (figure 4). Increasingly mould making industry will be more information-oriented, knowledge driven and as far as much of the daily routine operations will be automated, resources will be shifted towards technological and business innovation and productivity improvement.

4. CONCLUSIONS

As in the past DET will create the conditions to face the new competition requirements, but will create by themselves new challenges. Now the new digital technologies involve new ways of thinking and new ways of working, supporting mould makers capability to answer to the new global market needs, defining new business attitude and corporate behaviour, which have strong implications in the strategic, organizational and technological domains.

This process began with CADrafting and NC equipments, but it is now much more intense as far as it deals with communication, collaborative engineering platforms, and information and knowledge management, which involves all companies and requires new work procedures.

New digital technologies are needed to stay competitive even in traditional SMEs highly focused on manufacturing competences. Though digital technologies are not only a base to do in a more efficient way the things companies are used to do, they must be perceived as extensive innovation enablers, particularly in the way companies design their business.

5. REFERENCES

1. Henriques E, Peças P.; Rapid moulds manufacturing as a competitive opportunity. Int. Conf. RPD2004 2004 CD-Rom, Portugal, 2004.
2. Sohlenius,G.; Concurrent Engineering ; CIRP Annals 1992, vol. 41/1, pp. 645-655; 1992
3. Fallbohmer P, Altan T; Tonshoff HK, Nakagawa T. Survey of the die and mold manufacturing industry - Practices in Germany, Japan, and the United States. J. of Mat. Proc. Tech. 1996: 59: 158-168.
4. Henriques E, Menezes J, Peças P. Reflexões sobre novas estratégias competitivas no sector dos moldes e ferramentas. O Molde 2005: 68:38-40.
5. Tang D, Eversheim W, Schuh G. A new generation of cooperative development paradigm in the tool and die making branch: strategy and technology. Rob. and CIM 2004: 20:301–311.
6. Cunha, P.F. Duarte, J.C. "Development of a Productive Service Module Based on a Life Cycle Perspective of Maintenance Issues", CIRP Annals 2004, vol. 53/1, pp. 13-16, 2004

GENERATIVE PLANNING
IN A DET ENVIRONMENT

Michael F. Zäh, Markus Wiedemann and Henning Rudolf
Institute for Machine Tools and Industrial Management (iwb),
Technische Universität München, Germany
{michael.zaeh, markus.wiedemann, henning.rudolf}@iwb.tum.de

Knowledge based methods in the domain of process and factory planning could lead to substantial savings for products with a high number of variants and production facilities. Although knowledge based approaches are already state of the art in the engineering and data management of complex products, these methods have not yet been applied to the planning of processes and production facilities so far. The extension of knowledge based methods to the domain of process and factory planning could lead to substantial savings for products with a high number of variants and production facilities. The objective of this paper is to demonstrate the state of the art in process planning with special focus on a possible integration with factory planning. Based on the literature review and the requirements of modeling data for the domain of process and resource planning, a methodology is derived and a prototypical solution based on commercially available software is demonstrated. The result is a knowledge based planning method for products, processes and the necessary production facilities.

1. INTRODUCTION

The situation of production enterprises is characterized by shortened innovation cycles, a rapidly rising number of variants as well as an accelerated technological progress. In those increasingly satisfied buyer's markets, the customers demand shorter delivery times, have high requirements regarding quality and technical functionality of the products and expect favorable prices. The cost and time pressure resulting from this, force the enterprises to develop new solutions (Dombrowski, 1996). For this purpose it is necessary to increase in particular the efficiency of the conventional planning processes. However organizational changes will not be sufficient enough. Therefore new methods have to be established for production and factory planning.

In the next section the term DET will be defined and substantial components of this concept are introduced. Since the emphasis of this work is on assembly planning, the next section discusses the requirements of software systems and their present shortcomings. Based on this the necessity of an optimized planning procedure is derived. Finally this article presents a realization methodology for an integrated knowledge-based assembly planning for high-variant products.

2. STATE OF THE ART

2.1 Digital Enterprise Technology (DET)

DET is a fairly new concept in academia and industry that has caught a lot of interest in the last couple of years. It is defined as "The collection of systems and methods for the digital modelling of the global product development and realization process, in the context of lifecycle management" (Maropoulos, 2002).

The system providers UGS (eManufacturing Server – eM-Server) and DELMIA (Integrated Process Database – IPD) are the two market leaders in this segment (Köth, 2003). Both software systems are based on one central relational data base. Additional tools such as process planning or ergonomics simulation are linked to the central database. Thereby the use of a consistent data model can be ensured across the entire product development process. Thus distributed working in the enterprise network with always current data is possible. Figure 1 presents schematically the sequential use of possible DET tools. The emphasis of this work is on the range of process planning for assembly. Therefore the following sections particularly deal with these tools.

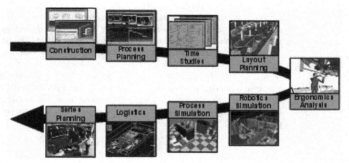

Figure 1 - Tools in the context of DET (Bley, 2004).

2.2 Assembly Planning Systems

The available software solutions for assembly planning of the above mentioned system providers are based on a systematic introduced by Jonas (2000) and Klauke (2002). As basis for the implementation of process planning, information from the domain of products, processes and resources have to be joined logically in a data model and illustrated in a semantically correct connection. Klauke (2002) clarifies in her publication the connection between the three entities (figure 2).

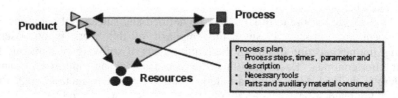

Figure 2 - Basic information for process planning (Klauke, 2002).

The elements product, process and resources represent the information of a work plan, in which the process steps with the necessary resources and products/parts are contained. The connecting lines between the individual elements represent dependences and illustrate in each case problems, which are to be considered in the context of production planning. On the basis of a linked storage the attached product and resources information can be made available over the inquiry of the processes.

The class "product" specified in figure 2 contains on the one hand the structure of a product, which can be illustrated for example over different modules. On the other hand it defines the characteristics of the objects e. g. the cost or the weight of components and higher-level information like tolerances. The structural configuration of the variants and/or alternatives is implemented by an association between individual parts and components. All assembly procedures, which will directly or indirectly contribute to the assembly progress, are administered by the class "processes". Just as the product, assembly procedures are illustrated hierarchically in different levels of detail. The structure of these processes is provided similarly to the product structure through a one to one relationship. Apart from the hierarchical arrangement on different levels additionally temporal relationships (sequentially, parallel, alternatively) between processes are to be considered, in order to provide a consistent planning. The assembly progression is documented by the characteristics "predecessors" and "successors". In the class "resources" the assembly plants and their components are administered. For example the description of an assembly line or cycles of provisioning are contained. The structure of the class is comparable with that of the product. It exists likewise a hierarchical structure, in which tooling and/or organizational units are represented by an identification number and an appropriate variant set.

The data models presented by Jonas (2000) and Klauke (2002) are the theoretical basis for comprehensive computer assistance. The illustration of planning contents is very time consuming due to the various classes and linkages. Particularly the variant management is supported only insufficiently by the available software systems. This circumstance is described in detail in the following section.

3. DESCRIPTION OF THE PROBLEM

In the currently available systems for assembly planning it is only possible to model a maximal structure and apply different filters to select different objects. This approach can be compared to a maximal process plan, in which certain process steps or machines are omitted, if certain filter conditions are not met. This concept only works for a limited number of variants and simple relationships between objects. The following section describes this problem based on the example of a table assembly with two different product variants (type A and type B).

Compared to type B additional process steps are necessary for the production of type A as shown in fig. 3. In order to consider this in the planning process, different variant filters can be attributed to the processes. Only if a relevant variant is selected these processes are chosen.

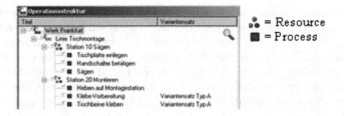

Figure 3 - Process structure in a process planning tool.

Planning a specific variant, the corresponding filter is selected and all elements that are part of other filters are omitted for this specific planning result. In this example step 2 and 3 at station 20 are only valid for type A as shown in figure 3, therefore they are removed for type B as depicted in the following figure 4.

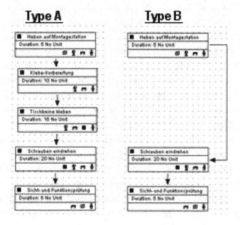

Figure 4 - Process structures for type A and B as a result of filtering.

According to Walter (2002) there are hardly any differences regarding version and variant management between both major system providers. It is demonstrated in a study on digital enterprise technologies that the fulfilment of these functionalities is only realized on a moderate level. A major cause for this is a lack of methodical support for the representation of knowledge by a procedurally programmed solution algorithm as it is the state of the art in current systems. Using a system based on a knowledge-based planning methodology, the functionality can be increased substantially, particularly in regard to the variant management.

4. KNOWLEDGE BASES SYSTEMS – RESEARCH OBJECTIVE

Knowledge-based planning is based on the generative principle. Herein influence parameters create the required result with the help of deposited knowledge. The suitability for daily use could be proven for variant management in PDM systems and for the generation of work plans with CAPP systems.

Knowledge-based systems with a rule-based knowledge representation have a long tradition in the scientific research of process planning systems (Zäh & Rudolf, 2005). The results of this work were having not been transferred into DET systems with a central data management yet. This is caused by the fact that the exclusive use of rules for the representation of knowledge is not sufficient to illustrate complex knowledge relations. Therefore further representation forms have to be implemented.

According to (Puppe, 1991) there is a dependency amongst knowledge applications and suitable concepts (figure 5). He distinguishes between the areas of diagnostics, design and simulation. Considering that process planning is the fundamental mapping between the domains of products, processes and resources it is very similar to the design process, mapping customer needs, functional requirements and design parameters (Harutunian, 1996). Therefore the same basic concepts should be applicable to the domains of design and process planning. Consequently, the methodology for process planning should be based on the concepts of rules, object-oriented representation and constraints. The relevant representation forms for the range of process planning are subsequently described in detail. The methodology should support a multiplicity of the presented representation forms.

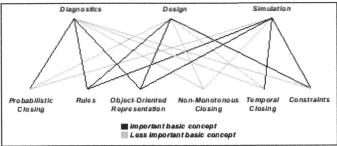

Figure 5 - Different concepts for knowledge applications (Puppe, 1991).

4.1 Rule-based representation

Rules are the most common form of knowledge representation in expert systems. They consist of a precondition and an action. The precondition describes in each case, when the rule may be used and the associated action is executed. Actions can be divided into two classes (Görz, 1995):

- Implications or deductions that affiliate the validity of a statement (e.g. "If A, then apply B").
- Actions that change a condition (e.g. "If A, then carry out B).

4.2 Object-based representation

Object-based representation is known to be a declarative system for describing, organizing and processing large amounts of knowledge. A first semantical order of the stored knowledge would be reached, if all statements about an object are combined into a frame (Puppe, 1991). The characteristics and behaviour of an object are held within a frame in different subjects, so called slots. Further frames with the same slots are produced by instantiation, thus representing the abstract object by a concrete instance, from a class frame. The structure of a frame is illustrated in figure 6.

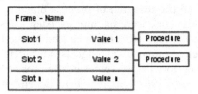

Frame - Name		
Slot 1	Value 1	Procedure
Slot 2	Value 2	Procedure
Slot i	Value i	

Figure 6 - Structure of a frame (Kurbel, 1992).

4.3 Constraints-based representation

Relations between variables can be represented by constraints. Constraints are particularly suitable for the representation of boundary conditions, which the solution of the problem has to fulfil in any case. Thereby a concrete problem solving is not specified. The goal is to find a solution by considering all relevant constraints (Puppe, 1991). In contrast to rules, which represent arranged connections, they express non-directional connections, which can be usually solved for each variable (figure 7).

> **Example for rules**
> $A => B$ „If A then apply B"
> No statement from the validity of B can be deduced on the validity of A
>
> **Example for constraints**
> $U = R \cdot I$
> If two variables are known, the third variable can be determined

Figure 7 - Difference between rules and constraints.

5. PROTOYPICAL IMPLEMENTATION

In order to demonstrate the efficiency of a knowledge-based system an assembly planning system, which illustrates tasks of planning of a DET-tool, was implemented in an object-oriented development environment. Günter (1999) has compared different development systems available on the market. Among other things a comparison of the different methods of knowledge representation being used by the individual systems was made. Due to the circumstances stated in the last section the development system camos. Develop is particularly suitable for the described purpose.

The emphasis of the development activity was to realize an automated generation of process plans for different product variants. The information about the product as well as the necessary processes and resources were already formally illustrated in a conventional assembly planning system. This basic information has to be provided to the camos. Develop system by a suitable and efficient procedure. Data has to be exported from the assembly planning system into an XML document. Afterwards this file is mapped to an XML data structure, which can be interpreted by camos. Develop. During this process the existing semantic links between the individual entities had to be preserved. This was achieved by the help of the integration software Microsoft BizTalk Server 2004.

In this first stage of development of the system, advantages could be determined in relation to the existing commercial planning systems apart from the simple and clear handling for different variants. For example assembly times per work station must no longer be deposited manually in the network. They were automatically generated due to the deposited program logic with selection of a specific variant. Furthermore the developed system allows a very flexible illustration of the variant structures. In conventional planning systems a very complex maximum structure has to be implemented with variant-specific processes, which can be filtered by corresponding variant codes (figure 8).

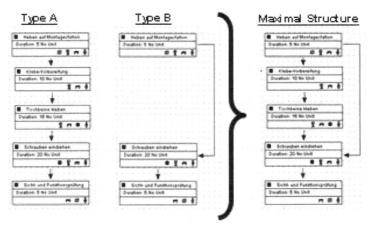

Figure 8 - Maximal structure of processes in a DET-tool.

Thereby the development effort increases substantially with a larger number of different variants and specific orders. The sequence of child elements can be generated in a knowledge-based system with the use of an index at run-time. This means that objects and their links do not have to be specified multiple times. With the help of an index the correct sequence, which is valid for the respective variant, can be generated using a rule.

6. CONCLUSION

The aim of this work is to show the enormous potential of generative planning functionality to be included in DET systems especially in the area of variant planning. To do so the state of the art in digital enterprise technology for assembling planning was shown. In the currently available systems for assembly planning it is only possible to model a maximal structure. The fact that different filters had to be applied to select different objects leads to the deployment of a new planning methodology. With this methodology planning content can be transferred and used in the developed assembly planning systems to support the planning task, especially for complex planning projects. This approach allows a semi-automated generation of plans for similar scenarios, instead of a manual one, which is based on copying and modifying existing projects. The realized advantages should be implemented in commercially available DET systems, which have their own advantages such as a high level of integration into simulation tools or factory CAD systems.

7. REFERENCES

1. Bley, H.; Reinhart, G.; Seliger, G.; Bernardi, M.; Korne, T.: Appropriate Human Involvement in Assembly and Disassembly. Proceedings of the CIRP Annals 2004: STC A 53/2/2004. Krakau 27.08.2004, pp. 487-510.
2. Dombrowski, U.; Tiedemann, H.; Bothe, T.: Visionen für die Digitale Fabrik.Zeitschrift für wirtschaftlichen Fabrikbetrieb 96 (2001) 3, pp. 96-100.
3. Görz, G.: Einführung in die Künstliche Intelligenz. 2. ed. Bonn: Addison-Wesley 1995.
4. Günter, A.; Kreuz, I.; Kühn, C.: Kommerzielle Software-Werkzeugefür die Konfigurierung von technischen Systemen. Künstliche Intelligenz 99 (1999) 3. pp. 61-65.
5. Harutunian, V., Nordlund, M., Tate, D., Suh, N., 1996, Decision Making and Software Tools for Product Development Based on Axiomatic Design Theory, CIRP Annals, Vol. 45/1: pp. 135-139.
6. Jonas, C.: Konzept einer durchgängigen, rechnergestützten Planung von Montageanlagen. PhD Thesis Technische Universität München (2000). Munich: Utz 2000. (*iwb* Forschungsberichte 145).
7. Klauke, S.: Methoden und Datenmodell der "Offenen Virtuellen Fabrik" zur Optimierung simultaner Produktionsprozesse. PhD Thesis TU Dresden (2002). Düsseldorf: VDI-Verlag 2002. (Fortschritt-Berichte VDI, Reihe 20, Nr. 360).
8. Köth, C.-P.: Geteilt durch zwei. Automobil Industrie 2003 (2003) 7-8, pp. 48-49.Köth, 2003.
9. Kurbel, K.: Entwicklung und Einsatz von Expertensystemen. 2. ed. Berlin: Springer 1992.
10. *Maropoulos, P. G.:* Digital Enterprise Technology - Defining Perspectives and Research Priorities. Proceedings of the 1st CIRP (UK) Seminar on Digital Enterprise Technology. Durham 16th – 17th September 2002, pp. 1-12.
11. Puppe, F.: Einführung in Expertensysteme. 2 ed. Berlin: Springer 1991.
12. Walter, T. J.: Einsatz von Methoden der Digitalen Fabrik bei der Planung von Produktionssystemen für die Automobilindustrie. PhD Thesis TU Clausthal (2002). Aachen: Shaker 2002. (Innovationen der Fabrikplanung und -organisation 6).
13. Zäh, M. F.; Rudolf, H.: Agile process planning based on the integration of process and factory planning. 38th CIRP International Conference on Manufacturing Systems. Florianopolis 16th – 18th May 2005.

ORGANIZATIONAL FUNCTIONS AND ENTERPRISE SELF-MAINTENANCE: A FRAMEWORK FOR INTEGRATING MODELLING, MONITORING AND LEARNING

David Aveiro[1] and José Tribolet[1,2]

[1] Organizational Engineering Center, INESC, Portugal
[2] Department of Information Systems and Computer Science, Instituto Superior Técnico,
Technical University of Lisboa, Portugal.
{david.aveiro,jose.tribolet}@ceo.inesc.pt

Process orientation is a major concern nowadays. For this reason there have been great advances in business process modelling as means to better understand and promote organizational operations and evolution. However, organizational functions such as logistics, quality, finance, etc. still exist and strongly influence aspects like change processes, or the structuring of organizational units even if a "process culture" is established. This paper proposes a framework for integrating modelling, monitoring and learning aspects associated with the functional dimension of the enterprise. This framework is based on: (1) an ontology proposed (in another forthcoming paper) for the functional dimension of an organization; (2) the fundamental concepts: entity, role and activity, that are the base for current research work by other authors, on modelling other dimensions or concerns of an enterprise architecture. Also an example of application of the framework is presented as a proof of concept.

1. INTRODUCTION

This paper proposes a framework for integrating the modelling, monitoring and learning associated with the functional dimension of the enterprise. This purpose comes in the context of research work done at Centro de Engenharia Organizacional (CEO) of INESC INOV, whose current view of organizational modelling is synthesized in the work of (Sousa et al., 2005), where key concepts for modelling the organization's enterprise architecture using the Unified Modelling Language (UML) are discussed. The authors argue that "modelling the multidimensional aspects of the enterprise should be organized into five architectural components: Organization, Business, Information, Application and Technological architectures. It is our purpose to further complement the above mentioned work, to incorporate the functional dimension of the enterprise. This paper aims at being a second step in that direction. As a first step, and for the clarification of the function concept, in another paper we abridged knowledge from diverse areas like management, biology and philosophy to arrive at an ontology that describes the main constructs of the functional dimension of an organization and their interrelation. Findings of this work important for the purpose of this paper are presented on section 2. In section 3, subsection 3.1, we introduce the fundamental concepts entity, role and activity, that are the base for current research work by (Sousa et al., 2005), on modelling other dimensions or concerns of an enterprise architecture. These concepts also serve as a basis for the framework proposed in this paper – in subsection 3.2 – with the purpose of integrating Sousa et al.'s current modelling methods, with the monitoring and learning aspects of the functional dimension of an enterprise. Subsection 3.3 clarifies the frameworks components and interrelations with an application example that serves as a proof of concept. Conclusions and future work based on work presented then can be found in section 4.

2. ORGANIZATIONAL FUNCTION: ONTOLOGY

In management/organization literature, the essence of the organizational function concept is not clear with several views and incoherencies in the use of the word. We can however infer one pattern: this word – *function* – is used to describe the aggregation of several processes into one more abstract macro-process, usually executed by an organizational unit (like marketing, logistics, IT, etc. But what is the added value of calling this macro-process a function? What properties emerge in a process that groups other processes, that justify calling it a function? To find out what these properties could be, we analysed perspectives on the function concept from biology and philosophy of biology and found that some seem to apply to organizations. In this section we cover a summary of the ontology that resulted from the thorough analysis of the several perspectives studied.

We propose an ontology for the organizational function concept, anchored on the fundamental concept of activity (we used the equivalent name: *process*). The word *function* has its root in the Latin word "function" which means functioning, which in turn means "doing well in a regular way". *Functions* are process interdependency relations that determine the nature of organizations as viable (cohesive) systems. *Processes* in an organization are all interrelated or interdependent in some way due to the intertwined nature of its operation. Changes in the characteristics of inputs or outputs of *processes* in an organization will affect in some way (dysfunctional or not) the operation of other *processes* elsewhere – process interdependence (Christensen, 2002) and non-locality (Chauvet, 1993).

In order for the organization to survive – maintain a capability of recursive self maintenance (Bickard, 2001) – certain *processes* (or parts of processes) will have to convey with the conditions on which the organization is able to maintain its cohesion and survive (primary goal of any organization). That is, an organization has to have processes (or parts of the processes themselves) which are dedicated to monitor key state variables and find out if they are in the state of "doing well in a regular way" – or in other words, respecting the established *norm* (Bickhard, 2002) or *goal* (Kueng and Kawalek, 1996) for them – and work as (or invoke elsewhere) *resilience* dynamics (Christensen, 2002), that is reaction mechanisms of the system to perturbations that move away from the *norm* and enter a state of dysfunction (converse of function).

If in a certain *process* there is a departure from the *norm*, this can be due to: an *expected exception* – the case in which previously existing *business rules* (Eriksson, 2000) (BRG, 2000) – methods embedded in the *process* – or other *processes* (invoked due to the *exception*) will work as a *resilience* mechanism to try to restore the *norm*; or an *unexpected exception* (Mourão and Antunes, 2005) – the case where the organization will enter in a dynamic space where *microgenesis* processes will occur (Bickard, 2001). They consist in heuristically, trough trial and error tentatives, based on past similar problem situations and analysis on its results, construct or change existing *processes* and/or *business rules* to circumvent or solve the problem that caused the *exception*. These *microgenesis* processes can be highly complex and unpredictable, depending on the degree of complexity of the problem that caused the *exception* and amount of *knowledge* necessary to investigate and understand necessary aspects of the problem. Just as the necessity of specialized *knowledge* (and its coordination) is at the genesis of the organization (Weeks, 2003) (Chandler, 1980), also specialized *knowledge* is at the heart of the micro construction (or change) of the organization, as a way of adaptation (realized in new resilience processes/rules) to new environmental conditions.

Summarizing, the ontology of an organizational function and its dynamics is depicted on figure 1. Given a *process* X, we can elicit an *organizational function* by stating the following interrelated artefacts: (1) a *norm* (goal value) for a certain state variable of the process; (2) which other *process* Y (or processes) depend on this *norm*, in order to remain *functional*; (3) the set of *business rules* (embedded in the process itself, or other processes) that work as *resilience* mechanisms to *expected exceptions* and try to re-establish the *norm* to the *process functioning,* either by internal measures, or by invocation of other processes that will make inputs of process X change in a way it returns to normal functioning (4) set of specialized *knowledge* related to *process* X and Y's domain, that is, information about business rules that: (i) worked or not in previous real (microgenesis) situations in the organization (ii) are best (or not so good or even bad) practices from theoretical (or real) situations accumulated in the memory of the agents executing the microgenesis processes (note that all these "theoretical situations" are patterns that had to be derived and elicited from previous real situations in real organizations as a result of a microgenesis process). This knowledge is valuable input for the *microgenesis*

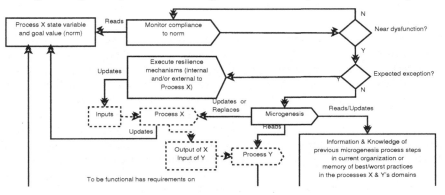

Figure 1 - Depiction of an organizational function's artefacts and dynamics.

process of treating *unexpected exceptions* that will select new successful business rules to be integrated in process X, or ultimately replace it.

3. FRAMEWORK FOR INTEGRATING MODELLING, MONITORING AND LEARNING

3.1 Enterprise architecture fundamental concepts

In this section we present the fundamental concepts – or primitives – for enterprise architecture modelling, that are defined in (Sousa et al., 2005):

Entity – An organization is composed of entities. Entities are nouns that have a distinct, separate existence, though it need not be of material existence. In enterprise modelling, an entity can be a person, place, machine, concept or event that has meaning in the context of the business, and about which some information may be stored because it is relevant for the purpose of the model. An entity is characterized by its attributes and methods. These features can be either intrinsic or extrinsic. Intrinsic features describe the entity in isolation, while extrinsic features arise from the relationships with other entities.

Role – A role is the observable behavioural of an entity in the scope of a specific collaboration context. Hence, a role represents the external visible features of that entity when it collaborates with a set of other entities in the context of some activity. Each role represents a subset of its external or extrinsic features in the context of a specific collaboration defined in a role model.

Activity – An activity is an abstraction representing how a number of entities collaborate through roles in order to produce a specific outcome. Similarly to an algorithm, an activity aims accomplishing some task which, given an initial state, will always end in finite time and in a recognizable end-state. An activity may also be functionally decomposed into a finite set of further activities, thus add detail to the specification.

3.2 Framework

In the context of the previously presented fundamental concepts, an *organizational function* is a special activity F that corresponds to the collaboration of the entities described in the following paragraphs.

An activity X, relates to a state variable a, on which an activity Y has requirements in terms of respecting a certain norm n that restricts accepted states or values for a, so that Y can remain functional. X can have an internal mechanism of resilience such that in the occurrence of an expected exception that endangers compliance to n (provokes an approach or entrance in a state of dysfunction), a certain set of business rules Ri will try to handle the exception and avoid dysfunction.

If we are in the presence of an unexpected exception that endangers compliance to n, the resilience mechanism can enter in a microgenesis (learning) dynamics that can change existing (or generate new) business rules that try to handle the exception and if successful, can be integrated in *Ri*. In case *Ri* cannot handle the exception (due to lack of knowledge or authority of the actors present in X's collaboration), actor *W*, responsible for monitoring *a*, will invoke activity *Z*, which constitutes an external resilience mechanism and implies a shift of control flow to the collaboration realized by *Z*. So that *X* can get functional again, *Z* may be able to handle and resolve the exception either by being able to change *X*'s inputs, or by also entering in microgenesis and for example, changing *X*'s own nature – algorithm, giving other kinds of inputs, etc.

Collaborations that execute microgenesis dynamics are, by nature, highly unpredictable and unstructured, but an important aspect to facilitate microgenesis dynamics is to keep a microgenesis log of steps taken (trial and error, justifications of decisions, etc.) until successful business rules are put in place that can resolve the exception. By nature (Bickard, 2001), this information is valuable for future microgenesis dynamics working on the dysfunctional activity. An essential role in microgenesis dynamics is of the knowledge of best/worst business practices associated with *X* or *Y*'s domains, that can be removed or instantiated according to the organizational scenario.

In failing to avoid dysfunction of *X* (*Z* itself is in a state of dysfunction), actor *W'* responsible for monitoring *Z* will have to invoke activity *Z'* and successively this pattern will have to repeat (hence the recursive nature of the organizational function concept) – eventually reaching the highest and ultimate (still internal) activity in the organization that can totally reconfigure the system (the *governance* activity) so that *X* can again return to a state of function, where the organization stabilizes (is able to maintain itself). In the case of (the *governance* activity) failing to do so, dysfunction can propagate to several other activities in the organization, eventually leading to its total collapse. In Table 1, these entities are further described, along with their roles in the collaboration that realizes the activity organizational function *F*.

Table 1 – Entities in the collaboration that realizes an organizational function F.

Entity	Description	Role
Activity X	The collaboration on which an organizational function (a collaboration itself, named F) is being elicited. From the point of view of the functional dynamics of F, X is an entity.	monitored
Activity Y	A collaboration that depends on good and normal outcome of Activity X.	dependent
Observable state a	A state variable a whose value depends on behaviour of Activity X, and on which activity Y has requirements, so that activity Y itself respects requirements on one or more state variables (a', a'', etc. whose value, in turn, depend on behaviour of activity Y) on which other activities will have requirements	observable state
Normative requirements on a: n	Allowed and/or disallowed states/values/variations for a that respect the norm of functioning in terms of requirements of Activity Y	business goal
Internal resilience mechanism Ri	Set of business rules established for Activity X, that work as an internal resilience mechanism, that is, contribute to the maintenance of normative requirements on a	internal resilience

Entity	Description	Role
Actor W	Entity that is monitoring Activity X. More than one Actor can be doing this (for example, the actor executing the activity can, himself be monitoring a)	monitor
Activity Z	Collaboration that is invoked (by Actor W) in case there is a departure from a's norm that Activity X's internal mechanism of resilience cannot withstand (activity is near, or already in the state of dysfunction), and therefore, constitutes an external mechanism of resilience	external resilience
Microgenesis Activity M	Collaboration with capacity to repair/replace Activity X (or other activities on which X inputs depend and are causing the dysfunction) in the case of unexpected exceptions	micro-generators
Microgenesis Information I	This entity has two aspects: (1) Microgenesis log, that is reasons why current internal and external mechanisms of resilience were chosen/selected (results obtained in face of other mechanism tried); (2) Memory of best/worst practices in Activity X and Y domains of knowledge	Organizational learning and knowledge

The invocation of resilience mechanisms can be characterized as *internal* or *external* and can be *proactive* or *reactive*. *Internal* is when activity X itself has embedded business rules as an internal resilience mechanism and actor with the role of executing it also has the role of monitoring a. *External* is when it's the activity organizational function F, executed by an actor with the role of monitoring X that detects dysfunction and activates resilience mechanisms. *Proactive* is when the exception that is (or is going to be potentially) disturbing normal functioning didn't yet provoked a departure from the norm and resilience mechanisms act immediately to avoid dysfunction. *Reactive* is when dysfunction has happened in X and is provoking an exception in Y (that depends on a, in turn dependent on X's behaviour) and Y's organizational function is invoking a certain collaboration context that will, for example, correct X's behaviour. To clarify the presented framework and its concepts, we now introduce, as a proof of concept, an example to show practical application and its potential usefulness.

3.3 Application example

Consider a retail company with the following activities: Activity X – Transport sunflower seeds; Activity Y – Sell sunflower seeds. If X is in a context of eventually failing to respect the norm n (arrive before 9h in the day after) for state variable a (estimated time of arrival) due to a severe traffic jam (expected exception) between store no. 4 and store no. 32, actor W (truck driver) with the role of executing X, and also the role of monitoring X, can, for instance (activate business rules belonging to Ri), accelerate the truck, or go trough a shortcut or alternative route to arrive on time (organizational knowledge that can or should be included in training or available to the actor). This is also an example of an internal and proactive invocation of a resilience mechanism.

If W encounters more traffic jams and keeps delaying (Ri not able to handle the exception), he can call the logistics centre, referring that he will not be able to arrive on time. This is an example of proactive invocation of an external mechanism of resilience, Activity Z – Manage fleet, now with the collaboration of Actor W' operator of the logistics centre of the company.

One outcome would be W' giving some advice on alternate routes for the truck driver to try (case of giving new inputs to X, whose executer W didn't have access to). Another outcome is W' to activate an alternate X - Send sunflower seeds by express mail - FedEx, (change in X's nature, with another instantiation). Another external proactive invocation would be the case of truck driver to be unreachable by mobile phone, but the logistics agent could be monitoring the truck by GPS system and detect the impossibility of arrival on time and activate alternate X as stated above.

Examples of application of microgenesis concept follow. If in store no. 32, Y approaches a state of dysfunction (a is number of packs in stock, n is have a minimum of 30) due to dysfunction on activity V - Replenish stock (in turn affected by a very unexpected exception of a devastating migratory hamster attack in the supplier's terrain), the salesman W will (proactively) invoke process Z – Manage stocks, which has the role of external resilience mechanism for Y's organizational function.

The inventory manager, executer of Z, enters in microgenesis mode, due to the unexpected nature of the exception and tries to construct alternative activities to solve or circumvent the problem. He contacted alternative suppliers, but they were also victims of the hamster attack. He then had the idea of checking if there was stock available on other stores. When he worked on other company five years ago, there was a process of shifting products between stores which wasn't a practice on his current company (case of application of tacit knowledge from the actor that corresponds to the current organization "learning") and then he had the idea to establish this activity, which turned out to be new business rules for activity Z that reflected on the construction of an alternative activity V, that previously only transported items between suppliers and stores and now transports items between stores. An example of using a microgenesis log would be registering the reason for choosing FedEx for alternative X: for example, a table with prices, showing it's much cheaper to send the packs by FedEx, than sending by UPS company. In a situation of necessity of changing X's nature this information can be useful for future decisions.

4. CONCLUSIONS AND FUTURE WORK

The proposed framework allows a separation of concerns between the modelling of operational aspects of collaborations as presented in (Sousa et al., 2005) and the interdependences, monitoring and learning aspects of collaborations inherent to the functional dimension of the enterprise. As an innovative contribution to the enterprise architecture modelling field, this framework, can be used as a basis to capture the dynamics of monitoring and evolution (or adaptation) of the enterprise, in face of its environment.

To capture and model organizational functions of activities is way to capture knowledge about resiliency solutions, that is, how to manage resources while facing disruptive deltas in certain processes that otherwise would remain tacit in the minds of human actors of organizations. It's also possible to capture information on which steps made current business practices successful (in situations of unexpected exceptions) and allow a more conscious process of evolution or adaptation to new unexpected environmental perturbations. That is, information of the process of learning of an organization can collected and reused in other learning situations.

Trough the elicitation of networks of interdependences between activities, it may also be possible to (automatically or semi-automatically) detect which processes are more vital and establish priorities for creating proactive mechanisms of resiliency that can prevent and avoid propagation of dysfunction in a timely manner.

To further develop current work, a graduate and an MsC thesis are currently ongoing. One has the purpose of extending a modelling tool to allow a coherent application of the proposed framework to model functional dependencies between processes. The other aims to create an intuitive tool for capturing, in real-time, structured information about dynamics of selection of new business rules (microgenesis dynamics) also for providing informational support to this dynamics.

5. ACKNOWLEDGMENT

Research work that led to results presented in this paper was possible thanks to the financial support of a PhD scholarship (Ref.: SFRH/BD/13384/2003) subsidized by "Fundação para a Ciência e a Tecnologia - Ministério da Ciência, Tecnologia e Ensino Superior" of the Portuguese government and by the European Social Fund.

6. REFERENCES

1. Bickhard M. H., The Dynamic Emergence of Error Avoidance and Error Vicariants, Journal of Experimental & Theoretical Artificial Intelligence, Taylor and Francis Ltd, 2001
2. Bickhard Mark H., Process and Emergence: Normative Function and Representation, Department of Philosophy, Lehigh University, 2002
3. Business Rules Group, Defining Business Rules - What Are They Really?, 2000
4. Chandler Alfred D., The Visible Hand: The Managerial Revolution in American Business, 1980
5. Chauvet G. A., Non-locality in biological systems results from hierarchy. Application to the nervous system., Institut de Biologie Theorique, Universite d'Angers, 1993
6. Christensen W. D. and Bickhard M. H., The process dynamics of normative function (The Philosophy of Biology), Monist, Hegeler Institute, 2002
7. Eriksson, H., Penker, M, Business Modeling with UML: Business Patterns at Work, OMG Press, Wiley Computer Publishing, 2000
8. Kueng P., Kawalek P., Goal-Based Business Process Models: Creation and Evaluation, Informatics Process Group (IPG), Department of Computer Science, University of Manchester, UK, 1996
9. Mourão, H. and P. Antunes, A Collaborative Framework for Unexpected Exception Handling, Groupware: Design, Implementation, and Use, Heidelberg, Springer-Verlag, 2005
10. Sousa P., Caetano A., Vasconcelos A., Pereira C., Tribolet J., Enterprise Architecture Modeling with the Unified Modeling Language, 2006
11. Weeks J. and Galunic C., A theory of the cultural evolution of the firm: the intra-organizational ecology of memes, 2003

DET: AN APPLICATION TO SUPPORT GLOBALIZATION AND SERVICE PROVIDING IN TOOLMAKING COMPANIES

Luís Mendes [1], Elsa Henriques[2], Manuel J. Fonseca[2] and Rui Soares[3]
[1]Partner Solutions, Portugal
luis.mendes@partnersolutions.pt
[2]Instituto Superior Técnico, Portugal
elsa.h@ist.utl.pt; mjf@inesc-id.pt
[3]Centimfe, Portugal
rui.soares@centimfe.com

This paper presents an application based on digital enterprise technologies to support both the business globalization and service providing in small and medium sized companies highly focused in production competences. The requirements and functionalise are discussed and the application to support the work environment, communication and remote access to information and in-site knowledge is overviewed. The application was designed considering the current work procedures in tooling industry and it allows tool makers staff, in their usual workstation, to interact with their in-site colleagues, clients or any partner at distant places and discuss technical problems, accessing and having available all the required information.

1. INTRODUCTION

Tool-makers have been facing huge challenges. They must provide extended quality services to their clients at a more and more reduced price and in a smaller and smaller timeframe. In this environment, teamwork within tool-makers staff and co-operation between tool-makers and clients (most of the time in different geographical locations) are vital to think ahead and to eliminate inefficiencies in the work progress related to delays in communication between the right interlocutors and in accessing relevant information and knowledge (seeking and retrieval) for in-time decision making.

Although each tool is a unique device produced in a one-of-a-kind manufacturing system, its production involves a common set of steps that happen concurrently rather than sequentially. From the request for a quotation (the traditional first step) to the tool trial out on production machines (the traditional final step) the building of a tool requires design and production technologies involving a high capital investment and a qualified labour force in which the tacit technological knowledge, highly dependent on a learning by doing process, is resident (Tang et al., 2004).

It is largely accepted that tool makers must accommodate new business strategies based on a closed interaction with their clients (Tang et al., 2004), frequently the tool user company, providing added value engineering services associated to the tool life cycle (Schuh et al., 2004) and targeted to the market real needs. Nevertheless, this new approach represents by itself a huge challenge. It requires a permanent interaction with a significant number of clients all over the world and even with partners and subcontractors at different levels in the value chain of the final products. The establishment of those relations requires a more permanent presence at the final parts fabricator site to assist the tool during its in-production phase, particularly in the tool trial out, maintenance procedures and troubleshooting events, and to identify new requirements and business opportunities in accordance to the clients' real needs. Since tool makers are small and medium size companies, this permanent presence represents a significant effort (Cleveland et al., 2002) which can be viewed at two levels. The immediate one is the significant financial effort, frequently difficult to support. The second one is related to the fact that this presence is relevant only if it is based on high level qualified human resources, which are scarce assets even at tool making plant.

The objective of the research work presented in this paper is to design and implement an innovative distributed and mobile engineering platform, based on information and communication technologies, which offers a more natural and user friendly approach to manage active and dynamic tool folders, allowing clients and field engineers to access tool-related information and tool related knowledge in several output modalities (e.g. audio, text, 2D/3D models, video, etc.). If such a platform is available the interface with clients and partners at their site or elsewhere can be made by personnel at lower levels of their learning curves maintaining the efficiency and the quality of the assistance as all the tool history data, tool maker knowledge and competences are available in real time in the background.

2. WORK PROCEDURES IN TOOLING COMPANIES

In order to support the definition of the Mobile Engineering functionalities and architecture, the first step of the work developed was to achieve a clear understanding of the current internal working procedures of a tool making company. This task was accomplished in Portuguese tooling industry and was supported on a formal questionnaire structured in the following topics: information and communication flow; work procedures; information systems currently used; most relevant problems and constrains regarding communication and information access.

Regarding the communication practices, tooling companies started in the recent past to use advanced tools as communication forms. The telephone, fax and the working meetings at prod are becoming less important with the growing use of informatics and communication technologies. The exchanges of e-mails are current and video-conference in general is emerging as a way to discuss projects within a virtual meeting. Although these technologies are owned by the most tool makers, a great barrier to their efficient use still remains, due mainly to the innumerable incompatibilities with client systems and to the current need to shift from the current workstation to a specific workplace where the communication devices are available.

The process of producing a new tool starts with a contact from a potential client requesting a quotation proposal (figure 1). Tool makers have a set of more or less stable clients, with whom they are used to work with. This scenario facilitates the communication between the intervening parts. The first contact to the client is made by telephone, fax or e-mail and the needed information to define the project requirements is transmitted by e-mail (even if it is not the most reliable tool for confidential information) or FTP servers (for large packages and/or for strictly confidential information). Having this information, usually the geometrical models and the technological information about the final product and the client production facilities, the tool maker can send a proposal document having a quotation, a delivery time and a technical overview of the proposed tool engineering solution.

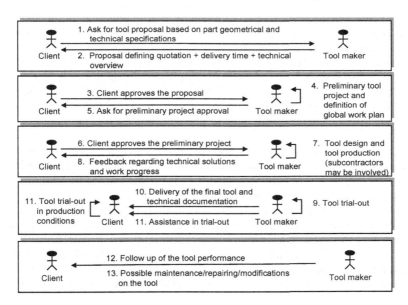

Figure 1 – Major actions on a tool development project (process iterations are not represented but currently occur at any stage).

If the client approves the provided proposal, the tool maker starts working on a preliminary project and on the work plan. The preliminary project can suffer several alterations and internal/external approvals, within a constrained timeframe, involving the tool maker and its client staffs. When the tool preliminary project is approved, it becomes the starting point for the development of the detail project where the tool is completely specified. Again the client has to acknowledge the rightness of the tool detail project to produce its product. The tool material list is build and the orders to the suppliers are emitted to buy the needed materials.

From this point on, the tool project manager coordinates all the decision making processes and handles all the generated information/documentation about the project. He also makes the bridge between the client, the toolmaker commercial, development and shop floor departments while the tool is not delivered to the client. A huge amount of information is managed and organized, making his job greatly dependent on his working capacity and coordination qualities. Indeed, the project manager spends a large percentage of his working time controlling the information and often the team management and the control of the work progress are neglected.

The tool trial is the production end stage. Once more, the project manager establishes the link with the client, following-up the trials. Frequently, re-work or fine adjustments are needed to guarantee the tool good functioning and/or to improve its performance. Finally, the tool and a set of tool related documents (CAD models, engineering analysis, quality plans, certificates ...) are sent to the client.

Nowadays, post-sale support is increasingly a differentiating factor among tool makers. Following-up the tool in the client's plant and the fulfilment of subsequent demands related to the maintenance support or even performance improvement are already current practices in the sector and are decisive factors regarding the establishment of long-term partnerships with clients. Telephone calls are usual the way to maintain the contact and follow the tool performance. However, even being expensive and representing a significant staff effort, when dealing with important clients, visits to the client site are done to stress the interest and the support from the tool maker.

During the development process the tool maker has to cope with a great amount of technical information about the final product and its materials, the tool design process, the design of auxiliary components and systems and the tool manufacturing process. They face a colossus job of keeping all the information and documentation organized, quickly accessible, wherever and whenever it is needed, and updated with the numerous modifications and iterations that happen all along the tool development process.

Although, PDM (Product Data Management) and PLM (Product Lifecycle Management) systems have been available for some years, such systems are not used in the tooling sector. The philosophy of PDM systems (Liu et al., 2001), with a long and unfriendly implementation process, compatibility problems and a rigid customized work-flow, does not support the degree of agility that the small tooling companies require to adapt to dynamic requirements within a short response time. Their unpredictability is quite difficult to structure in a PDM system, designed for large organizations with highly structured work procedures. In fact, some tool makers have access to advanced tools for communication and product information management, but two technical barriers still prevail. The first one is the small adequacy of the available systems, conceived for large companies dealing with mass production or large industrial projects, to the specificity of this industry. The second one is related to some technical incompatibility between different clients and tool maker's hardware and software systems.

3. MOBILE ENGINEERING CONCEPT

Despite the still common vision that the office or the factory is the place where the work is performed, nowadays many people work "off-site" in other environments. For instance, they can be in the clients or supplier's site, in the factory floor, in a hotel or even at home. The competitiveness of tooling companies in a global market requires from each company the agility to search for new business opportunities and to deal with dynamic client requirements and potential needs in order to establish a permanent relationship. In such context, tool makers must promote their engineering and technical staff mobility (e.g. tool designers; project managers and other specialized workers), providing them a work environment that allows the access in real time to tool projects information, the access to internal and external knowledge and the facility to have communication between workers in order to share the knowledge between the senior and junior staff. The concept behind the Mobile Engineering project is an effort to answer the staff mobility requirements mentioned above.

The Mobile Engineering platform is the materialization of the Mobile Engineering concept (figure 2). It integrates different Information and Communication Technologies (ICT) based systems to provide the access to the tooling company information and knowledge repository, to support competitive decision making processes and efficient after-sales engineering services, in a context where the workplace can be anywhere.

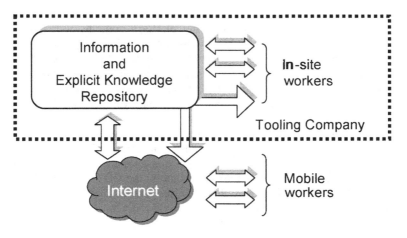

Figure 2 – Mobile Engineering Concept.

The success of such platform depends on the fulfilment of a set of functional requirements:

- Integrated IT environment compatible with the toolmaker working procedures;
- Central repository of information and explicit knowledge with the capability to store and organize in a hierarchical fashion all project documentation;
- Remote access to the central repository resident in the tooling company;
- Capability to work off-line if an internet connection is not available or has a low band width;
- Support for video and voice meetings among project participants;
- Support for virtual conferences involving shared visualization, manipulation and edition of digital geometric models;
- Security/integrity of the repository data by reliable and secure communications (authentication, encryption, integrity) and permission access control;
- Low implementation cost, simple administration and maintenance requirements and user-friendly interfaces with quick learning curves.

4. PLATFORM ARCHITETURE

The architecture of the Mobile Engineering platform contains four main blocks: Smart Field Manuals (SFM), CAD Annotation, Voice/Video Tools and the Commercial-of-the-Shelf (COTS) production software systems (figure 3). Each block has a counterpart on the user computer, called Mobile User Workspace, and on the tool maker back office, called the Mobile Engineering Central Services, which represents the central repository that is part of the Mobile Engineering concept.

The COTS Production software block represents the set of software applications used in the tool development process. Besides engineering software like CAD, CAE and CAM systems, this block also represents non-engineering software like word processing, spreadsheets, etc. The files generated by the COTS production Software are the main subject of the tasks done by the Smart Field Manual and CAD Annotation blocks.

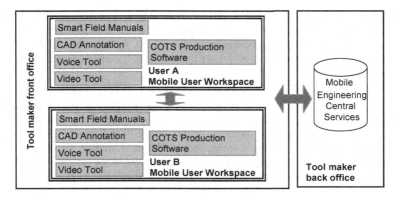

Figure 3 – Mobile Engineering architecture.

The Voice/Video system block is the application that allows the mobile users to communicate between themselves by voice or video using an internet connection. Since there are many communication applications freely available with excellent quality, an analysis of such applications was done in order to find out the most adequate one. Skype2 was selected as it is a free product, already used by some tool makers, has communication quality and is easy to install and operate.

The CAD annotation block provides to the tool engineers a flexible and simple system for visualization, edition and textual annotation on 3D geometric models in a mobile and shared environment. With this system the participants on a tool project can exchange ideas having as a starting point the tool 3D model, reducing the time needed to find the best solution for a geometrical/technological/engineering problem. Simultaneous with the CAD Annotation block, the Voice/Video system block can be used to improve the communication between the participants.

The Smart Field Manual (SFM) block creates and manages the central project documentation repository from the Mobile Engineering Concept. The projects documentation is organized in a set of Smart Field Manuals. A Smart Field Manual is the collection of all documents generated all along the tool life cycle (design, production, assembly and trial outs, delivery, operating conditions, maintenance). By a document it is meant a digital file, like a text file, a CAD or CAM file produced by the COTS Production Software block or by the CAD Annotation block. With the projects digital artefacts organized in SFMs, the tool makers have in a unique and secure location all the information related to all their projects, which facilitates the reuse of the past projects data in the development of new ones.

An SFM file besides its content (produced by COTS) has also indexing information (like name, client, comment) describing its content. The content of an SFM file can have multiple versions to accommodate the evolution of the tool project. To support concurrent project development a new version of the content can only be added by a user if no other user is also working on the same SFM file (check-in/check-out operations).

To organize the SFM Files there is the possibility to place them in a SFM Directory. SFM Directories can be organized in a tree structure. Each SFM Directory has also indexing information describing its content. SFMs, SFM Files and SFM Directories have a permission list which tells what users can view, delete or edit its contents.

The architecture of the SFM block follows the client/server pattern where the communication is done via web services. The client application is called the SFM Desktop and the server application is called the SFM Services. The SFM Desktop can work connected or disconnected from the SFM Services. To support the mobility and assuming that a connection to the tool maker back office may be unavailable or have an inadequate band width to support an efficient access to large files, the SFM block provides an off-line working mode where the content of SFMs can still be viewed and accessed disconnected from the central repository. The SFM Desktop is depicted in figure 4.

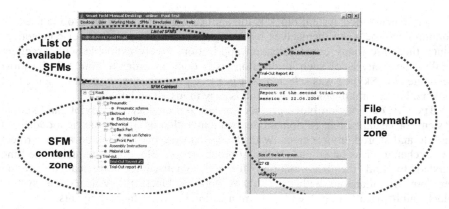

Figure 4 – Smart Field Manual Desktop screen-shoot.

The client is divided in three main areas. The top area lists the SFMs from the central repository to which the user has access when working in on-line mode or the ones available when working in off-line mode. The bottom area, displays the content of the selected SFM from the top area. The right area gives a quick overview about the indexing information of the SFM, SFM Directory or SFM File selected on the other two areas. The content of the SFM list and the content of each SFM are directly related with the permission rules applied to the user.

For a SFM to become available off-line it is necessary to apply to it the Subscribe operation while the SFM Desktop is on the on-line working mode. During the SFM Desktop off-line mode the SFM can be consulted and the content of the SFM Files can by changed by applying new versions to them. Once the SFM desktop is back to the on-line working mode, it is possible to update the SFM on the central repository with the new versions added to its SFM Files.

The SFM Services are located on the Mobile Engineering Central Services. Conceptually they are organized in six components:

- Content Storage Area: Abstracts the computer file system, where the SFM Files contents (and versions) are stored and retrieved;
- User Directory: Definition of users and what operations they can do on the SFM Desktop;
- Content Authorization Service: Rules what SFM, SFM Directories or SFM Files a user can view, edit, delete;
- Content Management: Implements the edit, view, delete operations on a SFM, SFM File and SFM Directory.
- Replication Management: In cooperation with the Content Management synchronizes the SFMs content when shifting from the on-line working mode to the off-line working mode and vice-versa.
- Communication Services: Provides the web services communication facilities between the SFM clients and the other SFM services components.

The development of the SFM Desktop and Services was based on Java open source projects. The products used were: Axis, Hibernate, PostgreSQL, Apache Tomcat, Apache Axis, HSQLDB and the Java Web Start Facility.

5. CONCLUSIONS

More than ever tool makers assume themselves as service providers with partners and clients are all over the world. But, to establish new businesses with far away clients and maintain long term partnerships and effective collaboration with them are perceived as huge barriers, difficult to deal within a scarce resources environment. The mobile engineering platform presented is an infrastructure that is being developed to provide close assistance to clients in distant places and to give an easy assess to information and to in-site knowledge wherever it is needed. Besides the remote access to the information repository, it provides each workstation with a collaboration environment where virtual meetings, integrating information access, CAD conference and video/voice communication can take place.

The human component in the implementation of communication and information management systems is quite difficult to unravel. Tooling companies have qualified technicians with a great ability to assimilate new technologies and work methodologies. However, they are highly focused on production competences and organization and information management issues are regarded as secondary and less relevant. If they are confronted with something new in this field, during the learning curve a rejection should be expected. So, all these new systems are being integrated gradually in a demonstrator company, in small task forces and pilot projects, to evaluate benefits and improvement potential and to eliminate possible rejections.

5.1 Acknowledgments

This research work has been sponsored by the EC through the 6th Framework Integrated Project – EuroTooling21.

6. REFERENCES

1. Tang D, Eversheim W, Schuh G. "A new generation of cooperative development paradigm in the tool and die making branch: strategy and technology" Robotics and Computer-Integrated Manufacturing 20 (2004) 301–311. ed. Elsevier.
2. Schuh G, Fricker I, Hagemann F. "Role Models For Mould Business in Europe", Conf. in Rapid Product Development RPD 2004, Marinha Grande, Portugal, 2004.
3. Cleveland M. "Competitive assessment of the die & mold building sector: a west Michigan perspective", http://www.rightplace.org/Info_Center/Library/News_Archive/2002_tooling_report.pdf , 2002.
4. Liu DT, Xu XW. "A review of web-based product data management systems," Computers in Industry 44 (2001) 251–262, ed. Elsevier.

TOWARDS AN OUT-OF-THE-BOX INTEGRATED SERVICES ENVIRONMENT

Rodrigo Castelo[1], Paulo Almeida[2] and Miguel Mira da Silva[1]
[1]Intituto Superior Técnico, Portugal
rodrigo@catastropha.org, mms@tagus.ist.utl.pt
[2]OutSystems, Portugal
paulo.almeida@outsystems.com

Although today a well-known Enterprise Resource Planning (ERP) System such as SAP can support many of the standard organization needs, the fact is that for many reasons most organizations prefer to change the ERP default configuration and/or complement the ERP with many other external applications, either existing or new ones. However, these external applications are still expensive to develop but especially to integrate with the ERP and even more expensive to change in order to support new business processes.
In this paper we present an integration tool that we developed for the OutSystems platform called Integration Studio. This tool completely automates the task of integrating OutSystems applications with .Net assemblies and relational databases. In addition, the tool was designed with an extensibility philosophy and was already extended to support easy integrations with SAP and Java. Other technologies, such as the Lightweight Directory Access Protocol (LDAP), will follow soon.
With Integration Studio, the OutSystems platform now supports not only the fast and easy creation and change of applications but also the easy integration of them with any other existing application in the organization. Furthermore, other non-OutSystems applications can also access the OutSystems platform (e.g. using Web Services) to easily integrate with any OutSystems or non-OutSystems applications. With Integration Studio, the OutSystems platform is now a fully automated Integrated Services Environment (ISE) that, unlike the existing products in the market, is extremely easy to learn and use.

1. INTRODUCTION

Engineers have the tendency to generalize solutions so they can be applied to multiple scenarios and situations. However, a solution must be concrete to become useful. The balance between generalization and concreteness is hard to achieve.

As a result of this dichotomy, some Enterprise Resource Planning (ERP) Systems have chosen one side and evolved to support a wide range of concrete business processes. Probably the best example of such an ERP is SAP. The result of its multiple concrete solutions is that, depending on the industry, the custom code of a SAP implementation can reach up to 60% (WestTrax, 2004). Not surprisingly, 20% of this custom code is just reinventing the wheel and could be replaced by native SAP code. This further supports the idea that offering a wide range of concrete solutions has limitations because such diversity is not scalable. On the other hand, these concrete solutions support so many business processes that, on average, a customer only uses 50% of the standard SAP code he paid for (WestTrax, 2004).

Another issue is that big ERPs address only the core business processes and companies need other systems to provide support for non-core processes and heterogeneous users. Also, there are many kinds of specialized systems, excellent in some industry specific tasks (SDCEXEC, 2005), which need to be integrated with the ERP. When trans-organizational processes need to be implemented to support the full chain of a product or service, these problems are even more aggravated.

These needed integrations are still complex and expensive. By 2000, 58% of the companies didn't have their new ERPs integrated with the previous existing systems, 23% because their attempts to integrate failed and 71% because they didn't even try considering the required time and costs (Themistocleous, 2001). The integration business alone moved $18 billion in 1998 and, at the time, it was predicted to move $34 billion in 2002 (Johnson, 2000). However, surpassing all expectations, it actually moved $65.5 billion in 2002 and is estimated to reach $82.8 billion by 2007 (AME, 2003).

Apart from the integrations problems, the development of custom applications is, in itself, a complex task. As an example, in Canada, by 1997, more than 75% of the Information Technology (IT) projects blew their schedules by 30% (KPMG, 1997). In the middle of the same decade, in the USA, 31% of the IT projects were abandoned before their completion and 52.7% cost more 89% of their predicted costs (StandishGroup, 1995).

Finally, as the businesses and chains evolve, the systems must evolve with them. The change of an ERP or even a simple application is known to be an even more complex task than its first implementation. Nonetheless, in an environment where the business rules and needs are constantly changing, organizations cannot wait nor afford the risk of such big projects and therefore do not change their applications, reducing their competitive advantage. This is why there is a broad market for systems that can be built in just a few weeks and disposed when they become superfluous or obsolete (Redshaw, 2005).

2. INTEGRATED SERVICE ENVIRONMENT

To solve the interoperability problems, an effort was started to create standards for different systems to communicate in a well-known way, detached from any proprietary technology. Nowadays, Web Services is the most commonly used standard to perform this task (Calladine, 2003) (Benfield, 2002).

Naturally, Web Services have evolved to become a central piece of another instance of a Service-Oriented Architecture (SOA), like the Distributed Component Object Model (DCOM) and the Common Object Request Broker Architecture (CORBA) were before them (Adobe, 2005).

A SOA has no accepted formal definition, nor a reference model. The OASIS, for instance, has been working on a SOA reference model (Adobe, 2005) and defines such an architecture as a system of components that offer a service which can be invoked by other components in compliance with a service contract.

Gartner, on the other hand, has been working on the definition of a methodology (Gartner, 2003) capable of surpassing the obstacles of creating, changing and operating enterprise applications by using a SOA. The definition of such a methodology involves the specification of the functional requirements that the tools must have, as the traditional application development tools are not suitable. This methodology for a Service-Oriented Development of Applications (SODA) has seven main aspects crucial for understanding the remaining of this paper:

- **Design**: Establishing how the requirements will be met or, in other words, defining the application architecture. A SOA relies on loosely coupled and coarsely grained components, multichannel access to services, process oriented design elements and early integrations.
- **Modeling**: Defining the application's structure in some modelling language, with three distinct phases: business modelling, application modelling and technical modelling.
- **Fabrication**: Creating the core service components of the application and the necessary integrations. This means writing code.
- **Assembly**: Aggregation of the service components, connection of their inputs and outputs and definition of its necessary translations. This can be performed with visual editors.
- **Orchestration**: Defining the processes flow along the services and how information and logic will flow through a given process. This can be performed with simple workflow managers.
- **Automation**: Hiding complexity and removing the need to write code by generating it automatically to map the model on some executable component, such as .Net or Enterprise JavaBeans (EJB), thus enabling less tech-savvy developers to work rapidly.
- **Variability and Rapid Change Maintenance**: Enabling changes to components that do not break the rest of the system. The variability of services should be encouraged and many small changes should be made continuously, rather than large changes sporadically. Usually, the variability of a system is inversely proportional to its automation.

From these seven aspects that support the full life-cycle of applications rises the notion of Integrated Services Environment (ISE). An ISE is not only a technology stack to support service-oriented and composite applications, but also a suite of tools to sustain their development. The more it supports the seven aspects of SODA, the more complete it is.

An ISE provides tools for the rapid development through composition and reusability that allow the applications to be easily changed. In addition, an ISE automates the deployment process, resulting in gains both in the development and the maintenance cycles. As a consequence, the development can be business-driven rather than technology-driven, meaning that developers can be focused more on the business processes themselves and less on the technological details.

SODA also stimulates Agile developments, materialized in shorter cycles, allowing feedback from real users to be incorporated into each new iteration and immediately validated. The application will therefore converge faster to a solution that satisfies the user's needs.

3. INTEGRATION STUDIO

The OutSystems platform is already an ISE, as recognized by Gartner in 2005 (Abrams, 2005). In fact, the OutSystems Hub Edition (OHE) provides an out-of-the-box ISE that supports the full life cycle of custom enterprise applications. But we believed that OHE could support SODA even better.

All the seven aspects of a SODA are covered by the OutSystems platform. Using an Agile methodology, OutSystems is able to fully model an application while its **Design** is provided by the OutSystems reference model. In fact, almost all the missing five aspects of SODA are combined in the **Modeling** one, as the **Fabrication** is fully **Automated** within OutSystems' scope and the **Assembly** and **Orchestration** are also performed in the same Integrated Design Environment (IDE) used to Model the application. This IDE is called OutSystems Service Studio (OSS).

Being a model, any OutSystems application can be visually changed and deployed again in a matter of seconds, supporting the seventh and last aspect of SODA: **Variability and Rapid Change Maintenance**.

Execution and deployment are orchestrated by the OutSystems Hub Server (OHS) that runs over standard Microsoft .Net or J2EE application server infrastructures.

According to Gartner, the **Fabrication** step includes the creation of adapters to integrate with legacy systems (Gartner, 2003). Going a step further, we wanted to apply the **Automation** principles to the creation of these integration adapters in order to speed it up. From the materialization of such goals, a new product named OutSystems Integration Studio was born.

4. IMPLEMENTATION

The current version of Integration Studio already supports the creation of adapters to integrate with .Net assemblies and relational databases. By stepping through simple wizards, the user is able to create a complete adapter and make that adapter available for use, in a completely automated fashion and without writing a single line of code, as this is a task performed by the tool.

Nonetheless, if more complex integrations are needed, Integration Studio allows the user to write code for them and provides help along this process by updating the adapter interface code according with the changes performed in its OutSystems Interface Definition Language (IDL).

Furthermore, Integration Studio was built with an extensibility philosophy based on plug-ins and provides a set of model objects, logic and user interfaces so that a new plug-in can be easily developed. This way, when developing a new plug-in, the effort can be put on creating the logic to expose to the user, via introspection, the interface of a foreign technology and on generating the adapter code between that technology and OHE.

In fact, with just two developers, new plug-ins to automate the creation of adapters for SAP and Java also by stepping through simple wizards was developed in less than two months each.

5. EVALUATION

In order to quantify the benefits of Integration Studio, we now briefly present a simplified benchmark.

Figure 1 shows the effort, expressed in seconds, of integrating with concrete .Net assemblies and relational databases, with and without Integration Studio. We define the complexity of a .Net method as the number of parameters a method has and the complexity of a database table as the number of columns a table has.

Considering that the process of exposing a .Net method or a database table to OHE is now automatic, there are gains in speed from 600+ seconds to just 20, for a complexity of 14 parameters or columns. The gains are proportional to complexity, because with automation, what was previously linear with the complexity is now virtually constant.

Obviously, no real integration takes seconds to perform. This benchmark only demonstrates that the time needed to perform the unitary tasks required to integrate with .Net assemblies and relational databases are drastically reduced. Having in account that these unitary tasks are performed multiple times for real integrations, the gains of using Integration Studio become visible.

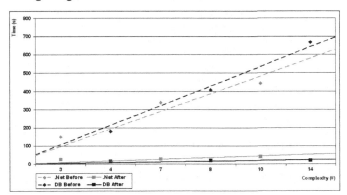

Figure 1 – Benchmark.

5.1. Benefits

With Integration Studio, OHE can aid organizations evolving their Information Systems (IS) towards a SOA, while still keeping their existing infrastructure, either composed of structural ERPs, specialized systems, or both.

Besides allowing the fast deployment of a SOA, OHE provides the means for delivering an IS infrastructure as Agile as the business demands, thus keeping the business requirements and technological solutions more aligned. The innovators can even migrate to OHE any obsolete or limited system, without any real impact on the business, following an iterative approach and without any rush, as the support for business agility was already secured. These organizations are known as the Next Generation Enterprises (NGE) (Umar, 2005) and are already sprouting.

By adding Integration Studio to the features of the OHE we expect, in the long term, to contribute to the reduction of the integration problems and, in the medium term, to deliver a system capable of handling heterogeneity without any need for a colossal, and therefore expensive, technological know-how, thus, setting a modus operandis for transforming the integration problem in the classical definition of a commodity.

With the addition of Integration Studio, OHE has extended all the benefits of an ISE to the domain of systems' integration. As the process of generating adapters for different technologies is automated, the same compose-and-reuse paradigm available inside the platform can now be used to access external systems.

6. DISCUSSION

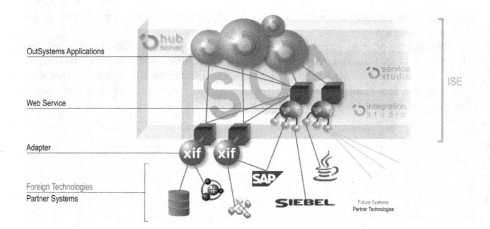

Figure 2 – OutSystems Out-of-the-Box ISE.

ISs have evolved from closed and complex structures towards open and simple ones. Like a newborn, ISs have learned over time to talk with each other and leave their autistic world, understanding that communication plays a crucial role in any successful network, capable of creating value through the combination of information from each of the parts.

There are many ways of solving the communication problems of ISs. The most broadly implemented is known as Enterprise Application Integrators (EAI) or Message Brokers (Khn, 2003). These kinds of systems tend to suffer from the "you-must-talk-my-language" syndrome. All foreign technologies need to use some adapter to communicate with their proprietary technology. Although technologically this could be a non-issue, EAIs can be considered a false answer to the integration problem because of the diversity of such solutions, like Jini* (Jai, 2000), CRISTAL (Gaspard, 2003) or iCell (Wu, 2004), to name a few. This further increases the problem, rather than solving it.

The problem with EAIs is not the pattern used to solve the communication issue (Vinoski, 2004), but rather the incapability of vendors to come to agreement on a standardized way to communicate. To solve this issue, the Web Services standards have emerged.

Web Services-based SOAs can now provide an interface that any technology can understand and use. This way, new applications can easily be incorporated into the existing infrastructure and reuse the processes already deployed, hence reducing the integration effort (Chung, 2004) (Peng, 2004).

There is still the problem of creating adapters to passive technologies, that is, technologies that wait for a request in order to provide a response. The creation effort of such adapters is solved and reduced by Integration Studio.

As depicted in figure 2, OHE can now also be considered as an EAI based on a standardized communication stack. With Integration Studio, adapters to the mentioned passive technologies can be automatically created as needed without any code writing, therefore allowing the use of specialized applications to create relevant data to feed decision support interfaces or control factory lines. Plus, all this can be achieved without the need for experts specialized on those applications.

By using the OutSystems platform, new applications that use existing applications can be easily and rapidly created to cover the on-going business needs, making information and functionality ubiquitous over the organization and across organizations. Also, these newly created applications can be changed with low costs and 100% uptime to support any functional change the business may require.

Furthermore, the specialized applications can make use of the newly deployed applications by using the Web Services standard.

By combining the power of a SOA with the principles of a standardized EAI, OHE can now be considered a state-of-the-art ISE supported by a standard reference model and a set of tools that allow both the visual creation and changing of new enterprise applications and the integration of existing ones.

6.1. Comparison

OHE is not the only platform that generically addresses all these issues. According to Gartner's 2006 Magic Quadrant for the ISE market, the closest competitor to the OutSystems technology is Skyway Software (Plummer, 2006).

The deployment and versioning of applications built with the Skyway technology are aided by the Skyway Director which supports J2EE containers from vendors such as BEA, JBoss and SAP (Skyway, 2005). These applications can be **Modelled** and **Assembled** using the Skyway Builder. The **Orchestration** is made using Web Services or Java Remote Method Invocation (RMI) and this tool also **Automates** the generation of J2EE compliant code.

Nevertheless, this **Fabrication** is not fully automated by the Skyway Builder as the integrations with external systems must be performed using Web Services or Java RMI and coded in the traditional fashion, therefore requiring expert knowledge. This is exactly where our proposed solution distinguishes itself from similar developments in the ISE/SOA direction as we have automated the fabrication of such integrations.

7. CONCLUSION

In this paper we introduced the existing major problems of ISs: the high cost to create and change custom enterprise applications and their integration with the existing applications.

The proposed solution for these problems involves the unification of an ISE with a tool capable of generating adapters to integrate with existing applications of different technologies. This proposal is concretized by OHE and the Integration Studio tool resulting of a research by the authors.

OHE already provides full automation, not inversely proportional to the created applications variability but independent from it.

Integration Studio extends OHE by applying the same SODA principles to the world of integration. The first version of this tool can integrate with .Net assemblies and relational databases just by stepping through simple wizards. Thus, the users can expose to the OutSystems technology the access to any functionality provided by those .Net assemblies and any information provided by those relational databases. Furthermore, Integration Studio was built with extensibility plug-ins architecture so that anyone can easily extend its functionality to integrate with all major technologies without writing a single line of code. Recently, support for Java and automatic integrations with SAP were added.

With Integration Studio, OHE tries to better solve the problems elicited above, allowing organizations to evolve towards a standardized and Agile SOA without the risk and expensiveness of huge infrastructural projects.

8. REFERENCES

1. Adobe. Service Oriented Architecture Whitepaper. March 2005.
2. AME. Slow growth in worldwide spending on systems integration services. April 2003. http://www.ameinfo.com/21935.html [Online April 2006].
3. Amjad Umar. IT Infrastructure to Enable Next Generation Enterprises. Information Systems Frontiers, 7(3):217-256, July 2005.
4. Benchiao Jai, Michael Ogg and Aleta Ricciardi. Effortless software interoperability with Jini* connection technology. Bell Labs Technical Journal, 5(2):88-101, April 2000.
5. Charles Abrams, David Mitchell Smith and Whit Andrews. How to Select Products and Services That Use Web Services Technology. Gartner, May 2005.
6. Daryl C. Plummer, David W. McCoy and Charles Abrams. Magic Quadrant for the Integrated Service Environment Market. Gartner, 2006.
7. Editorial Staff. ERP Alone Is Not Enough to Meet the Challenges of Performance and Compliance. Supply and Demand Chain Executive, 2005.
8. Gail Johnson. The Big Kahuna of IT Systems. Electrical Wholesaling, April 2000. http://ewweb.com/mag/electric_big_kahuna_systems [Online April 2006]
9. Gartner. Next-Generation AD Tools Will Bring SOA to the Mainstream. April 2003.
10. Gartner. The Integrated Service Environment Market Magic Quadrant. April 2003.
11. Harald Khn, Franz Bayer, Stefan Junginger and Dimitris Karagiannis. Enterprise Model Integration. Lecture Notes in Computer Science, 2738:379-392, October 2003.

12. J. Calladine. Giving Legs to the Legacy – Web Services Integration Within the Enterprise. BT Technology Journal, 22(1):87-98, March 2003.
13. KPMG. Survey. 1997.
14. Marinus Themistocleous, Zahir Irani, Robert M. O'Keefe and Ray Paul. ERP Problems and Application Integration Issues: An Empirical Survey. IEEE Publications, 9(9):9045, 34th, 2001.
15. Ruey-Shyang Wu, Shyan-Ming Yuan, Anderson Liang and Daphne Chyan. iCell: Integration Unit in Enterprise Cooperative Environment. Lecture Notes in Computer Science, 3033:962-969, April 2004.
16. Sam Chung, Lai Hong Tang and Sergio Davalos. A Web Service Oriented Integration Approach for Enterprise and Business-to-Business Applications. Lecture Notes in Computer Science, 3306:510, October 2004.
17. Sbastien Gaspard, Florida Estrella, Richard McClatchey and Rgis Dindeleux. Managing Evolving Business Workflows through the Capture of Descriptive Information. Lecture Notes in Computer Science, 2814:5-16, September 2003.
18. Skyway Software. Service Oriented Architecture: Realizing the Business Value. May 2005.
19. Steve Benfield and Peter Fingar. Managing Web Services. Internet World, 8(5), 62, May 2002.
20. Steve Vinoski. An Overview of Middleware. Lecture Notes in Computer Science, 3063:35-51, April 2004.
21. The Standish Group International, Inc. The Chaos Report. 1995.
22. Toby Redshaw. Selling to Optimal-Edge CIOs. SandHill.com, February 2005.
23. WestTrax Applications. The SAP ROI Debate: What Is The Real ROI From SAP? 2004.
24. Xin Peng, Wenyun Zhao and En Ye. Research on Construction of EAI-Oriented Web Service Architecture. Lecture Notes in Computer Science, 3032:592-600, April 2004.

SESSION 5

PHYSICAL-TO-DIGITAL ENVIRONMENT
INTEGRATORS

A CAD MODELLING SYSTEM AUTOMATION FOR REVERSE ENGINEERING APPLICATIONS

Jafar Jamshidi, Antony R. Mileham and Geraint W. Owen
IMRC, Department of Mechanical Engineering
The University of Bath, UK
{J.Jamshidi, A.R.Mileham, G.W.Owen}@bath.ac.uk

In the Reverse Engineering process, scanned data digitised by various scanning systems from the component geometry is used to regenerate the original design information. CAD model creation from such data requires numerous stages of modelling processes. Several algorithms for the modelling processes were developed and verified in the earlier stages of this research. In this paper the automation of these algorithms into a unique CAD modelling system is introduced. The system user can create a complete CAD model by integration and minimum manipulation of the high resolution scanned data, obtained using a high accuracy Coordinate Measurement Machine with touch probe, and low resolution scanned data obtained using a high speed Laser Scanner, rapidly and accurately.

1. INTRODUCTION

Reverse Engineering (RE) is the process of extracting design information from an existing part, for which such information is unavailable of mislaid. In order to digitise part geometry, various scanning systems are available in industry including the Coordinate Measurement Machine (CMM) with touch probe and the 3D Laser Scanner (LS). CMMs can create high accuracy data-points from the part surface, but when the number of the required data-points is large they are considered to be inefficient. On the other hand LS can rapidly create thousands of points from the part surface but in lower resolution compared to CMMs. In a typical component both high and low accuracy features can be seen. Therefore to have a fast and accurate scanning system, CMMs manufacturers have now equipped them with LS probe heads. However, the data integration of the two scanning systems is still in its early stages of development. For instance, several modelling processes are required for CAD model creation and this can be tedious, time consuming, and error prone.

In this paper the automation of the modelling algorithms, which were developed and manually verified in the earlier stages of this research, is introduced. Although the system is not fully automated, however, the user interaction with the system is minimised to a great extent. The system performs modelling processes based on the user's selection within the available options in each stage. Alternative options are created for features to enhance the flexibility where possible, i.e. the user can decide to perform some of the modelling stages with or without interaction with the system.

2. RELATED WORK

CMMs integrated with LS probe are now available in industry (Rooks, 2004). However, they are mostly used for individual probe usage or for basic applications such as part position finding (Chan et al, 2001) or for CMM probe guidance (Li and Liu 2003). In a different topology the LS is used as a separate device and the scanned data are used for CMM automated probe path planning (Shen et al, 2000).

It is proposed to integrate the scanned data between the two systems of LS and CMM with touch-probe. Bradley and Chan (2001) used the CMM touch probe to scan the feature boundary of complex surfaces for surface extraction from data cloud scanned by LS. Their method reduces the surface extraction time in the modelling process; however it is unable to create a complete geometry of inward sloping faces and also the precise touch probe data-points are treated in a similar way to the points in data cloud, not as high accuracy data-points.

If multiple probes or multiple sources of digitised data are used, the calibration of all the probing systems into a unique coordinate is necessary. Current practice is that different probes are calibrated prior to scanning to the same datum (Bradley and Chan, 2001). This method is rather inflexible due to the datum selection that is set to the centre of a single and fixed calibration ball attached to the CMM table. In another method, Shen and Menq (2001) have used the tip of the probe for 3D LS camera calibration with touch probe. Although this scheme results in accuracy of greater than 0.1mm, it is inflexible if the features on the part are far away from the initial calibration position.

Other research has attempted to create an automated measurement planning and digitisation system. Spyridi and Requicha (1994) have automated the CMM programming using the CAD model to generate the CMM setup, probe selection, path and direction. Despite the dependency on CAD model, which makes it unsuitable for RE applications, their method can be used for automation of post RE measurements on similar components.

In an ideal RE system, the complex geometric surfaces can be scanned with a non-contact LS in a very short time and leaving the accurate features for a CMM with touch probes. The scanning results then are required to be integrated together to create the CAD model. This requires faster and more accurate CAD modelling methods, as the existing modelling and optimisation processes are time consuming and/or not accurate enough for RE of components with precision features.

3. AUTOMATED CAD MODELLING SYSTEM

A general overview of the system is given in figure 1. In this method (Jamshidi et al, 2006) the sensitive features of the desired component are scanned using the conventional CMM with high precision (at *35μm*) touch probe in order to create CMM-model from the part geometry.

Sensitive features are the features that require more accurate dimensions and have tighter tolerances. However, for the RE problem, where the tolerance information is unavailable, these features can be identified visually through their surface texture and machining used (Jamshidi et al, 2006). If a feature on the component has for instance grinding surface finish, one can assume that such feature has precision dimensions and tolerance. Therefore such feature can be accounted for as sensitive.

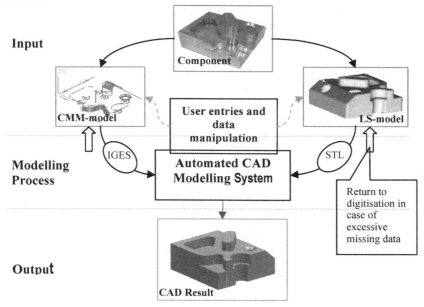

Figure 1 – Overview of the CAD modelling process in the system.

Any other features of the component are considered as non-sensitive, thus can be digitised rapidly by LS. If complete coverage scanning is required the part should be digitised from different scanning view angles. Individual scanned sections of the component from different view angles should be registered to a unique coordinate to create the LS-model. Such a model is then registered to the same coordinates system of the CMM-model for further modelling stages. Here the registration of the scanned models is an automated operation, which utilises 3-Coordinate Balls (3CB) (Jamshidi et al, 2005) and can be followed to the fine registration process (Jamshidi et al, 2006) if necessary.

Therefore the inputs of the automated system are the CMM-model, LS-model and the user inputs that are entered through selection options and user interaction (figure 1) during the CAD modelling processes. The level of user inputs and interaction varies depending on the geometric complexity of the component. This can be a minimum or no user manipulation, for components with simple and standard geometry.

4. DATA INPUT TO THE SYSTEM

The complete modelling processes take place in three software environments. For the work presented in this paper the Minolta Polygon Editing Tool, as the LS software, creates the triangulated mesh from the scanned data-cloud and exports the scanned section models into Stereolithography (STL) file format after the initial view registration and data-cloud reduction. The CMM-model is created using PC-DMIS which is standard CMM software. It is possible to create volumetric features using the measured data-points within PC-DMIS if necessary. Nevertheless, it is preferable to perform model manipulation in the CAD software environment as it has greater flexibility. The scanned CMM-model is then exported into IGES (Initial Graphics Exchange Standard) file format for importing to the CAD software.

The LS and the CMM stage models, as the main inputs of the automated CAD modelling system are imported into the desired layers of the CAD software. For this a consistent naming convention, as shown in Table 1, is used to automate the process. For instance the 3CB data-cloud in the LS-model of the first scanned view can be saved under "LS_3CB_V1.stl" name. This approach can assure that such data-cloud will be loaded to its assigned layer of the CAD environment, in the file import process.

Table 1 – Target layer assignment for imported and newly created entities.

Source	Data-cloud / Feature / Function			CAD
Object/Feature	View #	Import File Name	New Entity	Target Layer
Part	-	CMM-model.igs	-	20. CMM-model
Part	V1 to V20	LS-model_V1.stl to LS-model_V20.stl	-	30. LS-model to 49. LS-model
3CB	V1 to V20	LS_3CB_V1.stl to LS_3CB_V20.stl	-	50. 3CB to 69. 3CB
CMM-model	-	-	Large Scale	70. Selection
LS-model	V1 to V20	-	Selected Points	80. Redundant

The highlighted selected points in Table 1 are in fact sections of the existing data-cloud that are automatically selected as redundant points, therefore eliminated from the data-cloud. These points include the unreal data-points, which are the result of noise and reflection in the scanned LS-model (Jamshidi et al, 2006) and also the points on and around the sensitive features. The resulting empty space of missing information in the data-cloud will be filled by accurate features generated from the features in the CMM-model. The remaining data input in to the system are the user entries that can include surface finish and tolerance information, and any other user selections that are available via options in user menus.

5. INFORMATION FLOW AND OUTPUT

The information flow in the automated CAD modelling system is shown in figure 2. After the data input and registration, in Stage-3, the volumetric features are formed by using the high accuracy measured data gained by the CMM touch probe. In this stage the user selects the required measured features from the CMM-model in order to create the real feature. For example two circles and two planes are required for a straight cylindrical feature, or a set of three points can be used to create a particular plane.

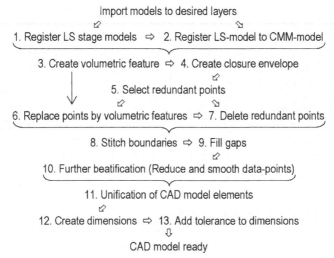

Import models to desired layers

1. Register LS stage models ⇨ 2. Register LS-model to CMM-model

3. Create volumetric feature ⇨ 4. Create closure envelope

5. Select redundant points

6. Replace points by volumetric features ⇨ 7. Delete redundant points

8. Stitch boundaries ⇨ 9. Fill gaps

10. Further beatification (Reduce and smooth data-points)

11. Unification of CAD model elements

12. Create dimensions ⇨ 13. Add tolerance to dimensions

CAD model ready

Figure 2 – 13 stages of automated modelling process in CAD environment.

The closure envelopes in stage-4 are the larger scale of the features from the previous stage. These closure envelopes are required for data-cloud selection by restraining the points in the neighbourhood of the sensitive features (Jamshidi et al, 2006). The selected points are considered as redundant and can be replaced by the high accuracy volumetric features, in stage-6.

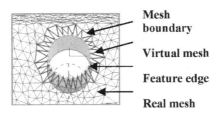

Mesh boundary

Virtual mesh

Feature edge

Real mesh

Figure 3 – Filling gaps between digitised models by virtual mesh creation.

In stage-8, the boundaries of the data-cloud are stitched, in a zigzag approach, to the boundaries of the appropriate features by a virtual triangulated mesh (figure 3). This process requires the user to rotate the model in the graphic view window so that the desired feature can be visible in a normal angle to the screen, and then the appropriate edge of the feature is selected by the user. Then the feature edge is divided by new points on the proposed edges in an automated mode. The stitching process starts by creating a line between the closest pair of points from the triangulated mesh boundary in LS-model and the feature edge. The next line begins from the end of the previous line to the closest point on the opposite model, i.e. if the line starts from LS-model the end of such line has to be located on the feature created or existed in the CMM-model. A virtual mesh surface is also added to each one of the newly created triangle sets. This can be a triangle with three straight lines or two straight lines and one curved line.

Stage-9 is an essential step for complete surface model creation, which is necessary for solid CAD model construction in stage-11. When the CAD model is completed the desired drawings can be created in which the dimensions on sensitive features are obtained from the existing measured data in the CMM-model. Initially the measured data are considered as nominal. However, this may not be optimal for components produced near to the acceptable boundary of their dimensions, i.e. close to upper or lower limit tolerance. Nevertheless, for the purpose of this paper the measured data are assumed as nominal. The final stage for CAD modelling includes adding tolerance to the dimensional features. This can be done automatically by the embedded tolerance approximation method (Jamshidi et al, 2006), or can be accurately determined, by tolerance accommodation analysis, and be added to the desired dimensions by the user.

6. EXPERIMENTAL RESULTS

For the validation of the automated modelling system, several components were reverse engineered, using the hardware and software described in Table 2. For the problem of model registration between the two scanned model types, an auxiliary 3CB, from which the coordinates' information is extracted, is used. The 3CB was fixed, by conventional clamping, in the scanning view of the LS in order to digitise its visible sections throughout the scanning process.

Table 2 – Systems used for the method experiments.

Hardware	Accuracy (mm)			Software
	X	Y	Z	
Minolta 900 Laser Scanner with Minolta tele-Lenz	±0.22	±0.16	±0.19	Minolta editing tool Version 1.1
Brown & Sharpe Global CMM with TP20 Renishaw Probe	±0.035	±0.035	±0.036	PC-DMIS Version 3.5 MR1 Beta
Auxiliary 3CB set	Ball Diameters = 28.63			Unigraphics NX3

Figure 4 illustrates a simple cubic component, which is fully digitised using the CAD modelling system. In this example it is assumed that only the diagonal holes are sensitive to the functionality of the part. The measured data in the CMM-model are used to create the hole features, which have the accuracy of micron level. Other sections of the part are left as triangulated mesh, as scanned by LS within an accuracy of *±0.22mm* (the accuracy level of LS). The registration process between the scanned models is done automatically.

Each hole is created as an internal cylinder from one circle and two planes representing the two ends of the cylinder. The closure envelopes, are created by increasing the hole diameters by *1.5mm* and adding *0.75mm* on either side of the cylinder. The orientation of the closure envelopes are intact with the same spatial location of the corresponding true hole features in the CAD model. The stitching process is then taken place after the deletion of the selected redundant points by closure envelopes. Finally the drawings are created including the dimension values.

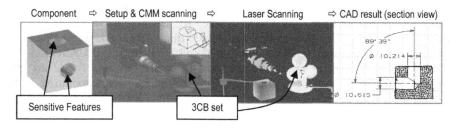

Figure 4 – RE of simple cubic part using automated CAD modelling system.

The second experiment is the RE of a sample component with more features, details of which are shown in figure 5. The overall geometry of the component is digitised by the LS from different view angles and registered to a unique coordinate system (figure 5, **A**). The complex geometry features of the component are exported to CAD software for data integration with model scanned by CMM (figure 5, **B**).

All the other features are assumed as sensitive and/or standard, therefore scanned by CMM. Volumetric features are created using the high accuracy features in CMM-model (figure 5, **C**). The final result with the CAD drawing is given in figure 5, **D**, which is a solid model combined of triangulated mesh and standard geometry feature. This model can be improved by beautification of the triangulated mesh then recreation of the solid model, and adding tolerance to the dimensional features.

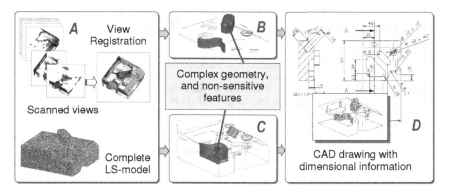

Figure 5 – RE of sample component using automated CAD modelling system.

7. CONCLUSION AND FURTHER WORK

In reverse engineering, data gained from different sources that have different resolution and accuracy level require to go through several modelling stages. In this paper, the automation of the previously developed modelling processes, which can be time consuming, tedious and expensive is introduced. By using this automated system, the user does not require extensive expertise for CAD modelling.

This system is most suitable for parts which have sensitive machined features and also complex but non-sensitive geometry on their casting surfaces. The results are reliable in accuracy due to the use of the actual measurement data in the sensitive features creation. No approximation is in place for sensitive and accurate features. Moreover, the resulting CAD model can include dimensional and approximated or actual tolerance information, which makes it more suitable for CAD CAM use.

Further development of the automated data-fusion method will focus on better accuracy and faster modelling processes, by employing more automation in the system. The system can also be integrated with automated system for machining process planning and measurement systems. Tolerance analysis can also be integrated into the system by parametric feature creation.

8. ACKNOWLEDGEMENT

The work has been carried out as part of the EPSRC E-IMRC at University of Bath under grant # GR/R67597/01. The authors wish to thank Phil Williams of Renishaw and Peter Smith from Konica Minolta Photo Imaging UK for their technical inputs.

9. REFERENCES

1. Bradley C and Chan V, "A Complementary Sensor Approach to Reverse Engineering", Dept. of Mech. Eng., Uni. of Victoria, Canada, Trans. of ASME, Vol. 123, pp74-82, 2001
2. Chan VH, Bradley C and Vickers GW, "A multi-sensor approach to automating co-ordinate measuring machine-based reverse engineering", Dept. of Mech. Eng., Uni. of Canada, Comp. in Ind., Vol. 44, pp105-115, 2001
3. Jamshidi J, Mileham AR, Owen GW, "A Laser Scanning Registration Technique for Reverse Engineering Applications", IMRC, Uni. of Bath, Int. Conf. on Manu. Research, Cranfield Uni., UK, 2005
4. Jamshidi J, Mileham AR, Owen GW, "A Proposed Data-cloud Reduction Method for Laser Scanned and CMM Data Integration", IMRC, Uni. of Bath, Int. Conf. on Manu. Research, John Moores Uni., Liverpool, UK, 2006, to appear
5. Jamshidi J, Mileham AR Owen GW, "Dimensional Tolerance approximation for Reverse Engineering applications", IMRC, Uni. of Bath, Int. Design Conf., Dubrovnik Croatia, May 15-18, 2006
6. Jamshidi J, Mileham AR, Owen GW, "High Accuracy Laser Scanned View Registration Method for Reverse Engineering using a CMM generated CAD Model", IMRC, Uni. of Bath, Int. Design Eng. Tech. Conf., DETC, 32nd Design Auto. Con., Philadelphia, Pennsylvania, September 10-13, 2006
7. Jamshidi J, Owen GW, Mileham AR, "A New Data Fusion Method for Scanned Models", IMRC, The University of Bath, JCISE Special Issue on 3D Computation Metrology, 2006, to appear
8. Li YF and Liu ZG, "Method for determining the probing points for efficient measurement and reconstruction of freeform surfaces", City Uni., Hong Kong, Measuring Sci. Tech. Vol. 14, pp1280-1288, 2003
9. Rooks B, "A Vision of the Feature at TEAM", Sensor Review, Emerald Group Pub. Ltd., Vol. 1, No. 2, pp137-143, 2004
10. Shen TS, Huang J and Menq CH, "Multiple-Sensor Integration for Rapid and High-Precision Coordinate Metrology", Ohio State Uni., Trans. on Mechatronics, Vol. 5, No. 2, pp110-121, 2000
11. Shen TS and Menq CH, "Automated Camera Calibration for a Multiple-Sensor Integrated Coordinate Measurement System", Ohio State Uni., IEEE Trans. on Robotics and Auto., Vol. 17, No. 4, pp 502-507, 2001
12. Spyridi AJ and Requicha AAG, "Automated Programming of Coordinate Measuring Machines", Comp. Sci. Dept. and Inst. for Robotics and Int. Sys., Uni. Of Southern California, IEEE, 1994

ADVANCED PROTOTYPING WITH PARAMETRIC PROTOTYPES

R. Anderl, K. Mecke and L. Klug

Darmstadt, University of Technology,
Department of Computer Integrated Design, Germany
{anderl, mecke, klug}@dik.tu-darmstadt.de

The "Parametric Prototype" has been developed as a tool for integrated parametric and physical shape representation to optimize styling and design. This tool will be applied in the early phases of the product development process at an appropriate level of detail, e.g. for the fast visualization of car parameters and proportions of the exterior car body. The development comprises a method that converses changes in the product model in a CAD system and the physical model bidirectional. Further the implementation of an interface between the physical shape presentation and the computer based representation has been realized.

1. INTRODUCTION

The competition on the automotive market has increased during the last decades. This can be explained by changes in the behavior of the class of consumers and the positioning of the automotive manufactures (Grabowski, 2002). Connected with this are saturated markets, especially in the automotive section (Kurek, 2004). The manufacturers have to adjust rapidly to changes in the demands of customers (Wagner, 2004). This results in a flood of new concepts and product variants on the manufacturer side (Ebel, 2004).

The applied process in the early phases of the product development process between styling and design is characterized by numerous virtual and physical models of the product. One possibility to create physical models from virtual models is Rapid Prototyping (Gebhardt, 2000). The reverse process, to create virtual models of real objects, can be performed by applying 3D scanning techniques. These transitions between physical and virtual reality, lead to so called media breaks. A possible consequence is the loss of data and data quality in the process.

This paper comes up with a solution how the physical process can be connected to the virtual process by an integrating application. Media breaks are avoided. Based on the methods of product data management, a form for the physical representation is developed at an appropriate level of detail. The parametric support of the process leads to a reduced number of iterations in the product development process. The term 'parametric' is extended in this case to the variance of physical objects, which size and shape is connected to parametric values, not only the virtual representation.

2. PRODUCT DEVELOPMENT AND STYLING

In the early phases of product development the styling of the product is dominant. This is especially true in the automotive industry where styling is essential for the success of a product. The styling of the automotive body shell is inevitable time consuming. Depending on the draft of the exterior styling, the tool design builds the forming tools, which is a time critical factor in the product creation process (Anderl, 2005).

The aim of the styling process is the development of several competing drafts, to scale presentation models. The presentation to the deciding committee leads to the final decisions over the final vehicle (Mischok, 1992).

The product development process with special consideration of the design demands for the following requirements, to reduce development time and costs while increasing the quality of the product:

- An efficient integration of computer based methods in the process.
- The creation of several design variants.
- The prevention of media breaks.

Contemporary traditional techniques dominate the state-of-the-art styling process. These techniques are characterized by artistic and technical skills (Spur, 1997). Despite a high number of iterations, there is no parametric tool, which can support a consistent presentation of the constantly changing models appropriately.

3. VIRTUAL AND PHYSICAL PRESENTATION

The term "model" is understood within the range of engineers according to VDI (German Association of Engineers) as an abstract representation of a product (e.g. by its data, characteristics or shape). The abstract representation of a product can be thereby both digital and physical. The expression "prototype" is also used for physical and digital representations of the product.

3.1 Physical models and prototypes

A physical model is an object or set of objects that is generated from a variety of materials to approximate an aspect of how a product concept will look like and perform. Synonymously, the term physical prototype is used. It is tested under a certain range of conditions to approximate the performance, constructed to control possible variety in the tests and it is used to communicate empirical data about the product so that development decisions can be made with high confidence and reduce risk (Otto, 2001).

Physical models and prototypes can be distinguished into six major classes, which are the proportion model, the ergonomics model, the design model, the functional model, the prototype and the product sample.

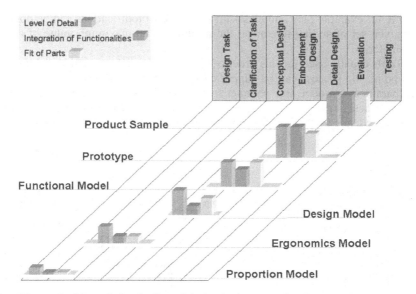

Figure 1 - Use of physical models in the product development process.

Figure 1 shows the allocation of physical models according to the product development phases, based on the VDI 2221 guideline (VDI, 1993) with the qualitative rating of the level of detail (left bar), the integration of functionalities (middle bar) and the fit of parts (Klug, 2004). Proportion models show the approximated outer shape of the product and its most important proportions. Numerous proportion models are generated during product creation, which leads to delays in the process.

3.2 Virtual Prototyping

Virtual prototyping refers to build a complete prototype assembly with geometric models of individual parts. Virtual prototyping systems allow the visualization of part assemblies and the feasibility check of proposed assemblies within production constraints. Through the assembly of an accurate virtual prototype, design flaws can be detected and design modifications performed (Lee, 1999). The virtual engineering process starts from geometric 3D-models, proceeds to the simulation of production systems and finally reaches the building of a digital mock-up, digital prototype or digital product (Klug, 2006).

All available physical and virtual models, methods and tools can not avoid a media break in the iterative product development process as a whole. From the requirement to make a physical model available for fast visualization of fundamental design characteristics, e.g. approximated proportions of vehicle, the parametric prototype has been developed at the Department of Computer Integrated Design (DiK).

The process of proportion definition can be defined on the basis of its input and output data. The input is the package data. The output is the freezed concept model. The package is defined as the process of transforming geometric and technical requirements, given by technical or ergonomic defaults and laws, and the styling theme, for example racy and classical. Aesthetical modifications can be done within the given set of styling tolerance; the minimum and maximum value of a package parameter.

Tools usually used for this process are full-scale sketches and sketch-models. At this point, the process can be supported by the parametric prototype, consisting of the parametric model and parametric mock-up. Figure 2 shows the generalized aesthetic design process referring to the FIORES report (FIORES I, 2001; FIORES II 2002) extended with the application of a parametric model and mock-up.

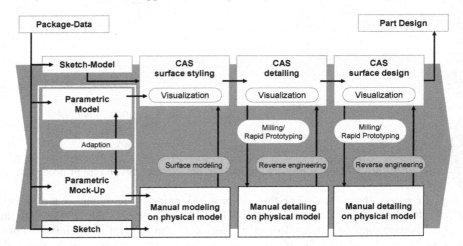

Figure 2 - General process chain with parametric model and mock-up in styling.

The parametric prototype can be defined as the set of a physical mock-up and a virtual model which are linked by an interface. Thus the parametric mock-up is a physical model which is used in the concept phases of the product development process for preliminary styling purposes. The outer shape of the parametric mock-up can be modified in a preset range by mechanical, electrical and control components in context to the parametric model.

4. THE PARAMETRIC PROTOTYPE

The concept consists of the virtual parametric prototype and the physical mock-up, which are connected via a hardware interface and software.

4.1 Conception of the virtual parametric prototype by segmentation

Based on the chosen parameters for variation of the car geometry, for example the total length, width, height or length font, rear, a concept for the segmentation of the car geometry is developed in this chapter by applying a number of half spaces. The complete object space is split into several primitive volumes, which are represented by simple sets. By applying these half spaces the orientation of planes can be considered (Spur, 1997).

The half spaces, with the definition of the inside, are representing the boundaries of the description of the volume element. For the generation of a fully described, topological-geometrical body, the surface description of the vehicle can be used. This can be done by using trimming and blending operations, applied on the planes and surfaces. Finally, the vehicle volume is described by several bodies, which are generated from spaces with multiple boundary planes.

In order to change the shape of the vehicle presentation by using the parametric prototype, several constrains have to be defined. These constrains are deduced by analyzing the directions of movement to change a specific measure. Based on this analysis, the partial volumes of the parametric prototype are combined to movement groups.

4.2 The parametric mock-up

Referring to the definition of a parametric Prototype, the mock-up serves as a physical presentation form. It can be changed in shape within a specific range by electrical, mechanical and control components. The parametric prototype is connected by a hardware interface, which passes the input signal on to the control components. Linear actuators and the framework enable the generation of a movement of the volumes by transforming signal and electric energy and represent the mechanical components. Sensors return the position of the volume elements to the control components. The output is the visual impression generated by the variation in form. A 'zero position' or undeformed neutral position is given by limiting switches of the linear guides.

4.3 Interface

To generate the control data, multiple steps have to be performed. The bases of these calculations are the different volume elements, defined by half spaces like described above. From the set union of half spaces and surface description, surface patches can be derived. These patches are used for the calculation of data of the displacement in one specific direction. To save the model specific segmentation, a special file format, base on the STL- file format, has been developed. Starting from these geometrical descriptions, the steps, input data, 'fitting', 'matching' and output of the control data are performed.

In the first step, the design data, that is supposed to be presented by the parametric prototype, has to be loaded into the system. The process 'fitting' is used to fit the geometric data into the space that the physical parametric mock-up can be adjusted to. For this procedure, translation, rotation and scaling transformations are applied. In the case that the design model contains a coordinate system according to the convention specified in DIN 70020, the fitting process is not needed.

The next step for the generation of the control data is the matching process. The surface patches from the segmentation process are fitted to the geometric data. The displacement gives the end position of the actuators. The process has to be performed for every patch representing a volume element of the physical parametric prototype. The control data is derived from the displacement information with additional information about the actuators, represented by the constraints. A graphical display of the overlapping surfaces is used as control output. The degrees of freedom of the actuators moving the surface of the physical parametric prototype are the parameters to be varied, while the geometry of the surface, represented by curvature and dimension are not to be changed. A mathematical criterion for the determination of the distance between the two surfaces has to be found. Several criteria are possible, e.g. the mean error minimization, squared error minimization, the Hausdorff distance or a Salient Feature Matching. The decision, which method suits the purpose best has to be made by the observer of the result.

The calculated data from the matching process represents the displacement of the volume elements. The control data is calculated form this data with additional information of the physical parametric prototype.

Depending on the situation it is necessary to move two actuators at the same time. Therefore two positioning procedures are needed. One realizes the movement of an individual block and one for the realization of a combined movement of two blocks.

Specific control libraries using USB are the interface between the control unit hardware and the personal computer. These libraries are loaded and called form the Software, which is performing and direction the calculations and the output of the data. The control unit provides the necessary electrical power to the actuators ant the status of the switches is monitored constantly and handed back to the controlling software.

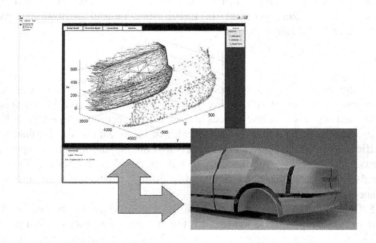

Figure 3 - Interaction of Graphical User Interface and physical parametric prototype.

4.4 The parametric prototype in action

Figure 3 shows the GUI and the physical parametric prototype. An export of native CAD or DMU data in a standardized geometric data format or starts the calculation software. Automatically, an additional user dialog is started. The user has to confirm the data. By doing so the described calculation steps are performed. In case the data set can not, or only poorly, be displayed the system outputs a warning message.

After that, the control data is calculated and send to the physical parametric prototype, which adjusts to the given geometrical representation, with the mechanical degrees of freedom as limiting factor. The control data can be distributed to several physical prototypes for collaboration to support video conferences.

5. CONCLUSIONS

Beside technical features, the styling of a product is very important for branding, and product differentiation, which are crucial criteria for the success of a product. This applies for the automotive industry in specific. The styling process in the early phases is characterized by generation of numerous models in virtual and physical reality. Transitions between physical and virtual reality world lead to media breaks. The claim for the application of virtual tools only is an approach to avoid these breaks, but an analysis of the state-of-the-art technology has shown that there are still immense deficits. The reason for that can be found in the insufficient development of styling tools. Designers are not supported to a desirable extent in their function, which leads to a rejection of these virtual tools and methods. Another reason is that the human perception of objects prefers physical objects, because of natural sensation. Therefore physical presentations are given a higher priority by the designer. Further, the support of parametrical tools is missing.

Based on the foundations of product data technology, an analysis has been performed on the existing tools and methods. Virtual and physical tools have been compared and differences, as well as possible interfaces have been shown. One possibility to generate a physical presentation form of virtual models is Rapid Prototyping. An inverse process, the generation of a virtual model from physical shapes, can be performed by 3D-scanning.

The developed concept introduces a new method and a new tool for a parametric support of the product development process. The method is based on a system of planes which define several half spaces. A number of constraint and parametric volume elements are defined this way.

The concept is put into practice by the construction of a physical parametric prototype and the implementation of a software interface. With these demonstration tools the analysis of proportions in the early phases of the product development process is possible. Integration in existing CAD- and CAS- systems, as well as information model in existing product data management systems is possible.

6. ACKNOWLEDGMENTS

Reiner Anderl studied mechanical engineering at the University of Karlsruhe where he reached his diploma in 1979. He worked as a research assistant from 1979 until 1984 at the Institut für Rechneranwendung in Planung und Konstruktion (RPK) of the University of Karlsruhe and received his doctor degree in 1984. From 1984 he took the position as technical manager of a medium sized company. Since 1985 he was working as chief engineer at RPK. In 1991 he achieved his habilitation and in 1992 the venia legendi which includes the authorization to teach CAD/CAM technology.

In April 1993 he received the professorship for computer integrated design at the Darmstadt University of Technology.

Prof. Anderl participates in the ESPRIT project 9049 PDTAG-AM (Product Data Technology Advisory Group - Accompanying Measure) and chairs a research group on product model development in the German QCIM project (Quality Management based on CIM). The ProSTEP association he has been elected as scientific advisor of the management board.

7. REFERENCES

1. Anderl, R.: Skriptum zur Vorlesung Produktdatentechnologie A: CAD-Systeme und CAx-Prozessketten. Technische Universität Darmstadt, 2005
2. Anderl, R.; Melk, K.; PFEIFER-SILBERBACH, U.; SCHÖFER, F.: Digital Mock-Up in der verteilten Produktentwicklung. In: CAD-CAM Report 6 (2004)
3. Ebel, B.; Hofer, M.; ALSIBAI, J.: Automotive Management. Berlin, Heidelberg, New York: Springer, 2004
4. Fiores I; Dankwort, W. (Hrsg.); PODEHL, G. (Hrsg.): Ein Protokoll zu FIORES - ein europäisches Projekt für neue Arbeitsweisen im Aesthetic Design. 2001
5. Fiores II; Dankwort, W. (Hrsg.): FIORES - CAD im Spannungsfeld zwischen Ästhetik und Design. Ein Hilfsmittel zur Bewahrung des Produktcharakters im Entwicklungsprozess In: Entwicklung im Karosseriebau. VDI-Verlag, 2002, S. 31–48
6. Gebhardt, A.: Rapid Prototyping. 2. Auflage. München, Wien: Hanser, 2000
7. Grabowski, H.: Rechnerunterstützte Produktentwicklung und -herstellung auf Basis eines integrierten Produkt- und Produktionsmodells. Ausgewählte Beiträge aus dem Sonderforschungsbereichs 346 der Deutschen Forschungsgemeinschaft (DFG). Shaker, 2002
8. Klug, L.; Anderl, R.: Virtual and Physical Mock-Ups - New Tools and Methods for the innovative Product Creation Process. In: 9th Seminário Internacional de Alta Technologia. Piracicaba, São Paulo (Brasil), Oktober 2004, S. 97–120
9. Klug, L.: Methodischer Einsatz von parametrischen Prototypen in der Produktentwicklung. Darmstadt: Dissertation Technische Universität Darmstadt, 2006
10. Kurek, R.: Erfolgsstrategien für Automobilzulieferer. Wirksames Management in einem dynamischen Umfeld. In: 6. Zulieferertag Automobil, RKW Baden-Württemberg, Stuttgart, 2004
11. Luddemann, J.: Virtuelle Tonmodellierung zur skizzierenden Formgestaltung im Industriedesign. Berlin: Dissertation Technische Universität Berlin, 1996
12. Lee, K.: Principles of CAD/CAM/CAE systems. 1. Aufl. Addison Wesley Longman, 1999
13. Mischok, P.; Albers, S; ROBB, D.: CAD im Flugzeugbau und Transportwesen. In: VDI-Berichte Nr. 993.2: Datenverarbeitung in der Konstruktion. Düsseldorf: VDI-Verlag, 1992
14. Otto, K.; Wood, K.: Product Design - Techniques in Reverse Engineering and New Product Development. Upper Saddle River (NJ): Prentice Hall, 2001
15. Spur, G.; Krause, F.-L.: Das virtuelle Produkt. Management in der CAD-Technik. München, Wien: Carl Hanser Verlag, 1997
16. VDI: VDI 2221: Methodik zum Entwickeln und Konstruieren technischer Systeme und Produkte -. Düsseldorf: VDI, Mai 1993
17. Wagner, R.: Automobilentwicklung in Deutschland - wie sicher ist die Zukunft? In: 6. Zulieferertag Automobil, RKW Baden-Württemberg, Stuttgart, 2004

ERGONOMIC EVALUATION OF VIRTUAL ASSEMBLY TASKS

M. Pappas, V. Karabatsou, D. Mavrikios, and G. Chryssolouris
Laboratory for Manufacturing Systems and Automation,
Department of Mechanical Engineering and Aeronautic,
University of Patras, Greece
{pappas, vasik, mavrik, xrisol}@lms.mech.upatras.gr

This paper investigates the use of Virtual Reality and Human Simulation technologies for the ergonomic evaluation of manual assembly tasks. Within this concept, a virtual environment has been developed for the realistic representation of assembly stations into which digital humans can be imported and be used in order to evaluate assembly executions, in terms of ergonomics aspects. The industrial need lies on the reduction of process time and on the ergonomic optimization of the assembly workstations. The use of this environment enables the identification of critical steps, during an assembly execution that causes stress to humans and results in increased assembly times and over wearied operators. A real life assembly task of a commercial refrigerator has been simulated and presented in order for its environment capabilities to be demonstrated.

1. INTRODUCTION

In modern manufacturing industries, the minimization of both product development cycle times and costs, is a strategic objective (Chryssolouris, 2005). In designing process workstations, such as the assembly ones, several physical prototypes and ramp-ups need to be built for the verification of human related factors. In complex manual tasks, the human involvement is very critical as it influences the feasibility, the cycle time, the working comfort and the safety of an operation. In manufacturing, in assembly and in related work, where human operators are involved, the flexibility that a human brings with it creates difficulties in modelling their behaviour. In this case, the interaction between humans and products, in all phases of the product life cycle, namely design, production, operation and maintenance must be studied. The easiness of assembling a product has to be taken into account at the early stages of its designing, where no physical models of the final product are available. Moreover, ergonomic problems in design demand empirical data on human capabilities and they have to be examined from the beginning as well (Chryssolouris *et al.*, 2003; Chryssolouris *et al.*, 2000).

Virtual Reality (VR) and Human Simulation offer a new tool that needs to be properly exploited in order for the Design for Manufacturing – Maintenance – Assembly – Disassembly techniques, to include the human behaviour, and the human dimensions, which up to now, have been difficult to incorporate (Lu *et al.*, 1999).

The use of such techniques provides a fast and flexible way of creating realistic virtual representations of complete assembly workspaces by integrating the human presence and the intervention into the form of digital mannequins as well as by supporting the optimization of the human-product-process relationship. These techniques have been explored, during the last few years, for the verification of the industrial processes. As a result, a number of VR and Digital Human based systems, oriented to assembly processes simulation, have been presented in the scientific literature (Gomes de Sa and Zachmann, 1999; Rajan *et al.*, 1999; Feyen *et al.*, 2000; Ottosson, 2002; Sundin and Medbo, 2003; Chryssolouris *et al.*, 2004).

In this paper, a virtual environment has been developed with the simulation of a real life assembly task of a refrigerator's assembly line. Videos for the assembly execution, by real operators, have been used in order for the critical body postures to be identified. Ergonomic evaluation of these postures is then performed with the use of digital mannequins. In this way, ergonomic parameters are calculated for each critical posture and any uncomfortable or stressed positions have been identified.

2. THE VIRTUAL ASSEMBLY ENVIRONMENT

2.1 Implementation environment

The virtual assembly environment has been developed with the use of the Division Mockup 2000i^2 platform for the development of Virtual Reality based applications (PTC website, 2006). Division SAFEWORK has also been used as the mannequin tool. Six default mannequins (5th, 50th and 95th percentile male and female) have been provided for the creation of any human being, by using the Human Builder option. The advanced anthropometry capabilities of the Human Builder option enable the direct control of 104 anthropometric variables as well as the somatotype of the SAFEWORK mannequin. The system currently "runs" on an SGI Onyx2 Infinite Reality2 RK Workstation. All the virtual parts of the environment have been designed with the use of the PTC's Pro/ENGINEER Wildfire 2.0.

2.2 Pilot application scenario

The pilot application scenario, selected to be an assembly station simulation of a commercial refrigerator assembly line, has been developed in order to demonstrate the VR environment capabilities. The increased stress and fatigue of workers, related to the tasks performed in this station, are the main factors for the investigation of their correctness from the ergonomic point of view. Therefore, the primary objective of this work is a human-centered evaluation of the assembly task and its further improvement, in case it is found ergonomically inadequate.

The general objective is to transfer the assembly task to a controlled environment, and to experiment with the current set-up in order to quantify its ergonomically related factors. This should minimize the pre-set "point factors", in our case being the time and the worker's fatigue. Figure 1a shows a snapshot of the real assembly performance. The virtual environment developed is shown in Figure 1b. The task to be analyzed is the assembly of the side glasses of the refrigerator.

 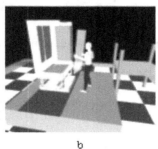

a   b

Figure 1 – The Real and Virtual Assembly Environment.

Based on the video of the real assembly performance available, this assembly task has been divided into five key-frames/postures during the simulation. These key-frames are:

- *Key-Frame 1*: The performer takes an appropriate body posture in order to grasp the side glass from the glasses bench and pulls it towards his body. He is leaning slightly to the front while his hands are grasping the glass from the front side. His legs are fairly straight and close to the bench (Figure2a).
- *Key-Frame 2:* The performer takes an appropriate body posture in order to pull off the glass. His spine is slightly bowed while the legs and feet are in a bended position allowing better support and balance. The left hand is in an elbow-upward position grasping the glass from the top while the right hand is straight and grasping the glass from the bottom (Figure2b).
- *Key-Frame 3*: The performer moves from the glass bench to the refrigerator. He is holding the glass while moving towards the refrigerator and rotating counter-clockwise. The various parts of the body take several positions of which the ones studied are the most stressing ones. His spine is fairly straight whilst his legs are slightly bended and so are his hands while holding the glass (Figure2c).
- *Key-Frame 4:* The performer takes an appropriate body posture in order to insert the lower corner of the glass into the refrigerator's side panel recesses. His spine and legs are straight and his arms bended so as to be allowed to grasp the glass in its middle from both sides (Figure2d).
- *Key-Frame 5:* The performer slides the glass through the recesses. He slightly bends forward while his left hand pushes the glass. His right hand is also pushing the glass from the inner side. His right leg is placed in front of the left thus, providing more leverage and balance (Figure2e).

Figure 2 – Key-frames of the side-glass real assembly process.

After all of the critical postures during this assembly task had been defined, the next step was to simulate these postures in the virtual environment with the use of digital humans and with ergonomic assessment

3. ERGONOMIC ANALYSIS

3.1 Digital Human description

The Division SAFEWORK was used for the performance of digital human simulation. This tool provides digital human models of different anthropometrics by using several databases. The one used for this simulation had all the characteristics of a real performer, as regards his body dimensions, and represented 50% of the global population in terms of a somatotype. The digital human was in the same five critical positions that the performer takes while assembling the refrigerator's side glasses. In figure 3, the digital human is performing the five key-frames of the assembly task. Posture and carry analyses were performed for the ergonomic evaluation of those postures required for the specific assembly task.

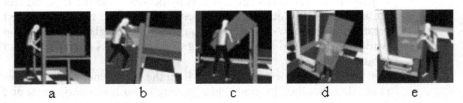

Figure 3 – Key-frames of the side-glass virtual assembly process.

3.2 Posture analysis

Posture analysis was performed for the five body postures of the digital performer, with the use of the GENICOM database for the angles limitations, provided by SAFEWORK.

Several body parts can be selected in the input box, for a specific posture, and a posture score is calculated by the system and is presented in a graphical mode. The color of the bar represents the comfort score of the current angle, whilst the percentage value indicates how close the current angle is to the optimum comfort value (10). The body parts and their respective degrees of freedom (DoF) that were selected to be studied in the frame of this work, have been presented in Figure 4.

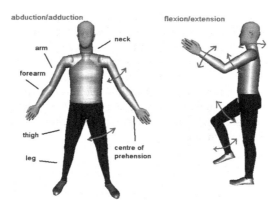

Figure 4 – Mannequin's body parts and their degrees of freedom.

For each posture and each body part studied, a posture score has been calculated based on the joint angles' values, in each of the five postures (key-frames). Posture analysis results of key-frame 4 are presented, as an example, in Table 1. Part of the graphical representation is shown in Figure 5, where the overall comforts score 42,3% is given.

Table 1 – Posture analysis results for the key-frame 4.

PART	SIDE	DOF	SCORE	PART	SIDE	DOF	SCORE
Neck	-	fle/ext	5/10	-	-	-	-
Thigh	right	fle/ext	0/10	Thigh	left	fle/ext	0/10
Thigh	right	abd/add	10/10	Thigh	left	abd/add	7/10
Leg	right	fle/ext	0/10	Leg	left	fle/ext	0/10
Arm	right	fle/ext	10/10	Arm	left	fle/ext	5/10
Arm	right	abd/add	0/10	Arm	left	abd/add	2/10
Forearm	right	fle/ext	10/10	Forearm	left	fle/ext	2/10
Wrist	right	uln/rad	0/10	Wrist	left	uln/rad	0/10

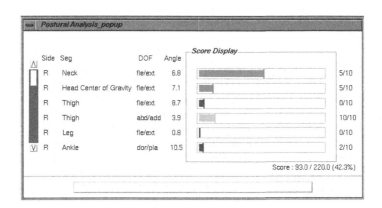

Figure 5 – Comfort scores window for key-frame 4.

A distribution of the percentage comfort score is presented in Figure 6, showing that postures 2 and 5 have low comfort scores, while posture 3 has the best score. A crucial factor that characterizes postures 2 and 5 is the fact that the performer tries to push or pull the glass by using a discomfort grasping strategy. The posture scores for the right arm and wrist are equal to zero in these postures. As for the overall comfort score, the fact that the performer not only does he have to carry the glass but also to rotate it from a sideward to an upward position, contributes negatively to the process ergonomics. This can be seen from the posture scores, being equal to zero, of the wrists as well as of the right arm and left forearm.

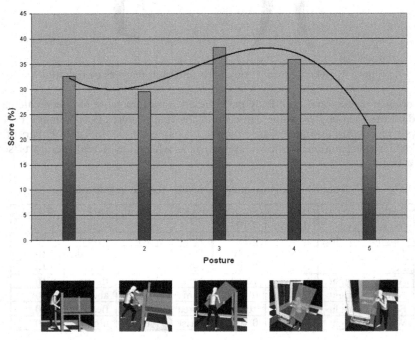

Figure 6 – Overall posture-based comfort diagram.

3.3 Carry analysis

Carry analysis was also performed by using the SAFEWORK's capabilities. Snook and Ciriello's 1991 general guidelines, included in the Liberty Mutual Manual Materials Handling Guidelines, were used for the analysis. The carry analysis dialogue box is shown in Figure 7. The input for this analysis includes: a) the frequency of the carry task, b) the distance of carry and c) the population sample, whilst the output is the maximum allowed load weight under these circumstances.

This analysis has been performed in order for one to study whether carrying a refrigerator's side-glass, weighing 16 kg, in the existing frequency, namely, one every 5 min, is ergonomically acceptable by a 50% sample of a male population in a carry distance of 2.1 m. After all calculations were made, the maximum weight allowed for this data was 33 kg, which was more than the real weight and thus, carry analysis has shown acceptable results for this carry task. Acceptable weights for all male percentiles are shown in Table 2.

Figure 7 – SAFEWORK carry analysis dialogue box.

Table 2 – Acceptable weighs for male population.

Male Percentile	Acceptable weight
10	48
25	41
50	33
75	26
90	19

4. DISCUSSION

This paper presents a straight-forward method for the ergonomic analysis of manual assembly tasks, with the use of Virtual Reality and Human Simulation techniques. This method is quite generalized and task-independent, and it could be used by engineers and process designers during the process design phase in order to evaluate assembly workstations from the ergonomic point of view. In order for the concept of the method to be analyzed, a pilot application has been thoroughly described, based on a real life assembly task of a commercial refrigerator. In the frame of this application, a virtual environment has been developed for the realistic representation of the assembly workstation in which digital human operators could be imported in order to evaluate assembly executions in terms of ergonomics aspects. The study of the results, having been derived from the posture and carry analysis, enables the identification of the critical points of the assembly procedure that provide stress to human operators and result in increased assembly times and over wearied operators. The critical identification points (for example key-frames 2 and 5 in the assembly task studied) also indicate where re-designing of the assembly procedure is required for both better ergonomics and efficiency.

5. REFERENCES

1. Chryssolouris G, Mavrikios D, Fragos D, Karabatsou V. A virtual reality-based experimentation environment for the verification of human-related factors in assembly processes. Robotics and Computer Integrated Manufacturing, 2000; 16(4): 267-76.
2. Chryssolouris G, Karabatsou V, Kapetanaki G. Virtual Reality and Human Simulation for Manufacturing. CIRP Journal of Manufacturing Systems, 2003; 32(6).
3. Chryssolouris, G, Mavrikios D, Fragos D, Karabatsou V, Alexopoulos K. "A hybrid approach to the verification and analysis of assembly and maintenance processes using Virtual Reality and Digital Mannequin technologies". In Virtual Reality and Augmented Reality Applications in Manufacturing. Nee AYC, Ong SK, London: Springer-Verlag, 2004.
4. Chryssolouris, George. Manufacturing Systems: Theory and Practice (2nd edition). New York: Springer-Verlag, 2005.
5. Feyen R, Liu Y, Chaffin D, Jimmerson G, Joseph B. Computer-aided ergonomics: a case study of incorporating ergonomics analyses into workplace design. Applied Ergonomics magazine, 2000; 31(3): 291-300.
6. Gomes de Sá A, Zachmann G. Virtual reality as a tool for verification of assembly and maintenance processes. Computers and Graphics, 1999; 23(3): 389-403.
7. Lu SC-Y, Shpitalni M, Gadh R. Virtual and Augmented Reality Technologies for Product Realization. Keynote Paper. Annals of the CIRP, 1999; 48(2): 471-494.
8. Ottosson S. Virtual reality in the product development process. Journal of Engineering Design, 2002; 13(2): 159-172.
9. PTC website: http://www.ptc.com/, accessed on-line: Oct. 2006.
10. Rajan V, Sivasubramanian K, Fernandez JE. Accessibility and ergonomic analysis of assembly product and jig designs. International Journal of Industrial Ergonomics, 1999; 23(5-6): 473-487.
11. Sundin A, Medbo L. Computer Visualization and Participatory Ergonomics as Methods in Workplace Design. Human Factors and Ergonomics in Manufacturing, 2003; 13(1): 1-17.

CAPTURING RESOURCE OPERATION KNOWLEDGE FROM RUNTIME DATA FOR PRODUCTION SUPPORT AND FEEDBACK TO DEVELOPMENT

Astrid von Euler-Chelpin and Torsten Kjellberg
Div. of Computer Systems for Design and Manufacturing
KTH – Dept. of Production Engineering, Stockholm, Sweden
{astrid.voneuler, torsten.kjellberg}@iip.kth.se

This paper describes the use of runtime data in two scenarios: to support the production, and to feed back resource operation knowledge to manufacturing system development. Challenges are discussed and some approaches are suggested. Raw data need to be synthesized into knowledge and analyzed within its specific context. A common ontology with shared concepts is needed for the whole manufacturing system life cycle. References need to be established between models from different contexts for increased accessibility.

1. INTRODUCTION

When the life cycle of products is becoming shorter, it is common that manufacturing resources must be reused for the next product variant in a changed process. When reconfiguring an existing system, it is important to start from an updated and accurate model of the manufacturing system. In addition, information about resource behaviour and capability in earlier manufacturing environments could be useful. This information can be extracted from runtime data gathered during production.

Many systems can gather runtime data and deliver trends and statistics in real time. This data could be used e.g. to aid continuous improvement (Mitsuyuki et al, 2003), or for simulating system behaviour (Ingemansson, 2004). Although there are many examples of using runtime data for operation and improvement, there seem to be little success in feeding back knowledge and experiences on a system level to development activities such as manufacturing system reconfiguration. In many manufacturing companies, there is no integration between development models and runtime data, as pictured in figure 1.

ISO/CD 18435 (Diagnostics, capability assessment, and maintenance applications integration) is an emerging standard that covers the use of operation data to improve execution and even manufacturing system design, with the focus on maintenance (ISO/WD 18435-3, 2004), (ISO/CD 18435-1, 2006). However, its scope is too narrow to support capability evaluation for reuse in a changed process. Also, it does not embrace the problem of how to use runtime data together with static models.

Life cycle information such as use, wear, and changes could extend the resource model, e.g. as in the Product Condition Model (Krause et al, 2004). The STEP standard ISO 10303-239 Product Life Cycle Support provides a standard for representing life-cycle information (ISO/TC184/SC4, 2005). However, the problem regarding feedback of runtime data to development remains.

Figure 1 – Information is reused within development and operation respectively, but little feedback goes from operation to development.

The purpose with this paper is to pave the way for the possibilities to feed back knowledge from the runtime environment also for manufacturing system reconfiguration activities. The more a resource is used, the more can be learned about its behaviour, e.g. unexpected maintenance needs, problems with a certain component, vibrations, dirt, wear, common causes of runtime stops, special actions to correct errors, etc. This knowledge could be utilized in many decisions regarding manufacturing system reconfiguration, such as:

- Evaluating what can be manufactured by the resources in the existing system according to new requirements
- Assigning the right resources to the right process operations
- Making more realistic production planning by forecasting realistic behaviour and performance, such as cycle times, cost, and accuracy
- Reusing the acquired knowledge for the development of the next system

In any of these examples, it is important that the manufacturing system models are up to date and reflect the reality. Thus, there is a need to not only update the manufacturing system models with changes but also to provide life cycle information such as use, wear and actual capability measured during production. Actual capability tells if each resource is likely to meet the demands and requirements set by e.g. a new product design.

In order to realize this, there must be a way to extract and synthesize knowledge from runtime data. Furthermore, there needs to be a way to relate the acquired knowledge from the runtime environment to the static models within manufacturing system development. These two approaches are elaborated within two scenarios:

- *Knowledge creation during operation*: Experiences regarding machine alarms are created to support operation and improvement work.
- *Knowledge feedback to reconfiguration activities*: Runtime experiences are presented for capability evaluation in decisions regarding reuse of resources.

2. REFERENCES BETWEEN MODELS AND ONTOLOGIES

2.1 The diversity of resource information

There are many resource models describing different aspects of the resource, e.g. what it is, what it does, or where it is used, each of which having different validity of the information. Some resource models can be considered static, such as the designed structure, designed capability and operation instructions. Models describing how a resource individual is used, e.g. a factory layout, are also static but only in a limited period of time. Whereas static models describe how things are supposed to be, the reality could be a little different. A model of a resource individual will need to be updated during its lifetime due to maintenance, repairs or other changes. Runtime data describes the resource in a matter of real measures, and this data is only valid within its specific runtime context. The validity differences are shown in figure 2. Clearly, the integration of information from different validity contexts is not easy.

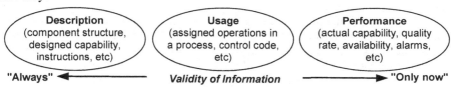

Figure 2 – Resource information in different contexts.

Runtime data can be gathered by monitoring systems and operators and refers to everything that can be measured and observed during production, including performance measures, events, and experiences (Euler-Chelpin et al, 2006). Events could be e.g. alarms, stops, maintenance, actions, and inspections. Experiences can be created systematically by synthesizing runtime data into interesting cases, such as alarm-cause-action groups, comparisons before and after improvement work, performance trends, etc.

The runtime data could only be interpreted correctly if sufficient context information is available. The context is described by the current configuration and the surrounding environment when the data was captured. A context model has been suggested (Euler-Chelpin et al, 2006) defining a process context, i.e. what feature and material is machined, and with which process and tool. Moreover, a set of measurable parameters such as temperature, humidity, states of components, etc, defines a snapshot of the environment at the time of measurement.

2.2 References to other models and a common ontology

In order to relate runtime data to development models, a shared ontology and referencing mechanisms between different models are suggested. Since there already are models describing the manufacturing system within the development environment, there should be an association between a resource occurrence in the runtime database and the occurrences of this individual in other models.

As a comparison, one could consider the referencing mechanism of Reference Data Libraries (RDL). RDL is used in e.g. the information standard ISO 10303-239

(Product Life Cycle Support) in order to separate contextual information from the core data, thus enabling better information integration between organizations exchanging information. Whereas the core model describes the main information types and their relationships, e.g. a product model, the reference data adds the context that enables the information to be interpreted in the desired way, providing true meaning of the information (Larsson and Kjellberg, 2006), (Rosén, 2006). Examples of reference data are business-internal definitions, identification mechanisms regarding e.g. products and parts, and refinement of taxonomies (Larsson and Kjellberg, 2006).

This principle could be extended so that not only contextual reference data could be accessible from the core model, but also other related models. Links such as "has occurrence in" and "is defined in" would keep resource models throughout the whole manufacturing system's life cycle coherent.

Figure 3 shows an example. An occurrence of a resource individual in a process plan has a reference to its definition in an ontology containing e.g. resource and process taxonomies. Similarly, runtime data could reference to definitions and taxonomies in an operation ontology that contains operation knowledge, e.g. alarm classifications. Furthermore, a resource individual in the runtime environment should be associated to the corresponding occurrences of the individual in the static environment, e.g. a process plan. Finally, a harmonization between the ontology's is required, thus forming a common ontology for the manufacturing system life cycle.

In the following sections, it is suggested how to create runtime experiences, followed by a discussion of how such experiences can be used in upstream activities.

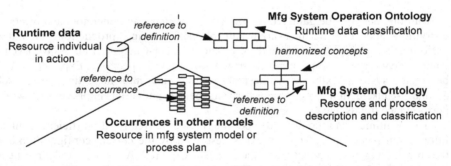

Figure 3 –References between different models and ontology's.

3. REPRESENTING RESOURCE OPERATION KNOWLEDGE - AN EXAMPLE USING MACHINE ALARMS

Since raw data is difficult to interpret, it needs to be synthesized into interpretable experiences. The following example uses machine alarms in order to create alarm experiences. It is assumed that machine alarms are logged automatically from the machine's control system. The alarms that need the operator's attention must be corrected with some actions, depending on the cause. Information about alarms, causes and actions could be formalized into facts and rules in order to become computer-interpretable (Euler-Chelpin et al, 2006). The concepts within the rules are defined in an operation ontology. The scenario is pictured in figure 4 and works as follows:

1. An alarm occurs that needs an operator's attention.
2. Known causes and suggested actions are automatically fetched by the use of rule-based reasoning. User interaction is needed if the machine needs to be observed to determine the cause. The provided actions are not necessarily comprehensive so additional actions might be needed.
3. In case of quality defects, the operator may have to search for the cause. In those situations, earlier experiences could guide the operator providing a base for case-based reasoning of the kind: What did we do last time and was it successful?
4. When the actions are executed, the operator writes all actions into the database, thus creating new cases and new experiences.
5. The experiences can be used to find preventive actions to reduce alarms.

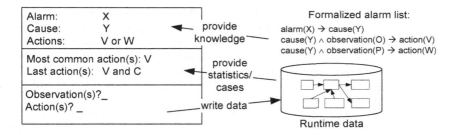

Figure 4 – Creation of alarm experiences using alarm knowledge and old cases.

In this way, the operator adds alarm experiences in the runtime database by the guidance of known rules, earlier experiences and statistics, and observations on the machine. Figure 5 shows a model of the resulting alarm experiences (Euler-Chelpin et al, 2006).

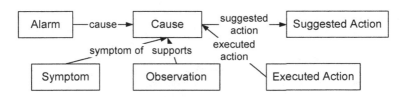

Figure 5 – Model of an alarm experience.

This approach has been tested in a Java program that uses JPL (Java Interface to Prolog) to communicate with a Prolog source. The Prolog source contains facts and rules about alarms, causes, and actions, and a goal-driven rule-based expert system algorithm (Luger, 2002). It reasons with the facts and rules and asks for observations on the resource in order to guide to the right cause and thereby to the right actions. The program also picks statistics from a runtime database for further guidance.

4. FEEDBACK OF RESOURCE OPERATION KNOWLEDGE FOR RESOURCE CAPABILITY EVALUATION

4.1 Difficulties interpreting runtime data

Alarms are one aspect of resource capability which could be useful during manufacturing system reconfiguration. When reusing resources, first the resource's theoretical capability has to match the new operations. Thereafter, one could evaluate the resource's actual capability from earlier operations (Holmström and Euler-Chelpin, 2004). The main resource capability can be defined by the supported processes and the resulting product transformations that are possible (Holmström and Kjellberg, 2004), (Kimura and Nielsen, 2005). The capability is further defined by properties in the technical specification such as maximum load, movement area, precision, etc. *Actual* capability, however, depends on the restrictions following the process, environment, and resource wear, and is measured during runtime.

However, since runtime data is valid only within a narrow context, it cannot easily be translated into general truths. One cannot assume that a machine behaves exactly the same when the process context is not the same. Perhaps one cannot even assume that two identical machines performing an identical process behave the same. Consequently, the evaluation of actual capability requires taking a lot of context information into consideration, as shown in figure 6.

The level of similarity could be everything from identical to completely different within each type of context aspect. Considering the large amount of context information needed, the comparison of runtime cases becomes complex. However, the use of standard processes, operations, tools, and features, defined in e.g. ontologies or data libraries, would keep the context definition in better control. In other words, if the manufacturing system is built up using pre-defined company standards, the context definition of runtime data will also be easier to define.

However, since the manufacturing system needs to be responsive to new demands and changed requirements, not only the context will change but also the way of interpreting the system's behaviour. Gathered data could be interpreted differently if performance targets or requirements on the system changes. Changing requirements and circumstances make interpretation of operation knowledge even more complex.

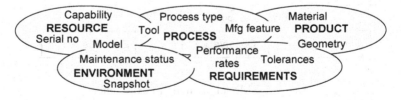

Figure 6 – A lot of information defines the runtime context.

4.2 A resource model enriched with life history and runtime data

Due to the complexity described above, an approach where a model of a resource individual is enriched with its life history and runtime data is suggested as a reasonable level for endeavouring better capture of operation knowledge. Computers can help gathering and creating data – the more synthesized into experiences the better – but in the end an experienced person is needed for interpreting this data in an appropriate way.

In other words, all relevant information needed for resource capability evaluation needs to be accessed and presented (see figure 7). This holistic resource view is enabled by the external referencing mechanisms described in Section 2.2, i.e. by the access of information from different resource models from all life cycle phases. The holistic view of resource capability includes information about:

- Theoretical capability: supported processes and catalogue properties
- Usage (and earlier use): process information
- Actual capability: measures and experiences within current or old contexts
- Life cycle data and condition: Maintenance, repairs, replacements, status

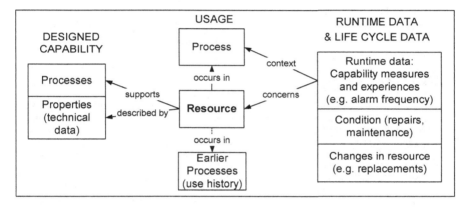

Figure 7 – A selection of aspects relevant for resource capability evaluation.

5. CONCLUSIONS AND FUTURE WORK

This paper presents an approach for better feedback of resource operation knowledge within manufacturing. With little work seen in using runtime data in the decision-making during manufacturing system development, there seems to be potential to improve knowledge management in this area.

Due to a complex context definition, the use of runtime data in a static context is complicated. The runtime data seems to become less interpretable the further upstream in the manufacturing system life cycle it is fed back. An initial step is to present runtime measures together with the necessary context information.

Data management during the operation environment is important since it is the foundation of the operation knowledge. Upstream activities would be able to interpret runtime data better if experiences are synthesized already at the operation level, such as the alarm example. By creating experiences, there is a possibility to reason with cases and patterns, although this is not an easy task considering the large amount of context information needed. However, the use of a limited set of standardized products, processes and resources defined in e.g. reference data libraries within a company would make the evaluation of context similarity simpler.

The feedback of operation knowledge requires that manufacturing concepts within both development and operation are defined in a common ontology. Harmonized concepts in all models during the whole manufacturing system life cycle would enable information integration and references between the models.

Many areas are left for future work. A guideline to determine the similarity of contexts is needed, as well as further synthesis of runtime data into experiences or cases within the operation environment. Also other scenarios could be included in the scope of the feedback. E.g. product design could use runtime data to analyse what design features are possible to manufacture in the current system.

6. ACKNOWLEDGMENTS

This is a continuation of work initiated during a research collaboration performed at the Dept. of Precision Machinery Engineering at University of Tokyo during 2005. The authors appreciate the financial support from STINT - the Swedish Foundation for International Cooperation in Research and Higher Education.

7. REFERENCES

1. von Euler-Chelpin, A., Kimura, F., Kjellberg, T., Nielsen, J., A Runtime Data Model for Capturing Operational Knowledge of Machining Resources, Proceedings of the 39th CIRP International Seminar on Manufacturing Systems, 2006, Ljubljana, Slovenia.
2. Holmström, P., von Euler-Chelpin, A., Manufacturing System Capability Representation with Runtime Information for Reliable Prediction of Produced Output, Proceedings of 13th Symposium of Product Data Technology Europe 2004, Stockholm, Sweden.
3. Holmström P., Kjellberg T., Modelling Manufacturing Resource Capability, Proceedings of the 37th CIRP International Seminar of Manufacturing Systems 2004, p. 79-82, Budapest, Hungary.
4. Ingemansson, A., On Reduction of Production Disturbances in Manufacturing Systems Based on Discrete-Event Simulation, Doctoral Thesis, 2004, Lund University, Sweden.
5. ISO/CD 18435-1, Industrial automation systems and integration – Diagnostics, capability assessment, and maintenance applications integration – Part 1: Overview and general requirements, dated 2006-01-31.
6. ISO/WD 18435-3, Industrial automation systems and integration – Diagnostics, capability assessment, and maintenance applications integration – Part 3: Enterprise and Manufacturing Operations Management Levels, dated 2004-03-18.
7. ISO/TC184/SC4, Industrial automation systems and integration - Product Data Representation and Exchange - Part 239: Application protocol: Product Life Cycle Support, ISO 10303-239, First Edition, 2005.
8. Kimura, F., Nielsen, J., A Design Method for Product Family under Manufacturing Resource Constraints, CIRP Annals 2005, STC Dn, p. 139.
9. Krause, F-L., Kind, C., Jungk, H., Holistic Product Condition Model, Proceedings of the 14th CIRP Design Seminar, 2004, Cairo, Egypt.
10. Larsson, M., Kjellberg, T., Towards a STEP based Reference Model for Manufacturing, Proceedings of the 39th CIRP International Seminar on Manufacturing Systems 2006, Ljubljana, Slovenia.
11. Luger, G.F., Artificial Intelligence – Structures and Strategies for Complex Problem Solving, Fourth Edition, Pearson Education Limited 2002, ISBN 0-201-64866-0.
12. Mitsuyuki, K., Reis, S., Kubota, F., Fukuda, Y., Arai, E., Manufacturing System Simulation Environment for KAIZEN Activities Based on Operation Data, Proceedings of the 36th CIRP International Seminar on Manufacturing Systems, 2003, Saarbrücken, Germany.
13. Rosén, J., Federated Through-Life Support, Enabling Online Integration of Systems within the PLM Domain, Proceedings of the 1st Nordic Conference on Product Lifecycle Management 2006, Gothenburg, Sweden.

ASSISTING MOULD QUOTATION THROUGH RETRIEVAL OF SIMILAR DATA

Manuel Fonseca, Elsa Henriques, Alfredo Ferreira and Joaquim Jorge
Instituto Superior Técnico, Lisbon, Portugal
mjf@inesc-id.pt; elsa.h@ist.utl.pt, jaj@inesc-id.pt

Moulds are complex devices and their quotation is one of the most risky tasks in mould industry. In this paper a digital work environment based on a computer assisted mould quotation tool is proposed in which all the relevant information is quickly available to assist a robust and rapid quotation. The tool involves a new way to directly access past quotations, designs and even manufacturing data based on the similarity of mould geometry and mould attributes. It applies new 2D/3D design concepts where sketches and text attributes are used to search for and access similar moulds. The main results from the analysis of mould quotation procedures and a preliminary tool prototype are presented.

1. INTRODUCTION

The quotation of complex moulds is one of the most difficult tasks in mould-making. Each mould is a unique device, where engineering solutions are implemented in accordance to the final part and moulding process requirements. It determines not only the efficiency of the mould manufacturing process but also the robustness and economy of the part moulding process (Wang, 2003). Though, if each mould is unique, the engineering solutions are frequently replicated in similar moulds. When facing a new project mould designers and mould quotation craftsmen start a reasoning process trying to remember a past similar mould. The idea is not to "re-invent the wheel" and not to star working on a "white piece of paper" but to work over validated past engineering solutions and cost data. In this reasoning process several problems arise. The first is that it is not clear what a similar mould is. The second can be expressed by the feeling "*I know I did something similar but I just can not remember neither what is it nor when was it*". The third is related to the fact that even if companies archive past data, those archives are frequently useless, due to the too long retrieval time and high probability of no succeeded search. This framework leads to:

- A long mould design process and long and ineffective quotation process due to the inefficient use of past information.
- Proliferation of design solutions some of them unproved and of poor quality.
- High dependence on knowledge "archived in human vaults" and high risk of knowledge lost with their leaving.
- Necessity of qualified craftsmen for quotation. Mould-makers are SMEs and staff qualification is highly dependent on a slow learning process and practice on job, so qualified personnel is a scarce resource (Henriques, 2004).

In fact a new way to design and directly access past quotations, designs, and even manufacturing data based on mould geometric and mould attributes similarity is required. This research work aims to develop a prototype tool based on digital technologies to support the mould quotation process. The tool applies new 2D and 3D design concepts where sketches and text attributes are used to search for similar moulds and access relevant mould quotations. The idea is to develop a digital working environment in which all the relevant information is quickly available to assist the budgeter in robust but quick quotations. This paper presents the main results from the analysis of the quotation procedures and a preliminary prototype, aimed to explore and validate concepts and approaches.

2. TASK ANALYSIS AND USER REQUIREMENTS

To get an overview and collect information from the mould development process several companies were visited and qualified persons involved in the mould quotation and design processes were interviewed. Currently, a typical mould company performs several hundreds of mould quotations annually, but only 5% to 10% of them evolve to production. The quotations are made mainly by senior budgeters, as they require a large experience and know-how involving not only cost estimation, but also facets in mould design, production engineering and management, and even marketing intelligence. The problem mould industry is facing now is that senior budgeters (knowledge vaults) are frequently getting retired and junior staff or commercial staff does not have enough know-how to perform reliable cost estimations. In addition, the pressure over costs promoted by the global competition and by the purchasing departments of large and global clients, focused on short term financial results, are demanding quick quotations and do not allow profit margins where unreasonable quotations could be accommodated without significant damages in the economical sustainability. In the industry survey different quotation methodologies were identified, based on two basic approaches:

1. Top-down approach – the quotation is built up based on the reasoning and accumulated experience (historic similar moulds "saved" as tacit knowledge). The focus is a synthesis competence only possible if a huge experience and tacit knowledge are present.
2. Bottom-up approach – the quotation is built up from a rough engineering solution upon which the aggregated cost and its parcels (materials, design, machining, trial-out) are identified. The focus is the analytical competences and requires the establishment of precise and formal procedures.

In both approaches some remarks were pointed out by budgeters: (1) they must deal with a constant trade-off between the speediness and the accuracy of the quotation; (2) formally (approach 2) or informally (approach 1), the mould design solutions are the basic reasoning to achieve the quotation; (3) formally or informally, the similarity to old moulds is a basic issue to support the quotation decision making process.

Depending on the project dimension, on its economical and technological risk and even on the negotiation process, the two approaches are often sequential in time. It was noted that the requirement of speediness privilege the top-down approach. Nevertheless, its success (accuracy in a range of +- 10% of the real cost of the mould) strongly depends on a qualified budgeter integrating commercial, engineering, production and costing competences.

2.1 Research Approaches and Quotation Commercial Systems

Some research has been developed in mould cost estimation. Most of the effort has been driven towards the part classification features and the effect of these features on the cost of the mould (Chen, 1999; Rosen, 1992). Wang et al (2003) proposed a case-based reasoning to look for similar old moulds in a case library and carry on the case adaptations to achieve accurate estimations. Fagade et al (2000) developed a method to evaluate the part complexity at the early stages of design. He used a complexity metric defined by the number of dimensions that uniquely define the part geometry and applied multiple regression analyses with the mean mould quotes and mean lead-times as dependent variables and a systematic combination of mould attributes (part envelope volume, complexity dimension, number of actuators, tolerances, surface finishing) as independent variables. From a set of 30 moulds Fagade concluded that these variables explain 91% of the mould cost and proposed multiple linear equations to estimate the mould final cost.

There are some commercial systems that support mould quotation process, such as ASAMould, Magics Tooling Expert, CalCard Pro Inject, CalcMaster. However, these systems are far from an extensive dissemination in the industry. One of the reasons given by mould-makers to explain the feeble dissemination of such systems is related to their complexity and difficult use, making any quotation a slow and complicated process. But, simultaneously companies refer the need for quotation tools easily adaptable to their business and their type of moulds. In fact two approaches have been developed in the quotation systems commercially available. One is what one can call automated mould engineering analysis. Starting from the part features effective engineering solutions are retrieved and used to elaborate the estimation. Nevertheless budgeters consider that is not possible to accept as adequate the solutions proposed because a lot of variables in the shop-floor and in the moulding process are not considered. The other approach is based on the fulfilment of an intricate list of parameters and so, to reach any simple estimation, an extensive effort is required. In general, this information is not sufficiently systematised and ready to be used. Moreover, frequently it is only possible to fulfil these parameters if a preliminary mould design is available. But when the percentage of quotations latter converted to orders is less than 10% the effort to do a preliminary mould design for any quotation is prohibitive. Companies refer that to work with current quotation systems high experience and qualified budgeters staff is needed. Though, if such staff is available they can undertake more rapid and accurate quotations using simple calculation templates prepared by them. On the other hand, these systems are expensive and need a continuous maintenance performed by technicians with digital technologies competences. In SMEs these professionals are a scarce resource as it is very difficult to support them financially.

2.2 Proposed Approach

A new tool to assist mould makers in the elaboration of rapid and precise quotations, providing an environment where similar historical data is quickly accessed to speed up initial stages of product and mould concept discussions, and to facilitate and increase the robustness of the engineering decisions during the preliminary development is the main driver of this research work. Two methods to access (search/retrieval) information associated to past moulds are provided. The first method is based on mould attributes, such as, client name, dimensions, type of mould, part name, etc. (figure 1). The second is based on geometric information of part drawings. Moulds always have associated part drawings in 2D or 3D, which can be used to index mould quotations in a database for later search and retrieval.

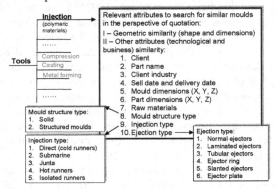

Figure 1 - Overview of the searching attributes.

This tool has the advantage of not modifying the current work methodologies. The idea is to develop a work environment for quotation, providing an effective access to morpho-dimensional and morpho-functional similar moulds produced in the company, to assist the budgeter in his decision making. Avoiding a strict framework, which has been the basic principle followed by other quotation tools develop for the sector, this approach can be viewed as a real human-centred quotation environment (figure 2).

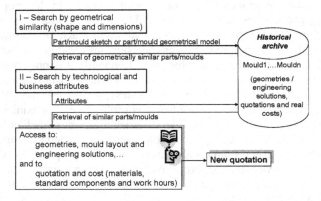

Figure 2 - Basic principles of the quotation assistance environment.

3. TECHNOLOGICAL DESCRIPTION

While searching using attributes associated to moulds is not very hard, since it is only textual, searching using the geometric information is not trivial. To support this, the quotation tool provides mechanisms for users to specify queries using free-hand sketches, which are then compared with the 2D or/and 3D drawings stored in the database. Moreover, techniques to simplify, index, search and retrieve complex 2D and 3D drawings were developed. It is important to notice that simple sketches drawn by users are compared with several complex CAD drawings. So, it is essential to use an efficient description mechanism to support this comparison. In summary, one can state that the main technological subject behind the quotation tool development is the retrieval of graphical information using sketches. In the remainder of this section the general architecture of the quotation tool is presented, followed by some research approaches related to 2D/3D drawing retrieval subject.

3.1 Prototype Architecture

The architecture of the quotation tool is divided in 2 parts. One where all information related to the existing moulds is processed (classification) and the other where a query is submitted and a result is received (retrieval). The classification consists in collecting the information and storing it in a database for further access. There exist two kinds of data to process: textual, that specifies information related to a mould, and graphical, which comprehends parts and moulds drawings. The textual data is manually classified while drawings are automatically processed. Figure 3 presents the steps needed to process drawings and generate descriptions suitable for further comparison to sketches. Firstly a set of simplification algorithms is applied to eliminate useless elements, such as, small area polygons, small lines or very near lines. This simplification reduces the number of graphical elements, making the comparison between sketches and drawings easier, and reducing the complexity of the structure that describes the geometry and topology of drawings. After simplifications, drawings are analysed extracting from them topological (spatial arrangement) and geometric information of their graphical elements. Features extracted and the textual information associated to the mould are then stored in a database for further searching and retrieval.

The searching and retrieval (retrieval part) is done using either the textual information or a sketch. When using textual information, the system compares the properties specified by the user to those stored in the database and returns moulds with similar properties. The retrieval process is very different when the search is performed with sketches (Figure 3). In this case the sketches are processed to extract features that can be compared to those previously extracted from drawings. Afterwards, algorithms to compare user's sketches to drawings in the database are applied. The system returns a set of moulds with similar drawings. From this set of moulds, it is then possible to consult all the associated information: drawings (2D/3D), quotation, real costs, client, etc.

3.2 Research Work on Geometry Retrieval

Content-based retrieval is currently a trend in multimedia information processing. Rather than manually generate text-based descriptions, content-based retrieval matches the query against an automatically generated representation of the content of the element to retrieve. There are multiple types of visual entities that can be retrieved based on their content. Here we analyze some content-based retrieval systems for 2D and 3D.

Gross's Electronic Cocktail Napkin (Gross, 1996) addressed a visual retrieval scheme based on diagrams to index databases of architectural drawings. Users draw sketches, which are compared to stored annotations (diagrams), manually produced by users. This manual annotation makes it difficult to scale to large drawing sets. The S3 system (Berchtold, 1997) supports the retrieving of CAD models of parts, described by their geometry (2D contour) and thematic attributes. S3 relies exclusively on matching contours, ignoring spatial relations and shape information, making this method unsuitable for retrieving complex multi-shape drawings. Park et al (1999) described an approach to retrieve complex 2D drawings based on the dominant shape. Objects are described by recursively decomposing its shape into a dominant shape, auxiliary components and spatial relationships, which are used to create a complex structure of graphs. The small set of base geometric primitives and the not-so-efficient matching algorithm, based on the breadth-first tree matching, make it hard to handle large databases of drawings. Elad et al (2001) presented a technique to search for similar 3D objects in a database, using VRML. Authors addressed the subjective matter of similarity, providing an approach based not only on geometric similarity but also letting the user influence subsequent searches by marking some of the results as "good" or "bad". The algorithm uses statistical moments computed from 3D objects' surfaces as features to define object signatures. Chen et al (2003) proposed a system for retrieving 3D models based on the visual similarity, using 2D projections. Authors encode multiple orthogonal projections of a 3D object using both Zernike moments and Fourier descriptors. Although a scheme to speed up the retrieval process is used, the comparison between the query and each model in the database is not avoided. Bespalov et al (2003) presented a preliminary framework for shape matching through scale-space decomposition of 3D models. The algorithm is based on hierarchical decomposition of metric data using spectral properties. 3D objects are mapped into binary rooted trees, recasting the problem of finding a match between 3D models as a simpler technique of comparing rooted trees. Funkhouser et al (2003) described a method for retrieving 3D shapes using textual keywords and sketches (2D/3D) or a combination of both. Their 3D shape descriptor is based on descriptive spherical harmonics invariant to rotations. Recently Lou et al (2004) developed an approach to search for 3D shapes, incorporating multiple feature vectors, relevance feedback, query by example, browsing and multidimensional indexing structure. As the system extracts four feature vectors it requires a large space to store the descriptors. To improve effectiveness, authors also proposed a multi-step similarity search, combining moment invariants and geometric parameters.

The majority of existing drawing retrieval systems use small databases (less than 100 elements), simple elements not representing real mould drawings and complex matching schemes (graph matching), making difficult the adoption of efficient retrieval algorithms.

4. PROTOTYPE DESCRIPTION

After identifying mould-makers needs, defining requirements (with them), and agreeing in the proposed solution, a prototype that allows searching for information about moulds using 2D sketches, drawings and textual queries was developed. The system for searching and retrieving moulds using 2D sketches is made of two prototypes, one to perform classification and another for retrieval. The prototype for classification processes automatically all drawings provided by the user, without any human intervention. The user only needs to give the location of drawings and the prototype does simplification, feature extraction and storage of logical information into the database.

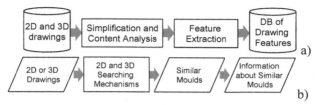

Figure 3 - a) Collecting information b) Searching/retrieving.

The prototype for retrieval, allows users to search and retrieve moulds, stored in the database by the classification prototype, using 2D sketches or an existent 2D drawing. It has a calligraphic interface divided in four main areas, one where users sketch an approximate drawing of what they want to find, another area with action buttons (right), an area for textual queries (left) and finally (on the bottom) the results area where similar drawings are presented to users (Figure 4).

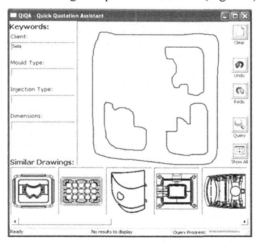

Figure 4 - Searching and retrieval of mould information.

Results are sorted by similarity, with the most similar on the left. To access all the information about a mould users only have to click on the desired result and the associated information is displayed. To search using an existent 2D drawing (from a CAD application), the user opens the file and then submit it as a query to the system. The rest of the process is similar to the use of sketches as queries. The prototype allows searching for a mould using only textual information, only geometric information (by sketches or CAD files) or a combination of both. Users can specify one or more textual attributes and then sketch a rough approximation of the desired mould. The system then combines the results from both types of information and presents the most similar results. Presently the system is completely operational in

2D. The development of the mechanisms to allow the classification, search and retrieval of 3D drawings has already started, being at present in a preliminary phase.

5. SUMMARY

This paper presents a research planned to develop a new tool to help mould makers in the quotation process. The solution provides an environment where mould budgeters can quickly access past similar moulds and consult them to support the decisions inherent to the cost estimation process. To that end, two retrieval mechanisms were combined based on drawing content and textual information. In this environment, mould-makers starting from the part (or mould) sketch (or CAD model) and from front end attributes can consult the historical data of the company and reuse engineering solutions achieved in the past, reducing the time needed to create a new quotation of a mould. In summary, the quick quotation tool, using cost and engineering solutions from similar projects, reduces the time needed to perform quick cost estimation, maintaining the accuracy and reducing the number of senior workers involved.

6. ACKNOWLEDGMENTS

We extend our thanks to all who contributed to this research, mainly to the industrial mould-makers and to the EC for the financial support of the EuroTooling 21 project.

7. REFERENCES

1. Berchtold S, Kriegel HP, 1997. S3: Similarity in CAD Database Systems. In Proc. of the Int. Conf. on Management of Data (SIGMOD'97), 564–567, Tucson, USA.
2. Bespalov D, Shokoufandeh A, Regi W, Sun W, 2003. Scale-space representation of 3d models and topological matching. In ACM Symp. on Solid Modeling and Applications, 208–215.
3. Chen D-Y, Tian X-P, Shen Y-T, Ouhyoung M, 2003. On Visual Similarity Based 3D Model Retrieval. Computer Graphics Forum, 22(3):223–232
4. Chen YM, Liu JJ, 1999. Cost-effective Design for Injection Moulding, Robotics and Computer-Integrated Manufacturing, 15, 1-21.
5. Elad M, Tal A, Ar S, 2001. Content Based Retrieval of VRML Objects - An Iterative and Interactive Approach. In Proc. of the 6th Eurographics workshop on Multimedia, 97–108.
6. Fagade A, Kazmer DO, 2000. Early Cost Estimation for Injection Molded Parts, J. of Injection Molding Technology, 4(3), 97-106.
7. Funkhouser T, Min P, Kazhdan M, Chen J, Halderman A, Dobkin D, Jacobs D, 2003. A search engine for 3D models. ACM Transactions on Graphics, 22(1)
8. Gross M, Do E, 1996. Demonstrating the Electronic Cocktail Napkin: a paper-like interface for early design. In Proc. of the Conf. on Human Factors in Computing Systems (CHI'96), 5–6.
9. Henriques E, Peças P, 2004. Rapid Moulds Manufacturing as a Competitive Opportunity, Int. Conf Rapid Product Development (RPD2004), Marinha Grande, Portugal.
10. Lou K, Prabhaka S, Ramani K, 2004. Content-based Three-Dimensional Engineering Shape Search. In Proc. of the 20th Int. Conf. on Data Engineering (ICDE'04), 754–765.
11. Park J, Um B, 1999, A New Approach to Similarity Retrieval of 2D Graphic Objects Based on Dominant Shapes. Pattern Recognition Letters, 20:591–616.
12. Rosen DW, Dixon JR, Poli C, 1992. Features and Algorithms for Tooling Cost Evaluation in Injection Moulding and Die Casting, Computers in Industry, 1.
13. Wang H, Zhou XH, Ruan XY, 2003. Research on Injection Mould Intelligent Cost Estimation System and Key Technologies, Int J Adv Manufacturing Technologies, 3:215–222.

DIGITAL ENTERPRISE TECHNOLOGY STUDIES OF THE SAARINEN ARCH

Lawrence Wolf, Joseph Huddleston, John Schleicher and Satish Palshikar
Oregon Institute of Technology, Freightliner Corporation,
Precision Castparts Corporation, Cascade Microtech Corporation, USA
Lawrence.Wolf@OIT.edu, JoeHuddleston@Freightliner.com
jschleicher@pcc-structurals.com, SatishP@cmicro.com

For their studio projects while learning DET, undergraduate and graduate students modelled the St. Louis Arch using the exact mathematical relationships of Eero Saarinen. They used that digital model to do finite element stress analyses for stresses, deflections, and vibrations. They investigated the challenging construction methodology used in building the Arch. They confirmed Saarinen's uniform stress assumptions using computing power that he never dreamed of. They checked out what was needed in the way of hydraulic force and piston travel to expand the two legs for "keystone" placement. They conceived and analyzed different tool-path strategies for the possible three- and five-axis cutting of exact physical models of that arch geometry. Most recently, using DELMIA to electronically model not only the tool path but also the machine tool operation and plant layout itself, precise 1/1000-sized models of the Arch are being cut and cast in aluminium and other materials. This paper is a follow-up of the paper submitted at the 2004 DET in Seattle entitled "CATIA Studies of the St. Louis Arch by OIT Students." As a final step, the studies are focused on a physical model to be produced with the assistance of Freightliner LLC - a DaimlerChrysler Company, and the Precision Castparts Corporation. The long-term institutional objective for the overall project was not just to have courses in DET but also to position DET centrally within the undergraduate and graduate manufacturing and mechanical curricula, and finally to use it to its full power and functionality.

1. INTRODUCTION

Two hundred years ago, Thomas Jefferson (then President of the United States of America) commissioned Lewis and Clark to conduct a 4000-mile exploration of the Western United States commencing in St Louis, Missouri, and extending to the Pacific Ocean near what is now Portland, Oregon. The famous St. Louis Gateway Arch (The Jefferson National Expansion Memorial), designed by Finnish architect Eero Saarinen, commemorates that exceedingly successful historical event.

During the past two-year Bicentennial Celebration of the Lewis and Clark Expedition, Oregon Institute of Technology students have been doing several related studio projects in the courses in which Digital Enterprise Technology is used as the primary laboratory resource tool. These studies began in courses using CATIA called "Solid Modeling," "Finite Element Analysis," and "Numerical Control Programming," which are upper-divisional courses in the BS degree Mechanical Engineering Technology and Manufacturing Engineering Technology programs. This past year they have been extended into post-graduate courses using DELMIA called "Automated Technology for Tool Path Generation," and "Plant Layout for Lean

and Agile Manufacturing," which are part of a new MS degree program in Manufacturing Engineering Technology.

The Jefferson National Expansion Memorial is also known as the Gateway Arch, and as the Saarinen Arch. It was designed by Eero Saarinen who won a design competition in 1948. Construction began in 1961. The arch was completed in 1965.

Saarinen's concept was to have a monument of elegance, grace, and beauty meeting the competition requirement of symbolizing a large gateway to the western United States. He devised a simple and structurally efficient form that was to receive the American Institute of Architects 25-Year Award in 1990.

It is the tallest monument in the USA and has no straight edges (see figure 1). It uses every ounce of material, with the exception of the internal elevators, for only one purpose. That purpose is nothing less than to defy gravity. Arguably it is the largest, if not the finest, example of "form follows function."

Figure 1 - Comparison of the Solid Model from the CATIA Screen to an Actual Photo. The CATIA image is an infinite perspective. The photo has some distortion due to the fact that it was taken with a 100-mm lens.

The Arch is a purely mathematical shape. The centroidal curve is a catenary:

$$y = 68.767\left(\cosh\frac{x}{99.668} - 1\right) \text{ft., or } 20.960\left(\cosh\frac{x}{30.378} - 1\right) \text{m.}$$

Where x and y are the horizontal and vertical positions, respectively, of points on the surface of the arch, and z is the distance outward from the plane of the centroidal curve, the inner surfaces of the arch have the curvatures $\dfrac{\partial^2 z}{\partial x^2}$, and $\dfrac{\partial^2 z}{\partial y^2}$, as well as the twist $\dfrac{\partial^2 z}{\partial x \partial y}$. A perfect subject for the study of CATIA!

The ARCH is 625 feet high by 600 feet wide at its base (190 x 183 m). The cross-section is an equilateral triangle. The side of the cross-section increases linearly with y. It is 17 feet (5.185 m) at the top of the arch and 54 feet (16.47 m) at the base.

Leave 3 lines space between the paper title and author name. Leave 5 line spaces between author affiliation and start of the abstract. Your paper should begin with a brief Introduction.

2. INTRODUCING THE STUDENTS

The students were working on the BS degree in Manufacturing or Mechanical Engineering Technology at Oregon Institute of Technology – Portland. They were third- and fourth-year students. They were employed as machinists, technicians, engineers, and managers. They were half-time students enrolled in evening courses in Solid Modeling, Finite Element Analysis, and Numerical Control Programming.

A studio approach was used emphasizing creativity. Each student had a door key and a password. Teamwork was encouraged. Mathematical theory was included along with demonstrations in CATIA. Students learned most actual CATIA from the program documentation, the textbook, and each other. While in the courses, they also did other "studios" in addition to the Arch.

3. FINITE ELEMENT ANALYSIS

A homogeneous solid structure was modelled rather than a stainless shell over concrete and a carbon steel undershell. This was a "first order" analysis. An effective density was used, which is the actual weight of steel plus the weight of concrete divided by the computed volume (44.9 pounds per cubic foot or 719.3 kg per cubic meter).

An effective modulus of elasticity was computed at the 300-foot-level (91.5 m) cross-section and was then used for the entire structure. The relationship for the effective modulus of elasticity is:

$$E_{effective} = \frac{A_c E_c + A_s E_s}{A} = 2.63 \text{ E6 pounds per square inch (18.12 E9 Pa)}$$

where: A_c = the area of the concrete,

A_s = the area of the steel,

E_c = the elastic modulus of concrete, and

E_s = the elastic modulus of steel.

3.1 Principal Stresses from FEA

The finite element analysis shows that Saarinen was correct (see figure 2). The dominant principal stresses are all compressive and for the most part constant (ranging from about 60 to 80 psi, or 0.413 to .551 MPa). They are essentially in the direction of the centroidal curve. The exception is on the inside corner near the base, due to Saarinen's probably not having considering the effect of the built-in condition at the base.

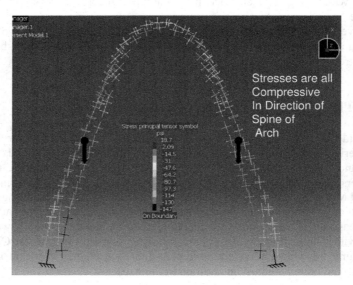

Figure 2 - The Principal Stresses Due to the Arch's Own Distributed Weight. The deformation is displayed with a high magnification factor that exaggerates the inward bending halfway up the Arch legs.

3.2 Arch Leg during Construction

The Arch leg was additionally modelled without support in order to determine the jacking force required to spread the legs apart for the insertion of the key section (see figure 3). In fact, from 300 feet (91.44 m) on up, the erection contractor used an expandable fixture to span across the two legs, thereby stabilizing the construction. The students determined that a jacking force of 1.19 million pounds (0.540 million kg) was required to spread the legs apart for the installation of the "key" segment at the very top.

3.3 Dynamic Analysis

The FEA analysis gave the first ten natural frequencies to be:
.568, .924, 1.072, 1.846, 1.943, 3.808, 3.244, 4.461, 4.742, and 6.459 Hertz.
The students studied and animated the higher-frequency mode shapes (see figure 4).

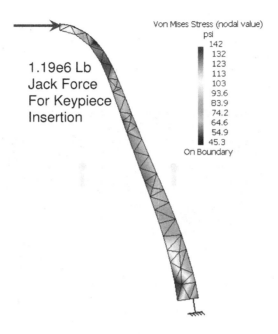

1.19e6 Lb
Jack Force
For Keypiece
Insertion

Von Mises Stress (nodal value)
psi
142
132
123
113
103
93.6
83.9
74.2
64.6
54.9
45.3
On Boundary

Figure 3 - One Leg of the Arch Showing Von Mises Stresses. The leg is shown deformed. The jacking force is shown as the big horizontal arrow.

First mode

Figure 4 - The Arch in the First Mode of Vibration. The first mode (.568 Hertz) is a cantilever vibration straight out in the z direction.

4. MACHINING THE MODEL

The numerically controlled milling functionality of CATIA was used to study various cutting strategies for machining a 1/1000-scale model of the arch. This screen (see figure 5) shows full five-axis milling using side-cutting. The students found it to be the most efficient way to machine the difficult "intrados" surface.

When the graduate students went on to actually make models using DELMIA, they used ball end milling because a Haase three-axis machine was the machine that was available to them.

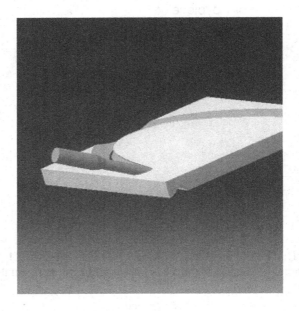

Figure 5 - CATIA Screen Showing the Milling of the "Intrados" of the Arch Using Side-Cutting. The outer part is the "good part." No fixtures are shown at this point.

4.1 Finishing the Job Using DELMIA

The students in the new MS degree program in Manufacturing Engineering Technology began working with DELMIA in their courses in "Automated Technology for Tool-Path Generation" and "Plant Layout for Lean and Agile Manufacturing." DELMIA, being fully associative with CATIA, allows the designers to reach right through it to CATIA in order to make changes in configuration and tool-path generation. DELMIA also adds the capability to include the actual machine on which the part is to be made. In this case the machine was a Haas three-axis milling machine (see figure 6). If the students wished to extend the project to design and to animate a manufacturing cell or an entire plant for production runs of the models, DELMIA would be able to assist in that as well.

The digital model was also converted to Solidworks for use at Precision Castparts and then to ProtoType for the creation of wax models to be used to make investment castings (see figure 7).

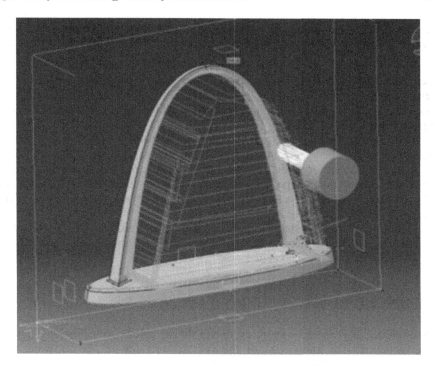

Figure 6 - Toolpath Generation Using a Ball Endmill in Three Axis
(courtesy, Freightliner Corporation).

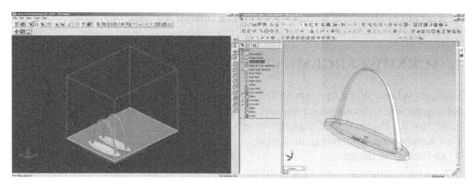

Figure 7 - ProtoType Layout (Left) and Solidworks Layout (Right).
These softwares were used for the model by investment molding
(courtesy, Precision Castparts Corporation).

At the time of this writing, actual models of the Arch are being machined at Freightliner and also cast at Precision Castparts. The job should be completed by the time of the actual DET conference in Portugal in September.

4.2 Strengths, Weaknesses, Threats, and Opportunities (SWTO) in Using DET (In this case CATIA and DELMIA) to Teach the Manufacturing Subjects Indicated

Strengths: Actual industrial PLM software; Awesome power; Cross-functionality of digital data sets; Associability between functionalities; Design closely coupled to manufacturing; Students reinforcing one another while learning; Increased creativity and excitement.

Weaknesses: Teaching end-to-end across functionalities can be overwhelming; Things take more time than expected; Frustration happens; No day is like any other.

Threats: The need for funding continuous improvement; The fluidity and variability of software, hardware, operating systems, and documentation; The possibility of "Bleeding edge" breakdowns and "train-wrecks"; The occasional corruption of files or settings due to inexperience.

Opportunities: An industrial-academic dialog is fostered; The DET is extendable to modeling of an entire factory; The global enterprise threshold is enabled; A multi-cad environment is easily envisioned.

5. CONCLUSIONS

1. Proficiency in concurrent engineering and digital enterprise technology can best be achieved with knowledge of the full functionality of the software, from modelling to manufacturing and analysis.
2. High-end software can tie all courses together if it is threaded throughout the curriculum, rather than being confined to special courses in using the software.
3. The digital data set becomes the common design authority for all functionalities.
4. Working in groups, in a studio fashion, is a catalyst for learning.

6. ACKNOWLEDGEMENTS

Students Whose Work Appears In This Presentation:
John Schleicher, development engineer
"Bo" Nonn, self-employed designer-inventor
Curt Kemper, manufacturing manager
Ryan Patterson, designer
Brian Fullbright, manufacturing engineer
The co-authors of this paper were also students in the MS degree program while this work was being produced.

Cooperating Corporations
Freightliner LLC - a DaimlerChrysler Company, Portland, Oregon, for donating the time on the Haas machine.
Precision Castparts Corporation, Portland, Oregon, for casting the model for investment molding.

SESSION 6

SPECIES – PRODUCTION SYSTEM EVOLUTIONS

SIMULATION OF THE MANUFACTURING PROCESS, GENERATION OF A MODEL OF THE MANUFACTURED PARTS

Frédéric Vignat and François Villeneuve
University of Grenoble, Laboratory 3S, France
{frederic.vignat, francois.villeneuve}@inpg.fr

Designing a new product in an industrial context supposes to be certain to be able to produce it according to a level of quality and controlled cost. To achieve this goal, it is necessary to simultaneously design the product and the process of production and to be able to simulate the envisaged process in order to predict the productivity and the quality that can be obtained. The proposed method is based on the generation of a virtual model of the manufactured parts (model MMP). The deviations of the manufactured surfaces of the MMP are expressed compared to the nominal part. These deviations are collected by simulation of the suggested manufacturing process. The range of variation of these deviations represents the 3d capabilities of the manufacturing means.

1. INTRODUCTION

To answer to an identified need, the designer creates a product. The use of CAD software has been generalized and the widely used concept of digital mock-up gives to the CAD model a central position. The CAD model a nominal model of the designed products and all the forecast simulations are made with this model. The manufacturing step of the product generates deviations and the consequences of these deviations have to be managed. It is necessary give limits to the deviations so that its influence on the product functionality is limited the requirements range. Several models to estimate the deviations generated by the manufacturing process and to evaluate its consequences on the cinematic functionality of the product have been proposed.

(Dantan and Al, 2000a) (Dantan and Al, 2000b) proposes to model the manufacturing process by gauges with internal mobility. They define three spaces gs, gi and gg for gauge situation, gauge intrinsic and gauge gap representing the variations due to the manufacturing process. The envisaged variations of these parameters determine a field of variation DM of the parameters of situation S and intrinsic I of the part. If this field DM is included in the D_{specif} field representing the field in which the functional specification is respected, it is possible to conclude that, for this phase, the selected process makes it possible to carry out suitable parts. The defined gauge can also be used like a manufacturing specification.

(Zhou and Al, 2003) use a vectorial model to describe the defects relative to a nominal model and gathers them in a state vector x(k). They then write that each manufacturing set-up generates defects which it classifies in three categories (see figure X): positioning defects which correspond to the positioning defects of a perfect part in an imperfect part-holder, machining defects corresponding to the defects of the machined surfaces relative to the machine and reference defects corresponding to the positioning defects of an imperfect part in a perfect part-holder. They then use matrices operators to combine the defects and to determine the state vector at the end of the set-up x(k+1).

(Tichadou and Al, 2004) propose a graph representation of the manufacturing process. This graph model the successive set-up and for each set-up the positioning surface and their hierarchy and the machined surfaces. This graph makes it possible to highlight the influential paths. They propose then 2 analysis methods. The first one uses a small displacements torsor model. The second one is based on the use of CAD software in which they model a manufacturing process with defect. They then virtually measure the realized part and check its conformity.

The common simulation and transfer tools assume that the form and orientation defects are negligible in front of dimensional defects. A vector can thus model each dimension. The projection of the vectors on the specified direction gives algebraic relations that can be used for the simulation or transfer purpose. The Δl method (Bourdet, 1973) and the tolerance chain are the main used methods using this model.

Usually, the designer indicates limits to the deviation by defining tolerances. (Zangh, 1996) describe the tolerances as a link between the product functional needs and the manufacturing cost. Specifications influence both the product and the process and the tolerancing activity has to be considered as a transverse one. Zangh proposes an integrated design approach where intermediate (functional) specifications are not used. He proposes to calculate directly the consequences of the manufacturing defects on the respect of the functional needs.

The model proposed in this paper can be used, in a classical way, to verify that the defects generated by the process are within the indicated tolerances. It can also be used, forgetting the tolerance intermediate step, to simulate directly the consequences of the defects on the utilization life cycle step of the product.

The MMP is constructed around the nominal model of the part. This nominal model can be positioned by a set of surfaces. The surfaces of the MMP are ideal surfaces associated to real surfaces by a criterion like least square. The deviations of these surfaces are described by a small displacement torsor. The parameters of these torsors depend on positioning and machining deviations and the limits on these parameters are expressed by constraints.

Containing defects parameters representing the main causes of process inaccuracy and constraints limiting the variation of these parameters, the MMP can be presented like the model of the manufactured parts.

2. THE GEOMETRICAL MODEL

The geometrical model used to describe the MMP is based on the definition described in (Bourdet et al, 1995) (Thiebaut, 2001) for the assembly analysis and extended by (Villeneuve et al, 2001) for the manufacturing process analysis. This model is based on an ideal part is a part made up of perfect form surfaces deviated relative to their perfect position. The surfaces of the ideal part are associated to the real one by a measurement and an association process. The geometrical description of the MMP is based on the nominal model of the part than can be issued of a CAD model. This nominal model is composed of:

- a global frame which can be constructed on associated surfaces
- nominal surfaces with for each surface:
  type of surface
  local frame
  boundaries (edges and vertexes)

The associated part is described relative to the nominal one by the deviation of each surface. Real surfaces are associated to ideal surfaces using a usual criterion like least square. In the MMP is described the deviation of these real surfaces relative to the nominal one by a small displacement torsor which structure depend on the surface type. For example for the plane 6 of the part, in a local frame (with Z local axis normal to the plane), the torsor is described figure 1. The 3 non-null values represent the potential defects of the surface and the 3 null values represent the invariant degrees of the surface.

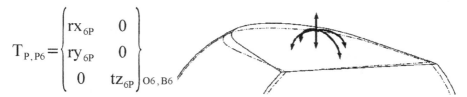

$$T_{P,P6} = \begin{Bmatrix} rx_{6P} & 0 \\ ry_{6P} & 0 \\ 0 & tz_{6P} \end{Bmatrix}_{O6,B6}$$

Figure 1 –Plane 6 displacement.

This model is also used to describe the process: the associated part-holder, the part positioning and the machining operations.

3. THE MODEL OF MANUFACTURED PARTS

The model of manufactured parts (see figure 3) is a representation of the set of produced parts including description of the process in term of geometrical deviations. It particularly describes the defects generated by the process, classify these defects and indicate the limits on these one. To illustrate the concepts presented in this paper, an example of realised part represented figure 2 will be used.

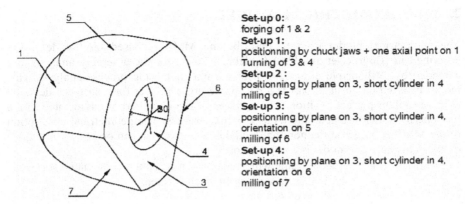

Figure 2 – Example of part and process planning.

The defects generated by a machining process are considered to be the result of 2 independent phenomenons: the positioning one and the machining one; accumulated over the successive set-ups. The combination of these two phenomenons can be made by summation; the result is the deviation of a realized surface relative to the part.

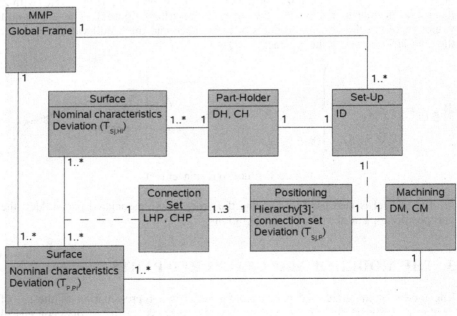

Figure 3 – Structure of the MMP.

The positioning deviation is the deviation of the nominal part relative to the nominal machine. The part positioning operation on the part-holder is realized by a set of hierarchically organized elementary connections. Each set determine part of the 6 degrees of freedom of the MMP in the 3D space. The positioning deviation is expressed by a small displacement torsor $T_{Sj,P}$ for set-up j. This deviation is function of the MMP surfaces deviation generated by the previous set-ups, the part-holder surfaces deviations and the link part-holder/part surfaces.

The part-holder surfaces deviations are described by small displacement torsors $T_{Sj,Hk}$ for surface k of the part-holder in set-up j. The parameters of these torsors (DH) are saved in the part-holder object of the MMP (table 1) and limited by constraints (CH) representative of the part-holder quality. These constraints are limiting one or a set of parameters together.

Table 1 – Part-holder description.

Set Up 3 : Part-Holder		
Surface	**Deviation DH**	**Constraints CH**
Plane 3S3	$rx_{3S3}, ry_{3S3}, tz_{3S3}$	$-0,0001 \leq rx_{3S3} \leq 0,0001$ $-0,0001 \leq ry_{3S3} \leq 0,0001$ $-0,01 \leq tz_{3S3} \leq 0,01$
Cylinder 4S3	$ra_{4S3}, rx_{4S3}, ry_{4S3}, tx_{4S3}, ty_{4S3}$	$-0,01 \leq ra_{4S3} \leq 0,01$ $\sqrt{(tx_{4S3} - 2,5\,ry_{4S3})^2 + (ty_{4S3} + 2,5\,rx_{4S3})^2} \leq 0,01$ $\sqrt{(tx_{4S3} + 2,5\,ry_{4S3})^2 + (ty_{4S3} - 2,5\,rx_{4S3})^2} \leq 0,01$
Line 5S3	ry_{5S3}, tz_{5S3}	$-0,01 \leq tz_{5S3} \pm 20\,ry_{5S3} \leq 0,01$

An elementary connection joins an associated surface of the part-holder and an associated surface of the MMP. The relative position of these 2 surfaces is described by a small displacement torsor $T_{Hk,Pi}$ called link torsor. The 6 parameters of this torsor are the link parameters (LHP). The LHP values depend on connected surfaces contact condition and can be calculated for each part/part-holder pair using positioning rules expressed by constraints (CHP). Two type of contact are distinguished: the floating and the slipping one. For floating contacts, the only constraint is non-penetration of the part in the part-holder and is determined on the boundary edge and vertex. For slipping contact the part is pushed on the part holder by a clamping strength. The constraint associated to this type of contact is a positioning function to maximise combined to non-penetration condition. The connection data are saved in the connection sets objects of the set-up (table 2).

Table 2 – Positioning description of the primary connection in set-up 3.

Set Up 3 : Positionning				Hierarchical set : 1		
Part-Holder surface	LHP	Type of contact	Positionning function	Non Penetration condition	Solution	MMP surface
Plane 3S3	lrx_{3S3} lry_{3S3} ltz_{3S3}	slipping	$-ltz_{3S3}$	$24,92\,lrx_{3S3} + 30\,lry_{3S3} + ltz_{3S3} \geq 0$ $38,44\,lrx_{3S3} + 6,58\,lry_{3S3} + ltz_{3S3} \geq 0$ $13,52\,lrx_{3S3} - 36,58\,lry_{3S3} + ltz_{3S3} \geq 0$ $-24,92\,lrx_{3S3} + 30\,lry_{3S3} + ltz_{3S3} \geq 0$ $-38,44\,lrx_{3S3} + 6,58\,lry_{3S3} + ltz_{3S3} \geq 0$ $-13,52\,lrx_{3S3} - 36,58\,lry_{3S3} + ltz_{3S3} \geq 0$	0 0 0	Plane 3

The deviation of the surface machining operation is described relative to the nominal machine by a small displacement torsor $T_{Sj,Pi}$ for the surface i realised in set-up j. This torsor is grouping deviation of the surface swept by the tool and cutting local deformations. The parameters of this torsor represent machining deviations (DM). They are limited by constraints (CM) representing the machines and tools capabilities. These data are stored in the machining object of the MMP (table 3).

Table 3 – Machining parameters description.

Set Up 3 : Machining		
Surface	Deviation DM	Constraints CM
	rx_6	$-0.0001 \leq rx_6 \leq 0.0001$
Plane 6	ry_6	$-0.0001 \leq ry_6 \leq 0.0001$
	tz_6	$-0.01 \leq tz_6 \leq 0.01$

For each surface, the positioning and machining effects are added and its deviation relative to the nominal part is determined and expressed by a small displacement torsor $T_{P,Pi}$ for surface i of the part like in figure 4 for surface 6 of the example figure 2. This deviation is stored in the surface object of the MMP.

$$T_{P,P6} = \begin{Bmatrix} Urz_{3S2} + ry_{5S3} + lry_{5S3} + rx_5 + rx_6 & 0 \\ \begin{aligned} & 0,86\,lrx_{10S1} - 0,86\,lrx_{3S3} + 0,5\,lry_{10S1} + 0,5\,lry_{3S3} \\ & -0,86\,rx_1 + 0,86\,rx_{10S1} - 0,86\,rx_3 - 0,86\,rx_{3S3} \\ & -0,5\,ry_1 + 0,5\,ry_{10S1} - 0,5\,ry_3 + 0,5\,ry_{3S3} + ry_6 \end{aligned} & 0 \\ 0 & \begin{aligned} & -1,73\,lrx_{10S1} - 6,49\,lrx_{3S3} - lry_{10S1} + 3,75\,lry_{3S3} \\ & +0,5\,ltx_{10S1} + 0,5\,ltx_{4S3} - 0,86\,lty_{10S1} - 0,86\,lty_{4S3} \\ & -8,66\,rx_1 - 1,73\,rx_{10S1} - 6,49\,rx_3 - 6,49\,rx_{3S3} \\ & +2,16\,rx_4 - 5\,ry_1 - 1\,ry_{10S1} - 3,75\,ry_3 \\ & +3,75\,ry_{3S3} + 1,25\,ry_4 - 0,5\,tx_1 + 0,5\,tx_{10S1} \\ & -0,5\,tx_4 + 0,5\,tx_{4S3} + 0,86\,ty_1 - 0,86\,ty_{10S1} \\ & +0,86\,ty_4 - 0,86\,ty_{4S3} + tz_6 \end{aligned} \end{Bmatrix}$$

Figure 4 – Deviation of a surface of the MMP.

4. THE PROCESS SIMULATION

The MMP construction is done through a simulation. The simulation is performed in two steps determining the effects of the 2 phenomenons. First, the MWP (Model of WorkPiece or intermediate MMP at the end of a set-up) from the previous set-up is positioned on the part holder. Then, the surfaces realised during the current step are machined.

The positioning is the result of the combination of parallel and hierarchically organised elementary connections between surfaces of a part-holder and surfaces of a part. A pair of surfaces, a connection type, a contact type and a potential contact zone defines a connection. The contacts are of two types, floating one and slipping one.

Each connection contributes to part of the 6 positioning degrees of the MMP and the links parameters describing this contribution are named determined. The connection also lives some degrees free and the links parameters associated to these degrees are named undetermined. The position of the MMP fixed by a connection n can be calculated by equation (1)

$$Pos[n] = T_{Sj,P} = T_{Sj,Hk} + T_{Hk,Pi} - T_{P,Pi} \qquad (1)$$

A rigid part position being unique in the 3D space, it is possible to express that expression coming from each connection is equal (2).

$$\forall \, n, m < \text{number of connections}: Pos[n] = Pos[m] \qquad (2)$$

This process called unification gives a system of 6x(number of connections − 1) equations that is solved to eliminate undetermined and over constrained links. The resolution of this problem (Villeneuve et al, 2005) gives the position of the MMP function of 6 piloting links. The values of these links depend on contact condition and part and part-holder surfaces deviation. This dependency is expressed by constraints function of the contact type like presented in chapter 3. The part position is being determined the surfaces can now be realised. The determination of the deviation of a realised surface relative to its nominal position is done by addition of positioning and machining deviation using (3).

$$T_{P,Pi} = -T_{Sj,P} + T_{Sj,Pi} \qquad (3)$$

This operation is repeated for the successive set-ups and leads to the construction of the MMP.

5. CONCLUSION

Verifying that nominal model of the product is a good answer to the expressed or implied needs is not sufficient. To be delivered, the products have to be manufactured and assembled. The manufacturing process generates deviation that have to be managed in order to be certain that the whole products are functional.

To approach this goal, a model of the manufactured parts with deviations is proposed. This model is a representation of the set of produced parts. It is generated by a simulation stage with the manufacturing means capabilities as input parameters.

This model can be used in an analysis stage to verify that the produced parts fit with the functional tolerances. It can also be used to perform assembly and mechanism simulation with deviated parts in a product life cycle engineering practice.

6. REFERENCES

1. Benea, R., Cloutier, G., Fortin, C.: "Process plan validation including process deviations and machine tools errors", Proceedings of the 7th CIRP Seminar on Computer Aided Tolerancing; pp. 191-200; Cachan 2001
2. Bourdet P.: "Chaînes de cotes de fabrication", Revue l'Ingenieur et le technicien de l'enseignement technique, No. 191, 1973
3. Bourdet P., Ballot E.: "Geometrical behaviour laws for computer aided tolerancing"; In: Proceedings of the 4th CIRP seminar on computer aided design; Tokyo, 1995

4. Dantan, J.Y., Ballu, A., Thiebault, F., Bourdet, P.: "Functional and manufacturing specifications –
    Part 1: Geometrical expression by gauge with internal mobilities"; In: Proceedings of the 3rd
    IDMME conference, Montreal; 2000
5. Dantan, J.Y., Ballu, A., Thiebault, F., Bourdet, P.: "Functional and manufacturing specifications –
    Part 2: validation of a process plan"; In: Proceedings of the 3rd IDMME conference, Montreal;
    2000
6. Thiebaut, F., "Contribution à la définition d'un moyen unifié de gestion de la géométrie réaliste basée
    sur le calcul des lois de comportement des mécanismes", PhD thesis, ENS de Cachan, France, 2001
7. Tichadou, S., Legoff, O., Hascoet, J.Y.: "Process planning geometrical simulation: compared
    approaches between CAD/CAM system and small displacement torsor model"; In: Proceedings
    of the 5th International Conference on Integrated Design and Manufacturing in Mechanical
    Engineering; Bath 2004
8. Vignat, F., Villeneuve, F.: "Simulation of the manufacturing process (2): Analysis of its consequences
    on a functional tolerance", Proceedings of the 9th CIRP International Seminar on Computer Aided
    Tolerancing, Tempe (US), 10-11 April 2005
9. Villeneuve, F., Legoff, O., Landon, Y.: "Tolerancing for manufacturing: a three dimensional model";
    International Journal of Production Research, Vol. 39, No8; pp. 1625-1648, 2001
10. Villeneuve, F., Vignat, F.: "Manufacturing process simulation for tolerance analysis and synthesis";
    In: Proceedings of the 5th International Conference on Integrated Design and Manufacturing in
    Mechanical Engineering; Bath 2004
11. Villeneuve, F., Vignat, F.: "Simulation of the manufacturing process (1): Generic resolution of the
    positioning problem"; In: Proceedings of the 9th CIRP seminar on computer aided design; Tempe
    (US), 2005
12. Zhang, G.: "Simultaneous tolerancing for design and manufacturing", International Journal of
    Production Research, Vol. 34, pp. 3361–3382, 1996
13. Zhou, S., Huang, Q., Shi, J.: "State space modelling of dimensional variation propagation in
    multistage machining process using differential motion vector", in: IEEE Transactions on robotics
    and automation, Vol. 19, No2, pp. 296-309, 2003

UML AS A BASIS TO MODEL AUTONOMOUS PRODUCTION SYSTEMS

Bernd Scholz-Reiter, Jan Kolditz and Torsten Hildebrandt
University of Bremen, Bremen, Germany
{bsr,kol,hil}@biba.uni-bremen.de

This article will investigate the suitability of the Unified Modelling Language (UML) for requirements analysis of autonomous logistic processes by a logistics domain expert. Such a model is the basis for subsequent implementation of the system consisting of software engineering and hardware configuration. Relevant parts of UML will be used to model an exemplary scenario which will form the basis to derive benefits and drawbacks of using the UML in this context. Suggestions on how the identified gaps can be filled will be presented in the paper.

1. INTRODUCTION

Enterprises are exposed to an increasingly dynamic environment today. Furthermore increasing competition caused by globalisation more and more requires gaining competitive advantages by improved process control, within and beyond the borders of producing enterprises. One possibility to face increasing dynamics is autonomous control of logistic processes, which is the main research topic of the SFB 637, the interdisciplinary research effort this work is based on. Autonomous control in this context means processes of decentralized decision making in heterarchical structures. It requires the ability and possibility of interacting system elements to autonomously make goal-oriented decisions. The use of autonomous control aims at a higher robustness of systems and simplified processes achieved by distributed handling of dynamics and complexity due to greater flexibility and autonomy of decision making. Focus of the SFB lies in the areas of production and transport logistics, so the system elements, making their decisions autonomously, are the logistic objects themselves (Scholz-Reiter, 2004).

In order to enable logistic objects to be intelligent they have to be provided with smart labels. While today's RFID (radio frequency identification)-chips have very limited capabilities with respect to energy, range, storage capacity and especially information processing (Finkenzeller, 2003), near future shall bring highly evolved smart labels that can provide resources alike micro computers to logistic objects. Nowadays RFID is already widely used in industry for identification matters and several visions for future applications exist (Fleisch, 2005), (Heinrich, 2005).

This paper presents a concept for modelling autonomous cooperating logistic processes. First section 2 gives a short overview of important aspects of the modelling method, especially the view concept to structure the model. Main section 3 discusses the notation for modelling the different aspects addressed in their respective views. It presents the appropriate notational elements of UML to be used in these contexts. Shortcomings of the UML notation to depict certain aspects of the autonomous logistics system are also presented in the context of the relevant view. The paper is concluded by a short summary and an outlook of future work.

2. MODELLING CONCEPT FOR AUTONOMOUS COOPERATING LOGISTIC PROCESSES

Creating models of autonomous production systems usually leads to a high degree of complexity, as does the creation of any comprehensive process model. Hence a view concept serves as a means to reduce the complexity constructing such a model (Scheer 1994). A fundamental distinction can be made between a static and dynamic (sub-) model. The static model describes the structure, the dynamic model the behaviour of the modelled system, according to the basic classification in UML (OMG, 2006) that is also appropriate here. In our proposed methodology we distinguish five different views, three in the static and two in the dynamic sub-model. In the static model we differentiate between a structure view, knowledge view and ability view. Process view and communication view are the different views of the dynamic model.

The *structure view* that shows the relevant logistic objects is the starting point. Besides objects and classes the structure view can show relationships between them, for instance in the form of associations or inheritance relationships. The *knowledge view* describes the knowledge, which has to be present in the logistic objects to allow a decentralized decision making. This view focuses on composition and static distribution of the knowledge while not addressing temporal aspects. The *ability view* depicts the abilities of the individual logistic objects. Processes of a logistic system need certain abilities, which have to be provided by the logistic objects. These abilities are supposed to be seen as abstractions of problem types and problem solving capabilities occurring in reality.

The *process view* depicts the logic-temporal sequence of activities and states of the logistic objects. Here the objects' decision processes can be modelled. The process view plays a central role connecting the views of the static model and depicting the behaviour of logistic objects, so far only viewed statically. The *communication view* presents the contents and temporal sequence of information exchange between logistic objects. Depicting the communication is especially necessary to show the interaction of autonomously deciding, otherwise only loosely coupled objects to model their interaction (Weiss, 2005).

In addition to the dynamic and static model just described we distinguish a macro and micro perspective. This distinction (largely independent of the distinction between the different views just presented) is also used in methods for software agent development (Weiss, 2000). The macro view describes the interaction between the autonomous logistic objects. To some extend, it shows an external view onto the system, its elements and their relations and interactions. On the contrary the micro view describes the actions within and composition of the autonomous logistic objects. For the micro-level especially the process, knowledge and ability view are relevant, while all views proposed are relevant for the macro-level. This means that the micro-macro perspective is orthogonal to the views described before. Nevertheless not all views use both perspectives to the same extend.

3. UML AS A MODELLING BASIS

3.1 Structure View

In the structure view class diagrams (see figure 1) are the most important diagrams. In general class diagrams support the modelling of system structure. Class diagrams describe the static elements, their fundamental characteristic and the relations between each other. Classes themselves are specified by attributes and operations. An attribute is a characteristic of a class that takes a concrete value in an object, which is an instance of a class. One kind of relationship between classes is generalisation. The central point there is the inheritance of the generalised class' structure, e.g. its attributes, to the specialized one. Associations describe the static relations between classes and are mostly explained by a name, association specific roles of the classes and multiplicities. Special associations are aggregation and composition. Both describe a part-of-relationship between two classes while the composition represents an existential dependency between a part and the whole it belongs to.

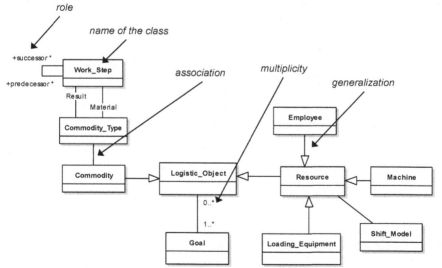

Figure 1 - Class diagram in the structure view.

For modelling autonomous logistics processes class diagrams provide the opportunity to picture structure and organization of the logistic system. Accordingly aggregation and composition can be used to model organisational units and generalizations to model the hierarchy of classes. Roles and names of associations support a better understandability of a model. The same applies for multiplicities which also provide a possibility of an early explication of structural constraints.

The exemplary class diagram in figure 1 shows an extract of the system structure. The central class *Logistic Object* is a generalisation of *Commodity* and *Resource*, whereas *Resource* again has specialisations *Employee, Machine* and *Loading Equipment*. The class *Shift Model* determines resource availability and therefore is an important factor for its capacity. Logistic objects are associated with goals and it is determined, that a logistic object may have multiple goals but have to have at least one.

3.2 Knowledge View

In the knowledge view class and object diagrams are the most important diagrams. These have already been sketched in the previous section. In the structure view the main modelling focus lies in the structure of the system and thus in the possible relationships of one element to another. The knowledge view addresses the content of elements already appearing in the structure view as well as of elements not specified yet. Furthermore this view provides information about the distribution of knowledge in the system. The knowledge distribution only shows a point in time, because no changes in time are described. The changes of knowledge distribution depending on time are looked at on an abstract level in the communication and process view but the concrete value of a system parameter arises during run time and is not specified beforehand. Modelling the knowledge distribution rather serves the purpose of assuring that the knowledge necessary for running the processes is present in the system and it is specified where it can be found.

One example for the knowledge view is the description and assignment of goals. In the structure view it is specified that a logistic object is supposed to have goals. In the knowledge view dedicated goals are assigned to the different logistic objects. This is possible on the class level for example when assigning the goal class *maximise utilisation* to the class *machine*, as well as on the object level when assigning goals with concrete parameter values to single machine objects.

For a clearly arranged overview of the durable aspects of knowledge distribution of the system, particularly the distribution existent in the initial state before run time, UML diagrams do not provide adequate notations. Therefore we use so called *knowledge maps* from business process modelling that have been enriched with elements from knowledge management (Allweyer, 1998).

3.3 Ability View

The ability view offers to model the autonomous system elements' abilities as abstract collections of different operations they are able to perform. This concept can be represented using UML-interfaces, which also allow generalisations between abilities and therefore creating inheritance hierarchies between the abilities. Interfaces and thus abilities can be shown in UML by class diagrams, already described earlier in this paper. The ability view therefore gives an overview of the abilities present in the system and their distribution to various objects.

A second aspect of abilities is the mapping between them and logistic objects, i.e. specifying which logistic objects have certain abilities. This is again shown in class diagrams and indicated by a special kind of relationship: the realizes-relationship between an interface and a class, graphically shown by a dashed line (with an arrow-head like a generalisation) from the interface to the class that offers the interface. How a class that implements a certain ability provides the necessary operations is not specified in the ability view, but the views of the dynamic model (process and communication view) instead as described in the following.

3.4 Process View

In the process view activity diagrams and state machines are used. Activity diagrams are constructed similar to Petri nets and provide a basis to model the processes possible at run time. They allow to specify particular operations or, on a higher level of abstraction, complete business processes. Activity diagrams are the diagram type most often used when applying the UML to business process modelling (Oesterreich, 2003).

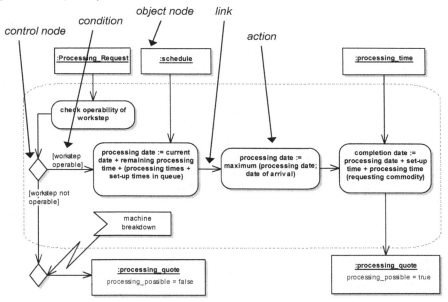

Figure 2 - Activity diagram in the process view.

First of all a number of actions characterising an activity are elements included in an activity diagram. These actions are connected by directed links which in combination with control nodes determine the control flow within a process and therefore possible sequences in which the action nodes are executed. Among the control nodes there are initial and final nodes, decision and merge nodes as well as fork and join nodes.

The exemplary activity diagram shown in figure 2 describes the internal handling process of a machine for a processing request. First the incoming request is checked whether the machine is able to perform the asked workstep. If the workstep is operable the machine calculates the earliest completion date for the commodity on the basis of its current schedule, the estimated arrival date of the commodity and the processing times. The process is completed by an outgoing message *processing quote* containing the estimated completion date for the requesting commodity. If the machine breaks down, the whole process is aborted and a negative processing quote is sent.

The state machine is another possibility to model the behaviour of a part of a system. There the behaviour is specified by possible sequences of discrete system states as well as internal or external triggers that cause a change from one state to another. States are connected by transitions in form of directed links. To model more complex relations between states the UML also provides pseudo states like an initial state, entry and exit point. Furthermore alternatives can be described by junction pseudo states or choice pseudo states. Parallelisation can also be expressed and is shown by forks at the beginning and joins at the end of parallel sections. These pseudo states can be connected with states and with each other.

3.5 Communication View

The communication view consists of two main components, the description of the message exchange between logistic objects and the description of the messages themselves concerning their structure and contents. For description of message exchange the sequence diagram is primarily applicable.

Sequence diagrams (see example in figure 3) provide a basis to illustrate communication processes within a system. They allow to model messages exchanged by communication partners in respect to their temporal and logical order. The communication partners are listed horizontally, the messages are ordered vertically. The messages themselves are symbolised as a directed link from the lifeline of the sender to the one of the receiver. Using so called combined fragments the message exchange process can be combined with rules to model for example alternative, parallel or optional message sequences.

Sequence diagrams provide vital instruments for modelling relevant aspects of autonomous logistic objects. So the information exchange necessary for solving a problem can be analysed and specified. That assures the availability of information needed during the runtime of the system and helps to allow an estimation of the communication volume.

The exemplary sequence diagram in figure 3 shows the communication between a commodity and a machine. The commodity executes a *processing request* whereon the machine answers with a *processing quote*. After the commodity has compared the quotes and selected one machine, the machine gets either a *booking request* or a *cancellation of the processing quote*.

One aspect that is not covered by the existing UML 2.0 specification concerns the exact determination of the number of messages in case of multiple communication partners. So the example in figure 3 does not determine, that the sum of the messages *booking request* and *cancel processing quote* is not allowed to exceed the number of requested machines. However such a determination would be useful to increase clearness and to allow enhanced plausibility checks at run time. A similar problem arises in the context of efforts to provide a better support of UML for concepts needed for agent-oriented software engineering (Bauer, 2005). There it is recommended to integrate notational elements in sequence diagrams similar to multiplicities in class diagrams. A similar mechanism is useful in our context of modelling autonomous logistics processes as well.

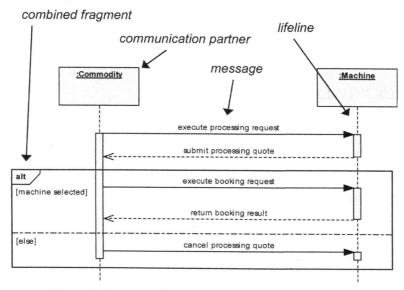

Figure 3 - Sequence diagram in the communication view.

The second main component of the communication view addresses the structure and content of the messages. For modelling the messages themselves class diagrams and object diagrams are adequate. An important part of specifying classes are attributes. In the example shown in figure 4 the message is described by the class *processing request*. There are four characterising attributes. The first attribute *sender* is of the type *commodity*. That way it is determined that processing requests can only be sent by a commodity or more precisely only a commodity can be put in as a sender.

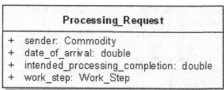

Figure 4 - class diagram in the communication view.

4. CONCLUSION

This paper investigates the use of UML to model autonomous logistic processes. Structured by a view model consisting of five different views, three static and two dynamic views, suitable UML notation to represent the elements necessary for requirement analysis to engineer such a system is presented as well as problems in using UML to show certain aspects are highlighted and solutions to adequately solve the problems are presented.

The work presented here is the foundation of a more comprehensive modelling methodology an overview of which is presented in (Scholz-Reiter, 2006). Further research will use the notation presented here to create a reference model of autonomous (production-) logistic processes, a procedure model to guide a modeller to efficiently engineer such systems. Furthermore a software tool is currently in development that will be specifically tailored to support our modelling methodology.

5. ACKNOWLEDGEMENTS

This research is funded by the German Research Foundation (DFG) as part of the Collaborative Research Centre 637 "Autonomous Cooperating Logistic Processes - A Paradigm Shift and its Limitations" (SFB 637).

6. REFERENCES

1. Allweyer, Th.: Modellbasiertes Wissensmanagement. In: Information Management 13 (1998) 1, pp. 37–45.
2. Bauer, B., Odell, J.: UML 2.0 and Agents: How to Build Agent-based Systems with the new UML Standard. In: Journal of Engineering Applications of Artificial Intelligence 18 (2005) 2, pp. 141–157.
3. Heinrich, C.: RFID and Beyond: Growing Your Business through Real World Awareness. Wiley Publishing, Indianapolis, Indiana, 2005.
4. Finkenzeller, K.: RFID-Handbook - Fundamentals and Applications in Contactless Smart Cards Identification, 2. edn. Wiley & Sons LTD, Swadlincote, UK, 2003.
5. Fleisch, E., Mattern, F. (eds.): Das Internet der Dinge - Ubiquitous Computing und RFID in der Praxis: Visionen, Technologien, Anwendungen, Handlungsanleitungen. Springer, Berlin, Germany, 2005.
6. OMG: Unified Modelling Language Specification (version 2.0). http://www.uml.org. Retrieved April 6th, 2006.
7. Scheer, A.-W.: Business Process Engineering – Reference Models for Industrial Companies, 2. edn. Springer, Berlin et al., 1994.
8. Scholz-Reiter, B., Windt, K., Freitag, M.: Autonomous Logistic Processes - New Demands and First Approaches. In: Proceedings of the 37th CIRP-International Seminar on Manufacturing Systems 2004, Budapest, Hungary, 19.-21.5.2004, pp. 357-362.
9. Scholz-Reiter, B., Kolditz, J., Hildebrandt, T.: Analysis and Design of Autonomous Logistic Processes. In: Proceedings of the 39th CIRP International Seminar on Manufacturing Systems, Ljubljana, Slovenia, 7.–9.6.2006, to appear.
10. Weiss, G. (ed): Multiagent Systems – A modern approach to distributed artificial intelligence. The MIT Press, Cambridge, USA, 2000.
11. Weiss, G., Jakob, R.: Agentenorientierte Softwareentwicklung. Springer, Berlin Heidelberg, Germany, 2005.

PROCESS ANALYSIS AND FLEXIBLE TRANSFER LINE CONFIGURATION

M. Rigamonti and T. Tolio
Dipartimento di Meccanica – Politecnico di Milano, Italy
massimo.rigamonti@mecc.polimi.it, tullio.tolio@polimi.it

The offer of the best machine tool configuration for specific customer's needs is a decisive factor to compete in the machine tool sector. Normally the offer is defined by the manufacturer mostly on the basis of his own experience and requires a considerable effort in terms of time and money while it leads to actual selling in a small percentage of the cases. Also, the knowledge related to the activity of offer preparation is not well formalized and this puts the company in a weak position in the case of retirements or job change of the experts. To address these problems, this paper presents a method for process analysis and transfer lines configuration. Results of the application of the method to a real case are reported.

1. INTRODUCTION

Currently manufacturing companies are under the intense pressure of global market competition. To successfully compete in such a situation companies have to continually release new products or modify the existing ones in order to meet the evolving requests of the customers. This strategy leads to a considerable reduction of product life cycle. As a consequence of this continuous change in the features of the products, production systems have to be properly configured or reconfigured to efficiently tackle the new production requirements.

From a system manufacturer point of view, system configuration is the cornerstone in the offer generation process to their customers. At present system configuration is carried out manually by experts that use their expertise to determine the most appropriate production resources required by each specific production problem. As systems configuration implies a huge set of decisions, it requires a considerable amount of time. It must be noted that only a small amount of offers, about 15%, are actually followed by an order, so the configuration phase is an expensive task for system manufacturers. Also, the knowledge related to the activity of offer preparation is not well formalized and this puts the company in a weak position in the case of retirements or job change of the experts.

Therefore there is the need of tools which support the configuration phase. In particular, this paper proposes an approach for automatic transfer line configuration. The method is based on process analysis to evaluate the manufacturing requirements, followed by a set-up planning and an equipment selection to define the configuration of the line.

2. OUTLINE OF THE PROPOSED METHOD

As transfer lines are dedicated manufacturing systems, their configuration is strictly dependent on the part mix to be produced. This high degree of customization allows these systems to obtain high productivity since high production rate and working accuracy can be obtained with relatively low investment costs. Conversely design cost, given the high degree of customization, tend to be pretty high. To face these problems modern transfer lines are designed according to modular design principles. Line configuration implies the selection of the number, characteristics and positioning of the modules the line is composed of. The combination of all these decision variables rapidly leads to an explosion of the number of feasible transfer line configurations. In other terms system configuration is very complex so hierarchical approaches are often used to face this complexity (Zhang, 2002), (Matta, 2005).

Therefore the proposed approach divides the configuration problem into two sub-problems which are hierarchically related. At the higher hierarchical level transfer lines are described by few decision variables, especially by the ones which mostly affect line investment costs. At the lower level the lines are described in a more detailed way by several decision variables in addition to the ones previously considered.

In particular in the present approach at the first hierarchical level the decision variable considered is the number of transfer lines necessary to process the production mix. The number of transfer lines is directly affected by the process analysis and in particular by the number of set-ups necessary to correctly manufacture the production mix. In fact especially in contexts characterized by high production rate each set-up is processed on a dedicated transfer line, thus reducing idle time due to line set-up. Once the number of transfer lines is defined, the decisions of the second hierarchical level are the number of working stations which compose the line and some technical characteristics of the machining units which equip each working station. In other words at the second level the production resources of the transfer line are selected.

3. PROCESS ANALYSIS

The production problem imposes some manufacturing requirements, which include the features to be realized. The features in turn imply the operations required to machine them. These manufacturing requirements directly affect both the set-up planning and the equipment selection phase.

The analysis of these manufacturing requirements is managed in the proposed approach by the ISO (14649) STEP-NC standard. The features of the workpieces are defined by STEP-NC as *Manufacturing Features* and each of them needs a set of *Machining Operations* to be processed. Furthermore according to this standard each *Manufacturing Feature* is combined with a *Machining Operation*, to be performed on the feature, to obtain the entity *Machining Workingstep* (MW). A MW, therefore, represents a precise operation a machine can make on a particular feature of the workpiece. In this study each MW has been characterized with information about the machining direction, which is the direction of the axis of the tool body that realizes the MW.

The MWs of the workpiece are often linked by technological priorities or tolerance constraints. In this regard the paper examines shape and position tolerance, these relationships are considered as precedence relationships. In particular precedence relationships have been classified in three types according to (Contini, 2004). Type 1 constraints refer to tight tolerance constraints which impose to process some MWs in the same set-up and in a defined sequence in order to ensure the maximum working precision thus avoiding repositioning errors. Type 2 constraints are technological constraints, which impose an order of execution of the MWs involved, but do not impose the sharing of the same set-up. For example drilling a workpiece imposes a previous milling of the surface involved. Finally Type 3 priorities affect manufacturing quality and efficiency, but are not essential for the correct production of the workpiece, so these relationships could be dropped if this allows to reduce the set-up number. An example of this type of constraints is the manufacturing of two nested pockets; the sequence of execution does not affect the machining feasibility but only the efficiency of the process itself.

4. SET-UP PLANNING

Set-up planning plays a key role in system configuration since it influences both production costs and quality. A reduction in the number of set-ups implies a decrease in the number of transfer lines necessary to correctly process the part thus reducing the investment costs. Also manufacturing quality improves due to the reduction of positioning errors which inevitably occur passing from one set-up to another.

4.1 Graph Based Approach to Set-up Planning

This paper proposes a graph based approach to determine transfer line set-up planning. Precedence constraints information, analyzed in the process analysis phase, is organized in an oriented graph usually indicated by the name of *Process Graph* (Yut, 1995), (Sarma, 1996). The nodes of this graph are the MWs, while the edges represent precedence constraints. The edges of the graph could be of different types according to the type of precedence constraints.

Set up planning is carried out considering each set-up of the workpiece as a group of MWs and therefore as a group of machining directions. However a group of machining directions represents a feasible set-up only if all its operations can be machined exploiting the degrees of freedom of the considered machine. Therefore initially the method creates groups of MWs which share the same machining direction and therefore are certainly accessible to the machine. To this purpose another oriented graph is created called *Direction Graph*. Each node of this graph represents a group of MWs, while each edge describes the precedence relations that exist among the MWs belonging to different groups, figure 1.

564

Digital Enterprise Technology

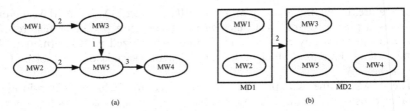

Figure 1 – *Process Graph* (a) and a corresponding *Direction Graph* (b).

This clustering allows to machine the created groups on a transfer line whose working stations are able to machine in only one direction. However, since each working station of a line is usually equipped with more than one production unit, the number of machining directions which could be processed in the same set-up increases. Therefore each set-up could be composed by MW belonging to different machining directions. In these cases the previous considered groups of MWs could be enlarged adding more machining directions.

Therefore the method, starting from the *Direction Graph* computes all the combinations of groups, so that each combination is an hyper-group which includes more than one machining direction.

Moreover the workpiece orientation affects the number of machining directions which could be processed at each work station of the line. So the method looks for alternative workpiece orientations in order to maximize the number of machining directions that are within the reach of the production units, thus going in the direction of minimizing the total number of set-ups. Alternative orientations are generated for each combination of groups taking into account the feasible directions of the machining units of the considered type of transfer line.

An accessibility analysis is then used to determine if the machine, exploiting its degrees of freedom, is able to reach all the machining directions of the considered combination. If this condition is satisfied with at least one workpiece orientation the considered combination of groups could be treated as potential set-up. The set-up plan is thus generated with the aid of an oriented graph called *Set-up Graph*. The nodes of this graph are potential set-ups, while the edges represent the precedence relationships among the potential set-ups. The presence of a cycle in the *Set-up Graph,* implies that the generated set-up plan is unfeasible, since it is not possible to establish the sequence of the set-up execution. So the method among a cyclical *Set-up Graph* selects the ones characterized by the minimum number of nodes, thus minimizing the number of set-ups.

These alternative set-up plans are then used as input data to the equipment selection module.

5. EQUIPMENT SELECTION

After a set of alternative set-up plans has been computed the configuration method proceeds with the equipment selection phase which selects the resources of the line.

In particular the equipment selection establishes the number of workstations of the line together with the number and the technical characteristics of the machining units that equip each working station.

This approach in particular refers to flexible transfer lines which are able to process different workpieces through appropriate line reconfigurations.

One of the key characteristics of the transfer lines is the possibility of processing different operations in parallel thus increasing the production rate. In particular different machining units in a given station can be simultaneously activated. Moreover each machining unit, if properly equipped, can perform more than one MW simultaneously.

To capture the system behaviour the MWs are clustered in blocks of operations, (Dolgui, 2006). Blocks are formed by operations which could be simultaneously machined by the same spindle. So the operations which belong to the same block have to share the same working feed and the same machining direction, and to respect some technological constraints imposed by the adopted tool.

The model assumes that blocks could be manufactured by different types of machining units characterized by different technical parameters, capabilities and investment costs. Moreover blocks processing time are deterministic and do not rely on the characteristics of the machining units.

The equipment selection module minimizes the investment costs by balancing the work load of the line and selecting the production resources avoiding capability excesses while satisfying the production rate imposed by the production problem and the technological constraints.

5.1 Problem formulation

This section presents the mixed integer programming model developed to face the equipment selection phase previously illustrated.

The problem is defined by the following parameters:

$BD_{b,d}$ = 1 if the block b must be processed by a machining unit belonging to the d direction; 0, otherwise (set-up planning output).

$WUBC_b$ = cost of the machining units equipped with the minimum technical characteristics required to correctly process block b.

TB_b = block b working time.

CT_p = cycle time imposed by the production rate of workpiece p.

$PREC$ = set of block couples related by precedence constraints.

ZN = set of block couples related by "negative zoning" constraints.

ZP = set of block couples related by "positive zoning" constraints.

The decisions variables are:

$WSB_{s,b}$ = 1 if block b is assigned to working station s; 0 otherwise.

$WUC_{s,d}$ = cost of the machining unit that equips direction d of working station s.

The model for transfer line configuration is presented in the following:

$$\text{Min } C\left(\sum_{p\in P}LT_p + \sum_{p\in P}\sum_{s\in S}WST_{p,s}\right) + \sum_{s\in S}\sum_{d\in D}WUC_{s,d}$$

subject to:

1. $WUC_{s,d} \geq WUBC_b \cdot WSB_{s,b} \cdot DB_{b,d}$ $\forall s \in S, \forall d \in D, \forall d \in D$

2. $\sum_{s\in S}\left[s\left(WSB_{s,b2} - WSB_{s,b1}\right)\right] \geq 1$ $\forall \left(b1,b2\right) \in PREC$

3. $\sum_{s\in S}WSB_{s,b} = 1$ $\forall b \in B$

4. $WSB_{s,b2} + WSB_{s,b1} \leq 1$ $\forall s \in S, \left(b1,b2\right) \in ZN$

5. $WSB_{s,b2} = WSB_{s,b1}$ $\forall s \in S, \left(b1,b2\right) \in ZP$

6. $WUT_{p,s,d} = \sum_{b\in B}\left(TB_b \cdot WSB_{s,b} \cdot DB_{b,d}\right)$ $\forall p \in P, \forall s \in S, \forall d \in D$

7. $WST_{p,s} \geq WUT_{p,s,d}$ $\forall p \in P, \forall s \in S, \forall d \in D$

8. $LT_p \geq WST_{p,s}$ $\forall p \in P, \forall s \in S$

9. $LT_p \leq CT_p$ $\forall p \in P$

The objective function is composed by two parts. The first part in brackets contains $WST_{p,s}$ and LT_p which represent respectively the working station time and the line time. $WST_{p,s}$ is the maximum of the machining unit times for each working station of the line. The term LT_p is the line time which corresponds to the maximum $WST_{p,s}$, i.e. the working station time of the slowest working station of the line.

The second part of the objective function considers the investment cost of the line which is the sum of the investment costs of the machining units.

Constraint set (1) ensures that the characteristics of each machining unit are appropriate to process the assigned blocks of operation. Constraint set (2) imposes the satisfaction of the precedence relationships. Constraint set (3) specifies that all the blocks that compose the problem must be assigned. Constraint set (4) represents exclusion constraints (Dolgui, 2005) and imposes that some operations cannot share the same working station. For example, roughing and finishing operations are usually manufactured in different working stations due to vibration and chip problems that could affect the quality of the machined surface. Inclusion constraints (Dolgui, 2005) are modelled by constraint set (5). These constraints are usually imposed when there are tight tolerance relationships that involve some operations of different blocks. Indeed the sharing of the same working station allows to avoid repositioning errors, thus ensuring the best precision that could be obtained. Constraint set (6) allows to compute $WUT_{p,s,d}$ as the sum of the block working time allocated to the same machining unit. Constraint sets (7) and (8) are necessary to determine the working station time and the line time. These time variables have to be considered in order to check if the line throughput satisfies the imposed production rate. To this purpose constraint set (9) ensures that the line time of workpiece p, is lower than the desired cycle time, thus assuring the attainment of the required production rate.

6. REAL CASE

The proposed method for flexible transfer line configuration has been applied to a real production case provided by an Italian manufacturer of transfer lines, Riello Sistemi S.p.A. This case refers to the configuration of a transfer line to produce a pick up steering gear holder, figure 2a, with a required production rate of 214 [piece/hour]. At the time of offer preparation, Riello S.p.A. already knew that some changes would occur to the pick up power train, implying some modification in the features of the steering gear holder. The new version of the same component is shown in figure 2b. The information available at that time said that production rate would not change passing from the first to the second version of the steering gear holder.

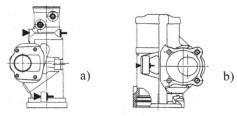

a)   b)

Figure 2 – First a) and second b) version of steering gear holder.

To compare the configuration obtained applying the proposed approach with the one proposed by Riello Sistemi, the same approach of the system manufacturer was followed.

The first step consists in the configuration of rigid transfer lines, i.e. systems equipped with the production resources necessary to manufacture one version of the steering gear holder. The configuration of the flexible transfer line is then determined starting from the rigid ones. In particular the number of lines of the flexible system is imposed by the workpiece version that needs the maximum number of set-ups to be processed. The same could be stated in regarding the number of working station of each line. The characteristics of the machining units are instead decided by the equipment selection module which considers simultaneously the manufacturing requirements of the two versions of the product.

Table 1 – System configuration: a) proposed approach and b) Riello Sistemi S.p.A.

Presented approach	N° working stations	N° machining units	Investment cost [Euro]		Riello Sistemi	N° working stations	N° machining units	Investment cost [Euro]
Line 1	11	28	368000		Line 1	7	19	246000
Line 2	5	8	120000		Line 2	11	17	258000
System	16	36	488000		System	18	36	504000

Table 1 compares some key characteristics of the configuration generated by the proposed approach with those of the configuration proposed by Riello Sistemi. It can be noticed that the configuration computed by the proposed approach has the same number of machining units and two working stations less than the real system, thus reducing the investment costs of the system.

The promising result obtained is due to the large number of alternative set-up plans generated by the set-up planning module which allows to explore a huge set of possible alternatives.

7. CONCLUSION

The present work proposes a possible solution to the problem of automatic configuration of flexible transfer line. The method could support the system manufacturer in the evaluation of alternative system configurations.

The proposed methodology starts with an analysis of the customer's production requirements following the ISO 14649 (STEP-NC) standard and thus considering both the technological and geometrical issues. These issues are then considered as input to the set-up plan module. A graph approach to set-up planning has been developed that generates, through an accessibility analysis, a set of alternative set-up plans characterized by the minimum set-up number. This set is useful evaluate different line configurations through the equipment selection phase. In this regard the methodology proposes a mixed integer programming model that minimizes the transfer line investment cost, selecting the most appropriate production resources for each working station of the line. The configuration method was applied to a real case, showing good agreement with the real configuration adopted by the system manufacturer.

8. REFERENCES

1. Contini P, Tolio T. Computer-aided set-up planning for machining centers configuration. International Journal of production research 2004; vol 42, n 17: 3473-3491.
2. Dolgui A, Guschinsky N, Levin G. A special case of transfer lines balancing by graph approach. European Journal of Operational Research 2006, 168: 732-746.
3. Dolgui A, Guschinsky N, Levin G. Exact and heuristics algorithms for balancing transfer lines which simultaneously activated spindle heads: A computational evaluation. Research report 2005.
4. Matta A, Semeraro Q. Design of advanced manufacturing systems. Springer 2005.
5. Sarma SE, Wright PK. Algorithms for the minimization of set-ups and tool changes in 'simply fixturable' components in milling. Journal of Manufacturing Systems 1996; 15: 95-112.
6. Yut G, Chang TC. An heuristic grouping algorithm for fixture and tool set-ups. Engineering Design and Automation 1995; 1: 21-31.
7. Zhang GW, Zhang SC, Xu YS. Research on flexible transfer line schematic design using hierarchical process planning. Journal of Material Processing Technology 2002; 129: 629-633.

SEQUENCE ANALYSIS OF FINITE POSITION MACHINE FPM

Jesus Trujillo[1], Enrique Baeyens[1] and Zbigniew Pasek[2]

[1]Universidad de Valladolid, Spain
jestru@eis.uva.es, enrbae@eis.uva.es
[2]Universtiy of Michigan, USA
zbigniew@umich.edu

Logic control is an integral part of manufacturing systems. The creation and debugging of the logic control represents a significant amount of the effort needed to design a large manufacturing system. Today's rapidly shifting markets have greatly reduced the life of a product design and the manufacturing system to produce it. As a result reconfigurable manufacturing systems are being developed which are capable of producing different parts over its life. These systems will need control logic, which is capable of being easily reconfigured as the system changes. This work describes the analysis of Finite Position Machines (FPMs) for reconfigurable manufacturing systems thought VS Tree method. VS tree allows to create feasible Pattern structures, whose basically are systems of communicating finite position machines which represent safe reactive processes and allow behaviour description.

1. INTRODUCTION

Today a vast of industrial logic controllers are performed under computer named programmable logic controllers (PLCs). The PLCs are specially designed to respond to use as controllers on industrial processes. A recent research work (Johnson, 2002) published on Control Engineering journal shows that 96% of those polled programs are using leader diagrams. Ones of principal inconvenient of leader diagrams are shown in the complexity of manufacturing systems. Several alternatives have been developed to lead diagrams to PLCs programming. In particular the standard IEC61131-3 publication and IEC61499 is directed to resolve some above problems (Lewis, 2001). The two formalisms more used for control manufacturing system are the finite states machine FSM and the Petri net (Genc, 2003; Park, 1999). However the real complex controller cases design though Petri net are few (Gollapudi, 2001).

The statechart are an alternative framework that allows to describe the behavioural of a complex system in a compact form (Harel, 1996; Hare, 1987). Similarly to a Petri nets they have a good concurrence. The complexity of semantic of execution does that the verification of control systems modelled with statecharts be a hard task (Gruer et al., 1998). On the other hand the supervisory control theory (Ramadge et al., 1987 and 1989) resolves problem in specific cases, when a supervisor creates exactly the desire behaviour in a close loop, even when the controller cannot control or observe all events (Cassandras, 1999; Kumar, 1995). SC theory could be not adequate to be used in developing of complex manufacturing control systems reading (Charbonnier et al., 1999). The principal reason is that the controllers of SC theory are designed to prevent the effects by already events despite of to try controlling the reasons that they create. This paper introduces the analysis of finite position machine (FPM) for studying system by behavioural description (Trujillo, 2004). A principal reason has been the behavioural description of logic control in complex manufacturing plants. The FSM framework is unavailable to represent adequately complex systems, since its required representation millions of states (Endsley, 2004). The finite position machine FPM has properties that allow developing a method thought VS tree, which identify all possible sequences in a control process. These sequences rapidly can be verified out-line, and composed in a safe and fast form obtaining feasible pattern sequences (Trujillo, 2004). Pattern sequences are capable to compose for a new control reconfiguration.

2. ANALYSIS OF A FPM

2.1 General

The majority of highly automated manufacturing process works cyclically, repeating manufacturing orders, in order to obtain products. The presence of non-repetitive lineal sequences is usually linked to the appearance of exceptions produced by conflicts, break downs or unexpected events. Therefore, in order to detect the presence of these conflicts, it is necessary to identify the appearance of sequences which break the operational cycle. With this in mind, it will be necessary to study the FPMs and to identify a priori the possible cycles that might appear. The appearance of cycles in an FPM is determined by their topological structure. Below, a condition is established which allows us to characterize the FPMs with cyclic processing.

FPM definitions: **Action:** An action consists of a tuple of five element formed of a set of a trigger, $A = (\tau, \pi^-, \pi^+, T, S)$. **FPM:** A deterministic FPM, denoted Σ, is a tuple of ten elements $\Sigma = (P, A, T, \rho, \varsigma, \tau, P_{G_{sa}}, P_{G_{ec}}, P_{G_{ic}}, P_{G_{vm}})$ produce the language $L(Gv)$ and marks the language $Lm(Gv)$. Where: $\rho : P \times A \to P$ or is the response of partial sequence ς : is the cyclic transition function or sequence of cyclic response $G_v, \varsigma : P \times A/T \to P$, $\tau_{G_{vo}}$ is the set of transition action triggered from Gv in position $p \in P_{Gv}$, as e.g., subset of AGv for which $\varsigma\, Gvo\,(p)$ is defined $PGsa$ initial position of complete sequence in an acyclic processing, $PGec$ initial position of external cycle Gv, $PGic$ initial position of internal cycle Gv, Pm is the set of marked positions, $P_m \subset P$. All details are in (Johnson, 2002).

2.2 Cyclicity Conditions

A finite position machine has cyclic processing if it satisfies the three propositions:
1) The number of actions η_A must be bigger or equal to the positions η_P. $\eta_A \leq \eta_P$

2) all positions P_n must have at least one arrival action π_{An}^+,

$$\forall \pi_{A_n}^+ \in P_n, \text{ when } \eta_{\pi_{A_n}^+} \geq 1,; n = 1, 2, \cdots$$

3) all positions P_n must have at least an exit action π_{An}^-,

$$\forall \pi_{A_n}^- \in P_n, \text{ when } \eta_{\pi_{A_n}^-} \geq 1,; n = 1, 2, \cdots$$

Below, we will establish the two conditions which allow us to obtain the cycles present in an FPM. We will begin by defining some concepts associated with the topographical structure of the machine.

2.2 Structural Elements of an FPM

The associated structural elements are defined as follows.

Node: In any position P_n of the machine, where three or more actions concur $\pi_{Ai}^-, \pi_{Aj}^+, \pi_{Ai+1}^-$ or $\pi_{Aj+1}^+, \ldots$, where $2 \leq \eta_A \in P_n$. When, with respect to the node, only two control actions π_{Ai}^-, π_{Aj}^+ at the same position, then this is named **junction position**.

Branch: is a set of actions which enclose two or more adjacent positions.
Loop: is a set of actions which forms a cycle. They could exist. **Unitary loops** formed by only one action whose starting and arrival positions are the same.
Lattice: is a loop which does not contain internal branches: i.e., actions neither leave nor arrive between the positions that form the loop, distinct from those included in the loop itself.
Tree: is all affinity set, where its branches contain all the nodes and junction positions, that does not contain any loop, there existing open branches, and consequently, it forms partial sequences of acyclic processing.
Chain: is all branch which does not form part of tree, but it has an affinity with it by one or other extremes.
Basic-loop: is a loop, which contains a single chain and all, or only part, of the tree branches are represented in it.
Affinity Structure: is that where its constitutive elements are formed by FPMs.

2.3 Example of an FPM plane

By means of the following example, the structural elements are shown corresponding to the FPM represented in figure 1 ~\ref{fig:1}

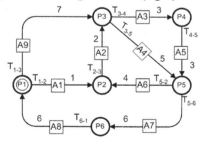

Figure 1 - Basic FPM.

1) The number of branches η_r is seven, identified in figure 1 by 1,..., 7. The actions A_3, A_5 in the positions $P_3 P_4$ and $P_4 P_5$ do not constitute different branches, but a single one, formed by the set $P_3 P_4 P_5, A_3, A_5$, where P_4 is a position of union, since only two actions concur A_3^-, A_5^+; similarly, it occurs for the position of union P_6 where A_7^-, A_8^+ concurs and where the branch is formed by the set $P_5 P_6 P_7, A_7^-, A_8^+$.

2) The number of nodes η_n is four and are represented by the positions P_1, P_2, P_3, P_5.

3) The number of loops η_l is twelve, as is shown in figure 2.

4) The number of loops η_b is four. These are shown in figure 1 by (a),(i),(k) and (l). N.B. None of the loops contain actions in their interior.

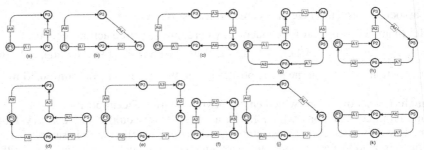

Figure 2 - ((a),...,(j)) Set of the twelve different loops which the FPM can build in figure 1.

5) Some trees of the FPM, to give an example, are (a) formed by the positions P1P3P2P5, (b) P1P3P5P2, (c) P1P3P4P5P2, (d) P1P3P4P5P2, (e) P1P2P3P5 and (f) P2P3P5P6P1.

6) The reference tree in figure 3, which chains are the branches between the positions P2P3, P3P5 and P5P6P1.

7) In a similar way, in figure 3 (f) is taken to be a reference tree, where a basic loop is formed, similarly, by the positions P1P3P4P5P6P1, since it only contains one chain between the positions P5P6P1.

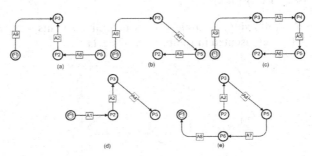

Figure 3 - Some trees corresponding to the FPM of figure 1.

2.3 Basic relation in the analysis of FPMs

Grouping together the relations given in the previous example, we obtain:
η_r = number of branches, η_e = number of chains, η_n = number of nodes, η_b = number of lattices, η_1 = number of loops.
- During the formation of a specific tree of an FPM, two nodes are chosen which are united by a branch, which afterwards add new branches. It can be observed that for every new branch that we incorporate, a new node will be added. In fact, it can be shown that the number η_r of branches of a specific tree is:

$$\eta_r = \eta_n - 1 \tag{1}$$

- If, to the tree considered, chains are added, every new chain is a new branch. Furthermore, as the number of branches is $\eta_{r'}$, where $\eta_{r'} = \eta_e$.
Adding the two previous expressions element by element, we obtain:

$$e = \eta_e + \eta_n - 1 \tag{2}$$

- For any FPM the number of branches is the same as the lattices, plus the number of nodes minus one,

$$n_r = \eta_b + \eta_n - 1 \tag{3}$$

- Considering a global structure formed by a set of independent S branches, by applying the previous expression \ref{e04003} to each of them for a specified tree of each branch, we obtain:

$$n_r = \eta_e + \eta_n - 1 \tag{4}$$

This is the equation which relates the number of branches, the number of chains, relative to a specific tree of each portion independently, and the number of nodes of the global structure of all the set, with the number of independent portions.

Below, we clarify this idea by means of an example. In the tree (f) in figure 1, it can be observed that the number of branches is $\eta_r = 3$ and the number of node $\eta_r = 4$. Therefore, the previous relation (1) is fulfilled where $3 = 4$-1.

In the tree considered, we include in it as many chains as considered necessary to form the primitive FPM calling η_r the number of branches added to the tree, equal to the number η_e of chains which have been placed in it. The result will be that the number of branches and chains added will be as indicated in figure (1), shown in red. This chain allows the closing of the tree, forming a loop and the rest of the chains added will coincide with three, corresponding to chains 2, 3 and 4.

FPM shown in figure 1 though equations (3) and (4) is easier to check the result of number of branches, nodes, chains and lattices. Let $A\{SP\}+(Pj)$ be the set of all the actions which starts from position Pj and arrive at any position of sequence SP and let A-(Pj) be the set of all the actions that begin from any position of the sequence SP arrive at the position Pj. For each position Pj and for each action Ak of an FPM, a numerical value can be associated with them, as was done in section~}, when position sequences were represented by recurrence rules. Let XP(Pj) and XA(A_k) be the numerical values associated with position Pj and with the action Ak. The associated numerical value can be associated with a weight or a dynamic characteristic that could temporally affect each action or position, such as for example, a specific priority in a process, when the action represents that process.

This characteristic will be of great importance in those cases in which the FPMs are used for simulating processes, as could be the case of the processes and operations which intervene in the productive process scheduling.

1) **Rule of position cycles:** *For any sequence of positions Sp of a FPM that forms a cycle, the sum of the numerical values associated with the starting actions minus the sum of the numerical values associated with arrival actions of all the positions of the sequence is zero.*

$$\sum_{P_i \in S_P} \left(\sum_{A_j \in \mathscr{A}_{S_P}} x_A(A_j) - \sum_{A_j \in \mathscr{A}_{S_P}} x_A(A_j) \right) = 0$$

2) **Rule of actions cycles:** For any sequence of actions S_A of an FPM that forms a cycle, the sum of the numerical values associated with the starting positions minus the sum of the numerical values associated with arrival positions of all the actions of the sequence, is zero.

$$\sum_{A_k \in S_A} \left(x_P(\pi^+(A_k)) - x_P(\pi^-(A_k)) \right) = 0$$

These two rules are dual, although the action rule is more simplified when the FPMs are defined in such a way that all the actions are different. If this supposition were not made several positions could have the same starting or arrival action and the duality would be complete.

Making use of these two rules, it is relatively simple to program an algorithm search which would allow us to obtain all the cyclic sequences on an FPM. Let us consider the machine in Fig. 4, where the numerical values have been defined of the positions and actions indicated in the following table:

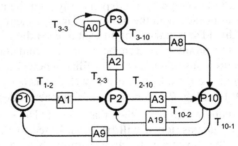

Figure 4 - Graphic of a FPM with cyclic processing.

Let the following sequences of positions be valid: S{P1}={P1, P2, P10}, S{P2}={P_2, P10}, SP3={P2, P3, P10} and actions: S{A1}={A0}, {A3,A19}, S{A2}={A1,A3,A9}, S{A3}={A2,A8}. In order to see which of these sequences are cyclic we apply the cyclic rules~\ref{le0401}. On applying the rule of position cycles we obtain: S{P1}=0, S{P2}=0, S{P3}=-11.

In order to deduced that all sequences form cycles except S{P3}. Now applying the rule of cycles of actions~\ref{le0402} can then be obtained, S{A1}=0, S{A2}=0, S{A3}=0, S{A4}=2.

We are able to deduce that all the action sequences form cycles except S{A4}. These two rules are important because the behaviour of a modelling system with an FPM is given by the sequences that it creates. Furthermore, the sequences can be composed amongst themselves, giving rise to more complex sequences. A modelling system with an FPM has a finite set of elementary, lineal and cyclic sequences whose composition completely characterizes the machine and which is denominated as elementary reference patterns of the FPM. The two rules studied in this section allow us to obtain and characterize simply the elementary working patterns of an FPM.

4. GENERATION OF VS TREE

The VS tree is formed by three basic levels: the axis level, the plane level and the order loop, lattice and closed loop level. The VS tree has the function of creating the basic structure, where all the possible loops that an FPM might contain are to be found.

4.1 Definitions in the generation of the VS tree

Axis: is the set of actions and positions which concur, forming a line which contains the positions of greatest confluence.
Plane: This contains the concatenate loops via common branches and which is initiated from a single axis, where other parallel loops cannot be given to those which exist.
Order loop: These are formed by lattices and are the result of all the possible combinations between the above lattices. Firstly, the FPM has to be ordered in order to obtain all the possible loops resulting from all the possible interactions which could take place in the FPM. For this, an ordering subroutine is used.

4.2 Algorithm of FPM ordering

For cases of an FPM macro-structure of great complexity, it could be possible to begin the process by identifying all the axes and obtaining all the relational combinatorial between them, and then to continue with the steps already taken.

The VS tree includes three fundamental concepts: on the one hand, the determinism of feasible structures, and on the other hand, the possibility of increasing or reducing elements corresponding to a structure, which determines an action that verifies the new extension adopted and, finally, it allows the rapid composition of structures for the creation of patterns.

5. CONCLUSIONS AND FUTURE WORKS

In this paper has been introduced the sequence analysis of finite position machine FPM. This analysis includes method to obtain all sequence possible easier and feasible form thought VS tree. VS pattern are safe structures that allow to compose faster control sequences for use and implementation on-line.

FPM is a new available framework to represent complex manufacturing system by faster and safer manner. This method allow to achieve that the patterns comply ones confidence margins, which this can determine that obtained properties in~\cite{TRU04}. They can warrant a feasible use of these reference patterns under optimal conditions.

5.1 Acknowledgments

This work has been supported in part by the Programa de Apoyo a Proyectos de Investigación del Ministerio de Educación y Ciencia, (VA-4875) and University of Michigan NSF Engineering Research Center for Reconfigurable Manufacturing Systems (NSF grant EEC-9529125)

6. REFERENCES

1. Cassandras C.G. and S. Lafortune. *Introduction to Discrete Event Sistems*. Kluwer Academic publishers, MA., 1999.
2. Charbonnier F., Alla H., and R. David. The supervised control of discrete-event dynamic systems. *IEEE Transactions on Control Systems Technology*, 7(2):175–187, March 1999.
3. Dietrich P., Malik R., Wonham W.M., Brandin B.A. Implementation consideration in supervisory control. In Caillaud B., Danrondeau P., Lavagno L. and X. Xie, editors, *Synthesis and Control of Discrete Event Systems*, pages 185–201. Kluwer, 2001.
4. Endsley EW. Tilbury DM. Modular verification of modular finite state machines. In *Proceedings of the 43rd IEEE Conference on Decisionand Control*, volume 1-5, Nassau, Bahamas, December 2004.
5. Genc S. and S. Lafortune. Distributed diagnosis of discrete-event systems using petri nets. In *Proceedings of the 24th International Conference on Applications and Theory of Peti Nets*, pages 316–336, Oulu, Finland, June 2003.
6. Gollapudi C., Tilbury D.M. Logic control design and implementation for achining line tested using Petri nets. In *Proceedings of the ASME-IMECE Dynamic Systems and Control Division*, November 2001.
7. Gruer P., Koukam A., Mazigh B. Modeling and quantitative analysis of DES: A statecharts based approach. *Simulation Practiceand Theory*, 6:397–411, 1998.
8. Harel D, Naamad A. The statemate semantics of statecharts. *ACM Transaction on Software Engineering and Methodology*, 5(4):239–333, 1996.
9. Hare D.l., Pnueli A., Schmidt J.P., Sherman R. On the formal semantics of statecharts. In *Proccedings of the Second Annual Symposium on Logic in Computer Science*, pages 54–64, Ithaca, NY, June, 22-25 1987. Computer Society Press.
10. Johnson D. Nano devices lead assault on traditional PLC applications. *Control Engineering*, 49(8):43–44, August 2002.
11. Kumar R. and Garg V.K. *Modeling and Control of Logical Discrete Event Systems*. Kluwer Academic Publishers, Norwell, MA, 1995.
12. Lewis R.W. *Modeling control systems using IEC 61499*. The Institution of Electrical Engineers, 2001.
13. Park E, Tilbury D.M., and Khargonekar. P.P. Modular logic controller for machining systems: Formal representation and performance analysis using Petri nets. *IEEE Transactions on Robotics and Automation*, 15(6):1046–1061, 1999.
14. Ramadge P.J.G. and Wonham. W.M. Supervisory control of a class of discrete event processes. *SIAM Journal of Control and Optimization*, pages 206–230, January 1987.
15. Ramadge P.J.G. and W.M. Wonham. The control of discrete event systems. *Proceedings of the IEEE*, 77(1):81–98, January 1989.
16. Trujillo J. *Finite Position Machine for Logic Control: Composition of Patterns in Reconfigurable Manufacturing System*. PhD thesis, University of Valladolid, Spain, 2004.

METHOD FOR INTEGRATED DESIGN USING A KNOWLEDGE FORMALIZATION

Alexandre Thibault, Ali Siadat, Régis Bigot and Patrick Martin
ENSAM, France
{alexandre.thibault, ali.siadat, regis.bigot, patrick.martin}@metz.ensam.fr

This paper presents a proposal for a method aimed to guide the designer within a context of product-process integration in forging design. The objective is not to generate but to assist the design of a product and its associated process planning. This method uses a decision support system called Ontoforge which is based on ontology for representing knowledge.

1. INTRODUCTION

The goal of this project is to conceive methods and computer tools to aid the design of a forged product by taking into account the competences and resources of the enterprise and the constraints related on the manufacturing process. For that, it is necessary to know not only the process knowledge but also the information concerning the resources (material, financial, human or of another nature), the product description during the design cycle and the production data.

The design aid computer tool called *Ontoforge* will be applicable to the forging domain, restricted to hot stamping, in order not to disperse into a too broad domain. However, this area could be widened in the future.

In the first section, the context of the project will be presented, before an example illustrates the kind of supported problems. In the third part are explained the mechanisms that intervene to supply the response to these problems. We discuss finally the benefits and drawbacks of the presented method.

2. SITUATION

The system proposed renders a service to the designer and/or to the manufacturer. It acts on the product data, the manufacturing process data and the resources data. Its aim is to make checks and proposals in respect to process knowledge and available resources.

2.1 Inputs

We place ourselves at the manufacturer point of view. The designer has already made some preliminary choices on the part design. That's why the design aid computer tool is supposed to intervene when the technical requirements have reached a certain level of precision: an incomplete specification of the part with mechanical functional characteristics already quantitatively defined. This specification is available for the geometry, the material or for other kind of data. The functions of the product won't be reassessed, only technical specifications could be changed in a certain range of value eventually defined by the designer. The precision level of this incomplete specification remains to be defined more precisely but we can already affirm that all the data necessary to do the morphological classification are required (see 3.1). The computer tool could also take into account a definition of the resources that are available in the manufacturer workshop (it can be the machines or the staff or any other type of resource).

2.2 Outputs

The goal is not to generate the manufacturing process like (Kim, 2000), but to assist the design of this one. In other words, the tool can make checks and proposals; the user has the possibility to consider or not those remarks. The checks and proposals are realized with the process knowledge and the available information that are filled in. Several sources are used to make it: the morphological classification (ADETIEF, 1974), the indicators presented by J.M. Arenas (Arenas, 2004), the availability of machines in the workshop, or some documents like norms.

3. A SIMPLE EXAMPLE

3.1 Introduction

The functioning of the application can be described with the following example: we consider a part whose draft geometry has been defined. First of all, in order to suggest some recommendations on the manufacturing process, the part is classified in a part family that is listed in (ADETIEF, 1974); this classification is oriented on the morphological point of view. A final processing is lead to know whether or not this part is manufacturable with the resources at disposition (the machines, staff…).

3.2 Automatic classification in a part family

A part is classified in a family according to the parameters enumerated on table 1.

Table 1 – Classification parameters.

Name of the parameter	Type
Existence of a central boss	Boolean
Bent part	Boolean
Existence of an opening	Boolean
Part with slender shapes	Boolean
Existence of a plate	Boolean

Name of the parameter	Type
Revolution part	Boolean
Complexity ratio	Real
Diameter/height ratio	Real
Diameter/Height of the boss (if exists) ratio	Real
Rectangularity ratio	Real
Section variation ratio	Real

After filling the parameters in, the recommendations are presented to the user, or if the manufacturing process is already partially defined, checks are realized that may cause alerts.

3.3 Automatic classification in relation to the available resources

This classification is realized with some parameters like material, size, etc... Two steps are required:

1) The user indicates the resources of the workshop, for example:
   Press1 {Max length = 300 mm; Max power=...; availability: ok}
   Press2 {Max length=400 mm; Max power =...; availability: out of order}
   The workshop is also able to manufacture only the parts that have max length less than 300 mm.

2) The user fills in the parameters of the part:
   If the parameter max length is equal to 305, the part would be classified in the category « parts not manufacturable by my workshop ». A proposal might be suggested: set the parameter max length at 300 mm (remember that we are in a design phase where the geometry isn't definitely set).

4. HOW CAN IT WORK

After explaining what is an ontology and what can be expressed with, we'll see how we can formalize the knowledge for our needs.

4.1 What is an ontology?

An ontology enables:
- To describe a knowledge field (ex: to belong to a certain part family, the part must have certain characteristics and this family implies some recommendations about the manufacturing process).
- To store a data structure and also the data (ex: in the ontology can be described a class named « Machine » that have for attributes: "name", "power", "availability", etc. and the user can fill in the fields with the corresponding data for his workshop).
- To define a common vocabulary for the field (in the form term/definition).

We must observe that the reasoning applied on the ontology rests on the open world assumption, i.e. all that is not asserted isn't assumed to be false. It implies that for certain instances of classes, the system cannot determine where to classify (we'll see it later).

4.2 Automatic classification

We'll illustrate the classification with the previous example (determination of the manufacturability of the part by the workshop). The ontology is expressed in OWL (Ontology Web Language) (Antoniou, 2004) with the OWL *Protégé* plug-in. Figure 1 presents the taxonomical hierarchy (based on the is-a relation) and the relations between the classes.

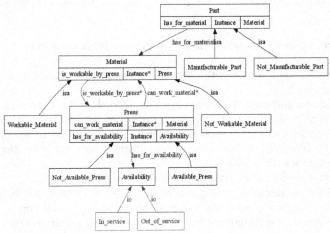

Figure 1 – Relations between the classes.

After having defined the taxonomy as well as the relations between the classes, it is possible to assert some restrictions on those relations (and then we can really talk about "knowledge"). These restrictions are used to define necessary and/or necessary and sufficient conditions to be instance of a class.

The Material, Press and Part classes are primitive classes, i.e. they have only necessary conditions. The other classes are defined classes: there exists for each of those ones at least one necessary and sufficient condition. Thanks to that, the classification in those classes is conceivable. On table 2 are presented the necessary and sufficient conditions for the defined classes.

Table 2 – Necessary and sufficient conditions on the defined classes.

Workable_Material	⊏ Material
	⇐ is_workable_by_press Available_Press
Not_Avalaible_Press	⊏ Press
	∋ has_for_availability {Out_of_service}
Available_Press	⊏ Press
	∋ has_for_availability {In_service}

Manufacturable_Part	⊏ Part
	⏟ has_for_material Workable_Material

Explanation for Available_Press:

⊏ Press: means that an instance of the Available_Press class must be also an instance of the Press class.

⏟ has_for_availability {In_service}: means that if an instance of the Available_Press class has a relation has_for_availability then this relation is necessarily associated to the instance "In_service".

If an instance verifies the two previous conditions then it is an instance of the Available_Press class.

It is important to remark that the properties has_for_availability and has_for_material are functional i.e. they accept a single instance for the range (for example a unique instance of the class Availability concerning the property has_for_availability). On the contrary, the property is_workable_by and its inverse property are not (actually a press can work with several materials and a material is workable by several presses).

This last remark has some issues in relation to the open world assumption; considering a class Not_Workable_Material defined as follows: an individual is an instance of the Not_Workable_Material if and only if it is an instance of the Material class and all the relations of type is_workable_by are pointing on instances of the Not_Available_Press class. But because that property isn't functional, it cannot be determined how many relations of this type really exist. Because it is assumed that what is not asserted may be true, it cannot be inferred that all the relations of this instances complies with the restriction. Then, it cannot be classified in this class (in the case of a functional property, there is no problem).

Example:

The instance "Steel" have only a single relation with « Press1 » which has_for_availability "Out_of_service". It cannot be inferred that this instance is of the Not_Workable_Material class; the contrary also cannot be inferred.

However, it is possible that some instances are classified in the Workable_Material class. It suffices that the instance has a relation is_workable_by with an instance of the Available_Press class.

Figure 2 presents a summarization of the situation.

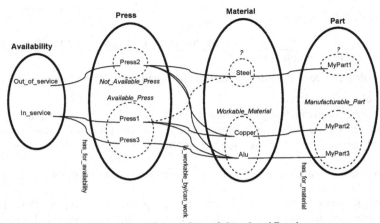

Figure 2 – Illustration of the classification.

The relation between Steel and Press1 isn't asserted but according to the open world assumption, it can exist, then it cannot be concluded that Steel is an instance of the Workable_Material class. MyPart1 has_for_material Steel, it cannot either be concluded something on its type apart that it's an instance of the Part class.

Fortunately the classes that are particularly interesting, that show the availability of the press, the workability of the material, and the manufacturability of the part are fully exploitable.

5. ADVANTAGES OF THIS METHOD

The information extracted from the above processing is the result of a classification. This result would of course be attained by a simple algorithm which would process the data. The interest for the use of an ontology is that it is not only consistent but also upward compatible and easily modifiable. Changing an algorithm implies coding, compiling, updating whereas the change of an ontology can easily be made with an ontology editor like *Protégé*. For instance, if some new parameters must be taken into account for a check on the part, we need just to add the appropriate structures in the ontology.

An ontology would permit to avoid the juxtaposition of several systems such as a xml database for the field terminology, an object database for representing the information concerning the manufacturing process, the product or the resources, and an expert system with a rule base for the field knowledge. Actually, an ontology can be used as an object database; a class diagram in UML can be transcribed in OWL (Falkovych, 2003; Colomb, 2004).

6. INCONVENIENCES

6.1 Database performance

Few similar projects have been carried out until now; we can mention the Kasimir project (D'Aquin, 2004) or also On-To-Knowledge and other different projects (Fensel, 2004; Davies, 2003; Sugumaran, 2002), then we don't know a priori what are the behaviour and performance of a database implemented on an OWL ontology. We can note however that there exists viable solutions for XML database and OWL is based on XML. Moreover an OWL ontology can be mapped in a relational database, so the problem can be less serious than we could think. In addition, we can cite a method for benchmarking Semantic Web knowledge base systems with respect to use in large OWL applications (Guo, 2005).

6.2 Some blocking points

Among the inconveniences, we can cite some limits of this recent technology: there is especially a blocking point, solvable but relatively embarrassing: the use of literals.

Until now, there is no way to use literals in restrictions. For instance, the following condition isn't expressible with OWL:
Relation: has_for_mass between an instance of the Part class and a numeric value
Condition: If x is-a Manufacturable_Part then x has_for_mass y with y < 150
However, this problem can be solved by creating interval classes (D'Aquin, 2004), for example: Mass_less_than_150, Mass_greater_than_150. Hence, if the user inputs the value 78 on the interface, the application would create an instance of the Mass_less_than_150 class that would be classifiable.
On the other hand, it is possible to express some knowledge with the Semantic Web Rule Language (Horrocks, 2005), that could accept the use of literals but this alternative hasn't be taken under consideration because until now there isn't any reason that can exploit the rules expressed with this language.

7. CONCLUSION AND PROSPECTS

We have seen on a simple and concrete example how to use an ontology for storing and exploiting knowledge. This use is realized with the help of an elementary processing: classification. We must be aware of some subtleties such as the open world assumption or the use of literals in order to control this classification. In addition, reflections must be made about the idea of using an OWL ontology like an object database.

Until now, the developments concerned:

- The creation of several demonstration ontologies to illustrate classification

- The creation of an ontology gathering the classes of a knowledge field (forging in our case) with their designation terms on several languages, and their definition (AFNOR, 1984)

- The integration in the previous ontology of the classes allowing the representation of a manufacturing process

The follow-up of this work consists essentially in developing a plug-in program in *Protégé*, that would permit to exploit an ontology according to our needs: creating instances of parts, defining the resources of the workshop, realizing checks on the parts, proposing some recommendations in relation to the manufacturing process. *Protégé* would remain the means to maintain and develop the ontology.

8. ACKNOWLEDGMENTS

This project is carried out in the common laboratory ENSAM-CETIM within the framework of a PhD Thesis financed by the CETIM organization. We thank particularly Mr. Patrick Marchand and Mr. Pierre Ravassard for their active collaboration.

9. REFERENCES

1. ADETIEF. "Classification morphologique des pièces estampées", 1974.
2. AFNOR. "Forge par estampage et matriçage", NF E 82-000, 1984.
3. Antoniou G, Van Harmelen F. "A Semantic Web Primer", The MIT Press, ISBN 0-262-01210-3, 2004.
4. Arenas JM, Sebastian MA, Gonzales C. "Parametric classification based on technico-economic approaches to optimize the design and manufacturing of hot forged parts", Journal of Materials Processing Technology, No150, 2004, pp. 223-233.
5. Colomb B, Hart L, Chang D, Kendall E. "OWL Full and UML 2.0 Compared", 2004, available at: www.itee.uq.edu.au/~colomb/Papers/UML-OWLont04.03.01.pdf.
6. D'Aquin M, Brachais S, Lieber J, Napoli A. "KASIMIR: Gestion de connaissances décisionnelles en cancérologie", Proceedings of 2ème colloque du groupe de travail C2EI, december 2004.
7. Davies J, Fensel D, Van Harmelen F. "Towards the semantic web", John Wiley & sons, ltd, ISBN 0-470-84867-7, 2003.
8. Falkovych K, Sabou M, Stuckenschmidt H. "UML for the Semantic Web: Transformation-Based Approaches", in Knowledge Transformation for the Semantic Web. Frontiers in Artificial Intelligence and Applications, IOS Press, vol. 95, 2003, pp. 92-106.
9. Fensel Dieter. "Ontologies: a silver bullet for knowledge management and electronic commerce", Springer-Verlag, ISBN 3-540-00302-9, 2004.
10. Guo Y, Pan Z, Heflin J. "LUBM: A benchmark for OWL knowledge base systems", Journal of web semantics, article in press, 2005.
11. Horrocks I, Patel-Schneider PF, Bechhofer S, Tsarkov D. "OWL rules: A proposal and prototype implementation", Journal of web semantics, No 3, 2005, pp. 23-40.
12. Kim DY, Park JJ. "Development of an expert system for the process design of axisymmetric hot steel forging", Journal of Materials Processing Technology, No 101, 2000, pp. 223-230.
13. Sugumaran V, Storey VC. "Ontologies for conceptual modelling: their creation, use, and management", Data & Knowledge Engineering, No 42, 2002, pp. 251-271.

AUTHOR INDEX

M

N

O

T

U

V

W

Z